CONTRACT BRIDGE COMPLETE

CONTRACT
BRIDGE
COMPLETE

By Ely Culbertson

Editor, BRIDGE WORLD MAGAZINE
Author of CULBERTSON'S SUMMARY
CULBERTSON'S SELF-TEACHER

Edited by JOSEPHINE CULBERTSON
and ALBERT H. MOREHEAD

THE JOHN C. WINSTON COMPANY
PHILADELPHIA · TORONTO

F-3-54

PRINTED IN THE U.S.A.

L. C. Card #52-14255

INTRODUCTION

By Albert H. Morehead

Some Facts for the Record

NOTE. Mr. Morehead is the outstanding authority on the history of contract bridge and other games. He is a former chairman and president of the American Contract Bridge League, bridge editor of *The New York Times,* and author of many books. As such he is eminently qualified to tell how the Culbertson System came about and what are the fundamental bids in contract bridge. THE PUBLISHERS

Almost from the day that it became the favorite card game of millions throughout the world, contract bridge has been synonymous with the name Culbertson. In some countries the game is simply called Culbertson. It is ironical to note that though so much of Ely Culbertson's recent efforts have been to create a system of international government, the most truly international of all laws is a different Culbertson law—the one applying to the bidding of bridge hands.

Only a handful of the millions of bridge players have any idea of the extent to which they are following "Culbertson law" each time they play bridge—even when they think they are playing some other system. The younger players take for granted, as though they were axioms that have always existed, certain bidding principles that were unknown before Culbertson first expressed them, in some cases almost thirty years ago. There are older players who were around when Culbertson (then considered a dangerous radical in the game) produced his first innovations back in 1923, but most of them have forgotten. It is all but incredible to most players, even experts, that the following were unknown or unhonored in the pre-Culbertson era:

The Bidding of Four-Card Suits

Introduced by Culbertson in 1923. Up to that time the minimum biddable suit had five cards and conservatives required that even a five-card suit contain at least one quick trick. Wilbur Whitehead, one of the great auction bridge authorities, wrote in the '20's: "The introduction by Ely Culbertson of four-card suit-bids is the greatest development of modern bridge."

The Approach Principle

This has become so much a part of the game that it no longer occurs to anyone that the "principle" requires a name at all. Yet before Culbertson, the "cheaper" notrump was the undisputed king, and countless games were lost through lack of any effort to find a trump fit.

The Principle of Economy of Bids

It was Culbertson who first taught that the bidding should be kept low at the start. Previously, believe it or not, the object had been to keep the bidding high so that the opponents could not overcall! What Culbertson actually taught bridge players, including the experts, was that the first object of bidding is to double the opponents and collect penalties; that the side with the preponderant strength can afford to keep the bidding low; and that by keeping the bidding low, this side will either reach its own best contract or can double the opponents if they step out. Self-evident, you may say; but the fact remains that no one thought so in those days.

The Forcing Principle

This, like several of the other Culbertson discoveries, seems like something everyone has always known, but it was originated and developed by Culbertson in California in 1927-1928, when it first became apparent that contract bridge would replace auction. It remains the dominant principle of contract bridge and it would be hard to conceive today of a system in which there are no forcing bids. From the forcing principle Culbertson derived scores of new methods including the forcing two-bid, forcing takeout bids and rebids, the overcall-in-the opponents'-suit-bid, and the many inferential forces that are now standard.

The Discovery of Distribution in Bidding

This is the least known, yet perhaps the most valuable, of Culbertson's contributions. Referring to Culbertson's discovery, R. F. Foster observed, in *Modern Bridge Tactics* (1924): "This matter of distribution has never been touched upon in any of the textbooks on auction, but I believe it will be the key to most of the bidding tactics of the future." Twenty-eight years after the fact, it seems incredible that the effect of distribution on bids was unrecognized until one man came along and told the world about it. Yet such is the fact, and for a number of years Culbertson's was a voice crying in the wilderness. As late as 1927, there were still experts who considered him a crackpot because he would bid more on a 4–4–3–2 than on a 4–3–3–3, more on a 5–4–3–1 than on a 5–3–3–2. Milton Work, the senior prophet of auction bridge, wrote, "Bridge is a game of aces and kings."

Revolution in Notrump Bidding

Ely Culbertson's technique of utilizing the distributional values not only revolutionized suit bidding, but notrump bidding as well. The classic theory and requirements for opening notrump bids, today standard in all systems and counts (balanced distribution, 3½ to 4+ honor-tricks or 16–18 points, three suits guarded, Q x in the fourth), were originated and introduced by Ely Culbertson early in 1934. Even the words *limit* bids, *balanced* and *unbalanced* distribution were coined by him as were so many other bridge terms in current usage.

The Honor-Trick Table

Of course, bridge was not then a game of Aces and Kings, but it was Culbertson who introduced the honor-trick table that was more flexible and gave quick-trick importance to un-supported lower honors, as Queens, Jacks and tens; who first pointed out the fact that there are a limited number of honor-tricks and by the "rule of eight" one can determine which side has the balance of power. Previously, even expert players had been guilty of such bidding absurdities as this:

SOUTH	WEST	NORTH	EAST
1 N T	Double	Pass	2 N T

—it never occurring to East that if he could make two no-trump, the penalty would be more valuable than the part-score, and that if he could make three notrump, the penalty would be more valuable than the game.

The Distributional Count

Culbertson's theories of distribution and balance of power led logically to the development of a method of counting actual winners at a given contract where, in addition to honor-trick a separate count was introduced for low cards in long suits and ruffers (distributional values). His wife, Josephine Cul-bertson, codified this discovery as the Distributional Count—still the most accurate way of valuing one's hand. This method, incidentally, later became the basis of the 4–3–2–1 point-count in suit-bids and various point-count methods.

The 4–5 Notrump Slam Bids

Culbertson first had the idea of using the 4–5 notrump level to show Aces wholesale. He published it in 1933. The first manuscript in which Easley Blackwood set forth his own theories presented them as "a development based on Culbertson's new idea." I know, because Blackwood sent that manuscript to me in 1934 for publication in *The Bridge World*.

Psychology in Bridge

Stating that contract bridge travels on two legs—the mathe-matical and the psychological—Culbertson integrated the scat-tered do's and don't's on bridge psychology into a psychological system of strategy and tactics. His chapters on psychology in the *Blue Book* and *Gold Book* are classic.

The One-Over-One

Culbertson did not name this; Theodore Lightner did. But Culbertson thought of it first. In the magazine article published in 1928, in which he first introduced the principle of the forcing bid, Culbertson gave a list of typical forcing situations—and look what led the list: "One partner opens with a suit-bid of one, and the other partner responds with a suit-bid of one." Yet within four years others were claiming the one-over-one as a bidding system of their own different from Culbertson's!

The list could be continued indefinitely. It would also include some impractical bids, proposed and soon abandoned; some excellent bids (like the asking bids) that at the time he failed to complete; and a host of bidding methods that were inescapable consequences of the basic principles, and that anybody might have thought of—given Culbertson's fundamental principles and specifics as a starting point. The fact remains that contract bridge today would be impossible without the theories and practical methods dicovered, developed and even named by Ely Culbertson. However, two facts must be made clear: Ely Culbertson is not the only man who has made important contributions to contract bridge as it is played today; and his creative mind did not create the Culbertson System System all by itself.

Who Created the Culbertson System?

As with most dynamic concepts, it is the joint creation of a single mind and of a collective mind. The System embodies the traditions and accumulated experience of whole generations of card players. In the course of its development, all the best minds of contract bridge contributed to it—those who were friendly or associated with Culbertson and worked with him, and also those who were unfriendly and trying to produce superior systems of their own. Theirs was the collective mind. The single mind was Culbertson's, and was essential. It is still essential. A committee cannot write a poem or compose a symphony—or create a system. Some dominant individual must be present to create, prod, suggest, and integrate. No one who was around at the time can doubt that in the case of contract bridge science, that individual was Culbertson.

The talent for organization is a rare one and an indefinable one. I am not sure just why Culbertson has it (though surely I know him as well as anyone does); I know only that he has it. Bertrand Russell, the Nobel Prize winner, recently wrote about him in connection with his creative work in a different kind of world system: "The most remarkable man I ever had the pleasure of knowing . . . I do not play bridge." Somehow, Culbertson not only produced a system but also organized another system to keep it in a continuous stage of growth and improvement.

Ethics in Bridge

I have written the foregoing because I think there has been of late too much tendency to overlook Culbertson's contributions, and to give other names to systems that are anywhere from 75% to 90% the Culbertson System. There is an unfortunate tendency of some American and British bridge writers to overlook the preponderant portion of their systems that is pure Culberston, or at least to give no credit to the original authors of the Culbertson System. In some cases they even convey an impression that the use of a point-count involves the abandonment of the Culbertson System. This is untrue. A point-count is not a system but simply another way of valuing the bids that make up a system. It is a different instrument playing the same music of the composer. Besides, the Culbertson Point-Count, which he has recently developed, bids fair, through its greater simplicity and accuracy, to take place among his major contributions.

A proper ethical code in any field of intellectual endeavor requires that due credit be given to anyone whose original ideas are used, borrowed, or extended. This is not a legal matter, for ideas cannot be copyrighted (and it is proper that they should not be; ideas should be the property of all). Hence, acknowledgment of the contribution of others is a debt of honor. In the case of bridge, it is elementary fair play to Culbertson and his lifework, and to the many others—writers, players, and teachers—who have been associated with him from time to time during that period. Yet in one of the point-count books—the one by Charles Solomon and Bennett Disbrow—I find credit to Culbertson only for devising the 4–5 notrump convention. In the books on point-count bidding by Charles Goren I find no mention of Culbertson's name, though Goren has not made any material change in his bidding methods since the days when his books were frankly written about the Culbertson System. True, Goren did credit Culbertson in his earlier books, and absence of credit in the Solomon-Disbrow and other books is, I feel sure, unintentional. Nevertheless, the beginning bridge player of today might pardonably get the idea that the authors of these books had originated and perfected a beautiful and harmonious system of contract-bridge bids and responses—a work of a genius; and that somewhere along the line a little guy named Ely Culbertson had helped out by proposing bids of four and five notrump to help in reaching slams.

To repeat, the Culbertson System is not the property of Ely Culbertson or any other individual. The authors of other bridge books have every right to write about it. It belongs to the players of the world. But the players themselves, millions of them, give credit to the man primarily responsible for the modern methods of contract bridge—Ely Culberston.

AUTHOR'S PREFACE

It is a fact attested by millions of players throughout the world that from the very beginning of contract bridge and up to today they have been weaned, taught and brought up on my basic books of contract bridge. First there was *Contract Bridge Blue Book,* published in 1930; then, in 1934, *Contract Bridge Red Book on Play.* In 1936 I combined the theory and practice of bidding and play in the *Gold Book of Contract Bridge* which like its predecessors went through innumerable editions.

And now, eighteen years later, appears my present basic work, CONTRACT BRIDGE COMPLETE. It incorporates the best collective experience of the best players and analysts of the world together with my own; the best features of the Gold Book; and the latest carefully tested developments of contract bridge.

It is not immodest to claim that CONTRACT BRIDGE COMPLETE, edition 1954 is the best complete work on contract bridge. The fact is—it is the *only* complete work on contract bridge in existence. There are here and abroad other books titled Contract Bridge Complete. Without exception they represent a perhaps too clever play on the word *complete:* they are "complete" in the sense that they give a smattering on Bidding, Leads and Play. The biggest of them contains only 185 pages of big print and fat paper on Bidding—adequate for a beginner, impossible for anyone who wants to understand contract bridge. Scores of important questions on bidding are not even raised, let alone answered.

Like chess, contract bridge requires a basic authoritative and comprehensive work on theory and practice of the game. Such is CONTRACT BRIDGE COMPLETE. Here a player, be he average or expert, will find, in a single volume, a scientifically unified view of modern contract bridge as a whole; and in the same work hundreds of questions which arise in the bidding, leads, the play, and the laws, will be answered and reasons given in simple language. Hundreds of selected hands and examples illustrate the bidding and playing situations.

One of the main reasons for the extraordinary place occupied by my basic books is that I have always had a double goal. On one side, I sought to *simplify* contract bridge methods by devising simple rules for beginners and average players, thus dramatizing the game for millions; on the other side, I sought relentlessly the winning methods for advanced bridge, adopting only methods calculated to win against the strongest opposition in championship (and money) games.

In 1951, with the help of some of the best players and analysts in the world, I undertook the task of revising and improving some contract bridge methods in the light of the most recent developments. As a result, two improvements of great importance, together with a score of minor improvements, were tested and adopted. They are now presented in CONTRACT BRIDGE COMPLETE. Among the improvements is the introduction of the Limit Two-Bid, which is the first real change in the Forcing Two-Bid in the last twenty-five years. Of the two major changes, one is intended principally for the beginner and average players; the other is for advanced and championship play. They are the New Point-Count Valuation and the New Asking Bid. In 1952 I published the Culbertson point-count valuation (the Rule of Three and Four). Although it was well received, I continued further to simplify it and make it even more accurate. At the time, I stated that there was much room left for improvement of all point-count methods and this included my own count based on 4-3-2-1. The 4-3-2-1 point-count has always been excellent for notrump valuation because it is simple and accurate. It was first made public by Milton C. Work and later published in my Blue Book (edition 1930) as an optional method in the Culbertson System.

In trump bids, however, a special count for distributional values
is indispensable in addition to the 4–3–2–1 count. And when
it came to the valuation of trump bids (especially in the raises,
which are the heart of trump bids) the best of current point-
counts, with all their deductions became slightly nightmarish
and, like all nightmares, mainly inaccurate. I am now in a
position to announce the definitive solution of the problem
of point-count in suit-bids—the Culbertson Point Count. The
count is an extension of the Rule of Three and Four, previously
published. In accuracy, it approaches, and sometimes rivals,
the precision of an expert player. Its greatest appeal, however,
is in its *simplicity*. By means of an utterly simple formula it
is now possible to make the most complicated raises (including freak hands) virtually *at a glance* and automatically. The
formula is so strikingly simple and startling that I repeat it
here: for raises you simply subtract your *shortest* suit (say a
singleton) from your trump length (say four trump) and the
difference (three points) is the number of distributional points
which, when added to your high-card points (4–3–2–1 count)
gives you the total point-count of your hand. Instead of an
assorted collection of extra points to be added and subtracted,
you only deduct one point if your hand contains no second
four-card or longer suit. Try this new formula right away and
you will see for yourself how you will bid more accurately and
yet save what amounts to many boring hours of needless counting. Revaluation of trump suits has been similarly simplified.
Now that the main objection to the point-count valuation is
removed, many of the players who still prefer the honor—and
playing—trick valuation (the favorite method used among
experts) might favor the point-count valuation (see slam
valuation) .*

$$13 = 5 - 1 = 4$$

	4 — 3	2 for short suits
7	5 — 2	1 for trump length
	6 — 1	1 for side lengths
	7 — 0	

Figure 13 is the number of cards in the hand, 5 is the trump length, 1 the shortest
suit, 4 the distributional tricks.

* Paradoxically enough, the simplest formula for raises in point-count valuation
is derived from a complicated mathematical formula. For a hand containing five
trump and a singleton, for instance, the formula for distributional points reads:

The second innovation presented in Contract Bridge Complete is also revolutionary, but its principal appeal is to advanced and tournament players, although even average players may greatly benefit. This is the New Asking Bid. Some of the features of the New Asking Bid were introduced before the war with considerable success, especially abroad. However, the New Asking Bid contains so many improvements and new features (such as the Trump-Asking Bid) that, far from being a revival, it is a new movement. In my considered opinion the New Asking Bid does for the solution of the chaotic problem of slam bidding what the new point-count does for valuation of trump bids. In the long, however, the New Asking Bid will have a more lasting effect on contract bridge bidding.

It will be clear to anyone who will read the chapters describing the New Asking Bid that, in advanced bridge, the side using the New Asking Bid will have a decisive advantage.

Although this edition of Contract Bridge Complete contains all the essentials of the new point-count method, it will profit the reader to consult for details and finer points my new book, exclusively on point-count, entitled *Culbertson Point-Count Bidding.*

For those who wish the basic facts for quick reference, there is my latest *Complete Summary of Contract Bridge,* which is derived from Contract Bridge Complete and which is the most popular bridge book ever written (5,000,000 copies sold). The *Summary* contains in summarized form all up-to-date developments, including the new point-count valuation and the New Asking Bid. One of the great advantages of the *Summary* (edition 1953) is that all bids are described in terms of point-count and honor-playing tricks, side by side. In this manner those who know only the honor-trick method can see at a glance the point-count equivalents and vice versa. There is also a *New Self-Teacher* for those who wish to learn by simple steps, illustrated by drills and exercises, and presented in both the honor-trick and point-count *equivalents.*

There is also the ever-present need for personal experience. A book is the experience of the *other* fellow. In order to get the indispensable personal experience and to have it properly interpreted for you, look for a teacher in the flesh and blood—

a relative or friend, if he *really knows,* or a professionally trained bridge teacher holding a certificate from the Culbertson National Studios.

The fates have decreed that I be the bridge doctor to millions of players. I remember the day, early in 1927, when there were only *two* who played the Culbertson System—Josephine and I. Today more than forty million players throughout the world play contract bridge, the greatest intellectual game of all time—a game equally thrilling to a beginner and to an expert who, too, learns every time he plays. And virtually all of them play Culbertson. My greatest asset is the confidence of bridge players. To justify this confidence is the purpose of my latest work, CONTRACT BRIDGE COMPLETE.

ELY CULBERTSON
Brattleboro, Vermont

ACKNOWLEDGEMENTS

To: Josephine Culbertson, the greatest teacher and twice international champion player, who contributed so much to the methods of the Culbertson System.

Albert H. Morehead, an outstanding analyst, who also, over the course of many years, has made major contributions to the Culbertson System, and who, together with Josephine Culbertson, has edited most of my books.

Theodore A. Lightner, whose contributions to the Culbertson System have extended from its earliest days right up to the present day. Mr. Lightner is more than a famous player: he is one of the outstanding theoreticians of the game. Particularly in this book his painstaking analysis of advanced bidding situations, viewed from the standpoint of a great expert, have been of utmost help.

Alphonse Moyse, Jr., my adviser and colleague for many years, and who has done such an outstanding job with *The Bridge World Magazine,* which he now publishes—and which is valuable to all bridge lovers.

Waldemar von Zedtwitz, many of whose original ideas were incorporated into the Culbertson System, including the famous "bust" two-notrump response to the opening two-bid.

Richard L. Frey, Myron Field, George Bard, Hy Lavinthal, Alfred P. Scheinwold, Samuel Fry, Jr., and other great players everywhere.

In a real sense, all great players, here and abroad, are in part creators of the Culbertson System.

I am also obligated, for this book, to the members of my immediate staff.

I heartily thank Professor Louis F. Woodruff of the Massachusetts Institute of Technology for his aid in mathematical questions.

CONTENTS

	Page
Introduction	iii
Author's Preface	x

Chapter   **Book I. BIDDING**

1. **The Culbertson Point-Count Method**	2
Mechanics of the Point-Count	6
The Point-Count at Notrump	7
Opening Bids of Two and Three Notrump	10
Opening Suit-Bids and Responses	12
Point-Count Requirements for Raises	15
Free Bids and Raises by Responder	17
Opening Two-Bids and Responses	23
Takeout Doubles and Responses	24
2. **The Bidding Process and Its Goals**	28
Tricks	28
Scoring and the Objects of Scientific Bidding	30
3. **Bidding Valuation**	33
The Three-Way Valuation of the Same Hand	34
4. **Honor-Tricks**	36
Culbertson Standard Table of Honor-Tricks	38
Rule of Eight	43
4–5–6 Table of Expectancies	46
5. **The Distributional Count**	49
Valuation of Declarer's Hand	53
Valuation When Raising Partner's Trump Bid	55

Chapter   Page

6. Partnership Language of Inferences 60

    The Approach Method 62

    The Limit-Bid Principle 62

    Inferences from Partnership Strategy 63

7. Opening Notrump Bids 66

    Opening One-Notrump Requirements.............. 66

    Rebids by the Opening Notrump Bidder........... 79

    When One Notrump Is Doubled or Overcalled....... 83

    Distributional Notrump Bidding................... 85

    The Opening Bid of Two Notrump................. 88

    The Three-Notrump Bid........................ 91

    An Alternative Theory of Notrump Bidding......... 93

8. Biddable Trump Suits 96

    Adequate Trump Support....................... 99

    Table of Biddable Suits........................ 101

9. Opening Suit-Bids of One 103

    Minimum Requirements 105

    Choice of Suits................................ 110

    The "Reverse" 113

    The Principle of Preparedness................... 115

    4-4-3-2 and 4-3-3-3 Minimums................. 121

10. Forcing Bids 123

    The Forcing Principle.......................... 123

    Bids That Are Forcing to Game................... 126

    Bids That Are Forcing for One Round.............. 129

    The Defenders' Forcing Bids..................... 131

    Summary of Forcing Situations................... 132

11. Opening Suit-Bids of Two 136

    Specifications for Forcing Two-Bids................ 138

    Responses to Forcing Two-Bids................... 143

Chapter	Page
12. Limit Forcing Two-Bids	146
13. Opening Pre-Emptive Bids	154
Opening Three-Bids	155
Opening Four-Bids	158
Minor-Suit Five-Bids	160
14. Responses to Suit-Bids of One	162
The Pass	163
The Raise	164
The Notrump Takeout	170
Suit Takeouts	175
15. The Passed Hand	184
Second-Round Bids by the Responder	186
16. Rebids by the Opener	189
When the Response Was Forcing to Game	191
Rebids After a One-Round Force	194
Rebids After One Notrump	196
Rebids When Partner Raises	198
Illustrated Summary of Rebids	200
17. Rebids by the Responder	208
Responses to Jump Rebids	208
Illustrated Summary	210
Guide to Game Valuation	215
18. The Intermediate Zone	216
Reading the Bidding	221
Preference Bids	224
Sign-Off of Rescue Bids	226
Where to Bid Game	230
19. Free Bids	236
Free Rebids	241
Bids Over Opponent's Takeout Double	242

Chapter   Page

20. Part-Score Bidding 244

    Part-Score Strategy and Tactics..................... 246

21. The Defenders' Bidding 250

    Strong and Weak Overcalls........................ 251

    Responding to an Overcall........................ 253

22. The Takeout Double 256

    Requirements for the Takeout Double.............. 257

    Responses to the Takeout Doubles................. 263

    The Penalty Pass................................. 267

    Rebids After a Takeout Double.................... 272

23. Strength-Showing Overcalls 277

    The Jump Overcall............................... 277

    The Immediate Overcall.......................... 279

24. The Penalty Double 282

    The Two-Trick Rule............................. 283

    Light Doubles 284

    Tight Doubles 287

    Penalty Doubles of Notrump Bids................. 288

    When to Redouble.............................. 291

    Summary of Doubling Situations.................. 293

25. Slam Bidding 296

    Mathematics of Slam Bids........................ 297

    Choice Between a Trump and a Notrump Slam..... 300

    When to Make a Slam Try....................... 301

    Controls 305

26. Direct Method of Slam Bidding 308

    Recognizing the Slam Zone....................... 309

    Direct Slam Tries 311

    Other Direct Slam Tries......................... 313

Chapter   Page

27. Conventional Methods of Slam Bidding 314

    Cue-Bidding to Show Aces......................... 314

    When to Make a Cue-Bid........................ 315

28. 4-5 Notrump Slam Conventions 322

    The Blackwood Convention...................... 322

    When Is Four Notrump Blackwood?............... 324

    Action by Responder 325

    Grand-Slam Bidding 326

29. The New Asking Bid 329

    Slam Valuation and the Asking Bid............... 335

    The Asking Bid Defined......................... 338

    The Agreed Suit 339

    Sign-Off 341

    Choice of Asking Bids.......................... 343

    The New Blackwood 4–5 Notrump................. 350

    The New Trump Asking Convention............... 350

    Blackwood and Asking Bids...................... 352

    Asking Bids in Opponents' Suits.................. 363

    Asking After an Opening Two-Bid................. 370

    When an Opponent Overcalls the Asking Bid........ 374

Book II. STRUCTURE OF BIDS AND PLAYS

30. The Safety Factor 380

    The Rule of Risk and Gain....................... 381

31. Scoring and Its Mathematics 384

32. Reading Distribution from the Bidding 391

33. What Is Duplication? 394

34. Duplicate Bridge Bidding.............................. 400

    Opening Bids 403

    Overcalls 407

    Choice of Contracts............................. 409

Chapter   Page

35. Psychology and Tactics................................ 412

      Concealing Weakness 412

      Trapping 414

      Bids to Misplace Cards......................... 418

36. The Personal Equation 420

      Playing Partner's Game......................... 420

      Opponents' Psychology 425

37. Modern Theory of Distribution 427

      The Law of Symmetry........................... 427

Book III. THE PLAY OF THE CARDS

38. The Winning of Tricks................................. 436

      The Principle of Promotion...................... 437

      Stoppers 438

      Guards and Suit-Distribution................... 438

      The Finesse 442

      Principle of Economy of Honors................. 445

39. Low-Card Tricks 448

      Long-Suit Establishment 449

      Short-Suit Establishment 449

      The Simple Probabilities 453

      Culbertson Standard Table of Finesses.......... 454

40. Communication Plays 459

      Entry-Making Plays 459

      Entry-Killing Plays 462

      Defenders' Entry Plays......................... 465

      Ducking 466

41. The Time Factor 472

      Time Valuation of a Long Suit 474

      Time Valuation of a Hand...................... 475

      Time Valuation of Ruffers 477

Chapter	Page
42. Declarer's Planning and Play	478
Advance Planning	479
Declarer's Play at Notrump	484
Trump Planning	486
Card Reading	493
43. End-Plays	498
The Squeeze	500
Typical Squeeze Positions	504
Trump-Reducing Plays	507
44. Safety Plays and Technique	511
45. Conventional Leads and Plays	516
Honor Leads	517
Leads to Show Long Suits	518
Short-Suit Leads	519
The Card to Lead	526
46. The Defenders' Game	528
Leads Against Notrump	528
Leads Against Trump Bids	531
Culbertson System of Leads	536
The Laws of Contract Bridge	539
Scoring Table	558
The Laws of Progressive Bridge	561
How to Run a Tournament	566
Index	569

CONTRACT BRIDGE COMPLETE

BOOK ONE

BIDDING

Card Sense is usually spoken of as one of the mysterious minor talents, an innate knack of grasping easily and applying in practice the logic of playing situations. Cards do have an inner logic and form a bizarre world governed by their own inexorable laws. But I do not believe in an innate faculty called Card Sense. Certainly a man is not born with an invisible deck of cards in the convolutions of his brain. Card Sense is largely an understanding of the spirit of cards, their remarkable structure and the few underlying principles that make up contract bridge.

CHAPTER ONE

THE CULBERTSON POINT-COUNT METHOD

The Story of the Point-Count

The point-count is older than auction or contract bridge. It was used first in whist by Dr. William Pole to determine, statistically, the relative trick-taking value of high cards. In auction and contract bridge the point-count was known as a notrump count, since it was used only for valuation at notrump bids where it possesses a high degree of accuracy.

In the Culbertson System the 4–3–2–1 notrump count, borrowed by Bryant McCampbell from Pitch and popularized by Milton Work, has been recommended since 1930 as an optional method to honor-trick valuation. Thousands of players have used it ever since and are still using it in conjunction with the honor-trick table for suit-bids. I wrote in the 1930 edition of *Contract Bridge Blue Book:* "A comparison will show that the 4–3–2–1 point-count as advocated by Mr. Work, or other similar point-counts, are for all practical purposes identical with the notrump valuation based on the Culbertson honor-trick count. The type of mind that thinks in figures will perhaps be happier with a point-count."

Milton Work attempted to adapt the 4–3–2–1 count to trump bids. He gave up, announcing that the count was not suitable for suit-bids. At the time he was right and for years I also opposed it as unsound. Recent developments opened the door to the application of the point-count to trump bids as well.

Various methods arose, most of them rigid and highly complex (unnecessarily so, as I found out later), but moving in the right direction. The most popular of them derived from the Culbertson valuation of distributional values.

Will a Point-Count Method
Replace the Honor-Trick Method?

There has been, and is, no thought of abandoning the honor-trick method of valuation in favor of some point-count. The honor-trick method is basic and inherent to contract bridge. Bidding is mental play. Bidding is a *prediction* (or a bet) that a number of tricks, as contracted for in the bid, will be made in the play. The honor-trick method derives from the direct count of winning (and losing) tricks in the bidder's hand—a method used, consciously or unconsciously, by virtually all expert players and which always will be used by the majority of players. It may be called a *natural* count. An Ace is valued as one trick in bidding, for the inescapable reason that it will win one trick in play.

This does not mean that a different method, based on a point-count valuation, cannot produce excellent results. There is room in the Culbertson System for both languages—the concrete language of tricks and the abstract language of points.

It seems to some innocent point-count enthusiasts (and to some not-so-innocent writers) that the use of a point-count involves the abandonment of the Culbertson System. Nothing could be further from the truth. The point-count is another method of valuation leading to the *same* bids on the *same* hands.

Charles H. Goren, in his excellent book, *Point Count Bidding in Contract Bridge* (Revised Edition), writes, "Let me make it clear that the point count is not a System. It is an approach; a simplified method for valuing one's hand. So you are not to feel that a new System is being foisted upon you." Mr. Goren, for a number of years a successful teacher of the Culbertson System, elsewhere writes: "The point-count valuation for suit bidding, as I have developed it, is almost a literal translation of the playing-trick table, with a few minor improvements."* The playing-trick table to which Mr. Goren refers is the table of the Culbertson Distributional Count.

The Babel of Point-Count Methods

Until today there has existed no standard point-count method of valuation. Instead, there are five entirely different types; and the 4–3–2–1 type, which is the most popular, has more than twenty different "varieties." The number of these "methods" is still growing, and with it grows the confusion and bewilderment of the players, who do not know who is right and which way to turn. The five basic types of point-counts and all the twenty-odd varieties of the 4–3–2–1 count seem to be agreed on one thing only: protected by the anonymity of the point-count, they preach and practice the Culbertson System in pointed disguise.

It is clear that there is a need for a new, improved method of point-count, preferably based on the popular and best-known 4–3–2–1 count. The new count, in order to become standard, would have to be simpler and more accurate than the preceding counts, particularly in suit-bids; and it must be designed from the standpoint of expert rubber bridge, while being adaptable to duplicate bridge.

Late in 1949, my associates and I began research to develop an improved 4–3–2–1 count. This book is the result of that research. We believe it fits the exacting specifications. We had the great advantage of coming into the field after all others and thus avoiding their errors, while profiting by their sound ideas. But much more than that was needed if we were to develop a point-count for suit-bids that would not collapse from the weight of its own complexities. The 4–3–2–1 count is at its best in notrump bidding; not much need be done to improve it there. But an opening notrump is a relatively rare bid. It is in the 4–3–2–1 count valuation for suit-bids and, particularly, the point valuation of distributional values (points for length and ruffing tricks) that the greatest improvement has been made by us.

---

* *The Bridge World,* January 1950.

From the standpoint of simplicity, the outstanding feature of the new Culbertson 4–3–2–1 count is the natural valuation attained by the use of the Culbertson Rule of 3 & 4 (the third and fourth card) for measuring the point-count value of an opening bid. Supplementing the Culbertson 3 & 4 rule, we have the Raise Rule, which is a simple and accurate formula based on the difference between trump-support length and the length of the shortest side suit. This revolutionary formula does away with the drudgery of counting points for doubletons, singletons or voids. No more do you have to make deductions for three-card trump support; or "promote honors" in trump support because of an inherent defect in an outmoded raise formula.

The Revaluation Rule, which applies after your partner has raised your suit, is a logical extension of the Culbertson Rule of 3 & 4. For the first time, point-count valuation for suit bidding has attained the accuracy of the Playing Trick Count, used the world over and offered to the public by this writer over twenty years ago.

On the Rapid Count of Points

In our continued quest for simplicity we turned our attention to one defect inherent in all point-counts: the sheer labor of arithmetic in adding up all those fours and threes and twos and ones after each deal.

The obvious short-cut in counting a hand's point-value is to learn and memorize the count of honor-combinations. There are not so many as to make this a great bother. The A-K-Q of a suit can easily be remembered as 9 points, and the mental effort is not much greater when one holds an Ace, a King, and a Queen in different suits. The same applies to K-Q, worth 5 points; A-Q-J, 7 points; to A-J, 5 points, and so forth.

Another difficulty inherent in the point-count method is to remember the formidable number of minimum-maximum requirements in points for various bids. We were baffled. The pages of point requirement demand the memory of a specialized robot. I, for one, could not remember them all, and am forced to *reconstruct* a particular requirement from the few basically logic assumptions. This was our clue to further simplification. Whenever possible, we tried to describe the simple processes behind the requirement, so that the reader may be able, himself, to reconstruct the requirements in points for various bids.

It is entirely possible for one player to use honor-trick valuation while his partner is using the point-count. In order to facilitate partnership (and opponents') understanding, we state many requirements in terms of both valuation methods.

The great weakness of many point-count players is their tendency to neglect the tactics of the penalty double. They are so intent on combining their hands for the best game bid that they forget that the biggest point-maker in bridge is a penalty double. To some extent, this defect is inherent in the structure of the point-count, where a concept of precise defensive valuation (defensive honor-tricks) is absent. To remedy this defect, at least in part, we have developed a special chapter on penalty doubles, a special rule based on the point-count.

In the rest of the book, we have tried to answer questions on the 4–3–2–1 point-count that were not previously answered or not answered satisfactorily. We devoted many pages to advanced valuation from the standpoint of expert bidding, both in rubber and duplicate bridge. We sought to achieve a greater simplicity than heretofore, and yet a greater accuracy.

The point-count has come of age. It is very well suited to certain types of players and to certain types of bids. If a player wishes to use point-count he will find in this book a careful, reliable guide. He will also find that he is in no way departing from the Culbertson System—and the latest methods of contract bridge.

Mechanics of the Point-Count

At the outset players must bear in mind that it is one thing to value a hand for a notrump contract, and quite a different thing to value a hand for a suit contract. The past failures of many point-count systems have been due largely to the fact

that their authors either ignored or discounted the vast difference between notrump and suit valuation.

In the Culbertson point-count method this difference is ad-
justed automatically by a simple formula, used in conjunction
with the ordinary count of high cards. This simple but amaz-
ingly accurate formula is the Culbertson Rule of Three and
Four for suit-bidding.

Before we take up this formula, however, let us thoroughly
examine the proper point-count approach to *notrump* bidding.

The Point-Count at Notrump

THE HIGH-CARD POINT-COUNT

$$\text{Ace} = 4$$
$$\text{King} = 3$$
$$\text{Queen} = 2$$
$$\text{Jack} = 1$$

In valuing a hand for notrump these important facts should
never be lost sight of: the pack contains 40 points in high
cards; and the average hand contains 10 points in high cards.
(The words "high cards," as used here and throughout this
point-count section, apply only to the four top honors in each
suit. If tens are important to the case at hand, they are mentioned specifically.)

In valuing a hand for an opening notrump, only the 4–3–2–1
count for high cards is used (with rare exceptions).

Before counting points, however, the player must determine
that the pattern of his hand is correct for notrump. The distribution must be balanced, that is, there should be no singleton, and certainly no void suit. At least three suits should be
stopped (a stopper is A x, K x, Q x x, or J x x x). Any doubleton suit must be headed by at least the Queen.

If these fundamental conditions are fulfilled, the player then
counts his high-card points, and if he has:

**Between 16 and 18 points—neither more nor less—
he should open the bidding with one notrump.**

Corrections

Although the high-card count is relatively accurate at no-trump, certain "corrections" are needed for full precision. These corrections are as follows:

If you hold all four Aces, add 1 point.

If you have Q J alone in a suit (without any small card) deduct 1 point.

The following are typical examples of one-notrump opening bids:

   ♠ A J 4   ♡ K 9 5   ◇ Q J 6 3   ♣ K Q 6

A minimum notrump opening—16 points.

   ♠ A Q 4   ♡ K J 5   ◇ Q J 6 3   ♣ K Q 6

A maximum notrump opening—18 points.

   ♠ A Q   ♡ K 10 3   ◇ A Q 8 4 2   ♣ Q 9 2

Despite the five-card minor suit, this 17-point hand is a better one-no-trump opening than a one-diamond opening.

Responding to a One-Notrump Opening

The responses to a one-notrump opening are carefully geared (as are all responses and rebids) to the expectancies, in terms of tricks, which various combined point-counts (for the partnership hands) figure to produce. It is vital for would-be point-counters to learn and remember these expectancies.

Twenty-six points in the combined hands are usually needed to provide a good play for game at notrump or a major suit.

With 29 points in the combined hands there is usually a good play for game at a minor suit, but in this zone it is still advisable to prefer a notrump game if the necessary stoppers are held.

With 33 points in the combined hands there is *often,* but not always, a good play for a small slam at notrump. At rubber bridge, particularly, care should be exercised by the partners if their bidding discloses only a minimum 33 points, *unless* one partner or the other has a five-card (or longer) suit to provide an extra trick or two.

With 37 points in the combined hands, a grand slam should

be considered, but here of course there must first be a careful check for the four Aces.

Requirements for Raises of Notrump

Just as the opening notrump bidder must have a balanced hand, so must his partner if he raises. With rare exceptions it is improper to give a raise on a hand containing a singleton.

With 8–9 points, raise to two notrump.

With 10–14 points, raise to three notrump.

With more points, make a slam try, as follows:

With 15–16 points, raise to four notrump.

With 17–18 points, raise to six notrump.

With 19–20 points, first bid three in a suit, then bid **six** notrump.

With 21 points, raise to seven notrump.

Examples of raises for a one-notrump opening:

   ♠ K 6 3   ♡ Q J 5 4   ◇ J 3 2   ♣ 9 7 6

Pass. Hand has only 7 points. Even if partner has the maximum 18, there figures to be only a sketchy play for game.

   ♠ K 6 3   ♡ Q J 5 4   ◇ J 3 2   ♣ J 7 6

Raise to two notrump on this 8-point hand.

   ♠ K J 3   ♡ Q J 5 4   ◇ Q 3 2   ♣ J 7 6

Raise to three notrump on this 10-point hand.

   ♠ K J 3   ♡ Q J 5 4   ◇ A Q 2   ♣ J 7 6

This 14-point hand typifies the maximum for a raise to three notrump.

   ♠ K J 3   ♡ Q J 5 4   ◇ A Q 2   ♣ Q 7 6

Raise to four notrump on this 15-point hand.

   ♠ K J 3   ♡ K J 5 4   ◇ A Q 2   ♣ A 7 6

Raise directly to six notrump on this 18-point hand.

   ♠ K J 3   ♡ K J 5   ◇ A Q J 2   ♣ A J 3

First bid three diamonds, then, regardless of partner's rebid, jump to six notrump on this 20-point hand.

   ♠ K J 4   ♡ A K 3   ◇ A Q 8 7 3   ♣ K 2

Jump straight to seven notrump on this 21-point hand. The fifth diamond counts 1 point. However, to be absolutely sure that the partnership holds all four Aces, use the four-club convention.

Special Considerations for the Raiser

The player who raises an opening notrump, in contrast to the opener himself, should add 1 point to his count if he holds a five-card suit headed by a King, Queen-ten, or better. Bolstered by the honor cards which he can expect the opener to have in that suit, responder must realize that the mere length in his suit increases the overall value of his hand. With an easily establishable six-card suit, responder should increase his valuation *substantially*, as follows: He should count 4 points for length, and add these 4 points to his high-card count. (With a seven-card suit, count 5 points for length.) Thus, if the opening bid is one notrump, and responder holds:

♠ 6 2   ♡ 7 4 3   ◇ A K 8 5 3 2   ♣ 8 4

he should count his hand at 4 for the Ace, 3 for the King, and 4 for the diamond length—a total of 11 points. If he had one more small diamond instead of a small heart, his count would be 12 points. In either case his proper response to one notrump is three notrump.

Opening Bids of Two and Three Notrump

To constitute a sound two-notrump opening, a hand must be balanced, with at least one stopper in *every* suit, and the point-count requirement for this strong bid is 22–24 points.

Examples:

♠ A Q 5   ♡ K J 6   ◇ A Q J 4   ♣ A J 8

A minimum two-notrump opening—22 points.

♠ A Q 5   ♡ A J 6   ◇ A Q J 4   ♣ A Q 8

A maximum two-notrump opening—24 points.

An opening bid of three notrump is, in its very nature, a mild slam invitation and requires 25–27 points in high cards.

Examples:

♠ K J 8   ♡ A K J   ◇ A Q 7 2   ♣ A Q J

A minimum three-notrump opening—25 points.

♠ K Q J   ♡ A Q 6   ◇ A K 8 4   ♣ A K J

A maximum three-notrump opening—27 points.

Responding to Bids of Two and Three Notrump

Responder should raise an opening two-notrump bid to three on as little as 3 points; he should give this same raise with as much as 8 points. In this latter case there does not figure to be a slam, since the maximum combined total will be only 32 points.

Examples of single raises of two notrump:

♠ Q 8 6 5   ♡ 7 4 3   ◇ 6 5 2   ♣ J 8 4

Minimum 3-point raise.

♠ Q 8 6 5   ♡ K 4 3   ◇ K 6 5   ♣ 8 6 4

Maximum 8-point raise.

With more than 8 points, the responder to a two-notrump opening should act as follows:

With 9–10 points, bid four notrump. Partner should bid six with 24 points, five with 23, and should pass with 22.

With 11–12 points, raise to six notrump.

With 13–14 points, invite a grand slam by bidding three in a suit, *then* jump to six notrump.

With 15 points, bid seven notrump.

Further examples of raises for two-notrump openings:

♠ K 8 6   ♡ Q 7 4   ◇ K J 8 7 2   ♣ 5 3

Raise to four notrump. The hand counts 9 points in high cards, plus 1 point for a five-card suit.

♠ A 9 5   ♡ K 8 4   ◇ K 7 3   ♣ Q 6 3 2

Raise to six notrump. The hand counts 12 points, and partner could not have had a two-notrump opening without at least two Aces.

♠ A 9 5   ♡ K 8 4   ◇ K 7 3   ♣ K J 3 2

First, jump to three clubs, then bid six notrump over any rebid partner makes. This hand counts 14 points.

♠ A 9 5   ♡ K 8 4   ◇ K 7 3   ♣ K Q 3 2

Jump straight to seven notrump on this 15-point hand.

If the opening bid has been three notrump, responder should:
Bid four notrump with 6–7 points;
Bid six notrump with 8–9 points;
Bid seven notrump with 12 points.

Examples of raises for three-notrump openings:

♠ K 10 7   ♡ 8 5 4   ◇ K 9 5 2   ♣ 5 4 3

Raise to four notrump—hand counts 6 points.

♠ K 10 7   ♡ 8 5 4   ◇ K 9 5 2   ♣ K 5 4

Raise to six notrump—hand counts 9 points.

♠ A 10 7   ♡ K 8 5   ◇ Q 9 5 2   ♣ K 5 4

Jump straight to seven notrump with this 12-point hand. Partner could not have had a minimum three-notrump opening without the three missing Aces.

The handling of six-card suits after an opening bid of two or three notrump is the same as after a one-notrump opening— that is, the responder places an arbitrary length-value of 4 points on such suits. (5 points on a seven-card suit.) In this connection, however, a warning must be issued. It is obvious that if responder's hand, opposite a two-notrump opening, consists of nothing but a six-card suit headed by the King, and an outside Queen, the 9-point count, expressed in terms of a mild slam try of four notrump, is illusory and therefore dangerous. For slam purposes, the suit must be strong enough to insure only one loser, at most.

A more important warning is this: *as a rule,* avoid direct jumps to slams in notrump. Whenever possible put the no-trump slam tries through the control-showing safeguards of trump bids.

For suit takeouts of notrump openings, see page 18.

Opening Suit-Bids and Responses

As previously stated, when a player values his hand for an opening suit-bid he must take into account his *distributional* assets as well as his high cards. After totaling up his points for honors, he should use the following formula to determine how many distributional points he has. Opener should count:

1 point for every card over *four* in his trump suit.
1 point for every card over *three* in each side suit.

These points are added to the high-card count, and the sum is the point-count value of the hand for a suit-bid.

CORRECTIONS

Opener adds 1 point for possession of all four Aces.

He deducts 1 point for a singleton King or a doubleton Queen-Jack.

He deducts one point if his hand contains one or more side-suit Queens or Jacks not supported by at least one other honor in a short suit. This does not mean a 1-point deduction for *each* unsupported Queen or Jack; it means a blanket deduction of 1 point for any number of such Queen or Jack holdings. For example, opener holds:

♠ A K 7 5 2   ♥ Q 4 3   ♦ A 6 4   ♣ J 2

The correct way of counting this hand is: 7 points for the A K of spades and 1 point for the fifth spade, 2 points for the heart Queen, 4 points for the diamond Ace, and 1 point for the club Jack. However, because the hand contains an unsupported Queen and an unsupported Jack in a short suit, there is an automatic 1-point deduction, and therefore the total point-count is 14 (15 minus 1).

Requirements for an Opening Suit-Bid of One

(For description of biddable suits, and the order in which suits should be bid, see page 96.)

Hands counting 14 points or more must always be opened in any position—first, second, third or fourth hand.

With 13 points, an opening bid is usually in order. The only exception is with a *bare* 13-point hand (usually distributed 4–3–3–3) which would become dangerous if opener were called upon by partner's response to make a rebid at the two-level.

With 12 points, an opening bid is proper with a *good* five-card suit (headed by at least the Ace-Queen) or a six-card or longer suit. In this 12-point category, however, the hand must contain 2 defensive tricks (combinations of honor-tricks such as A K, A Q, A, K Q or K x).

With 11 points, the bidding may be opened if the hand is bolstered with intermediate cards; for example, if the trump suit is something like A Q 10 9 7. Eleven-point hands must contain 2½ defensive tricks, as above.

Examples Illustrating the 3 & 4 Count for Declarer's Hand in Opening Suit-Bids of One

♠ A K 8 4 2	8 (7 + 1)	♠ 5 3	0
♡ 7 3	0	♡ 10 7 6 2	1
◇ J 10	1	◇ A Q 5	6
♣ K 8 4 3	4 (3 + 1)	♣ A K 6 4	7
	—		—
Bid one spade	13	Bid one club	14
♠ A Q 10 9 6	7 (6 + 1)	♠ A K J 7 3	9 (8 + 1)
♡ A 8 6	4	♡ 10 7 5	0
◇ 7 2	0	◇ K 3 2	3
♣ 5 4 3	0	♣ 8 7	0
	—		—
Bid one spade	11	Bid one spade	12

Responses to Opening Suit-Bids of One

Raises

The responder uses the Culbertson Short Rule for Raises in arriving at the proper valuation of his hand for a raise of partner's suit. It is the most valuable rule in trump bids. The application of this rule is extraordinarily simple and yet extremely accurate. In fact, I do not hesitate to state that this Rule of Raises not only rivals the precision of experts' valuation: it will liberate the bridge player from the drudgery and confusion of various point-count methods for raises heretofore proposed. Here is the rule:

In order to determine the total of distributional points (in long suits and ruffers) subtract your shortest suit from your trump length. The difference is the exact number of your *distributional points,* and this number, added to your high-card total, gives you the exact point-count of your hand for a raise of partner's suit-bid. There is only one deduction from the above total, namely, you deduct 1 point if your hand lacks a four-card or longer side suit. The corrections which you heretofore accepted as necessary with point-count are completely discarded by the use of this revolutionary formula.

Another way of expressing the *Shortest Rule for Raises* is as follows:

To your high-card total:

Add the difference in length between the trump length and the shortest side suit.*

Deduct 1 point if you lack a four-card or longer side suit.

In the examples under the next heading, the amazing simplicity and precision of the Rule of Raises will become obvious when compared to other, cumbersome methods.

Point-Count Requirements for Raises

(Assuming adequate trump support)

With 6–10 points, raise partner's suit-bid to two.

With 13–16 points, raise to three. For this double raise, you must have at least four-card trump support, usually J x x x or better, and at least 10 of your points must be in high cards.

A raise of partner's opening suit-bid of one to four is a preëmptive raise which should not contain more than 8 points in high cards. For this raise there should usually be five-card or longer trump support; any four-card support should be extremely strong.

Here, assuming an opening spade bid, are examples of how the responder counts his hand for raises:

	Points		Points
♠ Q 7 6	2	♠ K 8 5 2	3
♡ K 5 4 3 2	3	♡ Q 6 4	2
◊ 6 5	1	◊ Q 7 3	2
♣ J 7 5	1	♣ 9 5 2	1
Total	7	Total	7 (8 — 1)

1 point was deducted because the hand lacks a 4-card or longer side suit.

---

*If your shortest side suit is a void, and you have four trumps, you have four distributional points—the difference in length between the two suits.

	Points		Points
♠ 10 4 3 2	0	♠ K Q 7 3	5
♡ A 8 4 3	4	♡ 9	3
♢ 7 6 2	0	♢ A 8 5 4	4
♣ 5 4	2	♣ Q J 6 3	3
Total	6	Total	15

No corrections are needed in this case.

No corrections are needed in this case.

Other Responses to Opening Suit-Bids of One

The main body of this book, pages 162 to 175, gives specific advice on the nature of the response that should be made to partner's opening suit-bid, depending on the high-card and distributional strength of responder's hand. Consequently, we will here set down only the point-count requirements for the various types of takeouts.

With hands of only moderate strength (6–10 points):

Respond one notrump with 6–10 points in high cards. This response may be made on even 1 point less if the hand contains a ten in combination with a higher honor. Hands which constitute proper notrump takeouts are usually balanced, but there may be occasion, as the least of evils, to respond with a notrump to partner's suit-bid, holding a singleton in partner's suit.

Give a single raise of partner's suit—as immediately above. With five trumps, or with unbalanced distribution and adequate trump support, a shaded raise may be given on only 5 points.

Valuing Responder's Hand for a Suit Takeout

In valuing his hand for a suit *takeout,* responder proceeds as though he were the original bidder, counting 1 point for every card over *four* in his trump suit, and 1 point for every card over *three* in side suits.

Make a one-over-one response with as little as 5 points. If you must choose between this type of response and a takeout to one notrump, incline toward the former.

With hands containing 11–13 points you have enough for two encouraging bids. You may take out to a lower-ranking suit (two-over-one) or you may make a one-over-one takeout with the intention of bidding again. With a strong five-card suit or a good six-card suit, two-over-one takeouts may be shaded down to 9 points.

Hands containing as many as 11 points with good trump support for partner are usually too strong for a single raise and not strong enough for a double raise. In these cases efforts should be made to mark time on the first round with a one-over-one or perhaps a two-over-one takeout, with the intention of raising partner later.

Hands justifying strong responses contain 13 points and upward. Among these strong responses are:

Double raise in partner's suit (see page 167). The point requirement is 13–16, of which at least 10 points must be in high cards.

Jump takeout to two notrump. This bid shows stoppers in the three unbid suits, balanced distribution, and 13–15 points in high cards.

Jump takeout to three notrump. This is the same type of bid as the two-notrump jump, but the point requirements increase to 16–18.

Jump suit takeout. This response, forcing to game and usually implying slam aspirations, requires a minimum of 18 points. With a count of *only* 18–19, there must be either good support for partner's suit or an independent suit in responder's hand.

Triple raise in a major suit. This shutout raise is based on very strong trump support and, as a rule, freakish distribution, but no more than *8 points in high cards.*

Free Bids and Raises by Responder

When an opponent has overcalled partner's opening suit-bid of one, point-count requirements for free raises or other calls by responder obviously increase. Thus—

A free single raise of partner's suit requires 8–11 points.

A free bid of responder's own suit at the one-level requires a minimum count of 9 points. (*Exception:* 8 points if honor cards are all in one suit. Example: A Q J 7 4.)

A free bid of responder's suit at the two-level requires at least 10 points.

When responder's suit is higher-ranking than opener's, about 12 points are required for the free bid. Consider these two sequences:

NORTH	EAST	SOUTH	WEST
1 ♠	2 ◇	2 ♡	

NORTH	EAST	SOUTH	WEST
1 ♡	2 ◇	2 ♠	

In the first sequence, South's two-heart bid does not require a particularly strong hand because it allows North to rebid his suit at the two-level. In the second sequence, however, South's spade bid may force North to rebid at the three-level, and South needs a better hand to provide for this situation.

A free bid of one notrump over opponent's intervening call shows a balanced hand, at least one stopper in the opponent's suit, and 9–12 points.

A free bid of two notrump over an opponent's one-level overcall shows two stoppers in opponent's suit with at least 13 points, or one stopper with 14 points. A free non-jump two-notrump bid over opponent's two-level overcall requires 11 points with two stoppers in opponent's suit, or 12 points with one stopper.

A free double raise of partner's suit is the same as the double raise without the intervening call, except that in minimum, borderline cases responder should give a free single raise where he had intended to "shade" for a double raise.

Suit Takeout of Opening Notrumps

The takeout of an opening one notrump to two of a suit is forcing for one round in the Culbertson System. Usually, the responder will not take out to a suit except with an unbalanced hand (containing a singleton or a void) or with a hand so strong as to justify a *jump* takeout. For example, opposite a one-notrump opening responder might hold:

♠ A Q 10 9 5   ♡ 6 2   ◇ A Q J 3   ♣ 5 4

This hand is not unbalanced, yet with two good suits and with worthless doubletons in the other suits, a jump to three spades is the obviously correct action. This hand counts 15 points—6 for the spade honors and 1 for length; 7 for the diamond honors and 1 for length.

Suit takeouts at the two-level, though forcing for only one round, require at least 8 points, of which 6 points must be in high cards.

Special Treatment of Six-Card Suits

When the responder to a notrump holds a six-card or longer suit, special considerations apply. (See page 85.) Because the opening notrump guarantees some sort of fit with responder's suit, it is as though that suit had already been raised. As explained in the section devoted to notrump bidding, responder applies an automatic length-valuation of 4 points to a six-card suit opposite a notrump; 5 points to a seven-card suit—these in addition to the points for any high cards in that suit.

Six-card suits, particularly minor suits, in hands of balanced distribution often warrant notrump raises, but when the hand is unbalanced or when the weakness of the suit suggests that its establishment will be difficult at notrump, a takeout of the notrump is advisable.

Suppose responder holds:

♠ K 7 6 4 3 2   ♡ 6 5 3   ◇ 8 7   ♣ 6 4

Counting 4 points for the spade length and 3 for the spade King, responder values this hand at 7 points with spades as trump. This is not enough for a takeout to two spades—the minimum is 8 points—and since the hand is obviously not up to a notrump raise, responder's proper action is to pass.

However, if the spade suit were improved a shade, to K J 7 6 4 3, two spades should be bid. If partner raises to three spades, responder passes; and if partner rebids two notrump, responder bids three spades as a sign-off.

Opener's Revaluation

There is no need for revaluation by the opening *notrump* bidder except when he holds a five-card suit. After partner has raised, opener counts an extra point for the fifth card of that suit; he then applies his new total to the points announced by partner's raise, and rebids or passes in accordance with the known combined total of the hands.

In the case where partner has raised your suit, you now use the Revaluation Count, which is simply a logical extension of the Culbertson Rule of 3 & 4. You revalue your hand by adding 2 points for each card over four in the trump suit. This is the only difference to the way you count your hand for an opening bid. The valuation of high cards, and the 1 point for each card over three in every side suit, are identical with the Culbertson Rule of 3 & 4.

When responder did not raise but showed a suit of his own which the opener now wishes to raise, opener revalues his hand as the raising hand.

Opener's Rebids

After a single raise in your suit by responder, revalue your hand, and if it totals only 14 to 16 points, pass.

Rebid your suit if you have 17 points; there is a chance that partner has a near-maximum raise, giving you a combined total of 26 points—enough for a game in a major.

If your suit is a minor and your hand counts no more than 16 points, you should usually pass. Do not venture a two-notrump response unless you hold either a good rebiddable minor or good intermediates and stoppers in other suits. Promiscuous two-notrump rebids after a single raise lead to shaky three-notrump contracts, often with disastrous results.

With 17–18 points, after a single raise by your partner, rebid your suit at the three-level.

With 19 points, show a new suit, or bid two notrump, or jump to game in a major suit.

If partner makes a suit takeout, raise his suit, especially if it is a major, if you have 14 or more points apply the Short Rule of Raises.

With 17 to 19 points, give partner a double raise if his suit takeout was at the one-level. *If his suit takeout was at the two-level,* you know that he has a minimum of 10 points. With your 17 to 19 points you have together enough for a game at notrump, or a major suit.

You have three choices in responding. Choose the one that best fits your hand. With unbalanced hands (especially four of partner's trumps and a short suit) choose a raise.

With 16–18 points, raise directly to game if your partner's suit takeout was a major suit at the two-level. Jump to three notrump if you have necessary stoppers in side suits and a balanced hand, with at least 18 high-card points.

Jump, as a rule, to four in your partner's suit if it is a minor and your hand is unbalanced. This jump raise requires at least 17 points, and before giving this type of raise consider the possibility that the combined hands will more easily win nine tricks at notrump.

If partner's response was one notrump, raise to two notrump with a balanced hand and 18–19 high-card points. Partner, with 7–9 points, will bid three notrump.

If partner's response was a two-over-one suit takeout, a rebid of two notrump is proper if your hand is adapted to notrump and contains 16–17 points in high cards. You may modify this point requirement slightly, if it appears that you can count on one solid suit.

With 17–19 points, opener may reverse at the two-level. For example, opener holds: ♠ A K J 2 ♡ 7 5 ◇ A Q 9 5 4 ♣ K 3. The opening bid was one diamond (19 points) and the response was two clubs. Opener should now bid two spades. The same applies to a rebid of a new suit at the three-level—this also requires 18–20 points, minimum.

Powerful Hands—18 Points and Over

With 18–20 points and a notrump-type hand, make a jump two-notrump rebid over partner's one-over-one response.

With 21–22 points, jump to three notrump.

Powerful Hands: 19 Points and Over

With 19–22 points bid game in a major over partner's single raise. With 19–21 points (revalued) and a sufficiently strong trump suit, make a jump rebid to three in your original suit. This suit, however, should be strong enough so that two small trumps in partner's hand will be adequate support.

With 22–23 points and a trump suit strong enough to play opposite a singleton, jump to game in your major suit.

In other situations, with 21 points or over, a forcing rebid is in order, i.e., a single jump in a new suit.

Rebids by Responder
5–10 Point Hands

When responder's hand is in this minimum range, bidding is fairly simple. Responder has already made a limited bid; if opener makes an encouraging rebid he announces that he is nevertheless still interested in game. Responder should therefore bid again with 8–10 points but should decline all invitations with 6 points, and usually with 7 points. Only if opener has reversed over the original response of one notrump should responder continue to hold the bidding open with as little as 7 points.

When the bidding has gone: one of a suit by opener, single raise by responder, then a rebid of two notrump by opener, there is strong indication that opener may have a four-card suit. Consequently, if responder raised originally with only three trumps, the suit should now be abandoned. If responder has 8 or more points for notrump he should raise the two-notrump rebid to three, or should now show a new five-card suit.

With good four-card trump support and 8 or more points, responder should jump partner's original suit to four, over his two-notrump rebid.

When responder has made a one-over-one response with less than 9 points, or a two-over-one response on 9 points, he should as a rule pass partner's rebid, or give a mere preference unless partner has forced or made a very strong rebid.

11–12 Point Hands

This is the range of encouraging responses—hands strong enough to invite partner to bid game, but too weak to insist that game be reached. If partner makes a minimum rebid, you should make a further rebid encouraging him toward game.

13–17 Point Hands

This represents the game range if partner's opening bid is in the minimum range. In this zone you may have solved your problem by showing your strength on the first round, that is, by a jump in notrump or a jump raise. The further bidding is then up to partner. The only remaining problem will be whether to bid a slam if partner makes a slam try. If your hand is near the maximum (15–17 points), you bid the slam; if near minimum (13–15 points), you decline the invitation. If your first response was a one-round force, bid game or make a second forcing bid.

18 Point Hands and Over

This represents the slam zone. Your 18 or 19 points will not produce a slam if partner's hand is a minimum, but will bring the total up to 31 or 32, which is close enough to justify a strong try, leaving it to partner to bid the slam if he is a few points above a minimum. Responder's proper procedure is a game-forcing takeout in a new suit—a jump of one trick more than necessary to overcall.

In rebidding, the responder should revalue his hand in the same manner as the opener bidder. He should revalue his hand as dummy if he intends to support a second suit-bid by partner.

Opening Two-Bids and Responses

The Rule of 24

In appraising a hand for an opening suit-bid of two, forcing to game, use the 4–3–2–1 count for high cards, deducting 2 points if the trump suit is not headed by at least six points.

Add 1 point for each suit (trump or side suit) in which there are 100 honors; add 2 points for 150 honors.

Length Points:

Count 2 points for each card over *four* in every suit.

If the total count of the hand is 24 points or more, it is a forcing two-bid.

Responses to Two-Bids

With less than 7 points make a negative response of two notrump. With 7 points or more (shaded down to 6 points with a suit headed by A Q) make a positive response. Any positive response indicates the possibility of slam.

After a positive response by partner, the opening two-bidder revalues his hand by applying the Rule of Three and Four.

Takeout Doubles and Responses

The takeout double of a suit-bid shows a hand containing from 13 points as a minimum, up to as high as 20 or 21 points. The precise point-requirement is qualified by several factors, among which are the level at which partner will have to respond, and the distribution of the doubler's hand—whether or not it contains an independent suit that can be used as a rescue, in effect, of the perhaps-very-weak suit which partner must name.

With as little as 13 points it is proper to double one club because partner has the other three suits at his disposition, but the takeout double of one spade logically requires greater strength because partner will have to respond at the two-level (or with one notrump).

Ideal distribution for the takeout double of a suit is a singleton in that suit and four cards in each of the other suits. With this automatic support for any suit partner can mention, 13 points justify the double, but when the doubler has several low cards in the opponent's suit the risk is increased appreciably, and so the point-count requirement for the double should be increased substantially—to about 16 points.

It is also advisable to double for a takeout when holding values that cannot be adequately shown by a simple overcall. Thus, with such a hand as

    ♠ K Q J 6 4   ♡ A J 10   ◇ 6 3   ♣ K Q 4

if the opening bid on one's right has been a diamond, a club or a heart, the proper procedure is to double for a takeout, then to show the spade suit over partner's response (or to raise partner if he responds in spades).

Doubling a Notrump

The requirement for doubling one notrump is 16 points, minimum, and if the doubler is vulnerable it is well to increase this requirement slightly. However, possession of strong intermediate cards (tens or nines) may be viewed as additional protection. Note, however, that the double of a notrump carries entirely different emphasis and intent from that of a suit-bid. A notrump double is an implicit request for partner to pass for penalties, whereas the double of a suit-bid is a strong demand for a response. It is true that partner can, on his own initiative, take out the notrump double or leave in the suit double, but this does not alter the express objective of each type of double.

Responses to Takeout Doubles

The average player tends to undervalue his hand in responding to the takeout double. He does not seem to realize that when he makes a minimum response in a suit, he has actually made no bid at all, as far as showing any strength goes. If the doubler was working on the properly cautious expectation of finding responder with about 3 points in high cards, the responder must realize that an actual holding of 5 or 6 points represents additional values which only he can know about, and so, if the doubler gives a strong raise to responder's minimum bid, as in the following sequence

North	East	South	West
1 ♡	Double	Pass	1 ♠
Pass	3 ♠	Pass	?

West should go on to four spades with 6 points, including distributional points.

With a hand containing 8–10 points it is often wise to make a minimum response to the takeout double but then to bid again if partner takes *any* further action. However, with the maximum 10 points and a good major suit, the better bidding technique is to make a jump response to partner's takeout double. For example, if partner doubles one heart and you hold this 10-point hand

♠ A 7 5 4 3 2　　♡ 6 3　　◇ A 5 2　　♣ 7 4

a one-spade response does not announce your game-going values, nor does it offer anything like the proper encouragement to partner; consequently you must respond with two spades.

With 11 points or more, this jump response to a takeout double is mandatory. The jump is not actually forcing (and consequently does not require anything like the strength required for another jump bid) but it at least fulfills the primary duty of informing partner that responder holds 8 or more points *in excess* of opener's normal expectations.

Responses in Notrump

With one or more stoppers in opponent's suit, or at times with only a partial stopper such as J x x, the best response to partner's double may be one or two notrump. Even a one-notrump response is always a strength-showing bid and should never be used merely because responder's only length is in the opponent's suit.

With two probable stoppers in opponent's suit, responder should bid one notrump on about 7 points; with only one stopper or with a partial stopper, another point is required.

With 12 or 13 points and a sure stopper in opponent's suit, the correct response (assuming notrump distribution) is two notrump.

The Penalty Pass

Only with a truly strong holding in the opponent's suit is it correct to pass partner's takeout double, thereby converting it into a penalty double. If you have five trumps, they should be strong enough to invite the lead of a singleton in that suit by partner—in fact, the leave-in of a takeout double is in itself a strong suggestion that partner should lead the opponent's suit.

Rebids by the Doubler

If partner responded to the takeout double with a minimum bid, your assumption should be that he holds about 3 points— it is unduly pessimistic to assume that he has *nothing,* and equally optimistic to assume that he has more than 3 points. Consequently—

To raise partner's suit to the four-level, the doubler needs 22 or 23 points, and at least four trumps, including two honors.

To bid three notrump, the doubler needs 24 points, with either one stopper in the opponent's suit and a long suit (usually a minor) which can be run, or two stoppers without this particular sort of value.

To jump-raise partner's suit to the three-level requires 19 points in support; and to bid two notrump requires 20 points, with two stoppers in opponent's suit.

To bid two notrump over partner's forced response at the two-level is also a very strong bid—almost the equivalent of an opening two-notrump bid. With less than 20 points the proper course is an immediate overcall of one notrump, not a double.

To make a jump bid in another suit, after having doubled for a takeout, requires about 22 points, revalued.

A single raise of partner's one-level response requires about 16 points.

When partner has responded to the double of a one-spade bid with two clubs, or with a one-bid in the lowest-ranking suit possible, extra caution should be exercised in raising, since partner may have been forced to respond on a three-card suit.

Reopening the Bidding with a Double

A double which is made as a reopening bid can be and often should be shaded down to 9 or 10 points, although 11 points obviously offer greater safety. For example, the bidding has gone:

SOUTH	WEST	NORTH	EAST
1 ♡	Pass	Pass	?

East holds:

| ♠ K 9 5 4 | ♡ 6 3 | ◊ A J 4 | ♣ Q 8 6 3 |

East's best course is to double.

CHAPTER TWO

THE BIDDING PROCESS AND ITS GOALS

The road to the best final bid is strewn with the bones and boners of millions of pasteboard soldiers. Their commanders-in-chief, the players, are to be sympathized with rather than condemned. The strategical possibilities of this fascinating intellectual game are practically unlimited. Simple enough for a grown-up child and yet deep enough for a demigod, it has this in common with the strategy of actual warfare (which it so strikingly resembles in many other particulars): the side that makes the fewer blunders is victorious.

The blunders which in bridge may keep the player from the best final bid are his sins of commission and omission in *bidding*.

Bidding is a complex process consisting of *Valuation, Information* and *Strategy*. The object of bidding is to select the best final bid for the partnership hands. The best final bid may be a contract of one's own, or a double of the opponents' contract for penalties. Bidding, like play, is based on tricks.

Tricks

In bridge, "tricks of the trade" are tricks. Only Aces and top sequences are dealt ready-made; all other trick values must first be established or "refined" from the suits of various lengths in which the tricks are embedded and which are their raw material.

The true nature and behavior of a trick is still a mystery

even to most advanced players, for there is nothing more tricky than a trick. There are even more ways of getting tricks out of suits than of skinning a cat.

A player would be overwhelmed with their number and variety if it were not for the basic fact that there are only three *kinds* of tricks and that all plays (and consequently all bids) are reduced to these three units of measure:

1. Honor-tricks, made with cards of high rank.
2. Low cards established from four-card or longer suits. They are called *long* cards.
3. Ruffs, obtained by ruffing (usually in the dummy) a losing card with an otherwise worthless trump.

At notrump bids there are only two kinds of tricks, honor and long-card. At trump bids the ruffer makes its appearance.

♠ A K Q 4 3 2	**N**	♠ 8 7 6 5
♡ A 5 3	**W　E**	♡ 6
◇ A K	**S**	◇ 6 5 3 2
♣ K Q		♣ 10 8 7 6

In this example, if spades are trumps West will win the following tricks: he will win honor-tricks with the ♠ A K Q, ♡ Ace and ◇ A K. He will lose a trick to the opponents' ♣ Ace but will then win another honor-trick with his remaining club. His two small hearts he will lead and trump with East's spades, creating ruffing tricks. Finally, when he has led his three high spades neither opponents can have another spade and the ♠ 4 3 2 will win.

If the bid is notrump, West may still win his seven tricks with high cards and he will still win his three long-cards in spades, but there will be no ruffers because there is no trump suit and the two small hearts he must lose to the opponents.

A player is thus equipped for attack or defense with three different weapons. Because each of these weapons is drastically different from the others, *each will require a specialized technique of handling during the bidding or play.*

It follows that all the rules, methods, and conventions of bidding and play are grouped around the three different kinds of tricks. The main object in the partnership language of bidding is to convey to partner information about honor strength and suit lengths. Accordingly, you have bidding conventions that show the honor strength of the hand; other conventions that indicate the length of suits; and a third type of convention that shows voids and singletons.

Scoring and the Objects of Scientific Bidding*

In bridge the bids are measured with tricks but paid for in points. *Points* are therefore the stakes for which we play in bridge and the final criterion of bidding strategy and methods.

The bid that will secure the greatest number of points is the *best final bid*. It does not matter whether those points are secured by scoring game or rubber at one's own bid or by scoring an equivalent penalty against the opponents. In fact, it is preferable, as a rule, to take the penalty rather than a game or rubber even when the expected penalty is slightly below the value of the game.

When the opponents have entered the bidding, the question of what bid in the partnership hands is the best depends entirely upon what the opponents could score at their own declaration. Your best contract, for instance, may easily be to sacrifice 500 points, if by so doing you can compel the opponents to give up their vulnerable game. The yardstick, therefore, by which the partnership's expected gain or loss is measured, is the point value of the contract which you can make, or the contract which the opponents can make against you. If you can score 120 points for making four spades, and the game which you can win is worth 300 points, your total gain at your own bid will be 420 points. If instead of bidding you double the opponents and defeat them 300 points, you have *lost* 120 points. If you defeat them 500 points, you have gained 80 points, for at your own bid you could have made only 420.

Thus the advice "watch the score" is of far less importance than the advice to watch for the mathematical realities *behind* the score sheet.

The equity values of games are as follows:

Any first game........................ 300 points

Any second game in succession (when opponents have no game).................. 400 points

Any third game........................ 500 points

---

* Here I can give only the sketchiest of descriptions of the all-important question of mathematics of scoring. (See Mathematics of Scoring in Book II.)

To these invisible equity values add the points for tricks, overtricks and honors, if any. For instance, if you make the first game at three notrump, your actual gain is 400 points—300 for the equity value and 100 for the three tricks.

Game and not rubber is the *strategic unit* in bidding and it is against the full game value that the enemy's bids are measured. Thus, the best final bid is selected not merely from the partnership but from the four hands around the table.

It follows that the mathematical ratios in premiums and penalties automatically determine *bidding aims.*

First Object: *Penalties* from opponents which are either equivalent to or greater than the points which could be scored at one's own bids. However, when the partnership side is vulnerable and opponents are not vulnerable, the chance of setting them at least three tricks should be accepted instead of a game (but not instead of a slam).

Second Object: *Slam premiums,* failing which, *a game.* If game is too distant, a part-score (worth roughly 160 points counting the trick value) should by no means be despised.

Third Object: *Sacrifice Bidding.* When neither a penalty nor a game at one's own bid seems likely, there still remains a powerful objective: to push the opponents to an unmakable contract or to force them to accept a penalty which cannot exceed and may be less than the trick score they could have made.

Underlying all objects of bidding we find the *Principle of Safety* requiring that no bid should be made that, under reasonable conditions, risks an excessive penalty. Safety in bidding is explained in Part II.

Play Is the Thing

Bidding and play are not two radically distinct departments of the game, as is commonly believed. In order to reach the decision that led to the *bid* of three notrump, for instance, I must *mentally* play out the hand at three notrump, using roughly the *same technique of play as though the dummy lay actually exposed before my eyes.*

It might be said that bidding is a *prediction* that a number

of tricks as predicted by the final bid will be made in actual
play. A good bidder is a good prophet.

Bidding, therefore, is *mental play* where the same kinds of
tricks are won or lost in the player's mind as with the exposed
dummy, so that each deal of the cards is played twice—the first
time during the bidding, but with abstract *ghost* tricks, and
the second time with their concrete counterpart, the physical
tricks.

But it must be remembered that the dummy is not yet visible
and that the bidder must piece together the imaginary dummy's
honor strength and various suit lengths from partner's or opponents' bids.

To help partner locate the missing pieces in the puzzle of
the combined hands is the object of partnership bidding.

From the foregoing, it is clear that an understanding of the
play of the hand is the beginning and the end of all bidding.
The better the player, the more precise his bidding.

CHAPTER THREE

BIDDING VALUATION

In order to sell a hand at the bridge auction for the best price in the constantly fluctuating market of bids and counterbids around the table, the player must know its trick-taking values.

The first thing a player does after picking up his hand is to take stock of the kind and the number of tricks that Chance has allotted to him. The honor and length-bidding values, which are more or less expected to reproduce themselves in the play as actual tricks, are called *winners* or bidding tricks.

Bidding valuation can be defined as the *count of expected winners and losers at a specified bid.*

After the player has appraised the value of his own hand he communicates the good or bad news to his partner, awaiting his reply. Until he hears from his partner (or opponents) there are many elements about his own hand of which he is either ignorant or uncertain. He does not know, for instance, the number of supporting trumps and the total honor strength of partner's hand. The inferences drawn from his partner's and opponents' bids will throw new light upon the winners and losers in the player's own hand. It will enable him to *revalue* his hand and begin the second stage of valuation, which is called Combined Valuation and which consists in counting the expected winners and losers at a specified bid in the *combined* hands.

The object of single valuation is to determine the total *net worth* of the player's own hand. The net worth of any hand is determined by *assuming that all the important cards outstanding against the player's hand are held by the opponents,* and therefore counting as *losers* any card or combination of cards that is not a sure or a probable winner. The worth of the following hand is five sure winners, leaving eight losers:

♠ K Q J 10 9 ♥ 7 5 2 ♦ A 5 3 ♣ 7 2

To avoid hopeless confusion, a player must first find out the net worth of his own hand. To this he may add values *already shown* by partner. He may then bid for only the number of tricks warranted by the known total value of the combined hands. If he bids on values he has merely *assumed* that his partner holds, it will result in duplication of bidding. Partner cannot be expected to know that his hand has already been bid for him; and, seeing these same values, will make further bids on them, forcing the combined hands to a contract beyond their reach.

The Three-Way Valuation of the Same Hand

The total number of tricks or winners in the same hand increases or decreases according to whether the trump bid is *the player's own,* or in *support* of partner's bid, or has been made by the opponents.

It follows that the hand must be valued in three ways, and according to two standards of value: The value in *attack* (when played at one's own or at partner's bid), and the value in *defense* (when played against the opponents' bid). The following deal dramatically illustrates the vast differences:

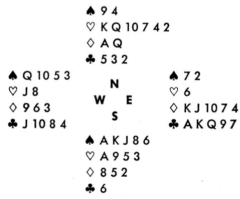

     ♠ 9 4
     ♥ K Q 10 7 4 2
     ♦ A Q
     ♣ 5 3 2

♠ Q 10 5 3   **N**   ♠ 7 2
♥ J 8   **W** **E** ♥ 6
♦ 9 6 3   **S**   ♦ K J 10 7 4
♣ J 10 8 4   ♣ A K Q 9 7

     ♠ A K J 8 6
     ♥ A 9 5 3
     ♦ 8 5 2
     ♣ 6

In this example South can make eight or nine tricks at his own spade bid. In support of his partner's heart bid there is a tremendous total of twelve tricks resulting in a slam—a significant lesson to selfish ones who always try to play their own hands. Against the opponents' club bid the value of the combined North-South hands suffers a terrific drop from a total of twelve tricks at hearts to a total of four tricks—the two top spades and the red Aces.

It seems almost as though the very spots on the faces of the cards were changed. Wall Street, in its wildest days of panic, does not approach such violent fluctuations of values as shown by a bridge hand every time the bidding shifts from a player to his partner's or opponents' hands and before the final bid closes the day.

The one type of winner whose value remains constant is the *honor-trick,* and this is the first aspect of bidding valuation that the bridge player must know or learn. Accordingly, we move on to honor-trick valuation in the next chapter.

CHAPTER FOUR

HONOR-TRICKS

Many honor combinations that are perfectly good winners at a partnership's own bids cease to exist when running the gantlet of the enemy's trump suit.

A sequence like A K Q J 10, *defensively speaking,* is worth only a "plus" more than A K 5 4 3. At your own bid the former suit will win five tricks and the latter but three or four. Against the opponents' trump contract the third lead of any side suit is likely to be trumped.

A *defensive* honor-trick or *defensive* winner is a card or combination of cards which may be expected to win a trick, even against the opponents' trump contract.* In defense, only the cream of honor-sequences is skimmed.

Not only Aces and Kings are counted defensively, but Queens, Jacks and even tens can be combined to form defensive combinations.

In the flux of constantly changing values of long and short suits, the defensive winners are the one relatively stable element. They are the cash, liquid assets of the hand, the gold standard of the Culbertson System. They furnish quick entries into partner's hand and at least a few always survive the worst distributional storms in the hands. This yardstick does even

---

* Throughout this book the term "honor-trick" is restricted to defensive winners. In speaking of honor-card valuation in attack (in declarer's or supporting hands) the term "honor-winner" will be used.

more. Since the two best top layers of the four suits are the
defensive tricks, it becomes possible to gauge at a glance the
approximate trick-winning expectancies not only against opponents' trump bids, but at partnership's own bids and at notrump. The Culbertson table of honor-tricks given on the
following page is standard and official with more than 30 million players throughout the world. It completely covers the
entire range of defensive honor values from an Ace-King-Queen
down to isolated Queens, Jacks and tens. Years of tests have
proved that it is simple and uncanny in its accuracy, while
remaining flexible.*

Except for Aces and King-Queens, honor-tricks are based on
the "finesse" value of honors, and all honor-trick values conform to the science of probabilities:

(1) The assumption that missing honors, if any, are held by
    the opponents and that their exact position is unknown.
(2) The assumption that the distribution of suits is not so
    freakish that honors are likely to be ruffed.

Accordingly, information disclosed during the bidding on
the position of outstanding honors and on suit lengths will
modify the defensive values of honors.

The Finesse Value of Honors

Most honor combinations depend on finesses for their definite values. For instance, A Q may take two tricks or it may
make but one trick, depending on the favorable or unfavorable *position* of the missing King, the chances of which are
roughly equal. It is worth, therefore, 1½ bidding tricks; K x
in a suit is worth ½ trick. A couple of K x's are worth one
"sure" trick, equivalent to one Ace or a K Q. The term "sure
trick" is used rather euphemistically, for there is only one thing
sure in bridge and that is that the losers must pay.

---

*It is important to remember that honor-trick valuation, unlike the 4–3–2–1
point-count, is designed as a double-edged weapon both for defensive valuation
(especially in penalty doubles) and for valuation at the partnership's own bids.

Culbertson Standard Table of Honor-Tricks

Defensive Winners Against Opponents' Bids

2 honor-tricks	1½ honor-tricks
A K in the same suit	A Q in the same suit
1 honor-trick	**½ honor-trick**
Ace alone or with others K Q in the same suit	K x (King with one or more lower cards in its suit, or K singleton*)
K J 10 in the same suit K x and K x⎫ or ⎬ in different suits K J and Q x⎭	Q J x in the same suit Q x and Q x in different suits

Plus Values

Two "plus values" = ½ honor-trick. Plus values are:

Any singleton or void. But not more than one singleton or void may be counted.

Queen in A K Q or in Q x (if not already counted as part of an honor-trick combination).

Jack held with a higher honor of the same suit (if not already counted as part of an honor-trick combination). But it is not advisable to count a plus value for the Jack in A K Q J or in Q J doubleton.

Thus:

A K Q is 2+ honor-tricks   A K Q and Q x = 2½ honor-tricks
K Q J is 1+ honor-trick   A J x and K Q J = 2½ honor-tricks
A J is 1+ honor-trick   A J x and K J x = 2 honor-tricks
K J is ½+ honor-trick   K J x and Q x = 1 honor-trick

The symbol "x" stands for any lower card of the same suit.

With all such finessable values the player must keep in mind the necessity of an entry in partner's hand. The A Q is worth 1½ honor-winners only if the bidding shows that partner's hand will have an entry.

Plus Values

A Queen with one or more small cards, or when backed up by the Ace and King of the same suit; sometimes a Jack when

---

* The honor value of a singleton King is reduced to a plus; but a plus value is regained for the singleton. A singleton or void in another suit should not be counted.

similarly supported; and such vague factors as "good distribution" or "hand solidity," are *plus values*. This important group of possible bidding tricks is situated between a near zero and a probable trick. I would be tempted to call the plus value a "quarter trick," but I have a horror of small mathematical fractions in bridge. They are usually so monstrously overprecise that they may become grossly inexact. Too weak to justify even the chance expectancy of a trick, the "plus" values when taken in the aggregate become very important. Two such plus values are worth *at least* ½ a trick, for in most cases I would rather have a couple of Queens than K x. Give me four plus values and I will undertake to win at least one and probably two tricks with them.

So in valuing your hand, whether for defense or for attack, do not overlook your plus values. A single plus value may in most cases be disregarded, but two or three plus values should be counted as ½ honor-trick, and three or four plus values should be counted as a full honor-trick. If you hold ♠ Q 6 5 2   ♡ 7   ♢ K Q J 3   ♣ A J 7 5, your four plus values bring the count of the hand up to three honor-tricks—enough for a bid!*

THE VALUE OF UNBALANCED DISTRIBUTION

For purposes of simplicity only, any singleton or void in the hand may be counted as a plus value.

Naturally a void does not "win a trick"; nor does a singleton, unless, by pure accident, it is a singleton honor. Bridge writers were for many years very strict in their injunction to the student: do not count a singleton as strength in your hand. Nearly all the early bridge authorities persisted in calling a

---

* The 4–3–2–1 point-count is in effect one trick for an Ace, ¾ of a trick for a King, ½ trick for a Queen and ¼ trick for a Jack. However, the "mathematical" precision of the count is an illusion unless it is corrected in individual hands. For instance, an A-K in the same suit, valued at 7 points (2 H.-T.), is worth considerably more than an Ace and a King in different suits, also valued at 7 points (1½ H.-T.). Q-x or the Q in the combination A-Q is valued at 2 points each; yet it is obvious that the former (a "plus" value) is worth considerably less than the latter (½ H.-T.). A J-x is not worth even ¼ of a trick; but in a combination such as A-J-x or K-J-x, the Jack is worth more than 1 point. Hence the importance of correction points to rectify the 4–3–2–1 valuation. In honor-trick valuation the plus values play the role of "correction points."

singleton a sign of *weakness* in declarer's hand, and in the late twenties a group of "authorities" produced this astounding advice: "With 4–4–4–1 or 5–4–3–1 hands, bid notrump! The singleton makes the hand *dangerously weak* for a suit-bid."

Yet a singleton or void is always a symptom of extra uncounted strength in the hand, both in attack and in defense. In defense it often leads to a ruff with an otherwise worthless trump—a clear gain of a trick. In attack, as the singleton or void will appear in hands of 4–4–4–1, 5–4–3–1, 6–3–3–1 or better distribution, it must always accompany some added length value in the hand.

Not to count the singleton or void in some way would lead to undervaluation, both defensively and in opening bids or responses. As a plus value, the worth of a singleton or void is properly expressed: somewhere between zero and a probable trick.

The Equivalence of Honor Values

Below this group of "plus" values, or intermediate values, there is still another group called the *minor intermediate* values, or "fillers." These fillers consist of isolated Jacks, tens and even nines.* They are too indefinite and variable to be counted even as remote tricks, and taken separately they are nuances. But their accumulated weight is of great importance and, together with "plus" values, accounts for the difference between a hand with "shape" to it and one that looks skinny.

For all practical purposes of bidding, Q J x is equivalent to K x of another suit and both are equivalent to an Ace or K Q; similarly, an Ace is equivalent to a K Q and together they are equivalent to an A K. The reader must be warned, however, that this basic principle of equivalence is not meant to be applied too rigidly and must be liberally strewn with "abouts" and "roughly."

There is another important reservation. As between two

---

* A nine, technically speaking, is not an honor-card but does in many cases become a ranking card. For instance, when the A, K, Q and J are eliminated by coverage, the nine will control the third round of the suit.

equivalent honor values, *the one containing more face cards is more valuable,* especially in attack.

In attack, the combination A J x (1+ honor-trick; two honor-cards) *may* win two tricks; but K Q J (also 1+ honor-trick, but three honor-cards) will *surely* win two tricks.

This advantage in face cards and other ranking cards is not so great with very long suits and freak distributions, but becomes tremendous with short-suited hands (usually distributed 4–3–3–3 or 4–4–3–2) that lead to four-card-suit bids or to no-trump bids. That is why you will find, in later chapters, that some hands fulfil the requirements for notrump bids only if they are bolstered by some minimum number of honor-cards.

Effect of Bidding Information

As the bidding is unfolded and the player learns more and more about the position and distribution of the unknown key cards and suit lengths, his original assumptions from the Standard Table will be confirmed or modified.

For instance:

♠ K x is worth ½ trick if the position of the ♠ Ace is unknown.

♠ K x is worth one trick if partner bids one spade.

♠ K x is worth *more* than ½ trick if spades are bid at the right.

♠ K x is worth *less* than ½ trick if spades are bid at the left.

♡ A K Q 9 2, originally valued as 2-plus defensive tricks, becomes worth three defensive tricks if partner repeatedly denies the suit.

♡ A K Q 9 2 will be worth at most two and perhaps only one defensive trick if partner vigorously supports the heart suit.

Practical Application of the Honor-Trick Table

The practical application of the Defensive Table comes up at every stage of bidding. It enables the player to estimate:

(1) The limit of the opponents' trump contract.
(2) The exact value of the hand when average, below or above average.

(3) The balance of strength in partner's and opponents' hands at any bid (Rule of Eight).

(4) The game, slam or no-game expectancy at partnership's own bids (Rule of Eight).

DEFENSIVE VALUATION OF OPPONENTS' TRUMP BIDS

To estimate the probable limits of the opponents' trump bid for the purposes of the penalty double and sacrifice overbids, the player adds his own honor-tricks to those shown by partner's bids (or assumed by inference to be held by partner). To these he adds the playing value of any trump tricks he holds (for instance, if the opponents are bidding spades ♠ Q J 10 3 are worth two tricks).

Subtracting the total from 13, he knows the approximate number of tricks available to the opponents.

THE AVERAGE HAND AND ITS WORTH

The following is a perfectly average hand from the standpoint of honors and honor-tricks:

♠ A 7 3   ♡ K Q 6 2   ◊ 10 9 5   ♣ J 8 4

It contains an Ace, a King, a Queen, a Jack and a ten, or exactly ¼ of all the honors. Because *too* average, such a hand is one of the rarest events in bridge. It is a purely abstract hand, something like the imaginary line of the Equator. Practically, however, this ideal average hand is of great value in serving as a *line of demarcation* between millions of hands below and above the average in honor strength. On the basis of the Table of Honor-Tricks, a perfectly average hand is worth 2 honor-tricks plus a Jack and ten, almost 2-plus tricks. Since all defensive honor values are interchangeable, we have a working equivalent of the average hand in terms of honor-tricks. A hand which is a Queen better than the average is worth about 2½ honor-tricks.

This basic assumption of the average hand furnishes the player with a remarkable yardstick for measuring the relative honor strength of any hand and, by means of the widely known Rule of Eight defined on page 43, will assist materially in estimating the game, slam or part-score expectancy of any bid.

The Rule of Eight

The defensive honor-tricks control the first two top leads or rounds and possibly the third lead of each of the four suits. Since each suit is worth from 2 to 2½ defensive honor-tricks, the deck contains about 8++++ honor-tricks, i.e., between 8 and 9 honor-tricks. As a rule, the materialization of the ninth trick will depend on a finesse. Hence, there are about 8½ honor-tricks which for simplicity's sake we shall call 8. This gives us the simple basis for one of the most valuable rules in Bridge—the Rule of Eight.

The total of defensive honor-tricks that will be won at any bid (trump or notrump) after each deal is about 8 out of the 13 tricks.

Aces will win 4 tricks, and the lower honors will win slightly less or more than 4 additional tricks. It does not matter how the honor values will combine, the final result will, as a rule, average around 8½ honor-tricks. Theoretically, it is possible to set up a hand that will show a count even of ten defensive honor-tricks. But it is sufficient for anyone to deal out a few hands and count the total of honor-tricks made after the play to notice that its number almost always varies between 8 and 9.

Since the number of defensive honor-tricks is constant, the more honor-tricks there are in one hand, the less there remain for the others, and vice versa. It is like four poker players starting a freeze-out game, each with an equal number of chips.

How to Determine the Balance of Strength in Partner's and Opponents' Hands at Any Bid

Add the minimum of honor-tricks shown by *partner's* various bids to the honor-tricks held in one's own hand; subtract from 8½; and you have the maximum number of honor-tricks held by the opponents.

A player calculates the honor strength in his partner's hand—even when partner has not bid—by adding to his own hand the defensive honor-tricks shown by *opponents'* bids.

The balance-of-strength principle is of great practical value in checking the weakness and strength of the enemy's and partner's hands. Take this situation:

North holds:
♠ Q 9 3
♡ K Q 8 4
◇ K 10 7
♣ Q J 6

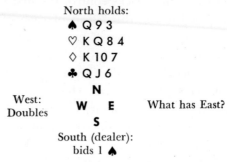

West:
Doubles

What has East?

South (dealer):
bids 1 ♠

South, for his bid, should be counted for 2½ honor-tricks or more. West, for his takeout double (page 257), has three honor-tricks. North has 2-plus honor-tricks, fortified by many *honor-cards*. South, West, and North have among them *at least eight* honor-tricks; East cannot have more than ½ honor-trick, and probably not that.

DETECTING A PSYCHIC

In the following situation, West-East, by applying the **Rule of Eight**, smoke out South's psychic bid with the greatest of ease.

North:
Passes

West:
Doubles

N
W   E
S

East holds:
♠ K J 7
♡ Q J 8
◇ K Q 9 6
♣ A J 10

South (dealer):
bids 1 N T

East passes for penalties, and South cannot have a good "out."

Many players have been astonished at the ease with which experts defend themselves against even the best-planned psychic bids. It seems that they calmly and unconcernedly wade through the psychic barrage as though the opponents were silent all the time. In fact, in many cases of awkward psychic bids the player is even helped. The answer to the question "How do the experts distinguish a bona fide bid from a psychic one?" is found in the application of the Rule of Eight and its principle of the balance of strength.

When to Expect a Blank in Partner's Hand

The Rule of Eight will help one to expect a blank in partner's hand and thus avoid a disastrous penalty.

North (dealer):
bids 1 ♠

West holds:

♠ A Q 7 4   **N**
♡ K 9 6 3   **W**   **E**   East passes
◇ A 8 5   **S**
♣ K 2

South
bids 2 N T

West takes no action, realizing that the North-South bidding indicates possession of five to six honor-tricks, and that East must therefore have a "bust."

The Rule of Eight in Slam Bidding

The Rule of Eight is also of great assistance in slam bidding.

For instance, partner opens the bidding with two hearts and you hold ♠ Q 7 6   ♡ Q J 6 3   ◇ K 9 5 2   ♣ K 4. You know the combined hands contain about 7½ honor-tricks and that the trump suit must be solid. At most there is one Ace out against the hand. A small slam must be certain.

Average Game and Slam Expectancies

The winning of tricks with low cards largely depends upon honors, which serve as indispensable stoppers and reëntries. It becomes, therefore, possible to use the Rule of Eight not only to measure the balance of defensive honor strength around the table, but to extend it for measuring quickly, and with fair accuracy, the chances for scoring one-odd, two-odd, game or slam, at trump *and* notrump. Of the thirteen tricks in the play of any hand, about eight are won with defensive honor-tricks and five with lower cards. This gives us a convenient yardstick of all trick values based roughly on the ratio of 8–5.

The following table of average expectancies is based on the count of defensive honor-tricks in combined hands; it shows when to expect a part-score, a game or even a slam. It applies both to trump and notrump bids, except that due to ruffing possibilities the expectancy at trump bids is usually one trick more than at notrump bids, even though the number of defensive honor-tricks is the same. This table cannot replace the more accurate valuation of hands by counting the honor- and low-card winners but it points out the approximate value of one's hand.

4–5–6 TABLE OF EXPECTANCIES

(Based on the Rule of 8)

4 **to 5 *bare* honor-tricks in combined hands.**
ONE-ODD ZONE. Hands containing about four honor-tricks lie on the line of demarcation between making one-odd and going down one. At suit-bids, one-odd can usually be made, and sometimes two-odd.

5 **to 5½ honor-tricks in combined hands.**
TWO-ODD ZONE. With only five honor-tricks, more than one notrump or two in a suit should usually not be bid unless the hands are well padded with plus values, or the suits "fit." However, a combined major suit of eight or nine cards may produce a game; and a notrump game should be bid if the partnership hands contain a solid or easily establishable five-card minor suit and stoppers in the other suits. (Possession of these values is revealed by proper bidding; see Chapter 18 on "The Intermediate Zone.")

6 **honor-tricks in combined hands.**
GAME ZONE. Six or more honor-tricks will, with rare exceptions, produce game in notrump or in a suit. The exception is six bare honor-tricks with no long suits or intermediate values. The word "bare" indicates a skinny type of hand with few intermediates or face cards.

6½-8 **honor-tricks in combined hands.**
SLAM ZONE. With 6½ or more honor-tricks, begin to think about a slam; but remember that it is still remote without freak distribution or long suits (see Slam Bidding). With eight honor-tricks you are in the Grand Slam Zone.

Illustrating the Table of Trick Expectancies

	Honor-Tricks
♠ A 7 3	1
♡ 10 5 4 2	
◇ Q J 9 6	½
♣ 10 7	

Honor-Tricks			Honor-Tricks
½	♠ Q J 6 2	♠ 10 5	
½	♡ K 8	♡ A Q 6 3	1½
	◇ 10 5 4	◇ 8 3 2	
1	♣ A 9 3 2	♣ K Q 6 4	1

N / W E / S

	Honor-Tricks
♠ K 9 8 4	½
♡ J 9 7	
◇ A K 7	2
♣ J 8 5	

It will be observed that East-West have a total of 4½ honor-tricks. They can make one notrump, winning four club tricks and three heart tricks after North and South have already taken four diamond tricks and the two high spades. In clubs, however, East-West can make two-odd, losing two spades and three diamonds.

Increase the combined honor-trick holding of East-West to five honor-tricks by adding the ◇ King or ◇ Q J x to West's hand and two notrump or three-odd in clubs can be made.

Again, strengthen the East-West hands by giving West the King of diamonds and the King of spades, making the combined holding six honor-tricks, and three notrump or four clubs will be produced. The notrump expectancy is therefore game.

Deduct ½ to 1 honor-trick from the combined total if holding 4–3–3–3 hand-pattern (especially for slam purposes) unless partner has shown a two-suiter.

Even with four honor-tricks a game at trump or notrump is not necessarily excluded with unusually favorable suit lengths. And in rare cases a game will not be made even with six or more honor-tricks. For instance,

♠ A K Q		♠ 9 6 2
♡ A K 6 3	W E	♡ 9 8 5 2
◇ A K 7 4		◇ 8 6 3
♣ Q 2		♣ 8 4 2

N / S

West is declarer at four hearts.

This hand is so hopelessly barren of distributional values that even the 6½ honor-tricks do not help much and yet a game should be bid, since nine times out of ten dummy will have something—a Queen, or a doubleton—that will make the game easy.

These average expectancies and zones are at best rough approximations and will lose all of their value if too blindly relied upon. The real value of the Rule of Eight is as a general guide, a compass indicating approximate location of strength around the table. The Rule of Eight has been a godsend to millions of average and advanced bridge players and its accuracy has been so remarkable that even expert players lean strongly upon it. As for the Standard Table of Honor-Tricks, it is, in my opinion, the indispensable measuring rod of all honor values in bidding, for masters and beginners alike. For it represents the train of subconscious reasoning of any expert.

CHAPTER FIVE

THE DISTRIBUTIONAL COUNT

Since counting in any form is a nuisance to most bridge players (and anathema to some) the Culbertson System expresses the requirements for nearly all bids and rebids in terms of honor-tricks or point-count. The need to count "winners" or "playing tricks" is thereby reduced to an absolute minimum.

The "4–5–6 Table" permits the player to judge roughly the bidding limits of the partnership hands, the Distributional Count permits him to *know*. Its accuracy is astonishing.

The value of the Distributional Count arises when a mere count of honor-tricks, and application of the 4–5–6 table, would not reveal trick-winning power that lies principally in distributional values.

For example:

♠ K Q J 4	**N**	♠ 8 7
♡ 8 7 6 3	**W E**	♡ K Q 9 5 4 2
◊ A Q J 5	**S**	◊ 7
♣ 5		♣ Q 8 6 2

West, who opens with one spade, has only the three honor-tricks he needs for a minimum bid. East, who responds two hearts, has scarcely the 1½ honor-tricks he needs for a two-over-one takeout. The combined total, 4½ honor-tricks, would not appear to put East-West in the game zone. Yet it is apparent that the East-West hands will win ten tricks at hearts, losing one spade, one heart and one club. Application of the Distributional Count will reveal this fact, for it will show that they have at least ten "winners" with hearts as trumps. Games on 4 or 4½ honor-tricks are admittedly rare, but when they are available it would be a shame to miss them.

The Distributional Count expresses in a few simple tables and formulas the entire process of bidding valuation. Many players at first find it difficult and troublesome to visualize the later play of the cards and thus determine the total of winners and losers in the hand. The Distributional Count expresses the same natural methods in a shorter way.

The Natural Method of Valuation
(Based on the Count of Winners)

One of the universal rules in contract bridge is that a player should pass, even with a fairly good hand, rather than bid one in a suit with less than two defensive honor-tricks. By distinguishing between the opening (primary) and the subsequent (secondary) bids, the player can often determine the minimum honor strength in partner's hand. Additional information on honor-trick strength in partner's hand is derived from various types of bids, such as forcing bids. In this manner the combined honor strength of partnership hands is unravelled by each partner in the course of bidding; and from this combined honor-trick strength, each partner draws his final conclusions as to the game, slam or penalty expectancies of the partnership hands.

This simple and flexible honor-trick method (based on the Culbertson honor-trick table) is not the only method of hand valuation. There is a second method based on a point-count of honors. But in addition to the honor-trick and point-count methods there exists a third method of valuation—a method which is more natural and superior to the first two, though more complicated. This is the method used by virtually all expert players, and by rank beginners who don't even know what an honor-trick or a point-count is.* This natural method is based on the count of *playing tricks* (winners) and is most accurately expressed by the Distributional Count. The honor-trick method is but a short-cut, a simplified version of the Distributional Count. The honor-trick method is remarkably

* Both the defensive trick concept and the point-count are relatively late arrivals on the stage of bridge. A great English player, Arnold Ward, was, I believe, the first to introduce the requirement of two sure tricks for opening bids.

accurate; however, as in the case of the point-count method (which is also quite accurate), it cannot entirely replace the natural method of bidding valuation. The reason is that this natural method mentally reproduces (and anticipates) the *actual play* of partnership hands at a given bid. That is why it always remains in the back of the mind of expert players. The expert players, as a rule, base their valuation on the convenient yardstick of the honor-trick method (or point-count); but in close situations, requiring greater precision, they fall back on the natural valuation of playing tricks.

What Is a Playing Trick?

Any card that is likely to win a trick is called a winner or a playing trick. A playing trick, therefore, can be an honor-card, a low card in a long suit, or a ruffer. There are two kinds of playing tricks: a *sure* winner, counted as one trick; and a *probable* winner, counted as ½ trick.

A card which is likely to lose a trick is called a loser and, as with winners, there are sure losers and probable losers. For instance, with A 3 2, the Ace is a sure winner; the trey and deuce are sure losers. With A Q 2, the Ace is a sure playing trick, the deuce is a sure loser, and the Queen is either a probable winner or a probable loser depending on whether your glands induce optimism or pessimism: either way it is worth ½ trick.

A Scale of Bids, Raises and Rebids
(Based on the Playing-Trick Count)

Generally speaking, the total number of playing tricks in any player's hand is announced by his bidding level. There are, for example, seven bidding levels from one heart to seven hearts. In the honor-trick method, different *kinds* of bids show a different number of honor-tricks from which we deduce the total playing-trick value of a player's hand. But in the playing-trick method we deduce directly the total number of playing tricks in the hand by the number of *times* (levels) the hand is bid. The exceptions occur after forcing bids, in sacrifice bidding.

or when the bidding level remains the same. For instance, if
the bidding is:

South	North
1 ♣	1 ◇
1 ♡	1 ♠

Each partner has bid twice, but since they remain at the bidding level of one, they do not *necessarily* show added playing-
trick values. In all other cases where a player carries the bid
to a higher level (thereby contracting to make more tricks) he
shows added playing-trick values.

*The total playing-trick worth of partnership hands is arrived
at by adding the playing tricks shown through partner's bids,
rebids or raises (bidding levels) to the playing tricks of one's
own hand.* The same process is used in the honor-trick method
(where the honor-trick values of the two hands are combined)
and in the point-count method (where the points for high-card
and low-card values are combined).

In the playing-trick method (the Distributional Count) the
playing tricks for each bidding level are shown by means of
a simple and logical scale of average expectancies. This is how
it works.

At any bid there are 13 winners distributed in the four
hands.* A bid of one-odd is a contract to win seven tricks out
of 13 for the partnership hands. Now, the *average* (not necessarily the most probable) way to distribute the 13 tricks around
the table is four tricks in one hand and three tricks in each
of the three remaining hands. $4 + 3 = 7 =$ one-odd. Four tricks,
therefore, is the average expectancy for any bid at the level of
one; and three tricks is the average expectancy in partner's
hand. These two average expectancies (the four and three) form
the basis of the playing-trick scale of bids, rebids, and raises
used consciously or subconsciously by all expert players and
by millions of others. In order to move to the level of two-odd
(a rebid) the declarer must have five playing tricks; six for
three-odd, seven for four-odd, etc. Similarly, in order to raise

---

* Actually, there are as a rule more than 13 winners, and out of this excess of
winners arises a fierce "struggle for survival" among the lowly cards of competing
suits seeking to be realized as actual tricks.

opener's one-bid to the level of two (eight tricks) the responder should have adequate trump support and about four playing tricks, which is one trick more than the first three tricks already included as an average expectancy in opener's bid of one.

Valuation of Declarer's Hand
(At Trump Bids)

Declarer, usually the opener, counts:

1. His honor-winners.
2. Long-cards in his trump and side suits.

He adds them together and that is the trick-winning value of his hand.

Honor combinations are counted at their full value, as explained below. Long-cards are counted in suits of four or more cards. The full explanation follows.

LONG-SUIT TRICKS

	In Trump Suit	In a Side Suit
A four-card length is worth...........	1 trick	½ trick
A five-card length is worth...........	2 tricks	1 trick
A six-card length is worth............	3 tricks	2 tricks
A seven-card length is worth.........	4 tricks	
An eight-card length is worth........	6 tricks	

DECLARER'S HONOR-WINNERS

The trump suit is usually controlled by declarer, who can draw out the opponents' trumps and remove the danger that the third round of a side suit will be ruffed. Therefore, A K Q, which is valued as only 2-plus honor-tricks against the opponents' trump bid because the Queen may be ruffed, becomes three full winners when declarer is estimating the tricks he will win at his own trump bid.

As a general rule, the total count of honor-winners in the hand can be determined quickly by using the table of defensive winners and adding the full honor value to the third round of a suit. For instance, A K Q or A Q J are worth respectively 3 and 2½ honor-winners. The exception is in the cases of four-card suits such as A K Q J (worth four winners) or Q J 10 9 (worth two winners). But with five-card or longer suits, such as A K Q J x x, the *fourth* honor-winner is not counted, to avoid duplication with length values (see below).

LONG-SUIT WINNERS

How to value the trump suit: Until partner has denied the suit (by refusing to raise) *every card over three in the trump suit is valued as one full winner.* Thus, the trump suit 9 7 6 4 3 2 is worth three winners for length; change the suit to A 7 6 4 3 2 and the value is four winners—the same three winners for length plus one for the Ace.

The long-suit values are based upon the mathematical expectancy that the remainders of a long suit will be divided more or less evenly. If I have A K 4 3 2, I expect that the eight other cards of the suit will be divided 3–3–2 in the other hands. If my partner supports the suit, he must have at least three of those cards. After I have led the Ace and King, only one card will remain with the opponents; I will lose a trick to it, but then I will have left two *long* cards, each worth a trick.

If partner supports the suit, declarer continues to count each long trump as one full winner. If partner fails to raise, declarer revises his valuation, considering the long trumps to be worth no more than long-cards in a side suit.

Solid trump sequences, however, are more easily valued by counting out the losers. Q J 10 9 8 2 is valued as four playing tricks, whether partner supports or not.

Valuation of Declarer's Side Lengths: Four-card, five-card and other *lengths* have a definite trick-taking value which must be added to the honor value of the suit and to the total winners of the hand. As with honors, the length winners are sure or probable, worth 1½ a trick.

As a rule, the side lengths are valued on the basis of the second most probable distribution.

Intermediate cards, the Jacks, tens and even nines, play an important rôle in the valuation of any suit. For instance, with ♡ K 5 3 2 as a side suit, I value the King as ½ trick and *the four-card length* as another ½ trick, giving me a total of one winner for the suit. If the suit were K 10 9 2 I would value it as 1½ winners, for the intermediates 10–9 are a mighty important factor.

It is important to remember that the establishable value of side suits depends entirely upon the strength and length of the trump suit. Unless the trump suit is strong and long enough to draw out the poisonous fangs of the opponents' trumps, the low cards of side lengths will be worthless. Their value appears when the opposing trumps disappear.

Valuation When Raising Partner's Trump Bid

When my partner makes an opening trump bid of one, I know he has at least four winners. When he makes an opening preemptive bid, or overcalls an opponent's bid, I will know approximately how many winners he has from the quantity of his bid.* By counting my supporting winners and adding them to his, I can judge how far my side can safely go.

As supporting hand, you count:

1. Trump tricks—high cards and long-cards in partner's suit, and ruffing winners due to short side suits.

2. Honor-winners in side suits.

3. Side suits (same as in declarer's hand). However, as a rule, count these only if you have four or more supporting trumps (see below).

Trump Winners

With four or more cards in the dummy the trumps have an intrinsic "promotional" value in addition to their ruffing value. They decrease the number of guards available to the opponents' honors, and make it easier for declarer to "drop" these honors. Hence, the "concealed" value of about ½ trick for a four-card trump length in the dummy.

Trump honors in the prospective dummy are also added tricks, since declarer usually assumes that they are held by the enemy. The J 10, the Queen and the King are valued some-

---

*It is unnecessary to count winners for opening one-bids and responses; a hand containing three honor-tricks and a biddable suit will automatically contain at least four winners (similarly for opening two-bids). But opening preëmptive bids, and defensive overcalls, require a definite number of winners depending on vulnerability and the bidding level.

what differently than usual. The J 10 and the Queen* are worth ½ trick each; the Q J and the King are worth practically the same as an Ace.

THE TRUMP LENGTH AND HONORS ARE VALUED:

Trumps	*Tricks*
Three cards or less....................................	0
Four cards	½
Five cards	1
Six cards	2
Add for Ace...	1
Add for King or Q J...................................	1
Add for Queen or J 10.................................	½*

RUFFING-TRICK TABLE

If the supporting hand has three or more trumps, and a short side suit—singleton, doubleton or void—he adds ruffing tricks according to the following table:

THE RUFFING TRICKS ARE VALUED:

	With 3 of Partner's Suit	*With 4 or More*
A doubleton (only two cards of a suit)	½ trick	1 trick
A singleton (only one card of a suit)	1 trick	2 tricks
A void (an absent suit)	2 tricks	3 tricks

When the hand contains two short suits, only one is counted—the shorter of the two.

This table reproduces the subconscious valuation of experts. It anticipates the actual play, assuming the best defensive play by the opponents. Assume that declarer has bid spades and dummy has ♠ J 9 8 and a singleton small heart. Even if declarer has three losers in hearts it is not probable that he will be able to ruff more than one of them, since the opponents, unless asleep at the switch, will lead trumps to prevent the second ruff. But if the dummy holds four trumps, declarer will usually be able to ruff at least two losing hearts even when the opponents lead trumps at every opportunity.

The table does not take into consideration a holding of two trumps with a short suit. (It is seldom that a player raises with only two trumps.) The

* The Queen is one full winner when partner has *rebid* the suit.

value of such a holding depends partly on how strongly declarer has bid his hand and his suit.

Two trumps and a void will usually be worth a full trick. Two trumps and a singleton may win a trick if declarer is strong enough to have made a jump rebid in his suit, but will be of little value opposite a weaker hand.

Suppose the bidding is:

SOUTH	WEST	NORTH	EAST
1 ♡	Pass	1 ♠	Pass
3 ♡	Pass		

North bids four hearts, holding:

| ♠ Q 9 7 6 4 2 | ♡ 9 3 | ◇ 6 | ♣ A 9 7 3 |

The singleton diamond is a positive value. It is more likely that South holds the ◇ Ace than that either opponent holds it; it is hardly to be expected that the opponents will open trumps and be able to lead them twice before South can ruff a diamond. If South's rebid had been merely two hearts, North would pass and the question of the value of the diamond singleton would never arise.

HONOR-WINNERS IN THE SUPPORTING HAND

In ordinary cases the supporting hand counts honor-winners at their full value, as the declarer does. But when declarer has shown a very long trump suit, as by making a preëmptive bid, the supporting hand should count his honors at their defensive value only.

When declarer has a very long trump suit, he will have short side suits. Suppose the responding hand holds ♡ Q J 10. His partner opened with three spades, meaning that in all likelihood he has seven spades. This leaves only six cards for him to hold in the other three suits together, and probably no more than two of them are hearts. If declarer has two small hearts, what does he care whether the responding hand has ♡ 4 3 2 or ♡ Q J 10? He must lose exactly two tricks either way. Counting his ♡ Q J 10 at their full value, the supporting hand would call them one full winner. He will be better off to call them ½ winner; even that may at times be too high.

WHEN SIDE LENGTHS ARE NOT COUNTED

Neither the declarer nor the supporting hand should count a side length that has been bid by an opponent.

The supporting hand should not count side lengths in any of the following additional cases:

1. When declarer has opened with a preëmptive bid, or has shown a two-suiter. In such cases, declarer will usually be very short (singletons or doubletons) in the side suits. His short side suits will be gobbled up by opposing honor-tricks before a long suit in dummy can be established and discards taken.

2. *As a rule, the supporting hand counts his side lengths only when he has four or more trumps.*

Suppose South opens with one spade and North holds:

♠ 10 8 7 6 5   ♡ A 6   ◇ 9 7 6 5 3   ♣ 2

The diamond suit is worth at least one trick for length. The combined hands should have enough trumps to draw the opposing trumps, and still leave two or three trumps in dummy. With these as stoppers in hearts and clubs, and as entries to lead and establish diamonds, South should be able to win at least one long-suit trick in diamonds. North counts 5 supporting winners: 1 for spade length, 1 for the ♡ Ace, 2 for the singleton club and 1 for diamond length.

If the side suit is solid or easily establishable (as A K 5 3 2 or Q J 10 9 5), *and if declarer has rebid his suit,* the supporting hand should count his side lengths even if he has only three trumps.

After bidding like this:

South	West	North	East
1 ♡	Pass	2 ◇	Pass
3 ♡			

North would be justified in counting 4½ winners (2½ for honors, 2 for length) for his diamond suit:

♠ 7 2   ♡ K 7 5   ◇ A K J 7 5 2   ♣ 6 3

South's jump rebid in the unsupported heart suit makes it clear that he has enough hearts to draw the opposing trumps, ruff a round of diamonds if necessary, and reënter dummy with the ♡ King to cash the remaining diamonds.

Counting 1 winner for the ♡ King, ½ for a doubleton with three trumps, and 4½ in diamonds, North has 6 winners. South, for his jump rebid, should have at least 7. The total of 13 does not necessarily mean a grand slam, or even a small slam, because North does not know that the required controls are present (see Slam Bidding); but North does know that the combined hands have enough winners to be in the slam zone. He makes a slam try by bidding five hearts (or by using an artificial slam convention, as described in Chapter 27).

REVALUATION OF THE HAND

A player values his hand first at his own bid; then, after his partner responds, he revalues it in support of partner's bid. His scale of values depends on the circumstances: At his own bid he counts honors, trump length and side lengths, but does not count ruffing values. As the supporting hand he counts ruffing values and, in most cases, side lengths.

CHAPTER SIX

PARTNERSHIP LANGUAGE OF INFERENCES

The structure of the language of bids is quite simple. In order to combine 26 cards for the best bid, partners must, as a rule, exchange three kinds of information—on the total *number* of tricks, on the minimum number of honor or defensive tricks, and on distribution of suits in the hands.

Inferences to show quantity, or the total of low-card and honor-tricks in the hand (playing tricks) are deduced by each partner from the number of *times* the bidding is raised to a higher level.

Inferences to show quality, or the total of honor-tricks in the hand, are drawn from differences in the *kind* of bid made, and from the bidding level. According to the kind of bid made, an opening bid, a simple takeout, a forcing takeout, a defensive overcall, a takeout double and so forth, and to the bidding level (one-odd, two-odd, three-odd, etc.) partners can determine the honor-tricks held by their side.

Inferences to show distribution (lengths of suits in the hand) are conveyed by almost any bid, side by side with quality and quantity inferences. The different trump lengths in declarer's hands, starting with four-card trump suits and on, will be shown by trump rebids and special bids such as opening bids of three or higher; the trump length and strength in the raising hand is shown or denied by raises or suit takeouts.

These three streams of inferences are generally found in a single bid, with the emphasis laid now on quantity, now on quality or distribution. For instance, an opening bid of one spade, when logically decoded, tells partner in two words, "One spade," an intricate story: 1. *Quantity*—I have at least four winners; 2. *Quality*—Among my winners I have at least 2½ honor-tricks; 3. *Distribution*—I have a minimum length of four spades.

Next, the language of bids tells much more through the silent language of indirect inferences in bridge, which are so called because their premise is not what partner actually bids, but what he fails to bid, and why. For example, I bid "One spade" and you raise my bid to "Two spades." Because you did not raise it to three or four spades; because you did not make any number of other bids, I deduce that you hold something like this:

♠ J x x x   ♥ x x   ♦ Q J x x   ♣ K x x

The Principle of Economy of Bids: Practically the entire structure of partnership language and strategy springs from the principle of Economy of Bids. Economy of Bids means economy of *time*. It is astonishing how much information can be packed into a single bid. The two partners may hold any one of millions of possible hands and yet, with the logic of inferences as clues, they join the two unknown hands for the precise bid.

The player must carefully avoid wasting precious rounds and, by thinking ahead, must so arrange his bidding sequence as to give and obtain the maximum of information at the lowest possible level.

Improper selection of opening bids and superfluous overcrowding of bids will rapidly exhaust the player's available rounds, compelling him to land for the final bid under zero ceiling in the fog of wild guessing. For example, with:

♠ A Q J 8		♠ 10 7
♥ 6	**N**	♥ A Q 9 5
♦ A Q 7 3	**W E**	♦ 10 6 2
♣ J 9 8 2	**S**	♣ K Q 6 4

Typical wasteful, jumpy bidding might go as follows:

WEST	EAST
1 ♠	2 ♡
3 ◊	4 ♣
?	

and only with excellent luck will any game contract be made. But orderly bidding would proceed to the logical contract as follows:

WEST	EAST
1 ◊	1 ♡
1 ♠	2 ♣
3 ♣	3 N T

The Approach Method

The principle of Economy of Bids leads to one of the most important practical applications in the strategy of bidding— the Approach Method.

In most cases an opening suit-bid of one will be the best preliminary description of the hand, permitting the partnership bidding to develop in a safe, easy and orderly manner, with all suits and notrump reserved as possibilities.

The only important exception to this rule is a range of hands containing exactly 3½ to 4 honor-tricks and 4–3–3–3 distribution or its practical equivalent. Here the opening notrump can do no harm. In fact, it becomes quite valuable as a *limit* bid.

The Limit-Bid Principle

Practically every bid carries with it the information that that particular hand has a certain *minimum* of honor strength and suit lengths. These *minimum requirements* as to honor strength or length of suits will vary greatly according to the particular kind of bid as recognized by its particular bidding level and position. You can jump your partner's opening three-notrump bid directly to six notrump if you hold two honor-tricks; but you cannot raise your partner's opening four-spade bid to six spades even with four honor-tricks. It all depends on the agreed *minimums* which are attached to every bid.

The Principle of Maximum Limits: It is also possible to limit the *maximum* of the hand and thus render the bidding more precise and at the same time more simple. These minimum-maximum limits of each bid form a logical series of inferences.

For instance:

SOUTH	NORTH
1 ♡	2 ◇ or 3 ♡ or 3 ◇

Any one of North's bids is forcing, but the two-diamond bid is forcing for only one round while the three-heart and three-diamond bids are forcing to game. The two-diamond bid shows a minimum of two honor-tricks, plus some distributional values, as does the three-heart bid, while the minimum of the three-diamond bid is 3½ honor-tricks plus good distributional values. The two-diamond bid has a top limit of about 3½ honor-tricks plus, and the three-heart bid is unlikely to exceed three honor-tricks, while the game-forcing three-diamond bid may contain every honor-trick in the deck that you do not hold yourself.

By bidding either two diamonds or three hearts, North gives his partner definite assurance that he is *not strong enough* to make a stronger bid such as three diamonds.

A bid is not only limited from the standpoint of honor strength, and sometimes suit lengths, but whenever possible the bid is restricted to one or two specific types of hand-patterns. Thus, notrump bids and responses, negative or strong, evoke a pattern of 4–3–3–3 or 4–4–3–2 in partner's mind; the suit response, especially when persistent, evokes the image of an unbalanced pattern, with trump length and a singleton lurking somewhere.

Inferences from Partnership Strategy

The most natural distinction between the various bidding situations is according to whether the player has *opened* the bidding, *responded* to partner's opening bid or is *defending* against opponents' opening bid.

The opening bid announces a hand which is above "average" either in strength or in length and usually in both. It announces the type of hand that is equally ready for attack (at the partnership's own bids) or for defense against the opponents' bids. The opening bid contains about three honor-tricks, and often more, which usually precludes any game for the opponents.

The responding hand can lean rather heavily upon the better-than-average strength shown by his partner. With as little as one honor-trick or some semblance of shape in the hand he can venture into the open. Two and one-half honor-tricks look quite promising; and three honor-tricks (provided the hands fit) ought to bring the game down always, with a slam not far off.

The defending hand has already heard the bad news. His strategy is dominated by the fact that the opponents have initiated the attack, presumably showing a fairly strong hand. The demon of penalty is at the heels of every bid he may make. But, although hopes for slams and games in minor suits are at the wrong end of the binoculars, the chances of major-suit and notrump games, especially the former, are by no means shut out.

In some cases the same strategical object will require a different kind of technique to interpret it. With

♠ —   ♡ A Q J 10   ◇ K Q J 10 8   ♣ A K Q 7

you make a forcing two-bid if you are the opening hand; you achieve the same purpose if you are the responding hand after your partner opened the bidding by jumping to three diamonds; if you are the defending hand against the opponents' spade bid you will bid over the opponents' one spade, *two spades* which is also forcing. The object in all three cases is the same—to show a very powerful hand. The technique and the bidding level differ.

It is only fitting that the most important bid of all—the penalty bid—has no specially assigned bidding level. It operates at every level, balancing the weight of all the other bids put together.

The inclusion of the penalty double completes the description of the beautifully logical instrument of bidding on which the player plays. Its scales are made up from various bidding levels. Its "octaves" are the bidding zones. Its notes are the bids which produce a different pitch of inferences as they strike this or that bidding level. Finally, the intensity of its tones and overtones is regulated by the levers of a few basic strategical conceptions—the Approach Principle, the Forcing Principle, minimum and shutout bids, and the penalty double.

CHAPTER SEVEN

OPENING
NOTRUMP BIDS

Notrump and trump bids, though in some respects similar, have several basic points of difference. Accordingly the requirements, responses and strategy of notrump are its own. And even valuation, though primarily a matter of defensive honor-tricks, must be considerably modified.

The main advantages of notrump are: one trick less for game; freedom from the plague of bad trump breaks; better promotion of Kings, Queens, Jacks and tens.

The disadvantages of notrump include: suppression of a great number of better-fitting game and slam trump bids due to the loss of bidding time; the inherent uncertainty of notrump, with the constant danger that an opposing suit of any length, if insecurely stopped, may be run against it; the absence of a number of trick-saving plays available in the more flexible trump bids.

The worst feature of the notrump has always been a contradiction in its very terms. If the opening notrump is weak, it serves as an effective shutout bid at the low level of one, but it then risks serious loss, when vulnerable,* through the devastating effects of the penalty double. If the opening notrump is strong, it acts as a naïve warning to the opponents not to commit suicide by overcalling.

There exists, however, a group of very important hands in

---

* See page 93 for optional non-vulnerable notrump.

which the opening notrump retains all of its advantages and eliminates most of its faults.

These hands, while not so strong that the opponents can be sure their case is hopeless, are not so weak that the penalty double is greatly to be feared. They are hands whose distribution is so sterile at trump bids that the cheaper notrump contract usually offers the best chance of game. And they are hands that might create bidding problems if the opening bid were one of a suit:

♠ Q 6 3   ♡ A Q 7 5   ◇ K Q 6   ♣ A 10 6

Suppose you bid one heart on this hand. If your partner's response is one notrump, you will be a little too strong to pass and a little too weak for a raise to two notrump (page 196). If your partner's response is one spade, you will be a little too strong for a rebid of one notrump or a single raise to two spades, and a little too weak for a jump rebid of two notrump.

By opening with one notrump, the most precise of all bids in bridge, you avoid these difficulties by informing your partner, in one bid, of both your strength and your distribution.

Opening One-Notrump Requirements

Open with one notrump, vulnerable or not vulnerable, only if holding: *A minimum of 3½ and a maximum of 4+ honor-tricks; stoppers in at least three suits, and preferably some honor-card in every suit; 4–3–3–3 distribution or its practical equivalent (a balanced hand with no doubleton weaker than Q x).*

The requirement of 3½ to 4+ honor-tricks must be strictly adhered to. The Culbertson 4–3–2–1 point requirements are 16–18 points. The following two hands show, respectively, the minimum and the maximum one notrump:

♠ A J 5   ♡ A 7 4   ◇ K J 6 3   ♣ K 3 2   (Minimum)
♠ A K 8   ♡ A Q 6   ◇ K 9 2   ♣ Q 7 5 4   (Maximum)

THE INFLUENCE OF HONOR-CARDS

The value of intermediate cards (fillers) such as Jacks, tens and even nines, is greater at notrump than at trump bids because these cards often control the third or fourth round and win tricks whereas at trump bids they would be ruffed.

The honor-trick requirement of 3½ to 4+ is based upon the expectancy that 3½ honor-tricks will be made up of six or seven honor-cards, as it usually is. A hand with 3½ *bare* honor-tricks is not strong enough for the opening bid of one no-trump; it is better to start with a suit-bid. *To bid one notrump on 3½ honor-tricks, you should have six or more honor-cards.*

♠ A 6 3	♡ A Q 7	◊ 7 5 4	♣ A 8 7 5	Bid one club
♠ K Q 6	♡ K 5 2	◊ A 7 6 3	♣ K Q 5	Bid one notrump
♠ A 7 6 5	♡ A 8 4	◊ A 6 2	♣ A 9 6	Bid one notrump*

A hand with four honor-tricks is best shown by a one-notrump bid even if, as in the case shown, there are only four honor-cards.

STOPPERS

Strictly speaking, a stopper is A x, K x, Q x x or J x x x—an honor that the opponents cannot drop by straight leads. The fact is, however, that a guarded King or Queen may be lost if the opponents can lead through it, and that there is little practical difference between Q x x and Q x or J x x, though the latter combinations are generally termed "partial stoppers."

A holding of J x x becomes a sure stopper if partner has Q x, K x, or 10 x x x. Likewise Q x is a stopper if partner has J x x. These are "combined stoppers." If a player waits to bid notrump until he has a sure stopper in every suit, he will lose many notrump games in which the combined hands stop a suit which neither of them singly can stop.

The holding of four small cards in a suit, though not a stopper at all, is immeasurably superior to three small cards and better than 10 x x. While this holding will not win a trick, it reduces the likelihood that an opponent has a long suit to run. Even better is 10 x x x.

It is not desirable to make an opening one-notrump bid with two suits unprotected, but a player should not hesitate to bid one notrump on such hands as:

1.	♠ 8 6 4 2	♡ Q J 6	◊ A K 7	♣ A Q 5
2.	♠ A 10 9 4	♡ J 5 2	◊ A Q 5	♣ A J 7

---

* With point-count valuation, four Aces in one hand are worth 1 additional point.

THE QUESTION OF BIDDABLE SUITS

Even if the hand has a four-card major suit, the notrump and not the suit should be preferred when the honor-trick and distributional nature of the hand are correct. Bid one notrump with

| ♠ A Q 10 9 | ♡ K 7 4 | ♢ Q J 3 | ♣ A 7 5 |

This is one of the few cases in our system where an opening suit-bid of one is disdained in favor of notrump. The system of responses to one notrump will usually make it possible to reach the major-suit contract if that would be a better spot to play for game. There are rare cases in which a preferable major-suit contract may be missed but these are greatly outweighed by the advantage of showing the hand precisely by the first notrump bid.

One notrump is not the preferred bid, however, in a hand containing a five-card major suit; or two four-card major suits; or a four-card major consisting of 100 honors.

4–4–3–2 AND 5–3–3–2 DISTRIBUTION

A doubleton suit consisting of a singly guarded honor, as Q x or K x; or of a tenace position such as A J or A 10, greatly increases in value if the opening lead comes toward it.

A doubleton K x or K J is not even a sure stopper unless the opening lead is made up to the King. A lead up to A J or A 10 makes it a double stopper if partner holds 10 x x or J x x respectively, or even 9 x x x; if the opponents can lead *through* A J or A 10 in such cases, the Ace will usually be the only stopper in the suit.

A doubleton Q x profits equally from having the lead come to it. If dummy has A x x, the Queen becomes a sure second stopper. If dummy has K x x, the lead makes the Queen a trick if the leader holds the Ace.

Hands containing such doubletons, provided the honor-trick holding is adequate and the long-suit strength is not concentrated in major suits, are good opening notrump bids. For example:

1.	♠ J 10 6 5	♡ A Q 3	♢ A J	♣ K J 8 7
2.	♠ Q 6	♡ A J 7	♢ A Q 5	♣ K 10 8 6 3
3.	♠ Q J 4	♡ J 10 3	♢ A K Q 5 2	♣ K 6

From the standpoint of the responding hand, it does not often make much difference whether the minimum suit holding in the opening hand is three small cards, or a doubleton as good as Q x. Either is adequate trump support for a five-card suit, if the responding hand chooses to insist on playing for game in a strong major. If the responding hand decides to risk a notrump game largely because he has a six-card suit such as K Q x x x x, he knows he will find at worst A x, or three cards which may be 10 x x or J x x. The chance of winning at least five tricks in the suit is good enough in either case to warrant the gamble.

OPENING NOTRUMP BIDS ON OTHER DISTRIBUTIONS

Occasionally, for psychological reasons of "changing pace" or when a strong minor-suit holding makes it apparent that three notrump will be the most likely contract if the hand reaches game, one notrump should be bid on a hand distributed 6–3–2–2 or 5–4–2–2.

In the case of the 6–3–2–2 hand, the long suit must be a strong minor—one that can probably be established without the loss of more than one trick. For example:

♠ Q 8 4   ♥ K 7   ♦ A Q J 9 8 3   ♣ A 10

One notrump should be bid on a 5–4–2–2 hand only when both long suits are minors:

♠ Q 6   ♥ K 5   ♦ A Q 7 6   ♣ A Q 8 5 3

Responses to an Opening One Notrump

The responding hand to an opening notrump bid is in a position almost unique in bidding situations. He knows precisely what his partner has. He can dictate the final contract. He is the captain of the hand from that time on, unless, by chance, the partnership gets into the slam zone.

The responding hand may draw the following inferences from his partner's opening one notrump:

1. The opener has at least 3½ honor-tricks. He may have 4+ honor-tricks but he does not have more.

2. The opener has at least three cards in every suit. (The possibility that the opener may have a doubleton is ignored, since a strong doubleton is usually equivalent to a weak three-card holding.)

3. The opener has at least one honor-card in any suit in which the responder may need it. (This is so nearly certain that the rare exceptions may be disregarded.)

From these inferences the responder may proceed to the following conclusions:

1. The responder can gauge the game or no-game expectancy on the basis of the Rule of Eight. With 2 honor-tricks he knows game is possible, with 2½ honor-tricks he knows it is probable, for the combined total must be 6.

2. If the responder has a playable five-card or longer suit, he will find adequate support for it in his partner's hand, and there is a 68% chance that the suit will produce two length winners.

3. The value of a King, Queen or Jack in the responder's hand is greatly increased when he knows his partner must hold at least one honor in that suit. For instance, Q x is only a plus value when partner's hand is unknown, but opposite an Ace it becomes ½ trick—as good as a King which is not known to be opposite an Ace—and should it be known that partner holds A K of that suit, *the Queen is equal to an Ace.*

THE EFFECT OF DISTRIBUTION

When both hands are of balanced distribution and one of them is 4–3–3–3, there is usually no extra trick available for trump bids. This is one of the basic principles of the author's theory of distribution. It is the exact reverse and complement of the Approach Principle. Boiled down, it comes to this:

With unbalanced distribution and a major suit, prefer a major-suit game to a notrump game.

With unbalanced distribution and a minor suit, bid the minor, but ordinarily play at notrump, if a game is to be reached.

With balanced distribution, prefer the notrump game in either case.

To illustrate: the opening bid was one notrump and the responder holds:

♠ A Q 5 4 2   ♡ 6   ◇ K 10 6 4   ♣ 6 4 2

He counts two long-cards in spades, and adds two for the spade A Q and 1½ for the diamond suit: total 5½. Counting his partner for four winners, he sees a combined total of 9½, enough to justify bidding four spades. Having an unbalanced pattern, he will arrange his responses so as to arrive at a four-spade contract.

Holding ♠ A Q 5 4 2   ♡ 6 3   ◇ K 10 6 5   ♣ 8 7 he again counts 5½ winners, but fears the quick loss of four tricks. Unless partner can raise spades, he will permit the hand to be played at three notrump.

In each case he will reach the most likely game if the opening hand is on the order of:

♠ K 8 3   ♡ Q J 9 4   ◇ A Q 7   ♣ K J 10

THE PASS

A hand with only 1½ bare honor-tricks, such as A-Q-x, and no six-card or longer suit, will not as a rule produce game opposite an opening one-notrump bid, but if the honor-cards count up to 8 or 9 points (for example, K-Q-x and K-x, or three Kings) then a single raise *is* in order. Examples of hands on which partner's notrump bid should be passed:

♠ A 6 3	♠ K Q 8 5 3	♠ 6	♠ 10 3
♡ 8 5 3 2	♡ 6 5	♡ K J 6 3	♡ 7 5
◇ K 8 5	◇ 8 6 4 2	◇ Q 10 7 4 2	◇ Q 9 7 6 5 3
♣ 9 4 2	♣ 8 3	♣ 8 7 4	♣ 6 4 3

THE SINGLE RAISE (POINT-COUNT, 8–9 POINTS)

Hands on which a single raise may be given to partner's one-notrump bid range in strength from 1½ to 2+ honor-tricks and may include suit lengths of five, six or seven cards.

Following are the types of hand on which a single raise should be given:

(a) 1½ to 2 honor-tricks, with strength in at least two suits.

A hand with two or more honor-tricks will usually include at least three or four honor-cards. With less than 1½ plus honor-tricks and no five-card suit, it is better to pass:

♠ 6 5   ♡ A K 7   ◇ 9 7 6 3   ♣ 8 5 4 2   Pass

or

♠ A 7 3   ♡ Q 6 3 2   ◇ 8 6   ♣ J 5 4 3   Pass

However, the presence of a stopper in another suit, or a five-card suit, will bring the hand up to the required strength; and with 2+ honor-tricks, even bare ones, the raise is required. Examples of sound raises:

♠ 6 5	♠ 6 5	♠ 6 3 2	♠ J 6 4
♡ A K 7	♡ A K 7 6 3	♡ A Q 6	♡ A J 7
◊ J 10 4 3	◊ 9 7 6	◊ 6 5 4	◊ K 3 2
♣ 8 5 4 2	♣ 8 7 3	♣ K 8 4 2	♣ 7 6 5 2

(b) 1½ honor-tricks when the strength is divided among three suits and is composed of five or six honor-cards.

The following hands count only 1½+ honor-tricks but are excellent raises to two notrump:

♠ K 10 3	♡ 9 8 5 4	◊ 7 3	♣ A J 7 2
♠ Q 10 5	♡ Q 7 6 3	◊ Q 6 2	♣ K 9 6

(c) 1½ honor-tricks in the hand, with a strong six-card suit, justify a raise.

The following hand is a poor takeout of two diamonds but an excellent raise from one notrump to two because you have a six-card suit headed by two honors.

♠ 9 4	♡ 6 5	◊ A Q 8 7 6 3	♣ 10 9 4

The Raise from One Notrump to Three Notrump

The double raise of partner's opening one-notrump bid follows the same principles as the single raise, requiring in each case ½ to 1 additional honor-trick. Summarized, the requirements for a raise to three notrump are:

(a) *2½ honor-tricks in three suits.* Jump to three notrump with (at least 10 points):

♠ A Q 7	♡ 9 4 2	◊ K Q 8 3	♣ 8 6 4
♠ Q J 6	♡ K Q 7 4	◊ K Q 8 5	♣ 8 2
♠ A K Q	♡ 10 8 4 3	◊ 10 6 2	♣ Q 8 7

(b) *2 honor-tricks* if the hand contains a six-card minor suit headed by ½ honor-trick or more.

Jump to three notrump with

♠ A 6	♡ 9 8 5	◊ K 8 7 6 3 2	♣ K 8

With such a hand, there is no sense in even mentioning a five- or six-card suit. When a hand justifies a raise, it should be given.

This is one of the most attractive features in our theory of distributional notrumps, for experience tells us that thousands of hands are butchered when apparently no one is to blame, the real reason being failure to understand distributional values. Hence, the apparently insane jumps to three notrump with solid major suits.

♠ A K Q J 6   ♡ 8 7 2   ◇ 9 5 3   ♣ 7 2

Five sure winners at notrump; partner has four. Do not bid spades, jump partner to three notrump.

The jump raise from one notrump to three is made on balanced hands with short suits. Unbalanced hands, especially those with five-card or longer suits, are better shown by a forcing suit takeout. When partner may have four honor-tricks, a hand with three honor-tricks and a good suit must put one in mind of a slam.

Suit Takeouts

A simple (non-jump) suit takeout of partner's opening one notrump may be made to offer a choice between a trump and notrump game, or to get out of a dangerous notrump contract into a safer trump contract. A forcing suit takeout (jump from one to three) announces a sure game and, in many cases, possibility of a slam. A direct jump to four of a major suit is a limit bid announcing that though the combined hands seem to have enough winners for game, they do not have enough honor-tricks for a slam; the opener is required to pass this response.

The Takeout of Two in a Suit

The simple suit takeout of partner's one-notrump bid, like a takeout of a suit-bid, is forcing for one round. Like any other one-round-forcing response, it does not require the responder to bid again when his turn, and it is not necessary that the bidding be carried on to game.

The suit takeout of two ranges in strength from a weak hand with perhaps only ½ honor-trick and a six-card suit up to a strong hand with as many as 2½ honor-tricks and a five-card suit.

The takeout is seldom made in a major suit without at least a five-card suit. The hand should contain 1½ to 2 honor-tricks; with 1½ bare honor-tricks it is better to pass one notrump, especially with balanced distribution.

Respond two spades with ♠ Q 10 8 6 5   ♡ 6 3   ◇ A J 7 5   ♣ 9 7. If partner can raise, a chance may be taken on game at four spades. If partner must bid two notrump, game is unlikely and it is better to pass.

Pass the one-notrump bid with ♠ A Q 6 5 3   ♡ 6 5 4   ◇ 9 4   ♣ 6 5 3.

Bid two hearts with ♠ 8 2   ♡ K J 10 8 5   ◇ K 5 3   ♣ Q 7 6, and if partner raises hearts, bid four; but if partner rebids two notrump, raise him to three notrump.

A four-card major may be bid when the hand contains two four-card majors:

Respond two hearts on ♠ A 10 6 3   ♡ K Q 8 5   ◇ Q 7   ♣ 8 5 2. The lower-ranking suit is bid so that partner may show a four-card spade suit if he has one; he might not bid a four-card heart suit over a two-spade response. If he can bid spades or raise hearts, the game should be bid in that suit. If his rebid is two notrump, it should be raised to three because the responding hand has the values required for a raise.

Except with freakish distributions, the only point to a minor-suit takeout is an effort to get into a major-suit game if one is available. Therefore a minor-suit takeout almost always implies four cards in at least one of the major suits.

Respond two diamonds with ♠ 10 9 6 3   ♡ J 6 2   ◇ A K 8 5 4   ♣ 7.

A four-card minor suit may be bid, even a very weak one:

♠ K 6 5 3   ♡ A 7 6 2   ◇ 5   ♣ Q 5 3 2   Respond two clubs. Because of the singleton diamond and absence of fillers in the hand, game at notrump is doubtful; while if the opener can rebid in a four-card major, there should be a game in the suit.

Whether his suit is a major or a minor, the responder's final decision on game or no game will be made far easier if he applies the Count of Winners (Chapter 5). The opening no-trump hand, with its 3½ to 4+ honor-tricks, will ordinarily produce 4 to 5 winners. Therefore the responding hand should decide on a major-suit game, even when his honor-trick holding seems somewhat deficient, if he has 5 to 5½ winners. In counting winners, he should keep in mind the increased prospects of his Kings and Queens through the knowledge that he will find a supporting honor in the notrump hand.

SIGN-OFF

There exist a number of hands which have no honor strength whatever, or ½ H. T. at the most, but which contain a six-card suit. At notrump, the suit is practically worthless. At a trump bid, it will produce three or four winners. When that suit is bid the first time, partner naturally does not know that the hand is blank and will probably rebid his notrump. The responder would now be in a worse situation than before if it were not for a special convention provided for just this type of hand.

The special convention brought in at this point is called the "Sign-Off Bid." *The sign-off is restricted to six-card or longer suits and to bidding situations in which the responding hand, having made a suit-bid at the level of two, rebids the same suit at the level of three.**

OPENER	RESPONDER
1 N T	2 ♠
2 N T	3 ♠ (sign-off)

Partner's notrump should be taken out into a six-card suit with ½ to 1 honor-trick, with the intention of signing off if he rebids two notrump, and of passing if he raises the suit to three.

Over one notrump, bid two hearts with:

   ♠ 7 2   ♡ Q J 8 7 6 3   ◇ 6 4 2   ♣ 8 6

With a totally worthless hand, it is unwise to start a sign-off immediately. Pass with

   ♠ 7 2   ♡ 10 8 6 5 3 2   ◇ 8 5 3   ♣ 4 2

—but if the notrump bid is doubled, bid two hearts.

BIDDING A 5–5 TWO-SUITER

The considerations which govern sign-off bidding apply also to hands with two five-card suits.

---

* Refer to similar situations on page 227.

A weak six-card suit will develop three trump tricks which would usually not be available at notrump, because of the lack of entries. This makes it worth-while to insist on playing the six-card suit even if you must raise the bidding level two steps (by signing off) to do so.

With two five-card suits in a weak hand, you gain two long-card tricks in the trump suit, and one or two additional tricks in the side suit—a gain in playing strength of three or four tricks; a net gain of at least one trick.

Even with a hand like this, bid two spades over partner's opening one-notrump bid:

♠ Q 8 7 6 3   ♡ 5   ◊ Q 8 6 4 3   ♣ 8 7

If partner bids two notrump, you next bid three diamonds. *Partner should then pass or show preference.*

Respond two hearts on this hand:

♠ 6   ♡ A J 8 7 6   ◊ 4 3   ♣ J 10 8 7 5

If partner can rebid by raising hearts, go on to four hearts; otherwise, bid three clubs on the next round.

With the following hand, which contains 5 to 6 winners, bid two spades over partner's opening one-notrump bid. If partner rebids two notrump, jump to *four* hearts on the next round:

♠ K J 8 7 5   ♡ K Q 10 6 3   ◊ 9   ♣ 8 2

It will be noted that the higher-ranking suit is invariably shown first. You do this regardless of the relative strength, because it then becomes much simpler for partner to show preference (page 112).

Forcing Suit Takeouts

The forcing takeout consists of a jump bid in any suit, exactly one trick higher than is necessary to overcall the notrump. Like all jump forcing takeouts, it unconditionally obligates both partners to continue the bidding until a game is reached. For instance,

OPENER	RESPONDER
1 N T	3 ◊ or 3 ♠

The opener must not pass short of game, even if he has made a minimum (or even a psychic) notrump bid.

A forcing takeout of a notrump bid does not require so much strength as a forcing takeout of an opening suit-bid. The opening notrump bidder shows at least 3½ honor-tricks, and if the responder has 2½ honor-tricks or more with a fair five-card or longer major suit or 3 honor-tricks with any biddable suit, he knows that the combined hands contain 6 or more honor-tricks, that a good fitting suit is available, and that in accordance with the schedule given on page 46 the hands are in the game zone.

The logical basis for a forcing takeout of a one-notrump bid may be *either* the possession of 6 or more honor-tricks in the combined hands, or the assurance of enough combined winners to guarantee a good chance for game in a suit.

For example, with ♠ K Q J 6 3 ♡ 8 ◇ Q 10 7 5 ♣ A 7 3, bid three spades over partner's one notrump. The bidding will probably stop at game, but if partner can rebid in diamonds it is worth a slam try.

With ♠ A 6 ♡ 7 2 ◇ A Q 10 8 5 3 ♣ K 5 4 bid three diamonds. After the opener's rebid, make a slam try, bidding 4 clubs (Gerber), checking on Aces. You would not want to be in a slam, off 2 Aces. If you are off only 1 Ace, then bid 6 notrump.

The Jump to Game

Some hands containing long major suits with six or more cards are too weak in honor-tricks for a forcing suit takeout, which may tempt the opener to make a disastrous slam try. Yet a very long suit will develop so many winners that game at a major is probable, while slam is out of the question and the hand will not even support a penalty double by partner if an opponent overcalls.

The responder should jump to game immediately in his major suit, holding:

At least a six-card major suit.
No more than 2 honor-tricks.
5½ winners with the major suit as trump.

With a seven-card suit the responder may be able to jump to game with as little as ½ honor-trick, and with an eight-card suit he may sometimes have no honor-trick at all. This response is quite a logical one, when the count of winners is considered.

♠ Q 10 9 7 6 5 4 3   ♡ 9   ◊ 6 4   ♣ 8 5

The spade suit will develop six sure winners, and the opening notrump bid has shown about four winners in the opener's hand. The total is ten, and four spades should be bid at once.

The jump to four in a minor suit should almost never be made, and a jump to five in a minor usually requires an eight-card suit. The hand should contain 7 winners. A slam is by no means out of the question if the minor suit is something like A K Q x x x x x. Therefore with a suit containing the tops the forcing takeout is preferable to an immediate game bid.

Rebids by the Opening Notrump Bidder

After partner's response, the opening notrump bidder becomes in turn the *responding hand*. His procedure will be governed by two principal questions:

1. "What does my partner already know about my hand and what else of value can I tell him?"

2. "What are the *minimum* and *maximum* values already shown to me by his response?"

Partner has for safety's sake already assumed a minimum such as

♠ K Q 3   ♡ A J 7   ◊ A Q 7   ♣ 8 7 6 2

Anything somewhat better than such a minimum is "news" and should be shown by the opener.

The Response Was Two Notrump

The opening hand should now:

(a) *Bid three in a biddable major suit*, if his distribution is 4-4-3-2.

As with ♠ A Q 6 2   ♡ K 6   ◊ A Q 5 4   ♣ Q 9 3

Here a bid of three in a suit is an indirect bid of three notrump. Since you have decided to bid three notrump anyway, why not show *en passant* a biddable four-card major suit?

If he happens to hold, opposite the hand just mentioned, ♠ K 9 7 3 ♡ A 7 4   ◊ K 6 3 2   ♣ 10 2, the game is best played at spades.

(b) *Bid three notrump* even with no better than 3½ honor-tricks provided they are distributed in four suits; and with any more than 3½ honor-tricks they may be held in only three suits.

(c) *Pass* only if holding the minimum of 3½ honor-tricks with one suit unstopped.

The Response Was Three Notrump

The opener must unqualifiedly pass, for slam is out of the question even with a maximum of 4+ honor-tricks. Partner cannot hold more than 3 honor-tricks, unless his distribution is insipid (or he would have forced).

The Response Was Four in a Major

Here again, the opener must unqualifiedly pass. The responder cannot have more than two honor-tricks and probably has no more than six winners; in neither respect will the combined hands reach to a slam.

The Response Was Two in a Suit

The simple suit takeout of a one-notrump bid, like the suit takeout of a suit-bid, has a wide range of values. The opener cannot tell whether the responding hand is weak, and intends to sign off; or is fairly strong, and intends to reach game. Therefore the opener shows what sort of notrump hand he has, and leaves the next decision to the responder. As opener, rebid as follows:

(1) With a maximum holding and two of the three top honors or A x x x or K x x x in partner's suit, you may jump to three notrump. However, it is better to raise partner—see (4) on next page. If partner's suit is a major and your hand contains a doubleton, bid four in the major, rather than three notrump.

(2) Bid *two* in a biddable four-card suit. This rebid does not increase the contract and should be made even with no added values. It is particularly desirable to show a biddable four-card major.

Having bid one notrump and received a response of two diamonds, the opener rebids two hearts on

 ♠ K 9 6 ♡ Q J 5 4 ◊ K 7 5 ♣ A K 2

Two diamonds may be rebid over a two club response, holding

 ♠ K Q 7 ♡ J 9 6 3 ◊ A Q 8 5 ♣ A 5

(3) Bid three even with a 4-card suit, to show a new suit if partner's takeout level so requires. However, prefer a two-no-trump response if holding a minimum one notrump.

Partner has responded two spades to your one-notrump bid. Rebid three clubs, holding

 ♠ Q 7 3 ♡ A J 5 ◊ A Q 8 ♣ K J 10 7

A strong five- or six-card minor suit may be shown at the three-level, even if there are only 3½ honor-tricks in the hand; for the fifth card in a strong suit is a probable additional trick, equivalent to the holding of an extra ½ honor-trick. Over the two-spade response the rebid would be three clubs on

 ♠ K 5 ♡ K 10 8 ◊ Q 10 6 ♣ A K J 4 3

(4) Raise a major or minor suit with A K x, A Q x or K Q x in partner's suit. Partner's two-diamond takeout should be raised to three diamonds, holding

 ♠ Q 10 5 ♡ K J 7 ◊ A Q 6 ♣ A J 6 4

The raise by the opener with A K x, A Q x or K Q x is a very neat one. Suppose your partner opens with one notrump and you respond two diamonds (intending to sign off later) with

 ♠ 5 2 ♡ 4 3 ◊ K 9 8 7 4 2 ♣ Q 5 3

But the opener raises you to three diamonds and now you know the combined hands have six sure tricks in diamonds with about 2½ honor-tricks outside. The 2½ honor-tricks should develop three winning tricks and you can without hesitation go to three notrump.

(5) Raise a major-suit takeout to three with four trumps.

If partner's response is two hearts, bid three hearts with

♠ Q 5   ♥ J 10 4 3   ♦ A K Q 6   ♣ A J 4

Temporarily, the responder will not know but that this raise was given with A K x, A Q x or K Q x, and may bid three notrump expecting that a long major suit can be run. But this will not trouble the opener, for if the responder bids three notrump it will be safe, with four-card trump support, to take him to four of his major suit.

(6) Bid two notrump on any hand that does not fit the requirements for a raise or suit rebid. Since the response was forcing for one round, it is improper to pass.

Partner having responded two hearts to your one-notrump opening, you rebid two notrump on

♠ A Q 5   ♥ 10 9 4   ♦ Q 10 7 3   ♣ A K J

THE RESPONSE WAS THREE OF A SUIT

The jump to three of a suit by responder is forcing to game. The opener knows the responder has about 2½ honor-tricks at least, and may have more. On the chance that the responder has a slam in mind, the opener should rebid so as to show, or deny, added values in his hand.

Added values may consist of a maximum (4+ honor-trick) hand; or of a good fit with the responder's suit, such as a doubleton with four trumps or with three strong trumps.

The opener's rebids are:

(1) With four honor-tricks, show a new biddable suit at the three-level even with 4–3–3–3 distribution.

Over a three-diamond or three-club response, bid three hearts with

♠ Q J 6   ♥ A K 4 2   ♦ K 5 3   ♣ A 8 2

(2) With four honor-tricks, raise partner's suit with any four trumps, or with strong three-card support such as K J x or better, even if your distribution is 4–3–3–3.

Raise a three-diamond response to four diamonds with

♠ K Q 6   ♥ A 7 6 5   ♦ K J 7   ♣ A J 5

(3) With 3½ honor-tricks, raise partner's suit, whether major or minor, with four trumps and a doubleton.

Raise a three-heart response to four hearts with

♠ A 4 3   ♥ Q 8 7 4   ♦ A K 10 5   ♣ K 9

A major suit may be raised with three-card trump support and a doubleton, even if the opening hand was near the minimum of 3½ honor-tricks; but a minor-suit jump takeout should not be.

Raise a three-heart response to four hearts with

♠ Q 2   ♥ K Q 6   ♦ A 7 6 3   ♣ A Q 9 6

But bid three notrump over three diamonds with

♠ A Q 6   ♥ Q 9 6 4   ♦ K 7 5   ♣ A J 6

(4) Bid three notrump on any minimum hand not meeting the requirements for a raise or suit rebid.

The reader need not learn or remember all the minutiae and shadings in requirements given above. My object was merely to trace the workings of an expert player's mind and to point out how an extra pip, a slightly different complexion of the cards, or a stray Queen, often directs the selection of the final bid. All the player needs to remember is the 3½ to 4+ honor-tricks in the opening hand, and the fact that the responding hand—knowing his partner *cannot* have more—is usually and solely in a position to decide if game should be reached.

When One Notrump Is Doubled or Overcalled

An opposing double of partner's opening one-notrump bid is a penalty double, but this should not frighten the responder into a panicky rescue. If he has any sort of strength, the opposing double offers an opportunity to increase the score of his side.

With 1½ to 2 honor-tricks, the responder should redouble; and this should be reduced to 1-plus or even 1 honor-trick if the responder has honor-cards in three or four suits. The partnership hands should readily make seven tricks at notrump; and if the opponents themselves take out the double into two of a suit, a penalty double should be very profitable.

Partner bids one notrump; your right-hand opponent doubles. Redouble with:

1.	♠ J 6 4	♥ Q 8 6 3	♦ Q 7	♣ K 10 5 4
2.	♠ 6 4	♥ K J 6 5 2	♦ A 5 3	♣ 7 5 2
3.	♠ 7	♥ 8 5 2	♦ A K 7 6 4 3	♣ 6 5 4

With one honor-trick or less, take partner out into *any* six-card suit; or into a five-card suit with unbalanced distribution. This applies whichever opponent doubles:

SOUTH	WEST	NORTH	EAST
1 N T	Double	?	

or

SOUTH	WEST	NORTH	EAST
1 N T	Pass	Pass	Double
Pass	Pass	?	

In either case, North bids two spades, holding

♠ 9 7 6 5 3 2   ♥ 7 3   ♦ 10 6 3   ♣ 8 5 or

♠ J 9 7 6 3   ♥ 7   ♦ Q 8 6 5   ♣ 9 6 2

Responder should not rescue the doubled one notrump in a four-card suit, no matter how weak his hand is. If he cannot bid a suit or redouble, in accordance with the requirements stated above, he simply passes.

Pass partner's doubled one-notrump bid, holding

♠ Q 6 5 3   ♥ 10 6 2   ♦ J 8 4 3   ♣ 7 6 or

♠ 7 6 3 2   ♥ 9 6   ♦ 8 6 3   ♣ 9 8 5 4

OVER AN OPPOSING OVERCALL

When partner's opening one-notrump bid is overcalled, the responder should think first of a penalty double. He knows his partner has 3½ or 4+ honor-tricks and at least three cards, or a strong doubleton, in the opponent's suit. Some of the most unusual doubling situations in contract bridge occur when an unwise player overcalls an opposing one-notrump bid.

South opens with one notrump; West bids two diamonds; North doubles, holding ♠ K 6 ♥ K 8 5 4 ♦ J 7 5 ♣ Q 8 7 2
North-South should get at least five tricks with honors and one sure diamond trick even if South has as little as ♦ Q x. Such hands will usually produce a two-trick set even if the defender who overcalled has strictly observed the Rule of Two and Three; yet if West has a strong diamond suit and an outside Ace he would probably be able to stop a notrump game.

If the responder bids a suit over the opposing overcall, it is a weak bid; *it is not forcing* because it denies the strength to double or raise the notrump, and the opener is expected to pass it as though it were a sign-off.

With a long suit containing the tops, the responder should raise the notrump bid even if he has no stopper in the opponent's suit; for there will be few cases in which the notrump bidder cannot stop the opposing suit at least once, and then run the long suit.

SOUTH	WEST	NORTH	EAST
1 N T	2 ♡	3 ◇	

North's hand:

♠ 8 6   ♡ 7   ◇ K 10 8 7 5 2   ♣ J 7 6 3

If North had a stronger hand:

♠ K J 8 4 3	♡ 7 2	◇ A J 6	♣ 9 6 2	Three spades
♠ 8 6	♡ K 6	◇ A Q 7 5 2	♣ 9 6 5 3	Two notrump
♠ 8 6	♡ 7 3	◇ A K 8 6 4 2	♣ 9 6 3	Two notrump

Distributional Notrump Bidding

1. OPENING ONE NOTRUMP; DISTRIBUTIONAL RAISE

♠ K 5 4	♠ A 6 2
♡ Q 10 7 5	♡ 8 3
◇ A Q 9	◇ K 10 8 7 5 4
♣ A Q 9	♣ 10 6

N
W   E
S

WEST	EAST
1 N T	2 N T
3 N T	

West, with 3½-plus honor-tricks, has added strength justifying a rebid. Eleven tricks at diamonds would depend upon a favorable lie of outstanding honors; nine tricks at notrump can be made with ease.

2. OPENING ONE NOTRUMP; MAJOR-SUIT GAME

♠ K 5 3	♠ Q J 8
♡ A Q J 5	♡ 9 7 4 2
◇ A J 7	◇ 3
♣ Q 10 6	♣ K J 7 5 2

N
W   E
S

WEST	EAST
1 N T	2 ♣
2 ♡	3 ♡
4 ♡	

East sees a possible game if West has a heart suit, but little chance of game at notrump, due to his lack of entries and the danger that the oppo-

nents can run diamonds. If West had a minimum hand, he could pass the
raise to three hearts. Having added values (in the strength of his heart suit,
and his many honor-cards) he bids game, which will depend at worst on a
favorable suit break or finesse.

3. Sign-Off with a Weak Six-Card Suit

♠ K 9 5		♠ Q J 6 4 3 2
♡ K Q 7	**N**	♡ 8 5 2
◇ A K 4 2	**W E**	◇ 8 6 3
♣ K 8 3	**S**	♣ 9

West	East
1 N T	2 ♠
2 N T	3 ♠
Pass	

West has 4 honor-tricks, but obeys the sign-off bid in spades. Three spades
can probably be made; in notrump, even one-odd would be doubtful unless
the spades are divided 2-2 or the Ace is a singleton.

4. Suit Takeout; Pass Short of Game

♠ K 7 3		♠ 10 9 6 4
♡ A K 5	**N**	♡ Q J 5 3
◇ J 10 7	**W E**	◇ A 9 4 2
♣ A 5 4 2	**S**	♣ 7

West	East
1 N T	2 ◇
2 N T	Pass

East, having 4½ or 5 winners in support of either major suit, explores the
possibility that West has a biddable four-card major. Since West has not,
East passes short of game.

5. Raise in Partner's Suit; Return to Notrump

♠ K 10 7 5		♠ 4 3 2
♡ A 8 5	**N**	♡ 9 6
◇ A K 9	**W E**	◇ Q 8 6 5 4 3 2
♣ Q J 6	**S**	♣ 7

West	East
1 N T	2 ◇
3 ◇	3 N T

East plans to sign off if West's rebid is two notrump. When West raises
diamonds, however, East knows he has ◇ A K x, and at least 1½ honor-
tricks outside. This should produce seven diamond tricks and two other
tricks, nine in all. East therefore bids game.

6. Raise in Partner's Suit; Major-Suit Game

♠ J 10 5 4		♠ K 8 7 6 3 2
♡ A K 5	**N**	♡ 8 4
◇ K Q 7 6	**W E**	◇ 9 3 2
♣ K 3	**S**	♣ Q 6

West	East
1 N T	2 ♠
3 ♠	3 N T
4 ♠	

East knows West may have A Q x in spades, and bids three notrump. West, not having that spade holding, now bids game in spades. The reason for raising a major suit with four trumps is that the final contract of three in the major is better than two notrump if partner is so weak that he must pass either bid. Four spades is not assured, but there is a play for it.

When the Distributional Notrump Is Not Used

Nearly every 4–3–3–3 hand or equivalent 4–4–3–2 hand is classified in one of the levels of notrump bidding, depending on the honor-trick holding. These are, however, subject to modification because different hands which count to the same number of honor-tricks—that is, which are of equal defensive value—vary greatly in playing strength depending upon their content of honor-cards.

A hand with five bare honor-tricks (♠ A 4 3 ♡ A 7 5 ◇ A 8 6 3 ♣ A K 9) is no better than most hands with about 4½ honor-tricks but seven or eight honor-cards (♠ K J 10 ♡ A Q 7 3 ◇ K Q 7 ♣ A 9 5). Most hands with five honor-tricks are one-bids in a suit, but some with eight or more honor-cards are good enough for a two-notrump bid (♠ K Q 9 5 ♡ A J 6 ◇ K Q 10 ♣ A Q J).

Hands containing 6½ bare honor-tricks may be no better than the average 5½ honor-trick two-notrump bid, and may be good for a bid of three notrump.

The Special Range of 4½–5 Honor-Tricks

Around the five-honor-trick level the greatest problem is caused by hands which are too strong for an opening one-notrump bid and yet too weak for a bid of two notrump. They contain 4½, 5 or 5+ honor-tricks with perhaps only six or seven honor-cards, or 5½ honor-tricks with one suit unstopped.

If one notrump were bid on such a hand partner might pass, expecting the average 3½-honor-trick holding in the opening hand, and a game would be missed. If two notrump were bid originally, partner might raise with far too little. In terms of 4–3–2–1 point-count, we are discussing hands with 19, 20 or 21 points.

Such hands are best opened with a one-bid in a suit, as they usually contain at least a *conditional* biddable suit. If partner is strong enough to respond at all (showing about one honor-trick) the opener can jump to two or three notrump, depending upon intermediates; if partner passes, game is probably out of the question.

♠ A Q 5   ♡ K J 7   ◇ A 8 5 4   ♣ A Q 6   Bid one diamond. The opener will make a jump rebid of at least two notrump.

The Opening Bid of Two Notrump (22–24 Points)

Make a bid of an opening two notrump in any position, vulnerable or not vulnerable, holding:

> 5+ *to* 5½+ *honor-tricks*
> *Balanced distribution*
> *No suit weaker than K x or Q 10 x*

A hand with 5+ bare honor-tricks *will not do*. It must contain at least 8 honor-cards, and preferably 9 or 10.

Ideal distributions are 4–3–3–3 and 4–4–3–2. A hand distributed 5–3–3–2 or 6–3–2–2 is a good two-notrump bid only if the long suit is a *minor* and is *solid or quickly establishable* (as A K J x x or K Q J x x).

Examples of opening two-notrump bids:

♠ Q J 6 5	♠ K J 3	♠ A J 7	♠ K 2
♡ A K 3	♡ A Q	♡ Q 10 5	♡ A J 10
◇ K Q J	◇ A K 3 2	◇ A K Q J 5	◇ K 2
♣ A Q 7	♣ A Q 3 2	♣ A 8	♣ A K Q 9 6 4

Note that with seven *quick winners* (as by holding a long, solid minor) 4½ honor-tricks are enough.

The opening two-notrump bid, though very powerful, *is not forcing*. Partner may pass with a blank hand.

Choice of Bids

The two-notrump bid is of great advantage on very strong hands which contain so many honor-tricks that there is danger of partner's passing an opening one-bid and yet whose distributional nature makes an opening forcing two-bid in a suit misleading to partner.

To bid two notrump with 4–4–3–2 distribution and any four-card major may keep the partnership out of a makable major-suit game. It should be done, however, when the hand is so crammed with top cards that there is grave danger of partner's passing an opening suit-bid.

♠ A K Q 7   ♡ A Q   ◇ Q 10 8 3   ♣ A Q 6

Bid two notrump, since one spade may be passed. However, with

♠ K Q 10 5   ♡ A 10 7 3   ◇ A K   ♣ A 9 5

one spade should be bid because the best play for game will be in a major if partner has four spades or four hearts.

Responses to Opening Two-Notrump Bids

An opening two-notrump bid may be passed, but only on a hand so weak that it is a near-Yarborough. The hand that passes two notrump probably has less than ½ honor-trick, and probably no five-card or longer suit.

Pass partner's opening two-notrump bid holding

	♠ 6 5 3	♡ Q 10 2	◇ 10 7 5 4	♣ 9 5 3
or	♠ Q 8 3	♡ 7 4	◇ 10 8 6 4 2	♣ 8 5 3

Raise partner's two notrump to three if holding about one-half honor-trick.

Bid three notrump with the following:

♠ K 8 5	♡ 7 6 3	◇ J 9 4	♣ 7 6 3 2
♠ Q 7	♡ 10 6 5 3	◇ Q 6 5	♣ 8 7 4 3
♠ 7 2	♡ 8 5 3	◇ 5 3 2	♣ K 8 7 6 3
♠ 7 2	♡ J 6 5	◇ 5 3 2	♣ Q 8 7 5 3

With two or more honor-tricks and no suit to bid, raise to four notrump. The combined hands are probably in the slam zone. The exception is when the responder has a 4–3–3–3 hand, when he should bid only three notrump on two bare honor-tricks, but raise to four with 2 plus–2½ honor-tricks.

SUIT TAKEOUTS OF TWO-NOTRUMP BIDS

Any takeout of partner's two-notrump opening with three of a suit is forcing to game. It may be made on a very weak hand, with which the responder expects to reach game; or on a very strong hand with which the responder expects to make a slam try or slam bid later.

The minimums on which three of a suit may be bid over partner's two notrump opening are:

(a) Any six-card major suit, regardless of honor-tricks.

(b) Any five-card major suit with ½ honor-trick in the hand.

(c) Any biddable minor suit accompanied by a four-card major, if the hand as a whole contains about one-half honor-trick.

A response of three spades would be made to partner's opening two-notrump bid, holding

| ♠ J 7 6 5 3 | ♡ 7 2 | ◇ K 6 4 | ♣ 8 7 3   or |
| ♠ 10 9 7 6 5 3 | ♡ 8 6 3 | ◇ 7 6 | ♣ 4 2 |

A response of three diamonds would be made to partner's opening two-notrump bid, holding

| ♠ 6 | ♡ Q 7 6 3 | ◇ Q 8 7 5 2 | ♣ 6 5 4 |

From these minimums the strength of the responding hand when he makes a suit takeout may range up to any maximum. The type of his hand will be shown by the responder's next bid.

With a six-card major suit and a trickless hand the proper treatment is to rebid the suit, even if partner's rebid is three notrump. Since the suit is a major, game will already have been reached, for the rebid will have been at the level of four.

With a six-card minor suit and less than ½ honor-trick (or the equivalent required for a raise) the two-notrump bid may be passed.

With a seven-card or longer minor suit, bid it; for five-odd can probably be made.

The Jump to Four in a Suit

A jump from partner's two notrump to four of a major or minor suit is a mild slam try, showing:

(*a*) A six-card or longer major suit headed by Ace or King with 1½ honor-tricks in the hand;

(*b*) A seven-card minor suit with 1½ honor-tricks in the hand. Even if partner has a minimum two-notrump bid, it should be easy to make five of the minor suit, and six is probable.

With only a five-card suit, or with a two-suiter, it is better to bid three of the suit first. After partner rebids, a second biddable suit may be shown if the responder has one, or four notrump (not conventional in this case) may be bid as a direct slam try.

Over partner's opening two-notrump bid:

1. With ♠ K J 10 8 6 4   ♡ 3 2   ◇ K 5 4   ♣ 7 3   Bid four spades.
2. With ♠ Q 8 7 6 2   ♡ 4 3   ◇ K Q 7 5 4   ♣ 9   Bid three spades. If partner rebids three notrump, next bid the diamond suit.

The Opener's Rebids

The opening two-notrump bidder should raise partner's major-suit takeout to game with any four trumps, and should show a biddable major if he can do so at the three-level.

Any suit takeout can be raised with only three trumps, if they are A K x, A Q x or K Q x; occasionally opener may stretch a point and raise with A J x or K J x.

When partner makes a slam try, the opener must remember that he has already shown at least 5+ honor-tricks, and without 5½ honor-tricks he must as a rule make minimum rebids. See Slam Bidding, Chapters 25 to 27.

The Three-Notrump Bid

The opening three-notrump bid is similar to the two-notrump bid, with slightly better honor-cards, specifically 25–27 points. On a 4–3–3–3 or 4–4–3–2 hand, the opener should have 6 to 6½ honor-tricks. When the bid is based primarily on a long, solid minor suit in a 5–3–3–2 or 6–3–2–2 hand, the opener should have eight quick winners.

Every suit in the three-notrump hand should be securely stopped if the opening lead comes up to it. The minimum doubleton holding is K x; the minimum three-card holding is Q J x—not Q 10 x as in the case of the two-notrump bid, for if an opening lead is made from A J x x x and the leader's partner has the King of the suit, Q 10 x may not be a stopper.

While it is technically a game bid, the opening bid of three notrump may more accurately be called a slam try. It is such a powerful bid that the sketchiest of support will turn it into a slam. For this reason, a forcing two-bid should be preferred when partner is a timid soul who "hates to disturb a game."

These are good three-notrump bids:

♠ A Q 6	♠ A J	♠ K 2
♡ A K 7 2	♡ K J 10 5	♡ A K 6
◇ K Q J	◇ A K Q 6	◇ K 2
♣ A Q 2	♣ A Q J	♣ A K Q J 8 3

Strictly speaking, three notrump should not be bid unless all four suits are stopped; but there are exceptions to everything. It is hard to think what to bid on the following hand, if not three notrump:

♠ A K Q   ♡ A K Q   ◇ A K 10   ♣ 8 5 3 2

SLAM TRIES OVER THREE NOTRUMP

The responder must resist the perfectly natural urge to pass simply because his hand is one he would ordinarily consider hopelessly weak. The opener will usually be able to win eight tricks, and most of them in top cards. The responder will probably be able to win a trick with a King or even a Queen. A hand with about 1½ honor-tricks and a five-card suit has four probable winners, which when combined with partner's eight will produce a slam (if the necessary controls are present). Two bare honor-tricks, even without a long suit, warrant a raise to four notrump.

Any takeout of partner's opening three notrump to four of a suit is a slam try. It may be made on a hand as weak as this:

♠ K J 5	♡ K 9 7 4 2	◇ 6 5	♣ 8 4 2	Bid four hearts
♠ 6 3	♡ 7 5 4 3	◇ A 8 7 6 3 2	♣ 5	Bid four diamonds

Whatever the response, the opener will carry on to a slam if he has the maximum of 6½ honor-tricks, but will make a minimum rebid (or pass, if the response was enough for game) if he has less.

OPENING NOTRUMP BIDS OF FOUR AND MORE

Any opening bid of four, five or six notrump is a slam try. Hands warranting such bids rarely occur, and require special treatment when they do.

An Alternative Theory of Notrump Bidding

The requirements for opening notrumps and responses in the preceding pages are based on the theory of strong notrumps introduced by this writer in 1934. The strong notrump theory is now an integral part of all systems of contract bridge whether they be based on honor-trick valuation or on a point-count. There is, however, an alternative theory of light notrumps, introduced by this writer in 1928, which is still used by a number of experts.

Both theories are based on the concept of balanced hand distributions (particularly 4–3–3–3). The difference between them is that in the strong notrump method no distinction is made between vulnerable and not vulnerable; while in the light notrump method the requirements for opening one-no-trump bids differ according to whether the side is vulnerable or not vulnerable.

No expert player indulges in a light notrump when vulnerable, except against weak opponents. The danger is that a light opening one-notrump bid when vulnerable might easily result in a disastrous loss when doubled by the opponents for business. This objection does not apply nearly so much, if at all, to light opening one-notrump bids when not vulnerable. Hence the point-count limits in the light notrump bids are:

For a non-vulnerable one notrump, 2½–3+ honor-tricks; 13–15 points.

For a vulnerable one notrump, 3½–4+ honor-tricks; 16–18 points.

The requirements for balanced distribution given for the

strong notrump method also prevail for the light notrump method.

Examples of light or weak non-vulnerable notrumps:

♠ A 9 8 2   ♡ K 7   ◇ K J 5   ♣ Q 10 8 2

2½ H.-T.—13 pts. Bid one notrump, not vulnerable.

♠ A J 7   ♡ A 6 4   ◇ Q 10 8   ♣ K J 5 3

3+ H.-T.—15 pts. Bid one notrump, not vulnerable. If vulnerable, bid one club on either of the two examples, above.

♠ K J 9   ♡ A Q 5 2   ◇ J 7 3   ♣ A Q 9

The count is 3½+ H.-T.—17 points. Hence the hand is too strong for one notrump, not vulnerable, and should be opened with one heart; vulnerable it is within the proper limits of an opening one notrump.

Responder should raise the non-vulnerable opening one notrump to two notrump with 2+ to 3 H.-T., 11 or 12 points; at times with 2 H.-T., 10 points. The opener will pass with 13 points and bid three notrump with 14 or 15. With 13–17 points, responder should bid three notrump. With 18 or 19 points he should try for a slam, and with 20 or more bid a slam.

With a five-card or longer major suit or with an unbalanced hand, he should make a forcing takeout with 13 or more points. A takeout of two in a suit is not forcing when this light opening notrump method is used.

The light notrump is an optional feature of the Culbertson System but the opponents must be informed of its use. The light notrump is not as popular as the strong notrump; it is more difficult to handle, since the partners must keep in mind two scales of values, vulnerable and not vulnerable. In most other respects the light notrump has distinct advantages over the strong notrump. The strong notrump, though artistically beautiful, occurs infrequently in the course of an evening's play. The light notrump is not only many times more frequent (and, therefore, of greater practical value) but is a powerful defensive bid, depriving the opponents of the valuable one-level and forcing them to climb to the level of two or three. The light notrump is annoying to expert opposition and is devastating to inexpert opposition. At the same time it conveys valuable information to partner, especially on distribution. It creates favorable situations for penalty doubles. One of the great advantages of an opening notrump bid is that hands containing tenaces (A Q, A J, K J, Q 10, etc.) are led up to, instead of being led through, as dummy. Use of the light notrump makes it possible to exploit a far greater number of these tenaced hands.

CHAPTER EIGHT

BIDDABLE
TRUMP SUITS

One of the greatest advantages accruing to the player who obtains the final contract is that he names the trump suit of his choice.

The first object of the bidder is to have *more* cards of his trump suit than any other player. If he does not hold at least four trumps some other player must have more than he. Therefore no suit can be considered biddable unless it contains at least four cards.

The second object of the bidder is, that even if another player happens to have as. many trumps they must not be as good as his. Therefore a minimum biddable suit must include certain high cards. The longer the bidder's trump suit, the less likelihood that another player will have as many, and the requirements in high cards are correspondingly decreased.

REGULAR BIDDABLE SUITS

The weakest suit that should willingly be bid is:
Four cards, headed by the Jack and at least one higher honor.
Minimum: Q J 3 2, K J 3 2, A J 3 2, etc.
Five cards, headed by the Queen (or any higher honor).
Minimum: Q 5 4 3 2, K 5 4 3 2, etc. Also, J 10 4 3 2, a J 10 being, usually, equivalent to a Queen.
These suits are biddable only once. Having made one bid

with such a suit, a player should not bid it again unless partner has raised, showing supporting strength in the suit.

A four-card length should not be bid a second time, even when partner has raised it, unless there is no other rebid available. Partner's raise may have been given with only a three-card trump holding such as Q 8 4, and it is seldom desirable to play a hand with a trump suit in which you hold only seven trumps to the opponents' six. Eight trumps in the combined hands, to the opponents' five, constitute a safe margin of superiority.

CONDITIONAL BIDDABLE SUITS

The strength or distribution of a hand may cause even weaker suits to be biddable. The following are "conditional" biddable suits. They are sometimes biddable, but only under certain conditions:

Four-card lengths: Q 10 3 2, K 4 3 2, A 4 3 2, or better.

Five-card lengths: 7 6 5 3 2, 10 7 5 3 2, J 5 4 3 2, etc.

The conditions upon which such a weak suit is biddable may be any one of the following:

1. When the hand also contains another biddable suit. The second biddable suit in the hand may be a regular or a conditional biddable suit.

Both hearts and diamonds are biddable in this hand:

♠ 6 5   ♡ Q 10 6 3   ◇ K 8 5 4   ♣ A K Q

2. When the hand contains *more* than the honor-trick minimum usually required for a bid:

♠ 6 5 4 3 2   ♡ A K 6   ◇ A K 6   ♣ 5 4

Here it is better to bid the spade suit, weak though it is, than to pass a hand with nearly half the honor-tricks in the deck.

3. When responding to partner's opening bid:

♠ A 10 5 3   ♡ 7 5 3 2   ◇ K 8 7   ♣ 4 3

Over partner's opening one-club bid, it is proper to bid the spade suit on this hand.

Rebiddable Suits

A five-card suit headed by K J or Q J 9, or by anything better, may be bid and then rebid once, even if partner has not shown support by raising. This type of suit is called a rebiddable suit. Examples: K J 4 3 2, Q J 9 3 2, K Q 4 3 2, A J 4 3 2, etc.

Any six-card suit is rebiddable and may be bid a second time without waiting for support from partner. This includes suits such as 9 7 6 4 3 2.

A four-card suit should not be rebid ordinarily, but four *honors* may be rebid if no better call is available.

The minimum rebiddable suits (K J x x x or Q J 9 x x) should not be rebid when another safe bid is available; but when a rebid is forced by the bidding situation, the above suits may be bid a second time in a pinch.

In this situation, South is forced to rebid:

South	West	North	East
1 ♠	Pass	2 ♣	Pass

He should rebid two spades on

♠ K J 8 6 5	♡ A 8 3	◇ A J 7	♣ 8 2

But if the bidding were

South	West	North	East
1 ♠	Pass	2 ♣	2 ♡

South should pass; East's overcall guarantees North another chance, and South's suit is too weak for a *free* rebid.

For a free rebid (page 241) it is desirable to hold at least a five-card suit headed by at least A K or any three honors: A K x x x, Q J 10 x x, or better. Even a six-card suit should be headed by one or two high cards: A x x x x x, Q 10 x x x x, etc.

Strong Rebiddable Suits

A suit containing about five and usually more trump tricks is called a *strong rebiddable* suit, and may be bid three times without support. The length of the suit may range from five to eight or even more cards:

A K Q J 7	A K Q 6 4 2	K 9 8 6 5 4 2
Q J 8 7 6 5 2	K Q J 7 6 3	

A five-card suit, however strong in high cards, is less desirable than a longer suit which is weaker in high cards.

Among the strong rebiddable suits are two types which have
distinct characteristics of their own:

Nearly solid suits, which are at least six cards in length and
are headed by four of the five honors; or are seven cards in
length and headed by three of the four top honors. The principal quality of such suits is that they contain not more than
one loser, except against extremely improbable division of the
remaining cards:

        K Q J 10 3 2   A K Q 10 3 2   A Q J 10 3 2
            A Q J 8 6 4 2   A K J 10 3 2

Ready-made (or "solid") suits go a step farther up the ladder.
They also are at least six cards in length, and cannot reasonably be expected to lose a trick:

        A K Q J 3 2   A K Q 5 4 3 2

Adequate Trump Support

The minimum biddable suits listed above could not safely
be handled if the bidder's partner were not strictly limited,
in raising, to hands containing *adequate trump support*. The
trump strength necessary to be considered adequate depends
upon the number of times the suit has been bid. Adequate
trump support for a suit which has been bid only once (and
must therefore be assumed to be a minimum biddable suit)
is: *Three cards headed by at least the Queen or J 10; or any
four small cards:*

    J 10 2   Q 3 2   K 3 2   A 3 2   or   5 4 3 2

Without so much in partner's trump suit a player should
not raise until he has heard his partner rebid the suit. The
responder should find some response other than a raise, and
failing to find one should pass.

Even though J 10 2, Q 3 2, K 3 2 and A 3 2 are adequate
trump support, the player should avoid raising immediately
when some other good bid is available.

Support for a Rebid Suit

When the trump suit has been rebid without support (that is, when it has been bid twice) partner is allowed to raise with slightly less: Q 2, K 2, A 2 or any three small cards. The greater strength which the bidder has guaranteed that he holds in his trump suit makes up for the lessened strength in the partner's hand. But with only two trumps, a rebid of notrump is to be preferred, if available.

A strong rebiddable trump suit, which can be recognized when it has been bid three times, actually is a safe trump suit without support, and partner can raise it with only one small trump in his hand.

The Bidding Level

Bidding a suit three times (that is, rebidding it twice) shows the same type of suit as an opening bid of three in the suit. When a player makes an opening suit-bid of three or four his partner may safely assume that he has a strong rebiddable suit, and may, in a pinch, raise with a singleton trump.

Similarly, when a suit is bid at the level of one-odd the assumption is that the suit contains but four cards. A bid at the level of two-odd usually shows a fair rebiddable five-card or longer suit, and partner may therefore raise with three small trumps or with Q x if his hand is strong.

This principle does not apply to a forcing two-bid or to a forcing takeout, which may be made at any level on a four-card biddable suit; nor does it apply altogether to overcalls and responses at the range of three in a suit.

When partner has opened with one spade, for example, and an opponent overcalls with two hearts, a bid of three clubs by the responder can be trusted to show a rebiddable suit, but not necessarily a strong rebiddable suit, and no raise should be given without three trumps or Q x.

When a Suit Need Not Be Biddable

The requirements given for biddable suits apply to cases in which the player bids a suit of his own free will. In one case— when a player is responding to his partner's takeout double (page 263)—he must often bid a suit which is not biddable. However, in this case partner will not expect to find a biddable suit.

Following is a table listing the types of biddable suits and necessary trump support. The requirements given apply only to trump strength; certain values in outside honor-tricks are equally necessary for most bids.

BIDDABLE TRUMP SUITS

For Bids, Rebids and Raises

Regular Biddable Suits

Suits which may be bid only once without support:

Q J x x	A K x x	A K Q x
K J x x	A Q x x	A K J x
A J x x	K Q J x	A Q J x
J 10 x x x	K Q x x	K x x x x
A x x x x	Q J x x x	A 10 x x x
	Q x x x x	

These suits should not be bid a second time unless partner has raised; and should be bid (for the first time) at the level of two only with very strong hands.

Adequate Trump Support

Trump holding necessary for partner to raise a suit which has been bid only once:

J 10 x	Q x x
A x x	K x x

or x x x x (any four trumps)

A double raise (from one to three) requires

Q x x x	J 10 x x

or x x x x x (any five trumps)

When no other bid is available, a double raise may sometimes be given with A K x, A Q x, K Q x, A J x.

Rebiddable Suits

Suits which may be bid twice, whether partner has raised or not:

K J x x x	Q J 9 x x	K Q x x x
	A J x x x	A Q x x x
	x x x x x x or better	
	(*any* six cards)	

Such suits, should, however, be bid a second time without support only as *forced* rebids and for *free* rebids you should have five cards headed by A K, Q J 10 or better; or any six cards:

A K x x x	Q J 10 x x	x x x x x x

Adequate Trump Support

When a suit has been bid twice without support, partner may raise with:

Q x	K x	A x

or x x x (any three trumps)

This usually applies also to a suit which is bid for the first time at the level of two.

A *double* raise may be given to a suit which has been rebid, holding:

Q x x	J 10 x

or x x x x (any four trumps)

Strong Rebiddable Suits

Suits which may be bid three times (or may be bid for the first time at the level of three or higher):

```
A K Q x x x              K x x x x x x
A x x x x x x            Q J x x x x x
          K Q J x x x
          A Q J x x x
10 x x x x x x x (any eight cards)
```

Nearly Solid Suits

```
A K Q 10 x x            A Q J 10 x x
A K J 10 x x            K Q J 10 x x
A Q J x x x x           A K J x x x x
A K x x x x x x         K Q J x x x x
```

(These suits are unlikely to lose more than one trick.)

Ready-Made Suits

```
A K Q J x x            A K Q x x x x
```
(These suits are unlikely to lose a trick.)

Conditional Biddable Suits

The following suits may be shown in very strong hands which contain no other biddable suit; or when there is another biddable suit in the hand; or in responding to partner's bid. They may not be rebid unless partner has raised twice.

```
Q 10 x x        K x x x        A x x x
     K 10 x x        A 10 x x
     x x x x x        J x x x x
```

Adequate Trump Support

A suit on which a preëmptive bid of three or four is made; or a suit which has been bid three times (rebid twice) without support, requires only

ONE SMALL TRUMP

in support. Partner may raise with a singleton, but should prefer some other bid unless his singleton is Queen, King or Ace.

Adequate Trump Support

Nearly solid and ready-made suits require no support in the trump suit, but partner should nevertheless not raise without at least one trump.

Adequate Trump Support

When partner has reason to fear that the suit may be a conditional biddable suit, he should if possible avoid raising with fewer than four trumps. With any four trumps he may raise.

CHAPTER NINE

OPENING SUIT-BIDS OF ONE

A player opens the bidding when he makes the first bid in any deal. His hand is known as the opening hand and he is known as the opener. The first bid is called the opening bid.

The opening bid is more than a contract to take a certain number of tricks. It has the added and equally important function of giving information to partner. The information given is that the opener has:

1. A minimum number of honor-tricks (defensive winners).
2. A minimum number of playing-tricks or expected winners at his own bid.
3. The bid also gives a rough clue to the distribution of the hand, due to the fact that the bid names a trump suit, guaranteeing a certain minimum length in that suit.

The approximate number of honor-tricks and winners and the general type of distribution will be set within narrow limits by the nature of the first call—whether it is a pass or a bid, and if a bid, whether a suit or a notrump bid of one, two, three or four.

THE PASS

A pass is not a bid, yet a pass by dealer (or by any other player when the bidding has not been opened) conveys a wealth of negative information to partner, from which the passing hand can be placed within the following limits:

1. *Honor-tricks:* Maximum three, which is improbable, down to minimum zero, which is equally improbable. Usually, from ½ to 2 honor-tricks.

2. *Distribution:* The greater the number of honor-tricks, the less the likelihood that the player holds any biddable suit. The pass may also, in first, second and third positions, be assumed to deny possession of a long, powerful trump suit containing as many as seven or eight winners, for on such a hand a preëmptive bid might be made regardless of honor-tricks.

It will at times happen that a player will pass freak hands containing very long suits (even up to a thirteen-card suit) and honor-trick holdings ranging up to three or even slightly beyond, for reasons of surprise strategy. He will do this rarely, and his partner will be wise not to expect any such contingency.

The Opening Suit-Bid of One

The opening suit-bid of one is the ideal bid. Rarely will the best final contract be apparent at the start of the hand, and the opening one-bid in a suit allows for the greatest possible exchange of information while keeping the bidding at the lowest possible level for purposes both of strategy and of safety.

Although it is the lowest bid, a one-bid does not show the weakest possible opening hand, particularly in honor-tricks. The playing strength of the hand is a secondary consideration compared to the vital necessity for making the opening one-bid show a fixed minimum number of defensive winners. This minimum should be better than an average share of all the honor-tricks around the table. According to the Rule of Eight there are usually 8 to 8½ honor-tricks in all; therefore the honor-trick requirement for an opening suit-bid of one is seldom less than 2½ honor-tricks, and usually three honor-tricks or more.

Any hand containing 2½ to 3 honor-tricks and a fair biddable suit will count to at least four winners.

Finally, the hand should contain a biddable suit, in which the opening bid will be made.

Minimum Requirements

Any opening one-bid in a suit shows at least:

3 honor-tricks with a four-card biddable suit or a weak five-card biddable suit, or sometimes with a three-card minor suit to the Queen or better. See page 121.

2½ honor-tricks with a five-card or longer rebiddable suit.

2+ honor-tricks with a six-card *major* suit.

The location of the honor-tricks does not matter, so long as *at least ½ honor-trick is outside the trump suit.* It may be that *all* the honor-tricks are outside the trump suit. The important requirement is that the hand as a whole must have the required minimum in honor-tricks, depending upon the length and strength of the trump suit, while its maximum may be 5½ honor-tricks.

These minimum requirements apply regardless of whether the opener is vulnerable or not, and whether he is dealer or in second, third or fourth position.

1.	♠ 10 7 5 4	♡ K J 6 5	◇ A K 6	♣ Q 2	bid one heart
2.	♠ Q 7 5 4 2	♡ K 3	◇ 9 7 5	♣ A K Q	bid one spade
3.	♠ K Q 10 8 5	♡ A 6 2	◇ Q J 8	♣ 5 4	bid one spade
4.	♠ K J 5	♡ 8 6 4	◇ A K 9 7 6	♣ 6 4	bid one diamond
5.	♠ Q J 9 4 2	♡ J 6	◇ K 6 5	♣ A Q 8	bid one spade
6.	♠ K J 9 7 6 3	♡ A 7	◇ K 5 2	♣ 8 3	bid one spade

The following hands are *unsound* opening bids because they do not contain enough honor-tricks.

1.	♠ A K 10 8 5	♡ 10 6 4	◇ Q 5 3 2	♣ 6	Pass
2.	♠ 9 7	♡ K J 8 5 4	◇ A 5 3	♣ K 6 4	Pass
3.	♠ Q J 6 5 4	♡ Q 6 3	◇ Q 7 5	♣ A 10	Pass
4.	♠ Q 6 3	♡ A K Q 5 2	◇ 8 4 3	♣ 10 2	Pass

No. 4 lacks the required ½ honor-trick outside the trump suit.

The following hands should be passed because they contain no biddable suit.

1.	♠ 9 5 4	♡ K 6 3	◇ A K	♣ 8 6 5 3 2
2.	♠ A 10 6 5	♡ 7 6 3	◇ A K 8	♣ 6 4 2
3.	♠ K Q 7	♡ K Q J	◇ 9 6 4 2	♣ Q J 3

The basic requirements for opening bids are flexible. At times hands containing slightly below the minimum requirements may be bid, and hands containing the minimum requirements or slightly more may be passed.

These modifications and exceptions are based upon considerations of psychology, playing strength, and position.

THE FACTOR OF PSYCHOLOGY

The honor requirements for opening bids may be shaded somewhat—but never very much—according to the psychology and skill of partner and opponents. The following hand, which does not contain 2+ honor-tricks, is a good example of the type of hand which may be bid when sitting opposite a very timid partner who otherwise may be fearful of entering the bidding and who in no case will be misled into contracting for a losing slam:

♠ A Q 10 9 5 4   ♡ K 8 3   ◊ 8 4   ♣ 5 2

A weak and sometimes even a "semi-psychic" bid is effective against the type of opponent who values his hand more with his ears than with his head and who is more likely to believe his opponents' bidding than the evidence of his own eyes. Such tactics are recommended, however, only for skilful players who are able to take care of themselves—and partner's possible enthusiasm—later in the bidding.

An occasional pass with an extreme type of freak is often very good strategy, leading an opponent later to make a losing penalty double. Holding

♠ —   ♡ A Q 10 9 7 6 5 4 3 2   ◊ Q J 6   ♣ —

there is little danger in passing, for one of the other players will surely open the bidding, and when such a hand is bid up to four hearts by slow stages there is an excellent chance that the opponents will double when they would not have doubled an opening four-heart bid. This, however, works only against inexperienced players.

THE TRAP PASS

Very rarely should an opening bid be passed, if the distribution of the hand is not freakish. To pass a hand like

♠ A Q 6   ♥ 7 2   ♦ A 10 6 5   ♣ K J 7 4

in the vain hope that the opponents will overbid and can be doubled is the height of guileless optimism. It is far more likely that a game will be lost because partner, holding a hand distributionally strong but weak in honor-tricks, must also pass and the opponents will not have enough strength to open the bidding. Such tactics as passing a strong hand in order to lay a trap can be attempted only against erratic players who open the bidding "on general principles," particularly in third position, and often in fourth position with the hope of "stealing a partial."

THE FACTOR OF PLAYING STRENGTH

The general playing strength of the hand has a particular effect on hands slightly below the minimum requirements in honor-tricks, but containing a fairly good trump suit and strong distribution.

It may be stated as a general principle that as the playing strength of the hand increases, the honor-trick minimums may be decreased, provided that in no case is an opening one-bid made with less than 2-plus honor-tricks, however strong the hand may be. The cases in which the honor-trick requirements may be revised downward because of playing-tricks are:

1. With five cards in one major suit and four in the other and with strong intermediates (Jacks, tens and nines) an opening bid is justified with about 2½ honor-tricks, even though neither of the suits is rebiddable.

♠ K 10 9 3 2   ♥ K J 8 7   ♦ A 6 3   ♣ 4   Bid one spade
♠ Q 9 6 5   ♥ K 10 9 4 3   ♦ A Q 6   ♣ 5   Bid one heart

2. With two five-card biddable suits, of which one is a major suit, the bidding may be opened with 2½ honor-tricks, even though neither of the suits is rebiddable.

♠ K 8 7 4 3   ♥ 9   ♦ Q J 6 5 4   ♣ A Q   Bid one spade
♠ A 10 6 5 4   ♥ Q 7 6 4 3   ♦ A 5   ♣ 8   Bid one spade

THE FACTOR OF POSITION

A player faces a different bidding problem in each of the four positions—first, second, third or fourth hand.

The problems of first and second hands are largely the same. Their principal fear is that partner will make a response which is forcing for one round, but which leaves them without a suitable rebid.

If there were not too many important exceptions one could state as a general rule that no hand should be opened *if it does not contain a rebid,* however slight.

♠ A K 6 5   ♥ 7 6 4   ♦ A 5 3   ♣ 9 4 2

If one spade is bid on this hand, and partner responds with two of any other suit, the opener could not safely raise, rebid his spade suit, or bid two notrump. A pass on this hand is therefore preferable.

For the same reason, a hand containing six small cards in a minor suit and 2½ bare honor-tricks may also be passed.

♠ 6 5   ♥ K 7   ♦ 9 8 6 5 4 2   ♣ A K 3

If an opening bid of one diamond is made and partner responds with one spade or one heart, a rebid of two diamonds would mislead him as to the strength of the suit; a rebid of one notrump would not correctly portray the distribution of the hand. If partner replied with one notrump, the opener could not safely pass, there being no assurance that his diamond suit would be of value at notrump; yet a bid of two diamonds might not be safe. Here again the player has the option of passing.

Most Aceless hands containing a bare 2½ honor-tricks should be passed first or second hand, even though they include a rebiddable suit and therefore the technical requirements for an opening bid.

♠ 7   ♥ K J 10 8 3   ♦ K Q J   ♣ 8 6 4 2   Pass

WHEN FOURTH HAND SHOULD PASS

The player in fourth position, when the other three players have passed, must decide not only whether or not to open the bidding for himself, but whether or not he should reopen for his opponents.

The requirements for opening bids as given apply generally to all four positions from first to fourth hand, whether vulnerable or not. Fourth hand should nevertheless pass hands containing the bare minimum requirements in the following cases:

1. When his strength is wholly in the minor suits, and he does not hold so much as adequate trump support for either major. In such cases, even though the strength is evenly divided between the two sides, the opponents with their major suits will be able to take the bidding away from the opener with his minor suits. The following hands should be passed fourth hand:

| ♠ 6 5 | ♡ 8 3 2 | ◇ A K 6 5 4 | ♣ Q J 3 |
| ♠ 8 6 | ♡ 7 4 2 | ◇ A Q 9 8 | ♣ A Q 6 5 |

2. When the opponents have a part-score, fourth hand should not open the bidding with the minimum of 2½ honor-tricks unless he has a strong trump suit of his own which he is prepared to rebid, or unless his hand is strong in intermediates and offers probable support for a suit partner may bid.

♠ 7 5	♡ A J 8 5 2	◇ A J 6	♣ 7 6 3	Pass
♠ Q J 7	♡ A Q 8 5	◇ K 7 4 2	♣ K 6	Bid one heart
♠ A K 10 6 4 2	♡ 5 4	◇ K 8 3	♣ 9 2	Bid one spade

Third-Hand Strategic Bids

The player who is third hand, when his partner has already passed and his own hand is below normal biddable strength, may reasonably expect that fourth hand will be strong enough to make a bid and that his opponents hold the major portion of the outstanding strength. In order to get in the first blow, to interfere with the opponents' bidding, and to indicate a favorable opening lead against an opposing notrump contract, the third-hand player can make a strategic bid on a hand containing 1½ to 2 honor-tricks and a fairly strong trump suit.

A third-hand strategic bid is best described as an *anticipated* defensive bid and is based more upon playing strength than upon honor-tricks. The hand should be safe under the Rule of 2 and 3 (page 381).

Third hand must remember that his partner will not know the bid is below the normal strength of opening bids and will respond as though to any opening bid. Of course, an intelligent partner will make allowance for the possibility of a weak third-hand bid, and will not jump to the sky just because he happens to hold a fair hand. But if the opener has too little, even a contract of one notrump or two in a suit may be badly defeated.

No strategic third-hand bid should be made when the suit is a ragged one and cannot stand an opening lead from partner. The following hands are typical of good third-hand strategic bids:

| ♠ K Q 8 7 5 4 | ♡ 6 | ◊ Q J 10 | ♣ 10 7 2 |
| ♠ 8 5 | ♡ Q 6 3 | ◊ A Q J 7 4 | ♣ J 10 8 |

Choice of Suits

The choice between two or more biddable suits in the opening hand is made by considering:

1. The length of the suits.
2. The rank of the suits.
3. The strength of the hand.

There is a further consideration which may outweigh all three of these mathematical guides, and this factor, though essentially a part of the third consideration, is important enough to warrant separate listing. It is:

4. The Principle of Preparedness.

We shall see later how the Principle of Preparedness may alter the normal choice of the opening bid if the hand includes less than four honor-tricks (or 3½ with well-padded suits). But first let us consider the factors that determine normal choice between two biddable suits.

LENGTH

1. With two suits of unequal length, the shortest being a five- or six-card suit, bid first the *longer*. (5 and 6, 5 and 7, 6 and 7.)

2. With one six-card or longer suit and one four-card biddable suit (a semi-two-suiter), usually bid the longer suit *twice* before showing the shorter,* and if the longer suit is seven cards or more, usually avoid showing the four-card suit at all.

Example:　♠ A Q 7 5　♡ 6　◊ A J 8 5 4 3　♣ Q 9

If partner responds with one heart to the opening bid of one diamond, rebid one spade rather than two diamonds.

---

* When a good four-card major may be shown by a bid of one, the four-card suit should be shown before the six-card suit is rebid.

3. With two biddable suits of five and four cards—the commonest type of semi-two-suiter—always bid the longer suit first if it is higher ranking. When the four-card suit is higher ranking it may sometimes be bid first—particularly with hands of less than four honor-tricks (or 3½ with strong intermediates). Consider the Principle of Preparedness before making the choice.

4. With two or three four-card biddable suits, the choice is governed by the Principle of Preparedness.

CHOICE OF SUITS OF UNEQUAL LENGTH

With 6–5, 7–6, 6–4, 7–4: Follow the Principle of Length regardless of honor strength.* In these distributional freaks lack of great honor strength is usually made up for by distributional values (winners), and it is of utmost importance to give the correct picture of length.

The Hand				Bid	Rebid
♠AKQ76	♡92	◇KQ8765	♣—	1◇	spades (twice)
♠986543	♡AKJ82	◇A	♣6	1♠	hearts
♠KJ74	♡A6	◇AQ7642	♣9	1◇	diamonds†
♠—	♡AQ63	◇AQJ8762	♣84	1◇	diamonds (twice)
♠KQJ853	♡—	◇—	♣A1076532	1♣	spades (twice)

With 5–4 Distribution: With four or more honor-tricks bid the longer suit first; show the four-card suit before rebidding the five-card suit. The choice with weaker hands is governed by the Principle of Preparedness.

♠ A K Q 6	♡ Q 9	◇ K Q 8 5 4	♣ K 3	Bid one diamond
♠ A Q 8 4 3	♡ K J 10 6	◇ A 7 5	♣ 4	Bid one spade
♠ 6	♡ K Q J 5	◇ K J 7	♣ A K 6 5 4	Bid one club

---

* Exceptionally, in a hand with minimum honor strength a strong five-card major may be bid in preference to a weak six-card minor.

† If partner's response is one heart, the first rebid is one spade. Otherwise rebid diamonds first (unless a pass is proper).

THE PRINCIPLE OF RANK

With two *five-card or longer* biddable suits *of equal length,* bid first the higher-ranking suit. There are two exceptions: (1) When the higher-ranking suit is weak (say, J x x x x); (2) when the opening bid is relatively weak (less than 4 honor-tricks) and the two five-card suits are spades and clubs.

♠ A K 7 5 3   ♡ 6 2   ◇ 8   ♣ A Q 9 7 4

It is better to be *prepared* on this hand by opening with one club. If partner responds with one diamond or one heart, bid one spade; and if partner persists, rebid spades, correcting the original wrong impression.

Thus, with

♠ A Q 8 5 3	and	♣ K Q J 7 6	Bid one club
♠ K 9 6 5 4	and	♡ A K J 10 5	Bid one spade
♡ K Q 7 6 3	and	◇ A K Q J 10	Bid one heart
♠ Q 6 5 3 2	and	♣ A K Q J 6	Bid one club

Bidding the higher-ranking suit makes it possible for partner to show preference (page 224) without raising the bidding level.

Suppose you hold

♠ Q 8 6 5 2   ♡ A K 8 5 4   ◇ K 3   ♣ 8

You open with one spade; partner responds one notrump. Now when you bid two hearts, partner can pass if he prefers hearts and can bid two spades if he prefers spades. In either case the best combined suit will be found at the two-level.

If you had opened with one heart, and then bid two spades over one no-trump, partner—if he preferred hearts—would have to bid *three* hearts to get back into that suit.

THE STRENGTH OF THE HAND

With two four-card suits, prefer as a rule the higher ranking whenever the hand contains four honor-tricks or more (3½ honor-tricks with well-padded suits or with strength in three suits). In all other cases choice should be made in accordance with the Principle of Preparedness.

I have stated that the Principle of Preparedness is essentially a part of the third factor governing choice of suits—the Strength of the Hand.

The reason why this principle is closely bound up with Strength is because of the quality and quantity inferences which are drawn from the *sequence* of bidding.

The "Reverse"

The bid of a higher-ranking suit by a player who has previously bid one of lower rank is called a "Reverse." This reverse when it occurs at the level of two or higher logically depicts a strong hand because it compels partner, if he wishes to express a mere choice for the first-mentioned suit, to climb to a still higher level.

SOUTH	NORTH
1 ◇	1 N T
2 ♠	

Of course South bid only two spades. He did not bid three. But suppose North has:

♠ 6 2   ♡ K J 3   ◇ 10 7 4   ♣ Q 8 6 4 2

South does not want to be left to suffer, with two little spades as trump support in North's hand. The diamond suit will be much better, and South naturally wants North to show preference and return to three diamonds.

This clearly announces greater strength than the opening bid might include if it were a minimum.

However, when the reverse occurs at the *same* level—the level of one-bids—it does *not* announce that the hand includes greater strength than shown by the opening bid itself (although the hand *may* contain added strength).

Thus:

NORTH	SOUTH		NORTH	SOUTH
1 ♣	1 ◇	or	1 ◇	1 ♡
1 ♡			1 ♠	

In these examples the reverse occurs at the *same* level and no greater strength than necessary for the opening bid itself may be assumed from the fact of the reverse.

After a game-forcing bid, also, the reverse by the opening

hand does not necessarily show any greater strength than if the
reverse had occurred at the level of one.

Example: SOUTH   NORTH
                        1 ◊   2 ♡
                        2 ♠

(Obviously, over a one-heart response the opening bidder could have
reversed at *one* spade. A similar situation may arise when partner has made
a free suit takeout—see page 239.)

What may the partner logically infer from these two different
uses of the reverse?

In the first example, he may expect greater strength than a
minimum—and he may also rely on the *count of length* given
by the bidding. North's first bid suit is *longer* than his second;
probably five and four; possibly six and five. In other words,
the choice of first bids has been normal because the strength
of the hand did not make necessary a modification of the Principle of Length.

But in the second examples, no such precise count of length
should be drawn. North's first bid suit *may* be longer than his
second, but the suits may be of equal length—if the strength
of North's hand was insufficient to warrant bidding in normal
order.

Assume that North, with suits of equal length, but with a
near-minimum, had chosen entirely on the Principle of Rank.
The bidding would then have gone:

NORTH   SOUTH   NORTH   SOUTH
 1 ♡   2 ◊   instead of   1 ♣   1 ◊
 3 ♣   1 ♡

A progression of two rounds, contrary to both the Principle of Economy
of Bids and the added strength requirements for the higher rounds. This,
though it does not actually bid the suits in reverse order of their rank, has
the same effect of forcing partner to make his choice at the level of three-
odd, and must therefore show at least as good a hand as the reverse shows.

Summing up the influence of the strength of the hand on
the choice of suits:

*Avoid the necessity for a reverse at a higher level if the hand
contains less than four (sometimes 3½) honor-tricks.*

With about four honor-tricks, or 3½ with well-padded suits,

the normal choice of opening bid (in accordance with principles of Length and Rank) should be followed even though this may necessitate a reverse in a higher round.

The Principle of Preparedness

Since the sequence of the bids interprets the strength of the hand, the probable second bid—the rebid—should usually be considered before the first bid is chosen.

The Principle of Preparedness therefore may *alter* the normal choice of first bids because the normal bid, if made, would become a distorted picture of the hand when modified by the rebid! This consideration and the Principle of Economy of Bids comprise the Principle of Preparedness.

WHY WE USE PREPARED BIDS

Modern bidding has made great strides, but perhaps it has grown too fast for its strength. We have established certain bids as forcing. Yet these bids—the one-over-one and two-over-one takeouts—may be made with very minimum values. At their weakest they may be "courtesy" bids, made solely to keep the bidding open. At their strongest, they are hands which almost warrant jump takeouts. To protect the weak "chance-giving" takeout, at the same time as we insure that the *powerful* takeout will be kept open, it is necessary for the sake of safety that the opening bidder can rebid over any one-round-forcing bid not only because he is *forced* to but because he was *prepared* to!

These, then, are the reasons why we employ the Principle of Preparedness in making the choice of first bids:

1. To economize on precious rounds of bidding.
2. To avoid *inferences* of added strength when rebidding.
3. To avoid forcing the responding hand to a level beyond the power of the combined hands.

HOW TO USE THE PRINCIPLE OF PREPAREDNESS

Practically the only interference of Preparedness with the Principle of Length comes in the bidding of hands of $3\frac{1}{2}$

honor-tricks or less, containing a five-card and a four-card suit.

With   ♠ A K 6 5   ♡ A 7 6 4 2   ◊ 9 3   ♣ 5 4

If we chose automatically by length we would bid one heart. Partner may respond two clubs or two diamonds, forcing us to rebid once. If we rebid two spades we *reverse* at a higher round, and partner, even with a weak hand, must now go to *three* hearts if he prefers that suit. So we conceal the true picture of *length* deliberately, to avoid a more dangerously false picture of *strength*.

NORTH	SOUTH
1 ♠	2 ♣ or 2 ◊
2 ♡	

Partner may now pass or he may express a preference for spades by going back to *two* spades.

With 5–4 Distribution and not more than 3½ honor-tricks, choose a high-ranking four-card suit in preference to a *touching* lower-ranking five-card suit.

♠ A Q J 8   ♡ A K 6 5 3   ◊ 7 2   ♣ 8 5   Bid one spade

♠ K 9 3   ♡ K Q 6 4   ◊ A J 10 8 5   ♣ 9   Bid one heart

Choose a lower-ranking five-card suit when the four-card suit may be shown in the same round (when the suits are not touching), or when a reverse at a higher round, if necessary, will be warranted because of strong support for partner's suit.

♠ A J 6 5   ♡ 9 2   ◊ 7 4   ♣ A K 8 5 3 Bid one club. If partner bids one diamond or one heart the reverse can be made at the same level—one-odd.

♠ K Q 9 7   ♡ 6   ◊ K J 10 5 4   ♣ A Q 8 Bid one diamond. Over one heart bid one spade. Over two clubs a two-spade bid is warranted by fine support for clubs.

With four honor-tricks or more, bid the longer suit first. Many players abuse the reverse principle, employing it to show strength at the cost of showing length. These players may bid a four-card minor suit before a five-card major, in order to make their second bid reflect their powerful high-card holding. This is entirely improper.

Also see page 112—the choice between spades and clubs with five of each.

Partner's Count of Length

When the opening hand reverses at a *higher* level, partner can usually expect that the first bid suit is the longer. A reverse at the same level does not necessarily indicate that the first suit is longer. The suits may be of equal length. For example:

South	North		South	North
1 ♣	1 ♡		1 ♣	1 ♢
1 ♠		or	1 ♡	

A rebid in a *lower-ranking* suit may possibly represent a longer second suit. For example:

South	North		South	North
1 ♠	1 N T		1 ♡	1 ♠
2 ♡		or	2 ♢	

But after a reverse, the first bid suit is almost always longer than the second.

South	North		South	North
1 ♡	2 ♣		1 ♢	1 ♠
2 ♠		or	2 ♡	

South's first suit is longer than his second suit unless the second suit is only a conditional biddable five-card suit.

(With ♠ 7 6 5 3 2   ♡ A Q   ♢ A K 7 5 3   ♣ A   Bid one diamond; over any response rebid in spades.)

Choice of Four-Card Suits

It is in the choice between four-card suits that the Principle of Preparedness has its greatest effect on the Principle of Rank— and it is here that the problem becomes somewhat more complex. The question involved is always that of the rebid, and the choice is therefore based to a large degree on which is the weakest (usually the shortest) suit in the opening hand.

The first step therefore is to expect that response for which we are the least prepared, and select the bid that gives us the soundest rebid over this anticipated response.

4–4–3–2 Distribution—Two Biddable Suits

As between two *touching* four-card suits, prefer as a rule the higher ranking. Spades adjoin or "touch" hearts, hearts "touch" diamonds, diamonds "touch" clubs.

| ♠ A J 6 5 | ♡ K Q J 7 | ◇ K 8 3 | ♣ 9 2 | Bid one spade |
| ♠ 7 3 | ♡ A J 7 5 | ◇ A K Q 4 | ♣ J 9 3 | Bid one heart |

Exception: Weak hands including four-card club and diamond suits may be bid one club. For example: ♠ 8 6 3   ♡ 10 7   ◇ A K 7 6   ♣ A J 9 4. If partner responds one heart or one spade we rebid one notrump. If we bid one diamond, should partner respond two clubs we are forced to raise to three clubs, a strong inferential try for three notrump (page 223), which the weakness of the hand makes unwise.

As between two non-touching four-card suits, prefer as a rule:

1. The most comfortable (round-saving).

   ♠ A K 8 3   ♡ 6 2   ◇ J 9 4   ♣ A Q 7 5   Bid one club

2. The prepared bid:

   ♠ J 6 2   ♡ A K 8 5   ◇ 7 3   ♣ A J 9 5 Bid one club. If partner responds one diamond we are prepared to rebid one heart. If partner responds one spade we rebid one notrump. But:

   ♠ 8 3   ♡ A Q J 2   ◇ K 9 5   ♣ K Q 6 4 Bid one heart. If partner responds one spade we are prepared to rebid one notrump or two clubs. If partner responds two diamonds we are prepared to rebid by raising diamonds. But it would be equally *safe* to bid one club; the only disadvantage being that a one-spade response would prevent our showing the heart suit.

3. When neither bid affords complete preparedness, which usually occurs with spades and diamonds:

   (*a*) Bid one spade when you have support for hearts.

   ♠ A K 6 5   ♡ J 10 3   ◇ K Q 8 4   ♣ 6 2

If partner's response is two clubs, bid two diamonds; if partner's response is two hearts, you may raise.

   (*b*) Bid one diamond with adequate support for clubs.

   ♠ A K 6 5   ♡ 6 2   ◇ K Q 8 4   ♣ Q 6 5

If partner responds one heart, rebid one spade; if partner responds two clubs, you may raise clubs.

(*c*) The stronger suit with minimum hands lacking support for hearts *or* clubs.

♠ A K J 6   ♡ 8 3   ◇ K J 10 5   ♣ 6 3 2

Bid one spade; if partner responds two hearts, a two-spade rebid, dangerous though it is, will be the least of evils.

4. With strength in three suits: Choose the prepared bid, including the possibility of two notrump as a rebid:

♠ A J 6 5   ♡ 8 4 2   ◇ K Q 7 6   ♣ A 8   Bid one spade

Obviously a bid of one diamond leaves only an unsound two-notrump or two-spade rebid over the possible response of two clubs. But if the response to one spade is two hearts, two notrump may be bid, as partner will have hearts stopped.

♠ K 8 5   ♡ K J 10 7   ◇ 6 2   ♣ A K 5 3   Bid one club

Show the hearts if partner responds one diamond; raise if partner responds one spade; pass a one-notrump response.

It will be noted that safety is always served by bidding one club if you have a club suit; when you lack a club suit, the higher-ranking suit is usually the preferred first bid.

But the reader is urged to treat each hand of this type as a separate problem. In many cases the choice may rest between two evils—and the best that can be done is to select the lesser. As a rule, the best suit is the one which does not carry the weak hand to the dangerous level of two- or three-odd.

4–4–4–1 DISTRIBUTION

When all three suits are biddable or nearly so, the choice is less difficult, from the standpoint of preparedness, than with two four-card suits. There is only one suit response for which we are not prepared and we need consider only the possibility of that response and a response of one notrump.

With three four-card biddable or nearly biddable suits, prefer, as a rule:

1. The highest when all suits are touching.

♠ A J 6 5   ♡ K 10 8 4   ◇ K Q J 3   ♣ 7   Bid one spade
♠ 8   ♡ K Q 6 5   ◇ A Q 7 2   ♣ K 10 6 5   Bid one heart

2. The most economical (round-saving) when the suits are
   not touching.

♠ A J 8 5   ♡ 6   ◇ K J 10 7   ♣ A 10 9 5   Bid one diamond

But: (a) The major when both majors are strong:

♠ K Q 10 6   ♡ A J 10 7   ◇ 8   ♣ K J 6 5   Bid one spade

(b) The lowest when both majors are weak:

♠ K 10 6 3   ♡ A 9 7 4   ◇ 6   ♣ A Q 10 3   Bid one club

We bid one club because if partner responds one diamond we can bid
one heart or one spade, but if partner responds one notrump we discard
any game hopes and pass.

Strengthen the example hands to four honor-tricks or more
and we make our choice on a different basis because we are
prepared to reverse if necessary.

♠ K Q J 8   ♡ A Q 9 5   ◇ 6   ♣ K Q J 2

Again we have two strong major suits but this time we bid one club, in
accordance with the Economy Principle. If partner responds one diamond,
we rebid one spade; and if partner then bids two clubs, two diamonds or
one notrump, we bid two hearts, thus showing all three suits below the
third round. But our great reason for this choice is that if partner bids one
notrump we can still bid two spades because the hand is strong enough to
warrant forcing the bidding to a higher round.

It will be observed that the Principles of Economy and Pre-
paredness are usually best served by the choice of that biddable
suit which ranks next below the singleton.

The Effect on Biddable Suits

Sometimes the one biddable suit in the hand offers no possibility of a sound rebid over partner's *anticipated* one-round-
forcing response. This has given birth to the much-abused
three-card minor-suit bid, often called—as though it were a
bidding system—the "Short Club." Experts fall back on this
bid of a three-card minor only when it is absolutely essential;
properly, they treat it as a necessary evil.

Many hands that are too strong to pass would be too weak
to rebid if the normal opening bid—based on biddable suit
requirements—were made. Other hands contain no properly

biddable suit, do not meet the requirements for one notrump, and yet are too strong to pass.

In some of these hands the problem may be solved by bidding a shaded four-card suit; in others, bidding a three-card minor suit is the only remedy.

The use of such a three-card suit is a "prepared" bid and should not be confused with the artificial club and diamond bids used in some systems to denote powerful hands and in others to denote sub-minimum protective third- or fourth-hand bids. Such bids are definitely losing bids, and systems based on them are unsound. They waste, needlessly, the most precious commodity in bridge—bidding rounds or *time*. They confuse the partner while opening the door to the opponents for low, cheap overcalls. There are no artificial opening bids in the Culbertson System. We do not *distort* the first bid to picture, by that one call, the general strength of the hand. We modify the first bid only so that later bids will *not* distort the picture of the hand's true strength.

THREE-CARD-SUIT BIDS

There are two sound reasons for the choice of the three-card minor as the "prepared bid." First: minor-suit openings offer partner easy opportunity to respond—and opening bidder opportunity to rebid—*at the one-level!* Second: partner is hardly likely to carry a minor suit to five-odd without at least five good trumps—in which case the suit is safely playable.

In order to assure this parallel—as well as to be prepared for a possible opening lead in the suit-bid—we set the requirements for the short minor suit as three to the Ace, King, or Queen-ten. (A x x, K x x, or Q 10 x.)

4–4–3–2 and 4–3–3–3 Minimums

The choice of the three-card suit is the only choice affected by the opening bidder's position at the table. Third or fourth hand, the use of the three-card suit is confined exclusively to those hands with no biddable suit and insufficient strength or incorrect distribution for opening with one notrump. Here there is no need for preparing the rebid, since partner's initial pass has removed the forcing character of the suit takeout.

Therefore, although there is little difference in the *strength* required for the opening bid first, second, third, or fourth hand, there may be a vast difference in the *choice* of what that bid should be when partner has not yet passed (first or second hand), and when partner has already passed (third and fourth hand).

The correct bidding of the following hands is given for first and second hand, as well as third and fourth:

Opening Bid, Holding:				First or Second	Third or Fourth
♠ A Q 6 3	♡ 8 7 5	◇ A 5 4	♣ K 8 6	1 ♣	1 ♠
♠ Q 9 5	♡ K J 6 3	◇ 8 5 4	♣ A K 8	1 ♣	1 ♡
♠ A 7 5 2	♡ K J 6	◇ A J 7	♣ J 5 3	1 ◇	1 ◇

CHAPTER TEN

FORCING
BIDS

The Forcing Principle*

At the start of the bidding the partners are in the situation of two allied armies groping in total darkness. Partner's (and opponents') honor strength and distribution or suit lengths are unknown. Almost any opening bid is a leap in the dark. The responding hand, though better off after receiving the first message from his ally, will as a rule need much more information before completing the maneuvers for the final position or bid at which to give battle. Hence the strategy of cautious advances by both partners, the scouting-approach bids pushed out ahead of the main body of hands as "feelers" to reconnoiter for game possibilities or to fall back on defensive positions.

It will at times happen that a glance at the hand will suffice to see a game and even the prospects of a luscious slam. Such a hand bristles with Aces and Kings and usually contains two or three suits with *untold* possibilities—untold because success will usually depend upon the selection of the right bid out of several bids available.

In all cases, without exception, it is important not to spurt wildly toward the goal like an untrained horse smelling its

---

* The Forcing Principle and various forcing bids were originated and developed by the author as a necessary and logical corollary of his Approach Principle. They are now standard and form the basis of every system without exception. The Culbertson System of Bridge is also called and known as the Approach-Forcing System, although this is not correct since it does not include the Culbertson System of Plays and Leads.

stable, but to double your caution. Here the principles of Economy of Bids and Approaching are more important than ever. The reason is that the greatest loss to players does not come from their bad hands but from their good hands. At the bottom of many of these disasters I find nervous, almost panicky leaps straight to game or slam. I have seen jerky, impulsive gambles with a dangerous trump suit ending in disaster when a game or a slam would have been assured in some other suit, had not additional information been suppressed. And back of this I find the fear, often justified only too well, that *partner may drop the bidding before a game or a slam is reached.*

It is the purpose of the Forcing Principle scientifically to approach a game or a slam by the utmost economy of rounds and yet to banish the fear that partner will prematurely abandon the bidding.

Forcing Bids Defined: The Forcing Principle requires that after certain special bids, called forcing bids, either partner must keep the bidding open *even without any, or added, values.*

Many years ago in auction bridge I held:

♠ —   ♡ K Q J 10   ◇ A K 5 4 2   ♣ A K Q 10

We were on the rubber game and the opponent on my right, a sound player, bid originally four spades. My partner was a relative stranger but looked intelligent. I bid five spades. Partner bid six clubs, holding:

♠ 8 6 5   ♡ 9 7 4   ◇ 9 3   ♣ 9 7 6 3 2

We made six clubs with a little luck, and a large profit.

That was the birth-cry of the Forcing Principle, years before contract bridge.

THE FORCING BIDS

In the opening hand the opening two-bids are reserved exclusively for the game-forcing bids. After the bidding has been opened, *any jump bid, when such a jump is exactly one trick higher than needed to overcall the last bid, is reserved for a game-forcing bid.**

---

* See also Chapters 11, 12, 16, 21, 23, 26, 27.

For instance:

	NORTH	SOUTH
	1 ♡	2 ♠ (forcing)
but not	NORTH	SOUTH
	1 ♡	3 ♠

It is evident that the lowest available berth that could be assigned to the game-forcing bids is a single jump.

OBJECT OF FORCING

There are three strategic objects of the Forcing Principle:

. 1. To choose or offer to partner a choice *for game* between one or more suits and notrump.

Partner has bid one heart; you bid *three* hearts with ♠ K J 6   ♡ Q 8 5 3 ◇ A 7 4 2   ♣ K 7, but you will pass a three-notrump rebid.

2. To determine, without risking a pass or contracting too high, whether partner has or has not a certain key card or cards necessary for a small or grand slam.

You hold ♠ A K Q 5 3   ♡ A Q 6 4   ◇ 7   ♣ Q J 10. Partner has bid one heart; you bid *two* spades; but hearts will undoubtedly be the trump suit at the final bid.

3. To determine, without risking a pass and yet without risking a possibly dangerous game contract, whether partner has added values over his minimum previously shown (in which case the game will be contracted for); or has but a minimum (in which case the hand is passed below game).

Partner has bid one heart; you bid two clubs with ♠ K 7 5   ♡ Q 6 3 ◇ 8 4   ♣ A Q 6 5 2.

Accordingly, there are three distinct kinds of forcing bids: the *game* force, the *slam* force, and the *one-round* force. In the *game* force, the bidding is kept open until some game is reached. In the *slam* force and *one-round* force the bidding is kept open temporarily.

When a forcing bid is made, the partner is under obligation to bid again. It is unconditional. "Theirs not to reason why, theirs but to do or die." It does not matter if the player who is forced to bid has an absolutely blank hand, or nothing "new" to show, or has made a psychic, or is convinced that his partner is a congenital idiot—the bidding must go on. People have been shot for less. This is the only meaning given to the word *forcing* in the Culbertson System. I do not deny that in certain rare cases a player may save a few hundred points by passing his partner's forcing bid, but this is a costly economy, for once partner's confidence is shaken and he has to take into his calculations even the remote possibility that partner may pass the forcing bid, the entire sequence of his bidding will take another and more unnatural course.

Bridge is full of bidding situations which are *"practically,"* *"almost,"* or *"semi-"* forcing bids. But with forcing bids there are no "ifs" and "buts." The pass ceases to exist.

The effect of a forcing bid is that partner must keep the bidding open.

South	West	North	East
1 ♠	Pass	3 ◇ (forcing)	Pass

South must bid

If South passed, West might close the bidding by passing and North would not get another chance.

When an opponent obligingly assures partner another chance to bid, there is no need to keep the bidding open for him.

South	West	North	East
1 ♠	Pass	3 ◇ (forcing)	3 ♡

South may pass

Since East has bid, North is sure to get another chance. South need not keep the bidding open for him.

A forcing bid is either *forcing to game* or *forcing for one round*.

Bids That Are Forcing to Game

When a bid is forcing to game it imposes simultaneously an obligation on both partners, the one who forces and the one who is forced. A "forcing situation" exists and both partners are supposed to continue the bidding until a game is reached or the opponents are doubled for penalties. Neither partner may pass unless an opponent bids, thus assuring the other partner another chance.

A bid of exactly one more trick than is necessary, whether an opening bid, a raise, or a rebid, and whether in a suit or in notrump, is, with rare exceptions, forcing to game.

When such a bid is not forcing to game, it usually carries a strength-showing message nevertheless and is non-forcing only in the sense that partner may pass it if his previous bid was not up to snuff.

Almost never will any real harm be done if a jump bid—provided it is a jump of exactly one trick—is treated as a forcing bid, since the hand shown is strong enough to stand an additional trick on the contract.

These are the bids that are forcing to game:

1. An opening two-bid in a suit. (However, see the "Limit Two-Bid," page 146.)

2. A jump takeout of partner's opening bid.

3. A jump rebid in a new suit by the opener, after his partner has responded to the opening bid.

4. In general, any response to a bid that is strength-showing but not forcing. Such a bid is deemed to accept the invitation to reach a game, so that thereafter neither partner may pass before game has been reached. To illustrate:

SOUTH	WEST	NORTH	EAST
1 ♡	Pass	2 ♣	Pass
3 ♡	Pass	3 ♠ (forcing)	Pass
4 ♣ (forcing)			

Once North responded to the three-heart bid (which he might have passed) a *forcing situation* was established. Now game must be reached.

Notwithstanding any forcing situation, a penalty double by partner may always be passed.

STRENGTH-SHOWING JUMP BIDS

The jump bids that are *not forcing* are:

1. A double raise of partner's opening minor-suit bid.

SOUTH	WEST	NORTH	EAST
1 ◇	Pass	3 ◇	Pass

South may pass

North has a fairly strong hand with powerful trump support, but his hand is unsuitable to notrump play or a major-suit takeout; and if South cannot bid notrump or a major suit, and is too weak to try for an eleven-trick minor-suit game, he may pass.

2. An opening bid of two notrump. (But this is a very strong bid, and is seldom passed—see page 88.)

3. A jump *rebid* in notrump, or in a suit previously bid by either partner.

South	West	North	East
1 ♡	Pass	1 ♠	Pass

2 N T
or 3 ♡ } Not forcing
or 3 ♠

These are strength-showing bids and urge North to go on to game, but he may pass if his first response was a minimum.

4. A jump response by a player who passed originally.

South	West	North	East
Pass	Pass	1 ♡	Pass

2 N T
or 3 ♡ } not forcing
or 3 ♢

South shows the maximum hand on which he could have passed originally. North, with a hand of genuinely biddable strength, should usually bid again; but North has the option of passing, knowing that South's hand is limited by his original pass.

5. A double raise over a takeout double is not forcing:

South	West	North	East
1 ♡	Double	3 ♡ (not forcing)	Pass

South may pass

North's bid is preëmptive and South should pass it unless he is strong enough to have bid over a (non-forcing) single raise.

6. A jump suit takeout over an opponent's takeout double is forcing for only one round:

South	West	North	East
1 ♢	Double	2 ♡	Pass

South must bid, but may later drop the bidding short of game.

7. When partner passes the opening bid, a jump rebid in a new suit is not entirely forcing.

South	West	North	East
1 ♡	2 ♣	Pass	Pass
3 ♢			

North may pass, but should raise with some distributional support for either of South's suits, even without an honor-trick in his hand.

Limited and Unlimited Forcing Bids

Some game-forcing bids are limited, some are unlimited. A limited game-forcing bid announces no aim beyond that of reaching game, and so is not forcing once game has been reached. An unlimited forcing bid hints at a slam and is forcing for at least one round even if game has been reached.

An opening two-bid in a suit, or a jump takeout or rebid in a new suit, is forcing for at least one round even if (with a part-score) game has been reached.

A two-notrump takeout or double raise of an opening bid is not forcing if it is enough for game.

North-South have 40 on score. The bidding:

South	West	North	East
1 ♡	Pass	2 ♠ or 3 ♢ (forcing)	
		2 N T or 3 ♡ (not forcing)	

Bids That Are Forcing for One Round

Some bids are forcing for one round only—that is, the player who forces demands one more chance to bid. He does not demand that a game contract be reached, but the necessity to respond once is just as great. The principal differences between these and game-forcing bids are:

(*a*) The partner, after making sure that the bidding is kept open once, may pass thereafter unless a new forcing bid is made.

(*b*) The player who makes the one-round-forcing bid does not obligate *himself* in any way. Even when he is given his chance to rebid, he is at liberty to pass, unless his partner's rebid was forcing.

Any suit takeout of partner's opening one-bid is forcing for one round.

South	West	North	East
1 ♡	Pass	1 ♠ or	
		2 ♢ (one-round forcing)	

But avoid confusion between this case and the following cases:

1. A non-jump *rebid* by either partner is not forcing.

SOUTH	WEST	NORTH	EAST
1 ◊	Pass	1 ♡	Pass
1 ♠ (not forcing)			
or 2 ♣ (not forcing)			

or

SOUTH	WEST	NORTH	EAST
1 ♡	Pass	2 ◊	Pass
3 ♣ (not forcing)			

2. A takeout of an opening suit-bid in a new suit is not forcing when made by a player who has passed originally.

SOUTH	WEST	NORTH	EAST
Pass	Pass	1 ♡	Pass
2 ◊ (not forcing)			

or

SOUTH	WEST	NORTH	EAST
Pass	Pass	1 ♡	Pass
1 ♠ (not forcing)			

South has in each case shown by passing at first that he has less than the strength needed for an opening bid. In view of this fact, North may decide that game is impossible and may pass the response.

3. A non-jump suit takeout is not forcing if it is enough for game:

North-South have 60 on score.

SOUTH	WEST	NORTH	EAST
1 ♡	Pass	2 ◊ (not forcing)	
		but 2 ♠ (forcing)	

4. A "free" suit response to an opening suit-bid of one is forcing, but a free response to an opening one-notrump bid is not:

SOUTH	WEST	NORTH	EAST
1 ♡	2 ◊	3 ♣ (forcing)	

but

SOUTH	WEST	NORTH	EAST
1 N T	2 ◊	3 ♣ (not forcing)	

In addition to the suit takeouts described above, any conventional four- or five-notrump slam try is forcing for one round. See Chapter 27.

The Defenders' Forcing Bids

The side that did not open the bidding must be more cautious in its forcing bids than the opening side. A defender knows that one opponent has about three honor-tricks against him. His partner may have a blank. Therefore a defender's bid is never forcing to game unless he has previously bid (or doubled) and his partner has responded. But the following defenders' bids are forcing for one round:

1. An immediate overcall in the opponents' bid suit.

SOUTH	WEST	NORTH	EAST
1 ♡	2 ♡		

This is the strongest bid a defender can make. It demands that East bid his best suit (other than hearts) or notrump.

2. An overcall of an opponent's preëmptive four- or five-bid with four or five notrump.

SOUTH	WEST	NORTH	EAST
4 ♠	4 N T		

or

SOUTH	WEST	NORTH	EAST
1 ♠	Pass	4 ♠	4 N T

This bid forces a response from partner in his best suit. It is at least as strong as an overcall in the opponents' suit, since it requires a response at so high a level. It could, of course, be classed as "forcing to game," since no response is possible below the game level.

An overcall of a preëmptive three-bid with three notrump is not a forcing bid.

3. A jump suit takeout of partner's overcall.

SOUTH	WEST	NORTH	EAST
1 ♣	1 ♡	Pass	2 ♠
			or 3 ♢

West must keep the bidding open for one round, but either partner may decide later to drop the bidding short of game.

4. A bid in the opponents' bid suit is usually forcing for at least one round, but there are exceptions (as explained on page 397).

A defender who has made an overcall in the opponents' suit can then force to game with a jump rebid in a new suit:

SOUTH	WEST	NORTH	EAST
1 ◇	2 ◇	Pass	2 ♡
Pass	3 ♠ (forcing to game)		

A jump response to a takeout double is not forcing; neither is a defender's jump overcall. Care must be taken to avoid confusion in these cases:

SOUTH	WEST	NORTH	EAST
1 ♣	Double	Pass	2 ♡
Pass	West may pass		

or

NORTH	EAST	SOUTH	WEST
1 ♣	2 ♡	Pass	West may pass

In either case, East could make a forcing bid by bidding two clubs.

SUMMARY OF FORCING SITUATIONS

Bids Which Are Forcing to Game

SOUTH	WEST	NORTH	EAST	
2 ◇				} Any opening two-bid.

SOUTH	WEST	NORTH	EAST	
1 ♡	Pass	2 ♠		
		or		} Jump takeout in a new suit.
1 ♠	Pass	3 ◇		

SOUTH	WEST	NORTH	EAST	
1 ♡	Pass	2 N T		} Jump two-notrump takeout.

SOUTH	WEST	NORTH	EAST	
1 ♡	Pass	3 ♡		
	but not			
1 ♡	Double	3 ♡		} Double raise in a major suit.
		or		
1 ◇	Pass	3 ◇		

SOUTH	WEST	NORTH	EAST	
1 ♡	1 ♠	2 ♠		Any bid in the opponents' suit, even
		or		if made by a player who has pre-
1 ♡	1 ♠	3 ♣	Pass	viously passed. (The exceptions are
4 ♣	Pass	4 ♡	Pass	noted on page 399.)
4 ♠				

SOUTH	WEST	NORTH	EAST	
1 ♡	Pass	1 N T	Pass	Jump rebid in a new suit after part-
3 ◇				ner has responded.
		or		
1 ♣	Pass	1 ♡	Pass	
2 ♠				

BY THE DEFENDERS

SOUTH	WEST	NORTH	EAST	
4 ♠	4 N T			Four- or five-notrump overcall of
		or		opponents' preëmptive bid.
5 ◇	5 N T			

SOUTH	WEST	NORTH	EAST	
1 ♣	2 ♣	Pass	2 ♡	A jump rebid in a new suit after
Pass	3 ♠			overcalling in opponents' suit.

Bids Which Are Forcing for One Round

SOUTH	WEST	NORTH	EAST	
1 ♡	Pass	1 ♠		
		or		
1 ♡	2 ♣	2 ◇		Suit takeout of an opening one-bid.
		or		
1 N T	Pass	2 ♡		

SOUTH	WEST	NORTH	EAST	
1 ♡	Pass	3 ♡	Pass	Any conventional four- or five-no-
4 N T	Pass	5 ♡	Pass	trump bid.
5 N T				

SOUTH	WEST	NORTH	EAST	
1 ◇	Pass	2 ♡	Pass	Any bid in a new suit when game
4 ♡	Pass	4 ♠		has been reached.

SOUTH	WEST	NORTH	EAST	
1 ♡	Double	2 ♠		A jump bid in a new suit over oppo-
				nents' takeout double.

SOUTH	WEST	NORTH	EAST	
1 ♡	Pass	2 ♡	Pass	A rebid by the opener in a new suit,
3 ◇				when partner has raised.

With a part-score, certain otherwise game-forcing bids become one-round forcing (page 129).

SOUTH	WEST	NORTH	EAST	
1 ♡	Pass	1 ♠	Pass	
2 N T	Pass	3 ♣		A response to an opening two-no-
		or		trump bid, or to a strength-showing
1 ♡	Pass	1 ♠	Pass	jump rebid. (But see also "Sign-off"
2 N T	Pass	3 ♡		and other weak rebids, page 226.)
		or		
2 N T	Pass	3 ♣		

SOUTH	WEST	NORTH	EAST	
1 ♠	Pass	2 ♦	Pass	After a game has been reached, any suit-bid which makes the contract still short of game.
3 N T	Pass	4 ♦		

See also The Forcing Pass, page 398.

BY THE DEFENDERS

SOUTH	WEST	NORTH	EAST	
1 ♡	Double	Pass	2 ♡	Cue-bid response to a takeout double.

SOUTH	WEST	NORTH	EAST	
1 ♡	2 ♡			Immediate overcall in the opponents' suit.

SOUTH	WEST	NORTH	EAST	
1 ♦	1 ♡	Pass	2 ♠	Jump takeout of overcall.

Bids Which Are Strength-Showing but Not Forcing

SOUTH	WEST	NORTH	EAST	
1 ♡	Pass	1 N T	Pass	
3 ♡				A jump rebid in the same suit.
or				
1 ♡	Pass	1 ♠	Pass	
1 N T	Pass	3 ♠		

SOUTH	WEST	NORTH	EAST	
1 ♡	Pass	1 ♠	Pass	A jump raise of partner's takeout.
3 ♠				

SOUTH	WEST	NORTH	EAST	
1 ♡	Pass	1 ♠	Pass	A jump two-notrump rebid.
2 N T				

SOUTH	WEST	NORTH	EAST	
1 ♡	Pass	Pass	1 ♠	Jump rebid in a new suit after partner passes opening bid.
3 ♣				

SOUTH	WEST	NORTH	EAST	
2 N T				Opening bids of two-notrump or higher.

SOUTH	WEST	NORTH	EAST	
1 ♡	Pass	3 N T		Jump notrump responses that are at game.

SOUTH	WEST	NORTH	EAST	
1 ♡	Pass	1 ♠	Pass	Jump preference raise of partner's suit.
2 ♦	Pass	3 ♡		

SOUTH	WEST	NORTH	EAST	
Pass	Pass	1 ♡	Pass	
3 ♡				Jump raises and notrump takeouts, when made by a player who has previously passed.
or				
Pass	Pass	1 ♡	Pass	
2 N T				

SOUTH	WEST	NORTH	EAST	
Pass	Pass	1 ◇	Pass	Jump suit takeouts, when made by a player who has previously passed; but if the opener had a genuine opening bid he should not pass.
2 ♡				

SOUTH	WEST	NORTH	EAST	
1 ◇	Pass	3 ◇		Double raise in a minor suit.

BY THE DEFENDERS

SOUTH	WEST	NORTH	EAST	
1 ♡	2 ♠ or			Single-jump overcall.
	3 ◇			

SOUTH	WEST	NORTH	EAST	
1 ♡	Double	Pass	1 ♠	A jump raise of partner's response to a takeout double.
Pass	3 ♠			

SOUTH	WEST	NORTH	EAST	
1 ♡	Double	Pass	2 ♠	Jump responses to takeout doubles.

SOUTH	WEST	NORTH	EAST	
1 ♡	Double	Pass	2 ◇	A jump rebid in a new suit after a takeout double.
Pass	3 ♠			

CHAPTER ELEVEN

OPENING SUIT-BIDS OF TWO

An opening bid of two in a suit is forcing to game, requiring partner to respond even with the weakest conceivable hand, and obligating both partners to continue the bidding until a game is reached or until a satisfactory penalty double of opponents is made. (See page 146, A Limit Two-Bid.*)

The purpose of the forcing two-bid is to make absolutely sure that, with certain powerful hands, neither partner will pass until vital information is exchanged for the selection of the best contract. In the days before the Forcing Principle was developed by this author, players who held powerful hands invariably found themselves between the devil and the deep blue sea: they either jumped to game, only to find themselves in the wrong contract for lack of time to exchange vital information about a better one, or they made a below-game bid, only to be left at the post by partner. In the philosophy of cards, a forcing two-bid is a device to *save time*.

By the same token, a two-bid should not be resorted to when a one-bid could do the job as well. The best *time-saver* and therefore the best bid in contract bridge is an opening suit-bid of one.

Hands containing five honor-tricks or less will not normally

---

* The obligation to reach game after a two-bid, like the obligation to respond to any forcing bid, is a matter of good bidding and not a matter of bridge law. Legally, a player cannot be forced to bid at any time. Occasionally, violation of partnership understanding yields a profit, but this is shortsighted economy because it risks more in loss of partner's confidence.

score game unless partner holds at least one honor-trick in addition. With one honor-trick he will usually respond to an opening one-bid, so that a two-bid with such hands is a losing bid, suffering a penalty when partner has nothing, and showing no gain when partner would have been able to respond to a one-bid anyway.

In this sense, a two-bid is a necessary evil. It must therefore be closely confined to the types of hands which cannot be adequately dealt with by an opening one-bid. There are two such types of hands: hands with powerful honor-trick strength and fair distributional values (strong suits); and hands with powerful distributional values (freak two-suiters or long solid suits) and fair honor strength. In the case of the former type of hand there is grave danger that partner may pass an opening suit-bid of one; in the case of the latter type of hand an opening two-bid, besides insuring a game, is better suited to slam development.

There is a third type of hand which, though powerful in honor strength (five or six honor-tricks) is so bereft of distributional values that it would be criminal to open it with a suit-bid of two, *even though there is a strong possibility that partner may pass an opening suit-bid of one.*

Here is an example of a "criminal" two-bid—a crime of which I, too, was guilty in the early unsophisticated days of two-bids:

♠ A K 3 2   ♡ A K 5   ◇ A K 8   ♣ 5 6 2

This hand should open with one spade. Certainly not two spades. If partner has a blank hand, there may easily be a three- or four-trick penalty at any game contract—a bidding crime. There is nothing more foolish in bridge than, with a powerful hand, to take a severe loss in reaching for a game.*

The dominant consideration of any two-bid is *safety.*

General Specifications of Two-Bids

An opening two-bid should seldom be even considered unless the hand *is not more than one trick short of a certain game.* The hand which justifies a forcing two-bid should, unaided,

---

* With the hand in question, I like a lead-deceiving one-club bid, with the intention of moving to game in notrump if partner shows a sign of life. But that's a horse of another color.

be reasonably sure of winning within one trick of the expected final contract (eight sure winners if able to stop at three no-trump; nine sure winners if necessary to go on to game in a suit).

Unbalanced hands are the ideal distribution for two-bids. Hands distributed 4–4–3–2 or 4–3–3–3, though strong enough for a two-bid, often can be better shown and can elicit more informative responses from partner if opened with a notrump bid of two or more (Chapter 7).

WHAT IS A STRONG SUIT?

The requirements in honor-tricks for a forcing two-bid will depend largely on the strength and length of the trump and side suits. Accordingly, the requirements vary from a minimum of 3½+ honor-tricks (with a powerful two-suiter) to 6 honor-tricks (with a balanced hand distribution and an average suit). How strong must a suit be? The answer to this question will in turn depend upon the length of a suit. As a rule:

A strong 4-card suit is one that contains three out of four top honors.

A strong 5-card suit is one that contains 4 winners (or 2 losers) based on the *next to worst* bad break. The next to worst bad break (or *normally* bad break) is usually four trumps with missing honors against the suit. For instance, ♡ A K Q 5 4 is a strong 5-card suit: it will win four tricks against ♡ J 10 3 2 in opponent's hands. But ♡ A K Q J 4 is a very strong or solid suit because it has virtually five sure winners against any trump distribution except five hearts to the ten.

A strong 6-card suit is one that contains four virtually sure winners (or two losers).

A strong 7-card or 8-card suit is one that contains five and six sure winners.

Specifications for Forcing Two-Bids

As a rule you will find that your hand is not good enough for a forcing two-bid unless you have at least the following:

5½ to 6 honor-tricks with strong four- or five-card suits:

| ♠ A K Q 6 | ♡ A K J 7 | ◇ A Q J 4 | ♣ 3 | Bid two spades |
| ♠ A Q 6 | ♡ A K 7 3 | ◇ 5 | ♣ A K J 10 3 | Bid two clubs |

5 honor-tricks with a strong six-card suit:

♠ A K   ♡ K Q J 7 5 3   ◇ 3   ♣ A Q J 10   Bid two hearts

5 honor-tricks with two strong five-card suits. They must
both be strong suits:

♠ 3   ♡ K Q J 10 2   ◇ A K Q 5 4   ♣ A Q   Bid two hearts

4+ honor-tricks with a strong seven- or eight-card suit:

♠ A 5   ♡ A K Q 9 6 5 3 ◇ 7   ♣ A 9 3   Bid two hearts

♠ A K 9 6 5 4 3 2 ♡ A 5   ◇ A 5 ♣ 2   Bid two spades

It will be noted that, as a general rule, the foregoing hands
contain 9 assured winners, i.e., are one trick short of game in
a major. No hand contains less than 4 honor-tricks. There is,
however, a small but important range of hands containing as
few as 3½+ honor-tricks which should be opened with a forcing
two-bid. Such hands belong to the family of powerful freaks.

HANDLING THE FREAKS

A freak may be defined as any hand containing a void or
two singletons.*

A hand-pattern such as 5–5–2–1 is *not* a freak, but the common garden variety of two-suiter. Even a 4–4–4–1, though somewhat feverish and wholly unlike her placid brother, the 4–4–3–2
is not a freak. But a 7–4–1–1, though beautiful in her sinuous
grace, is a freak; and so is the stolid and chunky 5–4–4–0.

The honor-trick requirements for the forcing two-bid with
strong freaks vary according to the number of sure winners in
the trump and side suits. The minimum honor-trick requirement is 3½ plus. In that case there must be 9 to 10 winners.
The trump must be a 6-card or longer suit with 5 assured
winners; the side suit must be almost as good. 3½ plus honor-
tricks is 15 to 16 points in high cards. The trump suit should
have the strength to withstand repeated ruffs. With 4 to 5
honor-tricks the hand may have as few as 8 winners provided
it has at least three first-round controls (Ace or void) and one

---

*I find nothing freakish in an eight-card suit by itself. It simply has a longer tail.

second-round control (a singleton or a K x). Here are some examples of two-bids on freaks:

♠ A K Q 8 4 3   ♡ K Q J 4 3 2   ◇ 3   ♣ —

Bid two spades. The hand counts up only 3½ plus, or 15 points in high cards, but it has about 10 winners. The hand will by itself produce game with any but a very abnormal break. If partner has anything at all it could produce a small slam, or even a grand slam. If partner responds to your two-spade bid with 2 notrump, bid three hearts. If partner's response shows strength, such as a raise to three spades, jump to four diamonds—an asking bid which is ideally suited for slam exploration, especially in view of the void in clubs.

It is true that if you bid one spade, the danger of the hand being left at one spade is not serious. The main reason for bidding two on this type of hand is that a forcing two-bid lends itself more easily and with a greater precision to slam bidding. (See Asking Bids and other slam conventions.) The precise responses to a two-bid are better adapted to exploration for slam. If on this hand you bid one spade and your partner responds, your subsequent bidding is bound to be jumpy and labored. No matter what you bid after one spade it would be difficult for partner to visualize such a freak as yours. You will too often end up with a four-spade or a four-heart bid when a slam is to be had for the asking. Besides, a one-bid will seldom save you a time-level * since you'll have to make a forcing rebid to three hearts if your partner responds with one notrump or two in a minor.

♠ A J 10 5 3   ♡ A   ◇ A Q 9 8 6   ♣ A x

Bid two spades. While this hand is not a freak, as defined, it requires the same treatment. Even if partner responds with two notrump, a couple of Queens may suffice for a game at three notrump or at spades. Admittedly, this hand may run up against that horrible situation where partner holds a blank heart-club two-suiter. But against this rare situation there is a greater gain from scoring games and slams which would other-

---

* I am forced to coin a term to express the time lost when a bidding level is shut out.

wise be missed. A raise to three spades may result in a small
or a grand slam—especially if asking bids are used.

♠ A Q J 5 3   ♡ A J 10 7 4   ◇ A Q 9   ♣ —

Bid two spades. This is one of the rare cases where the rule,
"More honor-tricks than losers," does not apply. The hand is
close, but I still prefer a two-spade bid.

It may be objected that a two-bid on this type of hand may
push partner into a *losing* slam by misleading him on the
honor-trick strength of the hand. It is difficult to see how an
alert player could be misled by a hand which, though slightly
shaded in honor strength, is considerably stronger in distributional value. A void is in most cases a better slam value than
an Ace. As for the danger of duplication of values, that always
exists. One of the advantages of the two-bid is that it is better
suited to explore duplication of values, especially when asking
bids are used. It has the added advantage of putting wise players
on the alert for this danger. Besides, it is a poor slam policy
for partner to rush into slam bids simply because he holds
some extra values. Except with weak players, it is more scientific to find out, as precisely as possible, about the first- and
second-round controls of the partnership's hands. Such methods
are available, especially in *asking* bids.

THE TWO-BID RULE

Before making a forcing two-bid, it is well to check up on
the hand by the application of this rule:

*You must have more honor-tricks than losers.**

Most hands that approach the two-bid stage are so solid that
the losers stand out and are easy to count.

♠ A 6   ♡ A K Q 10 9   ◇ A K J 10   ♣ 4 3

You have 5½ honor-tricks, counting "plus" values. Your
losers include two in clubs, one in spades, perhaps one to the
Queen of diamonds and one to the Jack of hearts. Total honor-

---

* From a practical standpoint it makes no difference whether you count honor-
tricks and winners and add them together ("Rule of Thirteen"), or count honor-
tricks and losers and compare them. Most players find it easier to use the rule
of "more honor-tricks than losers." I am indebted to Hy Lavinthal, on whose
original suggestion these rules are based.

tricks, 5½; total losers not more than 5. You have more honor-tricks than losers and should bid two hearts. If you hold:

♠ A K 10 6 5   ♡ A K 7   ◊ A Q 5   ♣ 7 3

You count two losers in clubs and one in hearts; one or two (say 1½) in diamonds; one or two in spades. You have at least 5½ losers; you have only 5½ honor-tricks. Not having more honor-tricks than losers, you must open with a one-spade bid despite your 5½ honor-tricks.

Losers are counted on the basis of a normal *bad* break. For instance, if opponents are assumed to have six cards in a suit, losers will be counted on the basis of a 4–2 division. The suit will not be expected to break 3–3 (a perfect division) nor 5–1 (an abnormal division).

Great losses come through automatically bidding two, and forcing to game, for no other reason than that a hand happens to have 5½—or even 6—honor-tricks.

For instance, ♠ A K 9 3   ♡ A K 10   ◊ A K 4   ♣ 8 5 4. Bid *one* spade. It is true the hand has 6 honor-tricks. But it also has seven losers. If you open with a forcing two-spade bid, you commit your side to game even though your partner may hold a trickless hand. With 7 losers, you may go down 3 tricks at notrump or 4 tricks in a major suit—a futile and disastrous loss.

It is also true that with 6 honor-tricks in the hand there is serious danger that your partner may pass if you open with one spade; a game in spades could be made if he has as little as ♠ J 10 8 3 and a singleton club. I concede that in rare cases a game may be lost by opening with a one-bid. Personally, I *like* to lose games occasionally.

Examples of Forcing Two-Bids

1.	♠ A K 10 9 7 6 4 3	♡ A Q 2	◊ K 6	♣ —
2.	♠ A K 10 8 7 6 3	♡ A Q J	◊ A 6	♣ 2
3.	♠ A K Q 7 6	♡ 6	◊ K Q J 10	♣ A Q J
4.	♠ A Q J 7 6 5	♡ A K 6	◊ K Q	♣ A 7
5.	♠ A Q J 6 2	♡ A K 6 3	◊ K Q 6	♣ A
6.	♠ K Q J 6 3	♡ A K Q 8	◊ A 7	♣ A 2
7.	♠ A K J 6	♡ A Q J 6	◊ K Q 10 7	♣ A

The following hands, despite their honor-trick strength, are *not* opening two-bids:

1. ♠ A K 6 5 3   ♡ A K 7   ◇ A Q 8   ♣ 6 2

2. ♠ A K 10 9 7   ♡ A K 6 5   ◇ A 5   ♣ 7 2

Responses to Forcing Two-Bids

The success of the forcing two-bid depends largely upon correct responses. The responses to a forcing two-bid are:

Pass—barred in all situations; except when the intervening opponent overcalls, in which case the pass is proper if holding less than 1½ honor-tricks.

If the bidding is:

SOUTH	WEST	NORTH	EAST
2 ♡	2 ♠	2 N T	

North, for his free two-notrump response, must have about 1½ honor-tricks including a spade stopper:

     ♠ K 10 6   ♡ 9 5   ◇ Q 6 4 2   ♣ Q J 5 3

With a weaker hand, North could pass, for South is already assured another chance to bid.

The fact that, due to an opponent's overcall, the responder may and does pass on the first round, in no way relieves either the opener or the responder from the obligation subsequently to keep the bidding open until game or its penalty equivalent is reached.

Two notrump—a blanket minimum response denoting a hand which contains less than one honor-trick and no long suit to show; or, if the hand does have one honor-trick, is not suitable to a raise or suit takeout.

Three notrump—a hand containing 1½ honor-tricks but no biddable suit or trump support. The 1½ honor-tricks should be divided among two or more suits.

Since the three notrump response to a forcing two-bid deprives the opener of his third level of bidding, the responder should avoid, if at all possible, bidding three notrump on bare 1½ honor-tricks.

A single raise shows adequate trump support with 1½ honor-tricks. As with the raise of an opening one-bid, the honor-trick requirement is decreased slightly when the distributional support is greater: With three trumps and a singleton, raise with one honor-trick; with four trumps and a doubleton, raise with one honor-trick.

Unlike the single raise of a one-bid, a single raise may be given to a two-bid when holding considerably more than the minimum requirements; for the bidding cannot die short of game. If partner opens with two diamonds, the best response on the following hand is a raise to three diamonds:

♠ 7 6   ♡ K 5 3 2   ◇ 8 7 5 4   ♣ A Q 6

The hand contains two honor-tricks, where only one is needed.

If the responding hand has better than a minimum raise, and also has a biddable suit, he should prefer to bid the suit first and raise later. He cannot give a double raise to show added strength, for the double raise carries a special message.

A double raise (from two to four) has a special meaning. Responder should give a double raise only when holding five trumps, or four trumps to the Queen; *he must not have a singleton or any honor higher than a Queen in his hand.* This is a neat little inference enabling the opener to stop dead in his tracks short of a dangerous slam, or, if strong enough to bid a slam without assistance, to decide whether to bid six or seven.

Caution: Do not use this weak double raise unless you are *sure* partner will not take it to be a sign of strength.

SUIT TAKEOUTS OF TWO-BIDS

A suit takeout is the preferred response on any hand that meets the requirements. This is not necessarily a strong hand. Much depends on the level at which the suit takeout can be made.

To bid a higher-ranking suit, which does not increase the bidding level, you need a biddable suit and:

1 honor-trick with a six-card suit;

1+ honor-trick with a five-card suit;

1½ honor-tricks with a four-card suit.

To show a lower-ranking suit a bid of three is required, and this response should not be made without 1½ honor-tricks; but any biddable suit, even a four-card suit, will do.

In the rare cases in which you may hold a strong hand and suit opposite partner's two-bid, it is unnecessary to make a jump response. Since the situation is forcing to game, you are sure to have another chance; and the jump response wastes valuable bidding time.

Any of the following hands justifies a suit takeout of partner's opening two-diamond bid:*

1.	♠ K 10 8 6 5 3	♡ 7 4	◇ 9 3	♣ 10 6 2	Two spades
2.	♠ A K Q 7 5	♡ K 6 5 2	◇ 6 3	♣ 8 2	Two spades
3.	♠ Q J 7 6 3	♡ 5 2	◇ 7 6	♣ K J 6 3	Two spades
4.	♠ 6	♡ A J 8 2	◇ 7 5 3	♣ 9 8 6 5 3	Two hearts
5.	♠ 6 5 3	♡ 9 7 5 4	◇ 3	♣ A Q 10 9 3	Three clubs

The following hands illustrate various responses to partner's two-heart bid:

1.	♠ 652	♡ 73	◇ 8654	♣ 9532	Two notrump
2.	♠ A65	♡ 42	◇ 8654	♣ 8653	Two notrump
3.	♠ K102	♡ 83	◇ 109642	♣ A74	Three notrump
4.	♠ 86	♡ Q32	◇ AJ7	♣ 109862	Three notrump
5.	♠ 87	♡ Q63	◇ K964	♣ 8643	Three hearts
6.	♠ 8	♡ 10976	◇ A862	♣ K853	Three hearts
7.	♠ 62	♡ J8753	◇ 1076	♣ 842	Four hearts
8.	♠ AQ65	♡ 96	◇ J874	♣ 832	Two spades
9.	♠ 87	♡ 93	◇ AQ9643	♣ 832	Three diamonds
10.	♠ 65	♡ 862	◇ AJ63	♣ Q852	Three diamonds
11.	♠ 632	♡ Q875	◇ 43	♣ Q652	Four hearts

It will be observed that you respond to a two-bid about as you would to a one-bid: If you would raise a one-bid, raise a two-bid; if you would make a suit takeout of a one-bid, make a suit takeout of a two-bid; but if you would pass a one-bid, you must still respond two notrump to a two-bid.

---

* Suit takeouts with six-card suits in weaker hands were formerly sanctioned, but were not widely practiced.

CHAPTER TWELVE

LIMIT FORCING TWO-BIDS
(For Advanced Bidding)

I am presenting here for the first time in twenty-six years an important improvement in the "Forcing Two-Bid." The New Bid, or to be exact, the New *addition* to the Forcing Two-Bid is called the Limit Two-Bid. Although simple enough, the Limit Two-Bid is so new that it should be reserved, to start with, for advanced bidding.*

A New Exception to the Forcing Two

Heretofore, the regulation opening two-bid was forcing to game (or a satisfactory penalty) on both partners, without exception. Now there is one exception, this: A rebid by the opener in the same suit and at the level of three is *not* forcing after a two-notrump response.

SOUTH	WEST	NORTH	EAST
2 ♠	Pass	2 N T	Pass
3 ♠			

South's three-spade rebid is *not forcing*.

Only a rebid in the same suit by the opener—and only after an original two-notrump response—justifies partner's pass short of game.

SOUTH	WEST	NORTH	EAST
2 ♠	Pass	2 N T	Pass
3 ♡ or			
3 ◇ or			
3 ♣ is forcing.			

---

* The Forcing Two-Bid and the Forcing Principle were originated and developed by Ely Culbertson, helped by his associates. For instance, the two-notrump response was originally suggested by one of the world's most brilliant players and creators of modern contract bridge, Waldemar von Zedtwitz, as a minimum response to an opening suit-bid of two.

Similarly, if partner responds with two notrump and bids thereafter, all the subsequent bidding by both partners is forcing to game.

Obviously, if South, after opening with two spades and hearing two notrump still sees game in spades, he jumps to four spades rather than rebidding three spades, and leaving to partner the decision to pass or to raise. On the other hand, if the opener has the type of holding (say eight winners) which, after the two-notrump response, cannot make game by itself, he may bid three spades, leaving to partner the option of passing with a near-blank or raising with something like three trumps and a singleton.

THE REQUIREMENTS FOR THE LIMIT TWO-BID

Generally, the requirements for the Limit Two-Bid are one winner less than for the regulation two-bid, i.e., about eight winners in the hand rather than nine winners. Thus there is a spread of about two tricks between a game and a bid in majors.

The minimum requirements are: About eight sure winners in the hand, including at least $3\frac{1}{2}$ plus in honor-tricks (15 to 16 points in high cards); the trump suit must deliver five sure winners. Usually it is a six-card or longer suit headed by top honors.

Here are some examples of the Limit Two-Bid:

♠ A K Q J 5 3   ♡ A 9 8   ◊ A 5 3   ♣ 6

This hand is an example of a perfect type of hand for a Limit Two-Bid. With its $4\frac{1}{2}$ honor-tricks and a powerful trump suit it is too strong for a one-bid (there is some danger that partner may pass a one-bid), and yet not strong enough for a regulation two-bid (only eight winners). If, after your two-spade bid, partner gives a positive response (any response but two notrump), you rebid your spade suit to three, and the bidding will proceed normally to game (or slam). The limit two-bid is treated like any regulation two-bid. If, however, partner responds negatively (two notrump), you still rebid three spades, thereby disclosing definitely that yours is a Limit Two-Bid. The decision whether to pass or go on is up to your partner.

♠ 7 2   ♡ A Q J 10 5 4 3   ◊ 5   ♣ A K 9

Open with two hearts. If partner responds with two no-trump, bid three hearts. Partner now knows that you have a Limit Two-Bid. With a blank hand, or a near-blank, he will pass, in which case you probably cannot make more than three hearts. If he holds as little as the heart King, or a couple of Queens, he will raise your bid to four, giving an excellent chance for game. One of the advantages of the Limit Two-Bid is that it will cut losses by stopping at the three-level if partner holds a blank, and if partner has anything at all, it will score games by encouraging a raise on values so slight that he could not respond to a one-bid.

♠ A K 10 9 5 3 2   ♡ K Q J 4   ◊ K 9   ♣ —

Bid two spades. If partner responds with two notrump, bid three spades. Partner will raise to four spades with as little as the ♠ Q and the ◊ Q, whereas a one-spade bid would be passed. If partner shows strength, you are in a slam zone.

The following type of hand is definitely *not* a Limit Two-Bid:

♠ A Q J 10 9 7 5 4   ♡ 5   ◊ 8   ♣ A J 6

An opening two-bid on this type of hand defeats the purpose of a Limit Two-Bid. A Limit Two-Bid is so-called, not only because it is limited to a one-round force when partner responds with two notrump, but also because it is limited to a definite minimum of honor-tricks, i.e., 3½ plus honor-tricks. This hand counts up to 3 plus honor-tricks (including a plus-value for a singleton)—a big difference. The correct bid with this hand is four spades in third position, and one spade in other positions. Four spades when third-hand is an excellent trap bid against the fourth-hand, and at the same time it does not shut out slams, since partner passed. In other positions bid one spade, followed by a bid of four spades, unless partner makes a strength-showing bid, in which case you can explore for slam controls (see Asking Bids and Blackwood).

A Limit Two-Bid makes no sense unless it is based on a definite minimum honor strength (in honor-tricks or high-card points). Furthermore, this honor strength must not be removed too far from the honor strength of regulation two-bids. The lowered honor strength in the Limit Two-Bid is compensated by the greater strength and length of the trump suit.

♠ A Q 10 8 6 5 2   ♡ 6   ♢ A K 7   ♣ K 5

Bid two spades. If partner responds with two notrump, bid three spades. If he passes, your best chance is for a part-score at three spades.

When you open with a Limit Two-Bid in a minor suit, you should be prepared to play the hand at three notrump, or be prepared to play the hand at five clubs or five diamonds in the event you receive a positive response from your partner. *With minor suits, to make a Limit Two-Bid you should have about nine winners.*

Responses to the Limit Two-Bid

After an opener rebids to three in a suit:

Pass with only a King or a Queen (except in the trump suit); or no raise.

♠ 9 2   ♡ 10 9 6   ♢ Q 9 5 3   ♣ 10 9 8 5

Partner opens two spades. Bid two notrump. If partner rebids to three spades, pass. If he bids three in any other suit keep the bidding open to game (or satisfactory penalty).

Keep the bidding open with a King and a Jack or with two Queens (4 points) or better.

♠ 10 8   ♡ 8 5 2   ♢ A 10 8 4   ♣ 10 9 7 6

Partner opens two spades. Bid two notrump. Opener bids three spades, raise to four spades. But if the rebid suit is minor, bid three notrump.

♠ 9 8   ♡ 8 5 3 2   ♢ K 10 3   ♣ Q J 9 3

Partner opens two spades. Bid two notrump and if he bids three spades, bid three notrump.

Raise partner's three-bid to four with King or Queen in trumps with outside Jack or Queen; or with three small trumps,

*a doubleton and outside King; or with three small trumps, a
singleton and outside Queen.*

| ♠ 9 5 2 | ♡ K 9 8 2 | ◇ 9 8 6 5 | ♣ 3 2 |
| ♠ 9 5 2 | ♡ Q 9 8 2 | ◇ 9 8 6 5 4 | ♣ 3 |

On either hand partner opens two spades. Bid two notrump
and if opener bids three spades raise it to four spades.

| ♠ Q 8 3 | ♡ 5 4 | ◇ J 10 9 5 4 | ♣ 7 4 3 |

Same as in the preceding two hands. ♠ Q is worth a trick
and a doubleton heart might produce a ruffing trick. With one
honor-trick in the hand and a five-card or longer suit headed
by a King or Queen-Jack show the suit in lieu of raising to four.

| ♠ 10 8 | ♡ K 9 7 6 | ◇ 8 3 | ♣ K 8 7 5 3 |

Partner opens two spades. You bid two notrump. Opener
rebids to three spades. Bid four clubs as an indirect raise.

The Limit Two-Bid and the Trump Suit

In the Limit Two-Bid the minimum requirement of at least
3½ plus honor-tricks (15–16 points in high cards) is inflexible
and should not be lowered. However, the requirement of five
sure winners in the trump suit is not so inflexible.

The Limit Two-Bid shows primarily a powerful trump suit,
able to stand on its own legs (five sure winners). There is,
however, a special group of hands in which the trump suit,
though strong, is not self-sufficient. In such hands the lesser
strength in the trump suit is compensated by the greater honor
strength in the hand. The requirements for the Limit Two-Bid
on such hands are:

Four winners in the trump suit and 4½ to 5½ honor-tricks.
For instance,

| ♠ A K 10 6 5 2 | ♡ 8 | ◇ A K J | ♣ A Q 5 |

This hand has the requirements for a regulation Forcing
Two-Bid and ordinarily it would be carried to a game in spades.
If partner holds as little as,

| ♠ J 9 7 5 | ♡ 9 8 5 4 3 | ◇ 6 3 | ♣ 5 4 |

or

| ♠ Q 7 | ♡ 9 5 4 3 | ◇ Q 10 6 3 | ♣ 9 8 6 |

game is certain and even a slam is probable! And yet with
five spades against this hand and finesses wrong, it will go down
in disaster. This hand was actually played and the two spades
bidder went down 1100 points. It is said that he threatened
to send me the bill for his losses on the perfectly justifiable
claim that his and his partner's bidding was blameless. Still,
few experts would bid one spade on this hand and assume a
grave risk of losing a game on this hand. The Limit Two-Bid
solves this awkward problem by insuring a good possibility of
game if partner's two-notrump response contains some values;
and if partner's hand is blank, it will at least reduce the loss.*

The advantages of the Limit Two-Bid are obvious to any
advanced player. It is also obvious that this Limit Two-Bid is
essentially different from a method of one-round Forcing Two-
Bids advocated by some writers, especially in England. In the
Acol system, for instance, *any* suit-bid at the level of three may
be passed by the player who responds two notrump to an opening two-bid in spades, hearts, or diamonds. Even with powerful
hands justifying a regulation two-bid, the opener must jump
to four, for if he bids three he may be left in. This means that
if the opener bids, say, two spades and the response is two
notrump, the opener cannot show his second heart suit at the
three-level, but must make a crippling leap to the four-level.
It is one thing to limit partner's option of pass at the three
level and after a rebid in the *same* suit; and it is quite another
thing to extend the option of pass to *rebids in new suits*. The
three-level is the most valuable level in the forcing bid mechanism, and its value becomes decisive when a necessity arises
of offering to partner a choice between various suits while still
below a game level. This is one of the main reasons for the
existence of the Forcing Two-Bid. And this alone is sufficient
to condemn any two-bid based on one-round forces. The introduction of an artificial two-club bid as an overall substitute for

---

* The foregoing hand is taken from Theodore A. Lightner's article published in
The Bridge World, October, 1951, issue. I must assume the sole responsibility for
the concept and the requirements of the Limit Two-Bid because they are my own.
But I am indebted to Mr. Lightner, whom I consider one of the few really scientific and practical theoreticians of contract bridge, for his assistance. He was the
first to advocate in print that a Forcing Two-Bid may be dropped short of game
under certain conditions.

the powerful hands so carefully differentiated in the Culbertson Forcing Two-Bid is a poor substitute. Besides, an artificial two-club brings its own complications and problems, among them the problem of *bidding time*. In most cases it needlessly wastes an entire bidding round (time-level) and mutilates the minor suits. It is not true, as claimed by some, that the artificial two-club bid with its artificial two-diamond response "does not lose time, in fact, it gains time." The fact is that the club bid loses a great many and most valuable time-levels.

ACE-SHOWING RESPONSES TO TWO-BIDS

A small sect of bridge players supports the idea that the re-sponder should forthwith proceed to Ace-showing cue-bids when responding to a two-bid. There are many varieties of the Ace-showing cue-bids; some are tied in with the artificial two-club bid and some are used with the regulation Forcing-Two.

I have never concealed my opinion of the Ace-showing cue-bids in general. Unlike the cue-bid in opponent's suit, the Ace-showing bids in all their 57 varieties are confusing, embryonic and time-wasting. When applied immediately after a Forcing Two-Bid they make even less sense. It is exactly like shooting sparrows with a cannon. Since this book purports to be a complete work on contract bridge, here is the outline of Ace-showing cue-bids after a Forcing Two-Bid. (See also Slam Bidding.)

The Ace-showing responses work as follows: With one Ace in a side suit, bid the suit of the Ace. With the Ace of trumps, raise once (some players raise with either the Ace or the King of trumps). With two Aces, bid four notrump. Without an Ace, usually bid two notrump, but jump one trick to show strength without an Ace. This follows the theory of the "Sims three-bid" that flourished in the early thirties but soon perished and was forgotten—not because there was anything wrong with it, but because players did not use it often enough to remember it betweentimes.

"WEAK" TWO-BIDS AND THE TWO-CLUB BID

A handful of players use opening two-bids in spades, hearts and diamonds as mild preëmptive bids, made on hands of 1½ to

2 honor-tricks with a fair six-card suit, like this: ♠ Q 10 9 7 6 3 ♡ 8 ◇ A J 5 4 ♣ 9 3.

A two-spade bid on such a hand works best when used by very good players against fairly weak players.

When the weak two-bid is used, an artificial two-club bid is the game force. It shows any hand on which a forcing two-bid might be made, and guarantees no specific holding in clubs— the bidder might even be void. The responder must bid two diamonds as an artificial denial bid if he has less than 1½ honor-tricks. From that point onward the bidding proceeds normally.

The two-club bid, while not unsound, offers no advantage; and any artificial bid is to be avoided if possible.

CHAPTER THIRTEEN

OPENING PRE-EMPTIVE BIDS

Opening bids of four, opening *minor-suit* bids of five, and to some extent opening bids of three, are preëmptive or *shutout* bids.

The purpose of such a bid is to make it difficult for the opponents to bid. If I open the bidding with "four spades," my opponents cannot enter the bidding without going as high as four notrump or five of a suit. They may have nearly all the honor-tricks in the deck, but with only one or two bids at their disposal they will have no *time* to exchange information. Except by blind stabbing they cannot reach a slam contract. With so few rounds of bidding available to them, they can seldom find their best trump suit, and may find themselves playing the hand at a contract of five diamonds with an unsatisfactory trump suit, when five or six could be made with hearts as trumps.

The distinguishing feature of the opening shutout bid is its weakness in honor-tricks. Naturally, with a hand strong in honor-tricks it is unnecessary to make a high opening bid (for, with so many honor-tricks against them, the opponents probably cannot make a game); and it is further undesirable to make a high shutout bid, because it robs the bidder himself and his partner of bidding time. *No bid is designed to shut out one's partner.*

Another distinguishing feature of the opening preëmptive bid is its long, powerful trump suit. With such a suit (something like Q J 10 9 7 6 5 4) the hand is obviously of little value unless that suit becomes trumps; so one might as well bid to the limit in that suit at once.

THE SAFETY FACTOR

The Sacrifice Principle is described in Chapter 29. Here, briefly, are the basic principles:

The purpose of a shutout bid is to prevent the opponents from reaching a game contract which, if bid in the right suit, they can probably make. It is losing strategy, however, to keep them out of a game if by doubling they can collect in under-trick penalties more than the game would be worth to them.

A game is worth to them, on the average, 500 points (see page 386 for exact value of game). Therefore, do not make a shutout bid if there is danger of going down more than 500 points.

This brings us to the Rule of Two and Three, which is: *Have at least within two tricks of your contract if vulnerable; within three tricks of your contract if not vulnerable.*

Then you can never be set more than 500 points (two tricks vulnerable or three tricks not vulnerable). Your loss, if doubled and defeated by that amount, is only as much as you would have lost anyway if your opponents had been permitted to bid and make their game.

Opening Three-Bids

The opening bid of three in a suit, especially in a minor suit, is not a very effective shutout because it is not a high enough bid. Care must be taken not to shut out partner if it is he, instead of the opponents, who has the game-going cards.

The danger is not very great when the three-bid is made in a major suit. If partner is strong, a contract of four in the major will likely offer as good a play for game as would three notrump. A minor-suit three-bid, however, may confront part-ner with a sheer guess; and he will have no time to explore the possibilities of different contracts, and still stay below the three-notrump level.

The requirements for an opening suit three-bid are:

A long, strong trump suit of at least six and usually seven cards; and

At least 7 winners if vulnerable, and at least 6 winners if not vulnerable.

Whereas any sort of long trump suit will do for a major-suit three-bid (for example, a seven-card suit like Q 10 9 8 6 5 4), a minor-suit three-bid should not be made without two of the three top cards in the trump suit. For example, K Q x x x x x.

Then, if partner has one of the three top honors in the minor suit, he can count on running the entire suit, six or seven winners, at notrump.

Examples of opening three-bids:

If vulnerable:

♠ 6	♡ KQJ8743	◇ J1095	♣ 6	Three hearts
♠ QJ107643	♡ 52	◇ KQJ	♣ 7	Three spades
♠ 6	♡ 54	◇ KQJ1063	♣ QJ104	Three diamonds

If not vulnerable:

♠ 10 9 6	♡ 2	◇ K 6	♣ K Q 10 8 6 5 2	Three clubs
♠ J 9 8 6 5 4 3 2	♡ 9 3	◇ —	♣ Q 8 3	Three spades

When you are third-hand, even a minor-suit three-bid may be made on a suit lacking the top cards. Partner, having passed, will not be strong enough to bid three notrump; and the three-bid may be valuable in keeping the opponents out of their best spot.

Responses to Opening Three-Bids

An opening three-bid shows a weak hand *and is usually passed.* It does not ask the responder to pass; the three-bidder, being human, hopes his partner will be strong enough to bid. But the responder seldom holds either the concentration of honor-tricks, or the perfect fit, that would warrant his bidding over such weakness as the opening three-bid announces.

A raise of a three-bid is based on the Rule of Two and Three. The opener has depended on his partner to supply two winners if vulnerable and three if not vulnerable. The responder counts his supporting winners and may raise once for every winner over two, if vulnerable, and for every winner over three, if not vulnerable.

In counting winners, the responder must limit himself to honor-tricks and ruffing tricks. He cannot expect that there will be time to establish any side suits. And seldom does a hand warrant raising a three-bid unless it includes at least one **and** preferably two Aces.

The following hand is a doubtful raise of an opening three-heart bid:

   ♠ Q J 6 3   ♡ 10 7 6 5   ◇ 4   ♣ K Q 8 2

Counting honor-tricks, trump tricks and ruffing tricks only, there are four winners in this hand. Partner has at least six if not vulnerable, seven if vulnerable; there should be enough tricks for game, with perhaps one to spare. But it does not help to have ten winning tricks if the opponents have already won four tricks. If partner, too, has an Aceless hand—which is not at all unlikely when he opens with a preëmptive bid—there will be no game.

Trump support is not so important when partner opens with a three-bid. Two small trumps are ample. A single Jack or Queen is as good as two trumps. Any of these holdings justifies a raise if there are enough winners in the hand. The following hands are good raises:

Raise three spades to four with:

   ♠ 6 3   ♡ A K 6   ◇ 7 6 5 3   ♣ A J 10 9

Raise a three-heart bid to four with:

   ♠ Q 8 6 5   ♡ 10 3   ◇ 5   ♣ A K Q 6 5 2

There is no reason to show the clubs on such a hand.

Three notrump is bid over partner's minor-suit three-bid with 2½ to 3½ honor-tricks, including the Ace, King or Queen of partner's suit. Three notrump is seldom bid over a major-suit three-bid.

Aces are important to the three-notrump takeout, as they are to the raise of a three-bid. The following hand is an excellent three-notrump bid when partner has opened with three diamonds:

   ♠ 10 7 6 3   ♡ A 6 2   ◇ K 5   ♣ A 9 5 3

If partner has seven diamonds to the A Q, the game can be run off except in the unlikely event that the defenders can start off with five spade tricks. But the following hand is a better pass:

♠ Q 8 3   ♡ K Q 5 4   ◊ K 5   ♣ Q 7 6 2

Even if the suit opened can be controlled, and seven diamonds run, the defenders will probably have the next five tricks in top cards. (And it may be only six diamonds.)

When the responder does bid three notrump over a major-suit three-bid, it is fairly obvious that he will have 3½ or 4 honor-tricks, or he will have a long suit of his own, something like this:

♠ 3   ♡ Q 10 9 5   ◊ A 10   ♣ A K Q J 8 5

Bid three notrump over partner's three spades, it being more likely that you will win nine tricks at notrump than ten tricks at spades, where there may be two spade and two heart tricks to lose.

A suit takeout of a three-bid should be made only in a suit that is close to self-sufficient itself, and a strong hand with at least 2½ honor-tricks. There is little reason to bid a suit over a major-suit three-bid; there is much reason to bid a strong major over a minor-suit three-bid.

With the following hand, raise three spades to four, but bid three hearts over three diamonds:

♠ 7 5   ♡ A K 10 9 6 3   ◊ 5   ♣ K J 7 6

Pass the following hand, whatever partner's three-bid:

♠ 7 5   ♡ A K 10 9 6 3   ◊ 5 2   ♣ Q 6 3

Game is unlikely, and it is probable that partner's suit is stronger than the hearts.

Opening Four-Bids

An opening four-bid is the same in a major or minor suit, with one exception. The major-suit four-bid may (but need not) have a little more in high cards.

A four-bid requires eight winners if vulnerable. Under the Rule of Two and Three, seven winners are enough if not vulnerable, but even when you are not vulnerable it is well to have eight winners, or at least a chance for eight winners (7½ winners, or an extra Queen or J-10).

The trump suit for a four-bid is almost never less than seven cards in length.

Here are two typical four-bids, respectively vulnerable and non-vulnerable:

♠ 5 ♥ K J 10 9 7 6 5 3 ♦ Q J 10 3 ♣ —
(Bid four hearts, vulnerable or not)

♠ 5 ♥ K J 10 9 7 6 5 3 ♦ Q J 7 ♣ 6
(Bid four hearts not vulnerable; three hearts if vulnerable)

The second of the two hands may lose six tricks, and go down three at four hearts; but there is a possible eighth winner (since the heart suit may develop seven tricks, losing only to the Ace).

With a ready-made suit, the major-suit four-bid is proper, the minor-suit four-bid should be avoided. That ready-made suit may mean seven or eight tricks at notrump, and it is unwise to start off at the four-level, committing the side to an eleven-trick game contract or none.

Bid four hearts, vulnerable, or not, with:

♠ 2 ♥ A K Q J 8 7 5 3 ♦ 6 5 ♣ 9 3

but pass with:

♠ 8 7 ♥ 10 9 3 ♦ A K Q J 8 7 5 ♣ 10

♠ — ♥ 7 ♦ K J 10 9 7 6 5 3 ♣ K J 10 6
(Bid four diamonds, vulnerable or not)

♠ Q 10 9 8 6 5 4 2 ♥ 7 ♦ K Q 5 ♣ 9
(Bid four spades not vulnerable; three spades or pass if vulnerable)

♠ 5 ♥ 6 5 ♦ K Q 10 9 8 6 5 4 2 ♣ 10
(Bid four diamonds, vulnerable or not)

Responses to Four-Bids

Partner must be very cautious about raising an opening four-bid past game. He may raise a minor-suit four-bid to game with three honor- or ruffing-winners, including two Aces, but should not raise any four-bid to six unless he has six quick winners when not vulnerable or five quick winners when vulnerable, including *three Aces*. He need have only two Aces if he has the King or Queen of the trump suit and a guarded King or a singleton in the fourth suit.

A conventional four-notrump bid (Chapter 28), if you are using one, should always be preferred to a mere raise of partner's major suit to five, and is usually better than a jump to six.

Partner opens with four hearts. Holding:

♠ K Q J   ♡ 6 5   ◇ A K Q 6   ♣ K Q 10 4 *Pass.* Partner should not be expected to hold two Aces.

♠ A 6 4 3   ♡ Q 5   ◇ A K Q 8 5 2   ♣ 5 *Bid four notrump* (conventional). If partner denies an Ace, stop at five hearts.

♠ K Q 7 6   ♡ Q 8 5 4   ◇ A K J 10 3   ♣ — *Bid six hearts.* Freak hands justify exceptional treatment.

♠ A K 10 5   ♡ K J   ◇ A Q J 8 5   ♣ A 5 *Bid four notrump, and go to seven if partner shows the ♡ Ace.*

Minor-Suit Five-Bids

An opening bid of five in a minor suit is, like the four-bid, a pure shutout bid. Following the Rule of Two and Three, it requires nine winners if vulnerable, and *about nine* winners if not vulnerable. However, when not vulnerable but holding eight sure winners and very freakish distribution, five in a minor suit may be bid, especially against strong opposition. The contract cannot be defeated more than 500 points, and will undoubtedly stop an opposing game.

♠ 6   ♡ 5   ◇ K J   ♣ A J 9 8 7 6 5 3 2
(Bid five clubs, vulnerable or not)

An opening five-bid in a major suit is not a shutout bid but a slam try.

THIRD- AND FOURTH-HAND PRE-EMPTIVE BIDS

In third position, *as a rare exception,* a player may sometimes make a four-bid with as many as 4-plus honor-tricks in his hand.

For example, a third-hand four-heart bid on a hand like this:

♠ K Q 6   ♡ A Q J 10 9   ◇ A Q 7   ♣ Q 2

Four hearts should be made, is likely to be as good a contract as any, and may induce an opposing four-spade bid.

This is purely a trap bid and, like all trap bids, entails some risk. (In this case, the principal risk is of missing a superior four-spade or three-notrump contract.) The great value of this trap bid is as a constant threat—the opponents will never know whether the third-hand preëmptive bid is a strong or a weak hand. Sometimes such a trap bid may be used when fourth-hand.

CHAPTER FOURTEEN

RESPONSES TO SUIT-BIDS OF ONE

The partner of the opening bidder is called the *responder,* and his bids are called *responses.*

There are "chance-giving" responses and "free" responses. The former term is applied to cases when partner has made an opening suit-bid of one, and the intervening opponent has passed. If the responder passes now, the other opponent may also pass and the opener may get no chance to rebid. While the responder is not literally forced to respond, he makes every effort to do so.

A "free" response is one made when the intervening opponent has overcalled partner's bid. In this case (described in Chapter 19) the opener will have a chance to rebid whether the responder bids or not. Therefore the responder need not make any undue effort to keep the bidding open.

The obligation to keep the bidding open, if possible, when partner makes an opening suit-bid of one, is very strong on the responder, for two reasons:

1. The opening hand *may* be packed with honor-tricks and reinforced with one or two powerful long suits, which the opener cannot show if the bidding dies.

2. The opener has already assumed a certain measure of strength in the responding hand. It is the job of the responder to confirm or deny this strength, and to show any additional strength he may have.

There are three kinds of strength the responder may show with his response to the opening bid:

1. Honor-tricks
2. Trump support and distributional (ruffing and long-suit) values
3. Expected winners in a biddable suit of his own.

There are four kinds of response with which the responder may show the nature of the strength he holds:

1. The Pass (denial of strength of any sort);
2. The Raise (trump support and distribution);
3. The Notrump Takeout (honor-tricks);
4. The Suit Takeout (a biddable suit of his own).

Finally, the *amount* of the strength held by the responder is generally shown by the quantity of his bid—whether he bids just as little as necessary, or jumps one trick, or jumps immediately to game.*

The Pass

To pass partner's opening suit-bid of one is the loudest warning in bridge. It shows a hand *so weak* that the opener should expect:

1. At most one honor-trick; usually less.
2. Less than adequate support for partner's suit; or, if adequate support (J 10 x, Q x x or x x x x) is held, very poor distribution, or a hand almost devoid of high cards.
3. No higher-ranking suit as good as A x x x x or K J 10 x x (five cards, headed by one honor-trick).

Some response should usually be made with as much as one honor-trick. Sometimes, it is true, a pass is made on a hand containing one honor-trick, but usually when it is a *bare* Ace, without a stopper in any other suit, and without distributional support for partner's suit.

The pass says, "Partner, my hand is so weak that no matter how strong you are I do not believe we should reach a higher (game) contract; and though a better part-score contract (a

---

* This does not mean, however, that the higher the bid the greater the strength shown, for some bids, being forcing. need not be high to show strength.

better suit fit) may be found, it is too dangerous to risk adding another trick to the contract trying to find out."

For example, holding the following hands the responder should pass his partner's opening bid of one heart:

♠ 8 4 3   ♡ K 8 5 2 ◇ 7 6 4   ♣ 10 9 7 —But add an Ace to one of the plain suits and he should raise

♠ 9 7 5 4   ♡ 8 7 4   ◇ J 6   ♣ K 5 3 2 —But add any King and he should bid one notrump

♠ J 10 8 6 3 ♡ 9 4   ◇ 8 6 3   ♣ 9 7 5 —But change a low spade to the ♠ King and he should bid one spade

♠ 7 5 2   ♡ 9 6   ◇ Q J 8 4 3 2 ♣ 10 7   —But change a small diamond to the Ace and he should bid two diamonds

The Raise

To raise is to increase partner's bid by one or more tricks in the same suit. There are the single raise (a raise to two); the double raise (a jump raise to three); and the triple or game raise (a raise to four).

SINGLE RAISES

A very weak raise may be given when the intervening opponent has passed. This is a "courtesy" raise and may conceivably be given with barely a single honor-trick in the hand, and as few as two winners.

Whether free or courtesy, every raise requires adequate trump support: J 10 x; Q x x, or any four trumps.

The number of winners in the hand is determined by counting the values in honors, long suits and short suits (Chapter 5). For those who find it easier to look only for the honor-tricks and trump support, *case methods* may be used.

Since length in trumps is more valuable than high cards,

and distributional (ruffing) support is equally valuable, the requirements for raises vary according to the distribution of the hand. The single raise requires:

1½ honor-tricks with adequate trump support; but
1 honor-trick with adequate trump support and a singleton, or
1+ honor-trick with four-card trump support and a doubleton.

These minimums apply only to cases in which the intervening player has passed. Typical minimum hands on which partner's one-spade bid may be raised to two are:

♠ Q 7 3 ♡ 8 6 5 2 ◇ A J 7 3 ♣ 9 6
(1½ honor-tricks; adequate trump support)

♠ J 10 7 ♡ 9 ◇ K Q 7 3 ♣ 9 7 5 3 2
(1 honor-trick, adequate trump support and a singleton)

♠ J 6 5 3 ♡ 9 2 ◇ A 8 6 ♣ 8 7 6 4
(1 honor-trick, four-card trump support and a doubleton)

From these minimums, the strength of the hand may range upward to 2-plus or 2½ honor-tricks—*but no higher.* The single raise is not forcing, and the responder does not take a chance on being passed out short of game when his hand is good enough for some stronger response. The maximum honor-trick holdings apply to hands of skimpy distributional support; when the distribution is good, 2-plus or 2½ honor-tricks may be enough for a double raise.

The following examples show the range of single raises of a one-spade bid, from weak to strong:

♠ 10 8 6 5 3	♠ Q 9 8 2	♠ A 9 6 5
♡ Q 6	♡ A K	♡ K 7
◇ A 6 5	◇ 6 4 3	◇ 9 8 6 5 2
♣ 9 5 2	♣ 8 6 4 3	♣ 10 7
♠ Q J 6	♠ A K 8 6 4	♠ J 10 5 3
♡ 8 5 4	♡ J 8 6	♡ Q J 5 3
◇ K Q J	◇ 6 5	◇ K 10 6 4
♣ 8 7 6 5	♣ 9 8 2	♣ 3

Whereas a single raise of a major suit is usually preferred to a minimum-suit takeout, a single raise should seldom be given to a minor suit if a major-suit one-over-one takeout is available.

Raise partner's one-diamond bid to two with:

♠ 8 6 4 3   ♡ A 5   ◊ K Q 6 5   ♣ 6 5 4

But bid one spade with:

♠ A 6 4 3   ♡ 8 5   ◊ K Q 6 5   ♣ 6 5 4

The barren distribution 4–3–3–3 is undesirable for a raise. On such a hand, a one-notrump response is preferred unless the honor-trick holding is near the maximum and includes four or more honor-cards to increase the playing strength of the hand.

If partner opens with one heart, prefer a one-notrump response holding

♠ A 6 3   ♡ K 8 4   ◊ 7 6 2   ♣ 10 7 5 3

Prefer a raise to two hearts holding

♠ A 6 3   ♡ K 8 4   ◊ K 7 3   ♣ J 8 6 5

The requirement that any hand, to raise, must contain adequate trump support is one of the most vital in bridge, yet even this rule may sometimes be relaxed when the responder, balked by the rules from any other response, must turn in desperation to the raise:

♠ J 6 5
♡ A 6 4 2   Partner has bid one spade. The hand, with 2+ honor-
◊ A J 7   tricks, is too strong for a bid of one notrump (page 170);
♣ 8 4 2   yet too weak for a response of two notrump. A single raise
                 (two spades) best portrays the hand.

♠ 10 7 3
♡ 2   Partner has bid one spade. A response of two clubs is
◊ J 7 4 3   barred (page 177); the hand is too weak. A response of one
♣ A 8 6 5 2   notrump is dangerous; the opponents may run the entire
                 heart suit. Raise to two spades.

Even when a single raise would be technically correct, a suit takeout is often strategically better (page 178).

Double Raises

A jump raise of partner's suit from one to three is called a double raise. In a major suit it is forcing to game. In a minor suit it is not forcing.

The major-suit double raise commits the partnership to game, and usually in the bid suit; therefore the regular adequate support (J 10 x, Q x x, and usually x x x x) is *not enough.* The trump support should be at least four trumps headed by the Queen, J 10 or better; or any five trumps.

The double raise usually shows at least five winners including 2+ honor-tricks or more; but as in the case of single raises, the responder may avoid counting winners by a *case method* of valuation. Under the case method, the minimum requirements are:

With five or more trumps, you need 2+ honor-tricks. Of these, at least 1+ should be outside the trump suit.

With Q x x x or J 10 x x, or better, in trumps, you should have at least 2½ honor-tricks; half of which, and usually more, should be outside the trump suit.

With only four small trumps (J x x x or weaker) the hand must contain at least 3 honor-tricks, all of which will obviously be outside the trump suit.

Partner having bid one spade, the following hands are typical sound jump raises to three spades:

♠ K 8 6 4 3	♠ K Q J 7	*♠ 8 7 6 5
♡ K Q 2	♡ A Q J	♡ K Q 8
◇ 8 3	◇ 7	◇ A 10 5
♣ A J 7	♣ 10 6 5 3 2	♣ A J 2

The responder must remember, however, that he is forcing to game and must be prepared to play for game opposite a weak opening one-bid. Therefore he should not jump his partner's suit to three without considering the following factors:

1. *With the bare minimum honor-trick requirements, any available suit takeout in a biddable or shaded suit should be*

---

* A case in which the double raise has fewer than 4 winners. The raise offers partner a chance to bid four spades with a five-card suit, and three notrump with a four-card suit. Some experts prefer to respond two clubs or two diamonds on this hand, and choose the next bid after hearing the opener's rebid.

preferred. Since this response is forcing for one round, the bidding will not die. At his next opportunity to bid the responder may raise his partner's suit.

Partner bids one heart. Holding

♠ A 8 5 4   ♡ Q 7 6 3   ◇ 9   ♣ A 6 4 2 *Bid one spade*. If partner rebids one notrump, two diamonds or two clubs, bid *three* hearts. If partner rebids two hearts, bid *four* hearts.

2. *With the principal honor strength of the hand in the trump suit,* and only one honor-trick or less outside, seek a suit takeout and if necessary give only a single raise.

For example, partner having bid one spade, raise only to two spades with

1.   ♠ A K 8 4   ♡ 6   ◇ 8 6 4 2   ♣ J 8 6 5
2.   ♠ K Q J 2   ♡ 7 3   ◇ A 5 4   ♣ 7 6 3 2

With ♠ A K Q 6   ♡ 7 5   ◇ K 7 5 4   ♣ Q 8 3, which is well over the minimum requirements, raise to three spades.

A double raise, though game-forcing, is a limited bid; and a forcing takeout should be preferred on any hand that meets the requirements (see page 179).

The minor-suit double raise is partly preëmptive in purpose. It may be made on a hand weaker in honor-tricks than the major-suit double raise. It should not usually be made when a sound suit takeout is available.

The requirements for this double raise are:

Strong five-card trump support (rarely, strong four-card trump support will do); and

1½ to 2½ honor-tricks.

By "strong five-card trump support" is meant a holding containing some top-card strength, such as A J 10 x x, and usually at least Q J x x x.

The following hand is a double raise of partner's one-diamond bid:

♠ 6 3   ♡ A 7   ◇ K J 10 6 5 3   ♣ 6 5 3

This hand is unsuitable to any response except a raise in diamonds; and a single raise would be far from enough to show partner the trick-winning strength of the hand. The double raise is the answer.

The bid is preëmptive, in that it may succeed in shutting out an overcall by fourth-hand; but by no means does it urge the opener to pass. On the contrary, the opener is expected to bid again if his hand was strong in honor-tricks (3½ to 4) or in distribution. But the non-forcing nature of the response permits him to pass rather than suffer the danger and futility of a three-notrump contract, or an eleven-trick minor-suit contract, on a hand that obviously is not going to make it.*

Having opened one diamond, and received a double raise, pass with:

♠ 8 7 5 4   ♥ 8   ♦ A Q 9 7 4   ♣ A 7 5

Other cases will be shown under "Rebids," page 193.

The double raise in a minor suit does not necessarily deny a biddable suit on the side, or four-card trump support for a major suit. The following are typical hands:

Raise partner's one-diamond bid to three diamonds with:

1.	♠ 6	♥ 4 2	♦ A K 6 5 2	♣ Q 8 7 4 3
2.	♠ A	♥ 6	♦ 10 9 7 6 4 3	♣ Q 8 7 4 3
3.	♠ 10 8 7 6	♥ 5	♦ K Q J 5	♣ K J 8 4
4.	♠ 9	♥ A 6 5 3	♦ K J 8 6 5	♣ Q 6 5

TRIPLE RAISES

A raise of partner's suit from one to four is a triple raise, sometimes called a game raise, and its principal purpose is to make it difficult for the opponents to enter the bidding. It is a shutout bid.

Being a shutout bid, the triple raise is limited as to honor-tricks, to reduce the danger of missing a slam, though its playing strength is unlimited.

The requirements by the case method are:

Jump partner's suit to four, holding *five or more trumps,* and

---

* Until 1949, the double raise in a minor suit was identical with the double raise in a major suit—forcing to game, and showing about the same sort of hand. It is admittedly desirable, for the sake of simplicity, to have all double raises mean the same thing. The less complications there are in bidding rules, the more attention a player can give to bidding strategy. But the nature of the Contract Bridge Scoring Table makes some differences necessary. During the years in which minor-suit and major-suit double raises meant the same thing, a double raise in a minor was almost never heard. A hand worth a game-force in a minor will usually be a better two-notrump or suit takeout. It is better to have a useful bid in your repertoire than an idle bid.

The experts, who are the most conservative of all bridge players, are coming around very slowly to the idea of making a minor-suit double raise non-forcing; but one by one they succumb and will continue to do so.

at least one honor-trick, but less than two honor-tricks, always including a singleton or void.

With 6–5–1–1 distribution, including six trumps, ½ to 1 honor-trick is usually sufficient.

Typical triple raises of a one-spade bid:

1. ♠ 9 7 6 5 2	♡ A 5	◇ 8 6 5 3 2	♣ 9
2. ♠ K J 6 5 3	♡ K 7 4 2	◇ J 8 3	♣ 6
3. ♠ J 9 8 6 5 4	♡ —	◇ 6 3	♣ Q J 6 5 3
4. ♠ Q 10 9 7 5 2	♡ 6	◇ 10 8 6 5 4	♣ 5

Hands distributed 5–3–3–2, such as ♠ K Q 7 4 3 ♡ 8 5 ◇ Q 7 5 ♣ 8 5 3, have too many losers, hence too few winners, for a jump to four. Prefer a single raise.

The raise of a minor-suit bid to four should not be attempted when there is any hope of making a game at notrump, for the three-notrump level is passed by the preëmptive raise. Hands offering a major-suit response to the opening minor-suit bid are also bad as triple raises. Only a hopeless freak, with no more than one honor-trick, calls for such a bid.

Raise one diamond to four with

♠ —   ♡ J 6   ◇ Q 8 7 6 5 4   ♣ K 7 6 3 2

The triple raise, while a weak shutout bid, must not be considered a "stop" bid. Its strength is limited, but very often the opener, with a powerful hand, will be able to make a slam try (Chapter 25).

A raise of more than three tricks (from one to five or six) should not be made, even in a minor where five-odd are needed for game. More scientific methods of reaching so high a contract are at the player's disposal.

The Notrump Takeout

To change the opener's suit by taking him out into another suit or notrump is called a *takeout*. The takeout, while it does not necessarily deny adequate support for the opener's suit, does say that in the opinion of the responder a better contract may be found.

A takeout in notrump portrays three qualities of the responding hand:

1. A minimum number of honor-tricks, the amount depending on whether the takeout is one, two or three notrump.
2. Balanced distribution, and therefore a desire or at least a willingness to play the hand at notrump.
3. Probable lack of a biddable suit and of sufficient trump support to justify a raise.

While a biddable suit may sometimes be hidden behind a notrump takeout, or adequate trump support may be included, the fact that the responder chooses to bid notrump means that he feels the notrump response best expresses the nature of his hand.

The responder has three available notrump responses:

1. One notrump, a negative response which shows a weak hand and little hope of game unless the opener has well above a minimum.
2. Two notrump, a forcing bid which must be carried to game (unless the responder has previously passed).
3. Three notrump shows a hand almost identical to an opening one-notrump bid (16–18 points), being limited to 3½–4 honor-tricks with 4–3–3–3 or 4–4–3–2 distribution.

ONE NOTRUMP

Lacking the requirements for a suit takeout or raise the responder should respond one notrump if holding:

1+ to 1½+ honor-tricks in the hand.

If the hand contains only 1+ honor-trick, there must be stoppers (such as J x x x, Q x x, K x or an Ace) in at least two suits, or at least 6 points in high cards.

If the hand contains 1½ or more honor-tricks, the strength may be (though it need not be) all in one suit.

In other words, a notrump takeout is made whenever the responder has one-plus honor-trick or more with a fair possibility of winning two tricks at notrump in his own hand. Such a hand may be very weak, as in the case of the hand containing one Ace and a Q x x x. Other hands, nearer to the maximum than to the minimum, may contain two honor-tricks, perhaps an Ace, a King and a Queen.

The opener will of course assume a near-minimum one-no-trump takeout, in order to be safe.

Partner having opened one heart, bid one notrump with:

1.	♠ K 10 2	♡ K 8	◇ 9 6 4 2	♣ 8 6 5 3
2.	♠ A Q	♡ 9 7	◇ 10 8 6 5 2	♣ 9 6 4 3
3.	♠ A J 6	♡ 5 4	◇ 9 8 7 6	♣ J 10 5 4
4.	♠ A 4 3	♡ 10 3 2	◇ 5 4 3 2	♣ Q 9 7
5.	♠ 8 3	♡ K 8 7	◇ Q 6 5 3	♣ Q 9 4 2
6.	♠ J 8 5	♡ 6 4	◇ K 9 6 3	♣ A 8 5 4
7.	♠ 9 6 5 2	♡ A K	◇ 7 4 3	♣ 8 5 4 2
8.	♠ Q 7 3	♡ Q 8	◇ Q 8 4 2	♣ J 10 6 3
9.	♠ A 10 8	♡ K 6	◇ K 5 3	♣ 9 6 5 3 2
10.	♠ 6 5 3	♡ 8 4	◇ 9 7 5	♣ A K 8 6 2

Hand No. 9 is the maximum on which to respond one notrump. With Q x x x x or better in clubs, or with anything more in honor-tricks, a suit takeout would be preferred. Hand No. 10, which meets the minimum requirements for a two-club takeout (page 177), is a better one-notrump bid because of its lack of intermediates.

Although the one-notrump response usually depicts balanced distribution, it must sometimes be made when the hand contains a singleton because there is no biddable suit or the biddable suit is not strong enough to show. When the hand has a singleton in a side suit, however, some other response should be sought and when the responder is void in any suit he should not bid one notrump.

Weak hands in general call for a one-notrump response even when containing a five-card biddable suit unless the suit can be shown at the level of one. A response in any lower-ranking suit requires a bid of two, and if the hand has less than two honor-tricks so high a bid is unsafe. But if the responder has a six-card suit, if he is strong enough to respond at all he should bid the suit.

It must always be remembered that one notrump is a negative response and in general should be used to show a hand which is weak and which is bid only to give the opener another chance. The Approach Principle applies to the responding hand so far as safety permits and whenever possible a player should avoid too brutal an admission of weakness by making a shaded suit takeout, particularly at the level of one.

For example, with ♠ Q J 6 3   ♡ 9 5   ◊ K 7 5 4   ♣ J 8 3 the proper response to partner's one-heart bid is one spade rather than one notrump.

Hands containing adequate trump support call for a one-notrump response only when the trump support is a three-card length (Q x x, K x x or A x x) and when the responder has less than 1½ honor-tricks, and no singleton.

The following hands are one-notrump takeouts of partner's one-heart bid:

| ♠ K 6 3 | ♡ Q 5 4 | ◊ Q 6 4 2 | ♣ 9 6 3 |
| ♠ 5 4 | ♡ A 6 2 | ◊ J 8 7 4 3 | ♣ Q 6 5 |

Two Notrump

A takeout of partner's one-bid with two notrump shows a strong hand and is forcing to game, unless the responder has previously passed. The requirements are:

3 to 3½ honor-tricks; 13–15 points.

Balanced distribution with (usually) no biddable suit;

At least two and usually all unbid suits stopped.

In hands fortified by the possession of stoppers in all three unbid suits, always provided that there are six or more honor-cards in the hand, the honor-trick minimum may be reduced to 2½. In forcing to game, the responder takes a heavy responsibility on his shoulders and must be sure a notrump game will be safe.

Another fortification for the minimum two-notrump response is a fit with partner's suit, something like A x, K x, Q J or three cards to an honor, making it probable that partner's suit can be established and turned into tricks at notrump.

The two-notrump response does not deny adequate trump support; in fact, it is just as likely as not to have support for partner's suit. With support such as Q x x the responder is barred from giving a double raise, yet a single raise may be passed by the opener and a game missed. A two-notrump response is often the solution.

Respond two notrump to partner's one-heart bid, holding:

1.	♠ A Q 6	♡ J 2	◇ K 10 5 4	♣ K 9 4 2
2.	♠ K J 5	♡ A J	◇ Q 10 5 4	♣ K 8 5 3
3.	♠ A 6 5	♡ 9 4 2	◇ A 7 4 3	♣ K J 10
4.	♠ A K 4	♡ 6 2	◇ A 7 6 2	♣ J 10 7 4
5.	♠ A J	♡ 8 5 4	◇ A 10 5 3	♣ A 7 5 2
6.	♠ K J 8	♡ A 10	◇ A Q 7 3	♣ 8 7 5 2
7.	♠ Q J 5	♡ J 6	◇ K 7 4	♣ A K J 8 3

Unless partner wishes to insist on a heart contract, No. 7 will surely be played at a notrump game. To show the club suit would unnecessarily enlighten the opponents.

The two-notrump takeout, though a strong bid and a game force, is by its nature a limited bid. It should seldom be made with more than 3½ honor-tricks for fear partner, visualizing the possible minimum, will jump to the conclusion that a slam is out of the question and will close the bidding at three notrump.

Three Notrump

The takeout into three notrump is a highly specialized bid to show:

(a) 4 honor-tricks (rarely, 3½) in four suits (16–18 points).
(b) 4–3–3–3 or 4–4–3–2 distribution.

With this limited range of honor and distributional values, the three-notrump response is so informative that it should be made even when holding a biddable suit or strong support for partner's suit.

The three-notrump takeout is a limit bid, its minimum and maximum being scarcely more than ½ honor-trick apart. Nevertheless, it is quite incorrect to get the impression, as do some players, that it is a stop bid. There is really no such thing as a stop bid unless, perhaps, it is a sign-off, and particularly not when the responding hand shows a minimum of 3½ honor-tricks. The three-notrump response is, however, very valuable in flashing a warning signal to partner when his own distribution is balanced and 7½ honor-tricks may not produce a slam.

The three-notrump takeout should rarely be made without at least a probable stopper in every suit. With one suit wide open, the two-notrump response is available.

The following hands justify a takeout of three notrump when partner has made an opening bid of one in any suit:

1. ♠ A Q 6   ♡ Q 5 4   ◇ K J 8 5   ♣ K Q 6
2. ♠ A 9 3   ♡ A Q 5   ◇ A Q 8   ♣ J 10 5 4
3. ♠ K J 10   ♡ Q J 10   ◇ A K Q 2   ♣ Q 8 6

The following hands are good three-notrump responses to partner's opening bid of one spade:

4. ♠ 9 5 4   ♡ A Q 6   ◇ A K 4   ♣ K 8 5 3
5. ♠ J 6 2   ♡ Q J 10 5   ◇ A K 8   ♣ K Q 7
6. ♠ A 9 4   ♡ K Q 8   ◇ J 10 6 5   ♣ A K 3

An immediate takeout of an opening suit-bid with four or five notrump should be avoided, a forcing takeout or other response coming first.

Suit Takeouts

A suit takeout is an overcall of partner's opening bid with a new suit. There are three varieties of suit takeout:

1. Forcing for one round—a bid of the minimum number required to overcall the opening bid.
2. Forcing to game—a bid of one trick more than necessary to overcall partner's suit.
3. Preëmptive takeouts—a *multiple* jump to four—sometimes a jump to three, if it is a *double* jump.

THE ONE-ROUND FORCE

To take out an opening suit-bid of one, the responder must bid one in a higher-ranking suit, or two in a lower-ranking suit. Either of these responses is forcing for one round, requiring at least one rebid from partner. The opener escapes this obligation to rebid only when the responder has passed originally or when the intervening opponent on his right makes some bid which assures the responder of a second chance.

WITH A HIGHER-RANKING SUIT

A takeout in a higher-ranking suit is known as a "one-over-one" takeout. It is forcing for one round, and has the widest range of values of any response, showing:

1. *A very weak hand with a five-card suit and 1 honor-trick, or a six-card suit and ½ honor-trick, in the hand.*

2. *A fair hand with a shaded or biddable suit and 1+ to 3 honor-tricks in the hand.*

3. *A strong hand with as many as 4+ honor-tricks, just under a jump game-forcing takeout.*

The following hands, on each of which the responder should take out partner's one-diamond bid with one heart, show the great range of the one-over-one:

1.	♠ 8 5	♡ K Q 9 7 2	◇ 9 6 3	♣ 7 5 4
2.	♠ 5 2	♡ K Q J 5	◇ 8 6 3	♣ 9 7 6 5
3.	♠ 2	♡ A 10 6 5 3	◇ J 10 6	♣ J 5 4 2
4.	♠ A 6 3	♡ A K 9 6 4	◇ 5	♣ Q J 6 5
5.	♠ A 6	♡ Q J 9 8 7 5 3	◇ A 9 8	♣ 10
6.	♠ A K 6	♡ A K J 5	◇ 7 6 3	♣ 9 5 2

Many hands containing support for partner's suit and enough strength for a single and even a double raise call first for a one-over-one response when one is available.

To facilitate the one-over-one takeout, the responder may respond even in a conditional biddable suit with the same honor-trick strength he would need to show a regular biddable suit. For example, partner having bid one heart, respond with one spade holding:

♠ A 10 6 3   ♡ 9 2   ◇ A 6 4   ♣ K 9 7 4

A one-spade response would also be made on a very weak hand such as the following:

♠ Q 8 6 3   ♡ A 9   ◇ 10 5 4   ♣ 6 5 3 2

With a 7-card major suit (but usually not with a minor) a one-over-one response should be made even if the hand technically does not contain any fraction of an honor-trick.

If partner opens one club, bid one heart with

♠ 7 3   ♥ J 10 8 7 6 5 3   ♦ 9 4   ♣ 10 5

but pass with

♠ 7 3   ♥ 9 4   ♦ Q 9 8 7 6 5 3   ♣ 10 5

WITH A LOWER-RANKING SUIT

The takeout with two of a lower-ranking suit falls into the same category as the one-over-one except that the minimum strength required cannot be quite so low, since the contract is increased. The requirements:

1½ honor-tricks with a strong six-card suit;

2+ honor-tricks with a five-card suit;

2½ honor-tricks with a four-card suit.

With less than these requirements the responder should find a possible raise or one-over-one takeout and, failing this, should bid one notrump. Even the 1½ honor-trick minimum to show a six-card suit may drive the partnership too high if the responding hand has no intermediates or support for the opener's suit, but since it is more disadvantageous to suppress information about a six-card suit, the lesser of the two evils is chosen.

These are the minimums; the maximum includes anything less than a forcing takeout (page 179).

The requirement of two honor-tricks may even be shaded somewhat to show a strong five-card heart suit (for example, one with 100 honors) over partner's one-spade bid. But it is undesirable to show a five-card minor suit in a minimum hand, and (especially when the distribution is balanced) a single raise or one-notrump response should be considered.

Thus, to partner's one-spade bid respond two hearts on:

♠ 6 3   ♥ A Q J 10 7   ♦ 8 6 5   ♣ 10 8 4   or
♠ 6 3   ♥ K Q J 8 7   ♦ K 7 3   ♣ 10 8 4

But bid one notrump, not two diamonds, on

♠ 6 3   ♥ 8 6 2   ♦ A Q J 8 5   ♣ Q 6 2

Raise to two spades on

♠ J 10 5   ♥ 6 3   ♦ A K 7 6 3   ♣ 9 5 2

The following hands are typical two-over-one takeouts of an opening one-spade bid:

1.	♠ 6 5	♡ Q J 6 5 4	◇ K 8	♣ A 7 6 3
2.	♠ 8 3 2	♡ 9 6	◇ A K 8 4 2	♣ K 6 5
3.	♠ Q 7 5	♡ K 6	◇ A Q J 5 4	♣ K 6 4
4.	♠ 8 6	♡ A Q 5 4	◇ K 8 2	♣ K 7 6 5
5.	♠ A	♡ A 8 5 2	◇ Q J 6 5	♣ 9 5 4 2
6.	♠ A 6	♡ A K 3	◇ Q J 8 5 2	♣ 7 6 5

In two other cases the requirements may be shaded.

1. Holding strong support for partner's suit, but not enough in honor-tricks for a double raise, show a five-card suit with about 1½ honor-tricks.

2. Holding about two honor-tricks with four-card support for partner's suit, responder may bid two in a conditional biddable suit such as Q 6 5 4.

In either of these cases, the responder, by first making a bid which is forcing for one round and at his next opportunity giving partner a single raise, shows the strength of his hand yet does not need to make a response which is forcing to game. Partner having bid one spade, the response on any of the following hands is two diamonds:

1.	♠ 7 6 5 3	♡ A 2	◇ A 10 6 4	♣ J 6 5
2.	♠ Q 8 5 4	♡ 6	◇ A J 7 3 2	♣ 9 6 3
3.	♠ A Q 5 4	♡ 7 2	◇ Q 9 6 5 3	♣ 8 5
4.	♠ 8 6 4 3	♡ A K	◇ Q 10 4 3	♣ 8 4 3

With a seven-card suit in the hand the requirement is decreased to one honor-trick, and sometimes less. With two suits divided 5–5 the requirement is only 1½ honor-tricks. With two suits divided 6–5 a takeout should be made with as little as 1 honor-trick.* With the hands below, take out partner's opening one-spade bid as follows:

Two clubs:	♠ 9	♡ 7 6	◇ 8 4 3	♣ K J 10 9 7 5 3
Two hearts:	♠ 6	♡ Q 10 8 6 4 2	◇ 5	♣ K 6 5 3 2
Two diamonds:	♠ 8 5	♡ 2	◇ K Q 8 5 4	♣ Q J 6 3 2

* With hands containing less than one honor-trick, a pass is always optional and usually preferable.

The Forcing Takeout

A takeout of partner's opening suit-bid of one with exactly one trick more than is necessary in another suit is forcing to game. Thereafter neither partner can allow the bidding to die until game (or a satisfactory penalty double) is reached.

Since a non-jump suit takeout which is forcing for one round is available, the forcing takeout should be made only with hands powerful enough to give practical certainty of game and fair hope of a slam. Such hands can be recognized as follows:

1. Hands with 3½ honor-tricks and a solid or nearly solid suit, or such strong support for partner's suit that a double raise could have been made.
2. Hands with 4 honor-tricks and adequate support for partner's suit.
3. Hands containing 4½ or more honor-tricks with any biddable (even a four-card) suit.

The jump forcing takeout may be at the range of two or of three, depending on whether responder's suit is higher or lower in rank than opener's suit. In either of these cases North's response is forcing to game:

South	West	North	East
1 ◇	Pass	2 ♡	

or

South	West	North	East
1 ◇	Pass	3 ♣	

Responses to partner's opening bid of one heart:

Two spades	*Three clubs*	*Three diamonds*
♠ A K 9 7 4	♠ 6 3	♠ A 5
♡ K 3 2	♡ Q 10 9 4	♡ Q 8 3
◇ A Q 8 5	◇ A 6	◇ A K 8 7
♣ 6	♣ A K Q 3 2	♣ K Q 6 3

Two spades	*Three diamonds*	*Two spades*
♠ A Q J 8	♠ —	♠ A K J 5 4 3
♡ Q J 6	♡ Q 9 7 4	♡ 2
◇ A K 6 2	◇ A K Q 6 4 2	◇ K Q 8
♣ K 10	♣ K Q 3	♣ A 4 2

A hand with long, powerful support for partner's suit and more than 3½ honor-tricks is usually too strong for a double raise and is best shown by a forcing takeout. If the hand contains no biddable side suit, a forcing takeout may be made in a strong three-card suit *provided it is lower-ranking than partner's suit.*

Partner opens with one heart. Respond *three diamonds* on

♠ A K 3   ♡ K Q 10 7 2   ◇ A Q 7   ♣ 6 5

If partner later raises diamonds, you can always take him back to hearts at the same level. It would be improper to bid two spades, for then you could be forced one trick too high in returning to hearts.

Pre-emptive Responses

A *single jump* takeout is a powerful forcing bid, while a *double jump* is a shutout bid.

1.	Opener	Responder		2.	Opener	Responder
	1 ♡	3 ♠			1 ♡	3 ♣

The three-spade response is a *double* jump, since two spades would have been a jump response. The three-club response is only a *single* jump. The *double jump* takeout is a shutout bid, showing a strong suit but a hand weak in honor-tricks; but, as the responding hand will usually have about 6 winners, the opener usually rebids.

The double jump to three of a suit should be avoided, except with an expert partner. Inexperienced players cannot be expected to distinguish the difference between the jump to three spades and the jump to three clubs, and will read them indiscriminately as forcing takeouts.

A double or triple jump to four of a suit is not so confusing to partner, and may be made as a shutout bid on a hand with seven (but not more than seven) winners, and with no more than 1½ honor-tricks.

The following hand justifies a jump to four hearts over partner's one-diamond bid:

♠ 6   ♡ K J 10 8 6 5 3 2   ◇ J 8 3   ♣ 2

This hand is so weak defensively that despite partner's opening bid the opponents may be able to enter the bidding and reach a game contract which they can make. The jump response of four hearts may prevent their finding a fit in spades.

The opener, when considering a slam try, must remember the weakness shown by this preëmptive response.

Choice of Suits in Responding

The responder, when he holds two or more biddable suits, should almost invariably follow the general rules covering the choice of suits (page 110).

These rules should be modified in the following cases:

When a four-card suit can be shown by a one-over-one response, while a five-card suit in the same hand would require a response of two, the one-over-one response should be preferred with hands containing two honor-tricks or less but the suits should be bid in normal order when holding more than two honor-tricks.

For example, partner having bid one heart, bid one spade with ♠ A Q 6 5 ♡ 7 2 ◇ K 8 5 4 3 ♣ 9 6; but bid two clubs when holding ♠ A J 6 5 ♡ 8 5 ◇ 7 3 ♣ A Q 6 5 4.

When making a one-round-forcing response in a lower-ranking four-card suit, the stronger of two biddable four-card suits should usually be chosen, since it is unlikely that both suits will be shown.

For example, partner having bid one spade, bid two clubs rather than two diamonds with ♠ 9 6 5 ♡ Q 3 ◇ Q J 8 5 ♣ A K 7 4.

When holding two four-card suits, either of which can be shown by a one-over-one response, the choice depends on the strength of the hand.

With two honor-tricks or less, bid one in the lower-ranking suit. This facilitates partner's making a rebid at the level of one.

Partner bids one club. Holding:

♠ A 10 6 3 ♡ 8 7 6 2 ◇ Q 9 7 5 ♣ 8 Bid one diamond. This permits partner to bid either one heart or one spade. Partner may have a four-card heart suit but a hand too weak for a "reverse" (page 113), and if you respond one spade he may be unable to show his hearts.

♠ A 10 6 3 ♡ K 8 5 2 ◇ 9 5 3 ♣ 8 3 Bid one heart. Partner can raise if he has hearts, and can bid one spade if he has a secondary spade suit. If you respond one spade, partner might be prevented from showing a four-card heart suit. If partner rebids one notrump or two clubs, you will pass on the second round whether your first response is in spades or in hearts, for this hand is too weak to try for game by showing a new suit (see page 209). Therefore the one-heart response provides the only chance of locating a 4–4 fit in either major suit.

With 2½ honor-tricks or more, show the two four-card suits in normal order (the higher-ranking first); for with this much strength you will wish to make a second bid on your hand, whereby you can show your other suit.

Partner bids one club. Respond one spade on

♠ A Q 6 3   ♡ K Q 8 2   ◇ 8 6 5   ♣ 8 3

Even if partner's rebid is one notrump or two clubs, you are strong enough to bid two hearts.

CHOICE OF RESPONSES

Many hands will fit the requirements for either of two responses. When this occurs, the choice is usually governed as follows:

1. Prefer a one-over-one takeout to a one-notrump takeout.

Partner bids one diamond. Respond one heart, *not one notrump,* on
♠ Q 6 3   ♡ K 8 5 4   ◇ 6 2   ♣ Q 7 5 2.

It must be noted that a one-over-one response does not guarantee any greater strength than a one-notrump response. It is incorrect to respond one notrump in the belief that your hand "is not strong enough to show a suit," if the suit can be shown with a one-bid.

2. Prefer a single raise to a minimum suit takeout.

Partner bids one heart. Respond two hearts, not two clubs, on ♠ 9 2 ♡ Q 7 4   ◇ 8 6 3   ♣ A Q 9 5 4.
Respond two hearts, not one spade, on ♠ A J 8 6 2   ♡ 8 6 5 3   ◇ 9 7 ♣ 8 3.

It will be observed that if you make a suit takeout in either of the foregoing examples, and if partner's rebid is two hearts, you will be somewhat too weak to make a try for game by raising to three hearts; yet if you pass and partner happens to have an unusually strong hand for a two-heart rebid, game may be missed. The single raise puts it up to partner: If he is weak he will safely pass, and if he has enough to bid again you will carry on to game.

With a stronger hand—about 2½ honor-tricks when holding three-card support for partner's suit, about 2 honor-tricks when holding four-card support—the suit takeout is preferred, with the intention of raising partner's suit on the next round.

Partner bids one heart. Holding:

♠ 6 5 3   ♡ 10 8 7 4 ◇ A Q 8 5 2   ♣ 6   Bid two diamonds.
♠ A K 7 5 ♡ K 8 6   ◇ 6 3   ♣ 9 7 5 2 Bid one spade.

A takeout in a major suit is always preferred to a raise when partner's suit is a minor:

Partner bids one diamond. Respond one spade on

♠ Q 8 7 5 3   ♡ 6   ◇ A 8 7 2   ♣ 9 5 4

The choice of responses on very strong hands is often based on slam-bidding considerations. See page 309.

When the responder has previously passed, his choice of responses may be different. This will be discussed in the next chapter.

Free Responses

In many cases the requirements for responses are different when the intervening opponent overcalls partner's opening bid. See Chapter 19 on "Free Bids."

CHAPTER FIFTEEN

THE

PASSED HAND

When a player passes at his first turn, he has given an eloquent warning to his partner; he has also made a very informative call. Throughout the auction, any bid he may make will be seen in the light of his previous pass, and will be limited by it. He may safely make bids he would not dare make had he not previously passed. They will not sound so strong now.

Responses to Opening Bids

An opening bid third- or fourth-hand is little different from any other opening bid; but the response to it may be decidedly different, because the responder passed originally and is known to have less than an opening bid. The various responses, and their meanings, are:

1. A one-over-one or non-jump two-over-one response shows the same minimums as though the responder had not passed; but the maximums are less, *and the responses are not forcing.*

Therefore, a shaded double raise should be preferred to a suit takeout of partner's major-suit bid. Partner may otherwise pass the suit takeout and never find out about the responder's trump support.

In this bidding:

South	West	North	East
Pass	Pass	1 ♡	Pass
1 ♠ or 2 ♣	Pass	North may pass	

South should bid three hearts, rather than one spade, holding:

♠ K J 6 5 3   ♡ K 8 6 4   ◇ K 8   ♣ 7 2

South should bid three hearts, rather than two clubs, holding:

♠ 6   ♡ 8 6 5 2   ◇ Q 5 4   ♣ A K 9 6 3

If South had not passed originally, these hands would be too weak in honor-tricks for a double raise. South would first respond in his suit, prepared to raise hearts on the next round. When South has passed, there may be no "next round."

2. A double raise of a major suit is not forcing when made by a player who passed originally. Therefore, with a hand that fully meets the requirements for a double raise (see page 167), the responder should raise to game at once.

To partner's third-hand one-heart bid, respond four hearts on

♠ A 6   ♡ K J 5 3   ◇ Q J 7 6 2   ♣ 8 4

It follows that a triple raise by a passed player shows a stronger hand in honor-tricks as well as in distribution than a double raise would; and the opener, if he has a very powerful hand, should remember this when considering a slam try.

3. A jump suit takeout, when made by a player who previously passed, is *not forcing;* but it shows a maximum pass— a hand that barely fell short of being an opening bid—and the opener is not expected to pass it if his own hand is fully up to opening strength.

SOUTH	WEST	NORTH	EAST
Pass	Pass	1 ♣	Pass
2 ♡			

South announces that he has a hand like this:

♠ 6 2   ♡ Q J 9 7 6   ◇ K J 5   ♣ A 6 4 (A good playing hand, but slightly short of 2½ honor-tricks)

Or a hand like this:

♠ 7   ♡ A Q 8 4 2   ◇ 4   ♣ Q 10 8 5 3 2 (A very good fit with partner)

Or perhaps like this:

♠ 6   ♡ K Q 10 9 5 3   ◇ K J 10 9 5   ♣ 7 (Such a powerful distributional hand that game is practically sure if North has full honor-trick values and any fit with hearts)

The only case in which the opener passes this jump suit takeout is when he has made a shaded third-hand bid (see page 109).

4. A two-notrump takeout is not forcing. It shows a hand of about 2½ honor-tricks, and conceivably as many as 3 honor-tricks, with stoppers in the unbid suits. The reason such a hand was not bid originally is, of course, that it contained no biddable suit.

A two-notrump takeout of partner's third- or fourth-hand one-diamond bid would show something like this:

♠ A K 4   ♡ 10 9 6 3   ◊ Q 7   ♣ Q 5 3 2

With a hand much weaker than this, it is better to make a suit takeout and see if partner can rebid. A two-notrump response to an opening bid, especially to an opening third-hand bid, is undesirable because the contract will be unsafe if partner has a weak hand, yet he may not be able to do anything but pass it. It must be remembered that a simple suit takeout of partner's bid, even when made by a passed player, may be fairly strong; something like

♠ K J 10 8 5   ♡ K 4 3   ◊ 7 2   ♣ Q J 8

Second-Round Bids by the Responder

There is a considerable difference between passing an opening bid that has not been overcalled, and passing an opening bid that has been overcalled. A "courtesy" response to an opening bid is made to keep the bidding open and often shows as little as one honor-trick; therefore failure to make such a response denies a holding of one honor-trick. But failure to make a free response, which requires 1½ honor-tricks or more, does not always deny holding a fair hand (though the opener, to be safe, must be prepared for a blank).

After this bidding:

SOUTH	WEST	NORTH	EAST
1 ♡	Pass	Pass	2 ◊
2 ♡	3 ◊		

North may raise with a trickless hand, if his distributional support is good; or with barren distribution, if he passed the opening bid with one or more honor-tricks. With either of the following hands, North should now bid three hearts:

| ♠ 6 3 | ♡ 10 8 5 4 | ◇ 7 6 5 | ♣ Q J 8 3   or |
| ♠ 9 5 3 | ♡ K Q 2 | ◇ 9 8 5 3 | ♣ 6 4 2 |

South cannot expect him to have more, for with more he would have given a courtesy raise to two hearts on the first round.

Having passed the opening bid, whether it is one of a suit or one notrump, a player may come in later without fear that his bid will sound stronger than his hand warrants.

SOUTH	WEST	NORTH	EAST
1 ♠ or 1 N T	Pass	Pass	2 ◇
Pass	Pass	2 ♡	

North holds: ♠ 6   ♡ Q J 10 8 5   ◇ 10 8 7   ♣ J 9 6 3

When the opener's second-round call is a takeout double, the responder should jump one trick in responding if he had a maximum pass on the first round. This may be a hand that looks very weak, but he must not fail to remember how weak his hand may have been, in view of his pass.

SOUTH	WEST	NORTH	EAST
1 ◇	Pass	Pass	1 ♡
Double	Pass		

The weakest bid North can make is two diamonds (which he should bid on a worthless hand that includes three or more diamonds):

| ♠ 8 5 | ♡ 7 6 4 2 | ◇ 9 6 4 | ♣ J 7 6 3 | Two diamonds |

Since a two-diamond bid may be so weak, a fair hand justifies a jump to three diamonds, or a jump response in a suit.

♠ K 8 6	♡ 7 5 2	◇ J 8 7 6	♣ 9 8 6	Three diamonds
♠ Q 10 9 6 4	♡ 8 5 3	◇ 9 2	♣ J 6 5	One spade
♠ Q 10 9 6 4	♡ 7	◇ 8 6 4	♣ Q 9 5 3	Two spades

When the responder merely refused to make a free bid, his jump response to a double should show 1 to 1½ honor-tricks.

SOUTH	WEST	NORTH	EAST
1 ♠	2 ◇	Pass	Pass
Double	Pass		

North first considers a penalty pass, of course, and will pass if his hand is:

    ♠ 6   ♡ A 7 3   ◊ J 8 5 4   ♣ Q 10 7 6 3

But if unable to pass, North takes out the double as follows:

♠ 8 6 2	♡ 7 5 2	◊ 9 4 3	♣ 7 6 5 2	Two spades
♠ Q 8 5	♡ K 6 3	◊ 9 4 3	♣ 7 6 5 2	Two spades
♠ 8 6	♡ K 9 8 6 5 2	◊ 7 3	♣ J 5 4	Two hearts
♠ 10 9 6 5 4	♡ Q 6 4 3	◊ 2	♣ 7 6 5	Three spades

When the opener's bid is a strength-showing bid (either a jump rebid, or a three-level bid) the responder, having passed, may and should raise or bid on the sketchiest of values.

SOUTH	WEST	NORTH	EAST
1 ◊	Pass	Pass	2 ♣
2 ♠	Pass		

North should raise to three spades on:

    ♠ 10 7 6 3   ♡ K 6 5   ◊ 9 4   ♣ 8 6 3 2

A jump rebid in a new suit by the opener demands a response on next-to-nothing:

SOUTH	WEST	NORTH	EAST
1 ♡	Pass	Pass	1 ♠
3 ♣	Pass		

If North passes, it means he has something like this:

    ♠ 8 6 5 3   ♡ 7 6   ◊ Q 8 5 4   ♣ 9 6 3

With even as much as this, North should bid:

♠ 9 6 5	♡ 10 7 3	◊ Q 8 5 4	♣ 9 6 3	Three hearts
♠ 9 6	♡ 10 7 6 3	◊ Q J 7 6	♣ 8 5 2	Four hearts
♠ 9 6	♡ 7 3	◊ K 8 7 5 3	♣ J 6 4 2	Four clubs

See also Chapter 19 on "Free Bids."

CHAPTER SIXTEEN

REBIDS BY
THE OPENER

When a response has been made to an opening suit-bid of one, the opener has another chance to bid. If the response was not forcing he must decide whether to pass or not; and if to bid, what to bid. If the response was forcing, assuming that the opponents pass, he must decide on the bid which best shows the type of hand he holds. Any second bid made by the opening hand is called a *rebid*.

The nature of the rebid will depend upon the bidding zone in which the opener's hand may be classified. The symptoms which will determine the proper zone are the general strength of the opener's hand and the maximum and minimum levels of strength which may have been shown by his partner's response.

CHOOSING THE ZONE

The general bidding situations which determine the proper zone of bidding and the opener's choice of rebids are as follows:

1. MINIMUM (PART-SCORE) ZONE

Situation: The response was one notrump, a single raise, or a preëmptive takeout. The opener has a minimum or near-minimum hand—this means that he could not remove an honor-trick, or a card of the trump suit, from his hand and still have an opening bid.

Object: Safety. If the response was a single raise, pass, since the contract is a safe one. If the response was one notrump, pass with a balanced hand and no six-card or longer suit. With a six-card trump suit, rebid the suit. With an unbalanced hand show a second biddable suit if lower-ranking than the first, or rebid a rebiddable suit; otherwise, pass.

2. INTERMEDIATE ZONE

Situation: The symptoms of this zone are of two kinds:

(*a*) The opener has a weak hand, but the response was a suit takeout (forcing for one round) which may show either a weak or a very strong hand.

(*b*) The opener has a strong hand, but the response was one notrump or a single raise, which may have been shaded.

Object: Information and safety.

(*a*) With a weak hand, the opener should try to show partner the distribution of his hand, by bidding notrump if he can do so at the level of one, by giving partner a single raise if he has adequate trump support, by showing a new lower-ranking suit, or by rebidding a rebiddable suit.

(*b*) If the opener is strong but responder may be very weak, opener should make a rebid which shows strength but which responder need not carry to game, unless he has rebid values of his own: a jump raise in partner's suit, a jump rebid of opener's suit, a bid or raise to two notrump, or a non-jump bid of a new suit at the level of three. Also included in this category are "reverse bids," which are explained on page 113.

3. GAME ZONE

Situation: Either partner makes a response which is forcing to game, or opener is so strong that game is possible even if responder has a weak hand.

Object: Security. The opener's first thought is to make sure the bidding will not be dropped short of game. If the response was forcing to game, the opener should simply make the rebid which best shows the strength and distribution of his hand. If the response is not forcing to game, the opener makes a forcing rebid by jumping one trick in a new suit, or bids game immediately in a suit or notrump.

4. SLAM ZONE

This does not mean a slam must surely be bid, but that the opener wishes to explore the slam possibilities before contenting himself with a game contract.

Situation: Opener has a strong hand *and* the response is forcing to game.

Object: Information and security. The opener tries to make some bid which will not risk having the bidding dropped at game and which will either give partner information or coax some desired information from him.

When the Response Was Forcing to Game

When the response to the opening bid was forcing to game the opening hand has little to worry about. He knows that the responder's hand is so strong that a game will be reached, so that the safety factor (the danger of being set) need not be considered and the only problem is how best to give as much information as possible about the nature of the hand.

RESPONSES TO A FORCING TAKEOUT

When the response is a jump suit takeout, which is forcing to game, the opener has only to look at his hand and choose any available rebid in the following order:

1. If he has a second biddable suit in his hand, he should bid the new suit.
2. Lacking a second biddable suit but with a rebiddable suit, he should rebid his suit.
3. With adequate trump support for responder's suit, he should raise. Added values justifying a double raise should not be shown at this point.

4. With very strong support for partner's suit, while it is seldom proper to give a jump raise, the opener may now try for a slam with a conventional four-notrump bid (Chapter 28).

5. Lacking any of these requirements, the opener should respond with the minimum number of notrump necessary, the minimum notrump bid being in this case, as in almost all cases, a negative bid.

For example, assuming the bidding to have been—

SOUTH	WEST	NORTH	EAST
1 ♣	Pass	2 ♠	Pass

South's rebid should be:

Three hearts, holding

♠ 7	♡ A Q 6 5	◇ K 8 2	♣ A J 10 7 5

Three clubs, holding

♠ Q 6 3	♡ 9 2	◇ A 7	♣ A J 10 7 6 3

Three spades, holding

♠ K 7 4	♡ 6 2	◇ A 9 8	♣ K Q 10 7 5

Two notrump, holding

♠ A 7	♡ K Q 6	◇ 10 8 5 4	♣ K J 6 2

With a near-minimum opening bid, the opener should sometimes fail to show a second biddable suit when it would carry the bidding to four-odd:

SOUTH	WEST	NORTH	EAST
1 ♠	Pass	3 ♡	Pass

South should bid three spades, holding

♠ K Q 10 6 5	♡ 8 2	◇ 7 6	♣ A Q 9 4

His hand is too weak for a bid of four clubs. This consideration also causes him to bid three notrump, rather than four clubs, holding

♠ K 8 7 4 3	♡ 8 5	◇ Q 10	♣ A K J 2

With added honor strength, he shows the second suit no matter what the necessary bid. He bids four clubs on

♠ K Q 10 6 5   ♥ 8 2   ♦ A 6   ♣ A Q 6 3

Rebidding Over a Double Raise

A double raise in a major suit is forcing and may not be passed short of game. The opener's choice of a rebid depends on his strength and his distribution.

The opener makes a slam try by bidding four in a new suit. With fewer than four honor-tricks, he should not usually make a slam try. If he does not make a slam try, he has only two rebids available: Four of his major suit, and three notrump.

Three notrump is the rebid on 4–3–3–3 or 4–4–3–2 distribution, with the honor-trick content of the hand distributed among the unbid suits as well as the bid suit:

You open with one spade. Partner raises to three spades. Bid three notrump with ♠ A J 6 2   ♥ Q 5   ♦ A 9 7 4   ♣ K J 6

Four of the major suit is the rebid with any hand—including a hand with a four-card trump suit—in which the distribution is unbalanced, or in which an unbid suit is not stopped.

You open with one spade. Partner raises to three spades. Bid four spades with:

♠ A K 6 5   ♥ A Q 7 2   ♦ 6 5   ♣ 9 4 3   or with
♠ J 7 6 5 2   ♥ A K Q   ♦ K 7 5 2   ♣ 6

A double raise in a minor suit is not forcing, but the opener should bid over it if he can. He should bid three notrump if his distribution is balanced and if he has stoppers, or partial stoppers, in the unbid suits. He should show a biddable four-card major if he has one.

The minor-suit double raise is passed only when the opener has a minimum hand, or a near-minimum, in honor-tricks; and his distribution is unbalanced, or his honor-tricks are concentrated in one or two suits, so that a three-notrump contract would be dangerous.

With unbalanced distribution and a long, strong suit, or a two-suiter, the opener may take a chance on playing at five of his minor suit for game.

You open with one diamond; partner raises to three diamonds. Your rebids on the various hands you may hold:

♠ K Q 6	♡ A	◇ K J 7 6	♣ J 8 6 5 2	Three notrump
♠ Q 10 6 4	♡ A 6	◇ A Q J 5	♣ 6 5 3	Three spades
♠ A K 5	♡ 5 2	◇ Q J 9 6 3	♣ 8 4 3	Pass
♠ 10	♡ K 3	◇ K 10 9 6 4 3	♣ A K J 7	Four notrump

Rebidding Over Two Notrump

When the response was two notrump, the opening hand should usually raise to three notrump with balanced distribution (unless the hand contains more than four honor-tricks and he wishes to make a slam try), but rebid his suit or a new suit with unbalanced distribution.

Even when the opener's distribution is balanced, if he has a rebiddable major suit, or a six-card minor, it should be rebid.

For example, when the opening one-spade bid has been taken out with two notrump, the opener should bid three spades, holding

♠ A J 10 8 5 ♡ 7 6 3 ◇ A Q 8 ♣ J 4

Having opened one diamond, over a two-notrump response:
Bid three notrump with

♠ A 6 4 ♡ J 3 ◇ A K 8 6 5 ♣ 9 8 6

Bid three diamonds with

♠ K Q 7 ♡ 7 3 ◇ K 9 8 7 4 2 ♣ A 8

Rebids After a One-Round Force

In general the opening hand, after a response to an opening bid, becomes the responding hand: his response to his partner's takeout must show his strength and the contract he prefers in accordance with his distribution.

Every rebid shows a certain distribution combined with a certain amount of honor strength. The rebid should be chosen primarily to show the hand's strength.

1. With a strong hand (usually one containing four honor-tricks or more) look for a strength-showing rebid: a bid of a new suit at the level of three, a raise of partner's suit to three, a rebid of two or more in notrump, or a jump rebid in the original suit provided it is a long, strong one.

2. With a weaker hand (usually one containing less than four honor-tricks) show a new biddable suit if it does not require a bid of three, give partner a single raise, preferably a raise to the two-level only, or make the minimum rebid in the original suit.

You opened with one spade; partner has responded two diamonds. Opponents pass. Your rebid:

♠ A Q 10 6 3   ♡ 9   ◊ 10 3   ♣ A 8 7 5 2   Two spades. Too weak to show a new suit at the three-level.

♠ A J 10 6 3   ♡ A J 5 4   ◊ 6 5   ♣ 8 2 Two hearts. No added strength is required to show a new suit at the two-level.

♠ A Q 7 5 3   ♡ 6 5   ◊ K 2   ♣ A K J 6 Three clubs. Too strong for a rebid of only two spades.

♠ K J 10 8 5   ♡ 7 4   ◊ K 10 6   ♣ A 8 3 Two spades. Too weak to raise partner's suit to the three-level.

♠ A K 9 8 5   ♡ A   ◊ K J 6   ♣ J 8 5 2 Three diamonds. Too strong for a rebid of only two spades.

Exact requirements for the various possible rebids are given in the Illustrated Summary on pages 200-207.

REBIDS IN NOTRUMP

With 4–3–3–3, 4–4–3–2, or 5–3–3–2 distribution, the opener has, in addition to his choice between suit-bids and raises, the possibility of a rebid in notrump.

A rebid of one notrump, when the response was a one-over-one, is a negative or minimum rebid. When the response was in a lower-ranking suit, however, the notrump rebid must be *two* notrump, which shows a stronger hand.

A notrump rebid at the level of one is made with any balanced hand containing 3½ honor-tricks or less, and with some hands containing four *bare* honor-tricks.

Two notrump is always a strength-showing rebid (see page 202) but it shows a stronger hand when it is a jump rebid made over a one-over-one response than when it is a non-jump rebid made over a two-over-one response.

You open with one diamond on

♠ A J 6   ♡ K 8 2   ◊ A K 7 5 3   ♣ J 8

If partner's response is two clubs, you rebid two notrump. But if partner's response is one spade or one heart you have not quite enough to bid two notrump, so you content yourself with a single raise in partner's suit.

REVALUATION FOR RAISES

When partner has made a suit takeout of the opening bid, and the opener has adequate trump support for the responder's suit, he may count his winners exactly as though he were the responding hand. His count of winners is based upon honor-, long-suit and ruffing tricks, which were explained in Chapter 5.

In general, a suit takeout of an opening one-bid shows at least three winners, and the opener should raise once if he has five supporting winners. To give a double raise the opener should have at least four trumps and one honor-trick more than he needed for his opening bid.

Without this additional honor-trick, the opener should not give a double raise without very strong distributional support— about 6½ or 7 supporting winners. For example:

Opening bid one heart, response one spade. Raise to three spades with

♠ Q 10 9 3   ♡ A K 9 6 5 2   ◊ K 3   ♣ 8

The rules governing the opener's double raises apply primarily to major suits. He should be careful not to raise the responder's minor suit to four, passing the three-notrump level, without at least seven supporting winners and four honor-tricks.

Requirements for raises in terms of honor-tricks and trump support are given on pages 202, 204 and 207.

Rebids After One Notrump

A response of one notrump is a minimum or negative response and is not forcing. The opener should consider the possibility of a pass as well as of a rebid. He should pass with any hand of balanced distribution and no six-card or longer suit when the hand contains only 3½ honor-tricks or less. He should pass a hand with unbalanced distribution unless he has a rebiddable suit, a second biddable suit, or an additional honor-trick.

The opener should rebid his suit even with a minimum if it is six cards long or longer.

A raise of partner's one-notrump response shows a *very strong* hand—4½ to 5 honor-tricks. (For the rebids see pages 201 and 203-205.)

Jump Rebids

A jump rebid to three in the major suit in which you opened the bidding signifies that game can be made unless partner has already shaded his first response. It is not absolutely forcing, but asks responder to bid again on the slightest excuse.

You open with one heart; partner responds one spade. You hold:

♠ 6 3   ♡ A K Q 8 5 2   ◊ A K 7   ♣ 5 2

There should be a play for game if partner has at least one honor-trick and two small cards in hearts. You rebid three hearts, urging partner to make another bid.

A jump by opener to four of his major suit is an even stronger bid, made when the opener does not wish to risk even the bare possibility that the responder will now pass. The opener, for a rebid to four spades, probably holds something like

♠ K Q J 10 8 6 4   ♡ 3   ◊ A K 7   ♣ K 5

Far from being a "hands off" or "stop" bid, this rebid shows so much strength that partner should make a slam try on a hand of moderate strength, perhaps with only 1½ or 2 honor-tricks.

However, the jump to game is less informative than the forcing rebid, which is a jump of exactly one trick in a new suit after partner has responded. In effect, the opener is making a "forcing takeout" of his partner's response.

The forcing rebid should be made when a game is probable mathematically (because opener has 5 or 5½ honor-tricks) or when game seems certain on fewer honor-tricks because of the hand's solidity.

If you open with one spade on

    ♠ K Q J 8 6 4   ♡ A K Q 7 2   ◊ 8   ♣ 2
 or ♠ A Q J 6   ♡ A K 10 2   ◊ A Q 9 5 ♣ 8

and your partner responds one notrump, your rebid is three hearts, forcing to game.

A jump rebid in a minor suit is somewhat different. It does

not promise so much general strength—in fact, it more or less denies a hope of game unless three notrump is the contract. The jump rebid in a minor suit is designed to show seven quick winners at notrump, contained in a long, solid minor suit with a side entry.

The following hands have long presented a troublesome rebidding problem:

1. ♠ J 6   ♡ K 9   ◇ A K Q 8 6 3 2   ♣ 9 8
2. ♠ 6 3   ♡ 10 9 3   ◇ A K Q 9 4 2   ♣ A 8

You open with one diamond; partner responds one spade. If partner has a fair hand, and diamonds break, a notrump game is practically sure. If partner has a weak hand, his strength limited to a trick or so in spades, game is out of the question and a contract of two notrump may go down two or three tricks. The opener hates to bid two diamonds, which sounds weak and may be passed; he hesitates to bid two notrump, which will be raised on a prayer.

The jump rebid to three diamonds solves this problem. If partner passes, you are in a safe contract. If partner can, he will bid three notrump and make it.

Requirements and illustrations of the opener's jump rebids appear on pages 205-206.

Rebids When Partner Raises

When partner gives a single raise to the opening one-bid, the opener should now count his winners. He must remember that the raise may be a shaded one; therefore caution is required in rebidding.

For those who measure all bids in terms of honor-tricks, the requirements are as follows:

With 3 honor-tricks and a six-card suit; or with 3½ honor-tricks and a five-card suit; or with 4 honor-tricks, even if the suit is a four-card suit; make some rebid. With less, pass.

If you find it easier to count your winners, the rebids are:

With 5½ to 6½ winners, the opener may now rebid to the level of three-odd, or bid two notrump.

With *seven* winners the opener may now rebid to the level of four-odd.

With 5½ to 6½ winners, the opener's rebid may be three in the same suit; two or three in a new suit; or two notrump, depending on his type of hand.

SOUTH	WEST	NORTH	EAST
1 ♡	Pass	2 ♡	Pass

3 ♡ ⎤
or 3 ◇ ⎦ are equivalent

South would bid three hearts holding

♠ 6   ♡ A Q J 7 5   ◇ K J 4   ♣ Q 10 6 5 = 6½ winners

He would bid three diamonds, holding

♠ 6 5   ♡ A Q 7 6   ◇ A K 4 3   ♣ Q J 6 = 5½ winners

and if North signed off by returning to three hearts, South would then pass.

South would jump at once to four hearts with

♠ A 5   ♡ A Q J 8 6 5   ◇ K J 10   ♣ 3 2 = 7½ winners

When a single raise has been given in a minor suit, the opener should prefer any new suit or notrump rebid. If he rebids his suit, it should be only because he has no other sound rebid (unless, with 8 winners, he can bid five of his suit).

Partner having raised the opening one-club bid to two, the opener would now pass, holding

♠ A.Q 7 6   ♡ K 7   ◇ 10 4 3   ♣ A Q 8 2 or
♠ 9 5 3   ♡ A 9 8 2   ◇ K Q 4   ♣ A 8 4   Pass

He would bid two spades, holding

♠ K J 5 3   ♡ A 6 3   ◇ 7   ♣ A Q 10 7 6

He would rebid his clubs with

♠ K Q 6   ♡ A 8 3   ◇ 3   ♣ K Q 10 9 6 5

A rebid of two notrump shows about four honor-tricks and probable stoppers in the unbid suits, whether the raised suit is a major or a minor. With five honor-tricks or with a solid minor suit, the opener should jump to three notrump, since the two-notrump rebid is not forcing.

Partner having raised a one-diamond bid to two, opener now rebids two notrump holding

♠ A J   ♡ A K 7   ◇ A 8 5 4 2   ♣ J 6 3

He jumps to three notrump with

♠ K 8   ♥ A 7 3   ♦ A Q J 9 5 4   ♣ A 7

REBIDS BY THE OPENING HAND
Illustrated Summary

I. Weak (Possible Minimum) Rebids

1. Rebid of One Notrump

Opener	Responder
1 ♥	1 ♠
1 N T	

The rebid shows: Opening hand is minimum or near-minimum (never more than 4 honor-tricks, probably less). Balanced distribution with no six-card suit. Opener may have a rebiddable heart suit, or a second biddable suit, or adequate support for spades; but with balanced distribution and no added values, prefers to emphasize the weakness of his hand. Examples:

♠ 8 5	♠ 6 2	♠ A 6 4
♥ A.Q J 7	♥ A K 7 5 3	♥ A Q 9 2
♦ K J 7 6	♦ A 5 4	♦ K 5
♣ Q J 4	♣ 9 6 2	♣ 8 7 4 3

With any one of these hands, opener would have passed a response of one notrump.

2. Two of a Suit Lower-Ranking Than Opener's First Suit

Opener	Responder
1 ♥	2 ♣
2 ♦	

The rebid shows: Opener may have a near-minimum hand with no more honor-tricks than he needed for his first bid. The diamonds may be a conditional biddable suit. Opener may have either balanced or unbalanced distribution. With a weak hand he may have a four-card heart suit and a five-card diamond suit (page 114). This rebid affirms or denies nothing except that opener is probably too weak to bid two notrump, raise to three clubs, or make any stronger bid. Yet his hand may be quite strong, with as many as 4+ honor-tricks. Examples:

♠ Q 6	♠ 9	♠ 8 5	♠ 9 6
♥ A Q 7 5 2	♥ A•10 7 5 3	♥ A.K 6 5	♥ K J 10 5
♦ A J 6 4	♦ K Q 10 7 5	♦ A 10 9 7 3	♦ K Q 5 4
♣ 5 4	♣ Q 2	♣ 4 3	♣ A 6 2

3. Two of a Lower-Ranking Suit When It Increases
the Bidding Level

Opener	*Responder*		*Opener*	*Responder*
1 ♡	1 ♠	**or**	1 ♡	1 N T
2 ◇			2 ◇	

The rebid shows: Opener has two biddable suits. He has either un-balanced distribution or at least ½ honor-trick above a minimum; other-wise, he could have bid one notrump (or passed responder's one-notrump takeout). In either case, this rebid shows slight added values in honor-tricks or in distribution. Examples:

♠ 8 6	♠ J 6 4	♠ 7	♠ Q 6
♡ A K 6 5 4	♡ A K 9 5	♡ Q J 10 8 4	♡ K Q 10 8
◇ K Q 10 5	◇ A Q J 2	◇ A K 7 5 2	◇ A Q 7 6 4
♣ 4 3	♣ 10 7	♣ 9 3	♣ J 7

4. Rebid of One in a New Suit

Opener	*Responder*
1 ♣	1 ♡
1 ♠	

The rebid shows: This rebid gives no specific information. Opener may have a minimum hand and, for purposes of safety, try to find the safest suit for a part-score contract; he may have a strong hand but less than the 4½–5 honor-tricks needed for a forcing rebid. Responder is expected to treat this about as an opening one-bid, except that he must assume that the spade suit is a four-card and possibly a weak one, and should not raise spades without four trumps or (rarely) three strong trumps (K Q x). Examples:

♠ A J 6 5	♠ K 10 8 7	♠ A K 8 6	♠ A 10 8 5 2
♡ 4 3	♡ J 5 2	♡ 7 4	♡ 6
◇ Q 6 2	◇ A	◇ K J	◇ 7
♣ A Q 10 6	♣ A J 10 7 4	♣ A K 8 5 2	♣ A K 8 4 3 2

5. A Rebid of Two in the Same Suit

1. *Opener*	*Responder*		2. *Opener*	*Responder*
1 ♡	2 ♣		1 ♡	1 ♠ or 1 N T
2 ♡			2 ♡	

The rebid shows: When it does not raise the bidding level, as in Figure 1, the opener's rebid in the same suit may not show any values either in honor-tricks or in distribution above a minimum opening bid. It affirms only a rebiddable heart suit, with possibly no more than 2+ or 2½ honor-tricks. In some cases a suit as weak as K 10 x x x is rebid.

When the rebid raises the bidding level, as in Figure 2, it means that the opener has either:

(*a*) A six-card trump suit.

(*b*) Unbalanced distribution with a five-card rebiddable suit; or

(*c*) About one additional honor-trick. Examples:

With ♠ 6 3 ♡ A K J 8 5 ◊ K J 6 ♣ 5 3 2, bid two hearts over two clubs; bid one notrump over one spade; pass one notrump.

With ♠ 6 5 ♡ J 10 8 6 4 2 ◊ A K 6 ♣ K J bid two hearts in either Figure 1 or Figure 2.

With ♠ 6 5 ♡ A Q 10 7 4 ◊ A K 5 ♣ J 7 3 bid two hearts in either Figure 1 or Figure 2.

With ♠ 5 ♡ A K 10 7 3 ◊ J 10 9 4 ♣ K 8 3 bid two hearts in either Figure 1 or Figure 2.

6. Raise of Responder's Suit to Two

Opener	Responder
1 ♣	1 ♡
2 ♡	

The rebid shows: Adequate trump support for hearts, and

(*a*) Four trumps, in which case the hand need contain no added values either in honor-tricks or in distribution;

(*b*) Three trumps with a singleton or an additional ½ honor-trick. Examples:

♠ 6 3	♠ 9 6 4 2	♠ K 8 5	♠ 8
♡ 10 7 5 4	♡ K 6 5	♡ A 6 3	♡ Q 5 2
◊ A 5	◊ A 3	◊ 7 2	◊ A K 6 4
♣ A Q 10 6 4	♣ A K J 5	♣ K Q J 5 2	♣ K 8 5 3 2

II. Strong Rebids (Some Added Values)

1. Non-Jump Rebid of Two Notrump

Opener	Responder
1 ♡	2 ♣
2 N T	

The rebid shows: About 4 honor-tricks or at least 16 points in high cards. Balanced distribution with probably a stopper or near stopper (Q x or J x x) in both unbid suits. Often as much as 4 or 4½ *bare* honor-tricks. With strong intermediates and a stopper in every suit opener may make this rebid with only 3½ plus honor-tricks. Opener does not deny a five-card rebiddable heart suit or adequate trump support for clubs. Examples:

♠ 9 6 5 2	♠ A 6 5	♠ K 6	♠ A 6
♡ A Q 10 3	♡ K Q 10 8	♡ A K Q 5 4	♡ A J 8 5
◊ A K 6	◊ 9 6 4 2	◊ K 8 3	◊ K 10 7 3
♣ K 3	♣ A Q	♣ J 9 4	♣ Q 10 9

2. Single Jump Rebid in Notrump

1.	Opener	Responder	2.	Opener	Responder
	1 ◇	1 ♡		1 ♡	2 ♣
	2 N T			3 N T	

The rebid shows: At least four honor-tricks with strong intermediates, probably 4½ honor-tricks (19–20 high-card points), and a stopper (usually a double stopper) in both unbid suits. Balanced distribution. *In Figure 1:* Perhaps adequate support for hearts, but not four hearts (with which a double raise would be made). Opener probably has no biddable spade suit or he would have bid one spade. *In Figure 2:* Opener may have only four honor-tricks, but A Q x, K Q x, etc., in clubs. Examples:

	In Figure 1			*In Figure 2*	
♠ K Q 6	♠ A 2		♠ A Q 6		♠ A 4
♡ Q 9	♡ A 6 3		♡ A J 10 6		♡ K J 7 2
◇ A K 8 4	◇ A Q J 6 3		◇ A K 7 4		◇ A 9 5 4
♣ K J 10 5	♣ K J 7		♣ J 10		♣ A Q 7

3. Single Raise of a One-Notrump Takeout

	Opener	Responder
	1 ♠	1 N T
	2 N T	

The rebid shows: 4½ honor-tricks. Balanced distribution with some strength (probably a stopper) in every suit. With only four honor-tricks, opener should have strong fillers. He may have a rebiddable spade suit or a second biddable suit, being *too strong* merely to bid two in the suit. Examples:

♠ K Q 6 5	♠ A Q J 7	♠ Q J 10 9 7
♡ K Q	♡ A 2	♡ J 10 6
◇ A 10 8 5	◇ A K 6	◇ A K
♣ K Q J	♣ 10 8 4 3	♣ A Q J

4. Raise of Responder's Suit to Three

1.	Opener	Responder	2.	Opener	Responder
	1 ♠	2 ♣		1 ♠	2 ♡
	3 ♣			3 ♡	

The rebid shows: Adequate trump support. With only three trumps the hand must contain an added ½ honor-trick. With four trumps, no added

honor-tricks required. Since the response of two in a suit usually shows a
five-card suit, opener may at times shade adequate trump support to J x x,
or, in a major, to x x x.

Bid three clubs with:		Bid three hearts with:	
♠ K Q J 6	♠ A J 8 5 4	♠ A Q 8 4 2	♠ K Q 9 6
♡ 9 8 5 2	♡ A Q 2	♡ 9 6 4 3	♡ K 9 7
◇ A 3	◇ 5	◇ A Q	◇ A K 8 5
♣ A 9 7	♣ J 9 7 4	♣ 6 3	♣ 7 3

5. Double Raise in Responder's Suit

1. Opener	Responder	2. Opener	Responder
1 ◇	1 ♡	1 ♠	2 ♡
3 ♡		4 ♡	

The rebid shows: Four trumps, a singleton and about 3½ honor-tricks
outside. With no singleton, the hand should contain at least four honor-
tricks. The takeout of two may be raised to game with only three trumps if
very strong (K Q x, A J x, etc.). On many hands which justify a double raise
consider some forcing jump bid.

Raise one heart to three with:		Raise two hearts to four with:	
♠ 9	♠ A 6	♠ K Q J 5 3	♠ K Q 5 4 3
♡ Q 10 6 5	♡ K Q 8 5	♡ 10 9 5 2	♡ A Q 7
◇ A K J 3	◇ A K 7 5 2	◇ A K 6	◇ 10 9 6 5
♣ A J 5 2	♣ 6 3	♣ 5	♣ A

Note: A minor-suit response should not be raised to four, passing the
three-notrump level, except with freak distribution (usually five trumps)
and four honor-tricks. *Note 2:* A double raise from one to three may be
given in a major or minor with only three trumps (A J x or K Q x) when
one suit is too weak to bid two notrump.

6. Rebid of Two in a Suit Higher-Ranking Than Opener's First Suit

1. Opener	Responder	or	2. Opener	Responder	or	3. Opener	Responder
1 ◇	1 ♠		1 ◇	1 N T		1 ◇	2 ♣
2 ♡			2 ♡			2 ♡	

The rebid shows: A four-card heart suit and a five-card diamond suit.
Usually at least four honor-tricks, or 3½ honor-tricks with both suits strong
in intermediates. With 6–5 distribution no added honor-trick is required.

Rarely, the hand will have a very weak (conditional biddable) five-card heart suit and a very strong five-card diamond suit. Examples:

♠ 6 3	♠ 7	♠ 6	♠ A Q
♡ A Q J 5	♡ A Q J 10	♡ K 10 8 6 5	♡ 9 8 7 5 2
◇ K Q J 6 2	◇ A K J 9 6	◇ A K 9 7 5 3	◇ A K Q 6 5
♣ A 7	♣ 10 4 3	♣ 2	♣ 4

With ♠ 6 ♡ K J 6 2 ◇ A Q 10 5 4 ♣ K J 6 (3+ honor-tricks) opener would bid two hearts over a takeout of two clubs, knowing that a safe final contract is available in clubs if responder cannot support hearts or diamonds.

7. Non-Jump Rebid of Three in a New Suit

Opener	Responder
1 ♡	2 ◇
3 ♣	

The rebid shows: About four honor-tricks except with two five-card suits (in which case 3½ honor-tricks are sufficient) or with strong support for responder's suit. Examples:

♠ A 6	♠ 9	♠ K 2	♠ 4
♡ K Q 10 5 4	♡ A Q 10 3	♡ A J 8 6 4	♡ K Q 8 5 3 2
◇ Q 6	◇ Q J 5 2	◇ 9	◇ 2
♣ A K 5 3	♣ A Q 7 4	♣ A Q J 7 4	♣ A K 7 5 3

III. Very Strong Rebids

1. Jump Rebid of Three Notrump

Opener	Responder
1 ♣	1 ♠
3 N T	

The rebid shows: About five honor-tricks, 21 points in high cards, with at least one stopper (Q 10 x or better) and usually a double stopper (K J x, Q 10 x x, etc.) in both unbid suits. Examples:

♠ K 4	♠ Q J 5
♡ A K Q	♡ K Q 7
◇ Q 10 5 3	◇ A K 6
♣ A K 7 5	♣ A Q 9 6

2. Jump Rebid in Opener's Major Suit

1. Opener	Responder		2. Opener	Responder
1 ♡	1 ♠, 1 N T or 2 ♣	or	1 ♡	1 ♠, 1 N T or 2 ♣
3 ♡			4 ♡	

The rebid shows: With a strong six-card suit, 4–4½ honor-tricks; with a seven-card suit, perhaps as few as 3½ honor-tricks. In any case, eight sure winners for a jump to three, 8½–9 sure winners for a jump to game. The jump to three may occasionally be made on a strong five-card suit (such as A K J x x or K Q J x x) with five honor-tricks. These are not forcing bids. Examples:

♠ K 6	♠ 9 4	♠ K Q
♡ A K J 9 3	♡ A Q J 7 6 5	♡ K Q 10 7 6 5 2
◇ A K Q	◇ K Q 7	◇ A 9 8
♣ 8 5 3	♣ A Q	♣ 2

3. Jump Raise of a One-Notrump Takeout

Opener	Responder
1 ♡	1 N T
3 N T	

The rebid shows: Five honor-tricks with a stopper in every suit. The hand should contain some added strength in fillers. Examples:

1.	♠ J 10 6 3	♡ A K 8 2	◇ A K 6	♣ A 5
2.	♠ A K	♡ Q J 10 5	◇ K Q J	♣ A 7 6 2

4. Jump Rebid in a New Suit (Forcing to Game)

Opener	Responder
1 ♡	1 N T, 1 ♠ or 2 ♣
3 ◇	

The rebid shows: Five honor-tricks with two biddable suits. Either great playing strength in opener's own suits or strong support for partner's suit. Since this rebid is forcing to game, opener should be sure of winning eight or nine tricks even opposite a shaded response. Examples:

♠ 6	♠ A	♠ Q 2
♡ A K J 7 4	♡ K Q J 5 3	♡ A K J 7 6 4
◇ A Q J 6 5	◇ A K 8 2	◇ A K Q 5
♣ K Q	♣ K 7 3	♣ 6

5. Raise of Partner's Suit from One to Four

Opener	Responder
1 ◇	1 ♠
4 ♠	

The rebid shows: Powerful spade support (such as K J x x) with about 4½ honor-tricks and an unbalanced hand or about 5 honor-tricks and a balanced hand. This bid is not often used because any hand so strong offers slam possibilities and a forcing rebid is usually preferable because it is more informative. See page 191. Opener would, however, raise to four spades as in the bidding above, holding ♠ Q J 10 6 ♡ K Q ◇ A K Q 7 5 ♣ K 7, because, lacking the important suit controls, he cannot expect a slam unless responder can make a conventional four-notrump bid.

CHAPTER SEVENTEEN

REBIDS BY
THE RESPONDER

The first response to an opening suit-bid of one is indefinite, like the opening bid itself. A suit takeout may range from ½ to more than 4 honor-tricks. A single raise may be as weak as 2½ winners, including less than one honor-trick, and as strong as 4½ winners, or 2½ honor-tricks. Even negative no-trump responses may vary by an honor-trick or so.

The responder, at his second turn to bid, gives a more definite impression of his general strength—

(a) by passing, or showing preference, if he has a weak hand and the opener's rebid was not forcing;

(b) by rebidding freely if he sees a chance of game.

Since the opening bid showed about three honor-tricks, the responder needs 2½ to 3 honor-tricks to try for game when the opener has made a minimum rebid. If the opener's rebid showed added values (that is, if he rebid two notrump, or reversed), the responder should consider game in sight if he has 1½ to 2 honor-tricks. If the opener has made a jump rebid, a lone honor-trick will do, with a bit of trump support.

Responses to Jump Rebids

If the opener makes a jump rebid in a new suit, it is forcing to game. No matter how weak the responder is, no matter how far he stretched to make his first response, he must bid again, and again if necessary, until game is reached.

The responder chooses his rebids as follows:

1. With a weak hand—about 1 to 1½ honor-tricks—show preference (page 224) or bid notrump at the lowest available level.

2. With a better hand—2 honor-tricks or more—show a new biddable suit or rebid a rebiddable suit. It is sometimes necessary to rebid a suit on a very weak hand, if it is unfit for notrump.

After this bidding:

SOUTH	WEST	NORTH	EAST
1 ♡	Pass	1 ♠	Pass
3 ♣	Pass		

North's rebids:

1.	♠ A J 7 5 3	♡ 8 4 2	◇ 6 3 2	♣ 7 5	Three hearts
2.	♠ K Q 7 3	♡ 8 7	◇ Q J 6 5	♣ 8 4 3	Three notrump
3.	♠ Q J 10 8 6 3	♡ 8 5	◇ J 6 2	♣ 10 3	Three spades
4.	♠ A J 5 4	♡ Q 6	◇ K Q 7 2	♣ 9 8 4	Three diamonds

If the opener's rebid is a cue-bid (in the opponents' suit) respond as to a forcing rebid, but see also page 314.

RESPONSES TO NON-FORCING JUMP REBIDS

The opener's jump rebid of two notrump, or of three in a major suit, is a strength-showing bid which the responder should pass only if he is very weak.

In response to a jump rebid in a major suit, a raise may be given with anything more than one honor-trick, and two small trumps are adequate support.

If you have responded one spade to partner's opening one-heart bid, and his rebid is a jump to three hearts, raise to four hearts with:

♠ A 8 6 3 2	♡ 6 4	◇ J 10 6	♣ 9 8 3, or even
♠ K 9 7 3 2	♡ 9 4 3	◇ 8	♣ 10 7 6 4

But pass with

♠ Q J 8 7 6 2	♡ 7	◇ 9 6 4	♣ Q 8 4

But a jump rebid in a minor suit, though it shows about the same number of winners as a major-suit jump rebid, does not promise so much general honor-trick strength. There *may* be only ½ honor-trick outside the trump suit.

The purpose of the minor-suit jump rebid is to reach a three-notrump contract where a long, solid minor suit will produce six or seven *quick winners.*

The responder should bid three notrump if he has:

About 1½ honor-tricks, *including an Ace,* with at least two of the unbid suits stopped. (Lacking an Ace, the responder should have all unbid suits securely stopped.)

At least two cards in the opener's suit. (With a singleton in the opener's suit, the responder should have two or more honor-tricks to compensate for lack of fit.)

After this bidding:

SOUTH	WEST	NORTH	EAST
1 ◇	Pass	1 ♡	Pass
3 ◇	Pass		

North bids three notrump with:

1.	♠ A 6	♡ K 8 7 5 2	◇ 5 3	♣ J 8 5 3
2.	♠ Q 6 5	♡ A 10 9 8	◇ J 3	♣ 8 6 5 4
3.	♠ K 9 8 4	♡ K J 7 6	◇ 5	♣ Q J 5 3

North passes with

♠ 8 7	♡ K 9 7 6 4 3	◇ 6 5	♣ Q 7 6

A rebiddable major suit should be shown with about 2½ honor-tricks. It forces partner to bid again and is forcing to game.

REBIDS BY THE RESPONDING HAND

Illustrated Summary

I. After One-Over-One Responses

The responder's one-over-one response guaranteed only 1 or 1+ honor-trick. Therefore with two or more honor-tricks responder has "added values" and should make a free rebid. With 2½ or more honor-tricks responder should make a try for game by rebidding in the three-level (or reversing, or bidding two notrump—see pages 222-223).

1. SOUTH	WEST	NORTH	EAST	
1 ◇	Pass	1 ♠	Pass	⎧ South has balanced distribution
1 N T	Pass			⎨ and about 3 honor-tricks or
				⎩ 13–15 points.

North should:

1. Pass with 1½ honor-tricks or less.
2. Bid a new biddable suit with a two-suiter.

3. Rebid a rebiddable suit with about 2 honor-tricks.
4. Bid two notrump with 2 honor-tricks, counting 11–12 points.
5. Jump to three in a rebiddable major suit with 2 honor-tricks.
6. With opening-bid qualities, make a jump bid in a new suit (forcing to game) or bid three notrump.

Pass	*Bid 2 ♣*	*Bid 2 ♠*	*Bid 2 N T*
♠ K J 8 6 4	♠ A 8 6 4 3	♠ K Q J 8 6	♠ K J 4 3
♡ K 6 3	♡ 7	♡ K 9 4	♡ Q 6
◇ 7 3	◇ 8 3	◇ 6 3	◇ J 6 3
♣ 8 5 4	♣ K 8 4 3 2	♣ 8 4 2	♣ A 10 4 2

Bid three spades with

♠ K Q J 8 6	♡ K 9 4	◇ Q x	♣ 8 4 2

Bid three clubs (forcing to game) with

♠ A Q 8 5 3	♡ K 5	◇ 8 2	♣ A J 10 6

2.

SOUTH	WEST	NORTH	EAST	
1 ◇	Pass	1 ♠	Pass	South shows only that his open-
2 ♣	Pass			ing bid included a second bid-
				dable suit.

North should:
1. Pass or show preference with 1½ honor-tricks or less.
2. Raise diamonds or clubs, or rebid as above, with 2–2½ honor-tricks.

Bid 2 ◇	*Bid 2 ♠*	*Bid 2 N T*	*Bid 3 ♣*
♠ Q J 10 8 6	♠ A Q 8 6 4	♠ A Q 10 8	♠ Q 10 8 6 3
♡ K 4 3	♡ 9 3	♡ K 6 4 2	♡ 10 8 4
◇ 10 8 7	◇ K 10 6	◇ J 3	◇ K 7
♣ 9 4	♣ 8 6 3	♣ Q 7 4	♣ A J 6

3.

SOUTH	WEST	NORTH	EAST	
1 ◇	Pass	1 ♠	Pass	South shows only that his open-
2 ◇	Pass			ing bid included a rebiddable
				diamond suit.

North should:
1. Bid two notrump with about 2 honor-tricks including Q x, J x x or better in hearts or clubs, and the other unbid suit securely stopped.
2. Otherwise, bid as above.

Pass	*Bid 2 ♠*	*Bid 2 ♡*	*Bid 2 N T*
♠ A J 8 6 3	♠ A Q 10 6 4	♠ A 8 6 5 2	♠ Q 10 8 3
♡ Q 5 4	♡ K 6 3	♡ K J 5 3 2	♡ Q J 4
◇ 8 6 3	◇ 9 2	◇ 9 6	◇ A 6
♣ 7 6	♣ 10 7 4	♣ 5	♣ J 10 8 6

4. SOUTH	WEST	NORTH	EAST	
1 ◇	Pass	1 ♠	Pass	South has a strong hand with 4 or more honor-tricks. He probably has only four hearts.
2 ♡	Pass			

North should:

1. Pass or show preference with less than 1+ honor-tricks.
2. Bid or raise with 1½ honor-tricks or more. A raise requires four hearts. A minimum notrump bid requires Q 10 x or better in clubs. With more than 2 honor-tricks, jump to game.

Bid 3 ◇	*Bid 3 N T*	*Bid 3* ♡	*Bid 4* ♡
♠ K 9 6 5 3	♠ K J 9 2	♠ K J 9 2	♠ K J 9 2
♡ 8 6 2	♡ Q 6	♡ 9 6 5 3	♡ Q 9 5 3
◇ 8 6 2	◇ 7 5 3	◇ 7 6	◇ 7 6
♣ K 4	♣ Q J 6 2	♣ Q 6 2	♣ A 6 2

5. SOUTH	WEST	NORTH	EAST	
1 ♡	Pass	1 ♠	Pass	South has a strong hand and needs only about two supporting winners for game.
3 ♡				
or 3 ♠				
or 2 N T				

North should:

1. Pass only with less than 1½ honor-tricks and no added values in trump support, trump length, or intermediates.
2. Otherwise, rebid. Any rebid is forcing unless it is enough for game.

Raise 3 ♡ *to 4 with*	♠ A 10 7 3	♡ Q 7	◇ 8 6 5 2	♣ 10 6 2
Bid 4 ♠ *over 3 with*	♠ K 8 7 6 2	♡ 8 7	◇ K 9 5 2	♣ 8 3
Raise 2 N T to 3 with	♠ K 10 5 4	♡ 6 2	◇ A 7 6 3	♣ 10 9 5

II. After Two-of-a-Suit Responses

The two-over-one response has already promised 2 honor-tricks, and the responder does not have added values unless he has 2½ or more honor-tricks, or strong support for partner's suit.

1. SOUTH	WEST	NORTH	EAST	
1 ♡	Pass	2 ♣	Pass	South has a rebiddable suit, but perhaps only 2½ honor-tricks; perhaps nearly 4 honor-tricks.
2 ♡	Pass			

North should:

1. Pass with 2 honor-tricks or less, unless able to raise or rebid in a suit because of distribution.
2. Raise with 4 winners; but if possible avoid raising with only Q x, K x or A x in hearts.
3. Bid two notrump or a suit with 2½ honor-tricks.

Pass	*Bid 3* ♡	*Bid 3* ♣	*Bid 2 N T*
♠ 8 6	♠ 10 8 6 3	♠ 9 7	♠ Q 8 6 3
♡ 5 2	♡ 9 4 2	♡ J 5	♡ Q 2
◇ 9 7 2	◇ A	◇ Q 6 3	◇ J 9 5
♣ A Q 10 7 6 3	♣ K Q 8 6 4	♣ A K J 8 6 2	♣ A K 9 3

2.	SOUTH	WEST	NORTH	EAST	South may have 3 to 3½ honor-tricks; but possibly only 2½ honor-tricks.
	1 ♡	Pass	2 ♣	Pass	
	2 ◇	Pass			

North should:

1. Pass or show preference with only 2 honor-tricks or less, unless able to raise hearts. It is futile to raise diamonds except with hope of a notrump game, or with 6 winners or more.

2. Otherwise, bid as above.

Bid 2 ♡	*Bid 3* ♡	*Bid 3* ◇	*Bid 2 N T*
♠ 6 5 3	♠ A 6 4	♠ 8 6 3	♠ A K 6
♡ 8 6 2	♡ 10 8 7 3	♡ Q 2	♡ 5 4 2
◇ 7 4	◇ 4	◇ A 8 5 4	◇ 7 4
♣ A K 7 6 3	♣ K Q 10 6 5	♣ K Q J 6	♣ Q J 8 6 3

3.	SOUTH	WEST	NORTH	EAST	South has at least 3½ to 4½ honor-tricks or 16–18 points in high cards.
	1 ♡	Pass	2 ♣	Pass	
	2 N T	Pass			

North should:

1. Pass only with a bare minimum.

2. Bid three notrump (or show a biddable spade suit) with 2-plus or more honor-tricks; or with anything more than a minimum.

3. Bid three hearts (forcing to game) with adequate support.

4. Bid three clubs with a six-card suit headed by 1 honor-trick, but no more than 1½ honor-tricks in the hand.

Bid 3 N T	*Bid 3* ♠	*Bid 3* ♡	*Pass*
♠ A 6	♠ K 10 4 3	♠ 8 6 5	♠ J 8 4
♡ 5 4 2	♡ A 6	♡ Q 7 5	♡ 7 3
◇ 7 3	◇ 5 4	◇ K 5	◇ 5 4 2
♣ K J 10 8 6 3	♣ A J 8 5 4	♣ A Q 8 6 2	♣ A K 8 7 2

4.	SOUTH	WEST	NORTH	EAST	South has 3½ or more honor-tricks with adequate support for clubs.
	1 ♡	Pass	2 ♣	Pass	
	3 ♣	Pass			

North should:

1. Bid three notrump (or show a spade suit, or show heart support) with more than 2 honor-tricks.

2. Pass (do not bid four or five clubs) if unable to make a major-suit or notrump bid, except with a very strong hand.

Bid 3 N T	Bid 3 ♡	Bid 5 ♣	Pass
♠ A 5 2	♠ 10 9 6 3	♠ 6 3	♠ 6 3 2
♡ 8 6 4	♡ Q 7 2	♡ 4	♡ 7 5
◇ Q 7	◇ 8	◇ K J 6	◇ 6 4
♣ A J 8 6 3	♣ A Q J 6 5	♣ A Q 10 9 7 4 3	♣ K Q J 8 6 2

III. After a One-Notrump Response

The response warned of weakness, and the opener expects to find only 1+ honor-trick. A rebid may be made on about 2 honor-tricks in two or more suits.

SOUTH	WEST	NORTH	EAST	
1 ♡	Pass	1 N T	Pass	South shows only that his opening bid included a rebiddable heart suit.
2 ♡	Pass			

or

SOUTH	WEST	NORTH	EAST	
1 ♡	Pass	1 N T	Pass	South shows only that his opening bid included a second biddable suit.
2 ◇	Pass			

North should:

1. Bid two notrump with 2 honor-tricks, 9–10 points, including Q x, J 10, etc., in at least one of North's suits.

2. Otherwise, pass or show preference.

Bid 2 N T with ♠ K 10 3   ♡ 6 5 2   ◇ A 8 4   ♣ Q J 8 5.

3. SOUTH	WEST	NORTH	EAST	
1 ♡	Pass	1 N T	Pass	South has 4½ honor-tricks with some strength in every suit.
2 N T	Pass			

North should bid three notrump with about 1½+ honor-tricks, 8–10 points, and pass with less.

Bid 3 N T with ♠ K 6 3   ♡ 7 2   ◇ A 8 6 3   ♣ J 10 4 3.

GUIDE TO GAME VALUATION

Here is a very rough guide, in terms of honor-tricks, for judging when partner's game invitation should be accepted; and for deciding when to invite game yourself.

Opening Hand

If partner makes a forcing bid:
BID. You have no choice.

If partner makes a three-level bid:
REBID with about 3-plus honor-tricks. Otherwise pass or show preference.

If partner makes a non-forcing jump bid:
REBID with about 2½-plus honor-tricks, or with trump support.

If partner makes a possible minimum bid:
REBID with about 3½ honor-tricks, or with strong trump support.

Responding Hand

If partner makes a forcing bid:
BID. You have no choice.

If partner makes a three-level bid:
REBID with about 1½ honor-tricks if your first response was 1 N T or a one-over-one; but if your first response was two of a suit, you need about 2-plus honor-tricks.

If partner makes a non-forcing jump bid:
REBID with about 1-plus honor-trick, or with trump support.

If partner makes a possible minimum bid:
REBID with more than 2 honor-tricks, or with 1½–2 honor-tricks and strong trump support.

CHAPTER EiGHTEEN

THE INTERMEDIATE ZONE

The intermediate zone of bidding is the keystone which holds up both the opening zone (one-bids and responses) and the end zone (game and slam bids). Unless the intermediate zone can be properly handled, correctness in opening bids is futile; and scientific slam methods lose accuracy because they are based on insecure premises.

A player becomes a winner when he is able to answer these two questions which occur in nearly all hands:

1. *When* to bid game—that is, will the combined hands win enough tricks?

2. *Where* to bid game—assuming that game is biddable, should the contract be in notrump or in a suit? If in a suit, what is the best trump suit?

Rarely can a bidder decide either *when* or *where* without knowing pretty well what his partner has. For example:

♠ A K Q J 8 7 5   ♥ 4   ♦ K J 10 9   ♣ 6

This is an exceptional hand on which a player may decide entirely on his own responsibility to bid four spades; especially so if his partner has passed, ruling out slam possibilities. But

1.	♠ A K 7 5	♥ A K 8 3	♦ A K Q 10	♣ 6
2.	♠ Q J 9 8 6 5 3	♥ K 8 3	♦ 7 2	♣ 10

On Hand No. 1, the question *when* is answered, for game should be bid; but *where* can be answered only after learning something about partner's distribution. On Hand No. 2, the apparent desirability of playing the hand in spades may answer the *where* question, but whether or not to bid game can be decided only when partner's bidding has revealed his general strength.

The ability to decide close questions in the intermediate zone depends upon an understanding of the meanings of partner's bids. Every bid in this zone should give some information about general strength and distribution. It follows that if a player can read his partner's bids, he also knows enough to make properly informative bids himself.

To bid correctly in the intermediate zone, and to understand correct bids made by his partner in this zone, the reader should acquire a full grasp of the bidding philosophy which may be divided broadly under the following three headings:

1. Valuation of the combined hands, including knowledge of what, roughly, is required to make a game at notrump and a game in a suit.

2. What constitutes a safe, and what constitutes an unsafe contract.

3. The principle that every bid must have a purpose. The greatest weakness of the average player is that he does not try to get under the surface of the bid, and determine what was his partner's reason for making it. This is one of the most fascinating studies in contract.

Hand Valuation

A rough idea of the trick expectancy of two hands may be had from the valuation methods already explained (pages 33-59). The honor-trick table, the Distributional Count, the Rule of Eight, the 4–5–6 table and the Culbertson point-count are as good as I have seen. Better than any is the playing-trick valuation. (See pages 49-55.)

The 4–5–6 table is a good guide because it is easy to remember, and because a fair knowledge of the bidding system will let you know, every time partner makes an opening bid or a response, about how many honor-tricks he has (at the least). After that, you need only remember that with no available

major suit in which to play the hand, you will need about
six honor-tricks to make game. With a fair fit in a major suit,
nothing exceptional, game on 5½ honor-tricks is quite likely.
With a very fine fit in a major suit, five honor-tricks should
be enough, and often 4½.

On this basis the player may classify his hand in one of the
zones of bidding. In the following examples, remember that
only the *hand-patterns* of possible North hands are shown. The
"x's," which usually represent very small cards, are used only
to show the number of cards in the suit, whether high or low.

SOUTH	NORTH	1. ♠ x x x x	2. ♠ x x x x x	3. ♠ x x x x
1 ♡	1 ♠	♡ x x	♡ x x x	♡ x x x x
2 ♡		◇ x x x x	◇ x	◇ x x x x
		♣ x x x	♣ x x x x	♣ x

South has an opening bid and a rebiddable heart suit. Little
more is known about his hand, except that he has at least 2½
honor-tricks, and may have 3½ or 4.

With Hand No. 1, North has only two hearts—no support.
Hope of game lies in notrump. If North sees a possibility of
a combined holding of six honor-tricks, he is still in the intermediate zone and should try to make another bid, but if North
sees no hope of the combined honor-trick total's reaching six,
he passes. That is, if North has about 2½ honor-tricks, he says
to himself, "*If* my partner has 3½ honor-tricks we may make
game, and on the chance that he has I will bid once more."

With Hand No. 2, North has fair support for a rebid suit.
He will bid again if he has about 2 honor-tricks and so sees
a good chance of there being 5½ honor-tricks or thereabouts
in the combined hands.

With Hand No. 3 North has very good support for hearts.
With about 1½ honor-tricks in his hand he will bid again, for
there may be a game if South has 3 to 3½ honor-tricks.

When there is trump support, the count of winners is equally
accurate, even more so, but many players do not like to count
higher than two. For them, let honor-tricks and distribution
suffice.

SAFE AND UNSAFE HANDS

A hand is *safe* when, whether or not the contract is made, it cannot be badly beaten by even a terrible break. A hand is unsafe when, if things go unexpectedly wrong, the contract can be defeated by four or five tricks.

It is seldom the high cards, Aces and Kings, in the hand which cause it to be safe or unsafe. High cards are only temporary barriers to the running of some long suit in the opponents' hands. Generally speaking, it is the combination of many trumps plus unbalanced distribution which forms a safe hand:

```
        ♠ K Q 8 6 3 2          ♠ J 9 7 5 4
        ♡ 6 5 2        N       ♡ 10
        ◇ 4 3 2     W     E    ◇ 9 8 7 5
        ♣ 7            S       ♣ J 8 3
```

This is a weak hand which must lose six tricks. At a four-spade contract it will go down three. But it is a safe hand because, whatever happens, it cannot go down more than three. Add a couple of Aces, say in hearts and clubs. Now the hand will go down only one at four spades. It probably cannot stop an opposing game in hearts, but it offers a cheap sacrifice with absolute safety. Now add the King of diamonds. There is a chance to make four spades. And if the chance fails, the risk is still negligible because the hand can go down only one. It is a typical safe hand.

An unsafe hand is typified by its short trumps or balanced distribution, or both.

```
        ♠ K Q 7 5             ♠ 9 8 6 3
        ♡ Q            N      ♡ 7 6 3 2
        ◇ A Q 4     W     E   ◇ 8 3
        ♣ K J 9 7 4    S      ♣ A 10 3
```

At a four-spade contract, this hand seems to have an excellent chance for game, good enough to warrant the bid. But it is still an unsafe hand. Suppose the trumps break badly, with ♠ A J 10 x in North's hand. Suppose North has the King of diamonds, and West guesses badly on the location of the Queen of clubs. This hand may go down four or five tricks doubled at four spades. It probably will not, but anything *may* happen.

It follows that you may bid more aggressively on a safe hand than on an unsafe one:

SOUTH	WEST	NORTH	EAST
1 ♠	Pass	2 ♣	2 ♦
2 ♡	5 ♦	?	

North holds ♠ 9 8 7 3 ♡ 6 4 ♦ A 2 ♣ K Q J 7 6, and doubles. There seems an excellent chance that five spades can be made, but if South happens to have a four-card spade suit and gets a bad break he will be down several tricks.

In similar bidding:

SOUTH	WEST	NORTH	EAST
1 ♠	Pass	2 ♣	2 ♦
2 ♠	5 ♦		

North bids five spades. With a rebiddable spade suit in South's hand, the hand can hardly be hurt even with bad breaks, and the excellent chance to make five spades is still there.

NOTRUMP HANDS

With very few exceptions, notrump hands may all be classified in the unsafe group. An unusually long suit, easily establishable, in an opponent's hand; together with an Ace or other sure entry card in a suit declarer must try to set up; these can pile up an impressive total of undertricks even when declarer's side has six honor-tricks or more.

About the only notrump hand which falls into the safe group, barring times when the partners have a near monopoly on the high cards, is one which includes a long, positively solid suit and quick, sure stoppers in the other suits. For example:

♠ A 6   ♡ Q J 3   ♦ A K Q J 8 6   ♣ K Q

This hand is pretty sure to win eight tricks, cannot fail to get at least seven, and with any help from partner will go game. It may go game without help from partner if the opponents make the slightest defense slip. But weaken any one of the stoppers in side suits; make the clubs K J instead of K Q, or the hearts Q 10 x instead of Q J 3, and automatically the hand becomes unsafe at notrump, for conceivably a suit of six or more cards could be run against it.

It may be accepted as a safe hypothesis that when a partnership can find some fair sort of trump fit, the same number of honor-tricks will produce one trick more at a trump than at a notrump contract.

This being so, it follows that a final contract of two in a suit is no more of an undertaking than a contract of one notrump. Further, it follows that *any bid of two notrump is equivalent to a bid of three in a suit,* showing about the same amount of strength because the two contracts are equally difficult to fulfil.

Reading the Bidding

Every correct bid must have one of two purposes:

1. To get out of an unsafe contract (a dangerous notrump or a bad suit fit) into a safer contract, though with no desire to increase the level of the bidding.

2. To get to a higher contract, in the belief that the important bonuses attending game or slam bids can be won.

If partner's last bid was made for purpose No. 1, be cautious, proceed on your own responsibility. If purpose No. 2 prompted his bid, stretch your hand to the limit in order to go farther.

How do you tell the purpose of partner's bid? Partly by the bidding situation, and partly by the level at which it is made.

Inferences from the Bidding Level

It is elementary that the bidding level alone cannot decide the strength or weakness shown by the bidder. A four-bid is sometimes stronger than a two-bid, sometimes weaker, depending on the circumstances in which it is made. There are, however, some cases in which the quantity of a bid is quite revealing.

Right or wrong, we play bridge according to a system in which the opening bid, and the response to it, carry us to the two-odd, or eight-trick level. Our system of one-round-forcing bids creates a situation in which, when I bid one in a suit, I am inevitably obligating my side to win eight tricks. Provided my partner responds (which he will do on the nominal value of one honor-trick) we must reach one notrump or two in a suit before we can stop. Remember, for trick-taking purposes one notrump and a suit-contract of two are about the same.

Therefore, up to the stage of two in a suit, we are in the

first phase of the bidding and all the bids are of an intro-
ductory nature, so incomplete in information as to be almost
meaningless. Being forced to arrive at one notrump or a two-
bid, the players may feel their way around, groping for a good
trump suit, without definitely committing themselves on how
much strength they have.

SOUTH	NORTH
1 ♠	1 N T
2 ◇	

South's two-diamond bid may have been made on a hand of better than
minimum strength, but again it may have been made simply because South,
even with small strength and no game expectations, does not have distribution suitable to pass one notrump safely.

In this phase of the auction, all bids are possible minimums.
They may be made for safety as well as for constructive purposes, and it is difficult to tell which. There is no definite
promise of strength beyond that which is required to open the
bidding, and to respond once. The auction is still in its blind
stages.

A non-jump rebid by either partner at the level of two is
not forcing. This is the time for the player to count up the
trick-taking possibilities, and if no game is possible, even though
partner have the maximum on which his bidding could have
been based, to pass.

THE FIRST SIGN OF STRENGTH

The first really encouraging bid which may be made by either
partner is a bid of three-odd in a suit *or its equivalent*.

Such a bid is not only a possible sign of strength, but a *sure
sign*. If the combined hands are hopelessly in the part-score
zone, one of the partners should have found it out during the
first phase of bidding, and passed safely at one notrump or a
suit-contract of two.

Even if a reasonably safe contract cannot be found without
getting up to a three-bid, it is better to play at an unsafe contract but at a lower level:

♠ 7 3   ♡ A Q 8 6 4   ◇ 6   ♣ A Q 8 6 4

South holds this hand and bids one heart. North responds two diamonds.
South *does not* bid three clubs. He would be risking a higher contract only

for a hope (not an assurance) of finding a better fit in clubs. North may prefer hearts to clubs; why get up too high? South's rebid is two hearts.

♠ 7 3   ♡ A Q 8 6 4   ◊ 4   ♣ A Q 8 6 4

South bids one heart, but this time North's response is one spade. This time, South shows his clubs, for he can do so at the two-odd level. This does not represent an increase in the contract, for the only available rebid of one-odd—one notrump—would be no safer than a contract of two in a suit.

Any time a player accepts the risk of a three-bid, he shows strength. Without strength, he would crawl into his sanctuary at the two-level. Therefore any three-bid is a game try, for there would be no sense in showing strength except to inform partner that game is welcome.

There is even a decided difference between these two cases:

1. SOUTH	NORTH	2. SOUTH	NORTH
1 ◊	1 ♠	1 ◊	2 ♣
2 ♠		3 ♣	

North's response in each case was forcing, so South had to find some rebid. In Example 1, South makes only a nominal rebid. He promises no extra strength, but does say that, while keeping the bidding at its irreducible level, he thinks a spade contract safer than a minimum contract in notrump or some other suit. In Example 2, however, South is making a strong bid. He has available a non-forcing, possible minimum rebid (two diamonds). This would permit the bidding to die in its first phase. Instead, South deliberately pushes up one trick higher.

If it be argued that South may not have a rebiddable suit, and therefore cannot bid two diamonds, I reply that South should have thought of that before. I refer the reader to the Principle of Preparedness in Chapter 9, and particularly to pages 118-119.

EQUIVALENT BIDS

I mentioned a bid of three in a suit "or its equivalent." The first equivalent bid that springs to mind is any bid of two notrump, two notrump being as hard to make as three with a trump suit. The other is a "reverse" (page 113).

1. SOUTH	NORTH	2. SOUTH	NORTH
1 ◊	2 ♣	1 ◊	2 ♣
2 N T		2 ♠	

In either case, South names a contract which will be unsafe if North cannot support it. Even with a weak hand, North may have to go to the three-level to get back to a safe trump contract. South has therefore taken the responsibility of a three-level contract.

Preference Bids

The need to get into a fairly safe trump suit accounts for the obligation to *show preference,* as strong an obligation on a bridge player as the forced response to an opening two-bid.

A sound bidder *must* understand preference bids and what they imply. He must equally recognize the necessity for them. Above all, he must realize that merely giving a preference places no responsibility on the responder.

*When one partner has bid two suits, the other partner must show which one he prefers.** His choice will be made as follows:

1. With equal length in each of partner's suits (as 3 and 3) he should usually prefer the first-bid suit, even though the second is stronger in high cards.

2. With greater length in one suit, he should prefer that suit, even though he has higher cards in the other. (He will prefer the suit in which he holds 6 5 4 to the suit in which he holds A Q.)

Preference is sometimes shown by bidding, and sometimes by passing, following these rules:

If you prefer partner's second-bid suit, and your hand is so weak that a pass is indicated, you show preference by passing; but

If you prefer partner's first-bid suit, even though your hand's weakness warrants passing, you do not pass. You return to partner's first-bid suit, at the lowest possible level. This is equivalent to passing.

Examples:

SOUTH	WEST	NORTH	EAST
1 ♠	Pass	1 N T	Pass
2 ♡	Pass	2 ♠	

This is no stronger than

SOUTH	WEST	NORTH	EAST
1 ♠	Pass	1 N T	Pass
2 ♡	Pass	Pass	

---

* Unless conditions and the strength of his hand warrant his bidding another suit, or notrump, in order to reach a contract he can consider superior to *either* of his partner's suits.

North's apparent bid of two spades in the first example is
not a bid at all. It means that North would have liked to pass,
but he knows spades to be a better trump suit than hearts.
He is not going to leave South to suffer in a bad heart trump
suit, when he can just as easily return the contract to a satisfactory spade trump suit. *But if he had preferred hearts he
would have passed.*

THE PREFERENCE RAISE

Therefore, when strong enough to raise one of partner's
suits, it is not sufficient merely to show preference. Partner,
knowing the bid may be equivalent to a pass, cannot be expected to read it as a raise.

If you have a real raise, jump one trick, provided you do not
shut out the still possible three notrump.

SOUTH	WEST	NORTH	EAST
1 ♠	Pass	2 ♣	Pass
2 ♡	Pass	3 ♠	

Showing preference when partner has bid two suits, of which
the second is obviously only a four-card suit, sometimes requires going one trick higher to show preference for the first-
bid, probably longer suit. One of the most nearly inviolable
safety rules in the game is not to support a four-card suit without at least four trumps in support, if any other sound bid
is available.

In this bidding:

SOUTH	WEST	NORTH	EAST
1 ♢	Pass	1 ♠	Pass
2 ♡	Pass		

North, holding ♠ Q J 8 6   ♡ K Q 5   ♢ 7 2   ♣ Q 6 5 3, should bid two
notrump rather than raise hearts.

With three cards of each of partner's suits it is customary
to return to the first-bid, and therefore the longer, suit, but
sometimes with very weak hands this rule is violated:

♠ J 6 5   ♡ 9 8 6 5   ♢ J 6 3   ♣ K J 10

The opening bid was one diamond, to which this hand made a one-
notrump response (this is the minimum hand on which such a response

should be made). Now the opener makes a rebid of two spades. He has only a four-card suit, but nevertheless it is quite proper to pass this hand. The bid is not forcing, and a three-diamond contract should be not more than one trick better than a two-spade contract, with more danger of being doubled.

Partner shows a 6–5 hand when he first bids a lower-ranking suit, then bids and rebids the higher-ranking suit:*

SOUTH	WEST	NORTH	EAST
1 ♢	Pass	1 ♡	Pass
1 ♠	Pass	2 ♡	Pass
2 ♠			

South must have five spades, to rebid them; therefore he must have six diamonds, or he would not have bid them ahead of the five-card spade suit.

Since a five-card suit may be supported with three small trumps, partner's five-card major suit should be preferred with three cards in each of his suits. This applies, however, only to strong combined hands offering a chance for game. When the partnership hands are weak, a combined eight-card trump suit divided 6–2 will usually play one or more tricks better than eight cards divided 5–3, and partner's six-card suit should be preferred even with a doubleton, if an opponent doubles the five-card suit.

Sign-Off of Rescue Bids

To "rescue" partner's opening bid, simply because of weakness in his suit, is one of the most tempting yet most dangerous bidding situations in contract bridge. The best rescue is a pass, which stops the bidding at a low level and warns partner of weakness. Any other bid should usually show strength.

The only exceptions occur in rare instances when the "rescue" inference is so clear that no possible misunderstanding can arise between partners, and then only when the responder can reasonably expect to win enough extra tricks at his rescue bid to justify increasing the contract.

One such exception (described more fully on page 76) occurs when a player takes out his partner's opening one-notrump bid with two of a suit; then rebids three of the same suit over

---

* See exception on page 112 in respect to spade-club two-suiters.

two notrump. This is the classic "sign-off." A similar message of weakness is given by a bid of three in a new suit over the two-notrump rebid. Thus:

South	North		South	North
1 N T	2 ♡	or	1 N T	2 ♡
2 N T	3 ♡		2 N T	3 ♣

Another exception occurs when the responder, over an intervening pass, gives his partner a single raise; and then, when opener rebids in a new suit, returns to the original suit at the lowest possible level.

South	West	North	East
1 ♠	Pass	2 ♠	Pass
3 ♣	Pass	3 ♠	

With his first response North gave tentative promise of strength. With his second, or sign-off bid, North said, "My hand is suitable for play only in this suit, and in addition I have a minimum or near-minimum hand. It is useless to try another suit, or to bid any higher in the same suit except on your own responsibility."

This sign-off is given only when the previous raise was a minimum or near-minimum.

North, holding ♠ K 8 6 3   ♡ Q 2   ◊ J 8 5 4   ♣ 7 6 3, would bid three spades.

It follows that the responder must jump to game if he had a sound raise in the first place.

Holding ♠ 8 7 6 2   ♡ A 3   ◊ Q 8 7 2   ♣ Q 5 4, North would jump to four spades.

Holding ♠ K 8 5   ♡ A 2   ◊ J 9 8 6 2   ♣ J 7 4, North would bid three notrump, warning that he has only three-card spade support, but showing added values by his failure to sign off.

Weak Rebids at the Three-Level

In the following bidding situation:

South	West	North	East
1 ♠	Pass	2 ◊	Pass
2 N T	Pass	3 ◊	

North's three-diamond rebid is not a "sign-off," but it is a weak bid; for with about 2+ honor-tricks North would raise to three notrump. Therefore North must have a hand such as

♠ 9   ♡ 8 7 6   ◇ A Q J 6 4 2   ♣ 6 4 2

The following situation shows a bid by the opener which, though weak, is not a "sign-off"; though it has been so classified for years:

South	West	North	East
1 ♡	Pass	2 ◇	Pass
2 ♡	Pass	2 N T	Pass
3 ♡			

By this third minimum bid in the same suit, the opener shows that his hand has no added values and that the principal strength is in a long, fairly weak suit unsuitable to notrump play. The hand is probably something like

♠ 5 2   ♡ K J 10 8 6 4   ◇ 6 3 2   ♣ A Q

However, this bid cannot overcome the fact that South has an opening bid and at least a six-card major suit; and the responder, with something like Q x in hearts and a very strong hand, should raise to four hearts.

A three-level bid is not strength-showing when the bidder has previously shown a weak hand. No bid in bridge has an invariable meaning; every bid may be modified and limited by the message conveyed in previous bids.

Usually the bid of a new suit at the three-level shows a strong hand and is an invitation to reach game. Sometimes, however, the bid cannot be so construed:

South	West	North	East
1 ♡	Pass	2 ♡	Pass
2 N T	Pass	3 ♣	

North was not strong enough to bid two clubs over one heart, though with his heart support he might have done so with as little as 1½ honor-tricks. Therefore North shows a weak hand containing a club suit; too weak to raise to three notrump, too weak to jump to four hearts; probably too weak (because of three-card heart support) even to return to three hearts. North's hand is something like this:

♠ 7   ♡ Q 8 5   ◇ 7 5 2   ♣ Q J 6 5 3 2

South is expected to pass the three-club rebid, and in most cases should do so.

Every bid must be measured by the strength it denies as well as by what it affirms.

South	West	North	East
1 ♣	Pass	1 ♦	Pass
1 ♠	Pass	2 ♦	Pass
2 N T	Pass	3 ♡	

The three-heart bid is a weak bid inviting a pass. North is too weak to raise to three notrump; he was too weak to show his heart suit by bidding two hearts over one spade. He has something like this:

♠ 6   ♡ 10 6 5 3 2   ♦ K J 8 7 3 2   ♣ 8

South's bidding has shown that he almost surely has three hearts, and he is expected to pass the three-heart rebid.

Guiding the Bidding

The only direct game-tries are bids at the three-level. The truth of this statement will become obvious when you consider that anything lower has already been classified in the minimum zone; anything higher *is* game.

But there are times when a furtive try for game may be made even at what is ordinarily the minimum zone, when the bidder thinks there is bare hope of getting somewhere, but is not confident enough to risk getting too high.

This bare hope arises from the fact that in such situations as the following, the information given by South is very indefinite, so that North is uncertain as to how far he can safely go:

South	North
1 ♡	1 ♠
2 ♦	

North holds ♠ K 10 8 7   ♡ J 5 2   ♦ A 8 6 3   ♣ 7 4

North prefers diamonds to hearts, but is not quite strong enough to raise either suit. Strictly speaking, he should pass two diamonds. However, if South has an unusually strong hand for a simple suit rebid, there may be a game. So North bids two hearts, which promises nothing but does keep the bidding alive a while longer. Now if South can bid once again—three hearts, perhaps, or two spades—North will go on to game.

When the responding hand bids a new suit, even at a minimum level, it may be a sign of strength:

SOUTH	NORTH
1 ♣	1 ♠
2 ♣	2 ♦

North cannot be "rescuing," for *it is never necessary to rescue
partner when he has rebid his suit.* North's strength may be
largely distributional, but if South can rebid North will be
able either to raise, to pass *safely,* or to rebid safely.

Nor is it necessary to rescue partner when he has bid two
suits:

SOUTH	NORTH
1 ♡	1 ♠
2 ♦	2 ♠

Again North shows strength, for with a weak hand he could
pass two diamonds or show preference for hearts.

Even with

    ♠ K J 10 7 6   ♡ 7   ♦ 8 2   ♣ J 8 5 4 3

North should not bid over two diamonds; he should pass.

Where to Bid Game

Usually, if a strong major suit is available in the combined
hands, and if the partners' strength makes a game contract
proper, they should bid game in the major suit.

If no major-suit game is available, game should usually be
bid in notrump, where only nine tricks are needed, despite
the fact that a strong minor suit may be available. The minor
suit will furnish tricks for notrump, and if game were to be
attempted with a minor trump suit, eleven tricks would be
required.

WHAT IT TAKES TO MAKE A NOTRUMP GAME

It is quite easy to say that six honor-tricks in the combined
hands will produce a notrump game, but it is possible to gauge
the notrump game possibilities of a hand much more accurately
if other factors are taken into consideration. After all, the object

is to win nine tricks, and sometimes six honor-tricks will not do it, while at other times fewer honor-tricks suffice.

In good notrump bidding, the following qualities of the hand are important:

1. Balanced distribution of suits and honor-cards.
2. Six honor-tricks, 26 high-card points, or an establishable long suit.

Mention of the strong suit is important, for a notrump bid of two or three is particularly unsafe if the bidder has no idea where his tricks are coming from. The strong suit being present, however, both the distributional and honor-trick requirements can be somewhat modified.

A notrump hand really should have some strength in every suit. By strength I do not mean a sure stopper. J x x, or 10 9 x, or four cards no matter how low, represent adequate protection in the notrump bidder's weakest suit. Then, if partner has something like Q x x, there is a strong probability that the suit is stopped.

Notrump distribution is said to be 4–3–3–3, 4–4–3–2, 5–3–3–2, sometimes 6–3–2–2. Many games will be missed if a player never bids notrump except on those distributions. I repeat that any one of the usual requirements may be modified if a long, strong suit is present.

South	North	South holds:	♠ A J 6
1 ◇	2 ♣		♡ K 4 3
2 N T			◇ A K J 10 8 5
			♣ 7

South has unbalanced distribution; but the diamond suit has such a good chance of being established and run, and North's bid gives such promise of taking care of the club suit, that South bids two notrump, trying for game, rather than rebid diamonds.

South	North	South holds:	♠ A Q 6 5
1 ♠	2 ◇		♡ K 6
2 N T	3 ◇		◇ K Q 7
			♣ K 10 4 3

North's three-diamond bid is not encouraging (page 227). South can be quite sure that the combined hands probably hold no more than five honor-tricks. But North undoubtedly has a six-card diamond suit, which if headed

by the Ace will produce six tricks at notrump. South can take a chance on
winning the three extra tricks. He bids three notrump.

SOUTH	NORTH	*North holds:*	♠ Q J 8 3
1 ◇	1 ♠		♡ J 6 5
1 N T			◇ Q J
			♣ A 8 5 2

South has made a minimum rebid, and probably has only three honor-
tricks. North's two honor-tricks offer a combined total of 5 or at most 5½.
But North has some strength in every suit, plus two honors which promise
that South can win several tricks with the diamond suit he has bid. North
raises to two notrump.

One thing for a player to keep in mind when striving for
game, and finding himself in the intermediate zone, is this:
If he seems to have a possible notrump game, but it is going
to be close, the number of Aces held by the partnership is
very important. Opponents' Aces are their sure re-entries. It
takes time to knock them out and run the tricks consequently
established. If there is only a hope of game at notrump on a
hand which contains no Ace, it is wiser to pass. Declarer and
dummy between them, except on hands of extreme strength,
should have at least two and preferably three Aces.

FINDING A MAJOR TRUMP SUIT

When the opening bid is in a major suit, and partner raises
it, the 4–5–6 Table or the count of winners decides the close
hands, while on many of them the first response is a double
raise and game must be reached.

When the responding hand does not justify an immediate
raise, the count of winners is not so easy to apply, for it is
difficult to tell how many winners opener has.

SOUTH	NORTH	*North holds:*	♠ A 9 7 6 3
1 ♡	1 ♠		♡ 8 6 5
2 ♡			◇ 6
			♣ K 10 9 5

North can barely support a rebid suit. Count his winners
and you find he has four; on the honor-trick basis, he can read
the combined total as possibly only 4½ or so, without a very
strong trump suit if South has only something like K Q x x x.

Yet South may have a maximum sort of two-heart rebid. Since there is a fair trump suit in the combined hands, though not necessarily a powerful one, North can take a chance on making another bid and raise to three hearts. This is about the minimum hand on which such a bid is proper. Usually, if there are only 1½ honor-tricks, the trump holding should be J 10 x or Q x x even when the suit has been rebid. With a singleton diamond you should pass.

THE FOUR-CARD MAJOR

When a player's strength indicates that a game may be possible, but no good trump suit has been found, he should look around for a major suit, and should try to show even a weak four-card major.

When holding four cards in support of a major suit-bid by partner, you will probably find that major suit to be the best spot in which to play the hand for game.

Here is how two partners "feel" their way into a suit:

	♠ 9 7 4 3	N		♠ Q 10 8 6
	♡ A 5	W E		♡ K J 7 6 2
	◇ A K 8 4 3	S		◇ Q 7
	♣ 8 3			♣ A 5

WEST	EAST
1 ◇	1 ♡
2 ◇	2 ♠
3 ♠	4 ♠

East, with 2+ honor-tricks and an honor in West's diamond suit, relished the idea of game. With his distributed strength a notrump game seemed the probable place for the hand, but first he investigated the possibilities in spades. Note that East's two-spade bid, a reverse bid, shows strength; for it would force West to the three-level to show preference.

West, having four trumps, raised spades and a four-spade contract was bid and made. At notrump, the opponents might very likely have established a club suit on the opening lead, and defeated the contract before East could find nine tricks.

WHEN THE ZONE CHANGES

This chapter has purposely been devoted only to bids which, though encouraging, are not forcing. When a player tries for game, if he is sure that a game should be bid he may protect himself against being prematurely dropped by making bids which force partner to keep the bidding open. Few bridge-table wails are sillier than the one that goes, "Oh, partner, I didn't think you would drop me!" Maybe "partner" was quite right to stop bidding. It is dangerous, and unfair to partner, to put the strain of bidding game on him if added strength in his hand is not necessary.

South	North	*North holds:*	♠ A Q 6 3
1 ◊	1 ♠		♡ Q 8 5 4
2 ♡			◊ 4 3
			♣ Q 6 3

South, by his reverse bid, has shown a strong hand, has encouraged a game contract, and has promised about four honor-tricks. North, seeing a fit in a major suit and a combined honor-trick count which is more than enough for game, has no reason to hesitate longer. He should next bid not three hearts, but four hearts.

South	West	North	East
1 ♠	Pass	2 ♣	2 ♡
2 ♠	Pass		

North holds ♠ Q 5 2   ♡ 5 3   ◊ A 10 5   ♣ K Q 10 6 2. He should not bid three spades, but should jump to four spades. This is one of the most misbid situations in contract bridge. South by making a free rebid (Chapter 19) has shown values in excess of his opening bid, and has promised a rebiddable suit. North does not want to stop short of game, so he should not merely raise to three spades and put on South the burden of deciding whether to go on or not.

South	North	*South holds:*	♠ Q 8 5 3
1 ◊	1 ♠		♡ K 6 2
2 ♠	3 ◊		◊ A K 7 6 2
			♣ 8

North is obviously trying for game—otherwise he could have passed two spades. But North's failure to make his rebid in spades warns that he has only a four-card spade suit and offers diamonds as possibly a safer suit. South, having four-card spade support (when he might have raised with three trumps), and having a sound bid and a sound raise, should jump to four spades.

The governing principle here is this: When a player makes a bid which is encouraging but not forcing, he tells his partner to go farther with anything more than has been guaranteed by previous bids, but to pass if his previous bids showed everything that he had. Sometimes bids are stretched and purport to show even a little more than the bidder actually has. In such cases, merely inviting him to bid game will get no response from him.

CHAPTER NINETEEN

FREE
BIDS

(*When Opponents Bid or Double*)

The forcing or non-forcing inferences of the various responses to opening suit-bids are not altered when the intervening opponent overcalls. The strength required for these responses must often be varied, however, because of the following considerations:

1. The fact that the opponent has made a bid or double guarantees that the opener will have another chance to bid whether the responder passes or not. This makes it unnecessary to keep the bidding open with highly shaded raises and takeouts.

2. The overcall may raise the bidding to a level at which the normal one-over-one takeout must be shown at two-odd, and the normal two-over-one takeout will require a bid of three. Since these takeouts are *still forcing for one round,* the opener may be hard put to find a safe rebid. Therefore a suit takeout at a higher level than the opener may have anticipated should be made only with somewhat better (an extra ½ honor-trick or an extra winner) than the minimum requirements laid down in the previous chapter.

The responses to opening suit-bids of one, assuming that the intervening opponent has overcalled, are as follows:

1. *Pass.* Extended to include
(*a*) Hands containing adequate trump support but less than four winners, including 1½ honor-tricks.

(*b*) Suit and notrump takeouts of one containing only 1½ honor-tricks or less; and all notrump hands lacking a stopper in the opponent's suit.

(*c*) Hands containing lower-ranking biddable suits but less than 2½ honor-tricks; or, in the case of six-card suits, 2 honor-tricks.

For example, partner having opened with one diamond and second-hand having overcalled with one spade, pass the following hands which would have justified responses had there been no intervening bid:

1.	♠ J 10 8 6	♡ J 7	◊ 9 5 3	♣ A 10 5 4
2.	♠ 10 7 5	♡ K J 7	◊ 10 7 3	♣ A 10 7 3
3.	♠ 8 6 5 3	♡ 6	◊ 9 5 4 2	♣ K 10 6 5
4.	♠ J 9 4	♡ A J 8 6 2	◊ 10 4	♣ J 7 2

2. *Raise.* Single raises should be made on the basis of one of the two methods already described—the count of winners or the case method. With four-card trump support, about 1½ honor-tricks are usually required; with three-card adequate (J 10 x or Q x x) support, 2 honor-tricks. When the hand comes to four winners but contains no more than 1 honor-trick, a pass is preferable.

The requirements for adequate trump support must be relaxed with hands containing 2 or 2½ honor-tricks and no available (or no safe) suit or notrump response.

Assuming the bidding to have been:

SOUTH	WEST	NORTH	EAST
1 ♠	2 ◊		

North holds ♠ 10 8 4 ♡ A 6 3 2 ◊ J 3 ♣ A J 5 3. A two-notrump bid, without a diamond stopper, is out of the question; and the hand is not strong enough to bid three clubs, which would force partner to rebid. The solution is found in a raise to two spades, which South has the option of passing if his hand is a minimum.

The double raise changes neither in its strength nor in its forcing nature regardless of intervening bids. A raise from one to three is modified only as follows:

1. Since the *shaded* single raise is abandoned when an opponent overcalls, any single raise therefore shows concrete values.

A *minimum* double raise need not be given, a single raise giving sufficient promise of strength.

2. When an opponent's overcall makes a raise to three the lowest possible raise, the responding hand may sometimes be stretched both as to trump support and number of winners. In such cases the raise from one to three is to be considered a single raise only and to show great strength the responder should jump immediately to four.

Assume the following bidding:

South	West	North	East
1 ♠	3 ♡		

North, holding ♠ Q 8 5 3   ♡ 6 2   ◇ K J 2   ♣ K 6 5 4, though he has only four winners, must raise to three spades rather than be shut out of the bidding. Holding ♠ K 6 4   ♡ 6 2   ◇ A 8 5 3   ♣ Q J 7 5, he likewise must bid three spades. Holding ♠ K 9 6 5 2   ♡ 3   ◇ A K 7   ♣ J 10 5 4, he should jump to four spades to convey the proper impression of strength. In this case the raise to four, being only a single jump, must be read by South as a strength-showing bid rather than a shutout. Of course, since a game has already been reached, it is not forcing.

If West's overcall in the example above had been only two hearts, making it possible for North to give a single raise, his raise on the following hand should be only to two spades.

♠ A 8 6 5   ♡ 7 3   ◇ A Q 6   ♣ J 6 4 3

A preëmptive raise to four remains the same if it is a skip of more than one trick (as, one spade by partner, two hearts by opponent, *four spades*).

Free Notrump Takeouts

The notrump takeout at all levels is controlled by the stringent requirement that the opponents' suit must be stopped; and any *jump* bid in notrump must show not one but two stoppers.

The responding hand must have at least two honor-tricks, distributed in three suits, including the opponents' suit. He may bid one notrump with as little as Q x x or J x x x as his stopper in the opponents' suit, but should prefer another bid, if one is available, unless his stopper is as good as the King. Point-count requirements: 9–12 points.

Opener having bid one heart and opponent having overcalled with one spade, bid one notrump, not vulnerable, with ♠ A 10 2 ♡ 7 3 ◇ K 8 6 4 ♣ Q 10 5 3. Vulnerable, the hand should contain added strength such as a Jack in any suit.

A two-notrump response, even though the opponent's overcall is at the level of two-odd and two notrump is the cheapest notrump bid available, is nevertheless a far stronger bid, requiring about three honor-tricks, or 13–15 points. These must include a stopper in the opponents' suit, and two stoppers are desirable unless a "fit" such as K x or Q J with partner's suit makes probable a plenitude of immediate winners. Though technically not forcing, because it is not a jump bid, it must be almost as strong a hand as though made without the opponent's bid.

A sound two-notrump response, when partner has bid one heart and opponent has overcalled with two diamonds, is ♠ K 10 3 ♡ 8 7 4 ◇ A Q ♣ A J 7 6 2. With a weaker hand the responder should try to find some other response.

A three-notrump response, if a jump bid, is just the same as though the intervening overcall had not occurred, with the one difference that it must include a sure stopper in the opponents' suit. Your hand should be the equivalent of an opening one notrump bid (16–18 points).

THE PENALTY DOUBLE

Before making a free notrump takeout in any case, and particularly when the opponents are vulnerable, the responder should consider a penalty double (see Chapter 24, with especial reference to "Light Doubles").

If partner's one-heart bid is overcalled by two diamonds, a two-notrump bid would offer far less chance for maximum profit than would a double on this hand:

♠ A J 6   ♡ K 5   ◇ Q 10 7 3   ♣ K 10 8 4

FREE SUIT TAKEOUTS

A non-jump suit takeout is still forcing for one round, despite the opposing bid (unless, of course, game has already been reached).* For example:

---

* A free suit takeout is not forcing when partner opened with one notrump—see page 84.

South	West	North	East
1 ◇	1 ♡	1 ♠ forcing	
		or 2 ♣ forcing	

South	West	North	East
1 ♠	2 ♡	3 ♣ forcing	

but

South	West	North	East
1 ◇	3 ♠	4 ♡ not forcing, because it is	
		enough for game	

A free one-over-one takeout shows a hand containing a biddable suit and about 2 honor-tricks; with a five- or six-card suit, 1½ honor-tricks will occasionally be enough to justify the response, provided they are fortified by some outside strength. A free bid at the one-level requires a minimum of 9 points.

♠ K 10 6 5 2   ♡ 8 6   ◇ K Q 7 5   ♣ 9 2 or
♠ A J 7 5   ♡ 7 4 3   ◇ Q J 5 2   ♣ Q 6 are enough for a *free* response of one spade, not vulnerable, when partner's opening bid has been overcalled. When vulnerable, the hand should have an extra plus value or one more card in the trump suit.

A free two-over-one takeout, because it is never made on a very weak hand, requires little more strength than when there is no intervening bid—*provided responder's suit is lower-ranking than partner's:*

South	West	North	East
1 ♡	2 ♣	2 ◇	

North may have

♠ K 7 2   ♡ 8 5   ◇ A Q 10 6 4   ♣ 9 6 3

But a free single raise, when available, is preferred to a free suit takeout on a near-minimum:

♠ K 7   ♡ J 10 5   ◇ A Q 7 6 3   ♣ 9 5 4   Bid two hearts.

When the responder's suit is higher-ranking than partner's, he needs more strength:

South	West	North	East
1 ♡	2 ◇	2 ♠	

or

1 ♡	2 ◇	3 ♣	

The opening hand may have been prepared to rebid over a response of one spade or two clubs, but has no safe rebid available when forced one trick higher. To allow for this,

North's response in each of the above circumstances should be stronger than usual, containing at least 2½ honor-tricks, or support in partner's suit:

1. ♠ K J 8 7 5   ♡ J 10 6   ♢ 5 3   ♣ A Q 7
2. ♠ A 8   ♡ Q 7 2   ♢ Q 6   ♣ K Q 10 8 4 3
3. ♠ 9 2   ♡ 6 5   ♢ A 7 3   ♣ A Q J 9 8 6

The responder should make due allowance for the opener's forced rebid:

SOUTH	WEST	NORTH	EAST
1 ♣	1 ♠	2 ♢	Pass
3 ♣			
or 2 ♡			

South may have had to bid three clubs on a suit (such as A J 4 3 2) he would not willingly rebid at the three-level. He may have bid two hearts on a hand which would not have been strong enough for a reverse had not North forced. The two-heart bid here does not show extra strength, for it is the "cheapest" rebid South has.

Free Rebids

Any time the opener rebids freely over an intervening over-call, as in a case like this

SOUTH	WEST	NORTH	EAST
1 ♡	Pass	1 ♠	2 ♣
2 ♢			
or 2 ♡			
or 2 ♠			

he shows added values—an extra honor-trick, perhaps, or equivalent values such as an unusually long and strong suit or very fine distributional support for partner's suit.

In the bidding example shown, South must hold:

♠ K 6	♡ A Q 7 2	♢ A Q 10 7 6	♣ 7 3	Two diamonds
♠ 5 2	♡ A Q J 10 9 7	♢ A 5 4	♣ 6 2	Two hearts
♠ K 6 3	♡ K Q 8 5 4	♢ A K 8	♣ 8 3	Two spades
♠ J 7 5 4	♡ A J 6 5 3	♢ A 9 3	♣ 8	Two spades

South would pass on

♠ A K 6   ♡ K J 10 6 3   ◇ 8 4 2   ♣ 6 5, for despite the high spades and rebiddable hearts the hand is about ½ honor-trick above a minimum and has no compensating distributional advantages.

South would pass on

♠ 6   ♡ A J 9 6 2   ◇ A 10 7 5 3   ♣ 8 2, for the two five-card suits do not represent added values; without them, the hand could not have been opened on so little honor strength.

Bids Over Opponent's Takeout Double

When an opponent doubles partner's opening suit-bid of one (for a takeout—page 257) he may show a hand as strong or stronger than the opening bid, a fact which must affect the responder's choice of responses.

With strong hands, two or more honor-tricks, redouble with distributed strength, and make a jump forcing takeout with a freak including 2½ or more honor-tricks.

With fair hands of 1 to 2 honor-tricks including a five-card or longer suit, *bid as though the double had not occurred.*

If your right-hand opponent has doubled partner's opening one-diamond bid, you should bid one heart with:

♠ 6 3   ♡ A Q 7 5 4   ◇ 6 4 2   ♣ Q 8 5

The suit takeout over an opponent's double is a denial of strength in a sense, since the responder cannot be strong enough to redouble. *Therefore it is not forcing* and in the case of a two-over-one response the minimum is reduced to about one honor-trick with a six-card suit.

Take partner's doubled one-heart bid out into two clubs, holding

♠ 7 6 2   ♡ 5   ◇ 6 4 3   ♣ K Q 10 8 6 2

This takeout escapes the danger that the double of one heart may be passed for penalties. With three-card heart support the responder would do better to pass the double:

♠ 7 6 2   ♡ 6 4 3   ◇ 5   ♣ K Q 10 8 6 2   Pass

With hands weak in honors but strong distributionally, *raise.* A single raise shows about four winners and usually four trumps. A double raise in this position shows about five winners and is *not a forcing bid.* Expressed in terms of honor-tricks: A double raise requires five trumps (or four strong trumps), a singleton and 1 to 1½ honor-tricks; a single raise is given on the minimum requirements stated (on page 164) for a raise if the opponent had passed.

With weak hands pass unless a raise can be given.

Assuming that partner has bid one diamond and intervening opponent has doubled:

♠ K1064	♡ K52	◇ A6	♣ J974	Redouble
♠ KQ63	♡ A974	◇ 7	♣ QJ52	Redouble
♠ K4	♡ AKQ9642	◇ —	♣ 9642	Two hearts
♠ Q65	♡ J843	◇ A6	♣ J752	Pass
♠ 62	♡ KQ874	◇ 963	♣ 1085	One heart
♠ 854	♡ 6	◇ Q9753	♣ QJ106	Three diamonds
♠ 4	♡ 864	◇ Q652	♣ J10943	Two diamonds
♠ 6	♡ 532	◇ 109765	♣ QJ76	Two diamonds
♠ 8	♡ QJ109763	◇ 82	♣ Q64	Three hearts

See pages 83-84 for the responder's action when his partner's one-notrump bid is doubled or overcalled.

CHAPTER TWENTY

PART-SCORE
BIDDING

A part-score affects the bidding in two ways. When your side has a part-score, the conventional meanings of some bids must be changed, since a lower contract will suffice for game. When either side or both sides have part-scores, your bidding *strategy* will change somewhat.

Forcing Bids in Part-Score Situations

1. An opening bid of one should be considered semi-forcing; the responder must of course pass a worthless hand, but should try to keep the bidding open with the slightest excuse, since at the risk of going down one extra trick the partnership may score a game.

With a part-score of 40, 50 or 60, a shaded raise to an opening one-spade bid should be given with ♠ J 8 5 4   ♡ 9 6   ◇ Q 5 3 2   ♣ 9 8 7, although this hand does not ordinarily conform to the minimum requirements.

2. (*a*) An opening two-bid in a suit, even if enough for game, is forcing for at least one round.

   (*b*) If responder makes any positive response (raise, suit takeout, or jump to three notrump) the two-bidder must rebid at least once. If responder makes a negative two-notrump response the two-bidder may pass.

   (*c*) If the two-bidder rebids in a new suit it is again forcing for one round; and thereafter whenever *either* partner bids a new suit, it is forcing for one round. If either partner rebids in notrump or in a suit already bid, it is not forcing.

(d) In order to make a forcing rebid in a suit which has previously been bid, the player must jump one trick in that suit.

A player should reduce the usual honor-trick requirements for a forcing two-bid—sometimes as low as 3½ honor-tricks—if he has a solid two-suited hand or freak; for he wants to advise his partner of slam possibilities.

For example, if North and South have a part-score of 70, an opening two-spade bid may be made on one of the following hands:

♠ A K Q 8 6 4 2   ♡ A 7 6   ◇ K 5   ♣ 3
♠ A K J 5 4   ♡ A Q J 10 7   ◇ K 6   ♣ 8

Only a one-spade bid should be made on the following hand, enticing the opponents to enter the bidding and be doubled:

♠ A Q 7 6   ♡ A 5   ◇ A K 8 4   ♣ K J 6

In general, an opening two-notrump bid or a jump two-notrump response (which are not forcing, of course, if they are enough for game) should be avoided. With hands of general strength it is best to keep the bidding low and give the opponents every opportunity to overcall.

A two-bid must be made on a hand as strong as the following, since it is unlikely that any other player will be strong enough to bid:

♠ A K Q 7   ♡ K Q J 5 4   ◇ A K 8   ♣ K

If the bidding, with a part-score of 60, is as follows:

South	West	North	East
2 ♡	Pass	2 ♠	Pass

The two-spade response is forcing for one round and South must bid again.

If South bids three hearts, three spades, or two notrump it is not forcing.

If South bids three diamonds, three clubs, four hearts, four spades, or four notrump, it is forcing.

3. A player may make a forcing takeout of an opening suit or notrump bid of one, or a forcing rebid over partner's response, despite a part-score.

The usual honor-trick requirements may be shaded by the responder with solid suits or two-suiters.

After the forcing takeout, the opener must bid at least once. If he bids a new suit or jumps one trick in his own suit, it is forcing for one round. As in the case of the opening two-bid, any bid in a new suit and any jump in a suit previously bid is forcing for one round thereafter. But if either partner simply rebids his suit or bids notrump, the other may now pass.

Having a part-score of 60, and partner having made an opening bid of one heart, bid two spades holding:

♠ K Q J 10 9 6   ♡ Q J 10   ◇ A 6 5 2   ♣ —

However, holding the following hand:

♠ A J 8 3   ♡ Q 6   ◇ K Q 7 5   ♣ A Q 7

only one spade should be bid; partner will not drop the bidding short of game and if the opponents overcall, they can be doubled.

4. Any opening three- or four-bid is purely a shutout bid. The common belief that a bid is strength-showing because it is more than needed for game is entirely incorrect.

5. A double raise in partner's suit, or a non-jump suit take-out which is ordinarily forcing for one round, means exactly the same thing with or without a part-score. These bids are not forcing, however, when game has already been reached.

Part-Score Strategy and Tactics

The average conception is that since a low contract means game, weak hands should be opened on advanced part-scores.

The superficiality of this idea is apparent to anyone who will take the trouble to delve further. The most determined defense is waged against part-score situations. It follows, since the possessor of a part-score *knows* he will be "pushed," that he must be well prepared for this pushing.

Shade your opening bids downward if your opponents have a part-score, and upward if you hold the part-score.

Consider this sub-minimum hand:

♠ A K 8 6   ♡ A 7 5   ◇ 6 3 2   ♣ 8 5 4

If the holder of this hand has a part-score, he is inviting defeat—possibly rout—by opening the bidding. He will have not only the opponents, but his own partner "pushing" him. He will not, of course, make another bid, but if partner holds a fair hand he will never be satisfied before the three-level, at least, is reached. And he will need a great deal better than a "fair" hand for this "minny" to bring in nine tricks!

Now for the other angle—opening the same hand *against* opponents' part-score.

It must be observed that, defensively, this hand is fully up to standard: that it should take three tricks against any adverse contract. Offensively, however, it is weak. If the hand is passed and the opponents open the bidding, it would be dangerous to overcall with only 3½ or 4 winners. Nor could partner be expected to risk an overcall on a hand like

♠ J 8 6 5 3   ♥ 6   ♦ A Q 9 7   ♣ 10 7 2

The opponents, therefore, may romp home at a low contract. But if you have opened with one spade, partner can safely raise you at least to a point at which you can take a cheap sacrifice—or drive the opponents too high and beat them a trick or two.

PANICKY BIDDING

The reaction of ninety players in a hundred, when faced with opponents' part-score, is to rush in and fight, regardless of position, and almost regardless of holding. Partners are forgotten: each feels that he and only he must be Horatio at the Bridge. Let us take one of the most typical situations.

Both sides vulnerable, East-West 40 part-score; the bidding has gone: North, one spade; East, two·hearts; South holds

♠ A 6 3   ♥ 7 5 2   ♦ Q 6 3   ♣ 5 4 3 2

and on the hysterical theory that the opponents are about to take the rubber with a measly two-heart contract, he bids two spades.

Quite obviously, no player, however expert, in the North position can tell whether the raise was sound or hysterical. Holding such a hand as

♠ K Q J 9 7 5   ♥ 6 4   ♦ A 10   ♣ A J 6

he cannot *assume* that South's raise was so bad that there will be no play whatever for four spades; to bid less than four on the next round would be ridiculously conservative.

Thus, since a free raise of partner's opening bid over an intervening bid is strength-showing, it remains that at all times, part-score or no part-score.

It is unavoidable that a part-score menace must influence the bidding, but only to induce the slightest of shadings. Thus if North bids one spade and East, with a 60 part-score, overcalls with two diamonds, South is more or less forced to raise on such a questionable holding as

♠ Q 10 6 5   ♡ K 8 6   ♢ 5 4 2   ♣ Q J 8

It will be noted that even this shaded free raise has more winners than the miserable one in the raise shown before. It naturally follows, in part-score situations, that the opening bidder must make some *slight* allowance for possible shading by partner.

To overcall the opponents' bids on an unplayable hand, simply because they have a part-score, is courting disaster. It is even more dangerous than when the score is blank, since the opponents need less than usual for game and may be underbidding slightly.

North-South have 60 part-score; South deals and bids one spade; West holds

♠ A 6 3   ♡ 7 2   ♢ K J 7 4   ♣ Q 8 6 2

and bids two clubs or two diamonds, in the belief that desperate measures are required. He will probably be doubled, if not immediately then later (for partner, encouraged by the overcall, will usually carry on), and the result will usually be disastrous.

Overcalls may, however, be made on certain hands which would be passed if there were no part-score:

North-South have 60 part-score; South deals and bids one spade; West overcalls with two diamonds, holding

♠ 6 3   ♡ 5   ♢ Q 10 9 7 6 5 3   ♣ K Q 9

The argument against overcalling on such a hand in normal circumstances is that there is too little to gain by the bid. Game is out of the question unless partner can enter the bidding on his own. If North becomes declarer partner may make a damaging opening lead from such a holding as ♢ A 2. But against the opposing part-score the bid is worth-while, if only to push the opponents a trick or two higher.

Takeout Doubles Against Part-Score Bids

When the opponents have a part-score neither trapping nor procrastinating tactics can be employed. *One of the most important functions of expert bidding is to relieve a partner from the intolerable burden of guesses and decisions.* Consider this situation:

Both sides are vulnerable: East-West have 60 part-score; East deals and bids one heart. South holds:

♠ K 10 7 2   ♡ K 8   ◇ A 6 5 3   ♣ Q 10 2

South has not quite the values for a sound takeout double. The situation, however, is desperate and it requires very little imagination on his part to foresee that, should he supinely pass, it will get worse instead of better. On a 60 score, West must consider the heart bid as a virtual force; surely he will scrape up, at the very least, a notrump response. What then will be North's dilemma, even if he holds a fair hand? He cannot be expected to bid at the two, possibly the three-level without knowing that South has good support for whatever suit he chooses.

To forestall such an outcome, South must double. Now North can enter the bidding with no worry.

CHAPTER TWENTY-ONE

THE DEFENDERS' BIDDING

A player who enters the bidding after one of his opponents has made an opening bid is called a defender. The defender enters the bidding for one of two reasons:

1. For defensive purposes: to conduct by judicious over-bidding a kind of guerrilla tactics with the object of intimidating the enemy; or, to point out to partner a possible opening lead against opponents' suit or notrump contract; or, to suggest a suit in which a possible paying sacrifice may be taken.

2. For aggressive purposes: to coax or trap the enemy into a penalty or to secure the contract for his side.

It may be stated as a general principle that when a player has a fairly strong hand he should, whenever safely possible, enter the bidding for one of these two purposes.

To pass for a trap, except with certain types of hand and in a few rare strategic circumstances, is a losing game.

The safety factor is nevertheless the principal one. The player should carefully learn and follow the Rule of 2 and 3, explained in Chapter 30, and quoted here:

When partner has made no bid, assume in his hand no more than two winners if vulnerable and three winners if not vulnerable.

In other words, for any defensive overcall the player should be able to win in his own hand within two tricks of his contract if vulnerable and within three tricks of his contract if not vulnerable.

Strong and Weak Overcalls

The defenders have the following bids at their disposal, depending upon the type and strength of the hand.

Minimum defensive overcalls show hands of about 1½–2½ honor-tricks which do not offer game unless partner can support freely.

A player should not, however, merely overcall if his hand is strong enough for any one of the strength-showing defenders' bids:

A jump overcall in a suit (one more than necessary) shows about 3½ honor-tricks and asks for a light raise.

A takeout double shows a hand with about three or more honor-tricks and strong support for two or three suits.

A jump overcall of four in a suit, or an overcall of three if it is a jump of more than one trick, is a shutout bid made on a hand with a strong suit but weak in honor-tricks.

A one-notrump overcall shows 3½–4 honor-tricks with balanced distribution and the opponents' suit stopped. (16–18 high-card points.)

An overcall in the opponents' suit or a notrump overcall of an opposing preëmptive four- or five-bid is an ultrapowerful hand, forcing to game.

Minimum Defensive Overcalls

Any defensive overcall should show, in addition to the winners required under the Rule of 2 and 3, about 1½ honor-tricks. In most cases the overcall also shows a five-card or longer biddable suit.

A defensive overcall of one-odd should be made:*

When not vulnerable with four winners, including about 1½ honor-tricks and a suit as good as Q 10 x x x or K Q x x.

When vulnerable, five winners, including 1½ honor-tricks and a suit as good as Q J 9 x x or A Q J x.

A strong four-card suit may be used only when the hand as a whole contains the required number of winners.

The requirement of 1½ honor-tricks may be shaded only

---

* See also "Reopening with an Overcall," page 262.

when the hand contains more than the minimum number of winners.

A minimum overcall of two-odd should be made with the following strength:

When not vulnerable, with five winners, including a fairly good five-card suit (A J x x x). The hand should contain 1½ honor-tricks or more. No overcall of two may be made on a four-card suit.

When vulnerable, the hand should contain six *sure* winners with a strong five-card suit (at least a rebiddable suit) and two or more honor-tricks.

Overcalls at the level of three or higher, when forced by the opponents' bidding (that is, when not jump bids) require more winners, depending upon the bidding level.

The following hands are proper overcalls of one-odd, an opponent having opened with one diamond.

Bid one spade with	♠ K Q J 10 7 6	♡ 9 4	◇ A 7 5	♣ 8 3
Bid one heart with	♠ 8 6 3	♡ A K Q 8 5	◇ 7	♣ 9 6 5 4
Bid one heart with	♠ 9 3	♡ A Q 7 5	◇ Q 6 2	♣ Q J 10 7

However, the last of the above hands should be passed if vulnerable because it does not contain enough playing strength. The following hands are sound vulnerable overcalls at the range of two, opponent having opened with one spade:

Bid two diamonds with	♠ 9	♡ K 6	◇ A Q J 7 4 2	♣ J 10 8 4
Bid two hearts with	♠ 6 5 3	♡ Q J 10 9 5	◇ A	♣ K Q 10 5

Pass with ♠ 9 6 ♡ A K 7 5 ◇ A 8 4 3 ♣ 5 3 2, because the hand, which contains three honor-tricks, has not enough winners for a vulnerable overcall either at one or at two.

Pre-emptive Overcalls

A distinction must be drawn between the overcall at the range of three when it is a jump bid and when it is necessary merely to overcall the last opposing bid. In this bidding:

South	West	North	East
1 ♡	Pass	2 ♡	3 ◇

East's bid of three diamonds is a regular overcall which does not guarantee any particular honor-trick holding, but merely the ability to win six tricks if not vulnerable, seven tricks if vulnerable. If the defender jumps unnecessarily to three, however, it is a different type of bid:

SOUTH	WEST	NORTH	EAST
1 ♡	3 ♣ Single jump overcall		
	3 ♠ Preëmptive overcall		

The single jump overcall (described on pages 277-278) is a strength-showing bid. The preëmptive overcall (any jump of more than one trick) is a weakness bid, designed to make it difficult for the opponents to exchange information.

In the example above, West needed at least six winners, not vulnerable, for his three-spade overcall; and seven winners if vulnerable, for preëmptive overcalls are strictly based on the Rule of 2 and 3; but there is no honor-trick requirement. West might have held, not vulnerable,

♠ Q J 10 8 7 5 3 2   ♡ 6   ◇ 5 4   ♣ 10 2

With more winners, a preëmptive overcall at the four-level may be made.

Over an opponent's opening one-spade bid, a non-vulnerable jump to four diamonds may be made on

♠ 6 3   ♡ —   ◇ K Q J 8 7 5 4 2   ♣ Q J 3

See also page 414, for a discussion of psychological preëmptive overcalling.

Responding to an Overcall

There is no pressure on the overcaller's partner to respond. The overcall shows limited strength—never a very strong hand. There is no reason to raise unless game is in sight, or unless to compete with the opponents for a part-score. There is no reason to "rescue" if you lack support, for the overcaller has already guaranteed relative safety under the Rule of 2 and 3.

In fact, in discussing raises of partner's overcall an about-face in terminology is required. A "free" raise is one given when there has been no intervening bid; but when the intervening opponent has bid, every effort should be made to raise partner's overcall and not let the opponents get an uncontested part-score or game.

It must be kept in mind that a vulnerable overcall promises at least one full playing trick more than a non-vulnerable overcall, and thus invites a lighter response.

RAISES OF OVERCALLS

The partner merely counts his winners (Chapter 5) and raises one trick for each winner over two, if vulnerable, and for each winner over three if not vulnerable. These should include 1½ to 2 honor-tricks. In competitive situations the honor-trick holding may be shaded, *but not the winners:*

SOUTH	WEST	NORTH	EAST
1 ♡	1 ♠	Pass	

East should pass, vulnerable or not, with

♠ K 10 8 3   ♡ 4 3 2   ◇ A 5 2   ♣ 6 4 2—only 2½ winners.

East should raise to two spades with

♠ K 10 8 3   ♡ 4 2   ◇ A 8 5 2   ♣ 6 4 2—4 winners—whether vulnerable or not.

Any overcall at the two-level shows at least a five-card rebiddable suit and may be raised on three small trumps.

SOUTH	WEST	NORTH	EAST
1 ♡	2 ◇	2 ♡	

Vulnerable or not vulnerable, East should raise to three diamonds with as little as

♠ Q J 7 3   ♡ 2   ◇ 9 6 3   ♣ A 10 8 6 4

A double raise of an overcall is not forcing. In counting winners for a double raise, it is best not to place too much reliance on long side suits. Thus, only a single raise is given to a vulnerable one-spade overcall with this hand:

♠ K 10 8 3   ♡ 4 2   ◇ A J 5 2   ♣ 6 4 2—4 winners, counting the four-card diamond suit,

while this hand would justify raising a vulnerable one-heart overcall to three, or a vulnerable two-heart overcall to game:

♠ A 6 2   ♡ 10 7 6 2   ◇ 5   ♣ K Q 9 5 4—4½ winners without counting the club length.

Suit and Notrump Takeouts

A suit takeout of an overcall shows that the partner is strong enough to make an overcall on his own responsibility, counting on the first overcaller for no more than 1½ honor-tricks. *A notrump takeout by the partner of the overcaller shows strength*—usually two or more honor-tricks.

South	West	North	East
1 ♠	2 ◇	Pass	

Vulnerable or not, East should

Pass, holding	♠ 6 5	♡ K 10 8 5 2	◇ 8 3	♣ K 7 5 2
Bid two hearts on	♠ 6	♡ K Q 10 8 5 4	◇ 7 5	♣ Q 8 6 3
Bid two notrump on	♠ A J 9	♡ J 10 5 3	◇ J 7	♣ K Q 9 5

If partner's overcall is doubled, one should rescue only if he has a long, fairly solid suit:

South	West	North	East
1 ♡	2 ♣	Double	

East passes with	♠ A 10 7 6 3	♡ 9 5 2	◇ Q 10 8 4	♣ 2
East passes with	♠ 9 7	♡ 9 5 2	◇ Q J 10 8 6	♣ 8 4 3

East bids two diamonds with

♠ 9 7   ♡ 9 5 2   ◇ Q J 10 9 6 4   ♣ 7 3—his hand is worthless at clubs and will produce four tricks at diamonds.

A jump takeout of partner's overcall in a new suit is forcing for one round. It requires 2½ to 3 honor-tricks and a strong suit:

South	West	North	East
1 ♣	1 ♡	Pass	

East, holding

♠ A Q 10 8 4	♡ Q J	◇ A J 6 2	♣ 4 3

should feel that with West able to overcall, a game is well in sight. East cannot tell, however, whether spades, hearts, diamonds, or possibly notrump would be the best contract. To assure himself of another chance to bid, East should now bid two spades.

CHAPTER TWENTY-TWO

THE

TAKEOUT DOUBLE

The defender whose hand in honor-tricks exceeds the usual sound opening bid has at his disposal a group of strength-showing bids of which the most valuable and most flexible is the *takeout double*.

DOUBLES CLASSIFIED

The literal meaning of a double is that the doubling player does not believe the opponents can make their contract, and wishes to increase the value of the undertrick penalties he expects to score. A double which is made for this purpose—that is, to penalize the opponents—is a *penalty double*.

Some doubles, however, are conventional bids signalling to partner a strong hand and requesting partner to take it out with a response which best shows the nature of his hand. This type of double is called a *takeout double*.*

The only time a player should even consider passing his partner's takeout double is when he is so strong in the opponents' trump suit and in general defensive strength that he feels certain the opponents will be defeated at their doubled contract.

---

* The penalty double is sometimes called a "business double," and the takeout double an "informatory" or "informative" double. By a few players they are called respectively "positive" and "negative." The terms given to them in this book are, however, more precise.

Definition of the Takeout Double

A double is meant for a takeout:

1. Provided partner has made no bid, double or redouble; and provided the doubled bid is a suit-bid of not more than three.

2. The double must be made at the player's first opportunity.*

3. A takeout double may be made by the player who has opened the bidding, provided partner has passed his opening bid and provided the opening bid was a *suit-bid of one*, not any notrump bid nor any suit-bid of two or more.

4. A player may repeat a takeout double when his partner, released by an intervening bid, has failed to respond to his first takeout double; but when partner passes the first double for penalties (page 267) it is construed as a response and any subsequent double by either partner is for penalties.

It follows that any other double is meant for penalties (Chapter 24).

Requirements for the Takeout Double

The takeout double is one of the most important of the prepared bids. An opponent has already opened the bidding, advertising possession of a hand which at the very least will probably win three defensive tricks. The opener's partner may sit behind the doubler with the balance of power. In the face of this opposing strength the defender, by doubling, commands his partner to bid with a possible Yarborough.

Before making a takeout double, the doubler should make sure that if his partner is forced to respond on a minimum hand his support for partner's suit will be such that the result will not be disastrous. If there is any suit in which partner may respond and which the doubler is not prepared to support strongly, then the doubler should have in his hand an "escape" suit—a rebiddable trump suit of his own into which he can

---

* Unless it is a double to reopen the bidding (page 262).

take out the response at a contract safe under the Rule of 2 and 3.

The requirements for a takeout double are:

3 honor-tricks divided in three suits; and if any one of the suits has less than four cards, the hand should contain strong intermediates.

3 honor-tricks in two suits, provided the hand has a rebiddable suit containing four trump tricks or more.

Exceptions are: When a hand is exceptionally strong in honor-cards, though having only 2½ honor-tricks, as in the case of Example 5, below, and also in occasional bidding situations that make a takeout double safer than an overcall would be.

MAJOR-SUIT SUPPORT

A takeout double always implies major-suit support.

When the doubled bid is a major suit, strong support in the other major may be expected by the doubler's partner. If at times such support is lacking, then the doubler will have equivalent values.

The following hands justify takeout doubles of an opponent's bid of *one heart:*

1. ♠ K Q 5 3   ♡ 7 2   ◇ A Q J 5   ♣ K J 10

Double; an ideal type of hand with 3½ honor-tricks and support for any suit partner bids.

2. ♠ A 8 6 3   ♡ 5   ◇ A 7 5 4   ♣ A 6 4 2

3+ honor-tricks, but very weak in intermediates. If vulnerable, pass; if not vulnerable, double.

3. ♠ 8 6 5 3 2   ♡ —   ◇ A K Q 2   ♣ K J 10 4

Double; an ideal hand since the five spades are as good support for a response in that suit as four strong cards would be.

4. ♠ K 10 5   ♡ 5   ◇ A Q J 6 3   ♣ A J 6 5

Double; though there are only three spades, the support for all suits is good and a takeout double best expresses the strength of the hand.

5. ♠ A J 10 9   ♡ 4   ◇ Q J 7 3   ♣ Q J 10 8

Double; though there are only 2½ honor-tricks, this is made up by excellent distributional support for every unbid suit and the many high intermediate cards.

The Strategic Double

When the doubler has strength in only two suits, with one playable trump suit of his own, he doubles because:

1. If his partner fits either of his two strong suits, that will make an ideal trump suit.
2. It is desirable first to show partner a hand stronger than could be shown by an overcall.

For example, holding:

♠ 6   ♡ A Q 7 3   ◊ A K J 6 5 4   ♣ 10 4

When an opponent bids one spade or one club, the proper action is to double. If partner responds in hearts, a game is very likely to be made. If partner responds in the weak club suit a prompt and safe rescue can be effected in diamonds. Meanwhile, partner knows that the doubler's hand has better than 2½ honor-tricks.

Other such hands justifying a double of a one-club bid are:

♠ K Q 10 9 8   ♡ A K 5 4   ◊ 6   ♣ 4 3 2
♠ A 6   ♡ A K Q 8   ◊ K Q 6 2   ♣ 10 4 3

Sometimes the "escape suit" is weaker—too weak, in fact, for an overcall. Holding about 2½ honor-tricks, with a five-card suit and support for the other unbid suits, a takeout double is the safest means of getting into the bidding. However, much depends on what suit is doubled, and what suit is the five-card suit.

♠ 5 ♡ K J 6 5 3 ◊ A J 8 4 ♣ Q 7 5 is a good double of one spade. A two-heart overcall would risk a costly penalty. If partner responds in clubs and is doubled, then two hearts may be bid; but in the meantime you will have given yourself an extra chance of finding the safest suit.

♠ Q 7 5 ♡ 5 ◊ K J 6 5 3 ♣ A J 8 4 is a good double of one heart. If partner responds in spades, it will be at the one-level and the opponents are unlikely to double.

♠ A J 8 4 ♡ 5 ◊ Q 7 5 ♣ K J 6 5 3 is a better spade overcall of one heart. You can't stand a two-diamond response.

♠ 5 ♡ Q 7 5 ◊ A J 8 4 ♣ K J 6 5 3 is a good pass of one spade. You can't stand a two-heart response.

♠ Q 7 5 ♡ A J 8 4 ◊ 5 ♣ K J 6 5 3 is a good double of one diamond.

The point is to be prepared for any response.

Strength in the Opponents' Suit

A player may make a takeout double with strength in the doubled suit when he is strong enough to rebid in notrump if partner's takeout is unsatisfactory; and also in those very rare cases when he is willing to play in the doubled suit despite the warning given by the opponent's bid.

Let us assume that first hand opens with one spade; second hand should double, holding:

♠ K J 10 9 7 6   ♥ A J 6 5   ♦ A 6   ♣ 5

If his partner replies in hearts, all is well; otherwise he can bid two spades. This will be a technically forcing bid, but will at the same time show *probable* possession of strength in the opponents' suit. Partner, holding support for spades, may and should raise; if the doubler does not actually have a spade suit he will have compensating strength in the responder's suit. It is also proper to double a one-spade bid with:

♠ A J 10   ♥ K J 10 4   ♦ A Q J 10   ♣ Q 5

He hopes for a heart response, can support diamonds, and can bid two notrump over two clubs. (NOTE: With an almost identical hand, but lacking the three tens, you would make an immediate overcall of one notrump.)

The Double of One Notrump

A sharp distinction must be drawn between the takeout double of a suit-bid and the double of one notrump.

In the face of the strength announced by the notrump bid— and the ease with which the opponents can profitably make a penalty double of partner's response, as explained on page 286—you will seldom have a hand on which you could safely make a *takeout* double of an opening one-notrump bid.

A double of an opening one-notrump bid with the following hand is not only futile but is courting disaster:

♠ A 7 5   ♥ A Q 8   ♦ 9 6 2   ♣ A Q 5 4

Though the hand contains four honor-tricks, it is just as likely as not to win exactly four tricks, with the additional disadvantage that any opening lead is likely to present declarer with an extra trick in the suit led. If partner were required (as in the case of takeout doubles) to respond in some weak four-card suit, he might go down, if vulnerable, 1100 points.

Therefore the double of a one-notrump bid is a *penalty* double, and is intended to be taken out only if partner has a long (at least a five-card) suit *in a hand too weak in honor-tricks to support the double.*

A double of an opponent's one-notrump bid requires:

About 4 honor-tricks in the hand (at least 16 high-card points) and

A strong (fairly solid) suit, usually a five-card suit, to open. An example would be A K x x x; or Q J 10 x x. Examples of hands on which to double one notrump.

1.	♠ K 6	♡ A 10 4	◇ A K Q 9 5 3	♣ Q 8
2.	♠ A K J	♡ Q J 10 9 8	◇ Q 5	♣ A 4 3
3.	♠ A Q 6 4	♡ K Q J 7	◇ K 2	♣ A J 6
4.	♠ A 8 3	♡ K Q 5	◇ Q 6	♣ K Q J 7 2
5.	♠ Q 9 8 6 5	♡ A Q 9	◇ K J 3	♣ A Q
6.	♠ 8 2	♡ A K Q 9 8 6 2	◇ K 6	♣ A 8

The Positional Factor in Doubles

When the opener's partner has responded to the opening bid, fourth-hand is faced with this situation: both opponents have bid. His partner, who has had a chance to bid, was not even strong enough to overcall. Here the danger becomes greater than ever that partner's hand may be completely worthless.

When the bidding is as follows:

South	West	North	East
1 ◇	Pass	1 ♠	

East should refrain from doubling on the following hand, which would have been a justifiable double for West to make over the one-diamond bid:

♠ Q 9 6 3	♡ K Q 6 5	◇ 8 2	♣ A Q J

However, with the following hand:

♠ Q 5	♡ A K 6 2	◇ Q 7 3	♣ A K 5 4

East has so many honor-tricks that he cannot afford not to give his partner some indication of his strength and should double.

A takeout double when the opponents have already reached a contract of two or three must be proportionately stronger than a takeout double of a one-bid.

REOPENING THE BIDDING

The situation when the opening bid has been passed by the opener's partner calls for special treatment.

In the first place, it is unlikely that the opponents have passed out a game hand at a one-bid. The defender's greatest risk in giving his opponents another chance to bid is that they will make a higher part-score.

In the second place, there is always a strong possibility that the other defender has passed a hand of better than average strength and yet too weak for an overcall or takeout double.* Such hands may be of two types:

♠ A 9 5   ♡ K 8 3   ◇ A 7 4 2   ♣ K Q 5

With this hand a takeout double of any opening bid would be dangerous, particularly when vulnerable, and the defender sitting second-hand would be forced to pass. The other type of hand is:

♠ K J 7 4 3   ♡ A Q 6   ◇ 5 4   ♣ K 8 5

When the opening bid is one spade the defender cannot double in second position, nor can he bid; therefore, he must pass and hope the opponents bid too high in spades so that he may double them for penalties.

In reopening the bidding the defender in fourth position may therefore double for a takeout with two honor-tricks and with strength in only two suits. His partner may take him out in a suit and make a part-score, and with strength in the opponents' suit his partner can make a profitable penalty pass of their one-bid.

A double of a one-notrump *response* which has been passed by the opener should be made with about 2½ honor-tricks, which may be reduced to two honor-tricks with a few Jacks and tens.

REOPENING WITH AN OVERCALL

When the fourth-hand defender has not the proper distributional type of hand for a double, but has a biddable suit with about 1½ honor-tricks, he should reopen the bidding with a simple overcall even though his hand is a trick short of the

---

* See also "Trapping," page 414.

safety margin required by the Rule of 2 and 3. Holding a strong suit and about 2½ honor-tricks, he should make a jump over-call of two.

SOUTH	WEST	NORTH	EAST
1 ◇	Pass	Pass	

East should double, holding:

♠ J 9 6 4	♡ K Q 5	◇ 10 3	♣ A 7 4 2 or
♠ K 6 2	♡ Q J 5 2	◇ A 4	♣ 9 6 5 4

East should bid two clubs, holding:

♠ 7	♡ K 5 4	◇ Q 3 2	♣ K 9 7 6 3 2

East should bid two spades, a jump overcall, holding:

♠ A Q J 8 4 3	♡ 7 2	◇ 8 4	♣ K J 7

Responses to Takeout Doubles

When one defender has made a takeout double, his partner is expected to respond by bidding his best suit. Unless released by an intervening bid he must not pass,* no matter how weak his hand is. The weaker the hand, the greater the necessity for taking out the double.

When the takeout double is passed by the next opponent, the doubler's partner must bid; therefore, his response is a *forced response*.

When the opponent bids over partner's takeout double, a pass is in order with a weak hand and a bid should be made only when holding some strength. A bid made over an inter-vening bid is therefore a *free response*.

Since the forced response cannot be avoided, the doubler's partner's only thought is what to bid.

CHOICE OF SUITS

The prime motive of the doubler's partner, when holding a minimum hand (from 0 to ½ honor-trick), is to get out of trouble as cheaply as possible.

First he looks for his longest suit. If he has only one suit of four cards or more, he takes out in that suit.

---

* Except with great strength in the opponents' suit (page 267).

The doubled bid is one heart. Holding:

♠ 6 5 2   ♡ 9 6 3   ◇ J 7 4 3   ♣ 10 8 4   bid two diamonds

Holding two suits of four cards or more, and ½ honor-trick or less, bid the one which can be shown more cheaply.

(a) If one of the suits can be shown by a one-bid, and the other requires a two-bid, take out with the one-bid.

(b) If both suits require the same number of tricks, show the lower-ranking.

The doubled bid is one diamond. Holding:

♠ 6 2   ♡ 8 7 4 3   ◇ 9 6 4   ♣ Q 8 6 3   bid one heart

The doubled bid is one heart. Holding:

♠ 6 2   ♡ 8 7 5   ◇ Q 10 6 3   ♣ 10 8 5 4   bid two clubs

The doubled bid is one club. Holding:

♠ 10 9 7 4   ♡ 6 5   ◇ J 6 5 3   ♣ 8 4 2   bid one diamond

This allows partner to rescue himself, if that is his plan, with a bid of only one heart. If the double were taken out with one spade, a rescue bid of two hearts would be necessary.

THE THREE-CARD SUIT

The most embarrassing situation that the doubler's partner can face is to have a weak hand with no four-card suit except the opponents' suit.

The doubled bid is one spade. The partner holds: ♠ J 7 4 3   ♡ 9 6 5 ◇ 8 6 3   ♣ 7 4 2. He cannot bid one notrump, which is a strength-showing response; he has no four-card suit with which to take out the double. *He must not pass.*

The solution of this difficulty is to bid the three-card suit which can be shown at the lowest level. In the example just given, the response would be *two clubs.*

The response of two clubs is not an artificial response. The doubler's partner does not bid two clubs merely because he has a blank hand. If he has a four-card unbid suit he should show it. If he has only two clubs and three diamonds, he should bid the diamonds. This will happen, however, only in the following two cases:

1. Doubler's partner holds five cards of the opponents' suit:
       ♠ 9 7 5 4 2   ♡ 8 6 5   ◇ 10 5 2   ♣ 6 3. The doubled bid
    is one spade. Respond two diamonds.

2. The doubled bid is one club. With ♠ 8 7 3 ♡ 9 5 4 ◇ 7 5 2
♣ J 8 7 6 respond one diamond.

In rare cases, holding a completely worthless hand, the
doubler's partner may bid a three-card minor suit rather than
take out with two of a higher suit.

The doubled bid is one spade; bid two clubs, rather than two hearts,
holding ♠ 9 7 5 ♡ 8 6 4 3 ◇ J 10 6 ♣ 8 5 2.

But if the doubled bid is one heart, bid one spade with

  ♠ 8 6 5 4   ♡ 8 6 3   ◇ 7 5 2   ♣ 8 7 6

Hands containing from ½ to 1-plus honor-tricks: With hands
containing more than ½ honor-trick there is little danger of
a disaster, provided the takeout double is a sound one. The
principal consideration of the doubler's partner is how best
to show the nature of his hand.

Usually he should simply bid his longest suit. The length
of the suit is more important than its high cards.

The doubled bid is one spade. Bid two clubs, holding

  ♠ 8 6   ♡ 9 5   ◇ Q J 10 7   ♣ 8 7 5 4 2

Bid two diamonds, holding

  ♠ 8 6   ♡ 9 5 4   ◇ Q J 10 7   ♣ Q 6 5 3

The Major-Suit Preference

The takeout double implies strength in the major suits, and,
if the doubled bid is a major, practically guarantees strength
in the other major.

Therefore, with a four-card major suit including a card as
good as the Jack, the major should be shown even when the
hand also contains a five-card minor suit.* Thus, the response
to a takeout double of one heart would be one spade on this
hand:

  ♠ J 9 7 3   ♡ 10 4 3   ◇ 6   ♣ A 8 6 4 2

This does not apply in the case of 6–4 distribution:

  ♠ J 9 7 3   ♡ 10 4   ◇ 6   ♣ J 10 8 7 4 2

* But if the hand is worthless and a response of two-odd is required, prefer a
five-card minor to a weak four-card major.

Bid two clubs, and show the spades later; then partner will be sure that the spades are a four-card suit.

When holding two four-card major suits, prefer spades even when the hearts are stronger; but prefer a five-card heart suit to a stronger four-card spade holding.

The doubled bid being one diamond, bid one spade with

♠ Q 8 4 2　　　♡ A J 6 5　　　♢ 6 4 3　　　♣ 8 7

Bid one heart with ♠ Q J 10 8　♡ 10 7 6 4 3　♢ 8 7　♣ 6 5.

THE NOTRUMP RESPONSE

A notrump response to a takeout double is always encouraging, showing at least one honor-trick and often more.

With a stopper in the opponents' suit, respond with one notrump (unless a major-suit response is available) provided the hand contains at least one honor-trick or a holding of K J x in the opponents' bid suit.

The doubled bid being one heart, bid one notrump with

♠ 8 6 4　　　♡ K 10 7　　　♢ K 8 5 4　　　♣ 6 5 2

This rule is not followed when the one honor-trick is the Ace of the opponents' suit, and the hand has nothing else of value, but does contain a four-card length:

♠ 8 6 3　♡ A 7 2　♢ 10 6 4　♣ 8 5 4 3—bid two clubs, not one notrump, over one heart doubled. With ♠ 8 6 3　♡ A 8 5 4　♢ 6 3 2　♣ 9 7 3 it is necessary to bid one notrump.

The one-notrump response may be made with only a partial stopper in the opponents' suit (J x x, for example, or 10 x x x) if the doubler's partner has 1½ to 2 honor-tricks and no five-card or strong four-card suit to show. Never make the one-notrump response if you have a more constructive bid.

The player who has made the takeout double should refrain from raising the notrump contract unless he himself has a stopper or partial stopper, such as Q x, in the suit adversely bid. Without this stopper, the doubler should rebid in some suit. Now, if the responder actually had the suit stopped, he may rebid notrump.

The doubled bid is one heart. With:

♠ K 6 5　　　♡ J 4 3　　　♢ A J 2　　　♣ 8 6 4 2

To respond with a bid of only two clubs would put fear into the heart of partner, who, being prepared for such a response on a weak hand, would probably pass and let the hand be played at two clubs. To respond with three clubs, thus giving the impression of strength by a jump bid, would deceive the doubler as to the strength of the club suit. The one-notrump response shows the strength of the hand and encourages the doubler to rebid. If the doubler, having a minimum, passes one notrump the contract (seven tricks) will probably be made even though the entire heart suit be run against it.

A response of two notrump to partner's takeout double shows about two honor-tricks, and must also guarantee a probable double stopper in the opponents' suit. (About 10–12 high-card points.)

The Penalty Pass

As a general rule, a double of one notrump should almost always be passed; a double of a suit-bid should be passed only when the penalty is sure and the chance for a game very remote. Nothing but extraordinary trump length justifies this pass.*

In counting up expected defensive winners against opponents' suit-bid, the doubler's partner adds his trump tricks and honor-tricks in side suits to three expected honor-tricks in his partner's hand; no more. Unless the total is at least seven tricks, do not pass.

Opponents' contract of one heart, doubled for a takeout by partner, may be left in with the following hand,

♠ 8   ♡ Q J 9 7 6 3   ◇ A 6   ♣ J 9 7 4

particularly when the opponents are vulnerable. A two-trick penalty (500 points) may be anticipated. If the opponents are not vulnerable the pass is still proper, but only because the game is uncertain and a two-trick set reasonably sure.

Procedure When Partner Doubles One Notrump

As a general rule the opening one-notrump bid shows a strong hand—4 to 4½ honor-tricks, or 16–18 points.†

The double of one notrump is primarily a penalty double, although technically it is a double for a takeout.

---

* A good rule is: Pass only when prepared for a lead in the opponent's trump suit. (Usually the penalty pass calls for this lead.)

† For "weak" opening one-notrump bids, see page 93.

The doubler's partner is aware that the double itself is as strong as the opening notrump bid, and is possibly of the same suit-pattern. (Actually, the double can be shaded to 15 points, directly *over* the notrump.)

This bidding situation demands that the partner of the doubler should make a penalty pass if his high cards, plus the high-card expectancy of the doubler, clearly demonstrate that his side has the balance of power. A combined holding of 5½ honor-tricks, or at least 22 points, counting high cards only, would constitute the balance of power.

Suppose your partner doubles an opening one notrump. If you make a minimum response in a suit, partner should realize, in view of the announced strength of the opening bid, that your suit takeout is based on little high-card strength and that you are co-operating by placing the bid in what you think is the best contract. *This minimum response to the double of one notrump is obviously not forcing.*

Partner doubles one notrump. With

♠ 6 5 2   ♥ 8 7 5 3 2   ♦ J 8 3   ♣ Q 7   Bid 2 hearts

With

♠ 6 5 2   ♥ J 8 6 3   ♦ J 7 5 4   ♣ 9 6

Pass and hope for the best. If an opponent redoubles, bid two diamonds.

In general, on any hand that clearly demonstrates that your partnership has the balance of power, pass for a penalty; *even if there is a redouble.*

The following hand is a borderline case, and you bid two diamonds only, because the strength is all in one suit. Your hand may be worth only one trick on defense if your partner does not lead diamonds.

♠ 7 5 2   ♥ 6 3 2   ♦ A Q 8 5 4   ♣ 7 6

With

♠ A J 9 5 2   ♥ Q 7 5   ♦ K 6 3   ♣ 9 7

pass for a penalty, because you have more than you need to guarantee the balance of power in your partnership's favor.

With freak distribution and two or more honor-tricks, make a jump suit takeout if game seems reasonably sure.

  ♠ A Q 10 7 6 3 2   ♡ K 8 7   ◊ 8 5   ♣ 3

Take out the double by bidding three spades.

Strength-Showing Responses

Holding over two plus honor-tricks, and a strong four-card suit or any biddable five-card suit, the doubler's partner shows his strength by making a jump response. At least 10 points in high cards. (Exception—6-card suits with less honor strength.)

1. When the jump response can be made at the level of two, it should be made with any biddable four-card suit, especially a major suit.

Take out partner's double of one heart with *two* spades, holding

  ♠ K J 6 2   ♡ 5 3   ◊ A Q 7   ♣ 10 8 6 4

2. When the jump response requires a bid of three, the suit should contain at least five cards.

The doubled bid being one heart, bid *three* diamonds holding

  ♠ 8 6 5   ♡ 6   ◊ A Q J 6 4   ♣ K 8 4 3

3. With a six-card suit, the response may be made at either two-odd or three-odd with only 1½ honor-tricks.

For example, take out partner's double of one spade with *three* hearts, holding

  ♠ 6 2   ♡ K 6 5 4 3 2   ◊ A 5 4   ♣ 7 6

The jump response to a takeout double is *not forcing*.

The "Cue-Bid" Response

If the partner responds by bidding the doubled suit, he is almost making a "takeout double" of his own. He denies great strength in the opponent's suit (with which he would have made a notrump response) and shows that he can support the other suits; the doubler may now take his choice.

This is a strong response, showing two or more honor-tricks. *It is forcing for one round.*

South	West	North	East
1 ♢	Double	Pass	2 ♢

East may hold ♠ 10 8 7 4   ♡ K Q 9 7   ♢ 4   ♣ A 10 7 3.

The Pre-emptive Response

Holding a six-card or longer major suit, with unbalanced distribution, a jump to game (four-odd) may be made with about one honor-trick. Usually this preëmptive response is made with seven-card or longer suits.

Respond four spades to a double of any other suit with:

♠ Q J 10 7 6 4 2   ♡ 8 5 3   ♢ 9 2   ♣ 8

Free Responses to Takeout Doubles

When the intervening opponent makes any bid over partner's takeout double, the doubler's partner is relieved of the obligation to respond. Any bid he makes at this point shows some strength.

In general these are the requirements for free bids when partner has doubled for a takeout:

1. *At the level of one:* bid a five-card major suit headed by ½ honor-trick, even with nothing outside.

2. *At the level of two:* Bid a five-card suit, major or minor, if the hand contains at least one honor-trick. Bid a six-card major suit headed by ½ honor-trick, even with nothing outside.

3. *At the level of three or four:* The hand should contain 1½ honor-tricks with any five-card suit; with a six-card major suit one honor-trick is enough.

Four-card suits require an additional ½ honor-trick in each case.

Assume that the bidding has been:

South	West	North	East
1 ♣	Double	1 ♡	

East may now bid one spade, holding:

♠ K 10 8 6 4   ♡ 6 5   ♢ 8 6 4 2   ♣ 6 3

He should not bid two diamonds unless he holds as much as

♠ K 9 6	♡ 7 4 3	◇ Q J 10 6 3	♣ 8 4
or ♠ K 10 6	♡ 7 4	◇ A 10 8 6	♣ 9 6 5 2

A one-notrump response in this case would show a stopper in clubs, but not necessarily a stopper in hearts (West's takeout double having implied sufficient heart strength to stop the suit). With no stopper in either suit, East should avoid bidding notrump. Any notrump bid at this point shows about 1½ honor-tricks:

| ♠ Q 6 | ♡ 7 4 3 | ◇ A J 8 | ♣ Q 9 6 4 2 | bid one notrump |

With four or more cards in North's suit, and 1½ honor-tricks, East should *double*.

| ♠ 6 3 | ♡ J 8 6 4 | ◇ A Q 6 | ♣ J 9 4 3 | double |

PROCEDURE WHEN THE TAKEOUT DOUBLE IS REDOUBLED

In this situation:

SOUTH	WEST	NORTH	EAST
1 ♡	Double	Redouble	?

East should now act almost as though North's redouble were a bid. In other words, with a weak hand East should usually pass; any bid he makes is in the nature of a free bid. He should take action as follows:

1. With a five-card suit and about ½ honor-trick in his hand; or with a six-card suit, no matter how weak his hand; East should bid his suit.

In the above bidding situation, East should now bid one spade, holding

| ♠ 9 8 6 5 3 2 | ♡ 7 4 3 | ◇ 9 6 | ♣ 5 4 |

East should bid two clubs, holding

| ♠ K 8 2 | ♡ 8 5 4 | ◇ 6 3 | ♣ 8 7 5 3 2 |

But East should pass, if he has a weak hand and no long suit:

| ♠ 8 6 4 | ♡ 5 3 2 | ◇ Q 8 7 2 | ♣ 9 4 3 | Pass |
| ♠ 9 7 5 2 | ♡ 7 5 4 2 | ◇ Q 6 5 | ♣ 10 7 | Pass |

The pass on weakness in this position often gives partner, who doubled, an opportunity to rescue himself from the redoubled situation with a lower bid than would have been possible had a weakness takeout been made. If in the above bidding situation East takes out with two diamonds on this hand:

| ♠ 10 9 5 | ♡ 8 6 4 | ◇ J 8 6 5 | ♣ 8 7 2 |

Then West, who may have little support for diamonds but a long, strong club suit, will have to bid *three* clubs. A pass by East permits West to take out the redouble with a bid of only *two* clubs.

2. Being warned that both opponents have fairly strong hands, the doubler's partner does not make a *jump* response over the redouble without about 2 honor-tricks and a fairly strong five-card or longer suit.

It is unnecessary to make a jump bid in this position without a strong suit, as any bid shows some strength.

In the above situation, East would respond *two* spades with

♠ A Q 10 6 5   ♡ 8 4 3   ◊ K 7 2   ♣ 8 4

3. A response of one notrump still shows a strong hand (never less than 1 honor-trick), but it should not be made over the redouble without a stopper in the opponents' suit.

East, in the bidding situation previously shown, should bid two clubs, not one notrump, with

♠ K 8 7   ♡ J 10 3   ◊ A 6 5   ♣ 10 6 5 4

WHEN THE REDOUBLED CONTRACT IS ONE NOTRUMP

As in all cases when a *penalty* double is redoubled, when one notrump is doubled and redoubled the doubler's partner should *pass* a strong hand. The pass in this position means that the doubler's partner is satisfied with the double and believes the contract can be defeated.

With one honor-trick or more, the pass is proper.

SOUTH	WEST	NORTH	EAST
1 N T	Double	Redouble	

East passes, holding:

♠ Q 8   ♡ K 7 4 3   ◊ 8 6 4   ♣ Q 6 5 2

With less than one honor-trick; or with one honor-trick or slightly more, but all his strength in one suit, the doubler's partner should take out the double in his best suit. (See page 268.)

Rebids After a Takeout Double

It is important in every department of bidding to avoid making two free bids on a hand which justifies only one. This error must be particularly avoided by the player who has made a takeout double.

Until partner confirms the possession of some strength by making a free bid, the doubler must assume his partner's hand to be an absolute minimum.

Therefore, having doubled and received a forced one-spade response, the doubler should raise to two spades but never to three or four spades, holding ♠ K J 7 5 ♡ A 6 ◇ K Q 9 2 ♣ Q 6 2. He must not fall into the error of raising as though his partner's bid were a free one. A three-spade raise would show something like ♠ A Q J 2 ♡ K J 4 ◇ A K 6 5 ♣ K 5.

The doubler's partner, if he is intelligent, will realize how strong the doubler must be to give him a double raise, and having been raised at once to three spades he will proceed to bid four spades with even so weak a hand as ♠ K 8 7 5 4 and nothing else.

In order to raise at once to four spades the doubler should be prepared to play at four spades with nothing more than four small cards of the trump suit in his partner's hand. This high requirement may, of course, be shaded when the doubler holds five cards of his partner's suit and knows that even though the high contract may not be made, it cannot be set badly; for example, having doubled one club and received a one-spade response, the doubler may raise at once to four spades with: ♠ K Q 8 7 4 ♡ A Q 10 5 ◇ K Q 6 ♣ 2.

The same situation should be kept in mind when the doubler, after receiving only a minimum response, bids two notrump, whether it is a jump bid or not. He can count on nothing from his partner and must be prepared to play the hand for eight tricks all alone or to rescue himself if doubled. The responder should raise with about one honor-trick.

Rebidding a Major Suit

The doubler's partner will respond on the supposition that he will find four trumps in either major. The doubler, remembering this, should not at a later stage bid a major suit unless it contains at least five cards. By doubling first and then bidding a major suit the doubler asks his partner for a raise with three small trumps and only about one honor-trick outside.

Jump Bid After Doubling for Takeout

A jump bid in a new suit by a player who previously doubled for a takeout is not forcing, but it shows a powerful hand which will produce game if partner has about a trick in support. This support may consist of either a high-card trick, or merely a distributional trick such as a singleton with three trumps or a doubleton with four trumps.

For example, South holds:

  ♠ K Q J 8 4 2 ♡ 7   ◊ K Q J ♣ A Q 5

 or ♠ A K Q 10 8 ♡ 8 4 ◊ A K J 4 ♣ K J

In this bidding sequence:

EAST	SOUTH	WEST	NORTH
1 ♡	Double	Pass	2 ◊
Pass			

South should now bid three spades with either hand.

If North holds:

  ♠ 9 7 6 3 ♡ 6 5 ◊ 10 8 7 5 3 ♣ 10 2

 or ♠ 7 6 3   ♡ A 5 2 ◊ 10 8 7 3 ♣ 10 3 2

he should raise partner to four spades; but with

  ♠ 7 6   ♡ Q 6 3 ◊ 10 8 7 5 3 ♣ 10 4 2

North should pass.

If South wants to make sure of reaching game, he must either bid the game, by himself, or cue-bid the opponent's suit.

Doubles of Preëmptive Three-Bids

The double of a preëmptive three-bid is a takeout double which requests partner to bid his best suit. The doubler must therefore be prepared to support any suit partner may bid, or hold an independent suit of his own.

Ordinarily, this double shows about four honor-tricks, but with a singleton in opponent's suit and good playing strength, the double may be shaded to 3½ honor-tricks. Conversely, with three cards in opponent's suit, about 4½ honor-tricks should be held.

It should be borne in mind that there is no perfect defense against preëmptive bids. Fair results on the average are all that can be expected. Possible gain must be weighed against possible loss in each individual case.

The following hands are good doubles of an opponent's three-spade opening. You can double with hands slightly weaker.

1. ♠ 6   ♡ A 10 8 4   ◇ K Q 9 8 3   ♣ A Q 10
2. ♠ 6 3   ♡ A Q 10 7   ◇ K Q 8 7   ♣ A Q 8
3. ♠ 6 3 2   ♡ K Q J 4   ◇ A Q 6   ♣ A Q J

The doubler's partner should take out the double except in two contingencies:

1. With his strength and length in opponent's suit, he should pass and thus convert the double into a penalty double.

2. With three or four cards in opponent's suit and a generally hopeless hand, he may pass as the lesser evil, rather than risk a probable severe penalty. Fortunately, the responder to such doubles is rarely in this unhappy position.

Barring these two contingencies, responder should take out in his best suit. With about two honor-tricks and a fair five-card major suit, or a six-card major with about 1½ honor-tricks, responder should jump to game (if a jump is needed, as with four spades over the double of three hearts).

In this sequence:

WEST	NORTH	EAST	SOUTH
3 ♡	Double	Pass	

South should pass if he holds:

♠ 9 4   ♡ J 5 4 3   ◇ 10 4 3 2   ♣ 9 5 4
or ♠ Q 5   ♡ Q J 8 7   ◇ K 5 3   ♣ 10 8 4 2

South should bid four diamonds with:

♠ J 4   ♡ 7 6   ◇ K 10 8 6 3   ♣ J 9 6 4

South should bid three spades with:

♠ J 9 6 3 2   ♡ J 5 3   ◇ 6   ♣ Q 8 3 2

South should bid four spades with:

♠ Q J 8 4 2   ♡ 9   ◇ A 9 7 4   ♣ K 3 2

The Double of a Four-Bid

The double of a preëmptive four-bid is a penalty double, but the doubler should nevertheless contemplate the possibility that partner may take out if he has a strong suit—particularly if the doubled bid is hearts and responder has spades. Consequently, though doubling primarily for a penalty, the doubler should have distributed strength, not a hand with all or most of the strength concentrated in opponent's suit.

About 3½ honor-tricks is the minimum for this double.

Partner should take out at the four-level with two honor-tricks and a good five-card suit, preferably a major suit, or with one honor-trick and a good six-card suit; or with any seven-card suit.

At the five-level, the takeout requires a strong six-card suit or a very strong five-card suit.

Double an opposing four-heart bid with:

♠ A Q 6   ♥ 6 2   ♦ K Q 5   ♣ A J 10 7 3

or ♠ A 10 6   ♥ A J 4   ♦ K 5 4   ♣ K J 6 2

The doubler's partner should take out to four spades with:

♠ J 10 8 5 3   ♥ 7 5 3   ♦ A 8 2   ♣ K 5

He should take out to five diamonds with:

♠ 8   ♥ 9 3   ♦ A J 10 7 6 3 2   ♣ 9 5 4

CHAPTER TWENTY-THREE

STRENGTH-SHOWING OVERCALLS

Most strong hands which the defender will hold he will show by the use of the takeout double. For other types of strong hands there are specialized strength-showing bids which show the hand type as well as the strength.

The Jump Overcall

A jump overcall *of exactly one trick* in a suit (as, *two* spades over an opponent's bid of one heart) shows a hand containing about 3½ honor-tricks, with:

1. *Two five-card or longer suits.* With such a hand a take-out double may lose a round of bidding.

2. *A hand containing one strong suit, and in all eight winners.*

The advantage of the strength-showing jump overcall is found in the following cases:

1. Suppose South bids one diamond and West, second-hand, holds:

♠ A K 10 5 4   ♡ A Q J 7 5   ◇ 6   ♣ 3 2

If West doubles, East's response will probably be two clubs. West must then bid two spades and risk having the bidding dropped (though East may have support for hearts); or bid *three* spades, which forces him to a game contract even though East may have no support for either suit.

The jump overcall shows one of the two suits and gives the proper impression of strength at the same time; it asks for a light raise, yet retains the advantage of being able to pass short of game if partner has a blank.

2. Suppose South bids one diamond and West holds:

♠ A Q 10 9 6 5 3   ♡ 6   ◇ A K 5   ♣ 3 2

If West doubles and East responds two clubs, West does not know whether East has a Yarborough, or something like x x x in spades and Q J x or a doubleton in diamonds, which would make game possible on a finesse. If West makes a jump overcall, bidding two spades, East will respond with the barest sort of support, and will pass safely if he has no support.

A single-jump overcall to three of a minor suit is a strength-showing bid, exactly as is the jump overcall in a major. But while in a major the jump overcall invites a raise, in a minor it invites a notrump response.

Therefore a minor-suit jump overcall practically guarantees a long, ready-made suit, with some high cards (not necessarily Aces or Kings) in side suits, and in all about eight winners.

Overcall an opponent's one-spade bid with three clubs, holding

♠ 6 2   ♡ Q 8   ◊ K J   ♣ A K Q J 7 4 2

The overcall may (rarely) be made on a nearly-ready-made suit with a stopper in the opponents' suit:

♠ A 2   ♡ Q 8   ◊ K J   ♣ K Q J 10 7 4 2

for if partner can bid three notrump he, too, must have a spade stopper, and the combined holding will provide time to establish and run the club suit.

Responding to the Jump Overcall

In general, some response should be made to a major-suit jump overcall when holding about one honor-trick. With some trump support (such as three small cards and a singleton) ½ honor-trick will do. A notrump takeout should include a stopper in the opponents' suit. A suit takeout shows at least 1½ honor-tricks.

If partner overcalls an opposing one-diamond bid with two spades, you should

Bid three spades with	♠ 8 6 4	♡ K 7 5 2	◊ 8 3	♣ Q J 7 6
Bid three spades with	♠ 8 6 4	♡ 6	◊ 9 8 5 3	♣ K 7 6 4 2
Bid two notrump with	♠ 8 6	♡ J 7 4	◊ Q 10 8 5	♣ Q J 6 3
Pass with	♠ 10 5	♡ 8 4 3	◊ J 9 8 5	♣ Q 10 7 6

With a sure stopper in the opponents' suit and a smattering of strength outside (in all, 1 to 1½ honor-tricks) respond in notrump to partner's minor-suit jump overcall. A suit takeout requires a strong rebiddable suit.

If partner overcalls an opposing one-heart bid with three diamonds, you should

Bid three notrump with	♠ J 8 5	♡ Q J 6	◊ 7 4	♣ A 8 6 5 2
Pass with	♠ Q 8 5	♡ Q 7 6	◊ 7 4 3	♣ Q 9 5 4
Bid three spades with	♠ K Q 10 8 6 2	♡ 7 4	◊ 8 3	♣ K 6 2

The Immediate Overcall

By far the strongest of all bids available to the defenders is an immediate bid of the suit which the opponents have already bid. It shows:

4½ or more honor-tricks. With a void in the opponents' suit, this may be reduced to 4 honor-tricks.

The Ace or a void (first-round control) or at worst a singleton, in the opponents' suit.

This cue-bid overcall is forcing for at least one round, and because of the strength shown it is usually carried on to game; but it may be dropped short of game if the responding hand is hopelessly weak.

In effect, this cue-bid is a gigantic takeout double; partner responds to it as to a takeout double; and the cue-bidder may force to game by making a jump bid in a new suit at his next turn.

A player might overcall an opposing one-club bid with two clubs on a hand like this

♠ K J 8 5 4   ♡ K Q J 6   ◊ A Q J 7   ♣ —

He does not double because he does not want to risk a penalty pass by partner.

There is no maximum strength for a cue-bid; it may be as strong as a forcing two-bid. Any of the following hands would justify a two-club overcall of an opposing one-club bid:

1.	♠ K Q 10 6	♡ A K Q 5 4	◊ K J 10	♣ A
2.	♠ A K 7 5	♡ K Q J 10	◊ K Q J 6	♣ 3
3.	♠ A K Q 10 5 4 2	♡ A Q J 6	◊ K Q	♣ —

THE FORCING NOTRUMP OVERCALL

As powerful in its way as the overcall in the opponents' suit is the notrump overcall of an opponents' preëmptive four- or five-bid.

SOUTH	WEST	NORTH	EAST
4 ♠	4 N T	Pass	

Now East is expected to respond as though to a takeout double; and in fact the four-notrump overcall *is* a takeout double; albeit an exceptionally powerful one. West's hand is probably on the order of

♠ 6   ♡ K J 10 9   ◇ A K Q 6   ♣ A K J 4

NOTRUMP OVERCALLS

Any overcall of an opposing bid with a notrump bid is equivalent to an opening one-notrump bid (16–18 points) and shows a strong hand, usually at least as strong as would be required for a takeout double except that the distribution is balanced and a substantial part of the strength is in the opponents' suit.

An opponent's bid of one heart may be overcalled with one notrump on any of the following hands:

1.	♠ Q 6 5	♡ A Q 6	◇ K Q J 8	♣ Q J 6
2.	♠ K 8	♡ Q 10 9 7	◇ A K 8 4	♣ A 6 3
3.	♠ A 9	♡ J 9 5 4 2	◇ A K 6	♣ K J 5

Partner should respond as though it were an opening one-notrump bid.

A notrump overcall at the two- or three-level is usually based on a strong minor of five or more cards, and must have enough sure winners to be safe under the Rule of 2 and 3.

South opens with one spade, West passes, North raises to two spades. East bids two notrump on

♠ K J 6   ♡ A 7 4   ◇ A K Q 9 5   ♣ Q 7

Partner should raise with two winners in high cards.

An overcall of an opposing preëmptive three-bid with three

notrump is not a "takeout" bid and partner is expected to pass unless he can see a probable game in a suit of his own.

South opens with three spades; West holds

♠ A 6   ♡ K 9   ◇ A K Q J 7 2   ♣ Q 10 6

The hand will win at least seven tricks, and the ♡ A in partner's hand will produce game.

Many fine players do, however, prefer to use this three-no-trump overcall as a signal to partner to take out, and a clear understanding on this point between partners is advisable.

CHAPTER TWENTY-FOUR

THE

PENALTY DOUBLE

The purpose of a penalty double is to defeat the opponents' contract and collect the maximum possible number of points in undertrick penalties. Any double is meant for penalties when it conforms to the following conditions:

1. *When partner has bid, doubled or redoubled; or has made a penalty pass of a previous takeout double.*
2. *Even when partner has not bid, if the double is not made at the doubler's first opportunity.*
3. *Whenever the doubled bid is in notrump, or is four of a suit, or higher.*
4. *When the player who doubles has made an opening bid in notrump or of two or more in a suit.*

PENALTIES VS. TRICK SCORES

Before deciding to make a penalty double of an opponent's bid the player should estimate the points he can score by doubling. He should compare these with the value of the part-score, game or slam he and his partner can bid and make.

A reasonably sure game should not be abandoned in favor of a penalty double unless the opponents can almost surely be defeated two tricks if vulnerable and three tricks if not vulnerable. Either counts 500 points, roughly equivalent to the actual value of a game. When the 500-point penalty can safely be expected, it is usually better to take the penalty than to bid game.

A *sure* small slam or grand slam should usually be preferred to any penalty double of non-vulnerable opponents. Under the present scoring, a team which is not vulnerable can profitably accept a seven-trick set to avert a vulnerable small slam, and an eleven-trick set (2100 points) to prevent a vulnerable grand slam which is worth at the minimum 2140 points. Provided the opponents play the hand in their best trump suit, it is almost incredible that they will be defeated by so much.

A part-score is worth roughly 160 points, and in theory it is better to defeat vulnerable opponents one trick doubled (200 points) except that, with a margin of only one trick, there is danger that something will go wrong.

The Two-Trick Rule

Any penalty double must be based on the expectancy of defeating the contract by two tricks. "Sporting" doubles on a margin of but one trick are never advisable.* Even when the opponents have bid a game it is not wise to double on a margin of one trick. Declarer may obtain from the double information which will enable him to locate an important honor, and by finessing for that honor he may make his contract.

CLASSIFICATION OF DOUBLES

Penalty doubles fall roughly into two groups:
1. Light Doubles.
A light penalty double is a double of an opposing part-score contract which, even if made, will not be sufficient for game. For example, if the opponents make one notrump or two diamonds undoubled they score 40 points; if they make two diamonds doubled they score 80 points, less than game. A light double must be a double of one in any suit or notrump, or of two in a minor suit.
2. Tight Doubles.
A tight double is a penalty double of an opponent's game

---

* Except in a duplicate game with match-point scoring.

bid, or a double of a part-score contract which, if doubled and
made, will give them game.

Light Doubles

The player who makes a light double thinks that the greatest
potential profits can be obtained from doubling the opponents,
but—usually because the bidding is still at a very low level—
he has not yet received enough information about his partner's
hand to be sure.

The light double is by nature tentative.*

Almost all light doubles are made when partner opens the
bidding and an opponent overcalls. The opening bid being
only partly informative, the responder cannot be sure of the
sort of hand his partner holds.

For example, consider the following bidding with East and West vulnerable:

SOUTH	WEST	NORTH	EAST
1 ♡	2 ◇	?	

North holds:

♠ A J 4   ♡ 6   ◇ J 6 4 2   ♣ K J 7 6 5

If South has two or three diamonds and three or four honor-tricks outside, West's two-diamond overcall can probably be defeated 500 or 800
points. If South has a long string of hearts headed by the Ace-King and
perhaps the King of spades on the side, the two-diamond bid may be made.
North cannot be sure which sort of hand South has, yet if he bids or passes
he has irretrievably lost his chance to double.

Waiting, as most players do, for a holding of five strong
trumps before doubling an opponent's overcall not only sur-
renders most of the best doubling opportunities but is also
futile. When ten or eleven cards of the same suit are divided
between two hands, the entire deal is probably so freakish
(see Law of Symmetry, page 427) that the opponents can readily
find a good escape suit in which they have fair trump control.

The light double may be effective even against a player
whose vulnerable overcalls conform strictly to the Rule of Two
and Three. Caught between two strong hands, without trump

---

* Hence it was formerly called the Tentative Double.

support or an entry in partner's hand, even a sound vulnerable
overcall may lose three tricks. A three-trick vulnerable penalty
is 800 points, which is greater than the value of any game.

The following hand seems to be a safe overcall of two diamonds, even
when vulnerable:

♠ Q J 6   ♡ 9   ♢ A K J 7 4 2   ♣ K J 5

But give partner a singleton diamond and no entry with which to finesse
and this hand may win only four or five tricks, yet the opponents probably
have not a game in hearts.

REQUIREMENTS FOR A LIGHT DOUBLE

Make a light penalty double of an opponent's vulnerable
overcall in the following circumstances:

*1. The opponents' contract, if made, must not equal a game
even at its doubled value.*

2. The doubler must hold about 2+ honor-tricks.

*3. The doubler must be short (usually no more than two
cards) in partner's suit if a major, and never more than three
cards in a major or minor.*

*4. The doubler must have at least 10 x x x or Q x x in the
opponents' suit.*

The fact that the doubler holds a biddable suit of his own,
even though it be a five-card major suit, should not deter him
from doubling provided the other conditions are fulfilled. The
following hands call for light doubles, partner having opened
with one spade and the next player having overcalled with
two clubs:

1.	♠ A 6	♡ Q 10 5 4	♢ K 10 3	♣ J 10 4 2
2.	♠ 7	♡ A K 8 5 4	♢ J 9 4 3	♣ Q 6 5
3.	♠ 5 4	♡ A K 6	♢ 10 8 4 3 2	♣ Q J 5

THE FACTOR OF VULNERABILITY

The requirements given above govern cases in which the
opponents are vulnerable and also cases in which both sides
are vulnerable. An expected two-trick set of a vulnerable player
is as suitable a choice as trying for a vulnerable game.

When the doubler's side is vulnerable and the opponents
are not vulnerable, a three-trick set is necessary to repay the

loss of the game. The requirements for the double must therefore be tightened up, not as regards honor-tricks so much as
regards trump strength.

Thus, double an opponent's two-diamond overcall of partner's one-spade
bid when opponents are vulnerable, holding:

♠ Q 6   ♡ K Q 7   ◊ Q 9 6 4   ♣ A J 4 3

But bid two notrump on the same hand when opponents are not vulnerable.

Double even when the opponents are not vulnerable, holding:

♠ 6   ♡ A K 5   ◊ Q J 8 3   ♣ Q 8 7 5 4

PROCEDURE OF DOUBLER'S PARTNER

When partner has made a light double, the opener should
usually pass when his hand is of balanced distribution (containing no void or singleton). He will then have at least two
cards in the opponents' suit and will be able to lead trumps,
preventing declarer's making his small trumps separately by
ruffing. The only time the double is taken out on balanced
hands is when the opener has a strong six-card major suit or
a hand containing two five-card suits and the minimum in
honor-tricks.

For example, partner's light double of two diamonds should not be left
in when the opening bid was made on ♠ 8 6 ♡ A K Q 7 4 2 ◊ 6 3
♣ Q 8 6. A rebid of two hearts is preferable.

*The opener should usually take out the double with a void
or singleton in the opponents' suit,* for in those cases his distribution is unbalanced and aided by 2½ honor-tricks in partner's hand is likely to produce a game.

THE LIGHT DOUBLE AFTER A NOTRUMP BID

The greatest opportunities for paying doubles occur when
partner has made an opening bid of one notrump and an opponent is so foolish as to overcall. The notrump bid gives so
much information that the responder can gauge the defensive
possibilities of the combined hands with extreme precision.

Consider the following case:

SOUTH	WEST	NORTH	EAST
Pass	1 N T	2 ♣	

East holds ♠ A 4 2 ♡ 10 7 5 3 ◇ K J ♣ 10 6 5 4. He knows that West has at least 3½ honor-tricks and at least ♣ Q x or three clubs. Therefore, East-West have between them five honor-tricks to North's three; and probably seven clubs to North's six. A big penalty is almost sure, whereas with only five honor-tricks and no long suit a notrump game for East and West would be unlikely.

The notrump bidder does not take out a penalty double of this type, for he has already given exact information on his hand and must assume that the doubler knows what he is doing.

Tight Doubles

A *tight double* announces that the doubler is convinced the opponents can be defeated enough to compensate for any makeable contract, and is willing to assume the risk on the basis of his own hand and what information he has already received about his partner's hand.

A tight double is based upon an actual count of defensive winners.

COUNT OF DEFENSIVE WINNERS

In valuing your hand for a penalty double,

1. Count your honor-tricks, exclusive of trump tricks.

2. Count as winners guarded honors in the opponents' trump suit and, whenever they are sure to develop, ruffers.

3. Add the minimum number of honor-tricks shown by partner's bids.

4. Subtract the total from 13, the difference being the trick-taking limit of the opponents. If this limit is at least 1½ tricks short of the opponents' contract—and if you cannot expect a greater gain at a bid of your own—make a penalty double. Of course a *sure* one-trick set is all right. Count as certain only sure trump tricks and Aces (except when there is an indication that an Ace may be ruffed).

Taking Out a Tight Double

Doubler's partner should be reluctant to take out a tight double. However, at the two-level, some protection must be given the doubler. A void in trumps is a highly unfavorable holding, and it is safer for the doubler's partner to take out unless he has about a trick more than the 2½ minimum. A singleton in the doubled suit is also somewhat unfavorable, and with 5–5–2–1 distribution, or a six-card suit, a takeout of the double is usually advisable.

At the three-level, a takeout of the double is rarely advisable—then, only when the hand has some feature of which partner is still unaware, and in addition, when a safe landing place is assured.

At the four-level, a singleton or void in opponent's suit is not unfavorable—it means that the opponent is going to get a bad break.

But the tight penalty double should be taken out when the doubler's partner has seriously deceived the doubler by a previous bid—such as making an opening bid with only 1 or 1½ honor-tricks in his hand—or when his distribution is freakish and his previous bidding has not revealed the fact. Holding a freak hand may justify taking out a penalty double in one of the following cases:

1. When a more advantageous trick-score can be made, but the doubler is not aware of it.

2. When the doubler is evidently counting on tricks which his partner knows he cannot win.

Penalty Doubles of Notrump Bids

The penalty double of an opening one-notrump bid is treated on page 260.

A double when an opponent overcalls partner's opening suit bid with one notrump is a light double, thus telling your partner that your side has the balance of power, either in high cards or in the clear ability to defeat the notrump overcall.

A double of a one-notrump overcall is based upon the Rule of Eight. The opening bid has shown 2½ honor-tricks. If the responder also has 2½ honor-tricks he knows that his side has 5 out of a total of 8½, and that the opponent has probably 3½ honor-tricks at most. With this advantage in honor-tricks, and with the added advantage of the opening lead, the one-notrump bid can probably be defeated by two tricks; and if partner has more than a minimum, the penalty should be three tricks.

Playing conditions will modify the Rule of Eight, which gives only a rough estimate of trick expectancy. If the doubler has a fit with his partner's suit, something like Q x x or J 10 x, and if his hand contains distributed strength with several tens and nines, he may double a one-notrump overcall with about two honor-tricks.

Though this is a light double, the opener is expected to pass it unless his distribution is highly unbalanced, consisting of a two-suiter or of one long weak suit which cannot be established at notrump.

DOUBLES OF NOTRUMP GAME BIDS

An opponent's three-notrump contract should be doubled when the defenders hold four honor-tricks, but rarely will they have this opportunity. Three notrump is a contract seldom attempted without at least six honor-tricks in the combined hands of declarer and dummy, leaving only 2½ or 3 honor-tricks as the portion of the defenders.

A player should not double· an adverse three-notrump contract, as a rule, unless he holds (or knows from the bidding that his partner holds) a leadable long suit and sufficient stoppers and entries to establish and cash it before declarer has time to win nine tricks.

When such a suit is available, value the defensive power of the hand as follows:

1. Decide upon the suit to be opened and estimate its combined length and strength in the partnership hands.

2. Determine how many stoppers declarer's side probably holds in the suit.

You will need as many entries as the number of declarer's stoppers, *plus one.*

The opening lead may be counted as one of the required entries. The other entries must be honor-tricks which the doubler holds or which he can safely assume that his partner holds. Also counted as an entry is a guarded honor in a suit which is one of declarer's strongest and which he will therefore have to establish.

Neither a count of honor-tricks nor accurate valuation of a long suit may be entirely relied upon in doubling a notrump bid. When declarer's side has a long established suit, he may be able to run off nine tricks before the defenders ever get the lead to make use of their own long suits or honor-tricks. When there is a wide-open minor suit, whether it has been bid by declarer's side or not, the prospective doubler must consider the fact that it may be the basis of the notrump contract, especially if strong opponents have apparently bid higher than their honor-tricks warrant.

The Effect of a Penalty Double on Leads

A double of a three-notrump contract (and in fact any penalty double of a notrump bid) strongly implies the fact that the doubler is dependent upon a strong suit to open. When he has bid a suit it is probably his own suit that he is planning to establish; if his partner has bid a suit, it is probably his partner's suit.

When your partner bids, then doubles a notrump contract, open his suit. If he has not bid, but you have, open your suit. If both of you have bid, choose as explained on the preceding page. With no strong suit, open a suit which dummy has bid but not rebid, and which declarer has not raised.

See also lead-directing doubles of slam bids, page 522.

The Effect of Leads on Penalty Doubles

No matter how good a chance you seem to have of defeating the opponents' notrump contract, unless you have the opening lead yourself you must take your partner's expected lead into consideration. If he is likely to make a lead which will nullify your chance of defeating the contract, you must refrain from doubling.

In the absence of any bidding information your partner will probably open his best suit against the doubled notrump contract, but if he has no fairly good suit of his own he will open some suit which has been bid by declarer's partner. His reason for doing this is that you would not have a safe double if there were great danger of dummy's long suit being run against you; therefore, you must have strength in that suit. In doubling you must therefore anticipate the danger or the possibility of a lead through dummy's suit and should refrain from doubling if you cannot stand that lead and yet defeat the contract; but should double more freely if that is the lead you most desire.

When dummy has bid two suits, partner's obvious choice would be what appears to be the weaker of these two suits— usually the one which dummy bid second.

Honor-Tricks and Penalty Doubles

A penalty double, like an opening bid, is based largely upon defensive honor-tricks. With nothing but length and strength in the opponents' trump suit one should almost never make a penalty double, particularly a light double. Partner may take the double out, and will be crucified at his own contract because your only strength is in the suit in which he is not interested.

If your partner bids one heart and an opponent overcalls with one spade, there is nothing worse than making a penalty double with a hand like:

♠ K J 10 6 4 2   ♡ 8 3   ◇ J 6 5   ♣ 9 7

The best procedure is to pass. Now if partner happens to be strong enough in the other suits to make a takeout double of the one-spade bid you are in a position to pass for penalties, and partner will not be deceived as to the nature of your hand.

When to Redouble

A redouble is a double of a double. It is the "you're another" answer to the opponents' assertion that they think they can defeat the contract.*

If a player redoubles and makes his contract, he gets four times the undoubled value of the trick score. For any over-

---

* See also redoubles of takeout doubles, page 242.

trick he makes he gets 200 points not vulnerable and 400 points vulnerable. On the other hand, if he is defeated at his redoubled contract, he loses heavily, the regular doubled penalty points being doubled again.

The question of whether or not to redouble depends upon considerations of (1) vulnerability, (2) the amount of the contract, and (3) safety.

1. Vulnerability. Unless an overtrick can be made, the player gains no more by making a redoubled contract when vulnerable than when not vulnerable; but if defeated at a redoubled contract his vulnerable loss is twice as great. Greater caution in redoubling is therefore required when vulnerable.

2. Amount of contract. The higher the contract the greater the possible gain by redoubling. Three diamonds, if doubled and made, score 120 points; if redoubled, score 240 points, a gain of 120. If the contract is defeated, the vulnerable loss will be 400 points for the first trick, instead of 200, a net loss of 200 points. In any close question a player stands to lose almost twice as much by redoubling a part-score contract and being defeated, as he can gain if he makes it; unless he must redouble to make game.

As a general rule, part-score and game contracts should not be redoubled when vulnerable unless the contract is reasonably sure, with an overtrick possible. They should be redoubled when not vulnerable if the contract is sure, irrespective of overtricks.

Any slam contract shows a much greater gain, particularly in major suits. Six spades bid and made count, if redoubled, 720 points in the trick score; a gain of 360 over the doubled score. The added loss by a one-trick defeat is still only 200 points, even when vulnerable, and 100 points when not vulnerable. Any major-suit or notrump slam should therefore be redoubled when there is a good chance of the contract's being made and no chance of its being defeated more than one trick.

Minor-suit slam bids and major-suit game bids score about the same number of trick-points. Whether or not to redouble is always a close question, and in general should be decided by the vulnerability conditions.

3. Safety. Whenever a player is doubled and nevertheless has a good chance to make an overtrick, there is something wrong. Of course, he may have freakish distribution for which his opponents were not prepared; and there is a further possibility that an opponent has made a stupid and hasty double. In most cases, however, it is wiser to give your opponents credit for their share of intelligence. There may be some almost inconceivably bad break of which you are not aware. A "safe" redouble means that the declarer has taken into consideration the most unusual bad breaks.

Factors of psychology and strategy sometimes make it unwise to redouble, because the opponents will become frightened and run to their own suit, whereas the player is better off playing at his own contract, doubled.

PENALTY AND TAKEOUT DOUBLES

Principal Takeout Double Situations

SOUTH	WEST	NORTH	EAST	
1 ♡	Double			West's first opportunity: partner has not bid.
SOUTH	WEST	NORTH	EAST	
1 ♡	Pass	2 ♡	Double	East's first opportunity: partner has passed.
		or		
1 ♡	Pass	Pass	Double	In this case the double may be somewhat shaded.
SOUTH	WEST	NORTH	EAST	
1 ◇	Pass	3 ◇	Double	East's first opportunity: partner has passed.
SOUTH	WEST	NORTH	EAST	
1 ♡	2 ◇	Pass	2 ♠	Although it is not South's first opportunity to *bid*, it is his first opportunity to *double*. Partner has passed.
Double				
SOUTH	WEST	NORTH	EAST	
1 ♡	Double	3 ♡	Pass	Repeating the takeout double; partner is again requested to bid, even though he did not have a free bid over three hearts.
Pass	Double			

PENALTY AND TAKEOUT DOUBLES—*Continued*

SOUTH	WEST	NORTH	EAST	
1 ♡	Pass	2 ♣	Double	A takeout double, because it is East's first opportunity. A very strong double.

SOUTH	WEST	NORTH	EAST	
1 ♡	Pass	1 ♠	Double	Asking partner to choose between the other two suits.

SOUTH	WEST	NORTH	EAST	
Pass	Pass	1 ♡	Pass	East's first opportunity to
1 ♠	Pass	Pass	Double	double spades. The required strength may be lowered, in order to reopen the bidding.

Principal Penalty Double Situations

SOUTH	WEST	NORTH	EAST	
1 ♡	1 ♠	Double		Partner has bid.

SOUTH	WEST	NORTH	EAST	
1 ♣	Pass	1 N T	Pass	West has passed previously. Hence he was trapping and
Pass	Double			doubles for penalties. East should take out only with a weak hand and a long suit.

SOUTH	WEST	NORTH	EAST	
1 ♡	Pass	1 ♠	Pass	If West were doubling for a takeout he would have doubled
2 ♡	Double			*one* heart.

SOUTH	WEST	NORTH	EAST	
2 N T	Double			If West is strong enough to force partner to bid at *three,* he can defeat two notrump.

SOUTH	WEST	NORTH	EAST	
1 N T	Pass	Pass	2 ♡	South's one-notrump bid has
Double				already depicted a strong balanced hand. The double is for
		or		penalties.
1 N T	2 ♡	Pass	Pass	
Double				

SOUTH	WEST	NORTH	EAST	
2 ♡	3 ◇	Pass	Pass	The opening two-bid was forcing to game. South can bid
Double				anything at this point—and partner must respond. Hence the double is for penalties.

SOUTH	WEST	NORTH	EAST	
1 ♡	Double	2 ♡	Pass	West's first three doubles are for takeout but his last double
Pass	Double	3 ♡	Pass	is for penalties. North should
Pass	Double	4 ♡	Pass	take out only on a very long
Pass	*Double*			suit.

PENALTY AND TAKEOUT DOUBLES—*Continued*

South	West	North	East	
1 ♥	Pass	Pass	1 ♠	Partner has bid. The double by North is a penalty double.
1 N T	Double			

South	West	North	East	
1 ♥	Double	3 ♥	Pass	The first double is for a takeout but the second is for penalties. If West were strong enough to force partner to bid game (but not to defeat the adverse four-heart bid) he should have cue-bid (page 279).
4 ♥	Double			

South	West	North	East	
1 ♥	Double	Redbl.	2 ♣	West's double is for a takeout. North's redouble is the equivalent of a bid. Hence South's double is for penalties.
Double				

South	West	North	East	
1 ♥	Double	Redbl.	2 ♣	Partner has bid.
Pass	Pass	Double		

South	West	North	East	
1 ♥	1 ♠	Pass	2 ♠	South has not doubled at his first opportunity.
Pass	3 ♠	Pass	Pass	
Double				

South	West	North	East	
1 ♥	Double	1 ♠	Double	West's double is for a takeout. But East's is for penalties—partner's double is the equivalent of a bid.

South	West	North	East	
1 ♥	Double	Pass	Pass	East has not bid, *but his penalty pass is equivalent to a bid.*
2 ◇	Double			

OPTIONAL DOUBLES

South	West	North	East	
1 ♥	Pass	4 ♥	Double	North's raise is preëmptive and it is East's first opportunity.

South	West	North	East	
3 ♠	Double			West is prepared for a pass, but East has the option of bidding.
		or		
4 ♥	Double			

South	West	North	East	
1 N T	Double			Although this is by definition a penalty double, partner has the option of taking it out.

CHAPTER TWENTY-FIVE

SLAM
BIDDING*

There is this in common between slam bids and part-score bids: both are deviations from the norm which is game. In both there is a touch of morbidity. The part-score bids represent dwarfish, arrested development of a game, a sort of cretinism due, if I may say so, to the subnormal "secretion" of distributional and honor values. The slam bids are abnormal in the opposite direction: they represent an overgrowth, a kind of gigantism, a sort of oversecretion of the "honor-roid" glands. Both require specialized technique of treatment.

At the same time, slam bids have their roots in lower bids and a slam bid may frequently begin with a bid of one-odd. A slam bid, in order to be successful, must be built on a firm foundation. Even a slight lack of precision in the initial stages of bidding, such as a careless trump rebid or a superfluous forcing bid, magnifies itself from round to round, growing from a whisper to a scream, louder and louder, until it shrieks into a disastrous slam bid. Thus, the sins of an evil opening bid may be visited upon the third and fourth generations of bids.

In a game of average or better-than-average players, if a player never bid slams he would be a heavy loser after but a few sessions. Although slams come up in about 5% of the deals, or, say, roughly every third rubber, their premiums are

---

* The theory and practice of slam bidding described below applies both to point-count and playing-trick valuation. However, the problems of controls, winners and losers are best expressed in terms of honor and playing tricks. For specifics on point-count valuation, see the first part of this book.

so great that they control about 40% of the player's total profit-and-loss column.

Mathematics of Slam Bids

The present small slam premiums are so computed as to be roughly equivalent or slightly more than the total value of a non-vulnerable or a vulnerable game.

1. *The value of the non-vulnerable slam premium (500 points) is almost exactly equal to the value of the first game.*

Suppose a player gambles for a small slam. If he makes it he gains 500 points extra; if he makes but five-odd and is set one trick, his loss is the value of the first game, say, at spades, worth about 420 points, plus 30 points for the overtrick he could have made, plus a penalty of 50 points if undoubled (and it is rare that a small slam is doubled), making a total of 500 points, which he gambled to make an extra 500 points. This offers an exactly even chance to win twice as much or nothing.

2. *If a player is vulnerable and opponents are not vulnerable, by trying for a slam he can gain about 100 points more than the value of his second game (see page 389) and if both sides are vulnerable he breaks about even.*

A blind finesse offers even chances for a full trick or nothing. Therefore, if a player will bid a small slam whenever he can account for eleven sure winners while the twelfth will hinge upon a finesse, he will mathematically neither gain nor lose by bidding a small slam.

It must be remembered, however, that in many cases it will not be necessary for the declarer to take a blind finesse: the declarer has at his disposal a number of plays such as the establishment of a second long suit, a ruff, a throw-in play or a squeeze that may easily eliminate the necessity of making a blind finesse. Hence this rule:

1. A small slam, vulnerable or not vulnerable, should be attempted whenever the estimate of combined hands indicates that the making of the twelfth trick depends upon only one favorable circumstance, such as a finesse.

2. A small slam should not be bid whenever it depends upon

more than one "50–50" circumstance, such as two finesses or a
finesse coupled with a favorable suit break.

	♠ A K Q J	N	♠ 9 8 6 4 2
	♡ A 6	W E	♡ K Q 7 3
	◇ K 7 4	S	◇ A
	♣ K J 10 5		♣ 9 8 7

WEST	EAST
1 ♠	3 ♠
4 N T	5 ◇

Now should West bid six spades or five spades? In this case he should bid
six spades. He knows (as the reader will learn when he reads about the 4–5
Notrump Convention, Chapter 27) that East has only one Ace. He knows
that the spade suit unquestionably will not lose a trick. He knows that East
has at least two honor-tricks. The small slam will probably depend on a
finesse. There are often chances to avoid a finesse. In this case, North may
lead clubs.

Change West's spade holding to ♠ A K 5 3 and he should bid only five
spades. He would require a trump break in addition to a finesse to make a
small slam.

Here the usual argument that a sure rubber "is in the pocket"
while the slam bid is a "gamble" is deadly fallacious. The
person who "pockets his sure rubber" will be forced to put it
up again at the very next deal; meanwhile he has lost forever
an opportunity to place his bet (every bid is a bet) at more
favorable odds than available to the opponents.

VALUE OF A GRAND SLAM

If on the rubber game I bid a grand slam and am defeated
by one trick, by losing a finesse, my loss is the value of a small
slam vulnerable plus 100 points (for an undoubled undertrick)
making a total of 1530 points. Had my finesse succeeded I would
have scored 2210 points, or 750 points more than I could have
scored by stopping at a small slam and making it with an
overtrick. In other words, I have risked 1530 points to gain
750 points, where the blind finesse offered but an equal chance
to win, very foolish odds indeed. Furthermore, a number of
end plays such as a throw-in play, where a trick is given up
in order to gain an extra trick, will not be available at a

grand slam bid. Therefore justifiable odds for a grand slam must be *better* than 2-to-1.

A grand slam should be bid when twelve winners are definitely certain and when the thirteenth winner will fail to materialize only in case of a very bad break. This rule is the same vulnerable or not vulnerable.

A seven-spade contract is justified with these hands, since the contract can be made unless North holds ♠ J x x x. The odds against this are better than 2 to 1. (See the table on page 453.)

SLAM MATHEMATICS READJUSTED BY PSYCHOLOGY

In considering when to bid a small or a grand slam, the mathematics must be drastically revised if the players around the table are of very unequal skill.

Logically, there is no such bid as a grand slam with a weak player if he plays the hand. This rule is indispensable for the weak player's own protection and benefit.

Regarding small-slam bids, there are two principal situations. In one, the player is paired with a weak partner against strong opponents; in the other a player is paired with a strong partner against weak opponents.

Outside of the question of the delicate plays involved in many slam contracts, the longer one plays with a weak player against strong opponents, the greater the mathematical probability of a disaster. Therefore,

With an inferior partner and superior opponents, a small slam should not be bid on an even chance, such as a blind finesse. With a superior partner against inferior opponents, a small slam should be attempted on slightly less than an even chance for success, and a grand slam with slightly less than a 2-to-1 chance.

Choice Between a Trump and a Notrump Slam

A slam bid at a suit is, as a rule, far more flexible, safer, and richer in potential tricks than a notrump slam bid. At a suit-contract, extra tricks are available through ruffs in the dummy; side suits may be established by ruffing the second and subsequent leads of the suit rather than finesse; a trump "strip play" (see Chapter 43) is available. Finally, the entire hand need not hang upon a single finesse which, if unsuccessful, offers the opponents a reëntry and may precipitate a catastrophic avalanche from their established suit.

With a few definite exceptions, all small slams and grand slams should be made at the best suit-bid rather than at notrump.

As a matter of fact, as soon as the slam possibility presents itself to a player he should cast about in search of the best fitting trump bid, be it even a minor.*

Examples of suit slams appear on pages 305-306.

When to Play a Slam in Notrump

A notrump contract rather than a suit contract is chosen for a slam only when:

1. The hands have no long trump suit, but are obviously so strong in honor-tricks and intermediates that the necessary twelve or thirteen tricks can be counted by process of elimination from the bidding. In such cases the only danger of losing the slam is by playing at a trump contract and finding five or six trumps in the hand of one opponent.

2. The combined hands contain four Aces, one long suit which will produce six or seven sure tricks, and a side suit which produce enough tricks to fill out the quota of twelve or thirteen. In such cases enough tricks for the contract are sure at notrump and seem to be equally

---

* This rule should be relaxed somewhat in duplicate match-point scoring where a more scientific slam bid in a minor suit may result in a lower score board as against a slightly riskier slam bid at notrump. Even in a duplicate game the best slam bid will prove, in the long run, to be the most secure slam bid and the present trend toward indiscriminate slams at notrumps is a losing policy.

sure at a trump contract *unless someone can ruff the opening lead.*

When to Make a Slam Try

A player should begin to expect a small slam when the previous bidding and his own hand indicate that the following essential factors must or may be present.

1. A trump suit is available in which there is no loser or at the most one loser.

2. The combined honor-trick holding of the partnership must be:

   (*a*) 6 to 6½ honor-tricks (29 to 31 pts.) if the hand of either partner is a freak. A freak is a hand which contains a void suit or two singletons.

   (*b*) 6½ to 7 honor-tricks (31 to 33 pts.) if the player's distribution is unbalanced (containing a singleton).

   (*c*) 7 honor-tricks or more (33 pts.) if the player's distribution is balanced (containing neither a singleton nor a void).

3. The combined hands must contain at least eleven winners.*

The player then looks at his own hand to see how many possible losers there are (see Plastic Valuation). He must still determine whether the losing cards in his hand will be covered by quick winners in his partner's hand. He will find out about these winners in his partner's hand by making a conventional slam try.

To make a grand slam the partnership must have primary control (ability to win a trick on the first round) in all four suits. To make a small slam the partnership must have primary control in three suits and secondary control (ability to win the second round of a suit, even though losing the first) in the fourth suit.

Before making a slam try the player counts his *quick* losers—cards which may be lost to the opponents the first or second time the suit is played. He estimates (conservatively) how many of these quick losers are presumably taken care of by his parner's honor-trick holding.

---

* In slam bidding it is easier to count losers than winners. The count of two losing playing tricks (honor or low card) in the hand shows eleven winners.

If there are only three possible losers, and if the combined winners and honor-tricks place the partnership in the slam zone, the player may make a slam try *if it will not force the partnership to a higher contract than four-odd.* Thus he retains the option of stopping at four of a major suit if partner does not hold the necessary controls to accept the slam try.

If only two possible losers are apparent, a slam try may be made which will force the partnership to a contract of five-odd. With only one possible loser, the slam try is safe even though it may force the partners to a small slam.

SOUTH	NORTH
1 ♠	2 ◇
3 ♠	?

There is a good possibility that South has a trump suit which will be made nearly solid with minimum support, and there is also some possibility that South has as many as five honor-tricks. Yet North, holding ♠ 5 2 ♡ Q 7 6   ◇ K Q J 9 4   ♣ Q J 2, should not try for a slam. His two honor-tricks, plus South's possible five honor-tricks, may give the combined hands a total of seven honor-tricks and place them in the slam zone. North's four diamond winners and one club winner may likewise give the combined hands a total of twelve winners. But North has too many losers to expect South to take care of them all. It is improbable that South can cover the two heart losers, one diamond loser, two club losers and any possible spade losers. North should not try for a slam but should simply bid four spades.

The subject of *controls* and the various types of *slam tries* are discussed in later pages.

THE QUESTION OF THE TRUMP SUIT

For slam purposes the trump suit must be solid or must contain not more than one loser. The responder should not consider a trump combination such as 9 7 5 3 or Q 5 4 as "adequate trump support" for slam purposes, unless his partner has rebid the suit; and even then such combinations should be viewed, if not with alarm, at least with suspicion. If one partner holds A K x x x and the other Q x x in the trump suit, there are 32 chances in 100 that one opponent will have J 10 x x or its equivalent. If your small slam bid requires a successful finesse, and you must further risk a bad trump break, mathematically you have a losing slam bid.

It does not follow that a slam should not be contracted for

with a four-card suit. Not to bid a four-card suit at all, for fear of possible unfavorable distribution, would be like jumping into the river to avoid the rain. It simply means that the most solicitous attention should be given to the trump suit in all slam valuation.

Choice of Suits for a Slam Bid

When there is a choice of suits the final trump suit should usually be the one which is most evenly divided between the two hands.

Thus, with two available trump suits, one divided 4–4 and one 5–3, the 4–4 trump suit should usually be preferred. The reason is that when each partner holds four trumps either is able to ruff losing cards and the other will still retain the maximum trump length. When the trump suit is divided 5–3, ruffs in the long trump suit usually add no tricks to the total, since these cards have their own independent value as long card winners.

Even when the same number of winning trump tricks can be developed in either suit, the suit divided 5–3 is likely to produce two discards if a plain suit, while the suit divided 4–4 will never yield a discard in either hand.

Consider the following hands:

```
        ♠ K Q 8 7 6                 ♠ A J 4
        ♡ 6 3            N          ♡ A 10 7
                      W     E
        ◇ A 5                       ◇ 4 3 2
                         S
        ♣ A Q 6 4                   ♣ K J 5 2
```

If spades are chosen as the trump suit no slam is possible. One heart and one diamond must be lost. If clubs are the trump suit a small slam is practically assured. Only all five missing trumps in one hand, or four clubs and a singleton spade, can defeat it. If clubs do not break 3–2, either a heart or a diamond can be ruffed before drawing trumps.

This choice of suits applies only to hands in which it is apparent that two trump suits of the required strength are available. When the solidity of one trump suit is doubtful but the other possible trump suit is assuredly solid, the solid suit should be preferred.

THE RULE OF EIGHT

The Rule of Eight is a simple and quick method to estimate how near one is to a small or to a grand slam. The player adds his own honor-tricks to the minimum number thus far shown by partner's bids. He subtracts the total from 8½. The remainder will indicate the probable maximum number of tricks the opponents can take. With a freak hand the 8½ total count may be reduced to 7½-8.

At trump contracts with a solid trump suit, 8½ honor-tricks warrant the expectation of a grand slam, unless the distribution is so barren (4–3–3–3 or 4–4–3–2) in each hand that the honor-tricks themselves are the only tricks that the player can expect to win.

The Rule of Eight is at best an approximation and must be replaced when approaching the slam by a precise count of total winners and by an elimination of losers which necessitate in most cases the use of special slam conventions. The Rule of Eight is of greatest value in telling the player when a slam is possible and when it should not even be considered. Similarly for the point-count method.

SLAMS AND DISTRIBUTION

Hands that will make slams with nothing but honor combinations and the trump suit are relatively rare. They occur only with freaks, pure cross-ruffs or unusually solid hands. As a rule, a successful slam must be fed with one or more low-card (distributional) tricks in side suits.

Some distributions are very dangerous for slam bids because they promise little, if any, of the necessary length values. Slam bids should therefore be tightened up with the balanced type of distribution and loosened up with the unbalanced type. With a 4–3–3–3, between 1 and 1½ extra honor-trick will be required; with a 5–3–3–2 about one extra honor-trick or slightly less; and a 5–4–2–2 should be reinforced with about ½ honor-trick.

All slam hands can be classified into the following three broad types:

1. Hands containing two or more principal suits (at least

two five-card or longer suits in the partnership hands), with singletons and three Aces or voids.

The next example is an exaggerated case of an ideal slam hand—a hand with two solid, long suits and first-round control in the fourth suit. Note please that against this hand there are more than three honor-tricks (♣ A K Q and ♡ K Q J) and yet it makes a grand slam if spades break 2–1 and diamonds 3–2 or 4–1.

	♠ A K 10 7 6 4	**N**	♠ 9 5 3 2
	♡ A 7 5 3	**W E**	♡ 6
	◇ 6 3 2	**S**	◇ A K Q 7 5
	♣ —		♣ 8 4 3

2. Hands containing a preponderance of ruffers and three Aces or a void.

The ideal exaggerated case of this type is the following pure cross-ruff:

	♠ K Q 6 5 3	**N**	♠ A J 9 7 4
	♡ A 8 6 3	**W E**	♡ 2
	◇ —	**S**	◇ Q 9 7 6 3
	♣ A 7 6 3		♣ K 2

With such types of hands the dummy usually has five trumps. As a rule, the ruffs alone will not suffice and there must be in addition either many fillers or a side length.

3. Hands containing only one principal suit but unusual strength in honors and intermediates, and, in most cases, four Aces.

	♠ K Q J 10 6	**N**	♠ A 7 5 2
	♡ A Q J	**W E**	♡ K 6 4 3
	◇ 9 4	**S**	◇ A 8 3
	♣ Q J 10		♣ A 7

When the player selects the proper trump suit and determines that he has more than enough winners for a slam bid, he has not yet touched the key-problem of slam bidding—the question of *controls*. Asking bids are ideal for the first and second types of hands.

Controls

At any trump bid you can have anywhere from thirteen to nineteen *sure winners* in the combined hands and yet make but eleven tricks. The hand shown on page 397 has seventeen winners, and yet it cannot make even a small slam.

A card or cards that can win the indicated lead of a suit (usually the first or second lead) is called a *control*.

	N		
♠ A K Q J 6			♠ 9 5 4
♡ 5 4	W	E	♡ A K Q J 3 2
◊ A 4 3			◊ 7 5 2
♣ Q J 2	S		♣ 5

West plays a six-spade contract. East's club singleton, combined with the ruffing power of the three small trumps, controls the club suit. West's diamond Ace, despite his two diamond losers, controls the diamond suit. Once West gets the lead he will draw trumps and run six heart tricks, discarding all his losers.

There are three degrees of suit control:

1. An Ace or a void is called *first-round* (primary) control.

2. A King or a singleton is called *second-round* (secondary) control.

3. A Queen or a doubleton is called *third-round* control.

It is assumed, of course, that enough trumps are available for suit controls.

THE TWO BASIC SLAM METHODS

The player should know how to observe the symptoms and diagnose slam expectancy as early as possible, in order to plan and coördinate his bidding. He must determine the specific winners needed in partner's hand to match his own losers and thus to find out about the essential twelve tricks and the essential control and so plan his bidding as to obtain (or give) the maximum information from partner.

In the Culbertson System there are two distinct methods of slam bidding, the Direct Method and the Conventional Method. In the direct method the presence or absence of controls in partner's hand is *deduced* from general bidding. The direct method, in addition to general inferences, makes use of a natural, clear-cut logic of the bid. For instance, your partner bids one spade and you raise it to five spades inviting him to bid six spades with anything better than a bare minimum.

The conventional method of slam bidding is based on artificial conventions such as the Ace-showing cue-bids, the cue-bid in opponent's bid suit, the 4–5 Notrump bids (Culbertson and Blackwood variants), the Gerber 4 Club and, last but the best, the Asking Bids. The purpose of these artificial bids is to find out specifically about Aces, voids and Kings (controls). Only with asking bids convention is one able to discover precisely not only the presence or absence of Aces, voids and Kings, but also about the location of singletons and even of Queens and doubletons (the *third*-round controls). Although the direct method is simpler it is far less precise than the conventional methods. Scientific slam bidding is impossible without good conventional methods.

However, the direct method is still preferable with partners who are confused by an artificial convention.

CHAPTER TWENTY-SIX

DIRECT METHOD OF SLAM BIDDING

The direct method is a natural way of bidding slams simply by a logical extension of the technique of bidding for game and without any special conventions. The direct method is based on general strength shown by partnership bidding and is greatly helped by the Rule of Eight or the point-count. The Rule of Eight shows that when the combined hands have seven honor-tricks, the opponents will *almost* never have two Aces. When it becomes apparent that a slam can be made except in the very unlikely event that the opponents hold two Aces, it becomes good "percentage" to bid the slam. For example:

SOUTH	WEST	NORTH	EAST
1 ♠	Pass	3 ♠	Pass

South holds:

    ♠ A Q 10 6 5 3   ♡ A K Q   ◇ K 10 6   ♣ 6

South has 4½ honor-tricks. North's double raise shows about 2½ honor-tricks, giving the combined hands probably a total of seven. It was previously stated (page 297) that a small slam is a good risk when there is approximately an even chance to make it. In this case, South can bid six spades and know that he has a far better-than-even chance to make it. Almost the only possibility of loss is that North's high-card holding for his double raise consisted of ♠ K, ◇ Q J and ♣ K Q, with or without the Jacks of spades and clubs. It is a slim chance, and there could be no possible objection to a direct six-spade bid by South—if there were no *sure* way to find out whether or not North has an Ace.*

Recognizing the Slam Zone

In nine out of ten slam hands, neither partner will be strong enough to make a two-bid, a forcing takeout, or a forcing rebid, and yet the slam should be reached if it can be made.

These slams cannot be reached, however, unless each player can read partner's bids so as to know exactly how strong partner's hand is and to recognize and diagnose the slam expectancies for combined hands.

Preparation for the ultimate slam contract often begins on the first round of bidding. For example:

South opens with one spade, and North holds:

♠ Q 8 7 3   ♡ A 8   ◇ K Q 10 7 5 2   ♣ 9

This is not a powerful hand, yet there are distinct slam possibilities. South may have virtually a minimum hand like this:

♠ A K 6 4 2   ♡ 7 6 5   ◇ A 6   ♣ 8 5 3

and yet a slam will be a laydown, barring freakishly bad breaks. North responds two diamonds and hopes for a chance later to find out about the high-card and distributional controls.

The choice between a suit takeout and a double raise, when the responding hand fits the requirements for both, is usually decided by the strength of the side suit. If the side suit is a long, easily establishable one, combined with strong support for partner's suit and some sort of control in one of the side suits, the responder's objective should be to give information which may lead to a slam contract.

Partner opens with one spade. You should bid two diamonds with
♠ Q 8 5 4 ♡ 7 ◇ A K Q 8 3 ♣ 9 5 3, because a slam is possible if partner has the top spades and the ♣ A; but you should jump to three spades on
♠ K J 8 7 ♡ K 8 ◇ A Q 10 6 ♣ 9 5 4, because there is no slam unless partner has added values and can make a slam try on his own. The honor-trick totals of the two hands are the same, but the second-hand shows no

---

* The only sure way is by a slam convention. In this case an asking bid will disclose one or two or no Aces; and (for a grand slam) a ♠ K with a ◇ Q in addition.

hope of developing twelve winners if partner has anything near a minimum bid.

In rebidding some national experts advise making a jump
rebid in a new suit even with a three-card minor—to keep the
bidding low for a slam.

West opens with one heart and East responds one spade. West holds:

♠ K Q 6 3   ♡ A K J 7 2   ◇ A 8 4   ♣ 6

This hand justifies a jump raise to four spades (page 207). But that bid
would be uninformative—it would advertise great strength, but would not
tell where the strength is located, and partner would probably be unable to
continue beyond the game level without guessing—something he would be
reluctant to do when it might mean jeopardizing the game itself.

West therefore makes a forcing rebid by bidding three diamonds. This rebid is safe, it is claimed, because West can always
return to spades if East raises diamonds.

I do not, as a rule, approve three-card suit-bids at a higher
level than one. I have witnessed time and again, disasters among
experts brought about by their own confusing acrobatics. However, I concede that for players who do not know Asking Bids,
the three-diamond jump bid by West on the hand in question
is the least of a choice of evils. For those who use the Asking
Bids it will not be necessary to dance like a pig on a rope. On
the hand in question the bidding will be classically simple.

WEST	EAST
1 ♡	1 ♠
4 ♣? Asking bid.	

If East responds with 4 Notrump (showing ♠ A and ♣ A)
West has a biddable small slam. But West is now interested
in a grand slam. If east has ◇ K and a ♡ Q or at least a
doubleton heart, the grand slam will be in sight. Accordingly,
West makes a *second* asking bid of 5 ◇ after East's 4 notrump
response—asking for information on *second*-round controls
(◇ K or ◇ singleton). If East now responds affirmatively (by
bidding 5 Notrump), West makes a *third* asking bid—asking
for information on *third*-round controls (♡ Q or ♡ doubleton)
by bidding 6 ♡. If East signs off with 6 ♠ the hand is played
at small slam; if he responds affirmatively (by bidding 6 notrump) West bids 7 ♠. Finally, if after West's asking 4 ♣ bid,

East does not show two Aces, the hand will be played at 4 ♠ or 5 ♠ or 6 ♠ depending on responses by East.

This hand shows both the superiority of a conventional over the direct method and of the asking method over the others.

Direct Slam Tries

When playing with a partner who does not know or does not use an artificial convention, the only method of slam bidding is the direct method. It is simple because based on natural, logical inferences. By the same token, its useful scope is very limited and, in addition, to play the direct method well requires a great deal of subtle imagination.

An unnecessary bid of five in a major suit, or of four no-trump, is an obvious slam try. But the distinction between an unnecessary bid and a competitive bid must be appreciated:

SOUTH	WEST	NORTH	EAST
1 ♠	2 ♡	2 ♠	4 ♡
4 ♠	5 ♡	5 ♠ Not a slam try	

North simply wishes to have the hand played at spades rather than let the opponents play it at hearts.

SOUTH	WEST	NORTH	EAST
1 ♠	Pass	2 ◇	Pass
4 ♠	Pass	5 ♠ Slam try	

or

SOUTH	WEST	NORTH	EAST
1 ◇	Pass	3 N T	Pass
4 N T Slam try			

In either of these situations there is no reason to bid more than game except as a slam try.

ACCEPTING THE DIRECT SLAM TRY

The direct slam try invites (does not compel) partner to bid six if he has somewhat better than a minimum hand. Not even an extra honor-trick is needed. An unrevealed plus-value, including a singleton; a good fit with partner's suit; even a minimum hand in which, however, the honor-trick values are Aces rather than other honor combinations, will justify accepting the slam try.

The Direct Method may be used in combination with a conventional method or alone. When used without a conventional method the direct slam try made by bidding five in a major suit as a rule, shows a shortage of controls and asks partner to go on to six if his values lie mostly in primary and secondary controls (Aces and Kings or singletons).

Even with a minimum hand, the partner should accept the slam try if most of the strength he has already shown is composed of top cards and not intermediate cards.

In the following bidding sequence:

SOUTH	WEST	NORTH	EAST
1 ♠	Pass	3 ♡	Pass
4 ♡	Pass	5 ♠	Pass

South will bid six spades on

| ♠ A 10 8 6 4 | ♡ 9 7 4 2 | ◇ A 7 | ♣ A 5 |

He has a minimum bid, but it includes three Aces.
South will bid six spades on

| ♠ A Q 10 6 | ♡ Q 6 4 3 | ◇ A 10 7 5 | ♣ 6 |

He has a minimum bid, but it includes two Aces and a singleton.
South will pass on

| ♠ A Q 8 5 | ♡ Q 9 7 3 | ◇ K Q J | ♣ 7 6 |

He has a minimum bid, only one Ace, no singleton, nothing he has not previously guaranteed.

A direct slam try in notrump is somewhat different. It usually means that the top cards, Aces and Kings, are accounted for, and that the slam will depend on the ability to win twelve tricks in the play. Intermediates (uncounted Jacks and tens) and long suits become the determining factor.

SOUTH	WEST	NORTH	EAST
1 ◇	Pass	1 ♠	Pass
3 N T	Pass	4 N T	Pass

North holds:

| ♠ A Q 9 7 5 | ♡ K 8 2 | ◇ Q 6 | ♣ 9 5 4 |

He knows the combined hands have 7½ to 8 honor-tricks (because South's jump to three notrump shows five honor-tricks—see page 197), and that there is no possibility of losing two quick winners to the opponents. But will the combined hands win twelve tricks? They will, if South holds:

♠ J 10   ♡ A Q 5   ◇ A K J 5   ♣ A J 10 7—five honor-tricks, nine honor-cards, a hand on which South should bid six notrump.

However, no slam is probable if South holds:

♠ J 2   ♡ A Q 5   ◇ A K 8 3   ♣ A Q 7 2—five bare honor-tricks, a hand on which South should pass because the three-notrump bid itself was a stretch, in respect to winners.

It should be noted that the four-notrump bid in this situation is not forcing or conventional, even if North-South are using a 4–5 Notrump Convention.

Other Direct Slam Tries

Other direct slam inferences are derived from bids which do not pass the game level, but which would be unnecessary if game were the only goal.

SOUTH	WEST	NORTH	EAST
1 ♡	Pass	3 ♡	Pass
4 ◇			

South's four-diamond bid cannot be merely a game-going bid since North has not only forced to game but has also established the fact that a playable major suit is available even if South has a minimum biddable suit. Therefore the four-diamond bid is a tentative try at a slam. But it is the mildest sort of try, for North, if he does not have substantial values over his double raise, can now go to four hearts and no bidding time will have been lost.

Of course, the assumption in this situation is that asking bids are not used. If asking bids are used (and they are far more preferable) the 4 ◇ bid would be an Asking Bid.

When no major-suit agreement has been reached, any bid which passes the three-notrump level is at least a slam *hint*.

SOUTH	WEST	NORTH	EAST
1 ♡	Pass	2 N T	Pass
3 ◇	Pass	3 N T will discourage South	
		4 ◇ will encourage him	

It is conceivable that the bidding will stop at five diamonds; but a minor-suit game contract of five-odd, requiring eleven tricks, is so close to the twelve-trick slam zone that any safe minor-suit game is a possible slam. An extra King in the hand of either partner, or even the holding of an Ace instead of a King-Queen, may permit the vital twelfth trick to be made.

CHAPTER TWENTY-SEVEN

CONVENTIONAL METHODS OF SLAM BIDDING

The conventional methods of slam bidding utilize certain bids (usually at the fourth or higher level of bidding) to show, not a playable bid, but the presence or absence of key-cards (controls) in various suits. The key-cards are Aces, voids, Kings, singletons and sometimes Queens and doubletons. The oldest and the least scientific of various slam bidding conventions is the cue-bidding to show Aces. Since this convention is surprisingly popular with some of the best players here is how it works.

Cue-Bidding to Show Aces

Indirect slam tries take one of two forms:

1. *Cue-bids.* A cue-bid is a bid in a new suit.* It can be recognized when the bidding situation makes these two things clear: The final contract will not be in the suit named by the cue-bid; and the information given by the cue-bid is not necessary to reach a game contract.

For example:

SOUTH	WEST	NORTH	EAST
1 ◇	Pass	1 ♡	Pass
3 ♡	Pass	4 ♣ Cue-bid	

With a satisfactory heart suit available, North can hardly be looking for a five-club contract. Since any bid over South's three hearts commits North-

---

* Not to be confused with a cue-bid in the opponents' suit, originated by this writer when he developed the Direct Method.

South to a game contract, North does not need to bid four clubs in order to show South game-going strength. Therefore four clubs is a slam try and a cue-bid, showing, as a rule, an Ace of clubs.

When to Make a Cue-Bid

A cue-bid is always a forcing bid, but never for more than one round.* A cue-bid calls for no conventional response. It merely offers certain information, for whatever use partner may be able to make of it. And the information it conveys is that a player is somewhat interested in a slam and to that end holds an Ace in the newly bid suit. Unfortunately most of the bidding levels used for the Ace-showing cue-bids are also the levels needed by a far superior convention—the Asking Bids. Therefore the Ace-showing bids and the Asking Bid are mutually exclusive and the player must make his choice between the two. Considering that the Ace-showing cue-bids offer the minimum of information with the maximum waste of bidding time; while the Asking Bids offer the maximum of information at a minimum cost of bidding time, the choice is not doubtful for anyone who will take the trouble to read up on Asking Bids.

There is nothing incompatible between cue-bidding and the various 4–5 Notrump Conventions. The latter show Aces wholesale; cue-bids show them retail (one by one), *often in bidding situations where it would be dangerous to bid four notrump and thus commit the partnership to a contract of five-odd.* All players who do not use Asking Bids must resort to cue-bids on occasion, whether they use a 4–5 Notrump Convention or not. After the first cue-bid, the bidding may develop in such a way that a conventional four-notrump bid can safely be used.

A player should make a cue-bid only if he has *all three* of the following intentions:

1. To indicate that he has hope of a slam.
2. To show partner the location of certain of his high-card strength.
3. To ask partner—if partner, too, considers a slam possible—to give further information on the location of his own high-card strength by making his own cue-bids only a sign-off.

---

* Except a cue-bid in the opponents' suit (page 317) which is forcing to game.

Order of Suits in Cue-Bidding

In choosing his cue-bid when he has two or more Aces to show, a player should generally choose the most economical way of showing them both, and this means he will first show the Ace that can be bid at the lowest available level.

West	East
1 ♠	3 ♡
3 ♠	4 ♠
5 ♢	

West probably does not have the Ace of clubs; if he had it, it would have been cheaper for him to show it than to show his diamond control.

Signing Off Over a Cue-Bid

There are two clear ways to sign off when partner makes a cue-bid:

1. Bid three notrump (if the bidding level is low enough, which it seldom is). *A four-notrump bid is almost never a sign-off.*

2. Return to the agreed trump suit.

For example:

South	West	North	East
1 ♢	Pass	1 ♠	Pass
3 ♠	Pass	4 ♣	Pass

The four-club bid is obviously a slam suggestion and a cue-bid, since the spade suit has been agreed upon.

If South now bids four hearts, he guarantees the ♡ A (or, in unusual circumstances, a void).

If South does not bid four hearts, *either he does not have the ♡ A or—if he does have the ♡ A—he does not want a slam.* South's bid of four spades is a sign-off; no desire for a slam.

An experienced player dislikes and distrusts cue-bids because they too often lead to horrible misunderstandings. A bid which is intended as a cue-bid may instead sound to partner like a genuine suit-bid, and partner may pass it. In other cases, a genuine suit-bid may sound to partner like a cue-bid, and partner will go slamming when the combined hands can barely produce game. Even with expert partners there is always a possibility of being left in with a mis-cued suit. Misty bidding is inherent in the Ace-showing cue-bids.

PSYCHIC CUE-BIDS

Some players make cue-bids in suits they do not control, in an effort to talk the opponents out of opening those suits against the ultimate slam contract.

For example, one partner opens with one spade and the other partner at some stage cue-bids in clubs on a hand like this:

♠ A Q 6 5   ♥ —   ♦ A K 9 5 3 2   ♣ 6 4 2

He expects to make at least a small and probably a grand slam if any suit but clubs is opened. In this hand, actually bid by a champion player, the psychic was disastrous. The Ace of clubs was promptly led.

It is my painful duty to explain in CONTRACT BRIDGE COMPLETE most every well-known bid even when I know it is cockeyed. However, I may add here that a psychic cue-bid in clubs on the foregoing hand is a naive give-away to any alert opponent, for no better bid could be found that would insure a club lead. Incidentally, if on this hand, my partner opens one spade, my next bid would be four clubs *asking* specific information about partner's holding in clubs. Depending on his answers to this and by means of repeat asking bids I shall know precisely whether to bid a grand slam, a small slam or simply sign off in spades. At the same time a safer and more convincing psychic bid is available when using the Asking Bid. Instead of making an asking bid of four clubs, a psychic asking bid of four diamonds could be made (depending on the mettle of the opponent) compelling partner to sign off with four spades, thus denying a fit in diamonds and inviting a diamond lead. The repeat asking bid could then be made in five hearts, further disguising the real weakness in clubs (see the Asking Bid).

CUE-BIDDING THE OPPONENTS' SUIT

Unlike the Ace-showing cue-bids, cue-bidding the opponent's suit is precise and clear-cut.

A bid in a suit previously bid by an opponent shows first-round control in that suit provided either partner opened the bidding. The bid is one of the oldest developed in the Culbertson System.

This type of cue-bid may be used either as the equivalent of a forcing takeout or rebid in the early stages of the bidding, or as a control-showing bid in the later stages.

For example:

SOUTH	WEST	NORTH	EAST
1 ♠	2 ♡	3 ♡ Shows Ace or void in	
		hearts	

or

SOUTH	WEST	NORTH	EAST
1 ◇	1 ♡	1 ♠	Pass

2 ♡ Shows Ace or void in hearts

or

SOUTH	WEST	NORTH	EAST
1 ◇	1 ♡	1 ♠	Pass
3 ♠	Pass	4 ♣	Pass

4 ♡ Shows Ace or void in hearts

When the bidding is opened by an opponent an *immediate* overcall in opponent's suit, though forcing to game is not a slam try. It simply shows a powerful hand and may even have a singleton or a doubleton in the opponent's suit. The question arises: suppose an opponent opened with a crazy psychic, say one heart with no heart suit. How could he be smoked out? The answer is that an overcall in the opponent's suit is *not* a cue-bid when *preceded* by a takeout double made by the overcaller. It shows, then, a real and a strong suit.

THE CASE AGAINST THE ACE-SHOWING CUE-BID

For two decades and more I have inveighed against the Ace-showing cue-bids. *I have not changed my opinion.* The fact that I am virtually alone among the writers in this belief does not in any way affect the logic of the arguments. My advice to advanced and expert players alike is still the same: avoid the use of Ace-showing cue-bids. With average and somewhat better than average players do not use them at all; instead prefer the Direct Method alone or with simplified asking bids. With advanced partners or experts, use, by all means, the Asking Bid with New Blackwood and New Culbertson 4–5 Trump Asking Bid. Of course if partnership does not know the Asking Bid, the Ace-showing cue-bids must be resorted to. But in that event, they should be used as described in these pages and with proper safeguards. But the sooner you drop their use (which is threatening to become a bridge plague) the better will be your slam bidding. The Ace cue-bids look simple; actually the method is a very complex mechanism. It is needlessly so, for it shows little more than what was already known by direct inferences. The method not only wastes the bidding time but is often vague and therefore dangerous. The profits of an entire evening may be wiped out by one of those horrible misunderstandings where a partner who cue-bids to show an Ace is left in to play with that Ace and nothing else . . . on perfectly logical grounds, of course.

The main reason that the cue-bid method is still used in the higher circles (the average players have too much uncorrupted sense to use it) is that some of the greatest players are using it. This only proves the well-known fact that many great players, though excellent at analyzing an individual hand, are poor on theory. To be a great theoretician one must be a great player; but it does not follow that all great players are great theoreticians. It is one thing to be a great racing car driver; but it is quite another thing to conceive and engineer the motor. The record shows that, with a few individual exceptions, the world's greatest all-around bridge players are Americans. I can testify to this because all of them play the Culbertson System at its best, though some of them, for reasons of vanity or ignorance of theory, will not admit it. In a special sense they could say that they play their own system since most of them have contributed in one way or another to the development of the Culbertson System. Like all great players they have their own variations and pet ideas—some good, some not so good, and some terrible. The Ace-showing cue-bid mania is their greatest weakness. The record of the championship games shows that the American experts who used the Ace-showing cue-bids (and, therefore, could not use Asking Bid method or even other methods) came to grief in slam bidding.

The following hand showed up in a great tournament, and nearly every expert pair that used Ace-showing cue-bids reached six spades:

<pre>
        ♠ Q J 8 6 4   ♠ 10 9 7 5 2
        ♡ A Q 10   N   ♡ 6
        ◊ 6   W   E   ◊ A K 5
        ♣ A Q 4 3   S   ♣ K J 7 6
</pre>

The bidding went something like this:

West	East
1 ♠	3 ♠
4 ♣	4 ◊
4 ♡	5 ♣
6 ♠	

Thus, after four bids (and two levels), they succeeded in locating three outside Aces and one King, but not the Ace and King of trumps—which is what really mattered. The reason is that in cue-bidding it is almost impossible for either partner to show specifically an Ace, let alone a King, *in a trump suit.* Such cases where the experts cue themselves to death are not infrequent in "super-expert" bidding. The fault clearly lies with the embryonic method of Ace-showing. As the experts proceed with solemn mien to hop from one suit to another they have the illusion of doing something deep and devastating. Actually they are bombarding sparrows with cannons.

The Asking Bid, the 4–5 Notrump Convention and other special slam conventions described in the next two chapters make it possible to locate *all* the Aces, and much more besides; to do this, frequently, with one simple exchange of bidding; and to do this with enough bidding time left over to do a scientific job of slam exploration. In modern bidding neither the Ace cue-bids nor the Direct Method could meet the bill.

The Direct Method, originally developed by the author early in 1928, is still used by many players. But it is too difficult for the average player and too simple for the expert. The average player cannot grasp all the delicate nuances of preliminary bidding upon which a slam is built; the expert, while thoroughly understanding all the positive and negative inferences that surround the slam bid, soon finds himself stumped by a great number of questions that can be answered only with the help of specially designed conventions. Thus, both expert and average player require more precise tools to take them out of the guessing zone and into a scientific zone of slam bidding.

CHAPTER TWENTY-EIGHT

4–5 NOTRUMP
SLAM CONVENTIONS

The Blackwood Convention

Back in 1932 this writer conceived the idea of showing Aces *wholesale* (two or more at a time) rather than retail (one at a time, as in cue-bidding). In order to accomplish this, an "idle" bid had to be found, that is, a bid which was of little or no use if used in a natural or non-conventional manner.

For this purpose the bid of four notrump was chosen, as in a great majority of bidding sequences this bid is unnecessary as a real bid of notrump. From this idea the original Culbertson 4–5 Notrump Convention was developed from which all other four-notrump conventions are offshoots. At the present time in the United States the Blackwood Four-Notrump Convention* is much the most widely used, and has been adopted as official in the Culbertson System.

The simple mechanics of this Convention are:

After a conventional bid of four notrump, partner *must* respond as follows. He must:

Bid five clubs if he holds no Ace.
Bid five diamonds if he holds one Ace.
Bid five hearts if he holds two Aces.
Bid five spades if he holds three Aces.
Bid five clubs if he holds all four Aces.

---

*Introduced by **Easley Blackwood** in 1934 and brilliantly analyzed in his book, *Bridge Humanics*.

These responses are invariable; the responder has no choice regardless of how strong or weak his hand is. All that matters is the number of Aces in the responder's hand. *Voids do not count as Aces.*

If, after partner's response, the four-notrump bidder now bids five or six in a suit, partner is required to pass. The one exception to this is where he has a void suit.

If, however, the four-notrump bidder now bids *five notrump*, he announces that the partnership holds all four Aces, and asks partner to show his Kings, as follows:

Six clubs shows no King.
Six diamonds shows one King.
Six hearts shows two Kings.
Six spades shows three Kings.
Six notrump shows four Kings.

The player who bids four notrump is the captain, and his partner must simply report on his Aces. After the bid of five notrump, however, *neither partner is the captain*, i.e., either player may determine whether a grand slam should be bid. The reason for this difference is obvious. The fulfillment of a small- or grand-slam contract is dependent on holding the necessary three or four Aces (barring void suits). However, no particular number of Kings is necessary in order to make a grand slam—two Kings, or conceivably even one, might be enough.

Where a minor trump suit has been agreed on, moreover, players will find it advantageous to use the new recommended responses which will enable the four-notrump bidder to show the possession of all the Aces without the chance of automatically going overboard. The correct bid to show all four Aces is five clubs—not five notrump. The bid of five notrump is undesirable for this purpose because it interferes with the normal operation of the Convention; the Blackwood bidder is denied the use of the five-notrump bid to ask for Kings. The apparent ambiguity in the use of the five-club bid to show *all* Aces or *no* Aces is only superficial. If the four-notrump bidder has one or more Aces, he knows that a five-club response cannot announce four Aces and consequently announces *none*. If the four-notrump bidder has no Aces and gets a five-club response from a partner who has bid strongly enough to invite the use of Blackwood, it is obvious that that five-club response shows four Aces.

A player holding all four Aces and wishing to ask for **Kings** should bid four notrump and then follow with five notrump.

The great popularity of this Convention is probably due to the fact that it is automatic and *specific*. As in the case of point-count it relieves the sense of insecurity that gnaws at the vitals of every bridge player by dispensing with the necessity to exercise judgment when based on a general principle. Actually this Convention, properly used, is a rather complicated one. It can be properly employed only in a minority of slam hands. In advanced bidding it can serve only as an auxiliary method to Asking Bids, and then only in a modified form. And finally, it is not usually a method of getting to slams—it is rather a method for staying out of unmakable slams. The Blackwood Convention merely assures the possession of the necessary controls. And even here it is rigidly limited to Aces (and rarely Kings) which it often shows at a level too high to be profitable. The great majority of slams which not only require information on Aces but on Kings, voids and singletons cannot be shown by Blackwood but by the Asking Bid.

Nevertheless, in the situations to which it properly applies, the Convention is one of special efficiency.

When Is Four Notrump Blackwood?

Of course the simplest and easiest method would be to make *every* bid of four notrump conventional. Unfortunately, however, this would not result in an effective use of the bid of four notrump. Although four notrump is an idle (unnecessary) bid in many sequences, in others it has an indispensable *normal* use; notably in hands where partner has bid notrump. Here it is invaluable as a simple invitation to partner to bid a slam if he has further values, or to pass if he has already shown his full strength. For example:

South, two notrump; North, four notrump.

All authorities agree that this bidding should not be Blackwood. For simplicity of presentation it is assumed here that players are *not* using the Asking Bid. It must be remembered that the Asking Bid is designed not only to determine the Aces, Kings and Queens in partnership hands, but voids, singletons and doubletons as well. Consequently, the role of Blackwood when used in conjunction with the Asking Bid is sharply restricted to special cases (see the Asking Bid).

Another situation:

South, one spade; North, three notrump; South, four notrump.

Here, although the opening bid was in a suit, the situation is almost the same as in the first example.

In this sequence of bidding the normal, non-conventional four notrump is of great use as a simple raise in notrump, indicating a hand not strong enough to bid six, but sufficient to invite partner to go on if he has a maximum holding. This is a frequent type of holding. The non-conventional use of the four-notrump bid here is necessary because it is the *only* bid which will invite partner to go on in notrump, yet allow him the option of passing.

Action by Responder

After a conventional four-notrump bid, responder may not pass. He must show the number of Aces he holds, regardless of the strength or weakness of his hand.

In only one situation does he retain the right to exercise independent judgment. This is where he has a void. He may not count the void as an Ace in making his conventional responses; but if he believes that it is highly probable that his void is not in the same suit as one of his partner's Aces, he may overrule partner's judgment and bid the slam. Before doing so, however, he should make the conventional response, showing his Aces, unless this response coincides with the agreed-on suit. Suppose the suit is diamonds, and responder has one Ace in addition to the void. If he bids five diamonds, partner may pass. Consequently, responder bids *six* diamonds, which tells partner he has a void as well as one Ace. In all other situations he first shows his Aces, and then perhaps overrules his partner's sign-off by going to six.

Grand-Slam Bidding

There are several different situations in regard to grand-slam bidding. The simplest is where the four-notrump bidder feels from his own holding and his partner's bidding that a grand slam is in the cards. However, it is just possible that part of partner's strength might consist of a King-Queen or King-Jack rather than the needed Ace. Instead of bidding seven immediately, he first finds out for sure, by initiating Blackwood, that all four Aces are held. Once this is ascertained, he simply puts the hand in seven. Just as with small slams, Blackwood should always be used, in preference to a direct bid of seven, if any possible doubt exists as to the presence of all four controls.

The next situation is where the four-notrump bidder feels sure of a small slam, and thinks a grand slam may be possible if his side holds all four Aces and if partner has sufficient Kings, or possibly other added values. If partner's response to the four-notrump bid confirms the possession of all four Aces, the Blackwood bidder explores the situation further by bidding five notrump. This bid announces the possession of all four Aces and requests partner to show his Kings, *unless there is some reason for not doing so.* In responding to the four-no-trump bid, partner has no alternative but to show his Aces— these are absolutely necessary for a slam (barring voids). But a singleton or a long suit may be just as good as or even better than a King. No particular number of Kings is needed for a grand slam, consequently, after the five-notrump bid, either partner is at liberty to bid the grand slam.

Fine Points

There are certain finer points which come up only rarely, but will then be important.

I. After a cue-bid in opponents' suit, a four-notrump bid asks partner how many Aces he has *exclusive of that Ace,* i.e., if he holds the Ace of opponents' suit he does not count it.

Some authorities apply this rule to any suit in which either partner has cue-bid. This, however, seems undesirable, as it is common practice to make such an intermediate slam try without the Ace in that suit; in fact it is quite possible that such a bid may show a second suit, or it might conceivably be a fake cue-bid to fool the opponents.

II. If an opponent puts in an interference bid over the four notrump, the responder may still be able to show his Aces as follows: pass shows no Ace; bidding the next-higher suit to opponent's suit shows one Ace, and so on.

III. Blackwood should *not* be used when the player himself holds three Aces. This situation illustrates an important point which is known to comparatively few players. Since partner of the Blackwood bidder is barred from reëntering the bidding (except with a void) he may hold a good slam hand and yet lack an Ace. There is no way for him to show it.

Where the bidding has been competitive and no slam is apparently in view, a bid of four notrump is not conventional, but merely an attempt to buy the contract at that level.

After an opponent's preëmpt at the four-level, a bid of four notrump requires partner to bid his best suit; *it does not ask for Aces.* This type of four-notrump call is really tantamount to a huge takeout double.

An *opening* bid of four notrump is not Blackwood.

Culbertson 4–5 Notrump

The original Culbertson 4–5 Notrump Slam Convention is the father of all 4–5 notrump varieties. It is still quite popular in many countries. I have good reasons to believe that the New Asking Bid, published for the first time in this book, will eliminate the Culbertson 4–5 Notrump. If not using the Asking Bid, the Culbertson 4–5 Notrump Convention is as follows:

A slam-try bid of four notrump is unconditionally forcing, and guarantees that the four-notrump bidder holds *three Aces,* or *two Aces plus the King of a bid suit* (any suit previously bid by himself or his partner).

His partner must respond *five notrump,* if he has two Aces, or if he has one Ace and the Kings of all bid suits. With one

Ace *or a void* in an unbid suit, he bids five of that suit. With the Ace of a bid suit, or the Kings of all bid suits, and with added values, he jumps to six in the best available trump suit. *To sign off* (and he must sign off if he has no Ace or void) the partner bids five in the lowest-ranking bid suit.

The sign-off does not imply any support in the lowest-ranking bid suit; the responder may even have a void in that suit.

SOUTH	WEST	NORTH	EAST
1 ♡	Pass	3 ◇	Pass
3 ♡	Pass	4 N T	Pass

South signs off by bidding five diamonds, *not five hearts,* on

♠ Q J 10   ♡ A K 8 5 4   ◇ 6   ♣ 7 4 3 2

For all South knows, North may have a solid diamond suit.

If a player bids four notrump and at his next turn five notrump, he shows all four Aces.

When the Culbertson 4–5 Notrump Convention is used, neither partner takes absolute control of the bidding. The four-notrump bidder shows certain values by his bid, and the responder shows certain values by his response. When either partner, on the strength of the information he already has, can jump to a slam, he does so.

The Grand Slam Force

This Convention is an optional part of the Culbertson System but only in advanced bridge. Today it has been superseded by a better method used in conjunction with New Asking Bids (see Trump-Asking 4–5 Notrump).

CHAPTER TWENTY-NINE

THE NEW ASKING BID

In this chapter I am going to present, for the first time, a definitive solution of the entire problem of scientific slam bidding—the New Asking Bid. The Asking Bid is a method of specialized bids and responses designed to uncover the presence or absence of Aces, voids, singletons, Kings (and even Queens and doubletons) for the purpose of precise slam bidding.

The old Asking Bid, introduced into the Culbertson System in 1936, has been widely and justly hailed as the most scientific slam method ever devised. At the time, however, it was not generally adopted. There were two reasons for this. At the time I was unable to complete and improve my work on the theory and practice of the Asking Bid, having been called into another field of activity. The Asking Bid concept was left half-finished; since it was my own brain child no one could do much about it. The second reason is that the public (and this includes many experts) were simply not ready. Though eminently practical, the Asking Bid was too startling an innovation. The World War further thwarted the development of the Asking Bid, and ruefully I wrote: "The Asking Bid is my greatest technical victory and my worst psychological defeat." But the psychological defeat was only temporary. Today the New Asking Bid, having been greatly improved, stands as the definitive solution of the chaos of slam bidding. I must express my appreciation to all those who kept the flame of the Asking Bid burning.

In South Africa a group of bridge intellectuals brilliantly

led by M. Sapire waged a successful battle for the Asking Bid. Throughout the European countries and especially in Scandinavia, the Asking Bid, with Blackwood as an auxiliary, is standard, even among average players. This is due to the efforts of Dr. Werner, captain of Swedish European championship team for 1952, and others.

The old Asking Bid withstood the acid test of years in spite of many defects. It was incomplete. But so great are the advantages of the Asking Bid that its defects were minor when compared to the gaping holes in other slam conventions, including my own 4–5 Notrump Convention. It should be remembered that, since its inception, the Asking Bid method had not been changed or improved. And yet there was much to be done. I was aware of it from my own analysis and from correspondence with the Asking Bid enthusiasts who offered suggestions and welcome criticism. Finally, in 1952, I was freed in part from a task in another field where a workable system was more important than in bridge. I began the job of revising and improving the Asking Bid, as a continuation of my original plan to devise a system for slam bidding that would be simple (because logical) and could really work.*

We already know that the *controls* include not only Aces and Kings but voids, singletons and in some cases even doubletons. From the standpoint of precise partnership information, all slam hands can be divided into two principal families:

1. Hands in which the slam depends upon key honor-cards, the Aces and in some cases the Kings.

2. Hands in which it is necessary to find a *distributional fit* in addition to the key cards.

---

* The plan to overhaul the slam bidding methods is, in turn, a part of the general task to overhaul gradually and bring up to date the various methods of contract bridge bidding, which are crying for improvement—a task which I and my associates undertook early in 1952. Except for the point-count movement, nothing new has been done in contract bridge in the last several years. And yet the great game, like all living institutions, has been moving ahead. Meanwhile, a number of barnacled conventions and localisms have accumulated which make the bidding not better but more difficult. They are now cleaned up. A number of worthwhile though minor improvements were adopted. The New Asking Bid, together with the Culbertson Point-Count Valuation and the Limit Two-Bid are among the major improvements in contract bridge, incorporated for the first time in CONTRACT BRIDGE COMPLETE.

Suppose you hold:

    ♠ A K Q 6 5   ♡ 6   ◇ A 9 7 5 2   ♣ A 5

With this hand you bid one spade and your partner raises it to three spades. He will not need much for you to make a small or even a grand slam. This is what he can hold:

Dummy No. 1:   ♠ J 10 9 8 7   ♡ A 8 5 4   ◇ 8   ♣ K 7 4

Then again, your partner may hold something like this:

Dummy No. 2:   ♠ J 10 9 8 7   ♡ A K   ◇ 8 6 4   ♣ K Q 6

Twist the bidding any way you like, use any system you like, and you will agree with me that there is no other method to reach a grand slam with Dummy No. 1 except the Asking Bid method. Many players will try for a small slam and lose it with Dummy No. 2.

I shall anticipate the presentation of the Asking Bid and show how the hand and the two dummies are handled by the Asking Bid method. With Dummy No. 1 (North) the bidding will run:

SOUTH	NORTH
1 ♠	3 ♠
4 ◇ ?[1]	4 ♡ [2]
5 ◇ ?[3]	6 ♣ [4]
7 ♠ [5] all pass.	

1. First asking bid for information about controls in the diamond suit and outside.
2. First response. Shows ◇ K (or singleton) and ♡ A (or void)—second-round control in the asked suit and first-round control outside.
3. Second (repeat) asking bid. South wants to know about his possible loser in diamonds (if North holds ◇ K x x) and in clubs.
4. Second response. Shows third-round control in diamonds (with ◇ K x x it would be a sign-off) and ♣ K (or singleton).
5. Now that every possible loser is specifically covered by North's responses, a grand slam is a virtual certainty.

With Dummy No. 2 the bidding would be after South's asking bid of 4 ◇ ?: 4 ♠ by North. All pass. The four spades is a sign-off showing at least two losers in Dummy's diamonds.

Scientific slam bidding is possible only if a logical method is designed to take care not only of Aces and Kings (this is easy), but of voids, singletons and even doubletons. Without some such method, slam bidding is a lame, half-blind affair. Virtually every slam bid has some distributional factor involved. The Asking Bid probes *both* the high card and distributional controls. Heretofore there has been no method to solve this problem of Distributional Slams, and that is the reason that slam bidding is still in a primitive state. It is largely a hit-or-miss affair. The would-be haymakers of prize-fighting are works of precision compared with the wild rushes of our experts at the hidden slam button. In the early days of Contract some superficially bright expert got the idea of showing Aces. Ever since, we have been breaking our necks "showing" all our powerful hands to helpless partners who, unable to visualize our hands, would sit squirming and hoping only that we shut up. It is ludicrous to keep on "showing" a hand bristling with winners to a partner whose hand is shot full of losers—in the hope that he will rise to the heights of slams. For a long time I could see no way out. And yet, I felt intuitively that there must be a way—a sort of Northwest Passage in and around singletons, voids or doubletons. Then, after one evening of foggy slam bidding, it occurred to me that something was woefully wrong with our slam exhibitionism. I came upon one startling fact. Every authority, without exception, bent his efforts to *show* his Aces. It then occurred to me that they were putting the cart before the horse and that instead of showing control in a strong suit, it would be better to *ask* your part-ner about controls in declarer's own *weak* suit! Why show? I asked myself. Why not ask? And out of this question came the Asking Bid which shows nothing but asks nearly everything. The New Asking Bid should become, on sheer merit, the domi-nant method for slam bidding in advanced or tournament play. The Asking Bid will enable players who are even slightly better than average to capture small and grand slams that had eluded them and save on unmakable slams. It is not true that Asking Bid is quite difficult and complicated; the Asking Bid is complex but simple. The responses are automatic and pre-determined. They can be memorized in a few concentrated minutes; and once learned, a new world of scientific slam bidding will be opened to those who learn them.

Of course, there remains much to be done for the future development of the Asking Bid. The Asking Bid is not merely another convention. It is a movement. But as it stands now, the New Asking Bid is worth all other slam conventions (including the previous Culbertson methods) put together. It is simpler, more comprehensive and yet far more specific than any other method or combination of methods. It not only succeeds brilliantly where all other methods fail in probing for voids, singletons and doubletons; it better achieves the goals of other slam conventions—the exploration for Aces and Kings. In my frank opinion, if the Asking Bid method fails now it will be only because it is too advanced for our generation of experts. Like certain chapters of my *Red Book on Play* it will have to wait for the next generation of players.

The New Asking method includes a number of new features. There is, for instance, a new convention to determine precisely *the key-cards* and the *length of the trump suit* held by either partner. The method is based, paradoxically enough, on the 4–5 Notrump (Trump-Asking Bid). This startling convention will please the players who have been stumped by the lack of precise information about partner's trump holding. The number of slams bid and lost, and of makeable slams not bid because there is no way of being certain of partner's trump suit is legion. The new 4–5 Trump-Asking Bid solves this problem. Furthermore, the scope of Asking Bids has been extended and their responses improved and simplified. The Blackwood, one of the few slam conventions which are retained, has been improved and fitted into the Asking Bid. For advanced players, new Asking Bids have been developed for use in notrump bidding, after the Forcing Two-Bid, the preëmptive bids, the cue-bids in opponents bid suits, and other special cases. Not the least of the services rendered by the New Asking Bid is the elimination of the whole slew of complicated and confusing slam conventions that have crept into the slam field. In the past some of them have rendered good service; today they have become unnecessary. Among these special conventions (to mention only a few) are the Culbertson 4–5 Notrump, the Grand

Slam Force (eliminated in favor of the new 4–5 Trump-Asking Bid), the Ace-showing cue-bids, the 4 Club (Gerber) bid, the Californian, the Herbert, and a swarm of other conventions of local usage, including the ultimate in *reductio ad absurdum* in slam bidding, the Solomon-Disbrow Two Diamond Convention.* The only special conventions retained as useful adjuncts to the New Asking Bid are the Blackwood 4–5 Notrump and the cue-bids in opponents' bid suits.

The New Asking Bid, however, does not eliminate the traditional, natural method of slam bidding based on the raise of the trump suit above the game level.

SOUTH	NORTH
1 ♠	3 ♠
5 ♠ A natural bid	

Five spades here is an example of direct method, simply asking North to bid six spades if he holds some additional values. The natural method can be used either with the New Asking Bid or without it. Thus, no one is forced to use the New Asking Bid. Players who either do not like or do not know the artificial slam conventions can always fall back on the natural method developed in the early days of bridge by this writer. With some types of partners this method, in skillful hands, is still the best one (and often the only one available). The Asking Bid also does not interfere in any way with slam bidding at notrump. In fact, it helps the reaching of notrump slams considerably (see Special Cases). All other basic methods of bidding are left intact by the Asking Bid. The Asking Bid works best with classic bidding that eschews artificial bids—for instance, after a Forcing Two-Bid. But it will also work well with the artificial opening Two-Club or with any other method. In fact, the possibilities of the Asking principle are so great that I can well imagine a system of bidding based on the Asking principle even to reach game. But this is for the future bridge analysts—long after I am gone, I hope.

The presentation below is in two parts: the first part is usable with a partner who is slightly better than average provided

---

* Some of these conventions are described in this book, not as a recommendation, but because the book bears the title CONTRACT BRIDGE COMPLETE.

he learns the steps, of course; the second part under the heading Special Cases in Asking Bids is for advanced and tournament play. To all players the New Asking Bid will open a door to the most thrilling bid in bridge—the scientific slam bid.

Slam Valuation and the Asking Bid

There are two basic requirements for any slam bid: the partnership hands must have the expectancy of twelve *playing tricks* for a small slam and thirteen for a grand slam; and there must be enough top playing tricks to insure control of the first and second leads (Aces, voids, singletons and Kings). The slam hands must have mass and "leaders" (controls). As I explained before, there are three ways of counting playing tricks for combined hands—by a direct, natural count of winners or losers (Plastic Valuation), by a count based on the honor-tricks (the Rule of 8, etc.) and by a count based on the point-count of high cards (33 points equals small slam, etc.). In a majority of cases, an honor-trick or point-count valuation is enough to reach a satisfactory slam bid without much ado. The control cards (Aces and Kings) generally will be found automatically in the honor or point-count valuation for slams. The point-count, though not as simple and rapid as the honor-trick count, is remarkably accurate. Many near-beginners and average players write to me that the Culbertson Point-Count has been a blessing to them. All they have to do is to add points shown by partner's bids to the count of points in their own hand and they have an automatic bid of game, small slam or grand slam—thus leaping over the years of drudging experience necessary to acquire a flair for slam bidding. All this is true only as far as it goes. If you are armed only with a point-count (or honor-trick count) you cannot get far in slam bidding. There are many hands which have the required count of high cards and distributional points for a slam bid, and yet they go down as the opponents turn up with missing Aces or other high cards.* Hence, the rigid necessity of special conventions, such as Blackwood, to make certain that the missing slam links (Aces and Kings) are

---

* Only in notrump bidding, where the high card point-count is "pure," is it possible to get an automatic point-count for slams. But such notrump hands come up once in a blue moon.

not in the enemy's hands. By checking his point-count total (or honor-trick total) with the controls, the player is a step higher in his climb to scientific slam bidding. But he is still far from his goal. There remains a most valuable and important group of slams that can be reached only through the Asking Bid. It is the family of *distributional slams,* where the dominant factor is not only the Ace-King controls (also reached by the Asking Bid) but the *distributional controls*—voids, singletons, and, in some cases, doubletons.

SOUTH	NORTH
♠ A K Q 9 6 3	♠ 10 8 7 5 4 2
♡ x x x	♡ —
◇ A 9 8 6	◇ K x
♣ —	♣ 10 9 8 7 5

These hands contain a cold grand slam. On a point-count valuation the bidding will reveal for both a measly 16 points in high cards; and if we count 6 points for North's void and 3 points for South's lengths, we still have only 25 points—not quite enough for a game let alone a slam. And as for controls, Blackwood or Ace-showing methods are useless. I shall anticipate the presentation of the Asking Bid and show how, by using new asking bids, it is virtually impossible to miss a grand slam.

SOUTH	NORTH
1 ♠	3 ♠
4 ◇ ? Asking bid[1]	4 ♡ [2]
4 N T [3]	5 ♣ [4]
5 ◇ [5]	5 ♡ [6]
5 N T [7]	6 ♡ [8]
7 ♠ ! [9]	

1. 4 ◇ is an Asking Bid, asking information about the diamond suit and outside strength, if any. There is no risk since a negative response brings South back to 4 ♠ which is the agreed trump suit.

2. 4 ♡ shows King of diamonds or a singleton and Ace of hearts or void.

3. A new Trump-Asking Bid to find out about any or all three top honors in partner's trump suit. The 4–5 Trump Asking convention is distinguished from Blackwood's 4–5 Notrump by the fact that it is used *after* any asking bid.

4. 5 ♣ is an artificial response to deny any of the three top honors in the trump suit. South, of course, is perfectly aware of it, but he is preparing the ground for a follow-up with 5 N T to find out about partner's *length* in trumps.

5. Second (repeat) asking bid. Since South already knows that North holds ◇ K or singleton he wants to know about *third*-round controls, i.e., singleton, K x or K Q.

6. North shows *third*-round controls in diamonds, probably K x or K Q. He could not have K x x—he would have signed off in 5 ♠.

7. 5 N T is asking about *length* in partner's trump suit. South will need at least five trumps to ruff out his losers.

8. A purely artificial bid to show a five- or six-card length in trumps. It has nothing to do with heart void.

9. Now that the asking bids have matched the six losers in South's hand, with scientific precision, with the six corresponding winners—a grand slam can be bid with virtual certainty.

It is not too much to claim that no method of slam bidding exists that can give so simply the precise and varied information as given here by the Asking Bid.

There remains one step more to be taken if a player wishes to bid slams scientifically. This step is possible, however, only to fairly advanced players. The step is, to base the slam bidding not so much on a point-count, nor on the Rule of 8, but on a far more precise count of playing tricks (Plastic Valuation), which is the specific count of winners and losers in the hand. In the bidding below a game level, the count of winners and losers is often difficult because the player's suits are full of gaping holes and there is not enough information from partner (and opponents) to fill in these holes adequately. But in slam bidding, where the strength is concentrated in partners' hands and the losers are relatively few, the playing-trick valuation is supreme. The whole problem is narrowed down to a few specific losers, where each loser is handled *individually* by matching it against the corresponding winner in partner's hand (seeking controls). Each loser has its own case history. Compared to this individual treatment of losers any method of slam valuation such as the point-count or honor-trick method which is based on a *total* count in the hands, is less accurate and less refined. This is why no expert player uses in his slam valuation the point-count or honor-trick method—except as a general

indication or check-up of conclusions reached by the favorite
method of *all* expert players—the direct count of losers and
winners. The Asking Bid works very well with any point-count;
but it works even better with the playing-trick valuation. My
contention that no expert player uses the point-count as his
principal method to reach slams will be disputed by some
writers. If they use some such method, then they are *not* expert
players. One cannot be a winning runner on crutches. Such
methods are valuable to average and to many of the advanced
players. But expert slam bidding requires something far more
refined and specific than a mere count of total points in hands.
Good slam bidding travels on two legs: ability to count your
losers; and ability to match your playing-trick losers with the
available winners in partner's hand. These available winners
or controls are best determined by the Asking Bid method, in
all three methods of valuation—the point-count, the Rule of 8
and the playing trick.

THE ASKING BID DEFINED

There is this essential difference between an Asking Bid
and any other suit-bid in bridge: an asking bid *asks,* not gives,
information about the asked suit. It is an artificial bid, telling
nothing about the bidder's holding in the asked suit, but requiring partner to give specific information about *his* holding.
As a by-product, the partner, in his answer on his specific holding in the asked suit, *also* gives information on his specific
holding in the *hand* (I have, in addition to the fit in the asked
suit, so many Aces, or a single Ace or a void, a King or a
singleton in the *unasked* suit or suits).

The Asking Bid can be clearly distinguished from a regular
suit-bid by means of the following simple formula applied to
the opening or responding hand:

*After a suit has been raised, any bid in a new suit at the
level of four or higher is an Asking Bid; or, if no suit has been
raised, any unnecessary jump in a new suit at the level of three
or higher is an Asking Bid.*

An *unnecessary* jump bid is a bid which is one trick higher
than necessary for a forcing takeout or a rebid, i.e., a *double-*

jump. Opener—one heart; Responder—three spades. Three spades is an asking bid. Illustrations of the asking bids:

SOUTH	WEST	NORTH	EAST
1 ♠	Pass	3 ♠	Pass
4 ♣? Asking bid			

The 4 ♣ bid is asking because (a) it is a bid in a new suit after a raise; and at the same time is (b) at the level of four. All asking bids, when made after a raise, are at the level of four or higher. Note that the Asking Bid completely eliminates the Ace-showing cue-bids and the Four Club Conventions. Their bidding levels are now occupied by the asking bids with far greater profit.

SOUTH	WEST	NORTH
1 ♡	Pass	4 ◊ ? Asking bid
		or
		3 ♠ ? Asking bid

Four diamonds or three spades is an asking bid because it is one level higher than necessary for a forcing takeout of South's opening one heart bid. This level of bidding was an idle level, that is, it was of little use; now the asking bids occupy it with excellent results. Note the Asking Bid is the only slam convention which, in many cases, initiates slam exploration at the level of three—a considerable gain of bidding time. Again,

SOUTH	WEST	NORTH	EAST
2 ♠	Pass	2 N T	Pass
4 ◊ ? Asking bid			

Three diamonds is forcing after an opening two-bid; therefore, four diamonds is asking.

THE AGREED SUIT

All asking bids are based on the *agreed* trump suit. The *agreed* suit is the trump suit at which the final contract is to be played.

*The agreed suit is always the one immediately preceding the first asking bid.**

---

* For an exception, see Blackwood and the Asking Bid.

South, one spade; North, four diamonds. The agreed suit is the spade suit. However,

SOUTH	NORTH
1 ♠	2 ♠
3 ♡	

Three hearts is *not* an Asking Bid because it is neither at the level of four (after a raise) nor an unnecessarily high jump. Therefore, there can be, as yet, no agreed suit. If South, instead of bidding 3 ♡, jumped to 4 ♡, he would thereby "agree" to the spade suit.

If two or more suits have been bid and raised, the one raised last before the asking bid is the agreed suit.

SOUTH	NORTH
1 ♠	2 ♡
4 ♡	4 ♠
5 ♣ ?	Asking Bid—agreed suit, spades

An unnecessary jump in a new suit, when no suit has been raised, is an Asking Bid setting the last bid suit as the agreed suit.

SOUTH	NORTH
1 ♡	1 ♠
4 ◇ ?	Asking Bid—agreed suit, spades

Three diamonds would have been a force to game; therefore the four-diamond jump was "unnecessary."

WHO IS THE CAPTAIN IN THE ASKING BID?

In the Asking Method the asker is not only the captain but an absolute dictator. Except for specifically defined responses, the partner of the player who makes the Asking Bid is silent to the end. He may not, after the asker bids his final contract, start a little asking on his own or increase or change partner's final bid. The basic rule after a forcing bid is that partner never passes; the basic rule after the final Asking Bid and response is that partner never bids. This rule of silence is based on the fact that the asking bids will pump out all the avail-

able information. It also prevents disasters arising from partner's sudden bursts of "initiative."

The following description of basic Asking Bids and responses
are for use with an average or expert partner. Later in this
chapter I shall describe the refinements for use in advanced
and tournament play.

Responses to the First Asking Bid

All Asking Bids are forcing for one round. The Asking Bid
and a response to it form a unit. Thereafter another Asking
Bid may be made, in the same or in a different suit, asking for
information—*information which had not been disclosed previously to the first asking bid.* The first asking bid and its
response are the core of the asking method. All subsequent
asking bids with their responses are conditioned by the first
response—by what was said or not said the first time in answer
to the first asking bid. The following schedule of 9 responses
gives the complete information on the responder's high card
and distributional controls in the hand. The schedule is held
together by inner logic, but a player will save time and confusion by memorizing it—a matter of a few concentrated minutes. All the asking bids below assume an opening suit-bid
of one and an asking bid made at the level of four.

Sign-Off

1. Lacking first- or second-round control in the asked suit,
the responder must sign off. He signs off by returning to the
agreed trump suit at the lowest possible level.

2. With second-round control (King or singleton) in the asked
suit, but no Ace or void outside, the responder must sign off.

These are the only two cases of a negative reply warning the
asker that either there are two or more losers in the asked suit
or, that the hand has no Ace or void.

South	North
1 ♠	3 ♠
4 ◇ ?	4 ♠ —four spades is a sign-off.

With any other holding, the response must be as follows, assuming that the asking bid was made at the four-level:

The Responder Holds	The Response Is
3. King or singleton in the asked suit, and one outside Ace or void.	Bid the outside Ace or void (except the Ace of the agreed trump suit). If holding an outside Ace *and* a void bid the Ace, suppress the void until a later round.
4. King or singleton in the asked suit, and Ace of the agreed trump suit.	With trump Ace jump one trick.
5. Ace or void in the asked suit, but no Ace or void outside.	Raise the asked suit.
6. Ace in the asked suit with one outside Ace; or King or singleton in the asked suit with two outside Aces.	Bid four notrump. (Aces only, not voids.)
7. Ace in the asked suit and two outside Aces; or the King or singleton in the asked suit and three outside Aces.	Bid five notrump. (Aces only, not voids.)
8. Same requirements as with four notrump (No. 6 above), and, in addition, a void in the outside suit.	Jump the outside void suit of one trick (single jump).
9. Same requirements as with five notrump (No. 7 above), and, in addition, a void in the outside suit.	Jump the outside void suit by two tricks (double jump).

Note. The numbers 8 and 9 are new bids. They are my favorites; but perhaps they are at their best with advanced partner.

Voids in the Asking Bid

A four- or five-notrump response to the first Asking Bid always shows Aces, never voids. With a void in the asked suit and an Ace outside; or with the Ace in the asked suit and a void outside: show the Ace or void, *depending on which is outside of the asked suit;* but do not bid four notrump. With a void in the asked suit and two outside Aces, bid four notrump, not five.

These are the nine basic steps in the first asking bid.

When the first asking bid is made at the level of three or

five, the response is the same as above, except that the response is, respectively, one level lower or higher.

SOUTH	NORTH
1 ◊	3 ♡ ? First Asking Bid

South now responds with 3 notrump instead of 4 notrump to show 2 Aces or as the case may be, bids four diamonds to sign off.

SOUTH	NORTH
2 ♠	3 ♡

5 ◊ ? First asking bid. Four diamonds would have been a normal bid. Five notrump response would show two Aces and a fit.

Choice of Asking Bids

When the player has decided that he is in the slam zone and can sound out the situation with an asking bid, he still has to use his head in deciding the suit in which he will ask for information. His objects will be:

1. With a borderline slam try, to retain the ability to sign off at game if partner cannot furnish the required information.

2. With a strong hand, with which he does not fear getting past game, nevertheless to arrange the bidding so as to obtain as much information in as few rounds of bidding as possible.

With very strong hands avoid choosing an asking bid where partner is likely to sign off.

One more general observation must be made on the "when" of the asking bids. That is: Don't use them if your partner cannot or will not make the correct responses. You cannot design any powerful machine which will not do harm if its power be expended in the wrong direction. However, the advantage of the New Asking Bid is so overwhelming and the pleasure of using it so dramatic that it will pay to urge your partner to learn it.

RESPONSES TO THE FIRST ASKING BID

(A Summarized Table)

Unless otherwise specified, the terms Ace and King in the table below include their *equivalents,* void and singleton, respectively. Assuming the asking bid was made at the four-level, responses are:*

The Responder Holds:	*The Response Is:*
1. Q J or less (2 top losers) in the asked suit; or, even with the King in asked suit, an aceless hand. Note. In the example on the right, spades is the agreed trump suit, 4 clubs? is the first asking bid, and the response is underlined.	SIGN OFF, by returning to the agreed trump suit at the lowest level. Ex. 4 ♣ ? <u>4 ♠</u> Sign Off
2. King in the asked suit and Ace outside (with trump Ace jump one trick).	Bid outside Ace. Ex. 4 ♣ ? <u>4 ◇ or 5 ♠</u>
3. Ace in the asked suit and no Ace outside.	Raise the asked suit. Ex. 4 ♣ ? <u>5 ♣</u>
4. King in the asked suit and 2 Aces outside; or Ace in the asked suit and 1 Ace outside (voids are not counted in N T responses).	Bid Four Notrump. Ex. 4 ♣ ? <u>4 N T</u>
5. King in the asked suit and 3 Aces outside; or Ace in the asked suit and 2 Aces outside (count only Aces).	Bid Five Notrump. Ex. 4 ♣ ? <u>5 N T</u>
6. Same requirements as with 4 N T and, in addition, a void in the outside suit.	Jump the outside void suit. Ex. 4 ♣ ? <u>5 ◇ or 5 ♡</u>
7. 3 Aces in the hand and, in addition, a void in the fourth suit.	Make a double raise in the outside void (usually to six). Ex. 4 ♣ ? <u>6 ◇ or 6 ♡</u>

Voids. With a King in the asked suit and an Ace *and* a void outside, show the outside Ace and suppress the void until a later round. With a void in the asked suit and an Ace outside, or with an Ace in the asked suit and a void outside, show the Ace or void, *depending on which is outside of the asked suit.*

---

* The same responses obtain when the asking bid is made at the three- or a five-level, except that they are proportionally one level higher or lower.

The Special Importance of Sign-Off Bids

The sign-off is made by rebidding the agreed suit at the lowest possible level. It generally announces a misfit, that is, two or more cards headed by a Queen or less. With a misfit this sign-off is imperative, regardless of the outside holding of the hand. However, an interesting situation may arise after a sign-off:

West	East
1 ♠	3 ♠
4 ♡?	4 ♠ Sign-off!

West, though knowing that East lacks the heart fit or an Ace, or both, nevertheless is not deterred from making another slam try, with the following hand:

♠ A K J 8 6 4   ♡ A Q J   ◇ 6   ♣ K Q 10

Knowing now that East lacks second-round control, West makes an asking bid in a new suit, bidding 5 ◇. East responds with 5 N T, showing a fit in diamonds and 2 Aces in the hand. After a sign-off to the first asking bid, a second asking bid in a new suit is treated like the first. Thus, in the space of two rounds of bidding, four different kinds of bids were made; the most detailed information was given; and all the time West was in a position to sign off at five-odd. West contented himself with a small slam, when many would bid a grand slam bid (38 pts.). The key to the bidding was the sign-off after four hearts. East's hand was:

♠ Q 9 7 3 2   ♡ 5 3 2   ◇ A K   ♣ A 8 7

Holding a singleton or the King of the asked suit, but lacking any Ace or void, the responder must sign off in the same way.

Strong but Aceless hands are most unusual and the normal assumption after a sign-off is lack of controls in the asked suit. In all such cases a sign-off is of great value as a block to unmakeable slams. The bane of slam bidding is the duplication of two losers in one hand with two losers of the same suit in the other hand. With the Asking Bid such duplication is immediately discovered by means of the sign-off. This is virtually impossible with any other slam convention. Equally impossible is to bid a small slam with two Aces missing, as happens to champion players who believe that their mystic intuition is stronger than the Asking Bid Method.

The following remarkable hand was played in the world

championship team-of-four contest in January, 1953, between the American team and the Swedish team, the European champions.

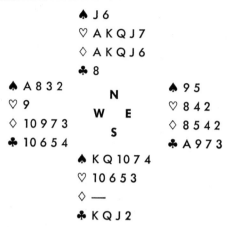

```
                          ♠ J 6
                          ♡ A K Q J 7
                          ◇ A K Q J 6
                          ♣ 8
        ♠ A 8 3 2                          ♠ 9 5
        ♡ 9                N               ♡ 8 4 2
        ◇ 10 9 7 3      W     E            ◇ 8 5 4 2
        ♣ 10 6 5 4          S              ♣ A 9 7 3
                          ♠ K Q 10 7 4
                          ♡ 10 6 5 3
                          ◇ —
                          ♣ K Q J 2
```

East-West vulnerable. North dealer. In Room One the Americans held the North-South hands. The bidding was (East-West not bidding):

NORTH Schenken	SOUTH Stayman
2 ♣	2 ♠
3 ♡	3 ♠
4 ◇	5 ♡
6 ♡	Pass

Luckily for North, East led a trump, giving North the contract. Nevertheless it is poor championship bidding. Even in moderately advanced bridge, a small slam bid with two missing Aces is deplorable slam bidding. In a world championship contest such bidding is definitely startling. What was amiss? The trouble was not with the players themselves, who are worthy champions, but with the defective tools they used. The first defective tool was the unrestricted two-club bid. As always happens when partner of the two-club bidder holds a higher ranking suit (in this case, higher than Schenken's heart suit), a precious round of bidding must be lost. In this case, Stayman lost two rounds of bidding by needlessly rebidding his spade suit. The real reason for the use of the two-club bid is that some experts, not realizing the value of the Asking Bid, hope that they can better "show" the shape and power of their hands for slam bids—a vain hope. Actually, any two average players using the Asking Bid will ferret out immediately the two missing Aces—a feat that two world champions could not accomplish without the tool of the Asking Bid.

The bidding should be extremely simple.

NORTH	SOUTH
(Mr. Average Player)	(Mrs. Average Player)
2 ♡	3 ♡[1]
4 ♣ ? Asking bid	4 ◇[2]
4 ♡ All pass	

1. South with a powerful hand keeps the bidding low to hear more from partner.

2. Shows clearly ♣ K plus void in diamonds; denies ♣ A and ♠ A. Therefore, North signs off at 4 ♡.

The same result would be secured if the bidding went:

NORTH	SOUTH
2 ♡	2 ♠
3 ◇	3 ♡
4 ♣ ? Asking bid	4 ◇
4 ♡ All pass	

In the other room, holding the identical hand, the Swedish European champions had the right tools—they used the Asking Bid—but one of the players (as it must happen to the best) went haywire. The bidding was:

NORTH	SOUTH
Anulf	Lilliehook
2 ♡	3 ♡
3 ♠ ?[1]	4 ◇
6 ♡[2] All pass	

Also down one trick

1. 3 ♠ is used as an asking bid, incorrectly, I believe. This shuts out many normal bids, which are useful. I restrict asking bids at the level of three to unnecessary jump bids.

2. North knew perfectly well that two Aces were against him, but he hoped to entice a diamond or a trump lead and make a small slam by discarding the club loser—a calculated, though desperate, gamble for a big swing.

SECOND ASKING BID AND RESPONSES

After first asking bid and response, a bid in any but the agreed trump suit is a second asking bid.

SOUTH	NORTH	
1 ♣	1 ♠	
3 ♠	4 ◊ ? *First Asking*	
4 ♡	5 ◊ ? *Second Asking*	

North's 4 ♡ is the first response. North's 5 ◊ is a second asking bid in the *same* suit (a repeat). If North bids 5 ♣ instead of 5 ◊ it would be a second asking bid in a *new* suit, even though it has been bid (not asked) before.

The object of second-asking bids is to secure essential information about second-round controls not previously disclosed. As a general rule, the first asking bid and response deal with first-round controls (usually at the level of four); the second asking bid and response deal with second-round controls (usually at the level of five); and the third asking bid and response deal with third-round controls (usually at the six-level).

The responses to all second asking bids deal almost exclusively with second-round controls (Aces not shown). Exception: If the response to the first asking bid was a sign-off, the second asking bid in a *new suit* is treated like the first asking bid (Aces must be shown).

The following are responses to the second asking bid—assuming a five-level.* Unless otherwise specified, the term, *King*, includes its equivalent, a *singleton*.

The Responder Holds		*The Response Is*
In Asked Suit	*Outside*	Sign Off.
1. Q J (or less)	no matter	Bid suit with outside King. With 2
2. King	King (except	Kings in side suits show one on next
3. King	agreed trump)	higher level to asking suit.
	King (trump)	Raise the agreed trump suit (usually
4. King	No King	to six).
		Bid 5 Notrump.

5. With 4 Kings bid the first pair of Kings. Follow up with a raise in the trump suit on the next asking bid.

---

* The same responses obtain when the first asking bid is made at a three- or five-level, except that they are proportionately one level higher or lower. When the King-showing responses are at a six-level, no outside King (or singleton) may be shown if it is above the sign-off level of the Asking bidder.

A Special Case. When the first response showed one outside Ace (or void) with King (or singleton) in the asked suit, the second response must be: Sign off with K x x or longer; give a positive response with K x, K Q, singleton or void (third-round controls).

Voids are treated like second-round controls. Raise a void suit only when it has been previously suppressed or not yet bid (see First Asking Bids). Whenever feasible it is best to keep the responses to the five-level.

THIRD ASKING BID AND RESPONSES

When second asking bid occurs at the five-level, the six-level is reserved for the *third* asking bid. *Purpose of the third asking bid is to find out from partner about his Queens or doubletons, which are third-round controls.* The object of the third asking bid, when at the six-level, is usually a grand slam, offering a foolproof method for reaching grand slams that heretofore were in a zone of wild guesses. There are third asking bids, however, which may occur at the five-level, when the first asking bid is made at the three-level. They are then most useful for small slams.

RESPONSES TO THE THIRD ASKING BID (AT SIX-LEVEL)

If responder holds no Queen or doubleton in the asked suit, he signs off. Voids or singletons are no longer counted.

If responder holds a Queen or doubleton in the asked suit *with* outside Queen (no outside doubleton is counted), he may show the outside Queen *en passant,* i.e., provided it is below the sign-off level—does not force the asker to a seven-bid in a suit or six notrump. Failing this (or with no outside Queen), the response is six notrump to show the Queen of the asked suit. The reason for this is that the asking bidder, in requesting information about the Queen in the asked suit is prepared for any answer, which is not the case with outside Queens.

The general range of asking bids is from the three- to six-level, inclusive. The *responses* may be in at the seven-range, but a *free* seven-bid is a final trump bid even when not made in the agreed trump suit.

The New Blackwood 4–5 Notrump

When used with the Asking Bid, the Blackwood is retained as an auxiliary to the Asking Bid, but modified as follows:

1. The Blackwood (and the nonforcing) 4–5 notrump convention is used only *before* any asking bid. The space for free 4–5 notrump bids *after* any asking bid is reserved for the Trump Asking Convention (see below).

2. There is always an *agreed* trump suit and it is always the *first* suit that has been bid by the four notrump bidder. South bids 1 ♠. North bids 3 ♡. South 3 ♠. North bids 4 notrump, which is Blackwood.
The agreed trump suit, however, is hearts, not spades. This is important. It is the first time in bridge that a deadlock, which often arises when each partner holds a powerful suit, can be broken at a sufficiently low level.

3. After Ace-showing response to Blackwood's 4 notrump, Kings can be explored either by a Blackwood 5 notrump or by a second asking bid (usually one level cheaper).

The New Trump Asking Convention

There has always been a crying need in slam bidding for a simple method to find out about the *specific* honors and length in partner's trump suit. This need has now been filled by the New Trump Asking Convention, as follows:

After any asking bid and response, a bid of four notrump is a trump-asking convention requiring partner to give information on the key-cards of the agreed trump suit. The responses (forced) are:

Five clubs, holding a Jack or less in trumps.
Five diamonds, holding one of three top honors (A, K or Q) in trumps.
Five hearts, holding two of three top honors (A-K, A-Q or K-Q) in trumps.
Five spades, holding all three of three top honors in trumps (A-K-Q).

The key trumps must be shown regardless of the trump length. If, after one of these responses, the four notrump bidder follows up with *five* notrump, he requests specific information on the *length* of partner's agreed trump suit. Partner's responses (forced) are:

Six clubs, holding three trumps or less.
Six diamonds, holding four trumps.
Six hearts, holding five or six trumps.
Six spades, holding seven or more trumps.

If for any reason the four notrump level cannot be used, then the five notrump is used in a manner similar to the four notrump (for honor cards) but without the follow-up for length.

The objection has been raised that Asking Bids, although brilliant, are relatively unknown and that, consequently, there are few partners with whom to play them. If we carry this objection to its logical conclusion, then all progress must stop. I have designed scores of new bids, and now they are played by millions. In fact, not so very long ago there were only two persons who played the Culbertson System—Josephine and I.

The point is not how old or new a bid is, but how good, and how much it is needed. Almost every bridge player has a partner with whom he plays regularly. A better bid is to their advantage. They adopt it, and soon the opponents do likewise. That is how superior bids spread in ever-widening circles, and that is how the New Asking Bids will become the new standard for winning slam bidding.

For thousands of couples who play their weekly match games and for all advanced players, the New Asking Bid will prove to be a nearly perfect method for making slams and for avoiding unmakable slams. The responses are automatic and easy to learn, in fact most anyone can learn them parrot-like in an hour or less and never forget them. For an advanced player, it should be easier to absorb these responses, as they are logical and each response flows from the former one.

Illustrative hand and finer points of the Asking Bid follow.

PRECISION BIDDING

♠ K Q J 8 6 4   N   ♠ A 9 5 3 2
♡ 7   W   E   ♡ J 9 6 3
◊ A Q 7 5 4   S   ◊ 8
♣ 9   ♣ A 5 2

The bidding:

WEST	EAST
1 ♠	3 ♠
4 ◊ ?[1]	4 N T[2]
6 ♠	Pass

1. If East lacks diamond control, West can stop at four spades. If East shows one Ace plus a diamond fit, West can stop at five spades, which will be absolutely safe. If East responds with four notrump, showing a diamond fit and two Aces, a small slam is secure; and if East holds a diamond fit and *three* outside Aces, West can confidently bid a grand slam.

2. The four-notrump response, showing second-round control of diamonds and two Aces, permits West to bid six spades. West does not care which Aces they are.

It will be noted that without the use of asking bids, West could never have located the diamond control, and would not even have known whether East held the Ace or some such holding as K Q J in clubs.

JUMP ASKING BID

♠ K Q 9 4   N   ♠ A J 10 3 2
♡ A   W   E   ♡ K 6 4 2
◊ A K Q 6 3   S   ◊ 5 2
♣ 8 4 2   ♣ K 7

WEST	EAST
1 ◊	1 ♠
4 ♣[1]	5 ♠[2]
6 ♠[3]	Pass

1. West, fearing East may have all of his strength in the major suits, asks about the club suit and simultaneously "sets" the spade suit.

2. Showing King or singleton club and the Ace of spades.

3. A small slam is safe since the diamonds will afford discards.

Blackwood and Asking Bids

Here are some new and old examples of asking bids as bid by the new and improved method. The following is a hand analyzed by Josephine Culbertson in which the players were

not using asking bids, but were using the regular Blackwood
Convention.

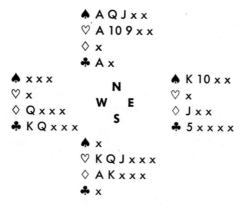

♠ A Q J x x
♡ A 10 9 x x
◇ x
♣ A x

♠ x x x
♡ x
◇ Q x x x
♣ K Q x x x

♠ K 10 x x
♡ x
◇ J x x
♣ 5 x x x x

♠ x
♡ K Q J x x x
◇ A K x x x
♣ x

As bid, using the Blackwood Convention:

South	West	North	East
1 ♡	Pass	2 ♠	Pass
3 ◇	Pass	4 N T	Pass
5 ◇	Pass	5 N T	Pass
6 ♡	Pass	Pass	Pass

The bidding stopped at the small slam although the grand
slam was unbeatable. North properly feared a spade loser.

Using new asking bids, the grand slam can be bid easily
and with complete certainty. The bidding would go as follows:

South	North
1 ♡	4 ♣ ?
4 ◇	4 ♠ ?
5 ◇	5 N T ?
6 ♡	7 ♡

Four clubs is an Asking Bid fixing hearts as trumps. *(There
is nothing to be gained by making a demand in spades.)* The
four-diamond response shows second-round control in clubs and
the Ace of diamonds. Four spades is a second asking bid. Five
diamonds shows second-round controls in spades and diamonds.
Five notrumps is a Trump-Asking Convention, asking, in this
case, for top honors in the agreed trump suit. If the 5 N T
were preceded by 4 N T, it would be asking for trump length.
Six hearts is an artificial response to show 2 out of 3 top honors

in hearts—K Q. With every possible loser specifically matched, North bids seven hearts which is a lay-down.

JUMP ASKING BID AFTER A RAISE

♠ A K Q 8 4	♠ J 9 6 2
♡ 3	♡ Q 10 5 2
◇ A 6	◇ 9 4
♣ K Q J 6 3	♣ A 8 4

WEST	EAST
1 ♠	2 ♠
4 ♣ ?[1]	5 ♣ [2]
6 ♠ [3]	Pass

1. West chooses to ask in clubs because the club Ace by itself makes a slam a good gamble; and if East can respond four notrump (two Aces) a grand slam is probable.

2. The raise in the asked suit shows the Ace (or a void) in clubs, and denies the heart Ace or void.

3. West takes the slight risk that East has seven minor-suit cards, in which case there may be a diamond as well as a heart loser. Since East is marked with four spades (by his raise) it is very unlikely that he will have only two hearts, for both opponents have passed a chance to bid the suit. Also, East may have the diamond King or Q J. There is far better than an even chance for six-odd.

HOW TO TRACE A K Q IN A SIDE SUIT

SOUTH	NORTH
♠ A K Q x x	♠ 10 x x x x
♡ x	♡ A x x
◇ J x x x	◇ A K Q x
♣ A x x	♣ x

The bidding:

SOUTH	NORTH
1 ♠	3 ♠
4 ♣ ?	4 N T
5 ◇ ?	6 ♣
6 ◇ ?	6 N T
7 ♠	Pass

It will be observed that every value in both hands, whether high honor or singleton, is necessary for the accurate bidding of the grand slam. South discovers the presence of all these values by the use of three asking bids. When North responds four notrump to the first asking bid of four clubs, he is showing two Aces and second-round club control, since South holds the other two Aces. When South asks five diamonds, North shows second-round diamond control and no third-round club loser by his six-club response. The grand slam is still not a make unless North holds Queen of diamonds, or A K bare, or Ace bare, or a void. There is still time for South to discover this without jeopardizing the small slam, and he bids six diamonds, asking for this third-round control. The six-notrump response shows that North has it, and the grand slam is on ice.

The time must come when the ridiculous guesswork of present-day slam-bidding is replaced by this superbly scientific accuracy!

How to Discover Seven Trumps Headed By A K Q in Partner's Hand

Suppose your partner shows a very strong trump suit and you hold a hand offering a grand slam provided partner's trump suit is absolutely solid. However, in support of his trump suit you have only a singleton Jack. The Trump-Asking convention solves this problem. After an asking bid based on the heart suit as the agreed trump, you bid 4 notrump. Partner replies with 5 spades. This shows A K Q in trumps. You now follow up with 5 notrump and partner replies also with 6 spades. This shows a 7 or 8 card *length* in hearts. Therefore he holds ♡ A K Q x x x x and you, with singleton Jack of hearts, know that his trump suit is absolutely solid.

Asking Bids Versus the Old-Fashioned Experts*

In *The Bridge World* of June, 1947, there appeared an article in which nine experts were approached for their opinions on the bidding of the following hand, to be considered on a non-double dummy basis:

West	East
♠ A 5	♠ K J 8 6 4 3
♡ J 7 5 3 2	♡ —
◇ A K	◇ 7 4
♣ A K 10 6	♣ Q J 9 5 2

* This remarkable hand and analysis is from M. Sapire's excellent booklet "Accurate Slam Bidding," published by *The Bridge World* magazine some time ago.

On this hand, seven clubs is almost a laydown, yet when it occurred in actual play, two expert players could reach only four spades! Of the nine experts who were approached for opinions, only two bid it alike, and while they all reached the small slam, only one of them considered that the grand slam could be bid!

In the consideration of the hand, Asking Bids were not even mentioned, hence one must conclude either that none of the players use Asking Bids, or that those who do could not apply them in this case. Yet I will proceed to demonstrate that two expert players, experienced in the use of Asking Bids, would reach the grand slam without the slightest difficulty!

This is how it would be bid:

WEST	EAST
1 ♡	1 ♠
2 N T	3 ♣
4 ◇	5 ♣
5 ♠	6 ♡
7 ♣	Pass

Two of the experts quoted by *The Bridge World* bid two notrumps after the one-spade response, hence this bid needs no justification. It is preferable to two clubs on West's powerful holding, and is virtually forcing. East's three-club bid makes West decide that the small slam is highly probable and the grand slam possible, and he proceeds to go into action with asking bids. But he has to use some ingenuity, as he cannot make an immediate asking bid in spades or hearts, as these are formerly bid suits. He makes the apparently useless asking bid of four diamonds, and gets the anticipated negative response. (The jump bid in diamonds is an asking bid fixing clubs as trumps by inference, since West could show a diamond suit by bidding three diamonds, to which East must respond.)

Now West makes his master bid, a subsequent asking bid of five spades. (Formerly bid suits can be used for making subsequent Asking Bids.) East responds six hearts, showing King of spades and Ace or void in hearts, making the grand slam almost a certainty. West assumes that East holds 10 black cards, hence there can be no losers in the red suits. But observe how he

finds out that East has King of spades, as East could be holding Q J x x x x. The grand slam could only fail if East held
♠ K J x x x   ♡ A x   ◇ x x   ♣ Q J x x, but his response to
two notrump would then not be three clubs. Furthermore,
the odds against partner's having this specific holding are more
than 3 to 1.

Bidding a Grand Slam After Making Five Asking Bids in One Hand

WEST	EAST
♠ A J x	♠ K Q x
♡ A K 10 x x x	♡ J x x x
◇ Q x	◇ A x
♣ A Q	♣ K x x x

The bidding:

WEST	EAST
1 ♡	3 ♡
4 ♣ ?	4 ◇
4 ♠ ?	4 N T
5 ◇ ?	5 ♡
5 ♠ ?	5 N T
6 ♣ ?	6 ♡
7 ♡	

Four clubs is the first asking bid, and the response of four
diamonds shows second-round club control and the diamond
Ace. The second asking bid is four spades, by which West asks
solely for second-round spade control. The four-notrump response by East shows second-round spade control. The five-
diamond bid is another asking bid, for second-round diamond
control, first-round control in diamonds already having been
shown. The five-heart sign-off denies second-round diamond
control. The fourth asking bid is five spades, which asks for
third-round spade control, second-round spade control having
been shown. The five-notrump response confirms third-round
spade control (the Queen). The fifth asking bid is six clubs,
asking for third-round club control, second-round club control
having been shown. The six-heart sign-off denies third-round
club control.

Now what has West discovered about his partner's hand as a result of all these asking bids? There are almost certainly no losers in hearts. His partner holds the King and Queen, or the King and only one small spade, hence there are no spade losers. His partner holds the Ace of diamonds but not the King, hence there is a losing diamond. But his partner holds the King of clubs *with at least two small clubs,* so this diamond can be discarded. West knows this by virtue of East's denial of third-round control in clubs. The grand slam can be bid and is almost certain to be made.

"Difference in Systems"

"On the following hand the United States team had no difficulty reaching a lay-down slam, while the Swedish pair stopped in game."

This is from a report by George Rapee in the *New York Times* on the World Championship match played by the winning American team-of-four against the Swedish team-of-four in January, 1953. Mr. Rapee, together with Theodore Lightner, was one of the members of the American team. One of the Swedish pairs played Culbertson combined with a highly artificial method they picked up in Italy. The method, called "EFOS," when tacked on the Culbertson System looks like a saddle on a cow. As a result their whole bidding went SNAFU. But the great significance of the hand cited by George Rapee is the bland assumption that the slam bidding by the American experts displayed an altogether superior system. Actually, as I will show, in the analysis below, the World Champions' bidding is a test case revealing the fundamental weakness of the American champions in slam bidding, and how it can be remedied.

Neither side vulnerable. South dealer.

SOUTH	NORTH
♠ K Q J 10 3	♠ A 9 7 2
♡ J 5	♡ A 8
◊ A Q 8 4	◊ K 9 2
♣ A K	♣ 10 8 7 3

SOUTH	NORTH
Crawford	Becker
1 ♠	3 ♠
6 ♠	Pass

The bidding was superficially impressive. In reality it was exactly on a par with the bidding of a near-beginner equipped with the Culbertson Point-Count (or Rule of 8). It must be remembered that the Crawford-Becker team is one of the few great pairs in the world, Mr. Crawford being noted for his brilliancy and Mr. Becker for his precision in bidding. Incidentally, it is fortunate that Becker did not use one of the current point-counts for his double raise. According to that count he has only 12 points—therefore not enough for a double raise. On the Culbertson point-count a double-raise is obligatory since North has exactly 13 points—11 points in high cards plus 2 points in low cards obtained by subtracting the shortest suit (the doubleton) from the trump length (see the Rule of Raises). After a double raise by Becker (North), a small-slam bid looked fine to Crawford (South) and he bid it and made it. What then was so very wrong with Crawford's bidding? The very wrong thing with Crawford's bidding is that his bidding was no better than that of any Culbertson near-beginner. With South's hand, Mr. Near-Beginner, using the Culbertson point-count, would know that North's double raise in spades shows at least 13 points. In his own hand he counts up 22 points— 20 points for high cards, 1 point for the fifth trump and 1 point for the fourth card in the diamond suit (Rule of 3 & 4). Adding both hands, he has a whopping total of 35 points, well within the small slam zone and even within hoping distance of a grand slam. Using the quicker, and also accurate, honor-trick method, the count of 7½ honor-tricks for combined hands leads to the same conclusion. In either case, Mr. Near-Beginner promptly bids six spades, just as Mr. Crawford did. It is little short of miraculous that Mr. Near-Beginner by using the Culbertson point-count arrives at a small slam as surely as Mr. Crawford, thereby bridging in a single leap the years of experience necessary to acquire an expert's finally attuned ear for slams. But it is a very sad miracle for Mr. Crawford. Mr.

Near-Beginner has been endowed with an exceptional point-count mechanism that does a lot of thinking for Mr. Near-Beginner and captures many slams with the precision of a robot. But this is not enough. There are many *other* slams which require more refined tools of precision (The Asking Bid) and which are beyond the capacity of Mr. Near-Beginner. That's where the expert comes in. Unfortunately, Mr. Crawford, unacquainted with the Asking Bids, has no choice but to rely on his own intuition. The best intuition in the world (and Crawford's is exceptional) cannot begin to compete with a clocklike, precision mechanism like the Asking Bid. As proof, here are three similar dummies. In each case, Crawford bids as he did, six spades. The results, however, are quite different.

Hand 1	Hand 2	Hand 3
NORTH	NORTH	NORTH
♠ A 9 7 2	(Becker)	♠ A 9 7 2
♡ A Q	♠ A 9 7 2	♡ A 8
◊ 7 6 3	♡ A 8	◊ K 9 2
♣ J 10 8 7	◊ K 9 2	♣ Q 8 7 3
	♣ 10 8 7 3	

SOUTH
(Crawford)
♠ K Q J 10 3
♡ J 5
◊ A Q 8 4
♣ A K

Each of the three North dummies rates a double raise in spades and in each case South (Crawford) bids six spades, side by side with Mr. Near-Beginner. It may be argued that Hand 1 "feels" wrong for a double raise and a waiting two-club bid would be preferable. In this case it makes no difference since South's hand is so powerful that without a special warning, that could come only from the asking bid, the final bid will be six spades. With Dummy 1, six spades by South is a poor bid despite the 35 points of Mr. Near-Beginner or Mr. Crawford's intuition. A diamond trick must be lost and two finesses must be right. With Dummy 2 (Becker) a six-spade bid is fine for Mr. Near-Beginner (his Culbertson robot clicked off an automatic 35 point-count for him); not so fine for Crawford. True, only a small slam should be bid, but Crawford failed to make at least a preliminary exploration for a possible grand slam. With Dummy 3, South's six spades is a poor bid indeed. The grand slam is cold. And, as I will show later, *it is easy to bid.* I can forgive the near-beginners for bidding only six spades. There is no way in which they can show the extra 2 points in the dummy for the Queen of clubs, and get 37 points; besides, they need a special kind of imagination for the count of the elusive losers which the Culbertson robot did not provide. For that, one needs the asking method plus a pinch or two of an expert's intuition. Crawford, however, slammed the door to the grand slam by his leap into six spades from Becker's double raise to three spades. Whenever I hear my partner make one of those herculean leaps (one spade—six spades is the worst), I wince. Why burn up the road? To the uninitiated these leaps may seem mighty dramatic, but it is poor bidding. Only a demigod (if he knows everything) can indulge in such short-cuts.

Crawford should have *expected* both the number 1 and the number 3 types of dummies from partner's double raise. All he needed for a sure grand slam, in addition to two Aces, was the King of diamonds and the Queen of clubs *with two small clubs.* Does this mean that Crawford is not as great a player as he is reputed to be? Not at all. Previously I analyzed a hand played in the same World Championship match by Crawford-Becker's teammates, Schenken-Stayman, where they found themselves in a small slam with two winning Aces against them. Both Crawford and Schenken are on my list of the greatest bridge players of all time. The trouble is not with them, the disease lies much deeper, and it is widespread. The fact is that the American expert players, though leading the world in other branches of contract bridge, are still in an embryonic stage in their slam bidding. They simply do not possess the necessary tools of precision for scientific slam bidding. The New Asking Bid fills this long-felt need. Here is how Crawford and partner would probably have bid his hand and dummies 1, 2 or 3 if they used the New Asking Bid.

Dummy 1

SOUTH	NORTH
Crawford	Becker
1 ♠	3 ♠
4 ◊ ?	4 ♠ Sign off
5 ◊ ?[1]	5 ♠ Sign off

1. North's 4 ♠ sign-off denies first- or second-round controls in diamonds. South's five diamond is a repeat bid asking for a doubleton diamond. He reasons he might still have a good gamble for a slam. North's second sign-off shatters South's last illusion. The hands play at five spades and make 11 tricks.

Dummy 2

SOUTH	NORTH
Crawford	Becker
1 ♠	3 ♠
4 ◊ ?	4 N T[1]
5 ♡ ?	5 ♠ Sign off[2]
6 ♣ ?[3]	6 ♠ Sign off[4]
Pass	

1. 4 N T response shows ♠ A, ♡ A and ◊ K or singleton.
2. South now is seriously thinking of the grand slam. His only loser to dispose of is a heart. Consequently he bids 5 ♡ asking for a second-round control in hearts.
3. In spite of North's sign-off, South still has a chance for grand slam if he can locate a ♣ Q. Accordingly he bids 6 ♣ asking for the ♣ Q.
4. North denies the ♣ Q (a club doubleton is highly improbable on the bidding). The hands play at six spades and make 12 tricks.

Dummy 3

SOUTH	NORTH
Crawford	Becker
1 ♠	3 ♠
4 ◊ ?	4 N T
5 ♡ ?	5 ♠ Sign off
6 ♣ ?	6 ♡ !
7 ♠	Pass

The bidding progresses in the same way as with No. 2 until North responds with 6 hearts to six-club asking bid. This response shows a ♣ Q and a ♡ Q or doubleton. South reasons that he can now discard the losing heart in his hand on the ♣ Q provided there are at least three clubs. If

North has only two clubs (South reasons again) then he must have five diamonds since North's 6 ♡ response showed a doubleton (with ♡ A Q plus ♣ Q, an Ace and a King there would have been a forcing takeout, most probably). With five diamonds headed by the King, South could still get rid of his losing heart on the fifth diamond. Therefore, either way a grand slam is safe. The hands play at a grand slam in spades and make thirteen tricks.

There is more to be done to improve the New Asking Bid and I expect the great players everywhere to correct and perfect the New Asking Bid. Enough has already been accomplished to warrant abandoning the present archaic and confusing methods of slam bidding and place them on a higher level of simple but scientific slam bidding based on the Asking Bid principle.

Asking Bids in Opponents' Suits

There are two situations when an asking bid is made in the opponents' bid suit: after an opening bid by partner and after an opening bid by opponents. Here I deal with the former situation.

When the opponents have entered the bidding, a player may find it necessary to make an asking bid in *their* suit. Since a bid in the opponents' suit is universally employed to show a void or the Ace plus excellent support for partner's suit, a player must jump the bidding to make an asking bid.

SOUTH	WEST	NORTH	EAST
1 ♡	1 ♠	3 ♠ ?	Pass

South must now make a conventional response, since North's jump in the opponent's suit is an asking bid. Without at least second-round control of spades, South must sign off at four hearts. With second-round control of spades (spade King or singleton) South bids the suit in which he holds the Ace: four clubs, four diamonds, or *five* hearts (jumping to distinguish from the sign-off).

In many cases the normal level of four is reached when the asking overcall is made:

SOUTH	WEST	NORTH	EAST
1 ♡	2 ◇	4 ◇ ?	Pass

Now South's responses will be at the usual levels. The situation is exactly as though North had raised hearts and had then made a normal asking bid in diamonds.

The asking overcall is used almost exclusively when a player has no fear except that the opponents may take two immediate tricks in their suit. He should remember that he is "setting" his partner's suit which may consist of only four to the Queen-Jack. For that reason, the asker must be ready to guarantee, opposite such a minimum trump holding, a trump suit which is strong enough for slam purposes.

Also, the asker should have a hand strong enough to warrant further action in the event that his partner's response is positive. Nothing is more ridiculous than for a player to make a slam try, only to collapse weakly when his partner shows enthusiasm.

Since many opening bids of one are made with only about four winners, the asker must have about seven winners to make up the required total of eleven. This usually takes the form of a long (generally solid) side suit.

If partner signs off, showing that he, too has at least two losers in the adverse suit, hope of slam is necessarily abandoned. The partners rest content with a game contract, thankful, nevertheless, for the weapon which disclosed the gaping pit before it was too late to draw back.

But when the response is positive, a slam is highly probable. After the asking overcall and its response, any bid (except the agreed suit) is a subsequent asking bid.

South	West	North	East
1 ♡	1 ♠	?	

North should bid:

Three spades	*Two diamonds*	*Three hearts*
♠ 5 3	♠ 5 3	♠ 5 3
♡ K J 9 6	♡ Q 9 6	♡ K 10 9 6
◇ A K Q 6 3	◇ A K Q 6 3	◇ A J 8 6 3
♣ A J	♣ A J 6	♣ A J

In the first example North has excellent support for even a weak trump suit. He has over seven winners in support of hearts and can almost guarantee a slam provided only that South can win the first or second spade lead.

In the second example, North lacks the trump support necessary for the asking overcall. The recommended response of two diamonds is a slight underbid, (North has the minimum for a game-forcing bid of three diamonds); but North may yet be able to make the asking overcall if South can rebid his hearts. North, therefore, tries to keep the bidding low.

In the third example, North has too few winners for an asking over-call. If South cannot make a slam try after the strong double raise, there is almost certainly no slam in the combined hands.

ASKING OVERCALL

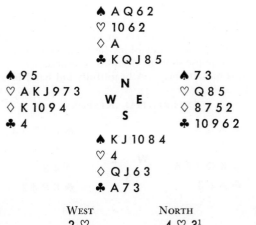

SOUTH	WEST	NORTH	EAST
1 ♠	2 ♡	4 ♡ ?[1]	Pass
5 ♣[2]	Pass	6 ♠[3]	Pass
Pass	Pass		

1. A slam is sure unless West can win two immediate heart tricks.
2. Showing the club Ace plus second-round heart control.
3. Knowing that South has the club Ace, North does not care whether his second-round heart control is the King or a singleton, because with a lead by West no more than one heart can be lost before discards are available.

ASKING OVERCALL PLUS THE TRUMP-ASKING BID

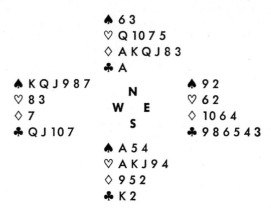

The bidding:

SOUTH	WEST	NORTH	EAST
1 ♡	1 ♠	3 ♠ ?[1]	Pass
3 N T[2]	Pass	4 N T[3]	Pass
5 ♡[4]	Pass	7 ♡ ! Final bid	Pass

1. Asking overcall.
2. Conventional response; two Aces, including Ace in the asked suit.
3. A Trump-Asking convention asking for top honors in hearts.
4. An artificial response showing A and K of hearts.
A grand slam is bid and made. A beautifully bid hand in modern dress.

INFERENTIAL RESPONSE

SOUTH	WEST	NORTH	EAST
Pass	1 ◇	1 ♡	1 ♠[1]
Pass	3 ♡ ?[2]	Pass	3 ♠[3]
Pass	4 ♣ ?[4]	Pass	4 ♡[5]
Pass	6 ♠	Pass	Pass
Pass			

1. Nearly a minimum free bid after an intervening overcall.
2. An asking bid in North's suit. This makes spades the agreed trump suit.
3. The sign-off; though East has second-round heart control, he has no Ace.
4. A subsequent asking bid.
5. The obvious inference from this bid is that East has second-round control both in clubs (the second asked suit) and in hearts (the first asked suit). If East had the heart Ace or void he would have bid four hearts over three hearts before. Lacking second-round club control he would have to sign off over four clubs.

THE OUTSTANDING BRIDGE HAND OF THE YEAR

Albert H. Morehead describes the following remarkable hand in the December 28, 1952, issue of *The New York Times:*

"The outstanding bridge hand of the year—or at least the one that most impressed this writer—was played in New York City and was reported by Lee Hazen.

"What makes the hand outstanding is that it defies constructive analysis: No generalized conclusion can be drawn from it
to help with similar bidding problems. This is the situation:

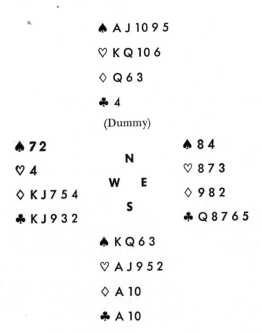

♠ A J 10 9 5

♡ K Q 10 6

◊ Q 6 3

♣ 4

(Dummy)

♠ 7 2

♡ 4

◊ K J 7 5 4

♣ K J 9 3 2

♠ 8 4

♡ 8 7 3

◊ 9 8 2

♣ Q 8 7 6 5

♠ K Q 6 3

♡ A J 9 5 2

◊ A 10

♣ A 10

North-South were vulnerable. The bidding:

NORTH	EAST	SOUTH	WEST
1 ♠	Pass	3 ♡	Pass
4 ♡	Pass	5 ◊	Pass
6 ♡	Pass	7 ♠	Pass
Pass	Pass		

"Experts generally agree with South's bid of seven spades.
Spades looked like the best suit, because North bid them first.

"Something went wrong, because it is apparent that North
could not make seven spades.

"In this case, however, a seven-heart contract would have
been a laydown. South would have discarded his ten of dia-

monds on North's fifth spade, trumped his ten of clubs in dummy, and won the remainder with top cards.

"The question is, how could South have known all this before making the final bid? There will be a lot of analyzing before a satisfactory conclusion is reached."

A satisfactory conclusion can be reached by means of the Asking Bid method. Here is the bidding.

NORTH (D)	EAST	SOUTH	WEST
1 ♠	Pass	4 ♡ ?[1]	Pass
5 ♠[2]	Pass	6 ♣ ?	Pass
6 ♠[3]	Pass	7 ♡ Final Bid	

1. South selects the heart suit for his asking bid because it is the key to the small or grand slam.

2. North shows the trump Ace and a second-round control in hearts, probably the King.

3. North's response shows ♣ K or singleton and ♡ Q. Doubletons in the outside suits are not shown. It is now certain that North holds ♡ K Q. It is also certain that North has no ◊ K, since North is required to show a ◊ K in preference to a Queen. Furthermore, the chances are substantial that North, to justify his vulnerable opening bid, has five spades at least. Thus, the Asking Bid method revealed that there are no losers in combined hands except ◊ 10 which can be discarded on the fifth spade. Hence a grand slam bid in *hearts*. In the Asking Bid method any free bid of seven (even though it be not in the agreed trump suit) is not conventional.

ASKING BIDS AFTER IMMEDIATE OVERCALLS IN OPPONENTS' SUIT

The second situation for asking bids occurs when an opponent opens the bidding. The immediate overcall in the opponents' suit by a defender is treated exactly as a forcing two-bid as regards asking bids and responses.

When an asking bid is made and partner holds the King or a singleton in the asked suit with an outside Ace, his preference is to show the outside Ace; but if he should hold no outside Ace, he must still respond with the required number of notrump.

The following is a beautiful hand to illustrate the modern bidding. My partner was Josephine Culbertson.

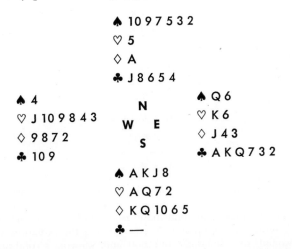

♠ 10 9 7 5 3 2
♡ 5
◇ A
♣ J 8 6 5 4

♠ 4
♡ J 10 9 8 4 3
◇ 9 8 7 2
♣ 10 9

♠ Q 6
♡ K 6
◇ J 4 3
♣ A K Q 7 3 2

♠ A K J 8
♡ A Q 7 2
◇ K Q 10 6 5
♣ —

EAST Dealer	SOUTH Ely Culbertson	WEST	NORTH Josephine Culbertson
1 ♣	2 ♣¹	Pass	2 ♠²
Pass	3 ◇³	3 ♡	3 ♠
Pass	5 ♡ ?⁴	Pass	6 ◇
Pass	7 ♠⁵	Pass	Pass
Pass			

1. A good forcing overcall. A takeout double is a poor bid since partner may make a disastrous penalty pass.

2. A very fine bid. There is no use getting excited by jumping, since the bidding cannot die here.

3. South naturally assumes from partner's two-spade bid that she may hold as few as four spades, nine-high. He therefore looks for a better fit in diamonds. So far the suit has not been set.

4. Five hearts is an asking bid, automatically setting spades as the agreed suit. South, in spite of his magnificent hand, definitely fears two losers—the heart King and the diamond Ace. If his partner holds a singleton heart, then a small slam is practically certain, and if his partner in addition holds the diamond Ace, then a grand slam is also practically certain.

5. Partner's six-diamond bid tells South that she holds the diamond Ace and the heart King or a heart singleton. Her free spade rebid must show at least six spades or five to the Queen. Hence a practically certain bid of a grand slam, in spite of the vulnerable opening suit-bid of one.

Discovering Second-Round Control in the Opponents' Suit

♠ K J 10 x x
♡ K x x
◊ Q J x
♣ x x

N
W   E
S

♠ A x x x x
♡ x x
◊ —
♣ A K x x x x

West opens one heart, North bids one spade, East passes. South can see a good play for the slam if North holds first- or second-round control in hearts, hence he makes an immediate asking bid of three hearts, fixing spades as the agreed trump suit. North, treating this situation as after a forcing two-bid, now responds four notrump, showing second-round control in hearts, and South bids six spades. With the lead coming from East, the contract is almost certainly a make.

Asking After an Opening Two-Bid

There must be a modification in the rules for asking bids when made by a player who has opened with a two-bid. The forcing two-bid is so strong that it often will lead to a slam, and asking bids will be of great value to the two-bidder.

The Problem of Aceless Hands

Here is logical modification in the case of asking bids as applied to forcing two-bids. We run up against a tremendous range of hands, especially after opening two-bids and other very powerful bids, where partner has no Aces and yet the meager balance of values—two or three miserable Kings or Queens, or a singleton—are decisive in the success or failure of a slam bid. Hence the following rule when responding to any asking bid:

After any opening bid of two in a suit, the response to an asking bid to show second-round control in the asked suit is
  (a) Outside Ace if available, failing which
  (b) The required number of notrump.

SOUTH	NORTH
2 ♡	2 ♠
4 ◇ ?	4 N T

North's four notrump shows either a singleton diamond or the diamond King. At the same time *it denies any Ace in the hand,* since the first preference in showing a fit is another Ace.

All other requirements and responses governing asking bids after an opening suit-bid of one, remain unchanged when the opening bid was two except the following:

Holding the King or a singleton of the asked suit and two Aces outside; or two Aces including the Ace of the asked suit, *jump* one trick in notrump.

A question may arise in connection with showing a single-ton after a forcing two-bid, which is a matter rather of common sense than of method. Your partner may have a singleton in the asked suit and only a singleton of trumps. In such cases your partner is expected to use a teeny bit of imagination. He should not give a positive four-notrump response with a single-ton of the asked suit and a singleton trump. That would be almost as bad as the story of a distracted act of a player who led a singleton for a ruff and forgot that he had no trumps.

In the foregoing example the usual 4 N T level is "usurped" to show at least one King. Consequently, the 5 N T level has to be used to show two Aces and a fit in the asked suit. Similarly if partner should hold three Aces and a fit—a most un-likely supposition after a forcing two-bid—he should bid six notrump, a safe enough bid after a forcing two-bid.

JUMP ASKING BID AFTER TWO-BID

♠ A K Q J 3 2		♠ 7 5	
♡ A	N	♡ 8 6 5 3	
◇ 7	W　E	◇ 9 8 4 3	
♣ A Q J 6 2	S	♣ K 7 5	

WEST	EAST
2 ♠[1]	2 N T
4 ♣ ?[2]	4 N T[3]
6 ♠[4]	Pass

1. Too strong for a Limit Two-Bid.
2. Asking for second-round control of clubs.

3. Showing the King. This is one case in which a positive response is given to an asking bid without an Ace or void in the hand—after an opening two-bid.

4. If East has a singleton club, instead of the King, he must have two trumps; otherwise he would have signed off. At worst, West will have a finesse for the small slam.

Asking Bids After Two Notrump Response to the Opening Two-Bid

There is another logical modification in the Asking Bids when an opening two-bid has brought a two-notrump response. For instance,

SOUTH	NORTH
2 ♡	2 N T
4 ◇ ?	

The two-notrump response shows as a maximum an Ace and a Queen or 1 plus honor-tricks (6 pts.). Consequently, the table of responses to the asking bid is rearranged as follows (assuming the first asking bid is made at the level of four):

I. *Responses to the First Asking Bid.*

With a Queen in the asked suit and an Ace (or void) outside, raise the outside Ace (or void) suit, including the agreed trump.

In all cases Queens are tied to Aces (or voids) which are shown by a raise.

A singleton (with two trumps) is equivalent to a Queen.

With a King in the asked suit and a King outside, bid the outside King; except that if the outside King is in the agreed trump suit you *raise* the trump suit (up to the level of six but no higher). Treat the Queen of the agreed trump suit as an equivalent of the King.

With a King (or singleton) in the asked suit only, respond with the required number of notrump.

Sign off with less.

II. *Responses to Second Asking Bids.*

Aces and Kings having been eliminated in the first responses, the second responses deal with Queens or doubletons (with three trumps). Sign off if holding no Queen or doubleton in the asked suit.

Show an outside Queen provided it is below the sign-off level.

With only a Queen in the asked suit, or no cheap Queen outside, respond with notrump.

III. *Responses to Third Asking Bids.*

These responses are valid only at the six-level and after the Queen of the agreed trump suit has been shown: show your Jacks in the same manner as the Queens.

Special Cases of Asking Bids

Championship play has produced many refinements of the asking bids. Advanced players will profit from a study of the special cases that follow.

AVOIDING DUPLICATION

How to show a void in the asking bidder's suit.

SOUTH	NORTH
1 ♠	3 ♠
4 ♣ ?	4 N T
6 ♡ ?	

A jump by the asker at the level of six (sometimes five) is a special case. Partner is required to sign off if holding an Ace in the asked suit. Otherwise his response is notrump.

Suppose South holds the following hand:

♠ K Q J 7 5   ♡ —   ◇ A K 6   ♣ K Q 8 6 2

He bids one spade, and North gives him a double raise to three spades. South now makes an asking bid of four clubs, and North's response is four notrump. North may hold:

1. ♠ 10 8 6 4 3   ♡ A K Q   ◇ 7   ♣ A 9 7 3
2. ♠ A 9 6 4   ♡ K Q J   ◇ 8 4   ♣ A 7 5 3
3. ♠ A 8 6 4 3   ♡ A K Q   ◇ 8 7 5 3 ♣ 9

If North has No. 2, seven spades can be made; if North has No. 1 or No. 3, six spades is the limit. South's problem is to find out which hand North holds.

The solution is in the double jump duplication-avoiding bid (for experts only).

ASKING BID DEFENSE AGAINST INTERFERENCE BIDS

At first it may seem obvious that, while partners are actively engaged in making asking bids and responses, the opponents will not stand idly by observing the proceedings with polite curiosity. It seems that they would and should try to block the exchange of information at least with an interference double.

And yet, to stand idly by is exactly what the opponents should do as their best defense against the asking bids. Let us take the following bidding situation:

SOUTH	WEST	NORTH	EAST
1 ♡	Pass	1 ♠	Pass
2 ◇	Pass	2 ♡	Pass
4 ♣ ?	Double	Redouble!	

West, by his double, is possibly trying to show to his partner that he holds fair clubs, but his main object is to "chop up" the messages being broadcast between South and North.

To double an asking bid is the worst thing that West could do. Its only effect is to *add* to North's collection of replies.

North will proceed in almost all cases as though the double had not been made, except that he may *gain* a round of bidding in the following cases:

To sign off, North will pass, instead of returning to the agreed trump suit. Therefore,

To show the trump Ace and the King or singleton of the asked suit, North may bid the agreed suit at the lowest possible level. He need not skip.

To show the King or singleton in the asked suit, but no Ace, North will redouble, instead of signing off as is usually required. This is valuable information, yet had West not doubled, North would have been compelled to sign off, at a higher level.

When an Opponent Overcalls the Asking Bid

When an opponent overcalls an asking bid with any suit-bid, he risks a penalty double and a large penalty. However, some freak hands will justify such an overcall. The asker's partner will proceed as follows:

1. If it is possible to respond to the asking bid at the same level as though the overcall had not been made, the usual conventional response to the asking bid should be made.

SOUTH	WEST	NORTH	EAST
1 ♠	Pass	3 ♠	Pass
4 ♣ ?	4 ◇		

North holds: ♠ Q J 7 5 ♡ A K 6 ◇ 5 2 ♣ K 7 4 2

North can bid four hearts, showing the heart Ace and second-round control in clubs, exactly as though West had not put in the four-diamond overcall. Therefore North should bid four hearts.

2. If ordinarily the asker's partner would have signed off to the asking bid, he should *pass* the opponent's overcall. This leaves his partner the option of making a penalty double.

The asker's partner may make a penalty double himself, *even though he holds a fit with the asked suit and sufficient values to make a positive response to the asking bid.* For example:

SOUTH	WEST	NORTH	EAST
1 ♠	3 ♣	3 ♠	4 ♣
4 ◇ ?	5 ♣		

North holds: ♠ J 8 7 5 ♡ 6 4 ◇ K J 6 ♣ A 10 7 3
He should double.

The player who has made the asking bid has an easy decision to make when the asking bid has been overcalled by an opponent. If his partner passes or doubles, the fit is probably lacking and a slam therefore being doubtful a penalty double will probably be the best final contract. With a freak hand, however, or when game seems certain and a satisfactory penalty doubtful, the asker can either continue the bidding in the agreed trump suit or make another asking bid.

A Tragedy to World Champions

The U. S. team-of-four champions were defeated in the preliminary match on the following remarkable hand played in August, 1953 in St. Louis. The losing team-of-four (John R. Crawford, B. J. Becker, Theodore A. Lightner, George Rapee, Howard Schenken and Samuel M. Stayman) are also the 1953 holders of the World Team-of-Four Championship which they won against the European champions (Swedish team-of-four led by Dr. Werner) in January, 1953.* By losing the U. S. Championship the present World Champions also lose the right to defend their world championship title in 1954. The team-of-four that won the preliminary match in St. Louis was the California championship team made up of Dr. Eduard Frischauer (a famous Viennese player), Ivan Erdos, Lewis Mathe and Meyer Schleifer. The knockout blow, however, was delivered not by them but by the World Champions to themselves with their antiquated methods of slam bidding. The hand is exceedingly interesting because it involves a very delicate and difficult choice between a small slam at notrump (which could be made) and a small slam at spades (which could not be made). It proves beyond any doubt that even one of the greatest pairs in the world (such as Crawford-Becker) are helpless unless they use a more scientific method of slam bidding—the Asking Bid.

The hand was:

SOUTH	NORTH
♠ A Q 9 x x x	♠ K J
♡ K 2	♡ Q 10 x x
◊ x x	◊ A K x x
♣ K x x	♣ A Q 10

South-North vulnerable, West-East not vulnerable, South is the dealer.

SOUTH Becker	WEST	NORTH Crawford	EAST
1 ♠	2 ♡ [1]	3 ◊ [2]	Pass
3 ♠	Pass	4 ♣ [3]	Pass
4 ♠ [4]	Pass	5 ♠ [5]	Pass
6 ♠ [6]	All Pass		

♡ A is led by West, wins first trick and second heart lead is ruffed by East, defeating the slam in spades. In notrump the slam is a laydown.

1. West held ♡ A J 9 8 x x x and his overcall is perfectly sound especially when not vulnerable.

2. Crawford, his side vulnerable and, he, scenting a slam, wisely refrains from taking a non-vulnerable penalty. He therefore makes a waiting bid of three diamonds.

3. After Becker's (South) normal rebid in spades, Crawford (North) reasons that his partner most probably holds ♠ A Q x x x x since there is not

---

* This event instituted in 1950 is not to be confused with the Schwab Trophy for world championship that was played previously and which is held by Ely Culbertson, Josephine Culbertson, Michael Gottlieb, Theodore Lightner, Albert H. Morehead and Waldemar von Zedtwitz.

much outside to justify an opening one-spade bid. Sure of the spade suit, Crawford proceeds with preliminary tests for a small slam. Aware of the ♡ Q 10 x x staring from his hand he proceeds with utmost caution. He bids four clubs, to "show" the Ace of clubs and indicate "a desire" for slam.

4. A more reckless player might have bid 4 N T to show ♡ K x and thereby avoided the future tragedy on this hand. But it is a dangerous plunge and besides, Becker reasons that West is not going to lead from ♡ A Q 10, Ace against a slam bid in notrump. A less experienced player might have bid five clubs "to show" the King of clubs. But Becker wisely ignores Crawford's desire and signs off with four spades.

5. After Becker's (South's) sign-off in four spades, Crawford makes what I consider a brilliant bid of five spades. Some experts criticized Crawford for not bidding Blackwood four-notrump to be followed by King-searching five notrump. This would have disclosed the King of hearts and Crawford could have then bid six notrump and made it. This is a better bid than supinely resting at four spades, but certainly not as good as Crawford's five spades. If South held no King of hearts, Blackwood could never show whether South held a singleton or a doubleton heart. Why should Crawford visualize a ♡ K x rather than a more probable singleton or doubleton heart? South, to justify his opening spade bid, could very well hold six or seven spades headed by A Q, ◊ Q J 10 and ♣ K J x with one or two hearts. At the same time, Crawford is perfectly safe at five spades even if partner holds a doubleton heart. Hence, a very fine bid of five spades by Crawford, virtually begging partner to bid six spades if he holds a singleton heart and sign off with a doubleton.

6. Becker's bid of six spades is irreproachable, as was his bidding throughout this sad hand.

Thus, both Becker and Crawford, bidding irreproachably and at times brilliantly, are forced step by step to the inexorable defeat where the great world champions went under. But what defeated them was not their individual errors nor that special bridge fate where a superior play loses. What led them to this defeat was, simply and obviously, a defective method of slam bidding. I will show now how, by using a better method, even Mr. and Mrs. Advanced Players Second Class, could not logically fail to reach a winning small slam at notrump (provided they memorize the simple and automatic responses to asking bids). Here is how the bidding would go on the same hand:

SOUTH	NORTH
♠ A Q 9 x x x	♠ K J
♡ K 2	♡ Q 10 x x
◊ x x	◊ A K x x
♣ K x x	♣ A Q 10

SOUTH	WEST	NORTH	EAST
1 ♠	2 ♡	3 ◇	Pass
3 ♠	Pass	4 ♡ ?[1]	Pass
5 ♠ [2]	Pass	6 ♡ ?[3]	Pass
6 N T	Pass	Pass!	

1. North's four-heart bid in opponent's heart suit is *an asking overcall* with spades as the agreed suit. Any jump overcall in opponent's bid suit (after partner opened the bidding) or, if partner's suit had been raised or rebid, any non-jump overcall in opponent's bid suit at the level of four, is an asking bid requesting information about the asked suit (in this case the opponent's hearts) and outside controls.* The asking overcall does not, as a rule, shut out the normal, traditional cue-overcall which is non-jump (not unnecessarily high) and which is usually made at the first opportunity. For instance, in the bidding above if North, after West's 2 ♡ bid 3 ♡ instead of 3 ◇ it would be a regulation cue-overcall indicating a void or Ace in diamonds and slam possibilities.

2. The five-spade response to the four-heart asking bid is regulation response to show (1) second-round control in the asked suit (♡ K x or ♡ singleton) and (2) the Ace in the agreed trump suit. At the same time it denies ♡ A.

3. North now knows that partner has either the King or a singleton heart. He could not have two smaller hearts because then South would have signed off with four spades. *The only problem North must now resolve is whether South holds King of hearts (in which case six notrump is the right bid) or a singleton heart (in which case six spades is the right bid).* Except with the Asking Bid there exists no method to solve this problem. With the Asking method the solution is very simple.

North makes *another* asking bid. A free asking bid at the *level of six* is reserved, as a rule, for information on the *third-round controls,* i.e., the Queen of the asked suit or doubleton. Failing to hold Queen or a doubleton in the asked suit the response is a sign-off. In this case South, holding a doubleton heart and *therefore K x of hearts, no more and no less,* makes a positive response of six notrump, which North naturally passes.

---

* The only difference in this situation from basic definition of when an asking bid is an asking bid is that the asked suit is opponent's and rebid of his suit by the opening bidder is enough to set the agreed suit.

BOOK TWO

STRUCTURE OF BIDS AND PLAYS

Before attempting a study of strategy and psychology in bidding, the player should be familiar with declarer's and defenders' leads and play. The average player is advised to read Book III on leads and play before taking up Book II. The more finished player should read Book II in its regular order and then read Book III for review and improved technique.

CHAPTER THIRTY

THE
SAFETY FACTOR

Self-preservation is the first law of bridge as of life. Safety, therefore, is the first and the last measure of any bid.

Avoidable loss comes from two sources: unjustifiable penalties, and failure to make the most of one's opportunities. I have tried to show throughout this book how to grasp and sometimes create opportunity. In bridge, opportunity knocks at every second deal and failure to grab it by the hair accounts for the invisible leak through which all the profits flow out.

MEASURING GAIN AGAINST RISK

Every bid is a bet. To be justified, the odds of any bet must be proportionate to the probable risk. The following bid is an utterly foolish bet:

South opens the bidding with one spade and West, though vulnerable, overcalls with two hearts. There are a score of reasons why this bid is a foolish bet. If partner is weak West will be doubled and lose 800 to 1400 points; the maximum he can gain is 620 points by scoring a game, a very remote possibility considering that South opened the bidding. Therefore, he gambles at least 800 points to win a part-score.

```
              ♠ 6 3
              ♡ Q J 9 5
              ◇ K Q 7 4
              ♣ Q 7 4
♠ 7 4            N        ♠ Q J 10 8
♡ A K 7 6 4   W   E      ♡ 8 3 2
◇ J 6 3          S        ◇ 10 9 8 5
♣ 10 6 3                  ♣ A J
              ♠ A K 9 5 2
              ♡ 10
              ◇ A 2
              ♣ K 9 8 5 2
```

The Rule of Risk and Gain

Before making any bid the player should apply the following simple rule of Risk and Gain:

First Step: Calculate roughly the reasonable maximum loss if the bid is unsuccessful.

Second Step: Calculate the probable gain of a bid. Compare the two. The "probable" gain of a bid may be points saved or points scored.

In calculating his risks the player should not, as a rule, expect the very worst. Except when the bidding so indicates, he is as unlikely to find partner's hand an absolute blank as to find it teeming with Aces and Kings. Somewhere, somehow a trick or a humble *trick-helper* will be found in his hand and players who habitually assume a maximum possible loss undershoot the mark as widely as the incurable optimist overshoots it.

If I hold ♠ A K J 10 8 2, for the purpose of bidding I am safe in valuing the suit as five sure winners. It is true that I may lose two tricks in the suit if an opponent's holding is ♠ Q 9 7 4 3, but to expect a blank hand (or a blank head) is disastrous in bridge. Curiously enough, it is the gloomy super-pessimist who always *gets* this type of monstrous distribution, just as it is the person who is terrified in crossing the street that most often gets killed.

The Rule of 2 and 3

It is evident that a player cannot know the safety margin of any bid unless he knows the minimum number of tricks that he has the right to expect in partner's hand.

This problem is successfully solved when partner has made some kind of bid. By adding the minimum number of winners shown by his bid to the winners in one's own hand one gets the total winners available and can then determine the limit of safety of his bid.

The real difficulty arises when partner has passed or has not yet bid. Caution demands that, except for special inferences drawn from opponents' bidding, the situation where partner has not yet bid should be treated as though partner had passed. In either case, should the player "play safe" and expect a near blank, or should he "take a flyer" hoping to find partner with fair help? The answer is: *He should do neither.* To expect too much would lead to severe penalties. To expect "nothing" in the dummy would result in an even greater evil—gross underbidding. The proper solution of this perplexing problem is to be found in this following Rule of 2 and 3:

When partner has passed or has not yet bid, the maximum expectancy of tricks in his hand should be two winners, if vulnerable, and three winners if not vulnerable. It follows that the bidder in order to be reasonably safe must have in his own hand the total of winners required by the contract *less two* or, as the case may be, *three* winners. Thus, to overcall the opponents' one-spade bid with two hearts, I must have at least six winners if vulnerable and five winners if not vulnerable.

The following table shows the number of winners required by the players at various levels of bidding:

Bidding Level	Winners Vul.	Winners Not Vul.
One-odd (not the opening bid)	5	4
Two-odd	6	5
Three-odd	7	6
Four-odd	8	7

The obvious exceptions to the Rule of 2 and 3 are:
(*a*) When the opponents do not know how to double for penalties, or are just naturally overpolite;
(*b*) When making an opening one-bid;
(*c*) When the bidding clearly indicates that partner, even though he passed, holds a fair hand; and
(*d*) When a sacrifice is advisable to stop a slam.

In many cases it becomes apparent that opponents are not likely to make game. In such cases the *safety margin* of expectancy in partner's hand (always assuming he has made no bid) is reduced as follows:

(1) If vulnerable, about one winner.

(2) If not vulnerable, about two winners.

There is no sense in risking a heavier penalty unless, of course, the player's own hand is so strong as to offer a fair chance for game. Moreover, it does not mean that judicious pushing of opponents should not be indulged in, especially when the bidding *overtones* make the player feel that the opponents will go on.

CHAPTER THIRTY-ONE

SCORING AND
ITS MATHEMATICS

The bid which, when compared with other possible bids around the table, is more likely to win the most points is the best final bid. If a contract of five diamonds can more probably be made than a contract of three notrump, the former is the best bid. To risk a safe game in a minor suit (worth roughly 500 points) for the sake of picking up a few extra points at a shaky no-trump is poor strategy, though a rather common failing.* The reverse is also true: not to risk a loss of 100 points or so in order to shoot at the game worth five times as much although in a less safe contract is equally poor strategy, and equally a common failing.

The player first determines the best bid available in partnership hands—be it even a part-score bid. *His second step is to compare the points he expects to score at his own bid with the estimated points that he can penalize the opponents; or the points the opponents can score at their best bid as against the points that they can penalize him.*

The best final bid, therefore, may range anywhere from a slam to a voluntary penalty when by so doing the opponents are prevented from scoring more points at their own bid.

A loss, for instance, of 300 points at a player's own bid is a splendid investment if his opponents are prevented from scor-

---

* The situation is different in duplicate with special match-point scoring, but even here the rubber bridge strategy should be modified but little and only when consistent with safety.

ing at their own bid a rubber worth 600 points. His net gain is 300 points. Never mind that the 300 points in penalties are reproachfully staring him in the face from the score sheet while the 600 points saved do not somehow seem to be in flesh and bones. These invisible items in the profit-and-loss column of scoring are nonetheless real, as we shall see below. On the other hand, a victory gained by taking a rubber worth 600 points is in reality a defeat in disguise when by so scoring an opportunity was lost, the opportunity to penalize the enemy's bid 800 points.

MATHEMATICAL REALITIES BACK OF THE SCORE SHEET

The tricks made and all penalties for undertricks are set up in black and white on the score sheet so that the player clearly sees his loss or gain. Not so with points to which the player is entitled for making the first or second game. Only a part of the total points is written on the score sheet, leaving the other and more important part as an invisible item that remains hidden in the mathematical clouds and turns up only at the end of the rubber.

The unscored part of the game value arises from the fact that, since two out of three games must be won to score and collect the rubber bonus, the player who wins the *first* game has mathematically greater expectations of winning the rubber. In the race for the goal, which is the rubber, the side that has won the first game will need but one more game to score the goal. Since the chances of getting a winning hand during the next or any subsequent deal are mathematically equal for either side, the side that has won the first game will collect the 700 rubber bonus *three times* as often as the side that requires two jumps to reach the same goal.* Accordingly, the winning of the first game confers an *equity value* definitely measurable in points so that, should one of the players drop dead just

---

* I receive many letters pointing out the apparent contradiction between the three-to-one expectancy of scoring the second game and the fact that by winning one out of two games the player, so to speak, is halfway advanced toward the goal. Actually, his advance after winning the first game is not half of the distance but three-quarters.

after scoring the first game, the opponents are obligated (only on the ground of mathematical morals, however) to pay his heirs not only the actually scored value but the equity value as well.*

This equity shifts in value according to whether the game is first game, second straight game, or rubber game.

EQUITY VALUE OF GAMES

1. Any First game .... 300 points
2. Any Second Straight game................................ 400 points
3. Any Rubber game (both sides vulnerable)................. 500 points

The 500 points for the third game represent the straight rubber premium, since all the advantages accruing to the side that wins the first game are cancelled when the opposing side wins the following game. Note also the important mathematical fact that the *equity* value of the second straight game is worth only 400 points, although the player who makes it will actually score a bonus of 700 points. It is here that so many good players fall into a mathematical trap: they frequently disdain a sure 500-point penalty simply to gamble for a fat-looking 700-point rubber, not realizing that the total value of the second straight game is but 500 points. It should be obvious that, after pocketing the 500-point penalty, the side that is one game ahead still has a three-to-one chance of scoring the rubber bonus.

The total point value of any game is obtained by adding to its *equity value* the trick points of the contract together with honor points and overtricks, if any. Assuming that there be no overtricks or honor points, the average trick value of a game contract is a few immaterial points over 100. Let's call it 100 for simplicity's sake, for the difference will in nowise

---

* The laws of the game recognize the equity value of allowing 300 points extra to the side that won the only game in an unfinished rubber. It is desirable for simplicity's sake that the future scoring should actually score the game and equity values after each game and remove the unnecessary mathematical puzzle of the invisible score which mystifies so many players. The best proof of how superfluous and complicated the present "part visible and part invisible" scoring is will be found in the fact that the original law-makers themselves committed during a period of several years the grievous mathematical error of allotting only 200 points for the winning of the only game in an unfinished rubber. This error was corrected only after a campaign by *The Bridge World Magazine.*

affect the bidding. We will then obtain the *total* (visible and invisible) values:

TABLE OF TOTAL VALUES OF GAMES

1. Any First game .... 400 points
2. Any Second Straight game............................. 500 points
3. Any Rubber game (both sides vulnerable)................ 600 points

FIRST PRINCIPLE: GAME VS. EQUIVALENT PENALTY

The knowledge of game values furnishes us with a fairly precise measuring-rod for comparing the expected penalty points with game points and then selecting as the final bid the one offering the greater number of points.

Assuming both the game and penalties are reasonably certain: *as between premiums at one's own bid and penalizing the opponents, prefer the penalty even though it may be somewhat less than the mathematical equivalent of the game.*

NOTE 1.—By "somewhat less" is usually meant a difference of about 100 points.

NOTE 2.—When a vulnerable side doubles non-vulnerable opponents in a low contract, it should be particularly careful to be assured that the expected penalty is at least three tricks.

This principle assumes partners of fairly equal skill. With a very weak partner or with a strong partner against weak opponents the procedure must be modified. With the former—exit; with the latter—prolong.

It follows from the first principle that if I am reasonably certain to take the rubber at four spades (worth 620 points) and, at the same time, am reasonably certain to defeat the opponents' four hearts by two tricks (worth 500 points), I shall prefer the penalty. The reason for this decided leaning toward penalties lies in the lower margin of safety of game bids as compared with penalty doubles. In doubling for penalties I expect at least a two-trick set, worth 500 points. This gives me a wide margin of safety, for in case of miscalculation the double will at worst produce a one-trick set. Game bids, even though reasonably certain, cannot be based on any such margin of safety.

Another important reason for preferring the penalty double is that the profits for making a game are distinctly limited, while profits from penalty doubles may expand into two-, three-

or four-trick sets, and with a panicky player or a distributional storm around the table, the penalty may spell a catastrophe for the enemy.

My records of several years prove that an expert player does not in the long run win many more rubbers than he loses. His tremendous aggregate profit comes from the fact that the rubbers he wins are fat and the ones he loses are skinny.

Second Principle: Sacrifice Bidding

A bid, where a player expects to be penalized but hopes by this means to prevent his opponents from scoring as many or more points at their own bid, is called a *sacrifice bid.**

Assuming that it is reasonably certain that the opponents will make their bid:

1. *As between allowing the opponents to score premiums at their own bids and forcing them through "sacrifice bids" to accept a proportionate penalty, prefer the latter, as a rule.*

2. *Even when the "sacrifice penalty" might be somewhat in excess (about 100 points) of the point value of opponents' bid, there is an advantage in so doing.*

When the overbidder is vulnerable, the extent of the overbid should be less than two tricks: the loss of the second trick should not be definite and may hang upon a finesse. The reason is the danger of incurring on doubtful hands a loss of three tricks doubled (800 points).

Mathematically, there may seem to be no sense in risking a penalty, since the opponents can score its equivalent in premiums. Actually, the advantage of deliberately forcing the opponents to the *breaking-point* of the hands is tremendous. One's opponents, instead of doubling as they should, may reach out for a higher contract only to be defeated. It is but human that when forced to guess the best of players may go wrong. The policy of deliberately overbidding will thus force the opponents to make hairbreadth decisions, stretching their hands to the breaking-point. This results in a gain for the scientific

---

* This principle of scientific overbidding, which in most books is tucked away in a very few paragraphs under the name of "flag flying," is one of the mainstays of the Culbertson System.

overbidder which, though not actually visible on the score sheet, is one of his principal sources of profit.

For instance, an ultra-conservative player allows the opponents to bid and score four spades vulnerable—a loss to him of 520 points, since he is not vulnerable. Had he bid five hearts, risking a deliberate loss of a maximum of three tricks not vulnerable, or 500 points, the opponents would have been faced with the alternative of doubling or bidding higher. If they double, the overbidder breaks about even. But if the opponents, fearing that they cannot set the contract by more than two tricks, decide to bid five spades, guess wrong, and go down one trick, now the net profit to the overbidder is:

520 points—value of the second successive game at four spades.
100 points—penalty for down one at five spades.
620 points—total net profit or about 65% of the average rubber.

There is a second advantage of a more subtle nature accruing to the aggressive bidder. The tactics of systematic overbidding keep the enemy under constant pressure, wearing down his morale. When the overbidding is skillfully mixed with real strength bids, the enemy may easily become confused. He may even begin to crack, if the scientific overbidding follows a definite psychological rhythm, expanding when the enemy does not double often enough and contracting when the enemy is too quick on the doubling trigger.

It goes without saying that defensive overbidding is dynamite. The principles of overbidding explained here are sound only with sound players, and are based on the assumption that partner is not a moron. The reader, I hope, will coöperate with me in hiding these inflammatory pages from some of his and my partners.

The Strategic Unit of Bridge

One of the costliest fallacies in bridge is to distinguish between the visible score sheet as "sure" and other mathematical gains as "probable." It is very difficult to convince even some expert players to give up a "sure" rubber for a penalty. "Why take chances?" they say. "The rubber is in the pocket and if you give up the rubber game for a penalty the opponents will go out on the next deal and then what good will it do you?" The fallacy lies in failing to realize that every new deal is an independent event offering exactly even chances for good or poor hands in the next deal. What happened in the past has no bearing whatsoever on the probability of the next event. When a coin is flipped and the head comes up ten times in succession, the chances that the head will come up on the eleventh throw are still exactly even.*

Much of the fog will be cleared up if a player realizes that in the course of his lifetime he will not have played a number of isolated rubbers, but one single unending rubber. The strategical unit in bidding, as in play, is *game,* not rubber. A rubber is simply an artificial abstraction. All bidding values and equities are measured in terms of the game, so that the player really plays for a stake of 400, 500 or 600 points, depending on whether the game is first, second straight or third.

---

* As a matter of fact, after a few throws, I would bet on "heads" on the possibility (remote) that the coin is defective.

CHAPTER THIRTY-TWO

READING DISTRIBUTION FROM THE BIDDING

There is a process of previewing the actual play of the cards by fitting your own hand to the picture of partner's hand as it is given by his—and sometime the opponents'—bidding. In this manner the gaping holes in the hand are gradually filled out and a composite picture of the partnership hands is painted— a beautiful intellectual process when done by an expert, each deft stroke of the brush producing a logical inference.

Every bid partner makes must tell something about his distribution. At first the information is meager. Suppose he bids one spade; all you know is that he has at least four cards in spades. His other nine cards remain a mystery. As partner rebids and rebids again, his distribution should become apparent within one or two cards, which is a reasonably low margin of error.

In general, when a player has bid three suits, or has bid strongly in two suits and has raised a third suit, it may safely be assumed that he has at most a singleton in the fourth suit.

Other cases in which a picture of partner's distribution is unveiled gradually as the bidding progresses:

South	North
1 ♢	1 ♠
2 ♡	2 ♠
3 ♣	

South has five **diamonds**, four hearts, four clubs *and a void in spades.*
(With four hearts, four diamonds and four clubs he would start off with **one**
heart.) North should merely bid three diamonds on

♠ A Q J 8 6 2   ♡ 9 5 3   ♢ 10 6   ♣ Q 8

He does not want to play a spade contract with a void in his partner's
hand.

SOUTH	NORTH
1 ♡	1 ♠
2 ♡	2 N T
3 ♢	

South has six hearts and four diamonds (with 6–5 or 5–5 he would have
shown the diamonds before rebidding the hearts). This leaves him only
three cards in spades and clubs together. North, holding ♠ A Q 7 5 2
♡ 9 5 ♢ 8 3 ♣ A 8 6 4 should bid three hearts. A notrump contract
would be dangerous, when neither partner can fill in the gaps in the other's
suits.

SOUTH	NORTH
1 ♣	1 ♢
1 ♡	1 ♠
2 ♠	2 N T
3 ♠	

South has 4–4–4–1, with a singleton diamond, or 5–4–4–0, with a void in
diamonds. North, holding

♠ Q 8 6 3   ♡ K 5   ♢ A 9 7 6   ♣ Q 10 4

should bid four spades. At three notrump he would have only one diamond
stopper, and the suit would probably be opened despite his bid.

READING THE OPPONENTS' BIDDING

When one opponent bids a suit (especially if he bids it at a
high level, or rebids it) and the other opponent raises it, partner's holding in that suit may usually be counted by simple
arithmetic.

North-South vulnerable, East-West not vulnerable. The bidding:

SOUTH	WEST	NORTH	EAST
1 ♡	Pass	Pass	2 ♠
3 ♣	4 ♠	5 ♣	

East holds:

♠ A K 9 6 5 2   ♡ A 8 3   ♢ 5   ♣ 9 3 2

South, who bid clubs at the three-level, must have five of them; North, for his raise to five, must have four; East has three. West has at most one club. Only one club trick can be lost.

South bids five spades, taking a vulnerable game rather than a penalty which will hardly exceed 300 points.

The defenders, too, can fit their hands together:

SOUTH	WEST	NORTH	EAST
1 ♠	Pass	2 ♡	Pass
3 ♡	Pass	3 ♠	Pass
3 N T	Pass	4 ♠	Double

East held:

♠ K J   ♡ A 8 7 5   ◇ A 6 4   ♣ 10 9 8 6

He counted North for four or five hearts and South, who had raised hearts, for three, so West must have a singleton or doubleton. North's insistence on spades marked him with the Ace or Queen, giving East a sure trump trick. East opened the ♡ A and led the ♡ 8, which West ruffed; won a diamond return and gave West another heart ruff; and finally won a second setting trick in spades.

Thus, with each new bid or pass the player's hand undergoes a plastic transformation resulting in a different type of mental play of the combined hands. In the few situations analyzed here it has been possible to cover only a small portion of the many clues which put the finishing touches on this fascinating process of Plastic Valuation and thus turn every well-bid hand into a thrilling victory of the mind over the unknown.

CHAPTER THIRTY-THREE

WHAT IS DUPLICATION?

"If one man can build a house in ten days, how long will it take two men to build the house?" is not quite as simple a problem as it sounds. Mathematically the answer should be "five days," but actually there are three big "ifs" attached to the actual problem.

1. *If* they do not duplicate each other's efforts.
2. *If* they do not duplicate each other's talents.
3. *If* they are able to work simultaneously.

The experienced builder calculates the work each man can do without being interrupted, and without interfering with another man's work. The experienced contract bridge player figures much the same way. In other words, they both try to avoid possible *duplication*.

There are three kinds of duplication in bridge:

1. Duplication of bids: Counting the same values twice; counting the values shown in partner's hand for your own bid—while he counts them for his; counting both length and ruffing values in the hand of the first player to name the suit, etc.

2. Duplication of values: Being able to win tricks in the same suit twice—once in either hand—while neither hand can win tricks in a second suit: e.g., a void in the suit in which partner has the Ace, etc.

3. Duplication of hand patterns: Exact or nearly exact suit distributions in the partnership hands, causing duplication of losers through inability to provide ruffers and long-card winners counted in the bidding.

DUPLICATION OF BIDS

One of the most common types of duplication of bids is where the player who has opened the bidding revalues his hand in support of partner's takeout, forgetting to deduct the winners which he promised by his opening bid and on which his partner is already counting!

For example, South bids one club with this hand:

♠ A K Q 6   ♥ 4 3   ♦ 7 5 2   ♣ K J 8 4

In honor-tricks he has only the minimum he has guaranteed by his opening bid. In winners he has about as many if the hand is played at spades as the minimum he has already shown at clubs. Yet, when his partner responds with one spade, he overlooks the fact that his great strength in spades has all been counted as part of his opening bid, and that actually the hand is no stronger than if he had held:

♠ K J 8 4   ♥ 4 3   ♦ 7 5 2   ♣ A K Q 6

He bids *three* spades and the panic is on. No matter how frantically he signs off later, the final contract will be highly unsatisfactory.

Another case of bidding duplicity comes when a player, after pushing his hand to the utmost to reach game, then makes a slam try on the same values.

NORTH	SOUTH
1 ♠	1 N T
3 ♥	3 N T
4 ♥	4 ♠
4 N T	

North's hand is: ♠ A K 8 4 3   ♥ A Q 7 6 5   ♦ 9   ♣ K 5. True enough, he has four honor-tricks and more. But he has already bid these values to the hilt in driving his reluctant partner to game. To make a slam with any hand that would be represented by South's weak bidding would be a miracle.

Beware of twice-told tales. If you have already told *your* story, any additions to it should come from your partner. Usually you will find him ready enough to speak whenever he has anything to say.

DUPLICATION OF VALUES

The one flaw in any method of valuation is the dread duplication of values; the overlapping of tricks which each player can legitimately count but which, because they occur in the same suit, duplicate each other's usefulness and leave gaping holes in other suits. Through these holes the opponents push their own tricks before the declarer can avail himself of possible discards—if, indeed, such discard opportunities exist.

Duplication of winners is not always disastrous; duplication of losers, unless discovered in time, invariably is.

```
        ♠ K J 10 8 6         N          ♠ A Q 9 7 4
        ♡ A K Q         W         E     ♡ 6
        ◊ Q 7                 S          ◊ K J 5
        ♣ 6 3 2                         ♣ J 9 5 4

        WEST                            EAST
        1 ♠                             3 ♠
        4 ♠                             Pass
```

West has 3½ honor-tricks; East has slightly better than the minimum required for a double raise. Yet a club opening—or a diamond opening and a club shift—must defeat four spades because West's strongest suit duplicates East's singleton. Move West's King-Queen from hearts to clubs; West now has a plus-value less in his honor-trick count, yet five-odd can be laid down.

Give West a stronger hand—enough to warrant a slam try—and note how, except with extreme skill or luck, a slam may be reached and lost because of duplication of losers.

```
   ♠ K J 10 8 6      ♡ A K Q      ◊ A Q 7      ♣ 3 2
```

There are very few players who could resist the temptation to bid six on this hand, when partner has given a double raise, yet two fast club tricks will beat it unless the Asking Bid is used.

The presence of void suits sometimes results in even more devastating duplication. For example:

```
        ♠ A 10 9 7 6 3       N          ♠ Q J 8 5 4
        ♡ K Q J         W         E     ♡ 6
        ◊ —                   S          ◊ A Q J 8
        ♣ K Q 8 4                       ♣ 9 7 2
```

The bidding must die at five, after East shows that he has no Ace but in diamonds, and five-odd cannot be defeated if no spade trick is lost. Here West can take out an insurance against duplication by making an asking bid of 4 ◊ (after 1 ♠–3 ♠). East's bid of 5 ◊ settles the issue.

DUPLICATION OF HAND-PATTERNS

The most unfortunate of all duplication is that of hand-patterns, for it may cause a vast difference between a perfectly legitimate count of winners in the bidding and the actual total which can be developed in the play.

WEST	EAST
♠ A J	♠ K Q

In this example, 1-plus winner in each hand (King-Queen, even though unguarded, is worth slightly more than one winner) results in not more than two possible winners in the combined hands. Add a low card to either suit and three winners must result.

This alone is catastrophic enough in close games or slams, but consider the tragedy of hands which so completely duplicate patterns as the following:

Expected Winners	WEST	EAST	Expected Winners
6	♠ A K Q J 10 3	♠ 9 8 7 6 5 4	2
0	♡ —	♡ —	3
1	◇ 10 9 6 5 2	◇ A K Q J 8	5
0	♣ 7 4	♣ 8 3	0

West's hand contains seven winners; East's ten—a total of seventeen. Yet with anything but a heart lead, East-West cannot win more than eleven tricks. In other words, six of these winners have vanished through the sieve of duplication. What has happened to them?

The two winners which East counts for length in the trump suit fail to materialize because, through duplication of pattern, West has six winners by length in his own hand. East's three ruffing winners in hearts disappear because West's hand includes no hearts to ruff. The one winner which West counted for length in diamonds does not materialize because East's pattern and solid suit have already accounted for all five available tricks in diamonds.

WARNINGS FROM THE BIDDING

Even without slam conventions the bidding may sometimes give helpful warnings of duplication.

NORTH	EAST	SOUTH	WEST
1 ♡	1 ♠	3 ♡	4 ♠
5 ♡	5 ♠	?	

South's hand is: ♠ 9 ♡ K J 8 4 3 ◇ A 6 4 ♣ K Q 7 5. Normally the value of his singleton spade with five trumps would be two winners. But from the opponents' bidding it is almost impossible that North could have three spades; in fact, it is doubtful that he has more than one.

Some Rare Bidding Situations

In a game so complex as contract bridge there are many thousands of bidding situations. Most of these can be classified according to type and grouped under one general principle or another. Some require their own independent treatment. Even in a book as nearly complete as this one the rules of bidding that are given leave some questions still in doubt.

Here are illustrated certain situations not specifically covered elsewhere.

THE FORCING PASS

In one of the rarest of the beautiful bidding situations, a pass is used as a forcing bid. It occurs when, after a series of strength-showing bids, one of the partners does not know whether the best course is to double for penalties or to bid again. He leaves the decision to his partner, who may be in a better position to judge.

SOUTH	WEST	NORTH	EAST
1 ♠	Pass	3 ♣	3 ◇
3 ♠	4 ◇	4 N T	5 ◇
6 ♣	6 ◇	Pass!	

North holds:

♠ A 6   ♡ A K   ◇ 7 3 2   ♣ K Q J 8 4 3

He knows the grand slam can be made in clubs if South holds the club Ace and a void in diamonds, and that six spades can be made if South holds a nearly solid suit, and that otherwise it will be necessary to double six diamonds and collect whatever penalty is available. When the bidding comes around to South he must bid six spades or bid seven clubs or double, but he must not pass.

In rare cases the fact that there is a part-score turns a pass into a forcing bid.

In the following situation, East and West have a part-score of 40 and North-South have a part-score of 60.

SOUTH	WEST	NORTH	EAST
Pass	Pass	Pass	1 ♠
Pass	1 N T	2 ♣	Pass!

Obviously, East would not have opened the bidding fourth-hand if he intended to let his opponents play at a two-club contract and get a game if they made it. West's notrump takeout may have been a trap bid and East passes to allow West to make a penalty double of two clubs if he wishes to do so. West must double or bid.

Genuine Bids in the Opponents' Suit

A bid in a suit the opponents have already bid is usually a conventional forcing bid rather than a genuine suit-bid. But there are rare cases in which a player wishes to play the hand in a suit which has already been bid against him. A bid in the opponents' suit may show a genuine suit if the player (or his partner) has:

(a) Previously made a takeout or penalty double of the opponents' suit.

(b) Passed at a previous opportunity, provided his partner has also passed.

South	West	North	East
1 ♡	Double	Pass	1 ♠
Pass	2 ♡		

West's bid is forcing but if East can support hearts he should raise.

South	West	North	East
1 ♠	Pass	1 N T	Pass
Pass	2 ♠		

Were it West's purpose to make a forcing bid, he could have bid two spades over one spade immediately. Evidently, he first made a trap pass of one spade, having a strong spade suit and hoping for a chance to make a penalty double of a spade contract later. Since this opportunity was not offered, he now wishes to play the hand in spades himself.

Large and Small Swings

Sometimes a player willingly accepts a loss rather than try for a possible gain.

South	West	North	East
1 ♡	1 ♠	3 ♡	3 ♠
4 ♣	4 ♠	4 N T	5 ♠
7 ♡			

West holds ♠ K Q J 10 6 4 3 2   ♡ Q 8 6   ◇ —   ♣ 8 2. West's Queen of hearts has a good chance to win a trick, but if it does not, North-South, vulnerable, will score 2410 points. At seven spades, West, not vulnerable, should be minus no more than 400 points. He bids seven spades to limit his loss.

CHAPTER THIRTY-FOUR

DUPLICATE
BRIDGE BIDDING

The popularity of duplicate contract bridge has grown steadily and rapidly since 1929, when the first contract bridge tournaments were held. The few thousand duplicate addicts of 1929 had become by today nearly two hundred thousand. This is a very far cry from over thirty million of rubber bridge devotees in the United States alone as officially estimated by the United States Playing Cards Association. Nevertheless duplicate bridge has its fascinating sides and most of the serious bridge players know and play it either regularly or occasionally.

The foundation of any bidding system, and its philosophy, rest squarely on rubber bridge scoring. The moment rubbers cease to exist, as in match-point duplicate,* there must be a readjustment of bidding and playing strategy and tactics.

MATCH-POINT SCORING

In duplicate bridge the trick-score, bonuses for overtricks, undertrick penalties and bonuses for slams are the same as in rubber bridge. Honors are not scored. Rubbers are not played, and there is consequently no rubber bonus. Instead, the bidding side scores (in addition to the trick-score):

500 for bidding and making game, vulnerable
300 for bidding and making game, not vulnerable
 50 for bidding and making any contract of less than game, with or without
    overtricks

---

* Ninety-nine percent of all duplicate games are scored by match-points, and in this chapter only match-point scoring is considered. In team-of-four matches scored by cumulative points the strategy and objectives are almost (though not exactly) the same as in rubber bridge.

All the scores made on each board (deal) are entered on a sheet and compared. The scores of North-South pairs are compared only with the scores of other North-South pairs, the scores of East-West pairs only with other East-West pairs.

A pair receives 1 match-point for each other pair which played in the same direction and got a lower score; ½ match-point for each other pair which played in the same direction and made the same score.

Observe the specimen "traveling score slip" illustration which lists all the results on a single deal played in an eight-table game. You will observe that the top score, North-South, went to Pair 3, which fulfilled a six-spade contract. Since there were seven other pairs, Pair 3 scored 7 match-points.

Pair 3's total score on this board was 1430 points, but it scored only 1 match-point more than Pair 12, whose total was 700 points; and Pair 12 got a full match-point more than Pair 8, which bid three notrump and made it with three overtricks, scoring 690.

In other words, Pair 3's 730-point advantage over Pair 12 paid it no more than Pair 12's 10-point advantage over Pair 8. We need look no further to find the difference in *objective* between match-point and rubber play.

THE BASIC DIFFERENCE

The mark of a great player in rubber bridge is grand strategy—maneuvers for a swing, the search for a killing bid. Although, in the course of the evening, he may lose more rubbers than he wins, a few killing rubbers, added to his total, will make him a good winner. The tactics in duplicate match point is to gain a series of small victories in a series of small battles. The 32 boards that he will play in the course of the evening means 32 separate battles in which it is immaterial whether a top score on the board is 20 or 2000 points. A slam at a riskier notrump is preferable to a sure slam at a minor suit.

TRAVELING SCORE (Mitchell or Howell)*

NORTH PLAYER only keeps score.
ENTER PAIR NO. OF E-W PAIR

Board No._____

N-S Pair	E-W Pair	FINAL CONTRACT PLAYED BY	NORTH-SOUTH		E-W Match Points	N-S Match Points
			Net Plus	Net Minus		
1	16	6♡-NORTH		100		0
2					1	
3	15	6♠-SOUTH	1430			7
4	7	4♡-NORTH	650			2
5					3½	
6	5	4♠-SOUTH	680			3½
7					5	
8	13	3 N.T.-SOUTH	690			5
9					3½	
10					6	
11	10	5♡dbld-EAST	500			1
12	2	6♡dbld-EAST	700			6
13					2	
14	9	4♠-SOUTH	680			3½
15					0	
16					7	

Form No. 134—Bridge World Accessories   Printed in U. S. A.

* For complete exposition of duplicate bridge my book *Bidding and Play in Duplicate Contract Bridge* by the same publisher.

This leads us to a statement of the basic difference between rubber bridge and duplicate bridge, when you are considering the advisability of any bid:

In rubber bridge you consider the *amount* of gain as against the *amount* of loss. In duplicate you consider the *frequency* of gain as against the *frequency* of loss.

Both sides are vulnerable. The bidding:

SOUTH	WEST	NORTH	EAST
1 ♠	2 ♡	Pass	Pass

South holds:

♠ A Q 8 7 4	♡ 7 4	◊ K 8 6 5	♣ A 7

At rubber bridge South would pass very, very rapidly. To rebid in such a situation is the mark of a losing player. What is there to gain by bidding? No more than a part-score, surely, when partner was too weak for a free bid. What is there to lose by passing? The unimportant part-score the opponents may make at two hearts. *What is there to lose by bidding two spades?* Maybe as much as 800 points, if East is loaded with spades and waiting for a chance to double. Why risk 800 points to stop a part-score?

But at duplicate bridge you do not sell out for two hearts. You bid two spades. The danger of being doubled and set must be accepted, for it is likely to occur only once in perhaps four or five deals. You cannot forego your chance at three or four good scores to avoid one bad score, no matter how bad that bad one may be. Partner may have a hand like

♠ J 6 3	♡ J 9 8 4	◊ Q 4	♣ Q 8 6 2

Though he could not raise freely, you can probably make two spades; East-West can probably make two hearts. They must not be permitted to score +110 when you can have the plus score for yourself.

The first thought of the duplicate player must be this: Never leave the opponents in a contract at which they can make a plus score if you can shift them into a contract at which they will make a lower plus score, or if there is a contract at which your side can make a plus score.

So that you may always know what contracts are available for your side, you should try to get into the bidding at duplicate as often and as cheaply as possible, even at some risk.

Opening Bids

There is a distinct analogy between duplicate bidding and part-score bidding. This argues for light opening bids. But the requirements for opening bids in the Culbertson System are already as low as possible consistent with soundness.

Therefore the same opening bid requirements should be adhered to in duplicate as in rubber bridge.

However, any hand listed as an "optional" bid (pages 106-108) should usually be opened in duplicate.

♠ A K 6 5   ♡ 7 6 4   ◇ A 5 3   ♣ 9 4 2

Most rubber bridge players will pass this hand in first or second position, because it provides no safe rebid if partner responds with two in a suit. In duplicate, however, one spade should be bid. You do not want to be shut out of the bidding if the opponents open it. You do not want to let the hand be passed out if your side has even a bare majority of the strength and can make a part-score; and your three honor-tricks suggest that this may be the case.

♠ 7   ♡ K J 10 8 3   ◇ K Q J   ♣ 8 6 4 2

This hand should be passed in rubber bridge because it has a bare 2½ honor-tricks and no Ace. In duplicate it is a biddable hand, especially in third or fourth position.

While in rubber bridge the opening bid requirements are the same in any position, it does after all take a sound hand for a fourth-hand bid. In duplicate, the bidding is often opened fourth-hand on a hand which would not justify a bid in first or second position.

♠ Q 10 6   ♡ K 5   ◇ A J 7 5 2   ♣ 7 5 4

This hand is worth a fourth-hand opening bid of one diamond.

The theory of the light fourth-hand bid is as follows: The strength is probably evenly divided between the two sides, since no one had an opening bid. Therefore, one side or the other can probably make a part-score. *At other tables the bidding may have been opened*—perhaps because someone chose to open a borderline hand which at your table was passed, or for any other reason. If you pass, letting the deal be passed out, you will have a bad score if the cards would have produced a part-score your way. If you bid and find that the opponents can make the part-score, you will have company because the same result will have been reached at other tables, and at worst you will have a few match-points.

This theory must not be carried too far. As long as you know that your partner will not fail to open on any hand of bare biddable strength, you may safely and profitably pass when you have a really weak hand:

    ♠ J 6   ♡ A 9 7 2   ◇ Q 8 6 4   ♣ Q 7 5

It is foolhardy to bid, third- or fourth-hand, with such a hand. The opponents must have more strength than your side, so the zero score you will get by passing the hand out should be your best result. Other pairs playing your way should have minus scores.

The question, "Who has the spades?" is even more pressing in duplicate than in rubber bridge. When the strength is evenly divided, the side with the higher-ranking trump suit can outbid the other side.

    ♠ 7   ♡ 10 5 4   ◇ K J 10 6 2   ♣ A 7 5 3

This hand is a fourth-hand pass. If the two suits were spades and hearts it would be an opening bid.

    ♠ 7 2   ♡ A Q 7 6 5 2   ◇ Q 8 4 3   ♣ 2

Bid one heart, third- or fourth-hand, on this, taking a chance that partner can stop an opposing spade contract; for if the opponents have diamonds or clubs they can be outbid.

The insistence on major-suit strength applies only to subminimum hands. Any hand with 2½ honor-tricks and a rebiddable suit, or three honor-tricks and a biddable suit, should be opened fourth-hand in duplicate whether the suits are majors or minors.

Both of these hands are listed (page 109) as fourth-hand passes in rubber bridge:

    ♠ 6 5   ♡ 8 3 2   ◇ A K 6 5 4   ♣ Q J 3
    ♠ 8 6   ♡ 7 4 2   ◇ A Q 9 8   ♣ A Q 6 5

Either warrants a fourth-hand one-diamond bid in duplicate.

Choice of Suits

At duplicate it is costly to let declarer make an overtrick, even at a minor-suit part-score contract, if the overtrick could have been prevented. Therefore borderline bids should be made with the future defensive play always in mind.

The following hand is a better heart bid than diamond bid in rubber bridge, but in duplicate it is best opened with one diamond:

♠ 6 3   ♡ 8 7 5 3 2   ◇ K Q 10 2   ♣ A K

RAISES

When partner has opened the bidding, the responding hand must often stretch a point to avoid being shut out on border-line hands.

♠ Q 10 6 5   ♡ 8 4   ◇ K 7 5 3   ♣ J 5 2

Partner bids one spade; second-hand overcalls with two hearts. In rubber bridge, you would pass; the hand is not strong enough for a free raise. In duplicate you raise freely to two spades. Otherwise the bidding may be at the three- or four-level when it reaches partner again. If he has a four-card spade suit he cannot dare rebid it without knowing you can support spades.

1. ♠ K 8 7 5 2   ♡ 7 4   ◇ 10 6 5   ♣ 7 6 2

2. ♠ A 5 4   ♡ 8 7 5   ◇ K 10 3   ♣ 8 6 5 2

These are hands on which you do not give partner a free raise if he bids spades and is overcalled. No. 1 has absolutely no defensive values; partner will make allowances for a possible shaded raise, but he cannot possibly expect as weak a hand as that. No. 2 has some defensive strength but little trick-taking support at spades, and it is better to let the opponents play the hand unless partner can rebid.

When partner has opened the bidding fourth-hand you must remember that he may have stretched a point to bid at all, and give him some leeway in your response.

If partner opens fourth-hand with one spade and you hold

♠ Q 10 8 6 3   ♡ 6   ◇ K 9 6 3 2   ♣ 10 5

the rubber bridge response of four spades is decidedly improper. A raise to two spades is ample.

Preëmptive raises in general should be avoided in duplicate bridge; even if partner's opening bid were made first- or second-hand, you would not give a jump raise on the hand above. It may prove desirable to stop at three spades, depending on the opponents' bidding, and a two-diamond response is prefer-able as a first step.

However, a hand so weak and freakish as the following warrants jumping partner's one-spade bid to four:

♠ 10 8 7 6 4 2   ♡ 7   ◇ J 9 8 3 2   ♣ 9

Unless partner has a strong hand and can make four spades, the opponents will be able to bid you up to where you would go to four spades as a sacrifice anyway.

Overcalls

In rubber bridge, one side or the other may never learn that it can make a part-score contract—it would be too dangerous to enter the bidding and find out—so the field is left to the other side by default. In duplicate the risk of being doubled must be faced and a player must often overcall when in rubber bridge he would pass.

Overcall an opposing one-heart bid with one spade on

♠ J 9 6 5 3   ♡ 7 2   ◇ A K Q 6   ♣ 7 4

except when your side is vulnerable and the opponents are not vulnerable.

This does *not* mean that the Rule of 2 and 3 should necessarily be set aside. The reason one passes the above hand in rubber bridge is not that he fears going down more than 500 points. Such a hand will usually win five tricks, and so will not go down more than 500 even if vulnerable. But in rubber bridge one passes because there is too little to gain from overcalling. No game is in prospect unless partner can bid on his own, and the diamonds offer defensive prospects against an opposing game contract. If the opponents can make a part-score, what of it?

But in duplicate, one must prepare early for a possible sacrifice, whether against an opposing part-score or against an opposing game. Therefore one may often overcall with no prospect except the hope of finding an excellent distributional fit with partner.

Holding ♠ 8   ♡ Q 10 8 6 5 3   ◇ K Q 7   ♣ 10 6 3 overcall a one-spade bid with two hearts, unless you are vulnerable and the opponents not. In rubber bridge you would pass.

Holding ♠ 9 7 5   ♡ 7   ◇ K 4 3   ♣ Q 9 7 6 3 2 overcall an opposing one-bid with two clubs *if* you are not vulnerable and the opponents are. In rubber bridge you would pass.

Sometimes the takeout double will prove to be safer than an overcall on a weak hand. In rubber bridge the takeout double is most valuable to show strength and signal game possibilities, but in duplicate the necessity for competing in the auction requires its use for no other reason than to learn partner's best suit, with perhaps only a future sacrifice in mind.

South	West	North	East
1 ♡	Pass	2 ♣	Double

East holds ♠ K J 9 7 6   ♡ 9   ◇ A J 6 5   ♣ Q 6 2.

If East passed, he might find himself with a bottom because his side could make some spade contract (or could profitably sacrifice in spades against an opposing four hearts). If East bid two spades, he might promptly be doubled and never learn that West had, say, a six-card diamond suit. The only safe action for East to take is the double.

It follows that a takeout double at duplicate must not be read as necessarily showing a strong hand until the doubler has confirmed it by some rebid.

VULNERABILITY

Nothing has greater influence on the choice of contracts in duplicate than the vulnerability conditions. The duplicate player must always be keenly conscious of who is vulnerable.

Sacrifice bids in duplicate are exact. There are no "approximate equivalents." You *must not* overbid by three tricks (500 points) to stop a non-vulnerable opposing game (400+ points). You *must* take every opportunity to go down 500 points when the opponents have a vulnerable (600+-point) game.

This consideration controls all penalty doubles. When not vulnerable, you hasten to double vulnerable opponents when a two-trick set is in prospect. When vulnerable, you refuse in most cases to double non-vulnerable opponents, especially at low contracts, when you are confident that you can make game.

You are vulnerable, opponents not vulnerable. Partner's opening spade bid is overcalled with two diamonds. You hold

♠ Q 6   ♡ A Q 7   ◇ K J 9 5   ♣ K 10 9 3

In rubber bridge you would double; in duplicate you bid two notrump because you cannot be confident of beating two diamonds 700 points, and a 500-point penalty would not be enough.

Especially in part-score situations, the Two-Trick Rule—page 283—is suspended in duplicate against vulnerable opponents, for a one-trick vulnerable set, if doubled, is 200 points—better than making any part-score.

SOUTH	WEST	NORTH	EAST
1 ♡	2 ♣	2 ♡	3 ♣
Pass	Pass		

East-West are vulnerable. North doubles, holding

♠ Q 8	♡ K 9 7 2	◇ K 10 8 3	♣ K 8 4

In rubber bridge he would bid three hearts. That contract can probably be made; three clubs can hardly be beaten more than one trick, and if by chance three clubs doubled is made North will have let the opponents make an undeserved game. The possible gain does not justify the risk.

But in duplicate North must not take a 140-point score when a 200-point score is within reach.

Of course, South (who knows that North has a close double, because North failed to double two clubs) will take out to three hearts if his hand threatens to be ineffective in defense against clubs.

Choice of Contracts

A successful duplicate player seeks to arrive at a normal final contract whenever possible. *It does not pay to play the Lone Wolf at duplicate,* gambling for top scores and risking bottoms if the gamble fails.

Victory in duplicate bridge, like victory in war, usually goes to the side that makes the fewest blunders. If you consistently arrive at sound contracts, you will be above average because some pairs will blunder into unsound contracts. But if you gamble on tops or bottoms, the tops and the bottoms will probably balance out to an average score, no more.

After this bidding:

SOUTH	WEST	NORTH	EAST
1 ♠	Pass	3 ♠	Pass
3 N T	Pass		

I have seen a player in the North position pass three notrump on a hand like

♠ K 9 7 6 3	♡ A 8	◇ K J 4	♣ 8 7 2

For a chance at 630 points (the score for four-odd at notrump) instead of the 620 points for four spades, he gambles on finding his partner with adequate protection in the wide-open club suit and a hand that will play equally well at notrump or spades. He knows four spades would be a safer contract, but he grasps greedily for those 10 extra points.

Sometimes a pass of this sort gains; more often it loses. When it loses, it is because North-South are in an *unnatural* contract.

There are nevertheless many cases in which a *sound* notrump contract is played at duplicate in preference to a suit contract which would perhaps be safer. This applies particularly to two-notrump contracts, which are seldom played at rubber bridge.

SOUTH	WEST	NORTH	EAST
1 ♣	Pass	1 ◇	Pass
1 N T	Pass	2 N T	Pass
Pass	Pass		

South holds:

♠ A 10   ♡ K 7 3   ◇ Q 9 5 2   ♣ A 10 8 4

In rubber bridge, South would have raised North to two diamonds instead of bidding one notrump; in duplicate he must think of the danger that North, with a weak hand, may pass either two diamonds or one notrump, and South must rush to get into the more lucrative notrump contract.

Three diamonds would probably be a safer contract than two notrump, but South has too much to gain by playing two notrump (120 points if made) as against three diamonds (110 points).

A major suit should be preferred, whenever available, to a safer minor suit, in choosing the final contract. Two of a major is as good as three of a minor (110 points each); three of a major (140 points) is better than four of a minor (130 points). Therefore, the major-suit contract is likely to be superior even if it plays a full trick worse than the minor.

SOUTH	WEST	NORTH	EAST
1 ♠	Pass	1 N T	Pass
2 ◇	Pass		

North would pass, at rubber bridge, on

♠ 10 7 3   ♡ 6 2   ◇ J 9 5 3   ♣ A 8 5 2

Why bid when game is out of the question and the diamond contract is safer?

But at duplicate North returns to two spades.

GAME AND SLAM BIDS

In rubber bridge you bid a game whenever you have a 50–50 chance to make it; even if the odds are somewhat against your making it (as when you need a 3–2 trump break plus a winning finesse) it is mathematically worth-while to bid the game.

But in duplicate with match-point scoring, it is an absolute toss-up whether you bid a game or stop at a part-score when game depends on winning a finesse.

And if there is even a slight edge against your making the game contract, it is better to stop short of it.

The question of slams is quite simple in duplicate. The rule, briefly and succinctly, is, "Don't bid them unless they are almost sure things!" If you fail to bid a slam that you can make, the chances are that you will have lots of company and your match-point score will not suffer greatly. If you bid a slam that fails to materialize, you will find yourself either a Lone Wolf or among an unselect few; in either case your match-point score on that hand will be very anaemic.

CHAPTER THIRTY-FIVE

PSYCHOLOGY AND TACTICS

While it cannot be denied that there is truth in the adage "God is on the side of the heavier artillery," it is of great importance to remember that artillery cannot place itself strategically, nor automatically time its firing to the highest degree of effectiveness.

So in bridge, a preponderance of high cards does not necessarily ensure victory. It must always be borne in mind that bridge, in its perfect simulation of warfare, provides opportunities for strategic, non-catastrophic retreats. To allow the enemy to withdraw is simply to offer him another battle, perhaps on ground advantageous to him. To penalize the opponents, unless the profit is at least equivalent to that voluntarily abandoned or forcibly snatched away, is defeat—not victory. This question of counter-compensation pervades the entire structure of competitive bidding.

Psychology at bridge can best be defined as the process of taking into consideration the *personal* element involved, viz.: the tendencies, idiosyncrasies and reactions of specific partners and specific opponents.

Concealing Weakness

A pass of partner's opening suit-bid of one is so patent a confession of weakness that it invites the opponents to enter the bidding—and perhaps reach a game or at least a profitable part-score. A one-over-one takeout, on the contrary, keeps the opponents guessing; for such a response may be made on a strong hand as often as on a weak. Fourth-hand, with a doubtful overcall, may pass rather than venture a bid and perhaps find himself between the nutcracker of two strong hands.

It may therefore be wise, *when not vulnerable,* to make a one-over-one takeout on a wholly unbiddable hand, rather than pass. Vulnerable, it is too risky to do this.

With ♠ K 9 8 6 4 ♡ 6 3 ◊ 7 5 2 ♣ 8 6 4, one may venture a one-spade response to partner's one-diamond bid, especially if not vulnerable against vulnerable opponents. If you are vulnerable, pass.

If your opponents observe you in such tactics a few times, they may perhaps be double-crossed later by *passing* partner's opening bid on a fair hand like

♠ Q 6 5   ♡ J 2   ◊ K J 8 7   ♣ K Q 10 4

An opponent may reopen the bidding and walk right into the double you have in store for him.

It is a much more difficult matter to conceal weakness than strength, when partner has opened on a part-score. Yet the greater the weakness, the more reason for its concealment. Suppose that North, on a 20 part-score, opens the bidding with one club. South holds

♠ 8 6   ♡ 7   ◊ Q J 10 6 2   ♣ K 7 5 4 2

Whether East overcalls the club bid or not, a two-notrump bid is made-to-order for South. South will of course run out of any bid North makes (such as three notrump, three spades or three hearts) to four clubs. A direct preëmpt by South of four clubs would stimulate rather than discourage the opponents.

Pre-emptive Bids—Honest and Fake

Since the very first days of contract, many self-styled theorists have delivered rousing philippics against preëmptive bidding.

Usually, I am not only tolerant of conflicting opinion—I try to profit by it! But I do not believe anyone who claims never, or seldom, to have been embarrassed, let alone obstructed, by adverse preëmptive bids. I have been seriously embarrassed on innumerable occasions; what makes *them* sacred? I should be very grateful if these profound players were to tell me what to do if the opening bidder preëmpts with three spades and I, next hand and vulnerable, hold something like this:

♠ 6 5   ♡ A K 7 5 3 2   ◇ A J 6   ♣ Q 4

Perhaps they would simply give the preëmptor a withering glance and bid four hearts in a loud, confident tone. If *I* bid four hearts, I'd do so shaking in my shoes.

PRE-EMPTIVE BIDS AFTER THE OPPONENTS HAVE BID

Generally speaking, it is futile to preëmpt after an opening bid by an opponent. He has already laid the line of communication to his partner; the information transmitted, while possibly incomplete, is usually sufficient for carrying-on purposes.

There are, however, opportunities for preëmptive coups when certain conditions prevail. With such bidding as

SOUTH	WEST	NORTH	EAST
1 ♡	Pass	2 ♡	

East may hold a hand like

♠ A K J 10 8 5 3   ♡ —   ◇ Q 8 4   ♣ Q 7 5

A preëmptive spade bid at this point may be highly provocative to the opening bidder, who is apt to regard it as an effort to keep him quiet. He may have planned either a three-heart or a two-notrump rebid over North's heart raise; a three-spade bid may spur him to four hearts. East's heart void indicates that such a bid may be eagerly welcomed by West, who may be "loaded" with hearts. I have heard this coup vulgarly but succinctly described as "dumping the opponents into partner's lap."

Trapping

Before discussing the various methods most effective in trapping the opponents, I had better digress a moment to scotch an impression that many badly informed players have concerning this type of strategy. I have been so often asked "Is it

ethical and sportsmanlike to 'lay for' the opponents?" that I
feel my reply must be recorded permanently.

It is entirely ethical and sportsmanlike to lay traps in bridge,
both in the bidding and in the play, *provided* such extraneous
and illegal devices as bluff hesitations, meaningful voice in-
flections, emphatic playing of signal-cards and a host of other
histrionic gestures contrary to the spirit of the game are not
employed.

The player who, either by a pass on a big hand or a psychic
bid on a poor one, succeeds in trapping his opponents, de-
serves full credit for his exploit; he has taken a serious risk,
and won out!

Now let us consider the various methods of trapping.

TRAP-PASS OVER OPPONENTS' BID

This is the most common type of trap. It is also the most
abused. One does not pass an opponent's one-bid for a trap
with a hand which justifies a sound bid or takeout double,
unless he is playing against the type of player who "always
keeps the bidding open for partner." But a trap-pass of, say,
an opponent's one-spade bid is good strategy holding a hand
such as:

♠ Q 10 6 5 3   ♡ A Q   ◊ K 6 5   ♣ A Q 2

If the bidding reaches two spades or one notrump, a penalty double
should be most profitable.

The trapper need fear only one thing: that the bidding will
not be kept open. And even then, no great loss should result.
If his partner has some strength, he will interject a bid largely
on suspicion.

THE TRAPPER'S PARTNER

Let us put ourselves in the East position on the following
bidding:

SOUTH	WEST	NORTH	EAST
1 ♠	Pass	Pass	?

East holds ♠ 6   ♡ K 10 9 6 5   ◊ K 9 4 3   ♣ J 7 2.

Not a very robust hand, to be sure, but it is just such hands that create problems. Shall we pass, satisfied that the opponents have stopped at one, or put in a bid to protect West if he is trapping?

These are the questions we must ask ourselves: First and foremost, what is the vulnerability condition?

It might be well to tabulate the vulnerability conditions under which trapping is and is not advisable:

Neither side vulnerable: trapping not usually wise.

Opening bidder vulnerable; trapper not vulnerable: ideal for trapping purposes.

Opening bidder not vulnerable; trapper vulnerable: very unwise to trap.

Both sides vulnerable: trapping may be wise.

When we, as East, have satisfied ourselves whether the correct vulnerability condition for trapping exists, we consider the distribution of our hand.

The singleton spade, with its implication of spade length in West's hand, must not escape notice. On a hand this weak, it is really the determining factor. Paradoxically to many players perhaps, the very lack of spade defense is the reason we should, with a good partner, keep the bidding alive. If our hand were like

$$\spadesuit\ 6\ 4\ 3\ 2 \qquad \heartsuit\ K\ 10\ 9\ 6\ 5 \qquad \diamondsuit\ Q\ 9\ 4 \qquad \clubsuit\ J$$

we should pass to the one-spade bid as fast as we can get the word out—the four spades in our hand make it extremely unlikely that partner has made a trap-pass.

SHIFT-BIDS

Most trapping tactics involve merely the use of that despised word "pass." Other trapping devices exist, notably the so-called shift-bid.

There are only a few situations in which shift-bids may prove valuable—*if properly timed against the proper adversaries*. Here is one:

SOUTH	WEST	NORTH	EAST
1 N T	Pass	2 ♣	

East, whose turn it is to bid, holds

♠ K Q J 10 8 6 ♡ K Q J 10 ◇ 7 5 ♣ 2

It is obvious that this hand should take eight tricks with spades as trump; it is very unlikely that the other two tricks necessary to a game contract will be found in partner's hand. The one hope of making a game is to be doubled at a two-spade contract. To trap such a double, East overcalls North's two-club takeout with a psychic bid of two diamonds. The notrump bidder, South, is very apt to double, whereupon East runs out to two spades. If he finds one of the opponents in a doubling humor, this apparent "rescue bid" may be doubled also.

It is unwise to get into a "doubling stride"; experts may double four or five successive bids and cannily pass when a new suit is suddenly brought out. The cards themselves—not vague suspicions—must guide doubles.

BIDDING OVER A TAKEOUT DOUBLE

The best opportunities for shift-bids occur after a takeout double. Since most bids (except redoubles) made directly over a double show weakness, it becomes comparatively safe to indulge in psychic or shift-bidding, provided, of course, that the bidder holds a good fit with partner's announced suit or an escape suit of his own.

Suppose South, not vulnerable, opens the bidding with one club and West, vulnerable, doubles for a takeout. North holds

♠ 8 6 2 ♡ 7 4 ◇ Q J 9 ♣ K 10 7 5 2

He is not only pitifully weak defensively, but in addition his club length is apt to kill some of South's tricks. Heroic measures are indicated. To preëmpt with four clubs is to court a severe penalty—and it may not even shut the opponents out of their likely game.

The best chance is a one-spade or one-heart bid. If East, the takeout doubler's partner, is not very alert, or is a timid bidder, the stratagem may succeed; at least it can hardly lose.

A psychic bid of one or two notrump is not good strategy; the former is not high enough to shut out a bid, and the latter is a little "too raw" to be successful. Alert players should rarely be taken in by shift-bids. The best defense against them is a quick penalty double.

Bids to Misplace Cards

A psychic bid calculated to assure the opponents that the sure tricks and solid suits staring them in the face are not there at all—are simply mirages—has not a very good chance of succeeding. Even the weakest players trust their own eyesight.

The only rational reason for psychic bids of all descriptions is to lead the opponents to think that their Kings and Queens are apt to be trapped by superior honors or that their suits will fail to break.

A bluff bid that has any sense must be provided with an emergency landing field. To pick up such a hand as

♠ 6 3 2   ♥ 8 7 5   ♦ 10 7 4 3   ♣ J 5 2

and open with one notrump on it, is to jump out of an airplane with an opened umbrella instead of a parachute; it *may* get you down safely, but the chances are a million to one against it.

If, however, against not-too-bright opponents, you pick up such as hand as

♠ 6 2   ♥ 8 5   ♦ K Q J 9 6 5 2   ♣ 7 3

an *overcall* of an opponent's bid with one notrump may have a beautiful result.

Doubling on Partner's Behalf

A situation that permits the exercise of the highest strategy is exemplified in the following hand:

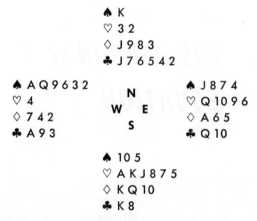

```
              ♠ K
              ♡ 3 2
              ◇ J 9 8 3
              ♣ J 7 6 5 4 2

♠ A Q 9 6 3 2          N          ♠ J 8 7 4
♡ 4                W       E      ♡ Q 10 9 6
◇ 7 4 2                S          ◇ A 6 5
♣ A 9 3                          ♣ Q 10

              ♠ 10 5
              ♡ A K J 8 7 5
              ◇ K Q 10
              ♣ K 8
```

The bidding (North-South vulnerable):

West (dealer)	North	East	South
1 ♠	Pass	2 ♠	3 ♡
Pass	Pass	3 ♠	4 ♡
Double!	Pass	Pass	Pass

West's double, which is certainly not justified by his holding, is based on the following reasoning:

Despite the fact that East could not have a big hand (witness his weak spade raise), even after South's vulnerable three-heart bid he showed he was not afraid of a heart game by again raising spades. He could not have great hopes of a game in spades, since West had made no rebid after being raised. Obviously, it would be inconsistent for East to bid up to four spades, considering his inability to give more than a minimum raise on the first round, and therefore he *must* be planning to double four hearts, if it should be bid. West makes the double himself so that South cannot place the heart honors.

CHAPTER THIRTY-SIX

THE PERSONAL EQUATION

The sum of all technical knowledge cannot make a master contract player. If it could, the greatest experts would be simply those players with the most retentive memories and instead of a magnificent scientific pastime, contract would be merely a glorified spelling-bee.

The personal element in contract is so pervasive that few intelligent bids or plays can be made without taking it into consideration. So true is this that a good bid or play may be reduced to a formula; thus:

$$\frac{\text{Bid or play}}{\text{Situation}} + \text{Partner's Psychology} + \text{Opponents' Psychology} = \mathbf{X}$$

With correct valuation applied to every element, X will of course represent perfection.

Whether a player is considering such an apparently elementary point as making an opening bid on minimum values, or attempting one of the bidding stratagems described in the last chapter, his decision must be guided by his partner's probable reaction.

Playing Partner's Game

There is widespread misconception of the proper technique to offset great aggressiveness or great timidity in a partner. A standard explanation for the failure to bid the full strength of one's hand is "but I didn't *dare* with so-and-so for a partner! We would have landed on the roof!"

The usual theory that with an aggressive partner one must be conservative and with a conservative partner one must be aggressive is completely fallacious. *The opposite is true,* paradoxical as it may seem. Let A, who is ridiculously optimistic, once see that you are "holding back" with him, and his bidding, far from coming down to earth, will soar to high heaven! If you pass his opening bid, he will "figure" that you were afraid to raise on a mere two Kings and a Queen; if you give him a single raise, he will assume you have about 2½ honortricks and good distribution.

Contrariwise, with B, the chronic underbidder, a few drastic overbids or over-raises on your part will send him scurrying to cover like a frightened chipmunk! And after that, nothing will convince him that he hasn't a wild man to contend with, and his timidity will become more and more acute until he automatically passes at every opportunity.

Since attempting to "compensate" cannot succeed, what course *should* be followed with extremist partners? None but this: meet them on their own ground! With A, bid aggressively; let him see for himself that you bid your own values up to the hilt and that, consequently, it will be fatal for him to do it for you. Scare him to death!

With B, be conservative. Let your bids, and particularly your raises, be so sound that he gains complete confidence; then he is apt to blossom like a shy flower.

Partner's Bridge Mentality

So far, we have discussed only partner's *disposition* with reference to his optimism or conservatism. Now we come to his *bridge mentality.*

With a stolid, unimaginative partner, there is no more sense in attempting a stratagem that requires coöperation than there would be in reading Einstein to a child. With him, the highest strategy is cut-and-dried, one hundred percent conventional bridge.

With such a partner, the technique of trap bidding (as de-

scribed on page 414) must be modified by the foreknowledge
that he cannot be depended upon for "protection." The Forcing
Pass (page 398) must be discarded entirely—there is too terrible a danger that when the bidding comes around to him,
he will simply pass. Far better to make a decision yourself,
even though the responsibility is logically his. Bluff notrump
bids (see page 418) are far too dangerous with a partner who
will never "let you off the hook"—who will keep bidding his
own suit till kingdom come.

PSYCHOLOGY OF DOUBLES

The fields of takeout and penalty doubles require the most
delicate readjustment according to partner's bridge intelligence. Take, for example, a situation such as this:

Both sides vulnerable, East deals and bids one club. You hold

♠ A K 6 2   ♥ A K 6 2   ♦ K 5 2   ♣ 4 3

You naturally double for a takeout. West passes and your partner responds with one spade. East passes and now it is up to
you again. What should you bid?

The proper bid ranges from two to four spades, depending
on the type of partner you have. With an expert, two spades
is strong enough to find out from him whether or not he had
a little bit better than a forced response. With an average
player, three spades is the best bid. He will require that much
encouragement to bid again if he holds such a hand as

♠ J 8 5 4 3   ♥ Q 7 5   ♦ Q J 6   ♣ 8 5

With a weak player, your best gamble is to jump (quite un-
soundly) to four. Should he hold the hand just described, or
even slightly better, he would pass to even a jump raise—on
the theory that "he hadn't a trick."

The subject of takeout doubles reveals amazing paradoxes.
A player who could not be bribed into opening such a hand as

♠ A K 10 4 3   ♥ K 10 6 2   ♦ J 7 5   ♣ 6

will smugly make a takeout double of an opponent's spade
bid on

♠ 5   ♥ Q 10 7 2   ♦ K 7 5 2   ♣ K 10 8 4

He will, if criticized, point righteously to his "excellent *support* for any other suit."

On the other hand, if you make a takeout double, and he holds

♠ K 10 9 8 6 2   ♡ Q 10 9 5 4   ◊ 5   ♣ 2

he will respond with one spade, and then later expostulate: "Why, I had only one King and one Queen in my hand!"

These are idiosyncrasies that only experience can discover; the point is that *all* of partner's "theories" must be carefully noted and filed away for future reference.

Partner's Morale

The question of morale is automatically solved for those who realize that partnership is simply a sporting proposition; we are drawn together for better or for worse, and, therefore, like true pals, should stand by each other cheerfully and courageously.

The practical attitude toward all partners should be that of a philosophical, sincere and sympathetic friend. Partner must never be allowed to feel that his loss is taken too hard by you. During bidding and play, partner, however weak, must feel that you sincerely respect his intelligence and efforts. Unless he is the veriest beginner, his bids must not be taken away from him on the silly ground that he would lose tricks in the play. He should be complimented if successful, and if he makes a blunder extenuating circumstances should be provided for him as an escape.

Partnership morale will always be maintained at a very high level if the following rule is obeyed to the letter: "Never reproach your partner if there be the slightest thing for which you can reproach yourself." Most disasters can be avoided by a good player if he takes care to foresee partner's possible mistakes.

This does not mean that partner should be unnecessarily flattered. Russians say very appropriately, "Praise the goat and next time she will refuse her milk." It is true that there are certain partners who can be brought out of their depressing fits only by a sharp word.

But recriminations, *even though one is quite right,* are like pouring water on flaming oil, and serious mistakes almost invariably follow. This is particularly true in the case of married couples.

How to Be Married and Yet Play Bridge

Some day I expect to turn into a poker Moses and lead millions of husbands now chained like galley slaves to the bridge table, into the promised land of a game in which the husband will regain his immemorial right to lose his own money without asking a special dispensation from his wife.

I observe with alarm the increasing hostility on the part of some husbands toward bridge, on the ground that it causes too many arguments and bickerings, due to a lack of benign tolerance from some womenfolk. It is characteristic of the American woman to be so enthusiastic about anything she undertakes—be it a husband, a home, a social movement, or a mere game—that she may become positively ferocious in her enthusiasm. And the poor husband suffers.

Granting even that the wholly self-assumed intellectual superiority of the average husband is most exasperating to any intelligent woman, it does not follow that the hubby should be mercilessly castigated because he is found inadequate in the subtle intricacies of a mere game! Women have leisure time to study and learn. It is too much to expect the same from the poor beast of burden who, harassed by worries of life which are more serious than the worries of a forgotten trump suit, slaves all day downtown to provide the wherewithal for the wife and kiddies (which includes bridge books for the wife). He cannot come home late and dead tired and become a bridge nonpareil overnight.

In my capacity as a bridge doctor I am often called into consultation. My advice to wives who are solicitous of real peace with their husbands is always this: *Let the poor devil alone!* Let him trump your Aces, pass your forcing takeouts, ignore your minimum responses, or mistake your opening two-bid for a pure shutout bid. After all, bridge is not the center of the universe. It is only a game. When it ceases to be a game, then it is time to quit either bridge or your husband.

Opponents' Psychology

The most essential point to determine in a given hand is whether it is more important to tell partner the whole truth, necessarily letting the opponents "listen in," or to mislead the opponents at the cost of misleading partner. The hand itself, and the situation, are the deciding factors. Take such a simple case as this:

With both sides vulnerable and North-South having a part-score of 20, North deals and passes; East passes and South holds:

♠ K J 9   ♡ K Q 10   ◇ A K Q 10 9   ♣ K Q

Here is a situation "made to order"! After partner's pass, a slam is remote, requiring an absolute minimum of two Aces in his hand, and therefore need not be given serious consideration. A much more profitable coup is possible, namely an apparently preëmptive bid of four diamonds! South need not worry that he is misinforming partner—he does not require North's coöperation on this hand. If West holds a fair hand (which the passes by North and East make likely) and is persuaded by the state of the score and South's "preëmptive" bid to overcall, he will probably be carried out on a stretcher!

A hand played by Mrs. Culbertson in the final round of an important tournament a few years ago portrays the fine art of using the simple truth as a double-cross:

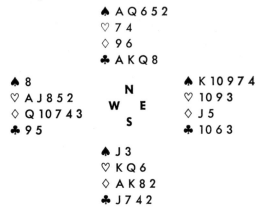

          ♠ A Q 6 5 2
          ♡ 7 4
          ◇ 9 6
          ♣ A K Q 8

♠ 8   **N**   ♠ K 10 9 7 4
♡ A J 8 5 2   ♡ 10 9 3
◇ Q 10 7 4 3   **W**   **E**   ◇ J 5
♣ 9 5   **S**   ♣ 10 6 3

          ♠ J 3
          ♡ K Q 6
          ◇ A K 8 2
          ♣ J 7 4 2

Mrs. Culbertson was South. The bidding was:

NORTH	EAST	SOUTH	WEST
1 ♠	Pass	2 N T	Pass
3 ♣	Pass	3 ◇	Pass
3 N T	Pass	Pass	Pass

No sooner was the final pass out of West's mouth than he fired a *diamond* as the opening lead! Mrs. Culbertson's three-diamond bid was the key-bid of the hand. Very shrewdly, she figured that West would regard the bid as an effort to stop a diamond lead, and she counted on his "not allowing himself to be fooled!"

Against that type of player, the *truth* was the most subtle double-cross!

CHANGE OF PACE

A truly great player is one about whom half of his partners swear that he is conservative, while the other half maintain that he is aggressive. He is in fact neither conservative nor aggressive, but is bold or cautious according to the bidding situations and partner's psychology.

Contract is a vast armory, in which weapons for every purpose, aggressive and defensive, are stocked. The password for admittance is knowledge; the selection of the right weapon requires imagination and experience; its actual use demands coolness and courage under fire!

CHAPTER THIRTY-SEVEN

MODERN THEORY
OF DISTRIBUTION

The Law of Symmetry

To say that mathematics is only a small part of bridge is not to impugn the validity of mathematical law, but the laws of simple probabilities must be modified and corrected when applied to cards. In calculating the probabilities of various hand and suit distributions the mathematicians presuppose an abstract perfect shuffle which is nonexistent in practice. This fact renders many of the current mathematical tables, which are sacred to so many experts, at best of problematical value.

The conditions governing simple probabilities in bridge or poker are somewhat similar to those governing the fall of loaded dice. A deck of cards is similarly loaded by the artificial selection of longest suits for trump bids, of smallest cards for losing tricks, and of biggest cards for the winners. Suppose that pure chance has dealt to a player

♠ A K Q 8 7 5 4   ♡ —   ◇ A K Q 3   ♣ 5 2

If the cards are not at all shuffled the next deal will be either extraordinarily "normal" or once more freakish. It will hardly be average and it will certainly not be due this time to pure chance. At a contract of six spades the player leads out seven rounds of spades. The first twenty-eight cards therefore form an artificial pattern, the characteristic feature of which is the abnormal condition that seven times in succession the first card of the trick is a spade. If the dummy holds four strong clubs, one of the opponents will cling to the bitter end with his four clubs, so in the last four tricks there will be at least eight clubs bunched together, and thus the artificiality of the pattern will be enhanced, unless the cards are shuffled to the point of wearing off their spots. Speaking scientifically, every deck of cards after a few hours of selective playing becomes, in the parlance of card sharps, "a cold deck." It is innocently stacked by the players themselves.*

The factor X—the artificially formed patterns and the imperfect shuffle—must be seriously reckoned with in calculations, and forms the basis of the Law of Symmetry.

The Law of Symmetry is not a law at all in the sense of a physical law. It is rather a loose collection of trends and tendencies which are implicit in the artificial formation of a deck of cards. As an auxiliary to the laws of probabilities it attempts in a quick and practical manner to correct roughly the errors in the application of simple probabilities caused by the artificial suit formations of the play. The Law of Symmetry can be defined as a guide for judging the types (balanced and unbalanced) of suit and hand-patterns in the remaining three hands or, if two hands are seen, in the two unknown hands.

There are three ways of determining the distribution of the unknown hands. First and most important, by means of card reading. Second, by means of percentages. Third, by means of the Law of Symmetry. The last method, though still imperfect, is the most fascinating of the three, for here a player attempts to penetrate the unknown hands by using only his own hand as a guide.

Thus, if you hold a 4–4–4–1 distribution you will consider it a very morbid symptom indicative of monstrous, cancer-like suit growths around the table. To start with, there must be somewhere a long suit to balance your singleton. If it is a five-card length, it means that someone else will have four or five

---

* Two or three master card players in the world have penetrated at least subconsciously to the bottom of cards. They not only remember the cards played in the present deal, but store in their minds the sequence of events in the preceding deal. Then, projecting the lay of cards of the preceding deal into the present deal, they attempt to pick up the broken bits and fragments that remained apparently intact after the shuffle and apply that knowledge to the wizardry of play.

of the same suit—at any rate something unbalanced. Similarly, the remaining suits must, so to speak, entwine themselves around your 4–4–4–1 hand-pattern. And as they do so they will naturally be packed so as to fit in more easily. Thus, if your hand is lopsided or cross-eyed, then the entire deck is very probably lopsided or cross-eyed. The fruit does not fall far from its tree.

When, however, you hold a hand-pattern belonging to the respectable but rather bourgeois family of balanced patterns, say the prosaic 5–3–3–2, this pattern symptom is nothing that is really alarming. At least one of the unknown hands, and at least one of the suits, will also be balanced, and probably other hands and suits as well.

The cards have their own laws of gravitation and their natural trend is along the lines of least resistance: some violent attraction such as an eight-card suit will cause abnormal perturbation throughout the deck, pulling the cards out of their natural orbits even though they be governed by the laws of great numbers.

There are thirty-nine suit or hand-patterns, starting with the most common, the 4–4–3–2, and ending with the patterns, such as 11–2–0–0, which, like the rarest of comets, gravitate on the outermost bounds of the distributional constellations— millions of light-deals away. In the Law of Symmetry we are not concerned, at least not directly, with the frequencies or probabilities of various suit or hand-patterns; we are mainly interested in their types. Thus the common balanced type of 5–3–3–2 is a blood cousin to the unusual but stodgy 7–2–2–2; while the unbalanced type 5–4–3–1 is intimately related to the swan-like grace of a 7–4–1–1. The balanced type is a hand or suit pattern which contains no singleton and usually no second long suit. The unbalanced type always contains a single-ton and usually a second four-card or longer suit.

Mathematically speaking, a 4–4–4–1 and a 5–4–3–1 are miles apart, the former occurring in three percent of all cases and the latter in thirteen percent. Actually, however, they are far more closely related to each other than a 5–4–3–1 is related to its mathematical counterpart, the 5–3–3–2, which occurs only a little bit more frequently.

Any suit or hand-pattern contains a long suit and its remainders. The remainders of a balanced type are called balanced and those of an unbalanced type are unbalanced. For instance, the remainders of 6–3–2–2 are balanced, while the remainders of 6–4–2–1 are unbalanced. The even number 2 is the dominant characteristic of balanced remainders and the odd number 1 distinguishes the unbalanced.

Typical Balanced Hand-Patterns

♠ K 7 4 2	♠ Q 10 8	♠ A K Q J 6 5
♡ A 6 4	♡ A K 4 3 2	♡ 4 2
◇ K 6	◇ 10 5	◇ 6 2
♣ Q J 10 7	♣ A J 9	♣ J 10 9

Typical Unbalanced Hand-Patterns

♠ K 7 4 2	♠ Q 10 8	♠ A K Q J 6 5
♡ A	♡ A K 4 3 2	♡ 4
◇ K 6 5 3	◇ 5	◇ 6 2
♣ Q J 10 7	♣ A J 10 9	♣ J 10 9 7

The suit and hand-patterns of any deal can be expressed in a special table (of which an example is given on this page below) which shows the distributions of the four suits in horizontal lines, and the distributions of the four hands in vertical lines. We can, therefore, call these distributions, in the terms of their arrangement in the table, as horizontal (the suit distributions) and vertical (the hand-patterns).

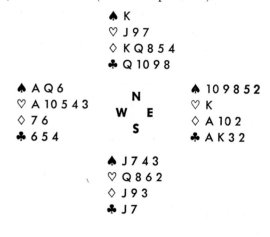

```
                    ♠ K
                    ♡ J 9 7
                    ◇ K Q 8 5 4
                    ♣ Q 10 9 8

     ♠ A Q 6              N        ♠ 10 9 8 5 2
     ♡ A 10 5 4 3                  ♡ K
     ◇ 7 6          W       E      ◇ A 10 2
     ♣ 6 5 4             S         ♣ A K 3 2

                    ♠ J 7 4 3
                    ♡ Q 8 6 2
                    ◇ J 9 3
                    ♣ J 7
```

HAND-PATTERNS
(Read down)

	SOUTH	WEST	NORTH	EAST
Spades	4	3	1	5
Hearts	4	5	3	1
Diamonds	3	2	5	3
Clubs	2	3	4	4

SUIT DISTRIBUTIONS
(Read across)

There often exists a striking parallelism or affinity between two balanced or two unbalanced suit and hand-patterns. Thus, if one hand is balanced it is probable that somewhere around the table there is another balanced hand. This does not mean that the correspondence is exact, but simply that the various types of kindred distributions, like gloves, are apt to come in pairs. So if you see a 5–4–3–1 in your hand, its brother or cousin hand-pattern is probably hiding around the corner.

What is far more extraordinary is that, in addition to the correspondence between two related hand-patterns, there is a close correspondence between at least one hand-pattern and a suit pattern. Thus, if you hold a 5–3–3–2 type of hand-pattern there is very probably somewhere a suit also distributed 5–3–3–2 or in a similar balanced fashion. It is also extremely likely that the balanced type is formed by the remainder of your own long suit. Again, if you hold a 6–4–2–1 hand-pattern, there is a suit somewhere which is distributed in a similar unbalanced manner, and it is quite likely that this "affinity" suit is your own. In other words, the remainder of your six-card suit will probably be unbalanced.

The above facts may be summarized in the following two theorems:

(1) A balanced hand-pattern is generally accompanied by at least one other balanced hand-pattern, and an unbalanced hand-pattern is generally accompanied by another unbalanced hand-pattern. The more unbalanced the pattern, the greater the expectation that another hand will be of the same type.

(2) A balanced hand-pattern is generally accompanied by a similar balanced pattern in at least one of the four suits, and an unbalanced hand-pattern by a similar unbalanced pattern

in some suit, usually the one in which the hand in question is
the longest. The more freakish the hand-pattern, the greater the
expectancy of a similar freakish distribution of the longest suit.

It will be noted that in the deal previously shown South's hand is 4–4–3–2,
and so is the club suit; West's hand is 5–3–3–2, to which the distribution of
the diamond suit conforms; the other two hands and the other two suits are
5–4–3–1. Here there is perfect symmetry; for every hand-pattern there is an
identical suit distribution.

The Law of Symmetry is chiefly useful in teaching one when
to expect the unexpected. In the play it is particularly valuable
as a basis for deciding, in borderline cases, when to finesse and
when to play for the drop, and, even more, when to plan the
play on the basis of bad breaks. In bidding its greatest value
is in serving as a warning to watch one's step when holding an
unbalanced pattern, where the danger of unfavorable breaks is
increased, while with a balanced pattern the expectancy of an
average break is increased.

For instance, I pick up

♠ A K 9 6 4 3   ♡ 5   ◇ A Q 7 5 4   ♣ 8

It would be the height of naïveté to lean too heavily upon
the expectation of "average" break of either of my long suits.
I would accordingly conduct the bidding very gingerly; my
spade suit may break evenly, but if the diamond suit breaks
5–5–2–1 then the spades will follow it. Take out this hand from
the deck and deal the remaining thirty-nine cards, observing
what happens.

If I hold a seven- or an eight-card suit I expect one or two
other very long suits. With a hand-pattern 7–4–1–1 I am not
so happy about my seven-card suit, for it is astonishing how
often it will break 7–4–1–1. It is one thing to hold ◇ A K Q 3 2
with a 5–4–3–1 hand-pattern and quite another thing if the
hand-pattern is 5–3–2–2.

The hand-pattern 4–3–3–3, while it usually indicates a number of 4–4–3–2's, 4–3–3–3's, and 5–3–3–2's around the table,
is sometimes the most deceiving symptom of all. It may be the
tail end of violent distributional storms which are raging in
other hands. It is the peculiarity of the 4–3–3–3 hand that it

often serves as a joiner between the freakish and normal distributions. Hence in bidding I am always careful to step lightly with a 4–3–3–3 unless well heeled.

Once more the reader should be warned that these theorems merely express trends, and not certainties or even strong probabilities. To use the Law of Symmetry as the main guide in the bidding and play would be disastrous: but to use it as a prop, a practical aid to the bidding and playing inferences as well as to the theory of percentages, is definitely valuable.

The Law of Symmetry deals principally with distributions rather than with individual honors, and this aspect of it is the only one with which we shall concern ourselves in this volume. It may be well in passing, however, to note that there are also remarkable correspondences between honors, which suggest that the law may have a much wider application. For instance, if a player holds a singleton King it will happen much more often than probability warrants that another singleton King is in the offing.* Similarly with Queens and other singleton honors. Sometimes, by a strange quirk of suit formations, a singleton honor may evoke a singleton lower honor or vice versa. Even more extraordinary are the cases where a solid sequence in one suit evokes a solid sequence in another suit or a long suit, full of holes, in one hand is in touching affinity with an identical long suit, which is full of identical holes, in another hand.

---

* I am aware that psychologically we are apt to be more struck by the unusual than by the usual and therefore to remember it better, while forgetting the tremendously more numerous instances which did not attract particular notice. To be certain of my conclusions I have for a period of years made actual tests, and am convinced that this is not a psychological illusion.

BOOK THREE

THE PLAY
OF THE CARDS

Bidding is only mental play, and its
efficacy can be demonstrated only by
the actual results when the cards are
played out and the tricks won and
lost. In the final analysis, the principles
of card-playing must be thoroughly
grasped before the ultimate precision
in bidding is possible.

CHAPTER THIRTY-EIGHT

THE WINNING
OF TRICKS

While there are dozens of plays in bridge, there are only three ways of winning tricks.

The first kind of trick is called an honor-trick.* The second kind of trick is called a long-card trick. The third kind of trick is called a ruffer. The second and third kinds of trick are won with low cards, and are a direct result of differences in suit-lengths around the table.

```
                K Q J
                  N
      A 4 3 2   W   E   7 6 5
                  S
                10 9 8
```

West can win the first trick with his Ace, because it is the highest card of the suit. North loses the first trick to the Ace, but now his Queen and King are the highest cards remaining and win tricks for him. These cards win tricks because of their rank.

After the first three tricks have been won by high cards, West has one card of the suit remaining, which, when led, will win a trick (unless trumped) because no higher card of the same suit remains to capture it. This is a *mass* element—pure length value.

North won two tricks, both honor-winners. West also won two tricks, one an honor-winner and one a long card. It follows that the total trick-taking possibilities of any long suit are the sum of ranking and long cards of that suit.

---

* An honor-card is technically a ten or higher card. Often a nine or lower card may win a trick by virtue of its rank, when the higher cards have been played. Such cards, honor or lower, which may win or promote the winning of a trick, may be called "ranking cards."

The same principle applies in the case of ruffing tricks, which are the result of a void in the suit led and a card of the trump suit with which to win the trick.

The Principle of Promotion

As each high-ranking card is played to win a trick, or is "captured" or "dropped" by a still higher-ranking card, all the remaining cards of the same suit move up one step in rank.

If on the first trick the King is played and the Ace captures it, the Queen controls the second round of the suit. If the Jack, Queen, King and Ace all fall together on one trick, the ten has in one operation become the most important card of its suit.

A player should always consider the promotional value of his honors. He can make the Principle of Promotion operate in his favor:

(1) By forcing his opponents to use two ranking cards to effect the capture of one; and

(2) By preventing an opponent from covering (capturing) his own ranking card whenever possible.

1.	A Q 8 2		2.	A 4 3	
	N			N	
K 6 4	W E	10 7 5	5 2	W E	K 10 9 8
	S			S	
	J 9 3			Q J 7 6	

In Figure 1, South leads the Jack. If West plays low, North can also play low, for the Jack will win the trick. Next South will lead the three, West will play the six, and North will win with the Queen. The Ace remaining in North's hand, East and West will never win a trick. If West had covered the Jack with his King, the Ace would in turn have recaptured the King; but since two of North-South's high cards fell at once, East's ten would have been promoted to second rank in the suit and would have won the third trick.

In Figure 2, if South plays the Queen and allows East to capture it with his King, East will still have 10 9 8, only two of which can be captured by North's Ace and South's Jack. East must win two tricks. If South plays to prevent the capture of his Queen, he can win three tricks against East's one. First, a low card is led to the Ace; then a low card is led from the North hand toward South's Queen and Jack. If East plays the King, South plays low and retains the two highest cards, both of which will win tricks. If East plays low, South wins with the Jack and still has the Queen, which can be promoted to winning rank by another lead from the North hand.

Stoppers

A suit such as K Q J 10 9 may properly be counted as four sure winners. The opponents' Ace, being the highest card, cannot be prevented from winning, but when the Ace has been played the other four cards, by the Principle of Promotion, will have become so many Aces.

Yet, while the Ace is held by an opponent, the suit K Q J 10 9 will not win a single trick. Before the cards of this suit can be cashed in as tricks the Ace must be removed. The run of the suit is *stopped* by the Ace.

A stopper is a card or combination of cards which can win a trick and which must be removed before other cards of the same suit can be established and turned into tricks.

The plays of suit establishment consist in removal of stoppers. There are as many methods of play in suit establishment as there are kinds of stoppers.

Guards and Suit-Distribution

A card which accompanies a higher card of the same suit is called a *guard*. In Q 3, the three is a guard. Each additional small card constitutes another guard. In J 8 6 4, the Jack is "three times guarded."

By giving up the worthless cards which guard it for the opponents' valuable cards, a ranking card is promoted into a winner. A King needs but one guard; a Queen needs two guards; a Jack, three.

When a ranking card is not accompanied by as many guards as there are higher honors in the opponents' hands, it will "drop" on the lead of a higher honor.

In the example shown, the Queen in West's hand is not well enough guarded. South, employing one of the most common methods of suit establishment, leads out the spade Ace and King. West's Queen drops, setting up the Jack in South's hand. Transfer one of the low spades from East's hand to West's, and West could have followed to each of the first two leads with low cards. South's play for a drop would have failed, for at the third trick West would have had the Queen, stopping the suit.

```
              ♠ 7 4 3
                 N
      ♠ Q 6   W     E   ♠ 8 5 2
                 S
              ♠ A K J 10 9
```

Straight Leads from Sequences

Previously it was stated that "there are as many methods of play in suit establishment as there are kinds and combinations of stoppers." Broadly speaking, there are two kinds of stoppers: strong and probable.

Strong stoppers are practically sure tricks—an Ace, K-Q, Q J 10, J 10 9 8 or other solid honor combination. Unless they can be ruffed, these stoppers are not to be prevented from winning tricks, provided they are held in a suit the opponents must establish.

Probable stoppers are guarded honors such as K x, Q x x, or similar combinations which may, as will be seen later, be trapped by the opponents.

In the case of a strong stopper, the only means of eliminating it is by sacrificing a trick to it—a sort of exchange of prisoners. This is the simplest type of suit establishment, and is used when holding a strong sequence.

Three or more cards of the same suit, in consecutive order of rank form a sequence. Thus, K Q J 6 5 or Q J 10 8 3 are suits headed by sequences. A two-card combination such as K-Q, though technically "in sequence" is known in bridge terminology not as a sequence but as "equals." The value of a sequence is that all its cards are equals, so that the lowest card of the sequence assumed a rank equivalent to that of the highest.

With such combinations as these:

K Q J	Q 10 6	Q 6 5	J 10 9 8	6 4 2
N	**N**	**N**	**N**	**N**
W E	**W E**	**W E**	**W E**	**W E**
S	**S**	**S**	**S**	**S**
4 3 2	J 7 3	K J 7	5 3 2	Q J 10

Lead out one of your equals; allow an opponent to win with his higher card. If your remaining cards are not yet established, lead another one when you regain the lead, and so on until your suit is established.

Position

Usually a suit is not headed by a strong sequence, but by some broken honor combination from which one or more honors are missing. In such cases, the question of whether or not a trick must be lost to a missing honor depends upon how well it is guarded and upon its *position*.

A card which is not the highest of its suit loses its value when it must be played before an opponent holding a higher card plays. But when the opponent holding the higher card must play first, the secondary card, provided it is guarded, will win a trick.

When the cards are divided as in the following diagram, South will win three tricks, capturing every trick but East's Ace, *if East must play first to every trick:*

$$\heartsuit\ 5\ 4\ 3$$

$$\text{N}$$

$$\heartsuit\ 6\ 2 \quad \text{W} \qquad \text{E} \quad \heartsuit\ A\ Q\ 10\ 8$$

$$\text{S}$$

$$\heartsuit\ K\ J\ 9\ 7$$

But so tremendous is the positional value of cards that East would win every trick if South were repeatedly forced to play from his own hand.

Apart from the method of leading out strong sequences, the two forms of establishing honor-tricks are plays for a drop (based on the supposition or hope that the opponents' honor is unguarded) and finesses (based on the hope that the missing honor, while guarded, is in a position disadvantageous to its holder). The player chooses between these alternative methods after determining how much likelihood there is of finding the honor guarded.

A card that is not the highest of its suit can be captured by playing for a drop if it is alone or insufficiently guarded. A play for a drop consists simply in leading out high cards, hoping that an opponent, forced by the laws of the game to follow suit, must play his lower-ranking card.

J 10 8 6 5			J 10 8 6 5			J 10 8 6 5	
	N			N			N
Q 3 W	E	—	K W	E 9	— W	E	K 9
	S			S			S
A K 9 7 4 2			A Q 7 4 3 2			A Q 7 4 3 2	

In the first example, South has only to lead out his Ace and King; he knows the Queen will drop, establishing the Jack, because only two cards are outstanding. In the second example if South leads his Ace, playing for a drop, he will win all the tricks, for the King is unguarded. But in the third example, if South leads his Ace, East will follow suit with the nine and win a trick with the King; whereas if North leads the five and East plays the nine, South can win the trick with his Queen and save the Ace to capture the King later.

The play for a drop is easy to execute; the only difficulty is in knowing when the missing honor is likely to be unguarded. Below are the logical steps that take place in every player's mind when he is deciding how to play a suit:

Culbertson Rule of Five Steps

Assume the dummy to be exposed, and consider declarer's and dummy's cards as the same suit.

1. Subtract the combined length of the suit in their hands from 13, and divide the remainder by 2 (as nearly as possible).
2. Assume that the highest-ranking outstanding card is held by the opponent who has the longer portion of the suit.

Usually the first two steps will be the ones to follow in deciding whether or not the outstanding honor is sufficiently guarded, or is insufficiently guarded and will drop.

3. Consider that one opponent has one card more than his half, and the other opponent one less.
4. Place the two highest-ranking cards outstanding in the hand of the opponent who holds the longer portion, and if possible protect against losing to both these cards.
5. Now assume the worst possible division and look for a safety play (Chapter 44).

To Illustrate the Rule of Five Steps

♠ K 9 5 3

N
W　E
S

♠ A J 7 4 2

STEP 1. 5 plus 4 equals 9, subtracted from 13 leaves 4 cards in the opponents' hands. Four divided by 2 equals 2.

STEP 2. With two cards in each opponent's hand, the holdings are Q x and 10 x. The Queen will drop on leads of the Ace and King.

STEP 3. If the outstanding spades are divided in the next most probable way, one opponent holds 3 and the other 1.

STEP 4. Placing both the Queen and ten with the three-card holding, one opponent has Q 10 x. If East has this holding, a finesse to the Ace-Jack will succeed.

STEP 5. If either opponent holds Q 10 8 6: suppose West holds it and the King is first played; West will now hold Q 10 8, and South A J 7 4. Due to West's position (playing after South, when dummy leads the suit) West will win two tricks. But if the Ace is first played, East will fail to follow suit and West can be held to one trick. Likewise, if East holds Q 10 8 6 and the Ace is first played, East can win only one trick, for the Jack is in position to play after East, and cannot be captured by East's Queen.

In this case, South can utilize the most favorable division (2–2) by playing for a drop, and likewise guard against the worst division (4–0) by first playing the Ace from his hand.

The table of probabilities (page 453) will serve as a constant check on the results of the Rule of Five Steps.

The Finesse

When probabilities do not favor the play for a drop, the alternative method is a finesse.

THE FINESSE DEFINED

A formal definition of a finesse is: *An attempt to win a trick with a card which is not the highest of the suit led.*

A strategic definition of a finesse is: *An attempt to win a trick by utilizing the possible favorable position of one or more higher cards in the opponents' hands.*

DIRECT AND INDIRECT FINESSES

All finesses belong to one of two fundamental types, direct (attacking) and indirect (defensive).

1. An indirect finesse is used when the finesser wishes to avoid having his ranking card covered by an opponent.
2. A direct finesse is used when the finesser wishes to force the opponents to cover his ranking card.

FIGURE 1	FIGURE 2
Q J 6	Q 4 3
N	N
8 5 2 W E K 4 3	K 9 2 W E J 10 5
S	S
A 10 9 7	A 8 7 6
This finesse is direct, or attacking	This finesse is indirect, or defensive

In Figure 1, North leads the Queen. If East plays low, the Queen will win the trick. If East covers, South recaptures with the Ace and has promoted the Jack and ten to winning rank.

In Figure 2, if North led the Queen and South played low, West would win with the King; but likewise, if the East-West cards were transposed and North led the Queen, North would cover with the King and after South won with the Ace, West would hold the winning cards for the next two tricks, the Jack and ten. South would win only one trick. Therefore South plays an indirect finesse by laying down the Ace first, then leading toward the Queen. If West plays low the Queen wins, if West plays the King the Queen controls the third round. South and North win two tricks.

A finesse against one outstanding card is a simple finesse.

1. 3 2	2. 4 3 2	3. Q 6 2
N	N	N
J 10 W E K 6	A 9 7 W E Q 8 2	A 8 3 W E K 10 7
S	S	S
A Q	K J 10	J 9 4

When North leads and South plays the lower card of the tenace, the cards of the tenace assume the function of *equals,* and the value of the tenace is equivalent to the value of a sequence.

When the tenace is accompanied by one or more equals of the lower tenace card, as in Figure 2 above, the finesse may be repeated by leading again toward the tenace. Sometimes an outstanding honor is well guarded at the start, but one or more finesses remove the small cards which guard it and then a play for a drop will succeed.

DIRECT SIMPLE FINESSES

When the cards of a tenace are not in the same hand, the

tenace cannot be turned into a sequence by finessing unless at least one equal of the lower tenace-card is held.

```
1.      J 6 3          2.      J 10 6          3.      J 10 5
          N                      N                        N
10 8 4 W   E K 7 5     9 5 2 W   E K 7 4      A 8 3 W    E Q 6 2
          S                      S                        S  .
        A Q 9                  A Q 3                    K 7 4
```

In Figure 1, North's Jack does not increase the winning power of South's tenace, for if the Jack is led East's King will cover it and West's ten will win a trick. In Figure 2, North has the ten as well as the Jack, and if East covers the Jack, North will win the third trick. In Figure 3, South can win only one trick; a direct finesse can be made against East's Queen once but not twice. If North held J 10 9, two finesses could be taken.

DOUBLE FINESSES

When there are two intervening key cards outstanding, two separate finesses may be made against them, known as a double finesse. The double finesse consists of two steps, of which the first step has the simple effect of reducing the situation to the common denominator of the simple finesse.

In this diagram, the King and Queen are held by the opponents. The Rule of Five Steps reveals the probability that neither honor will drop, so if South led the Ace he would lose two tricks. Using the double finesse method, North leads the three, East plays low, South plays the ten, and West wins with the King. The position is now the same as though South held A-Q and

```
        9 4 3
          N
K 6  W    E  Q 7 5
          S
       A J 10 8 2
```

East the King, for the Principle of Promotion has made South's A-J the best and third-best cards of the suit, and East's Queen the second best. North again leads, and when East plays the seven South wins with the Jack. His loss, played this way, is only one trick. An identical situation is found in the diagram below, except that when East holds both missing honors

```
        9 4
          N
6  W      E  Q 7
          S
        A J 8 2
```

South's finesse of the ten on the first round wins the trick, and South later takes a simple finesse against the King, losing no trick in the suit; if the honors are split, South will lose one finesse, but win the other. In playing such a combination it is better to finesse the ten on the first round in an attempt to win all the tricks, except when anxious to clear the suit as soon as possible.

```
        9 4 3
          N
8 2  W    E  K J 6
          S
       A Q 10 7 5
```

A *triple finesse* is a play against three outstanding cards. Again, it is a problem of bringing about the simple finesse position.

1.		A J 9		2.		Q 10 4	
		N				N	
Q 10 6	W	E	K 7 3	K J 5	W	E	A 9 8
		S				S	
		8 5 4 2				7 6 3 2	

In Figure 1 South leads low, West low, North plays the *nine*. This forces East's King and the remaining cards leave West's Queen trapped in a simple finesse. The play of the nine is a finesse within a finesse—seeking to make North's J-9 combination act as equals, so that it will be as though North held A J 10. In Figure 2, a finesse of the ten on the first round draws East's Ace and later a lead through West's King yields a trick.

Principle of Economy of Honors

Much of the play of declarer and defenders consists in the struggle to force opponents to give up their ranking cards for small cards. Even with seemingly solid sequences, every effort should be made to lead toward a guarded high card or sequence. Especial care is required when leading toward a tenace.

1.		8 7		2.		10 4 3	
		N				N	
9 6 5 3 2	W	E	A	9 7 5 2	W	E	K
		S				S	
		K Q J 10 4				A Q J 8 6	

Though Figure 1 is an exaggerated case, it happens frequently. If South leads a card from his powerful sequence it will fall to the Ace and West, with the guarded nine, will have a stopper; if the first lead is made by North, South may throw his small card on the Ace and win four tricks.

The ten in Figure 2 is a *ranking card;* let it be covered by East, and a brand-new stopper is created in West's hand.

A simple rule for beginners (and some experts) is:

When playing to a finesse, *play the lowest,* except when prepared to stand for the cover (that is, when holding in either hand the card next lower than the card led).

When to Cover an Honor

When declarer or dummy leads an honor to a finesse, by covering it with a higher honor you will either win the trick or force declarer to use two honors to capture your one. If you or your partner hold any ranking card in the suit, this wholesale use of declarer's honors will hasten the promotion of yours by one full step. Therefore you should cover an honor whenever you hold, *or your partner may hold,* any ranking card whose promotion to a winning position will thus be made more rapid.

An honor led must not be covered when it is evident that no trick may be promoted for yourself or partner.

1.	AJ7	2.	AJ108	3.	AJ109
	N		N		N
K85	W E	Q96	K52 W E 9764	K653 W E	874
	S		S		S
	10432		Q3		Q2

In Figure 1, South leads the ten. West, by covering, can promote East's nine to third rank in the suit, causing East to have a perfect tenace over North's Jack; if West failed to cover the ten, East's nine would never be promoted and on the next round West's King would be finessed. In Figure 2, South leads the Queen; West, though he cannot see South's or his partner's hand, knows that East may hold a card higher than dummy's eight. By covering the Queen, West can promote the nine in East's hand two steps at once, so that it will control the fourth round. In Figure 3, West should not cover because dummy's suit is solid; East cannot hold any card which may be promoted.

When one of two equal honors is led from dummy, do not cover; the second honor, if led, can be covered with equal effect. Likewise, when declarer leads an honor which *may* be one of equal honors, do not cover unless the card led, if not covered, would win the trick.

1.	A87	2.	A87
	N		N
K43 W E 1065		Q43 W E K962	
	S		S
	QJ92		J105

In Figure 1, South leads the Queen. If South is the dummy, West knows he should not cover, since dummy also holds the Jack. If West covered,

North would win the Ace and lead back toward the J 9, successfully finessing East's ten.

In Figure 2, South leads the Jack. West should play low; and if the Jack is finessed to East's King, South cannot finesse again, for West would cover the ten and establish East's nine. If West covered the Jack, the first honor led, North's Ace would win and the ten could be established for a second North-South trick by a lead through East's King.

THE TWO-WAY FINESSE

Many combinations offer a choice between two types of finesses:

1.	◇ A J 6	**2.**	◇ J 10	**3.**		◇ Q 10
	N		N	West	N	
	W E		W E	Leads	W E	
	S		S	◇ 4	S	
	◇ K 10 2		◇ K 5			◇ A 2

In Figure 1, shall the finesse for the Queen be taken through East or through West? In Figure 2, shall the Jack be led and finessed, hoping East has the Queen and the Jack will force out the Ace; or shall South put up the King, hoping East has the Ace? In Figure 3, shall North's ten be played, hoping West has the Jack, or shall North's Queen be played, hoping West has the King?

The disclosures through bidding often *place* the outstanding high cards (Chapter 42). In other cases, declarer must resign himself to a guess.

CHAPTER THIRTY-NINE

LOW-CARD
TRICKS

In the preceding chapters our only interest in low cards was as guardians to their masters. We will now take up the technique of establishing tricks from low cards, consisting of long cards and ruffers.

Long-Suit Establishment

A card of a suit remaining in one hand, after all the opponents' cards of that suit have been played, is called a long card. A four-card suit is the shortest length which can produce a long card.

Most long suits combine the rank and mass elements. A suit such as A K 4 3 2 contains both honor-winners and long cards. The Ace and King will win tricks because of their rank. Later, the three and deuce may win tricks because of the length of the suit.

1.	6 5 4		2.	9 8 7	
	N			N	
J 10 9	W E	8 7	A K Q	W E	J 10
	S			S	
	A K Q 3 2			6 5 4 3 2	

In Figure 1 South leads the Ace, King and Queen, which eliminate the opponents' cards. The 3-2 are now established. At first glance it seems that the A K Q have made the suit, but it is only a case of optical illusion in bridge. The two long cards were always there and made themselves, by virtue of greater length. In Figure 2, three leads will still establish two long cards for South, but they will be losing leads.

To establish a long suit, first make the correct play to develop what tricks you can with honors—by leading out a sequence, by playing for a drop, or by finessing, whichever is proper. You are at the same time eliminating cards of the suit from your opponents' hands. When you have exhausted the possibilities of your honor-tricks, proceed to establish your long cards by sacrifice.

THE USE OF PROBABILITIES

The most even division of the opponents' cards is not always the most probable—see the table on page 453. It is of great value to know what chance of success a suit-establishment play has, in order that a proper choice may be made between alternative lines of play.

```
              ♠ 7 5 3
              ♡ A J 10
              ◇ 8 5 4
              ♣ 7 6 3 2
♠ 9 8 4 2              ♠ 10 6
♡ Q 7 6       N        ♡ K 9 5 2
◇ J 9      W     E     ◇ Q 10 6 2
♣ Q J 10 9    S        ♣ A 8 4
              ♠ A K Q J
              ♡ 8 4 3
              ◇ A K 7 3
              ♣ K 5
```

In this hand, South is declarer at three notrump, so he needs nine tricks. West leads the Queen of clubs, East wins the Ace and returns a club. South takes the King—one trick. He can also win four high spades, two high diamonds and the heart Ace. He must establish one more winner. In diamonds he has a possible long card; but probabilities do not favor a 3–3 division of the outstanding diamonds. In hearts there is a possible double finesse to add the ninth trick. Probabilities favor finding the missing heart honors so divided between the opponents' hands that the double finesse may be expected to gain a trick. South chooses the finesse in hearts and makes his contract.

Short-Suit Establishment

Three or fewer cards of the same suit are called a short suit, or remainders. Short suits have their value at trump bids, where they give rise to ruffers.

A trick made by ruffing a losing card with an otherwise worthless card of the trump suit is called a ruffer.

A ruffer adds an extra trick only when the card ruffed would otherwise be a loser, and when the trump used for ruffing has no independent value as a high card or long card. If either of these conditions is missing, the ruffer does not gain a trick but is only a *duplication play*.

1.	2.	3.
♠ 10 9 8	♠ 10 8 7	♠ A K Q
♡ 3	♡ 3	♡ 3
◇ K Q 10 4	◇ K Q 10 4	◇ K Q 10 4
♣ A 6 5 4 2	♣ A 6 5 4 2	♣ A 6 5 4 2
DUMMY	DUMMY	DUMMY
DECLARER	DECLARER	DECLARER
♠ A K Q 5 4	♠ A K Q 5 4	♠ 8 7 5 4 3
♡ A 6 2	♡ A K Q	♡ A 6 2
◇ J 7 5 2	◇ J 7 5 2	◇ J 7 5 2
♣ 7	♣ 7	♣ 7

In Figure 1 declarer, after taking the heart Ace, will ruff the ♡ 6 2 with dummy's spades, which are trumps. This creates ruffers, since declarer's hearts would otherwise be lost and dummy's spades would otherwise fall valueless when declarer plays the ♠ A K Q. Declarer cannot make ruffers by cashing dummy's club Ace and then ruffing a small club in his own hand; for, if the opponents' spades are normally divided, 3–2, they will fall when declarer leads his high trumps, and the low spades in declarer's hand will win tricks as long cards.

Likewise, in Figure 2 it will not help declarer to ruff his hearts, which will win tricks when led, if unmolested; and in Figure 3, though declarer's hearts are losers, to ruff them with dummy's spades will be sacrificing the tricks which the high spades in dummy would have won when led.

The method of establishing a ruffer is a very simple one: the short suit (doubleton or singleton) is led until a void is created. Then, if the suit is led by another player, a trick may be won by ruffing it. Even a three-card suit may eventually make possible a ruffer, if partner has four cards of the suit and its division makes the establishment of a long card impossible.

RUFFING OUT STOPPERS

The ruffing process allows plain suits to be established with no loss or with minimum loss despite powerful stoppers in the opponents' hands, because the losers can be ruffed.

At the right is shown a case in which a trick would ordinarily be lost to East's Queen before the long cards in diamonds could be established; but in this case, after the Ace and King have been played South ruffs a third round of diamonds with the ♠ 6, killing the value of East's stopper and establishing the long diamonds without loss.

```
                    ◇ A K J 6 3
                        N
    ◇ 10 7 5       W    E    ◇ Q 8 2
                        S
                    ♠ 6 (trump)
                    ◇ 9 4
```

At times a finesse may be taken against an opponent's high card by combining the powers of a sequence, a void, and the ruffing power of the trump suit.

In the example shown, spades are trumps; the club King is led from the North hand. If East plays his Ace, South ruffs with the ♠ 4 and the ♣ Q J are established; if East does not play his Ace South has no need to trump, but can discard a loser from another suit, for the King will win the trick.

```
                    ♣ K Q J
                        N
    ♣ 7 3 2        W    E    ♣ A 6 5
                        S
                    ♠ 4
                    ♣ —
```

In effect, this method of play is no different from a finesse in which South holds the ♣ Ace, East the ♣ King and North ♣ Q J 10. The relative value of the cards is the same, with South's trump acting as a super-Ace.

THE DANGER OF OVERRUFFS

Knowledge of probable suit-distributions is of as great importance in the use of ruffers as in the establishment of long suits. An attempt to ruff a losing card with one of dummy's small trumps must always be attended by the fear that an opponent, being also void in the suit, can snatch the trick away from dummy by playing a higher trump. Especial care should be taken to ruff with *as high a trump as can conveniently be spared.*

However, when two or more ruffers will be needed, do not make the typical beginner's mistake of ruffing too high the *first* time, and low the second time.

```
                          ♠ K 9 4
                          ♡ Q 7 6
                          ◇ 5 3
                          ♣ A J 6 5 2
        ♠ J 10                              ♠ 8 5 3
        ♡ A 10 4            N               ♡ K J 9 5 3
        ◇ J 9 8 6      W         E          ◇ Q 10 7
        ♣ K 9 7 3          S               ♣ Q 8
                          ♠ A Q 7 6 2
                          ♡ 8 2
                          ◇ A K 4 2
                          ♣ 10 4
```

South, playing a spade contract, plans to ruff two diamonds. Since the spade King will be needed to draw trumps, the two ruffs must be made with the ♠ 9 and ♠ 4. The first ruff should be with the ♠ 4; the second ruff will be with the ♠ 9, which East cannot top. If only one ruff were necessary, the ♠ 9 would be used at once, for fear East had originally held only two diamonds.

The Simple Probabilities

SUIT DIVISIONS		
If you and your partner together hold in one suit:	**The cards of that suit in your opponents' hands will be divided:**	
6 cards	**4–3**	62 times in 100 deals
	5–2	31 times in 100 deals
	6–1	7 times in 100 deals
	7–0	Less than 1 time in 200 deals
7 cards	**4–2**	48 times in 100 deals
	3–3	36 times in 100 deals
	5–1	15 times in 100 deals
	6–0	1 time in 100 deals
8 cards	**3–2**	68 times in 100 deals
	4–1	28 times in 100 deals
	5–0	4 times in 100 deals
9 cards	**3–1**	50 times in 100 deals
	2–2	40 times in 100 deals
	4–0	10 times in 100 deals
10 cards	**2–1**	78 times in 100 deals
	3–0	22 times in 100 deals
11 cards	1–1	52 times in 100 deals
	2–0	48 times in 100 deals

DIVISIONS OF OUTSTANDING HONORS		
If opponents hold 2 honors:		
They will be divided 52 times in 100 deals Both will be in one hand 48 times in 100 deals		

If opponents hold 1 honor:	Guarded Once	Guarded Twice
If they have: 3 cards it will be	52%	22%
4 cards it will be	40%	38%
5 cards it will be	28%	40%
6 cards it will be	18%	54%

HAND-PATTERNS
(Distribution of four suits in one hand)

Balanced Patterns	Frequency*	Unbalanced Patterns	Frequency*
4–4–3–2	22%	4–4–4–1	3%
4–3–3–3	10%	5–4–3–1	13%
5–3–3–2	16%	5–5–2–1	3%
5–4–2–2	11%	6–4–2–1	5%
6–3–2–2	6%	6–3–3–1	3%
†5–4–4–0	1.20%	5–5–3–0	0.90%
7–2–2–2	0.50%	6–5–1–1	0.70%
		6–4–3–0	1.30%

* Approximately.   † A balanced freak.

Culbertson Standard Table of Finesses

	You and Partner Hold		Opponents Hold	First Lead	First Play	Second Lead	Second Play
	You	Partner					
SIMPLE FINESSES	K-x	x-x	Ace	Partner x	You K		
	Q-x-x	A-x-x	King	Partner A	You x	Partner x	You Q
	A-Q	x-x	King	Partner x	You Q		
	A-K-J	x-x-x	Queen	You K	Partner x	Partner x	You J
	A-x-x	Q-J-x-x	King	You A	Partner x	You x	Partner J
	A-K-x-x	J-x-x	Queen	You A	Partner x	You x	Partner J
	A-Q-x-x	J-x-x	King	Partner x	You Q		
DOUBLE FINESSES	A-Q-10[1]	x-x-x	K-J	Partner x	You 10	Partner x	You Q
	A-J-10[2]	x-x-x	K-Q	Partner x	You 10	Partner x	You J
	K-J-x[3]	x-x-x	A-Q	Partner x	You J	Partner x	You K
	Q-J-x	x-x-x	A-K	Partner x	You J	Partner x	You Q
	K-10-x	Q-x-x	A-J	You x	Partner Q	Partner x	You 10
	A-x-x	Q-10-x	K-J	You A	Partner x	You x	Partner 10 or Q[4]
	A-10-x	Q-x-x	K-J	Partner x	You 10	or as Type 2 above	
	A-J-x	x-x-x	K-Q	Partner x	You J		
	A-K-10	x-x-x	Q-J	Partner x	You 10[5]		
TRIPLE FINESSES	A-Q-9	x-x-x	K-J-10	Partner x	You 9[6]	Partner x	You Q
	A-J-9	x-x-x	K-Q-10	Partner x	You 9	Partner x	You J
	K-J-9-x	x-x-x	A-Q-10	Partner x	You 9	Partner x	You J
	K-10-x	x-x-x	A-Q-J	Partner x	You 10	Partner x	You K
	Q-10-x	x-x-x	A-K-J	Partner x	You 10	Partner x	You Q
	Q-x-x	J-9-x	A-K-10	Partner x	You Q	You x	Partner 9

NOTES REFERRING TO TABLE OF FINESSES

[1] With nine cards in combined hands, play Q on first round to lose one trick; also see Safety Plays (Chapter 44). [2] This procedure is correct with ten cards or less in combined hands. [3] If only one trick can be lost in suit, either King or Jack may be played on first round. [4] If combined hands hold the 9-spot as well, two finesses should be taken. See Safety Plays (Chapter 44). [5] Only when right-hand opponent is marked with Q-J. [6] If right-hand opponent plays Jack or ten on first round, cover with Queen.

Illustrating the Principle of Promotion

FINESSING

As each high-ranking card is played, every lower card of the suit moves up one step in rank. A three can be a "high card" if the only other card of the suit remaining is the deuce.

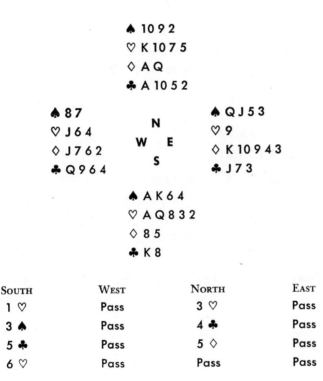

		♠ 10 9 2		
		♡ K 10 7 5		
		◇ A Q		
		♣ A 10 5 2		

♠ 8 7   ♠ Q J 5 3
♡ J 6 4   ♡ 9
◇ J 7 6 2   ◇ K 10 9 4 3
♣ Q 9 6 4   ♣ J 7 3

♠ A K 6 4
♡ A Q 8 3 2
◇ 8 5
♣ K 8

SOUTH	WEST	NORTH	EAST
1 ♡	Pass	3 ♡	Pass
3 ♠	Pass	4 ♣	Pass
5 ♣	Pass	5 ◇	Pass
6 ♡	Pass	Pass	Pass

THE PLAY: FINESSE AGAINST A FIVE

West opens the eight of spades, dummy plays the nine, East the Jack, and South the King. Three rounds of trump are taken ending in the dummy and the ten of spades is led. East covers with the Queen, South wins with the Ace, and West drops the seven. The six of spades is thus the master card of its suit after only two rounds have been played! Moreover, the fall of the seven assures declarer that East has the remaining spades, the five and the three. Dummy is therefore entered with the Ace of clubs and the deuce of spades is led. When East plays the three, South finesses the four. He then discards dummy's losing diamond on the six of spades, thereafter ruffing out his losing diamond for thirteen tricks.

Suit Establishment

PLAY FOR A DROP VS. FINESSE

Even when the odds favor a play for a drop, tactical considerations may make a finesse necessary.

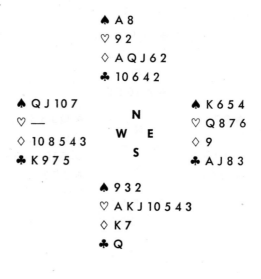

♠ A 8
♡ 9 2
◇ A Q J 6 2
♣ 10 6 4 2

♠ Q J 10 7
♡ —
◇ 10 8 5 4 3
♣ K 9 7 5

♠ K 6 5 4
♡ Q 8 7 6
◇ 9
♣ A J 8 3

♠ 9 3 2
♡ A K J 10 5 4 3
◇ K 7
♣ Q

NORTH	EAST	SOUTH	WEST
1 ◇	Pass	1 ♡	Pass
2 ◇	Pass	4 ♡	Pass
Pass	Pass		

THE PLAY: SAVING A STOPPER

West opens the Queen of spades, dummy winning with the Ace. In addition to the losing club and spade, declarer can afford to lose one trump trick, provided it be lost while dummy still has a trump to stop the spade suit. Despite the combined holding of nine trumps, therefore, declarer must not only abandon a play for a drop but must also forego the standard safety play of taking the first round of trumps with the Ace and finessing on the second round.

The ten of hearts is finessed at the second trick. When West shows out, dummy is entered with a diamond and a second trump finesse is taken. Trumps are then cleared and the King of diamonds is overtaken by dummy's Ace, so that the Queen of diamonds may be led to furnish a discard.

Suit Establishment

ECONOMY OF HONORS

Every effort should be made to avoid having high cards covered by opponents' higher cards, by leading toward even a seemingly solid sequence.

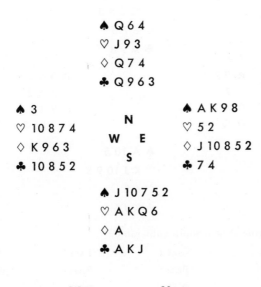

```
                    ♠ Q 6 4
                    ♡ J 9 3
                    ◇ Q 7 4
                    ♣ Q 9 6 3
      ♠ 3                          ♠ A K 9 8
      ♡ 10 8 7 4         N         ♡ 5 2
      ◇ K 9 6 3       W     E      ◇ J 10 8 5 2
      ♣ 10 8 5 2         S         ♣ 7 4
                    ♠ J 10 7 5 2
                    ♡ A K Q 6
                    ◇ A
                    ♣ A K J
```

SOUTH	WEST	NORTH	EAST
1 ♠	Pass	1 N T	Pass
3 ♡	Pass	3 ♠	Pass
4 ♠	Pass	Pass	Pass

THE PLAY: LEADING TO A SEQUENCE

West opens the three of diamonds, declarer winning with the Ace. South leads a small trump and dummy's Queen is taken by East's King. East returns a small diamond, and South, unwilling to shorten his trump suit, discards the Queen of hearts. West wins with the King of diamonds and returns a club. Dummy puts up the Queen in order to lead a trump. East plays the eight of trumps and South wins with the ten. When West shows out, the wisdom of South's plan becomes apparent, for only by leading again from the dummy can he avoid the loss of two more trump tricks. Dummy is entered once more with the Jack of hearts, which would not have been an entry had South not saved the heart six. Another trump lead limits East to his Ace.

Suit Establishment

THE BACKWARD FINESSE

Card-reading proves that a normal finesse will lose, but declarer, by a "backward finesse," wins the trick anyway.

```
                    ♠ K Q J
                    ♡ Q 6 4 3
                    ◇ 8 7 5
                    ♣ A 9 8
  ♠ 9 7 4 2                        ♠ 8 6 3
  ♡ 7              N               ♡ A 5 2
  ◇ A K Q J 10   W   E             ◇ 9 4 3
  ♣ Q 7 4          S               ♣ 10 5 3 2
                    ♠ A 10 5
                    ♡ K J 10 9 8
                    ◇ 6 2
                    ♣ K J 6
```

The bidding (North-South vulnerable):

WEST	NORTH	EAST	SOUTH
1 ◇	Pass	Pass	Double
Pass	2 ♡	Pass	4 ♡
Pass	Pass	Pass	

East opens the nine of diamonds, declarer losing two tricks and ruffing the third. A heart lead is taken by the Ace, East returning a spade. Two rounds each of trumps and spades are taken, after which declarer has to run the club suit without loss. East would not have passed the opening bid with the Queen of clubs as well as the Ace of hearts. The normal finesse, therefore, cannot win. The Queen will not drop, for East has followed to three rounds of each suit and cannot have more than four clubs. West must therefore have at least three clubs to the Queen.

South's Jack of clubs is led. West covers with the Queen and North's Ace wins. The nine of clubs is returned, both East and South ducking. The backward finesse thus enables declarer to make his contract.

CHAPTER FORTY

COMMUNICATION PLAYS

A card which wins a trick on a lead by partner or an opponent is called an *entry*. The winning of a trick opens the door, so to speak, into the hand. With the winning of a trick the player obtains the privilege of leading to the next trick—an all-important privilege when there are winning cards to be taken, or a tenace in partner's hand that demands that the lead be toward it.

The object of communication plays is to maintain entries in partnership hands and cut off entries in opponents' hands.

Entry-Making Plays

A card which may win a trick on a finesse is a probable entry. If the finesse wins, the means of entry is automatically included. The purpose of the finesse as an entry play, however, is entirely apart from the purpose of the finesse as a suit-establishment play.

In the diagram shown, North-South have three sure tricks in hearts, but if three entries to the North hand are vitally necessary (in order that another suit may be led three times by North) South must play the ♡ 3 and finesse for the Jack by playing North's ♡ 10. If West has the Jack, the extra entry has been found.

```
        ♡ A K 10
           N
      W         E
           S
        ♡ Q 4 3
```

Ruffing entries, likewise, while mechanically the same as any ruffing trick, have a different purpose.

♠ J 4 3
♡ 7
◇ A K Q 8 4
♣ 10 9 4 3

In this example, it is South's lead. North needs to have the lead, so that two diamonds may be cashed for discards of South's club losers, and so that a finesse may be taken against the spade King. To create an entry in the North hand, South takes the heart Ace, then leads the heart King. North ruffs, thereby obtaining entry.

```
        N
    W       E
        S
```

♠ A Q 10 6 5 2
♡ A K Q
◇ —
♣ A K 7 5

UNBLOCKING

A suit is *blocked* when one partner holds a card which would win over the opponents' cards, and with which he wishes to win the trick; but his partner, with nothing but higher cards in that suit, has no choice but to take the lead away from him. To avoid blocking a suit, a player should resort to an unblocking play; that is, he throws a higher card than necessary in order to avoid being left in the lead.

```
              ◇ 7 6 5 2
                 N
◇ J 10 8      W     E      ◇ 9 4
                 S
              ◇ A K Q 3
```

When the North hand should lead, the ◇ 7 is allowed to win the fourth round; when South wants to keep the lead, North unblocks by throwing the ◇ 7 6 5 on the Ace, King and Queen when they are led. Now North has the ◇ 2 and South the ◇ 3, and South can cash his long diamond and yet keep the lead.

Whenever it is possible, the entries needed to establish a suit should be found in the suit itself, so that other winning cards may be kept to act as stoppers.

```
1.      Q 3           2.      A 5           3.      J 9 6
         N                     N                     N
    W        E             W        E             W        E
         S                     S                     S
      A K 7 4 2             K Q J 4               A Q 10 2
```

In Figures 1 and 2, if one of South's honors is led first, North must win the second trick and South will need to reënter his hand with a side entry* to continue establishing the suit. In these and similar cases North's honor should be led first. In Figure 3, if North leads a low card and South finesses the Queen or ten, though the finesse may win, North must regain the lead to make another finesse. If North first leads the nine, South plays the deuce and North, if the finesse wins, remains in the lead. Now North can lead the Jack and South can throw the ten under it; and though East have the King three times guarded, North can lead to three successive finesses without losing the lead.

The trump suit offers many opportunities for unblocking.

♠ 6 5 3

N

♠ J 9   W   E   ♠ 10 2

S

♠ A K Q 8 7 4

With spades trumps, if South ruffs an opponent's lead he must be careful not to ruff with his lowest spade. It will cost him nothing to ruff with the seven or eight. Then two rounds of spades clear the suit, and North has an entry by taking South's ♠ 4 with the ♠ 6.

DUCKING

To postpone the winning of a certain or possible trick by purposely playing a low card of the suit led is called ducking. The mechanics of the ducking play ordinarily consist in conceding a trick (which must be lost sooner or later in any case) to the opponents at an early stage, conserving one or more winning cards of the suit with which to enter the hand later.

1. A K 8 6 4 3	2. A 7 6 5 4	3. A Q 6 5 4
N	N	N
W E	W E	W E
S	S	S
7 5 2	8 3 2	8 3

If in any example the suit is established in the usual way, by taking in the available honor-tricks and then giving up a trick or tricks to establish the long cards, North cannot later cash the long cards without a side entry. If a trick is ducked on the first round (in Figure 1) a subsequent lead by South

---

* A side entry: an entry in a suit which is not the player's strongest; used, commonly, to get the lead and immediately lead some other suit.

will enable North to run the entire suit, even if they were divided 3–1 in the opponents' hands. In Figure 2, against the expected 3–2 division, North must duck twice, taking the Ace on the third round to run the remainder of the suit.

Figure 3 is rather a desperate case, but if North has no side entry and the suit must nevertheless be brought in to make the contract, the first round is ducked entirely, and on the second round the Queen is finessed. If West had the King, and if each opponent had three cards of the suit, it will yield four tricks.

Timing of Entries

A card which wins a trick is not an "entry" in the full meaning of that term if the player winning the trick has no need to lead. The proper timing of entries consists in winning tricks when the lead will be of value.

1.	♡ 9 4 3	
	N	
♡ Q **W** **E** ♡ K 7 6 2		
	S	
	♡ A J 10 8 5	

2.	♡ A 6 5	
	N	
♡ 7 **W** **E** ♡ J 9 8 2		
	S	
	♡ K Q 10 4 3	

In Figure 1 the proper play is to take two finesses, as has been shown. South expects a 3–2 division of the East-West hearts, but should guard against a 4–1 division by first leading the ♡ 3 from dummy and finessing the ten. When the time comes to take the second finesse, the ♡ 9 is led from dummy, and wins the trick, leaving dummy in the lead for a final finesse through East's King.

In Figure 2, South expects to play for a drop, but will of course finesse if West shows out on the second round. The first trick should be taken by the Queen or King, then a heart led to the Ace; if West shows out, dummy will have the lead and a finesse may be taken forthwith. If the Ace were used to win the first trick, West's singleton would not be revealed until the second round, and a side entry to dummy would be needed for the finesse.

Entry-Killing Plays

The Hold-Up

The hold-up play consists in refusing to take a trick with a stopper in the opponents' suit, until one opponent has no card of that suit in his hand.

```
                    ♠ 10 6 2
                    ♡ A 9 5
                    ◇ 7 5
                    ♣ A J 7 4 3
     ♠ K 9 3              N              ♠ J 8 5 4
     ♡ 10 8 2          W     E           ♡ J 7 4 3
     ◇ K Q J 8 4          S              ◇ 10 9 2
     ♣ 6 5                                ♣ K 9
                    ♠ A Q 7
                    ♡ K Q 6
                    ◇ A 6 3
                    ♣ Q 10 8 2
```

South is declarer at three notrump, against which West opens diamonds. South allows West to win two tricks in diamonds, taking his Ace on the third round. Now he finesses for the King of clubs, losing to East; but East has no more diamonds and West has no immediate entry, so South makes his contract.

In this case the hold-up play was assured of success, because only East could get the lead. Had the Ace of clubs, instead of the King, been in the opponents' hands South could only have hoped that East would hold it.

A hold-up play may be made with two stoppers, to slow up the establishment of a suit.

In the example shown, West leads the ◇ Queen and South refuses to win in either hand. The next diamond lead he wins. Now, if he must relinquish the lead to East, no diamond can be led to knock out his second stopper. West, to establish and run the suit, must have two side entries.

```
                    ◇ K 6 2
                       N
     ◇ Q J 10 9 5   W     E   ◇ 8 4
                       S
                    ◇ A 7 3
```

The following are cases in which a hold-up play may be used, even at the apparent sacrifice of a trick:

```
        ♡ 7 5                        ♡ 7 5
           N                            N
♡ A 10 8 6 4 2  W   E  ♡ J 9   ♡ A 10 8 6 4 2  W   E  ♡ Q 9
           S                            S
        ♡ K Q 3                      ♡ K J 3
```

When West opens the ♡ 6 and East puts up his honor, South should hold up, playing the ♡ 3, *if it is East who must be given the lead;* he does not know that East has a doubleton heart, but his only chance to shut out West's suit is to exhaust East's supply of hearts while retaining a stopper. But if West is to get the lead in the course of South's suit-establishment plays, or if either opponent is equally likely to get the lead, South must win the first trick. While West is in the lead South's guarded honor will be a second heart stopper.

When Not to Hold Up

The cases in which a hold-up play should not be made are: when the hold-up will sacrifice a sure trick in the suit led; and when the suit opened, while dangerous to declarer, is not so dangerous as another suit to which the opponents may switch. For example:

FIGURE 1				FIGURE 2		
	♠ 8 7				♠ 10 7	
West	N	East		West	N	East
Leads	W E	Plays		Leads	W E	Plays
♠ 6	S	♠ Q		♠ 3	S	♠ Q
	♠ K 5 4				♠ A J 4	

In Figure 1, if South does not win the first trick East may immediately lead through the ♠ King to an Ace-Jack holding in West's hand, and South will never win a trick. In Figure 2, South by winning guarantees himself two spade tricks, the Jack and ten being equals against the King; if he ducks he may get but one spade trick.

The Bath Coup

The most effective of all hold-up plays is known as "The Bath Coup."

1.	♡ 7 4 2			**2.**	♡ A 6 5	
	N				N	
♡ K Q 10 9	W E	♡ 8 6 5		♡ K Q 10 9	W E	♡ 7 4 2
	S				S	
	♡ A J 3				♡ J 8 3	

Figure 1 is the classic Bath Coup. West leads the King and South lets him hold it. Now West cannot continue hearts without leading into a tenace. To establish the Queen, East must get the lead, using an entry for the purpose; and meanwhile South will have had time to find some means, if any exist, for ridding himself of the losing ♡ Jack. Figure 2 shows a situation in which a hold-up when the King is led serves the same purpose. If in either case the ♡ Ace were played on the first trick, East could lead hearts on gaining the lead and West would win two tricks.

Defenders' Entry Plays

UNBLOCKING

Most of the defenders' unblocking plays do not differ from the unblocking plays of declarer.

1.	♣ 6	2.	♣ Q 6
	N		N
♣ A K Q 4 3 W E ♣ 10 9 8 2		♣ A 9 7 5 4 W E ♣ J 10 3	
	S		S
	♣ J 7 5		♣ K 8 2

In Figure 1, on West's leads of the ♣ A K Q, East must throw the ♣ 10 9 8, allowing West to win the fourth trick and remain in the lead to take the fifth. In Figure 2, dummy's Queen is put up to win West's lead of the ♣ 5. East unblocks with the Jack, so that on the next round, if East leads through South's King, South cannot cover and block the suit.

The following standard play combines the functions of a ducking play and a deceptive play:

1.	♡ 6 4	2.	♡ 6
	N		N
♡ J 9 7 3 2 W E ♡ A Q 5		♡ J 9 7 3 2 W E ♡ A Q 5	
	S		S
	♡ K 10 8		♡ K 10 8 4

West opens the ♡ 3 against a notrump contract, and East, despite the old "third-hand high" rule, plays the Queen. In Figure 1, if West has no entry, the only hope of bringing in the suit is that South, fearing his King will never win a trick unless he grabs it, will fail to hold up. If East played the Ace and returned the Queen, South would hold up. In Figure 2, if East has no entry, the play of the Queen is the only means of establishing the heart suit. If South wins it, West later gets the lead and puts East in with the Ace to lead through South's 10 8. If South holds up, he can never win more than one heart trick.

This play is also proper when East's holding is A J x or A J 10.

TIMING OF ENTRIES

When, in defense against notrump, the defenders are trying to establish a long suit, the defender who holds the shorter portion of that suit should try to get the lead with his entry cards as soon as possible; saving his partner's entries for the time when the suit is established.

In the diagram at the right, the contract is notrump, the North hand being dummy. West has
opened the ♠ Queen and dummy's King has
won it. Now a small heart is led from dummy
and East should play the King! South may
have another spade stopper and a heart holding such as Q J 10. Let him knock out West's
♡ Ace first, and the spade suit will be lost. If
East gets the lead first and plays spades, the suit
will be established while West still has the heart
entry. Even if West does not hold the ♡ Ace,
there are few possible cases in which East's play of the King can cost a trick.

```
                          ♠ K 6
                          ♡ 8 4 3 2
                          ◇ Q J 9 7
                          ♣ K 10 6

                                        ♠ 9 7 3
                              N         ♡ K 9
                          W       E     ◇ 10 6 5 3
                              S         ♣ J 8 4 2
```

Ducking

The defenders' ducking plays are of the utmost importance.
Their purpose and their execution are identical with declarer's
ducking play.

```
1.              ◇ 8 7                2.        ◇ K 10 6
                  N                              N
     ◇ A 9 6 4 2  W    E  ◇ K 5 3      ◇ 9 2   W    E  ◇ A Q 8 7 4
                  S                              S
                ◇ Q J 10                       ◇ J 5 3
```

In Figure 1 West opens diamonds, East taking the King and returning the
five. West, lacking an entry, must allow South to hold this trick so that if
East has an entry he can continue diamonds when he gets in. In Figure 2,
East gets the lead, diamonds not yet having been led. He simply leads a low
diamond into dummy's tenace, and now if West leads diamonds later, East
can run the suit. If on such a holding West opens diamonds, East, if he lacks
an entry, ducks and saves his tenace.

BLOCKING PLAYS

Putting up an honor second-hand is essential to success in
all positions such as this one. When dummy holds any four
or more cards headed by A J 10, second-hand, holding an honor,
must put up the honor when the suit is led.

In this case, South leads the ◇ 7 and
West plays the King. If the Ace wins,
there is no entry to the long suit. If
North ducks East has the suit stopped
again and still there is no entry.

```
              ◇ A J 10 4 3
                  N
     ◇ K 6 5   W    E  ◇ Q 8 2
                  S
                ◇ 9 7
```

The fact that dummy seems to hold an inviolate entry card,
such as an Ace, must not cause the defending team to lose

hope. The following example is an illustration of the heroism of pasteboard armies, in which a King gallantly sacrifices himself to block a suit.

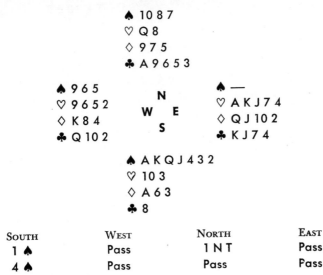

♠ 10 5 2
♡ 9 6 5
◊ K Q J 7 5
♣ A 5
(Dummy)

Opening
Lead
♡ 2

♠ J 9 7
♡ A 4 3
◊ A 6 4
♣ K 4 3 2

Against three notrump, East wins the first trick with the heart Ace and lays down the King of clubs as fast as he can get it out of his hand. It is an entry-killing play which cannot fail, because dummy has only two clubs. If he takes the Ace his entry is gone; if he ducks East continues clubs. Now East holds up the diamond Ace and the suit is lost to declarer unless he has four.

Hidden Trump Entry

Count the number of entries needed to each hand. Make any play necessary to establish the necessary entries, even when it involves the loss of a trick if unsuccessful.

♠ 10 8 7
♡ Q 8
◊ 9 7 5
♣ A 9 6 5 3

♠ 9 6 5
♡ 9 6 5 2
◊ K 8 4
♣ Q 10 2

♠ —
♡ A K J 7 4
◊ Q J 10 2
♣ K J 7 4

♠ A K Q J 4 3 2
♡ 10 3
◊ A 6 3
♣ 8

SOUTH	WEST	NORTH	EAST
1 ♠	Pass	1 N T	Pass
4 ♠	Pass	Pass	Pass

The Play: Unnecessary Finesse

West opens the deuce of hearts, East winning with the Jack and cashing the King. The Queen of diamonds is returned and South wins with the Ace. Declarer's only chance of avoiding the loss of two diamond tricks is to establish a club by ruffing. Four entries to dummy are required, of which only two or three are at first glance apparent. But an apparently unnecessary finesse provides him with the necessary extra entries.

Declarer leads a club to the Ace and ruffs a low club with the spade Jack. The spade deuce is led and when West plays low, dummy finesses the seven. Another club is ruffed with the spade Queen. The three of spades is led for a second trump finesse and another club is ruffed by the spade King. The last low spade is led to the ten and the thirteenth club is led, giving declarer the vital diamond discard.

Deschapelles Coup

The Deschapelles Coup is the sacrifice of an unsupported honor; when the opponents capture it, a card in partner's hand becomes an entry.

♠ 8 5 4
♡ A 7
◇ A Q J 6 4 3
♣ A 9

♠ Q J 10 9 6		♠ K 3
♡ Q 5 2	**N**	♡ K 6 4 3
◇ 7	**W E**	◇ K 10 5 2
♣ 8 6 5 2	**S**	♣ 10 4 3

♠ A 7 2
♡ J 10 9 8
◇ 9 8
♣ K Q J 7

North	East	South	West
1 ◇	Pass	2 ♣	Pass
2 ◇	Pass	2 N T	Pass
3 N T	Pass	Pass	Pass

The Play: Leading a King to Slaughter

West opens the Queen of spades, East covers with the King, and South ducks. East continues the spades, South ducks again, and West wins with the nine. The Jack of spades is led, South winning with the Ace. The diamond finesse is taken and loses to East's King. Knowing that West's only possible entry is in the heart suit, East leads the King of hearts. Regardless of declarer's subsequent play, he cannot run nine tricks without permitting East to win with the diamond ten; and when this is done, South leads a heart to West's Queen. West then runs his spades.

The Shutout Play

At trump contracts, dummy's suit may be killed by leading the suit until declarer has no more.

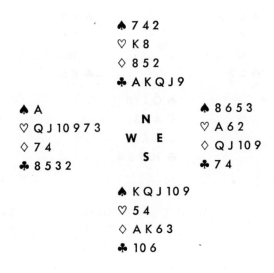

♠ 7 4 2
♡ K 8
◇ 8 5 2
♣ A K Q J 9

♠ A
♡ Q J 10 9 7 3
◇ 7 4
♣ 8 5 3 2

♠ 8 6 5 3
♡ A 6 2
◇ Q J 10 9
♣ 7 4

♠ K Q J 10 9
♡ 5 4
◇ A K 6 3
♣ 10 6

SOUTH	WEST	NORTH	EAST
1 ♠	2 ♡	3 ♣	Pass
3 ◇	Pass	3 ♠	Pass
4 ♠	Pass	Pass	Pass

West opens the Queen of hearts and after cashing two heart tricks the defenders lead a club. The Ace of spades is knocked out and West leads a second club. At this point declarer is helpless. He is unable to obtain discards on the clubs, since East will ruff; and he cannot draw trumps and subsequently reënter dummy.

The Bath Coup

The Bath Coup gains time by causing the opponents to waste an entry before they can establish their suit.

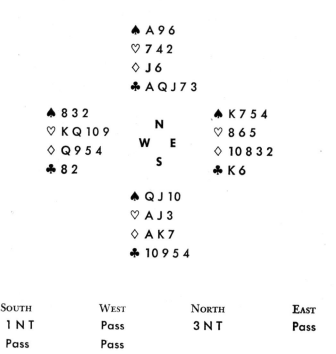

♠ A 9 6
♡ 7 4 2
◇ J 6
♣ A Q J 7 3

♠ 8 3 2
♡ K Q 10 9
◇ Q 9 5 4
♣ 8 2

♠ K 7 5 4
♡ 8 6 5
◇ 10 8 3 2
♣ K 6

♠ Q J 10
♡ A J 3
◇ A K 7
♣ 10 9 5 4

South	West	North	East
1 N T	Pass	3 N T	Pass
Pass	Pass		

West leads the King of hearts and South plays low.

To avoid leading into a tenace, West shifts to a spade. Dummy ducks and East wins with the King. A heart is returned and South plays low. West wins with the ♡ Queen and knocks out the Ace, but South can now take the club finesse without losing another heart trick.

If South had won the first heart, West could have run three tricks whenever East got the lead.

Ducking to Save an Entry

The effect of the ducking play is to postpone taking a high card until it is needed as an entry.

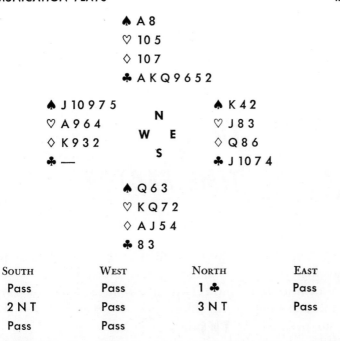

♠ A 8
♡ 10 5
◇ 10 7
♣ A K Q 9 6 5 2

♠ J 10 9 7 5
♡ A 9 6 4
◇ K 9 3 2
♣ —

♠ K 4 2
♡ J 8 3
◇ Q 8 6
♣ J 10 7 4

♠ Q 6 3
♡ K Q 7 2
◇ A J 5 4
♣ 8 3

SOUTH	WEST	NORTH	EAST
Pass	Pass	1 ♣	Pass
2 N T	Pass	3 N T	Pass
Pass	Pass		

West opens the Jack of spades, dummy playing the eight and East winning with the King. A spade is returned to dummy's Ace. Dummy must immediately lead a low club. Regardless of subsequent defense, declarer wins at least six club tricks, two spades and the Ace of diamonds.

CHAPTER FORTY-ONE

THE

TIME FACTOR

The Time Factor may be defined as the general principle in play that the establishment and winning of tricks is subject to a definite time limit. This time limit is determined by the number of stoppers held by one side in relation to the number of stoppers held by the other.

When a partnership has no stopper, it cannot win a trick, however many high cards and long cards it may have been able to develop previously in the play of the hand. The problems of play are therefore primarily the problems of timing, of holding on as long as necessary to stoppers which will prevent the opponents from winning the rest of the tricks.

A stopper may be a high card or a trump. A trump is a super-stopper; it will interrupt the run of any suit.

In the example shown spades are trumps, and South is declarer. West opens the King of hearts, then leads the Jack of spades. A rapid count of his resources shows South that by establishing the diamond suit he can win four diamond tricks, five spade tricks (with the expected 3–2 division) and two club tricks. He has no need to create ruffers by ruffing his losing hearts. Yet he cannot draw trumps; for dummy's small spades are his only means of stopping the heart suit. While he does not wish to ruff hearts in order to win tricks, he must be prepared to ruff hearts to stop the suit. South wins the spade lead in dummy with the King, and immediately proceeds to establish his diamond suit by straight leads. Once the diamond Ace (the opponents' last stopper) is gone, South can draw trumps and run the remaining tricks.

♠ K 6 4
♡ 4
◊ Q 10 9 7 5
♣ A K 9 6

```
       N
   W       E
       S
```

♠ A Q 5 3 2
♡ Q 6 5 3
◊ K J
♣ 10 8

In the example shown, East takes the Ace of diamonds, South unblocking with the King. East now leads a spade and South wins. If West follows, the last trump is drawn and the losing hearts are discarded on the established diamonds. If West fails to follow on the second trump lead, the trump suit must once again be abandoned in favor of diamond leads. And if East ruffs the third round of that suit, South overruffs and continues his policy of not drawing trumps by entering dummy with a club to continue the diamonds.

The play of most hands involves the establishment of two or more suits. In the course of establishing these suits the lead must be given up to opponents' stoppers.

Declarer's choice among various suit-establishment plays is a matter of discriminating between cases in which his establishable cards are valuable principally as tricks, and the cases in which they are more valuable as stoppers. Declarer should avoid any suit in which he will develop more tricks for his opponents than for himself.

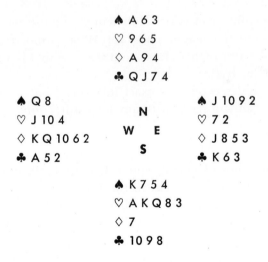

♠ A 6 3
♡ 9 6 5
◇ A 9 4
♣ Q J 7 4

♠ Q 8
♡ J 10 4
◇ K Q 10 6 2
♣ A 5 2

♠ J 10 9 2
♡ 7 2
◇ J 8 5 3
♣ K 6 3

♠ K 7 5 4
♡ A K Q 8 3
◇ 7
♣ 10 9 8

South is declarer at four hearts, against which West opens the ◇ King. The Ace wins and three rounds of hearts clear the suit.

It is obvious that South could continue to win tricks without interruption for several plays. He could cash the Ace and King of spades. He could lead diamonds from dummy and ruff, or he could simply lead out his long hearts. But all these cards are stoppers. They must be kept to hold the opponents at bay while South establishes the club suit. By leading clubs South will force out the Ace and King, and when East and West, in the lead with these cards, play back spades or diamonds South has winning cards with which to stop them from winning tricks. One of South's losing spades can then be discarded on the last club.

Time Valuation of a Long Suit

Timing in suit establishment consists of a count of the tricks it is necessary to lose to opponents because they hold stoppers in the suit, and the count of the entries required to regain the lead each time.

The club suit held by West in the following diagram will not win a trick:

```
        ♠ 8 4 2                    ♠ A 7 5 3
        ♡ 10 5          N          ♡ A 8 4 3
        ◇ 9 3      W         E     ◇ 10 7 6 5
        ♣ K Q J 10 9 8    S        ♣ 6
```

West's opening lead is the club King, establishing the club suit. But there the matter ends, for West cannot regain the lead to make use of his clubs: and East, with his two Aces, has no club to lead.

In order to determine the exact number of entries required to establish and win tricks with any long suit, count as follows:

The Rule of X-Plus-1

1. The number of entries you will need is the number of estimated losing tricks in the suit (X), plus 1.
2. The opening lead (or the right to play first) is counted as one of the required entries, and therefore the formula is applicable to all positions from first- to fourth-hand.

In cases where partner has one or more cards of the long suit to lead, his entries are interchangeable with the entries in the leader's own hand. When partner has no card of the long suit, or when his cards can be removed by a hold-up play, the entries must be in the leader's hand.

An entry, in this case, must usually also be a stopper, or partner must have a stopper with which to get the lead and the leader an entry with which his partner can put him in.

♠ 9 5 3
♡ 8 2
◇ K 7 4
♣ A J 10 9 6

♠ K 10 6   **N**   ♠ Q 7 2
♡ A 10 6 5   **W   E**   ♡ K 9 3
◇ Q 9 2   **S**   ◇ J 10 3
♣ Q 8 5   ♣ 7 4 3 2

♠ A J 8 4
♡ Q J 7 4
◇ A 8 6 5
♣ K

The contract is notrump, with South the declarer. West opens the ♡ 5, East winning with the King; East then leads the ♡ 9, and South covers with the Jack, West ducking. South, in the lead with the ♡ Jack, applies time valuation to his strongest suit, clubs.

Using the Rule of Five Steps, South determines that the ♣ Queen will probably not fall on leads of the King and Ace. One trick must therefore be lost to establish the club suit. Applying the Rule of X-Plus-1:

X equals 1.

1 plus 1 equal 2 entries required to establish and cash the club suit.

To create a second entry to dummy, South leads the club King and overtakes with the club Ace. Now the suit is established by leading the Jack and letting West win with the Queen. Finally, South regains the lead with a *stopper* in whatever suit West chooses to lead, and puts North in with his *entry*, the diamond King, to utilize the rest of the club suit.

Time Valuation of a Hand

Before deciding which suit or suits to establish, declarer counts the number of times he must lose the lead to an opposing stopper. Then he counts the winners they can establish and win with this number of entries.

Having completed his time valuation, declarer should make his establishment plays in the suit or suits which will not allow the defenders to find the setting tricks.

```
                          ♠ K J 3
                          ♡ 10 5
                          ◇ A 9 6 4
                          ♣ K 10 5 2
          ♠ 7                  N           ♠ 9 8 6 2
          ♡ A K J 8 6 4                    ♡ Q 9 7 3
          ◇ Q 10 2        W       E        ◇ J 8 5
          ♣ A 7 6             S            ♣ 9 4
                          ♠ A Q 10 5 4
                          ♡ 2
                          ◇ K 7 3
                          ♣ Q J 8 3
```

    South is declarer at four spades; West wins the first trick with the heart
King and then leads the heart Ace. South, who could stop the suit by ruffing,
sees that he must later lose a trick to establish clubs. After losing that trick,
he must be careful still to have a heart stopper. His only available heart
stoppers are his trumps. If he can draw the opponents' trumps in three
rounds, he will have that stopper; if it requires four rounds, he must either
fail to draw trumps, leaving an opponent the means of stopping the club
suit; or use up his own last trump, giving up his means of stopping the
heart suit.

    To increase his stopping power, South saves all five of his trumps, discard-
ing a diamond on the second round of hearts. Now dummy's trump suit
serves to stop hearts, preventing a continuation of that suit. Either the defenders must set up South's clubs for him, or must give him the lead in diamonds, where he is adequately protected. He can draw trumps, establish
clubs, and still have a trump to stop the hearts.

    At notrump contracts time valuation is similar:

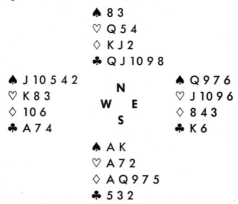

```
                          ♠ 8 3
                          ♡ Q 5 4
                          ◇ K J 2
                          ♣ Q J 10 9 8
          ♠ J 10 5 4 2        N           ♠ Q 9 7 6
          ♡ K 8 3                          ♡ J 10 9 6
          ◇ 10 6          W       E        ◇ 8 4 3
          ♣ A 7 4             S            ♣ K 6
                          ♠ A K
                          ♡ A 7 2
                          ◇ A Q 9 7 5
                          ♣ 5 3 2
```

    South is declarer at three notrump. West opens a spade, South winning
with the King. Being able to count eight winners, South must establish one

more. In clubs he can establish it by straight leads, and entries are plentiful to dummy, but time valuation shows this to be a losing play. The opponents must be given two entries before the clubs can be established; with these entries they can first knock out South's last spade stopper, and then run the established spade suit. In hearts a trick may be found by an indirect finesse. The success of this finesse is doubtful, but the extra trick, if the heart suit will produce it, can be made with the loss of only one entry. To balance this losing trick, South has a remaining spade stopper. Time valuation having shown him the proper point of attack, he leads a low heart toward the Queen.

He does not first lay down the heart Ace, though this play was recommended in Chapter 41 as protection against loss to an unguarded King. In this case, the heart Ace is South's only sure heart stopper, and he must keep it until forced to use it, or until by playing it he will win a trick which makes his contract.

Time Valuation of Ruffers

The ruffer is a combined unit, consisting of two parts—the losing card to be ruffed and the worthless trump. To determine the number of ruffers you can win, count the number of worthless trumps, then count the number of losing cards that can be ruffed. The smaller number is the number of ruffers.

The hand which must lead the losing cards needs exactly as many entries as the number of available ruffers. The entries must be available *after* the void is created.

The opponents' best defense against a ruffing game is to lead trumps every time they get the lead. Therefore, assume that with every entry they have they will lead a trump. Count the number of losing leads necessary to establish the void *and* to develop the necessary entries. Deduct this number from the number of available trumps before counting the expected ruffers.

One opponent, however, may not have a trump to lead when he gets the lead; and, in certain circumstances, one or both may be unable to lead a trump without leading into a tenace.

♠ K 10 6

N

♠ Q 5 4   W   E   ♠ J 7

S

♠ A 9 8 3 2

If either opponent leads spades he sacrifices the combined stopper.

CHAPTER FORTY-TWO

DECLARER'S PLANNING AND PLAY

The paramount objective of declarer's play is to make the tricks required by the contract, be it a part-score, a game, or a slam. No contract should be given up as hopelessly lost unless all possibilities—including end-plays and psychic plays*—have been eliminated.

When it is evident that the contract cannot be made, the object of play will be to minimize the possible loss. Here the technique of play will be the same, except that declarer will have no definite number of tricks to strive for, but will play to win as many tricks as he can *with safety*.

The safety factor demands that certain contracts be abandoned because, though there be some outside chance of its being made, the loss if that chance fails will be too great to risk. In the typical situation declarer has three choices:

To make his contract if a gamble is successful;

To be set several tricks if the gamble fails;

To be set one trick by playing safe.

In making his choice declarer must be guided by the chances for and against the success of the gambling play, and the points he can gain or lose, always keeping in mind the invisible score— the points which do not show immediately on the score sheet.

---

* A psychic play is one whose object is to mislead the opponents and cause one or both of them to make a mistake.

Let us assume, for instance, that declarer is playing a four-spade contract, not vulnerable, but doubled. In dummy he has A-Q of a plain suit, and does not know the whereabouts of the King. The opponents have an established suit in which declarer has no stopper, not even a trump. If declarer finesses and the finesse wins, he makes his contract. If the finesse loses, the long suit will be run against him and he will be down four tricks.

If he refuses the finesse he is surely set one—100.

If he finesses and wins he makes 240 for tricks; 300 for the invisible value of the game; 50 points bonus; and he *saves* 100 that he would have lost. Total, 690.

If he finesses and loses he loses 700.

Here his possible gain is 690, his possible loss 700, on an exactly even bet. Having more to lose than to gain, he should play safe, taking the one-trick set. But if the most he could be set, even if the finesse lost, were three tricks, 500 points, he should gamble the extra loss against the chance of making his contract, and take the finesse.

PLAYING FOR OVERTRICKS

To make extra tricks should be the object of play only when the chance of losing the contract is very remote. I purposely avoid the usual injunction *"Never* risk the contract for over-tricks." An overtrick is worth, on the average, at least 25 points. Only when the odds are overwhelmingly in favor of a certain line of play may the game be risked for an overtrick.

Advance Planning

The indispensable factor in the correct play of the hand is planning.

The first step is to take stock of the available forces by counting the number of winners and losers in the combined hands. The united hands will, as a rule, contain a number of sure winners, a number of unavoidable losers, and a number of possible losers, some of which can be turned into winners by skillful play.

As a general rule, the losers should be counted at trump

bids and the winners at notrump bids, but there are some important exceptions. The winners should be counted at trump bids:

1. With pure cross-ruffs, when the trumps in the two hands are to be made separately by ruffing.
2. With powerful hands, containing a solid or nearly solid trump suit and a solid or nearly solid side suit.
3. With very weak hands, when the total resources consist of a few Aces and Kings, and one or two possible ruffs. Here, to count nine losers instead of four or five winners would be very inefficient.

At notrump contracts the winners are always counted, but especially at slam contracts the declarer at notrump should check his count by counting the losers.

Declarer should not lose sight of the fact that a possible winner may not get a chance to win a trick.

♠ 10 8 7 6
♡ 5
◇ K Q 7
♣ K Q J 9 8

Here is shown a hand in which South can establish four spade tricks, two diamond tricks and four club tricks by straight leads. He can ruff two or three hearts in dummy. The total count of winners is 13 or 14. Yet three tricks must be lost to Aces, so declarer can win at most 10 tricks. Here the value of checking the losers against the winners, both by an actual count of opposing stoppers and by time valuation, is apparent.

```
        N
      W   E
        S
```

♠ K Q J 9 5
♡ A 4 3 2
◇ J 10
♣ 10 7

The Culbertson Rule of Notrump Planning is divided into three reviews. Each review is subdivided into steps which portray the subconscious thought process of a nearly perfect player.

THE FIRST REVIEW

The first review is an estimate of the resources of the hand—the tricks that can be won with high cards and that can be developed from high or low cards by suit-establishment plays.

STEP 1. Study the card led—it probably has some conventional meaning (Chapter 46) which will guide you in estimating the chances for success of any suit-establishment play in that suit.

STEP 2. Starting with the suit led, count the immediate winners (cards which will win tricks without any preliminary suit-establishment plays, and without giving up the lead) in all four suits. In each suit, count on the basis of the combined length and strength of your and dummy's hands. Then deduct the number of immediate winners from the total number of tricks you need to make the contract, and you will know how many additional winners you must establish.

STEP 3. Study all four suits to determine how many additional winners may be established in each. In the first count, consider only honor-winners establishable by straight leads, and long cards which can be made if the opponents' cards are divided in the most probable (not necessarily the most favorable) way. *Then* consider a finesse, or a play for a drop, or long-suit establishment, which may succeed if the position or division of the outstanding cards is favorable.

THE SECOND REVIEW

The second review is a revaluation of the establishable winners by time valuation and a count of entries.

STEP 4. Take the suit in which you can establish the greatest number of winners. How many times must you lose the lead to establish this suit? How many winners can the opponents establish and win with this number of leads? In counting the opponents' potential winners, include any Aces or other immediate winners which *they* hold, and which they can take whenever they are ready and have the lead.

If time valuation shows that the best suit you have cannot be established without losing the lead too many times, consider another suit from the standpoint of time valuation. Another suit may produce fewer eventual winners, but may be establishable in *less time*.

STEP 5. Usually one opponent is more "dangerous" than the other—he may hold established or establishable trick-winners, or he may be in position to lead through a tenace. Look for an entry-killing play to keep that opponent out of the lead as much as possible.

STEP 6. Count the entries you need for each projected suit-establishment play. Then look for possible entries, and if they are not readily available plan entry-making or entry-saving plays.

But do not give up a valuable stopper, by using it as an entry, unless it is absolutely necessary.

THE THIRD REVIEW

The object of the third review is to plumb the depths of the hand to safeguard a sure contract or to find hidden means of making a doubtful one.

STEP 7. Safety plays. With the contract apparently assured, look for ways to protect the counted winners against abnormally bad breaks.

STEP 8. End-plays. Especially when the contract is doubtful, but sometimes only to make an overtrick, look for an end-play situation and try to play the hand so as to retain the chance of making it.

STEP 9. Psychological plays. When all other resources fail, look for a sheer bluff play or stratagem which may lead the defenders to make a mistake and give you one or more tricks.

Do not play from dummy to the first trick until you have completed the three reviews.

ILLUSTRATING THE THREE REVIEWS

No matter how cut-and-dried even the play to the first trick may seem, it is worth-while to pause and plan the future play of the hand. When declarer cannot hope to win the first trick, his three reviews of the hand may lead him to try a false-card which will work. At the right is shown a hand which South plays at three no-trump. West's opening lead is the ◊ 6. South, before playing to the first trick, applies the steps of planning. The results are as follows:

♠ J 9 5
♡ J 5 2
◊ Q 3
♣ A J 6 4 3

West   N
Leads W   E
◊ 6   S

THE FIRST REVIEW

STEP 1. The card led is probably from a long suit of five or six cards. Possibly it has only four cards.

STEP 2. South can immediately win one trick in diamonds, two in clubs, one in spades and one in hearts. He needs nine for his contract. 9 — 5 leaves 4 tricks he must find.

♠ A 10 3
♡ A Q 10 4
◊ K 8 4
♣ K 10 2

STEP 3. Assuming a 3–2 division but a losing finesse for the Queen, the club suit will produce two additional winners; the heart suit at least two, even if the finesse fails; the spade suit one with a double finesse. If the heart finesse wins, another finesse may be taken against the King, adding at least two tricks without losing the lead. If the club finesse wins and the suit breaks, the suit will develop five winners, three more than the counted immediate winners in that suit. Finally, if West has the Ace of diamonds, dummy's Queen will win the first trick, leaving South the guarded King to stop the suit provided East never gets the lead.

THE SECOND REVIEW

South now knows that he must establish four winners by various sorts of suit-establishment plays; that the club suit will produce a maximum of three, more than any other suit is likely to produce. He now applies time valuation.

STEP 4. In establishing the club suit, no more than one trick need be lost. If South succeeds in stopping the diamond suit and still retaining a diamond stopper, the opponents cannot do more than take their diamond Ace when they get the lead in clubs; but if South proves to have only one diamond stopper, his only hope is to shut out the player holding the long diamond suit.

At most, three extra tricks can be found in clubs. South will need another trick. If he seeks it in hearts, and the finesse works, the lead need not be lost; if the finesse fails, the opponents will get the lead. However, the spade finesse cannot fail to give up the lead, and can produce at most one additional trick; therefore South must face the need for taking the heart finesse.

STEP 5. If South can surely keep East out of the lead, he should put up the Queen of diamonds on the first trick, for if it holds the trick South's King will be a sure second stopper. But if East must be given the lead, South should play low from both dummy and his own hand until forced to win a diamond trick; by using the hold-up play he may exhaust East's supply.

Checking up on the club suit, South finds that he can make an entry-killing play against either opponent at will. But in hearts, if he loses a trick, it can be only to West.

South therefore determines to play dummy's diamond Queen hoping that to establish their suit the defenders must at least give him a second diamond trick.

STEP 6. If South is to finesse a club into West's hand, he must lead from the dummy, which requires an entry. The diamond Queen, assuming it wins the first trick, provides that entry.

A lost finesse limits the club suit to four winners, meaning that two finesses will be needed in hearts. Where are the other two entries? The club Ace is one of them. The other is supplied by leading the ♡ Jack for the first finesse.

If the diamond Queen does not win the first trick (if East has the Ace and plays it) then South's plan will be a hold-up play with the King of diamonds, and a club finesse through West.

South has now sketched out his plan of play on an *if* basis, his plan depending upon whether or not the diamond Queen wins the first trick.

STEP 7. There is no available safety play.

STEP 8. End-plays (covered in Chapter 43) may possibly be developed, but it is too soon to judge.

STEP 9. No specific plan for deceiving the opponents need be formed on this hand.

South now plays the Queen of diamonds from the dummy, the entire plan detailed above having consumed about ten seconds. The complete deal:

```
                    ♠ J 9 5
                    ♡ J 5 2
                    ◇ Q 3
                    ♣ A J 6 4 3
    ♠ Q 7 4              N          ♠ K 8 6 2
    ♡ 7 3                           ♡ K 9 8 6
    ◇ A 10 7 6 5 2    W     E       ◇ J 9
    ♣ 9 8                S          ♣ Q 7 5
                    ♠ A 10 3
                    ♡ A Q 10 4
                    ◇ K 8 4
                    ♣ K 10 2
```

The ◇ 6 is opened, dummy plays the Queen, East unblocks with the Jack and South plays the four. The ♣ 3 is led from dummy, East playing the five, South the ten and West the eight. After the clubs are run, the Jack of hearts is led and South makes three heart tricks, easily sufficient for his contract.

•

Declarer's Play at Notrump

The whole body of notrump play is built around the long suit or suits in the combined hands. From the standpoint of declarer's play, a long suit is not a four-card length in his own hand but a length of at least seven cards in the combined hands. A 5–1 or 6–0 division may, it is true, develop long cards, but unless the long suit is plentifully equipped with tops the time factor usually prevents the suit's establishment. With a suit divided 4–2 or 3–3 in the partnership hands no long card is possible and to lead the suit will establish long cards for the opponents instead of for declarer. With suits divided 4–3, 5–2, 5–3 (or better) in the hands of declarer and dummy the problem of play is usually a matter of choosing among several such suits.

Choice of Suits

When two long suits are available, and only one is needed to make the contract, the choice is determined, as in most bridge problems, by the time factor. As a rule it will be found preferable to establish the suit in which the opponents can surely win tricks with their stoppers, whether you lead the suit yourself or not. The other suit, which contains a greater number of immediate winners, can be attempted later if the plans for establishing the first suit went wrong; and at this point the suit with more tops will provide its own entries and stoppers.

A second and often a more important consideration is to keep a close check on the opponents' entries. When one opponent is more dangerous than the other, the suit should first be attacked which will keep the dangerous adversary out of the lead.

When the two suits are not of equal length, expediency often determines the choice—declarer first attacks the suit in which he can establish more winners.

West opens a spade against three notrump, and declarer wins the trick by putting up dummy's Queen. His count of winners shows him that he needs two additional winners; his time valuation shows him that he can afford to give up the lead only once. The only chance of developing two winners with one loss of tempo is to play for a 3–3 diamond break. The odds favor a 3–2 club break and are against the diamond break, but the danger that the defenders can establish and cash the setting tricks with two entries is too great. South therefore plays the King, Ace and a small diamond.	♠ Q 6
	 ♡ 7 2
	 ◇ A 8 7 5 4
	 ♣ K 7 6 3
	       N
	 W E
	       S
	 ♠ A 8 5
	 ♡ A J 10 5
	 ◇ K 3
	 ♣ A 9 5 2

When time does not press and either of two suits will produce the needed winners, choose the one which is more likely to break favorably. The table of probabilities on page 453 is an invaluable guide in such choices.

When the contract depends upon trying to establish a long card or finessing for a missing honor in another suit:

1. If the finesse, if successful, does not involve the loss of a trick (that is, with A-Q or another tenace which has been promoted to equivalent rank) *try for the long card first*. If you cannot establish the long card you can always try the finesse later.

2. If the finesse involves the loss of the lead whether successful or not (that is, with K J 10 and x x x, etc.) follow the line of play which has mathematically a better chance of success. The odds on a single finesse are 50–50. They favor a double finesse (A J 10 and x x x) by 3 to 1. The odds are *against* the establishment of a long card from a combined length of seven cards, but favor the establishment of a suit whose combined length is eight cards or more. The bidding and previous play may give information which alters these percentages up or down.

The Waiting Game

Sometimes—rarely, but it happens—declarer has no establishable long suit. In such cases, when his strength in the other suits lies in broken strength and no solid sequences, he must play the waiting game.

· The waiting game consists simply in throwing the opponents into the lead as often as possible and letting them lead to one of the tenaces.

Trump Planning

With the play of trump bids the declarer ascends into a higher and far more complex technique. The trump suit introduces into the play a third kind of trick—the ruffer—and a second kind of stopper and entry, the trump suit.

The Rule of Trump Planning, like the notrump rule, is divided into three reviews.

The First Review

STEP 1. Starting with the suit led, count the number of tricks you must lose immediately—tricks the opponents can win without knocking out one of your stoppers.

STEP 2. Count the possible losers in combined hands—losing cards in suits which you have stopped temporarily, or immediate losers which the opponents cannot take until they get the lead. Add your sure and possible losers, and compare the total with the number of tricks you can afford to lose.

STEP 3. Look for a suit in your hand or dummy in which long cards or high cards can be established; if the other hand is short in this suit, it can discard one or more losers.

You will not gain by discarding a loser from dummy on a *long card* unless dummy has more trumps than are needed to draw the opponents' trumps.

But you can gain by discarding one or more losers from dummy on established high cards in your hand, if it can be done while dummy still has trumps which can be turned into ruffers.

STEP 4. Look for a short suit in dummy, and for worthless trumps; apply time valuation (page 477) and decide whether or not you can make ruffers.

STEP 5. Consider a finesse or a play for a drop to establish a card *which you cannot discard or ruff.*

THE SECOND REVIEW

The first review has allowed you to take stock of your resources. The second review considers these resources from the standpoints of time, entries and probable holdings of opponents.

STEP 6. Apply time valuation to every proposed plan of play. Count the number of times the opponents can get the lead and the tricks they can win when they have the lead.

If you plan to discard losers on high cards, remember that the high cards must be established and the discards taken before the opponents can establish and win their own tricks. If the opponents establish their tricks on the opening lead, you must be able to take your discards without losing the lead. If you still have one stopper in the opponents' suit, you must be able to establish your high cards for discards with only one loss of the lead.

If you plan to discard losers on established long cards carefully time-value the trump suit. You must have enough trumps to stop the opponents while you are establishing your long cards, and you must generally be able to draw trumps before using the long suit.

If you plan to make use of ruffers, remember that the opponents will probably lead trumps every time they have the lead. Then proceed to Step 7.

STEP 7. Almost every suit-establishment play requires that the lead come from a certain hand. To discard a loser on an established card in the other hand, you must put the lead in the other hand. To lead losing cards and ruff them, you must have entries to the hand which holds the losing cards. Count the entries required for every proposed line of play, and look for plays to create more entries.

Above all things, look ahead in your suit establishment. Do not go through the waste effort of establishing a long suit for later use unless you carefully save an entry until such time as the long suit is established.

THE THIRD REVIEW

STEP 8. With the contract assured, look for a safety play to protect against bad breaks.

STEP 9. Especially if there is doubt as to making the contract, look for an end-play.

STEP 10. When all other resources fail, look for some means of bluffing the opponents into making a mistake.

Then play from dummy to the first trick.

ILLUSTRATING THE THREE REVIEWS

The hands shown are to be played by South at a contract of four spades. West's opening lead is the Queen of diamonds. After a brief glance at the lead, South plans his play:

♠ Q 6 5 2
♡ K J 8 5
◇ 7 5 3
♣ K 3

THE FIRST REVIEW

STEP 1. There is an immediate loser in diamonds, if the opponents take their Ace, and an immediate club loser whenever they wish to take the Ace.

STEP 2. A second loser is evident in diamonds, but need not be lost until the opponents have knocked out the King. A spade trick must probably be lost, for South cannot clear the suit by finessing unless East has a doubleton King. If the club Ace kills dummy's King, the Queen will win the second round, but South will have remaining two clubs which will be losers unless they can be ruffed, or unless the Jack drops or is finessable. There is no loser in hearts.

N
W   E
S

♠ A J 8 3
♡ A Q
◇ K 8 2
♣ Q 10 7 5

STEP 3. There is no long suit in the combined hands, except the trump suit. The heart suit, however, can win four tricks with high cards. Since South has only two hearts, there is a possibility of discarding two losers.

STEP 4. South can use two of dummy's small trumps to ruff his losing clubs, and his own trump suit will be long enough, in normal circumstances, to draw trumps and to retain one long trump to act as a stopper. However (applying the Rule of Five Steps), one opponent has only three clubs, and may be able to overruff the dummy on the fourth round.

STEP 5. The spade finesse may be attempted, but it is unlikely to gain a trick, since the opponents will probably exact one spade trick regardless of who holds the King.

If South decides that he probably cannot ruff out both clubs, he can try a finesse against the Jack of clubs; if the club King wins the first trick in that suit, he can take a free finesse, without risking the loss of an extra trick.

THE SECOND REVIEW

Since nothing can be done about the first diamond trick, a small diamond is played from dummy. East takes the Ace and returns the ◊ 9. South wins with the King.

STEP 6. The opponents now have one trick, and hold an established diamond which South cannot stop—if they get the lead. Having counted that he must lose tricks in spades and clubs, South cannot afford to lose a second diamond trick. Therefore, he cannot give up the lead, to establish his club ruffs, or risk giving up the lead by finessing in spades, until he has discarded his diamond loser. He must at once lead three rounds of hearts and throw off the diamond. *But—*

STEP 7. If South cashes his ♡ A Q, how will he get to dummy? No entry can be established without losing the lead, whereupon the opponents will take a diamond trick. Therefore, South must create a quick entry to dummy by taking the heart Ace and overtaking the Queen with dummy's King. This he does. Now he leads the Jack and gets rid of his diamond.

Now the problem of entries remains. South would like to lead a club from his hand toward the King, but dummy is in the lead. South cannot get the lead except by ruffing a diamond, which would sacrifice a trump valuable as a stopper, or by leading a trump.

If South leads a trump and takes the Ace, it is a sure entry; but then, when the opponents get in with the club Ace they may lead the King and a small trump, leaving dummy with only one trump to ruff clubs.

Another entry consideration is the avoidance principle. South does not want East to lead, for East may have the last outstanding heart. On a heart lead South would ruff, but West might overruff.

The best chance of shutting East out, attempting to create an entry, and taking the best chance of avoiding a spade loser is to lead a small spade from dummy and finesse. If the finesse wins, South will clear the club suit and ruff two clubs, resigning himself to the loss of one, but only one, spade trick. If the spade finesse loses, and West returns a trump to shut off club ruffs, South can win the trick and dummy will still have two trumps to ruff clubs, with the option of the club finesse. If West leads a diamond, South's small trump stops the suit.

THE THIRD REVIEW

STEP 8. The contract cannot be made without good breaks, so no safety play is available.

STEP 9. No end-play is likely to develop, but South's plan of play cannot be altered on a bare hope in any case.

STEP 10. There seems to be no available opportunity to false-card or make any other deceptive play.

The complete deal, and South's play of it, follow:

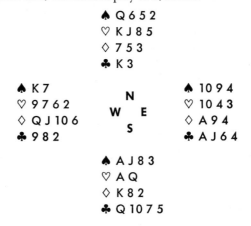

♠ Q 6 5 2
♥ K J 8 5
♦ 7 5 3
♣ K 3

♠ K 7   ♠ 10 9 4
♥ 9 7 6 2   ♥ 10 4 3
♦ Q J 10 6   ♦ A 9 4
♣ 9 8 2   ♣ A J 6 4

♠ A J 8 3
♥ A Q
♦ K 8 2
♣ Q 10 7 5

West opened the Queen of diamonds. East took the Ace and returned the nine, South winning. South led the Ace of hearts, then the Queen. Dummy took the heart King and led the Jack, South discarding a diamond.

Dummy led the ♠ 2, East played the four and South the Jack. West won with the ♠ King and returned the ♠ 7. South won with the Ace and led a club, the ♣ King falling to East's Ace. East returned the ten of spades, dummy's Queen winning.

Dummy led the club three, and East played the four. The Rule of Five Steps convincing him that the Jack was unlikely to fall on the next round, South finessed the club ten. The ♣ Queen and the remaining spades won the last tricks.

TRUMP MANAGEMENT

A troublesome problem for all players is "When shall I lead trumps? When shall I postpone leading trumps?"

During the play, a trump in either hand may be "busy"—it may be needed, now or later, as a stopper, entry, guard or ruffer.

Other trump cards will be idle; they will have no function, now or later, as stoppers, entries, guards or ruffers.

Do not draw out your busy trumps! If the time comes when your suit-establishment plays are completed, and the opponents' strong suits are no longer dangerous, then trumps can be led.

Draw out immediately all your idle trumps! They are doing you no good, and they will eliminate from the opponents' hands trump cards which may serve them as added stoppers, entries or winners.

In the example shown, the game is made by saving a busy trump. South plays four spades, and West leads the diamond Ace, following it with the Queen, which South trumps. South finds that he has more than enough trumps to stop the diamond suit, so that his trumps are not busy. North's two small trumps are not busy as they are not needed as stoppers, entries or guards.

♠ Q 7 5
♥ 8 6 3
♦ 7 4
♣ K Q J 6 2

      N
 W   E
      S

♠ A K 9 6 3 2
♥ A Q 5
♦ 3
♣ 10 5 4

South lays down the Ace and King of spades. One opponent shows out, meaning that the other opponent still has a trump. There is danger of a club ruff, but South cannot lead another trump—dummy's Queen is busy, for it is needed as an entry to the club suit.

South proceeds to lead clubs and establish the suit by driving out the Ace. The opponent who holds the third trump may get a ruff, it is true; but then dummy gets the lead with the spade Queen and South's two hearts are discarded on the remaining clubs. Without entry to the club suit, South would have had to try the heart finesse and be defeated if it failed.

When the opponents, after the trump suit has been led, have remaining one or more high trumps, declarer should be guided as follows:

If his own lower trumps are not busy, he should lead them and allow the opponents to take their master trump at once.

If his lower trumps are busy, he should lead other suits and if possible force out the opponents' master trump by letting them ruff his winning cards in other suits.

The Cross-Ruff

The important considerations of the ruffing game are:

1. Count the tricks that can be won by ruffs and high cards in other suits, and be sure they are enough.

2. Count the entries needed in both hands, and establish the entries, as often as possible, *first*. Usually the ruffs in each hand will provide entries.

3. *Cash all idle top cards in trump or plain suits*, before starting the ruffing process. This is important, yet must

be followed intelligently. Do not cash a top trump if
it frees a master trump for the opponents, with which
they can get the lead and shorten your trump length in
both hands.

The reason for cashing idle cards—those not needed as entries
—in side suits is simple: while you are ruffing plain suits, the
opponents may discard on the plain suits their losers in other
plain suits. When later you try to cash your top cards, the
opponents will be void and can ruff. However, this rule must
also be followed cautiously; be *sure* of your entries before cashing top cards in plain suits.

The most effective cross-ruff is one in which all ruffs are
made with high trumps. No overruff is possible, and each
winning ruff is its own entry.

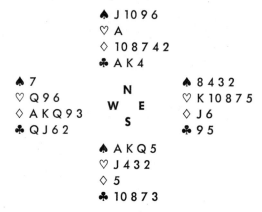

```
                      ♠ J 10 9 6
                      ♡ A
                      ◊ 10 8 7 4 2
                      ♣ A K 4
    ♠ 7                                      ♠ 8 4 3 2
    ♡ Q 9 6              N                   ♡ K 10 8 7 5
    ◊ A K Q 9 3      W       E               ◊ J 6
    ♣ Q J 6 2              S                 ♣ 9 5
                      ♠ A K Q 5
                      ♡ J 4 3 2
                      ◊ 5
                      ♣ 10 8 7 3
```

South plays four spades; West opens the diamond King and, seeing the
dangerous cross-ruff impending, switches to the spade. South counts his
tricks: he will win this spade trick, can win two club tricks and one heart,
and can ruff three times in each hand, total six: ten tricks. He needs three
entries to each hand for the three ruffing leads, and will procure these
entries by ruffing. He does not need the top clubs as entries or stoppers. He
cashes the top clubs and the heart Ace, then leads diamonds and hearts
back and forth, ruffing as he goes.

If South neglected to cash both clubs at once, East would discard a club
on the third round of diamonds. South could then never get more than one
club trick.

Dummy Reversal

As a rule ruffing with the long trump suit does not gain a
trick, and should be avoided except when the ruffing trick

provides an entry or a stopper, or serves to ruff out a long suit. An exception exists, however:

♡ A J 3

N

♡ 10 5 2   **W**   **E**   ♡ 9 6

S

♡ K Q 8 7 4

When no ruffs are possible in the North, or dummy, hand, South's maximum number of heart winners would seem to be five, the length of his suit.

If, however, South is short in a suit which North can lead, and if South can ruff three leads of this suit, North's hearts will win three tricks and can even draw the opposing trumps. The total tricks will then be three in each hand, a total of six.

This type of play will be overlooked consistently by those who consider the dummy only an adjunct to declarer's hand, and do not realize that the hands, in a practical sense, are interchangeable.

Card Reading

There are two objects in card reading:

1. To determine the position of the missing key-cards of each suit.
2. To determine distribution of the outstanding cards of each suit.

Very often it is possible to gauge precisely the cards an opponent holds in a suit he has bid. Of course, it does not necessarily follow that because a player has bid spades he must hold the spade Ace, but it is very likely that he does rather than a sketchy suit such as Q x x x x. A come-on signal will likewise serve to place a high card or cards in the hand of the signalling player unless, of course, declarer must suspect that his intention is deceit rather than the giving of information to his partner. A suit may be placed not only from the bidding but from the stronger influence of leads which show length (page 518) or the exact information as to the original suit holdings which is available when any player shows out. The method of placing a single suit is:

1. Assume the probable number of cards that a player must have had to bid; or to make a certain lead; or take the exact number of cards he was shown to have had originally when he fails to follow suit.

2. Add that number to the combined holding of your hand and dummy, and subtract the total from thirteen. The remainder is the length of that suit in the other opponent's hand.

The rules for counting out the distribution of an entire hand are very similar to the rules for suit placing. The repeated operation of the latter rule finally yields an accurate count on the entire missing twenty-six cards rather than on one-fourth of them. In both hand and suit placing a player will usually find it easier to reconstruct the unknown hands on the basis of their original thirteen-card holdings rather than by deducting cards already played.

The steps in hand placing are:

1. From any information, sure or probable, at your disposal, reconstruct as many suits in one opponent's hand as possible.

2. Add each separate suit holding to the total in your hand and dummy, and by subtracting from thirteen place the remaining cards of each suit in the other opponent's hand.

3. When three suits can be placed, their total subtracted from thirteen gives the length of the fourth suit in an opponent's hand, after which Step 2 will give the number of that fourth suit in the other opponent's hand.

4. When only one or two suits can be placed, and there is no available information on the other suits, assume that they are divided as evenly as possible.

Declarer's Play

When the previous play has shown that a finesse, if attempted, will lose, declarer may resort to a ducking play commonly known as the "obligatory finesse."

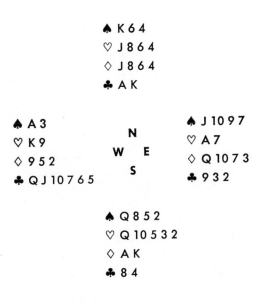

♠ K 6 4
♡ J 8 6 4
◊ J 8 6 4
♣ A K

♠ A 3
♡ K 9
◊ 9 5 2
♣ Q J 10 7 6 5

N
W E
S

♠ J 10 9 7
♡ A 7
◊ Q 10 7 3
♣ 9 3 2

♠ Q 8 5 2
♡ Q 10 5 3 2
◊ A K
♣ 8 4

South	West	North	East
1 ♡	2 ♣	3 ♡	Pass
4 ♡	Pass	Pass	Pass

THE PLAY: OBLIGATORY FINESSE

West opens the club Queen, dummy winning. Dummy leads a trump, East winning the Ace and playing another club. Dummy wins and leads another trump, which West wins. Now West leads a diamond. South takes the diamond King and leads a spade. West plays low and dummy's King is put up, winning the trick. A spade is led back from dummy and though East plays the Jack, South ducks. East's failure to win the first spade trick marks West with the spade Ace. South could not gain by playing the spade Queen, for it would surely be captured. When South ducks, West must play the Ace nevertheless, establishing South's Queen. South loses only two heart tricks and the Ace of spades, making four hearts.

Declarer's Play of Trump Bids

The declarer must realize that the dummy hand is not merely an adjunct to his own hand and that the dummy's short trump suit may sometimes be used to draw the opponents' trumps.

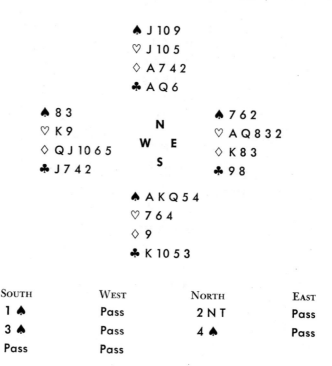

♠ J 10 9
♡ J 10 5
◇ A 7 4 2
♣ A Q 6

♠ 8 3
♡ K 9
◇ Q J 10 6 5
♣ J 7 4 2

♠ 7 6 2
♡ A Q 8 3 2
◇ K 8 3
♣ 9 8

♠ A K Q 5 4
♡ 7 6 4
◇ 9
♣ K 10 5 3

SOUTH	WEST	NORTH	EAST
1 ♠	Pass	2 N T	Pass
3 ♠	Pass	4 ♠	Pass
Pass	Pass		

THE PLAY: DUMMY REVERSAL

West opens the diamond Queen, dummy's Ace winning. If South draws trumps at once he can win five spade tricks, one diamond and three clubs. His tenth trick will materialize only if the clubs break 3–3. South cannot ruff a fourth club in dummy because East would ruff one of his high clubs on the third round. South can, however, develop the necessary ten tricks by ruffing three diamonds in his own hand and drawing trumps with dummy's ♠ J 10 9. Therefore, after winning the first diamond in dummy South immediately ruffs a diamond with the spade Queen. He leads the ♠ 4 to dummy and ruffs another diamond with his spade King. He re-enters dummy with the ♠ 10 and ruffs the last diamond with his last spade, the Ace. Now the dummy gets the lead again with the club Ace, draws the last trump with the spade Jack, and leaves two high clubs to win South's ninth and tenth tricks.

Declarer's Play

CARD READING

From leads, plays and especially from discards (when one opponent shows out) estimate the distribution of each suit in the opponents' hands.

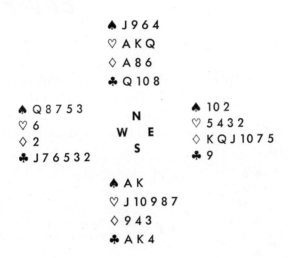

```
                    ♠ J 9 6 4
                    ♡ A K Q
                    ◊ A 8 6
                    ♣ Q 10 8

  ♠ Q 8 7 5 3          N          ♠ 10 2
  ♡ 6              W       E       ♡ 5 4 3 2
  ◊ 2                  S          ◊ K Q J 10 7 5
  ♣ J 7 6 5 3 2                   ♣ 9

                    ♠ A K
                    ♡ J 10 9 8 7
                    ◊ 9 4 3
                    ♣ A K 4
```

NORTH	EAST	SOUTH	WEST
1 ♣	1 ◊	1 ♡	Pass
2 ♡	Pass	4 ♣	Pass
4 ◊	Pass	5 ♡	Pass
6 ♡	Pass	Pass	Pass

THE PLAY: "MARKED" FINESSE

West opens the deuce of diamonds (obviously a singleton), dummy winning with the Ace. The Ace and King of hearts are led and when West shows out, East is marked with ten red and (consequently) three black cards. Trumps must be drawn, so the heart Queen is cashed and declarer enters his hand with the Ace of spades to lead the Jack of hearts, dummy discarding a low diamond. The two black Kings are led and when East follows to both, the location of every card is marked. The low club is led and the ten is finessed. The Jack of spades is returned, South discarding the Ace of clubs. West wins with the Queen and must yield entry to dummy with a spade or club, affording discards for South's losing diamonds.

CHAPTER FORTY-THREE

END-PLAYS

The term "end-play" applies to three types of plays which occur late in the play of the hand. The first is called the "throw-in." An opponent is forced to win a trick when he must make a lead which costs him a trick. There are three typical throw-in situations:

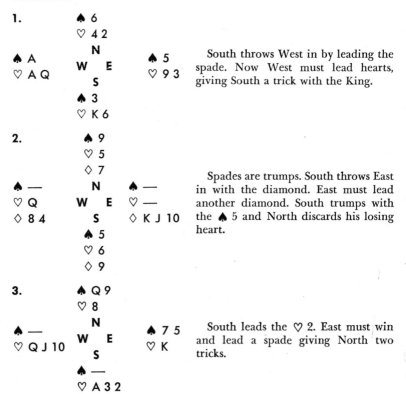

1.

	♠ 6	
	♡ 4 2	
♠ A	N	♠ 5
♡ A Q	W　E	♡ 9 3
	S	
	♠ 3	
	♡ K 6	

South throws West in by leading the spade. Now West must lead hearts, giving South a trick with the King.

2.

	♠ 9	
	♡ 5	
	◇ 7	
♠ —	N	♠ —
♡ Q	W　E	♡ —
◇ 8 4	S	◇ K J 10
	♠ 5	
	♡ 6	
	◇ 9	

Spades are trumps. South throws East in with the diamond. East must lead another diamond. South trumps with the ♠ 5 and North discards his losing heart.

3.

	♠ Q 9	
	♡ 8	
♠ —	N	♠ 7 5
♡ Q J 10	W　E	♡ K
	S	
	♠ —	
	♡ A 3 2	

South leads the ♡ 2. East must win and lead a spade giving North two tricks.

Declarer first establishes a throw-in card, one which only the desired opponent will be able to win, and one which he *must* win.

The Throw-In Card

The following are infallible throw-in cards:

1. ♠ 4 3 2	2. ♠ 4 3 2	3. ♠ 4 3 2
North	North	North
South	South	South
♠ A Q 9	♠ A J 10	♠ K 10 7

In any case, North leads; if East plays a high card South covers, if East plays a low card South plays the ♠ 9 in Figure 1 and the ♠ 10 in the other two.

The Stripping Process

Stripping consists in making sure that the opponent has no exit-card. A card which will not win a trick, but which, when led, will not cause the unnecessary loss of a trick, is an exit-card.

1.

```
            ♠ 8 5 3
            ♡ —
            ◇ Q 6
            ♣ 4
♠ —                        ♠ —
♡ K 10    N                ♡ Q 6 3
◇ K 8   W   E              ◇ J 9
♣ Q 10     S               ♣ 6
            ♠ 10 7 2
            ♡ —
            ◇ A 5
            ♣ 3
```

2.

```
            ♠ 8
            ♡ A K J
            ◇ 8 2
            ♣ —
♠ Q J                      ♠ A
♡ 9       N                ♡ Q 8 7 6 3
◇ A Q   W   E              ◇ —
♣ Q        S               ♣ —
            ♠ 9 6 3
            ♡ —
            ◇ 6 4
            ♣ 3
```

Spades are trumps.

Here is a case in which South has stripped his and dummy's hands. West, thrown in by a club lead, can make no lead without losing a trick.

No trumps.

Here is a case in which South has stripped his opponent's hand. East, thrown in with the spade, must lead to dummy and give up three tricks.

Timing is not a serious consideration when declarer is equally willing to throw in either opponent—when he has a combination such as A 10 x in one hand and K 9 x in the other; or when he has Q x in one hand and A x in the other, and will have a chance to finesse if the suit is led by an opponent.

The Squeeze

Elsewhere I have discussed the principle of idle and busy cards.

A busy card is one which will have a definite duty in the play of the hand, either as a stopper or as a guard to a stopper. Every busy card is equivalent to one full trick. If I hold A K J and my opponent holds Q 3 2 he may as well throw away the Queen as the deuce. A "squeeze" is a play which forces an opponent to throw a busy card.

The success of a squeeze play is dependent on:

1. A stripping process which removes from the hand all non-essential cards.
2. Entries.
3. Position.

THE STRIPPING PROCESS

A card in an opponent's hand is not, strictly speaking, busy if his partner can also stop the suit. He can throw away a card which may seem to be a stopper and yet declarer will not profit. The first thing for declarer to look for is two suits in which one opponent has the *only* stoppers. These are his busy cards. When he can be forced to discard one of these cards he is squeezed.

The second problem of declarer is to remove from that opponent's hand all idle cards. Declarer simply counts up the number of cards required by this opponent to stop the two suits, and then plans to reduce him to that number of cards.

When the opponent has been stripped to busy cards only, declarer must still have a winner to lead which the opponent can neither follow to nor ruff.

Finally, declarer must be able at the time he applies the squeeze to win all but one of the remaining tricks.

1. ♠ A J
    ♥ K 2
    ♦ —

  ♠ K Q   **N**   ♠ 5
  ♥ A 6   **W   E**   ♥ 8
  ♦ —   **S**   ♦ 7 3

    ♠ 3
    ♥ 5 2
    ♦ A

2. ♠ A J 6
    ♥ Q
    ♦ —

  ♠ K Q   **N**   ♠ 5 2
  ♥ A K   **W   E**   ♥ 6
  ♦ —   **S**   ♦ 9

    ♠ 10
    ♥ J 4
    ♦ A

In each case there are no trumps and South leads the ♦ Ace, a card that West can neither follow to nor ruff. Nevertheless, there is no squeeze in this case. In Figure 1 West has an idle card, the ♥ 6 which he can throw away. In Figure 2 West's cards are all busy but South does not hold all but one of the remaining tricks. In the following example it will be seen that the squeeze is present because both conditions are fulfilled.

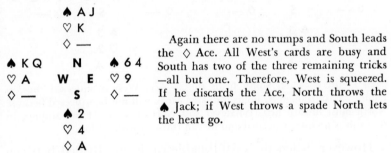

    ♠ A J
    ♥ K
    ♦ —

♠ K Q   **N**   ♠ 6 4
♥ A   **W   E**   ♥ 9
♦ —   **S**   ♦ —

    ♠ 2
    ♥ 4
    ♦ A

Again there are no trumps and South leads the ♦ Ace. All West's cards are busy and South has two of the three remaining tricks —all but one. Therefore, West is squeezed. If he discards the Ace, North throws the ♠ Jack; if West throws a spade North lets the heart go.

Therefore an essential part of the stripping process is to count up the number of top tricks in the combined hands and if the number falls short of the required all-but-one, *then purposely and immediately lose that many tricks.* In losing tricks be careful to lose the trick in a suit in which you still retain a stopper, and also be careful that when the opponents get the lead they cannot knock out an entry essential to the squeeze.

ENTRIES

A player does not have to worry much about keeping a stopper when declarer has no entry to the suit he is trying to stop. An essential part of the squeeze is that after the squeeze has been effected and the opponent has discarded a stopper, there must be an entry to whatever card has been established by his discard.

Obviously the hand which wins the squeezing trick will remain in the lead so the important thing to remember is that an entry must be kept to the hand that does not win the squeezing trick.

POSITION

When both establishable cards, which the opponent is trying to stop, are in the same hand (declarer or dummy) there will be no squeeze unless the opponent plays *before* that hand.

1.

```
                ♠ K
                ♡ A J
                ◇ —
   ♠ A          N          ♠ 6
   ♡ K Q      W   E        ♡ 5 4
   ◇ —          S          ◇ —
                ♠ 3
                ♡ 2
                ◇ A
```

2.

```
                ♠ K
                ♡ A J
                ◇ —
   ♠ 6          N          ♠ A
   ♡ 5 4      W   E        ♡ K Q
   ◇ —          S          ◇ —
                ♠ 3
                ♡ 2
                ◇ A
```

In Figure 1, when South leads the ◇ Ace, West is squeezed; but in Figure 2 East, though he holds the same cards, will not be squeezed because North must discard first. Whatever suit North discards, East's stopper in that suit is no longer needed and he can throw it without loss.

However, when the establishable cards are divided between declarer and dummy it does not make any difference which opponent holds the stoppers because declarer and dummy will both have superfluous cards and neither will be forced to let go an essential card. Note in the diagram that when South leads the ◇ Ace North can fearlessly discard the ♠ 3 and yet East is squeezed because if he throws his spade stopper

```
                ♠ 3
                ♡ A J
                ◇ —
   ♠ 6          N          ♠ A
   ♡ 5 4      W   E        ♡ K Q
   ◇ —          S          ◇ —
                ♠ K
                ♡ 2
                ◇ A
```

South remains in the lead to cash the ♠ King before taking the ♡ Ace.

Sometimes to effect a squeeze declarer must cash the master card of a suit so that the hand which held it may later discard freely. By so doing he *seems* to be setting up a trick for the opponents. The seeming sacrifice strikes the fancy of most players and a play of this type is known as the Vienna Coup (page 509).

VARIATIONS

The mechanism of the squeeze is essentially simple because the same underlying principles apply to all its forms.

There are many variations of the squeeze. The "matrices" shown and described on the following pages illustrate the typical end positions of the squeeze in its different forms.

Typical Squeeze Positions

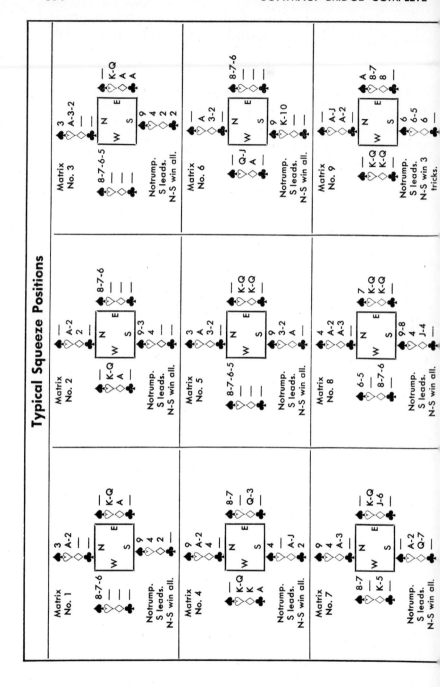

Typical Squeeze Positions (Continued)

Matrix No. 10

North: ♠ 3 ♥ A-2 ♦ 5-4
West: ♠ 8-7-6 ♥ — ♦ — ♣ K-6
East: ♠ — ♥ K-Q ♦ A ♣ 8-7
South: ♠ 9 ♥ A-2 ♦ 4 ♣ A-Q

Notrump. S leads. N-S win 4 tricks.

Matrix No. 11

North: ♠ K ♥ A-2 ♦ 6 ♣ 2 — ♠ A-2 ♦ K-Q-J
West: ♠ 4 ♥ K-Q-J ♣ A
East: ♠ Q-3 ♥ 6 ♦ A-2

Notrump. S leads. N-S win 4 tricks.

Matrix No. 12

North: ♥ A-2 ♦ 2 — ♥ K-7 ♣ A
South: ♠ Q-8 ♥ A — ♦ 9 ♥ 4 ♣ 2

Notrump. S leads. N-S win all.

Matrix No. 13

North: ♠ 8 ♥ Q-7 ♣ A
West: ♠ — ♥ 4 ♦ 2
East: ♠ 9 ♥ A-2 ♦ 4
South: ♠ K-8 ♥ K-8

Notrump. S leads. N-S win all.

Matrix No. 14

North: ♠ J-1-6-5 ♦ A
West: ♠ 3 ♥ A-K-2
East: ♠ 9 ♥ 4 ♦ 2 ♣ 2
South: ♠ Q-8-7 ♦ A

Notrump. S leads. N-S win all.

Matrix No. 15

North: ♠ K-Q ♥ K-Q — ♠ 6 ♥ 3-2 ♦ 3
South: ♠ A ♥ 3-2 ♣ 9 — ♠ 8 ♥ 8 ♦ 8-7

Spades trump. S leads. N-S win all.

Matrix No. 16

North: ♥ Q-7 ♦ Q-7-6 ♣ 8-7
West: ♥ A-2 ♦ A-2 ♦ A-6-5
East: ♠ 9-8-7 ♥ 4-3 ♦ 4-3
South: ♠ K-8 ♥ K-8 ♦ K-Q-J

Spades trump. S leads. N-S win all.

Matrix No. 17

North: ♠ 8-7 ♣ A-K
West: ♥ A-2 ♦ 3-2
East: ♠ 9 ♥ 4 ♦ 4 ♣ 3
South: ♠ K-Q ♥ A-K

Notrump. S leads. N-S win 3 tricks.

Matrix No. 18

North: ♥ 4 ♦ Q-J-8 ♣ A
West: ♠ 3 ♥ 3 ♦ A-3-2
East: ♠ 9 ♥ K-4 ♣ K-Q
South: ♠ 8-7-6 ♥ A-K

Notrump. S leads. N-S win 4 tricks.

Explanation of Squeeze Positions (Matrices)

1. South leads ♠. East's discard establishes a red deuce.

2. South leads ♠ 9. If West discards ♡, dummy discards ◇ and vice versa.

3. South leads ♠. If East discards ♡, dummy's suit is established. If East discards an Ace, South cashes the winner thereby established, squeezing East once more.

4. South leads ♠. If West discards ♡ or ♣ a deuce is established; if ◇, there is a finesse against East's Q.

5. South leads the spade, next the Ace of East's discard; then the other Ace, and the remaining card is a winner.

6. South leads ♠. North discards same suit as West.

7. South leads ◇ Q, West covers and North wins with A. North leads ♠ and East is squeezed.

8. South leads ◇ 4 to ◇ A and cashes both spades, North discarding ◇ 3. East is squeezed.

9. South leads ♠. West is squeezed.

10. South leads ♣ Q, West winning. South then cashes both black winners. East is squeezed.

11. South leads ♠, East winning. East's return permits South to cash a spade and a diamond. West is squeezed. If East does not take ♠ A, North leads ♣ 2, South discarding ♡. On ♡ return East is squeezed.

12. South leads ♠. West must discard ♡, so North discards ◇. Then East is squeezed.

13. South leads ♠. West must discard ♡; dummy discards ◇. The ◇ A is cashed and East is squeezed.

14. South leads ♠. West must discard ♡ and East is squeezed.

15. South leads ♣. If East discards ♡, South cashes ♡ A and dummy is good; if East discards ◇, North ruffs ◇ and South hand is good.

16. South leads ♠. If West discards ♣, a club-ruff establishes winner. If West discards otherwise, North discards same suit and that A is taken. The ♣ A is cashed, South discarding from other red suit. A club is ruffed and the last trump led, the situation then being similar to Matrix No. 12.

17. South leads ♠. If West discards ♡, North's deuce is established. If West discards ◇, dummy discards ♡ 2 and South leads ◇.

18. South leads ♠. East's only safe discard is ♡ 4. South then leads ♣.

Trump-Reducing Plays

The least difficult branch of end-plays is the trump-reducing play. It is, however, much revered because one of its variations is known as the Grand Coup.

The purpose of a trump-reducing play is to utilize a trump tenace which cannot be used for a finesse because there is no trump in the opposite hand to lead.

1.

```
              ♠ 6 3
              ♡ —


 ♠ 8 7      N      ♠ —
 ♡ —     W    E    ♡ K J
            S


              ♠ —
              ♡ A Q
```

2.

```
              ♠ 6 5 3
              ♡ —
              ♢ —


 ♠ 8 7      N      ♠ —
 ♡ —     W    E    ♡ K J
 ♢ 10       S      ♢ 2


              ♠ —
              ♡ A Q 8
              ♢ —
```

Hearts are trumps, with South holding the major tenace over East. No finesse is possible because dummy has no trump, but if dummy leads a spade, East must trump and South by overtrumping wins the last two tricks.

Here South has the same major tenace over East, but when dummy leads a spade East discards a diamond. South must win the trick and then, being in the lead, must allow East to win with the ♡ King. Here South lost a trick because he had too many trumps. Hence the name trump-reducing play.

The execution of the trump-reducing play depends upon precise timing, which is usually nothing more or less than precise counting:

1. Count the number of trumps held by the defender, then deduct them from the number of trumps you hold yourself. The difference is the number of trumps you must remove from your hand by ruffing.

2. The number of entries to dummy required is the same as the number of times you must ruff, plus one.

The diagrams previously shown make it obvious that the final position must be created by means of the stripping process common to all end-plays. In the trump-reducing plays the stripping consists in removing all cards except trumps from the hands of both declarer and the defender who holds the guarded trump card. The stripping is very simple—in addition to ruffing the required number of times, declarer leads out all plain-suit cards he holds, winning them, of course, if possible, but allowing the adversaries to win them if it is necessary. The final entry to dummy, which will allow the decisive lead to be made when all but trumps are gone, must carefully be retained.

In cashing winners in plain suits, declarer must be extremely cautious, for a void suit in the hand of the adversary who holds the trumps will permit him to ruff, and now he has won his trump trick and the trump-reducing play has gone for naught.

When one of the cards ruffed by declarer to reduce his trump length is a winning card, the play is called the Grand Coup. This is the only respect in which the Grand Coup differs from any other trump-reducing play—the card ruffed must be able to win a trick on its own. If two winning cards are ruffed, it is a Double Grand Coup; there are rare cases of the Triple Grand Coup, while the Quadruple Grand Coup occurs even more rarely than a hand with thirteen spades.

ILLUSTRATIONS OF END-PLAYS

Grand Coup

The Grand Coup is a trump-reducing play in which declarer, in order to shorten his own trump length, must ruff one or more *winning* cards. When *one* winning card is ruffed, it is a Single Grand Coup; ruffing *two* winning cards makes a Double Grand Coup, etc. In the following example of the Grand Coup, declarer shortens his trump length by *two* cards, each time ruffing a card which would otherwise be a winner.

```
                    ♠ Q 9
                    ♡ A K Q J
                    ◇ K J 10
                    ♣ 8 5 4 3
    ♠ 8                            ♠ K 7 5 4
    ♡ 8 7 4 3 2       N            ♡ 10 9 6
    ◇ 9 7 4 3     W       E        ◇ 8 6 2
    ♣ A K 6           S            ♣ Q 7 2
                    ♠ A J 10 6 3 2
                    ♡ 5
                    ◇ A Q 5
                    ♣ J 10 9
```

South	West	North	East
1 ♠	Pass	2 ♡	Pass
2 ♠	Pass	2 N T	Pass
4 ♠	Pass	Pass	Pass

West opens the club King, and East-West take three club tricks. East returns a heart, won by dummy's Jack. Now the Queen and nine of spades are finessed, both winning. The heart Queen is led from dummy and South ruffs it. A small diamond puts dummy in with the ten, and South ruffs the King of hearts.

Next the diamond Queen is led and overtaken by North's King. Now dummy leads the heart Ace. If East ruffs, South can overruff; therefore East discards his last diamond and South discards the diamond Ace. When dummy now leads a diamond, East must ruff and South overruffs, winning the last two tricks and making four spades.

The Vienna Coup

The Vienna Coup is the play of the highest card of a suit, temporarily establishing an opponent's card, only to squeeze him into discarding it (or another equally valuable card) later. The Vienna Coup is used when the *position* of the opponent's cards would otherwise make a successful squeeze impossible.

```
            ♠ 6 2
            ♡ A K 9 7 2
            ◇ A 7 4
            ♣ Q 8 5
♠ 9 7 3              ♠ 10 5
♡ 3           N      ♡ Q J 10 8 5 4
◇ J 10 9 5   W   E   ◇ 8 3
♣ K J 9 6 3     S    ♣ 10 7 4
            ♠ A K Q J 8 4
            ♡ 6
            ◇ K Q 6 2
            ♣ A 2
```

North	East	South	West
1 ♡	Pass	2 ♠	Pass
2 N T	Pass	4 N T	Pass
5 ♡	Pass	5 N T	Pass
6 ◇	Pass	7 ♠	Pass
Pass	Pass		

West opens the three of hearts, dummy's Ace winning. South cannot establish the heart suit for a discard because he lacks entries to dummy, and cannot ruff his losing diamond because unless the suit breaks 3–3 (in which case he has no need to ruff) one of the opponents can trump the third round. Therefore South plays for a squeeze. He runs six spades, saving two hearts, two diamonds and two clubs in dummy. Then he lays down the club Ace (Vienna Coup). He then enters dummy with the diamond Ace and leads the heart King, discarding his club. West cannot hold the club King and yet keep the diamond suit stopped. If West discards the club King, it establishes dummy's Queen. If West discards a diamond, all South's diamonds are good.

CHAPTER FORTY-FOUR

SAFETY PLAYS
AND TECHNIQUE

To the master player the so-called brilliant coups are essentially simple and he is far prouder when he can say that his technique on the simpler plays is flawless. Technique in its highest form is exemplified in the actual cards chosen in the handling of a single suit and the order of plays in the handling of an entire hand. Many of the proper technical plays in single suits are known as safety plays because they take into consideration the most unexpected pranks of distribution and guard against them.

The following plays are justly called safety plays because they cannot lose, and may gain.

1. J 7 6 5 2	2. Q 6 5 2	3. 7 4 3
N	N	N
W E	W E	W E
S	S	S
A Q 9 8 4	A K 9 7 3	A Q 6 5 2

In Figure 1 South should decide to finesse for the King, on the basis of the Rule of Five Steps, and in leading to the finesse he should play the Jack. If East covers and West shows out, a finesse against the ten is marked. If East shows out the Jack is allowed to lose to the King so that the Ace and Queen will clear the suit later. In Figure 2 the Queen is the first play, so that if West shows a void two finesses may be taken against East's J 10 x. In Figure 3 the normal play, which is entirely wrong, is to lead a small card from dummy and finesse the Queen. The correct first play is not a finesse but the Ace. With five high cards outstanding, South's two honors cannot possibly drop them all, so one trick must in any case be lost. If South by any chance allows his Queen to be killed by a singleton King, East, whose original holding was J 10 9 8, will win two more tricks and South, for all his long suit, can make only two tricks against the enemy's three. The first play of the Ace will guard against the singleton King and a later lead from dummy toward the Queen will offer South every possible advantage of a finesse with the added ability of ducking if by card reading South decides that West's original holding may have been King doubleton.

The following plays typify the "percentage play":

1. A 10 6 5	**2.** A 9 3	**3.** Q 10 6
N	N	N
W E	W E	W E
S	S	S
K 9 7 4 3	K J 6 5 2	A 9 8 4 2

In Figure 1 the loss of two tricks can surely be avoided by leading low from either hand and finessing the nine or ten; but if the top card is played from either hand first and the wrong opponent is void, two tricks must be lost. In Figure 3 percentage favors taking two finesses and thereby avoiding a guess. This is a trick I learned years ago from a Frenchman who knew nothing else about bridge. I introduced it to the bridge players of this country after a tremendous tussle with the old guard, who for years had been first laying down the Ace, then leading low toward the Queen, then guessing. Figure 2 offers a safety play to lose no more than one trick by first leading the King, then low toward the A 9, and finessing the nine if West follows. (If West shows out the Ace is played and the nine led back toward the Jack.) The "normal" way of cashing the Ace and then finessing loses two tricks when West holds Q 10 x x.

Other typical long-suit holdings in which there is a "right way" to play are:

x x x

A K J x x

Lead the King. Then lead the second round from North. If East follows, finesse the Jack. If this should lose, the Ace will clear the suit. This method of play avoids losing a trick to a singleton Queen in West's hand.

x x x

N
W   E
S

A Q 10 x x x

To avoid losing two tricks: Lead a small card from the North hand and if East plays a low card, play the Ace. If East plays the Jack, finesse the Queen. If neither missing honor falls on the first round, reënter the North hand and lead toward the new combination.

K x x

N
W   E
S

A 10 x x x

Lead the King; then a small one from North. If East plays low, finesse the ten. If this should lose, the Ace will clear the suit. The finesse saves a trick if East started with Q J x x. Win the second trick if East plays high.

Q 10 x x

A K 9 x x

Lead Ace (or King). If either opponent shows out, a finesse is established against his partner. If the first trick is won by the Queen, West will make a trick if he holds J x x x.

10 x x

A K 8 x x

Lead the Ace. Then lead low from South if (a) East drops an honor, or (b) West drops the nine or an honor. If either started with four: in (a) the ten will make a trick; in (b) a third-round finesse is taken through East.

Q 10 9 8

A x x x

Lead the eight. If East follows, take two finesses through him. If East shows out, win with the Ace and lead through West's King-Jack.

A J x

K 9 x x x

Lead the Ace. Then enter the South hand and lead low. Play the Jack unless West plays the Queen. If West started with Q 10 x x, the Jack makes; if East, a third-round finesse picks up the ten.

Sometimes the absence of entries or the pressure of time will alter the recommended technique.

Declarer's Plays at Notrump

An equally important branch of bridge technique is the proper play from dummy to the first trick at notrump contracts.

With the following suit holdings, assuming that the opening lead is a low card, the proper first play is always dummy's lowest card.

1. 10 2	2. 10 3 2	3. Q 2	4. Q 3 2
N	N	N	N
W E	W E	W E	W E
S	S	S	S
A J 3	A J	A 10 3	A 10

5.	Q 2	6.	Q 2	7.	K 2	8.	A J 2
	N		N		N		N
	W E		W E		W E		W E
	S		S		S		S
	K 10 3		J 4 3		J 4 3		K 9 3

9.	A J 2	10.	K J 2	11.	10 3 2
	N		N		N
	W E		W E		W E
	S		S		S
	10 3		10 3		K J 4

I use the word "always" in the full realization that it should be taboo in bridge books and that even in the cases above there may be exceptions.

The following combinations are usually pure guesses.

1.	Q 2	2.	Q 10	3.	K 6	4.	10 6 3
	N		N		N		N
	W E		W E		W E		W E
	S		S		S		S
	A 10		A 2		J 5		K Q 5

In each case, when West leads a low card, unless South has some indication from the bidding he may as well toss a coin. Usually it is safer to play the leader for the higher of the two outstanding cards and therefore to play the Queen in Figures 1 and 2, the King in Figure 3 and low in Figure 4. But I don't want to be blamed if these plays go wrong, and particularly in Figure 4 declarer is up against it. If he thinks that East has either the Ace or Jack he should play low, but if he thinks West is leading from the Ace-Jack, he should put up the ten and hope it wins the first trick.

Finally, the most commonly overlooked technical plays of all occur when the long suit is not in the leader's hand.

1.		Q 6 5			2.		K 6 3		
		N					N		
	9 2	W E	A J 10 8 7			10 5	W E	A J 8 7 4
		S					S		
		K 4 3					Q 9 2		

In Figure 1 when West opens the nine either as a short-suit lead or in response to a bid by East, dummy should play the Queen and kill an entry unless declarer is positive that West will never again have the lead.

In Figure 2, when West opens the ten, dummy's King should promptly cover and South will have a beautiful tenace over the Jack.

The many other cases in which there is a tremendous amount of difference between playing one card and another can often be worked out by a few seconds of thought at the time.

CHAPTER FORTY-FIVE

CONVENTIONAL
LEADS AND PLAYS

The defenders' game has two branches:

1. Information—painting a picture of the hand to partner so that the two hands can be combined for a single purpose as effectively as can declarer's and dummy's hands.

2. Strategy—selecting a point of attack or, when it is not safe to attack, waiting until the proper time to make the most of whatever establishable tricks are available.

The selection of a card to lead or to play for the purpose of giving information is governed by the alphabet of conventional plays. The selection of a particular suit to lead is governed by the strategy of leads.

The Alphabet of Conventional Plays

Every card that is played, whether in leading, in following suit, or in discarding, conveys a number of inferences which tell the story of the closed hand. Whether a card is played with intent to win a trick or not, it simultaneously fulfills its function of being a signal to partner. Most of these signals are not arbitrary but have their basis in logic and natural inferences.

Signals may be divided into three general categories: Signals to show honors; signals to show long suits of four cards or more; and signals to show short suits of three and fewer cards. These signals may be given in four different ways: by means of leads; when discarding; when following suit; and when winning a trick.

Honor Leads

Since it is not safe to lead an honor except from a sequence and then rarely from a sequence of only two cards, any lead of an honor may naturally be expected to show a *leadable sequence* in the player's hand. A leadable sequence consists of:

1. A three-card sequence headed by an honor (K Q J, Q J 10, J 10 9, etc.) or
2. Two touching honors with a third card one step lower (K Q 10 or Q J 9 or J 10 8).

When leading a suit headed by a leadable sequence lead the top of the sequence, regardless of the length of the suit. When the suit is not headed by a leadable sequence the proper lead is in most cases a low card.

Certain sequences are intermediate or middle sequences: K J 10 9, A 10 9 7, K 10 9 2, Q 10 9 2, etc. With such combinations the highest card of the suit is disregarded and the top of the sequence is led; but here the rule of leadable sequences varies. With three ranking cards in a suit it is proper to lead one of them, even though the intermediate sequence itself does not contain a third card in sequence or within one step of the sequence.

1.	K J 5	2.	6 3
	N		N
Q 10 9 6 W E 7 2		A J 10 8 5 W E 7 4 2	
	S		S
	A 8 4 3		K Q 9

In Figure 1 the lead of the six by West allows South to win the first trick with the eight and by finessing for the Queen, win all four tricks; the lead of the ten assures West of a trick, and if East had the King dummy's Jack would be caught. In Figure 2, the lead of the Jack forces out one of South's honors and if East gets the lead West can run the entire suit; there is the further advantage that if North had the Queen and East the King the Queen would be trapped on the first trick.

The phrase "middle sequence" denotes a sequence headed by an honor; K 9 8 7 6 is not a middle sequence and the proper lead is the **fourth-best**.

It follows from all this that the lead of any honor in an unbid suit guarantees the next lower honor in the suit and denies the next higher honor. The one exception is in the case of the Ace-King. From Ace-King the proper lead is the King and not the Ace. The purpose is to make it easy for partner, when he sees the King win the first trick, to know that the leader also has the Ace.

The lead of an Ace therefore does not show a sequence but probably denies one. When a player leads an Ace his next highest card in the suit is probably the Queen or lower. The one exception is when he has a doubleton Ace-King. Then he leads the Ace and follows it immediately with the King, showing his partner that he has no more and can ruff a third round.

Against notrump bids the rule of leadable sequences is followed quite closely and the fourth-highest card is led even from suits headed by A-K. Against trump bids it is not safe to lead a low card from Ace-King and risk having an honor-trick ruffed later. Likewise, except in the cases of strategical under-leads, it is not safe to lead low from an Ace against a trump bid and is even more unsafe to lead low from a King-Queen.

At notrump the lead of an Ace is purely conventional, showing a long powerful suit and asking partner to unblock (and at the same time to give information) by playing his highest card of the suit led.

Leads to Show Long Suits

From a suit which contains four cards or more and is not headed by a leadable sequence the proper lead is the fourth-best card. For example, Q 10 8 6 4, K J 9 5 2; and at notrump, A K 6 5 3 or K Q 3 2. Having led the fourth-best, follow it whenever possible with the next lowest card and then with a still lower card if any. Partner can then obtain a precise count of the number of cards held in that suit by the leader.

The Rule of Eleven

The use of the fourth-best rule makes possible the Rule of Eleven, which was worked out in 1889 by R. F. Foster and later independently discovered by E. F. M. Benecke of Oxford, England.

When the card led is the leader's fourth highest of a suit, subtract the denomination (number of pips) of the card led from 11. The result is the total number of cards, higher than the card led, held by the three other players.

The reason that the Rule of Eleven works is that the cards of a suit are a series of numbers with the lowest number 2 and the highest, the Ace, being equivalent to 14. As in all numbers in series, any number subtracted from the highest number gives the total number of higher cards in the series. In bridge, since three of these higher cards are held by the leader, three is at once deducted from 14 and then by deducting from 11 one gets the number of cards in the other three hands.

Short-Suit Leads

From a worthless short suit the highest card is usually led; from any doubleton the highest card is led. With three cards in an unbid suit, lead low from K x x, Q x x or J x x. It is better to make partner think that you have a four-card suit than to sacrifice the honor. With A x x the Ace should be led unless a deceptive under-lead is to be attempted. With 10 x x the lowest is led against a suit-bid but the ten against notrump.

With a *worthless* three-card suit, provided the middle card is sufficiently high not to be confused with a fourth-best lead, as in 9 8 2 or 9 7 2, the middle card may be led against a suit-bid so that on the next play the leader may use his higher card to show his partner that he did not have a doubleton.

In a suit partner has bid, from three cards to Ace, King, Queen or Jack, the highest should be led against a suit-bid but the lowest against notrump. The reason for the low lead against notrump is that declarer probably has one or two honors in the suit, as in the diagram shown, when a low lead by West allows South's 10 to be trapped but the lead of the ♠ Jack would give South two stoppers.

```
          ♠ 7
          N
♠ J 4 2  W   E  ♠ A Q 9 8 3
          S
        ♠ K 10 6 5
```

With any three-card suit containing two touching honors, such as K Q x or Q J x, the conventional lead is the top.

Following Suit and Discarding

Whereas the highest card of a sequence is led, when *playing* to a trick with intent to win the trick, the lowest of touching cards should be played. If your partner leads a suit in which you have A K Q, win with the Queen and not with the King or Ace. The play of any card denies a lower card which would fulfill the same purpose; with Q 10 9 8 7, if your partner leads a low card of the suit and dummy, with J x x, plays low, you play the seven.

DISCARDS

Discards, or follow-suit plays of lower cards are of two types, positive (encouraging) and negative (discouraging). The encouraging or come-on method is an unnecessarily high card. The discouraging or stop method is the play of the lowest available card.

Usually a card such as a 7, 8 or 9 will be encouraging and a 2, 3 or 4 discouraging; but when partner has no lower card than the 7 or 8, he has no choice but to use it as a stop-signal; and when he cannot spare a higher card than the four he may have to play it as a come-on and hope it is read. The partner must systematically analyze such discards by the "rule of missing pips"; he counts the number of pips on the discarded card and checks up in his own hand and dummy for lower cards if any. If there are no missing lower cards, the discard is undoubtedly negative; but if there is a lower card outstanding which may be held by the player or declarer, the discard may be a come-on; and if there are several outstanding lower cards it almost surely is a come-on.

THE ECHO

When a single card cannot be clearly read as a signal, a player may employ the echo or high-low. First he plays a card which is not his lowest, and follows it at his first opportunity with a lower card of the same suit. This is unmistakably a come-on signal provided partner watches the sequence of the plays.

Another valuable use of the echo is to show distribution. In following to a long suit which declarer is trying to establish, play your lowest with exactly three cards of the suit but echo if holding two or four cards of the suit.

1.　　　K Q J 10 5　　　　　2.　　　K Q J 10 5
　　　　　　N　　　　　　　　　　　　　N
　6 4 2　W　E　A 8 7　　　　　6 2　W　E　A 8 7
　　　　　　S　　　　　　　　　　　　　S
　　　　　9 3　　　　　　　　　　　　9 4 3

In Figure 1 South leads the nine and West plays the deuce. East, knowing that West has three cards of the suit, holds up his Ace once but wins the second trick. If he held up twice South would get an extra trick. In Figure 2 West plays the six on the first play and the deuce on the second. East knows he should hold up twice and win the third round.

THE TRUMP ECHO

In signalling with the trump suit a different sort of distributional echo is used, exactly the opposite of the one just explained. Here a player with three trumps plays high-low, and with two trumps plays them in normal order, the low one first.

Thus, a player holding 7 4 2 in trumps will play first the four and then the deuce, whether he is following suit or ruffing. This shows that he has at least one more trump.

THE SUIT-PREFERENCE SIGNAL

During the last few years an auxiliary signalling method known as the suit preference signal* has become very popular. This signal is so devised as never to interfere with the normal conventions of leads and plays previously described, and can

---

* The suit-preference convention was submitted in manuscript form to *The Bridge World Magazine* by Hy Lavinthal in the winter of 1932–33, long before it was known or played by any expert players to my knowledge. Since then other players have claimed credit for originating it and it is of course quite possible that they came independently to the same conclusions as Mr. Lavinthal.

therefore be unusually effective. The suit preference signal is based upon the fact that usually a defender, when faced with a difficult choice of leads, knows that his choice lies between two suits and only two.

An unnecessarily high card used in leading, discarding, or following suit, asks partner at his first opportunity to lead the higher of the two suits other than trump* and other than the suit in which the signal was made.

1. The opening leader holds a trick on which his partner shows out. He now plans to lead the suit again for his partner to ruff. If he wishes his partner to return the higher of the two suits in question, he now leads an unnecessarily high card; if the lower of the two suits, an unnecessarily low card.

2. The opening leader holds the first trick and a view of dummy makes it obvious to both partners that he will now switch suits. His partner's play to the trick he wins is not a come-on or stop-signal but an indication of whether he should switch to the higher or lower of the two possible suits.

3. In discarding, a player throws an unnecessarily high card in a suit in which he obviously cannot be signalling. This discard indicates his preference between the two suits other than the suit he discards and the suit on which he discards.

4. Finally, any play of a high card which can be read as not meaning any of the signals described in the previous pages calls for the higher of the two leadable suits, and vice versa.

LEAD-DIRECTING DOUBLES

A double of a slam contract asks partner to make an unnatural lead. That is, it cautions the leader not to open a suit-bid by either defender nor a trump. This usually narrows the

---

* At notrump contracts a suit in which declarer is so strong that to lead it would be futile is automatically eliminated from consideration; at trump contracts, the trump suit.

choice down to one of two other suits, and the leader selects the suit from the texture of his hand, plus bidding inferences.

With great length in some suit, for instance, the leader may expect that the double was based on a void in that suit and ability to ruff it. In other cases the leader may have a singleton and his partner a trump stopper. If the singleton is in a bid suit, the doubler may have inferred that it would not have been opened without the double.

A double of a three-notrump bid often indicates a safe opening lead (page 290).

Hands Illustrating the Suit-Preference Signal

1. Suit-Preference Discard

```
                    ♠ K 8 5
                    ♡ J 7
                    ◇ K 8 4
                    ♣ Q J 10 8 4

    ♠ Q 6 2                         ♠ J 9 4
    ♡ A 9 5 4          N            ♡ 10 6 3 2
    ◇ Q 5 3        W       E        ◇ A J 10 2
    ♣ 9 5 2            S            ♣ 7 3

                    ♠ A 10 7 3
                    ♡ K Q 8
                    ◇ 9 7 6
                    ♣ A K 6
```

South	West	North	East
1 N T	Pass	2 N T	Pass
3 N T	Pass	Pass	Pass

West opens the ♣ 9, having no favorable long suit to lead. South wins and lays down the heart King. West takes the Ace and East plays the ♡ 2. Since East obviously does not want clubs led, and can hardly want a continuation of hearts (the suit South first seeks to establish), East's discard of the ♡ 2 may be read as indicating a preference in the other two suits, spades and diamonds. It being his lowest heart, it calls for a lead of the lower of these suits, that is, diamonds. West leads the diamond Queen, the proper entry-saving play designed to keep West in the lead in case dummy's King is not put up. Whatever dummy plays, East can run four diamond tricks and defeat the contract immediately.

2. A Lead to Show Suit Preference

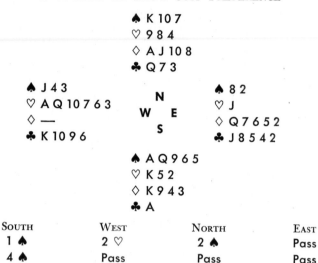

```
              ♠ K 10 7
              ♡ 9 8 4
              ◇ A J 10 8
              ♣ Q 7 3

  ♠ J 4 3                      ♠ 8 2
  ♡ A Q 10 7 6 3    N          ♡ J
  ◇ —             W   E        ◇ Q 7 6 5 2
  ♣ K 10 9 6        S          ♣ J 8 5 4 2

              ♠ A Q 9 6 5
              ♡ K 5 2
              ◇ K 9 4 3
              ♣ A
```

SOUTH	WEST	NORTH	EAST
1 ♠	2 ♡	2 ♠	Pass
4 ♠	Pass	Pass	Pass

West opens the heart Ace. When East plays the Jack, West knows he can ruff the second round. After ruffing the heart Jack, East of course will not lead a trump, but in choosing between diamonds and clubs, he will be more likely to lead a club than to lead into dummy's strong diamonds. West therefore leads the heart Queen to the second trick, and East ruffs with the ♠ 2. West's lead of an unnecessarily high card having indicated to East a preference for the higher of the two minor suits, East now returns a diamond and West ruffs. East then ruffs another heart and West another diamond, defeating the contract by two tricks. Had East first led clubs instead of diamonds, South could have made his contract.

3. Showing Suit Preference When Following Suit

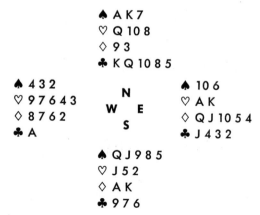

```
              ♠ A K 7
              ♡ Q 10 8
              ◇ 9 3
              ♣ K Q 10 8 5

  ♠ 4 3 2                      ♠ 10 6
  ♡ 9 7 6 4 3       N          ♡ A K
  ◇ 8 7 6 2       W   E        ◇ Q J 10 5 4
  ♣ A                S         ♣ J 4 3 2

              ♠ Q J 9 8 5
              ♡ J 5 2
              ◇ A K
              ♣ 9 7 6
```

NORTH	EAST	SOUTH	WEST
1 ♣	1 ♦	1 ♠	2 ♦
2 ♠	Pass	4 ♠	Pass
Pass	Pass		

West opens the club Ace, which is obviously a singleton because otherwise he would not open dummy's bid suit. Since East has bid diamonds, West plans to switch to diamonds, hoping to find East with an entry in that suit. However, East plays the club Jack on the Ace. This unnecessarily high card indicates a preference for the higher of the two suits other than trumps. West therefore shifts to hearts rather than to diamonds. This starts a cross-ruff which enables East-West to win six tricks instead of three.

The Card to Lead

The following table assumes that you have already selected a *suit* to lead (Chapter 46) and indicates only the proper conventional *card* to lead.

CULBERTSON STANDARD TABLE OF

Conventional Leads

HOLDING IN SUIT	LEAD AT SUIT-BIDS	LEAD AT NOTRUMP
A-K-Q-J *alone or with others*	K, then J	A*, then J
A-K-Q *with 3 or more others*	K, then Q	A, then K
A-K-Q-x-x *without a reëntry*	K, then Q	Fourth best
A-K-Q-x-x *or* A-K-Q-x	K, then Q	K, then Q
A-K-J-x-x-x *or more*	K, then A	A, then K
A-K-10-x-x-x *or more*	K, then A	A, then K
A-K-J-10-x-x *with a reëntry*	K	A
A-K-J-10 *alone or with others*	K	K
A-Q-J-x-x-x *or* A-Q-J-10-x-x *with a reëntry*	A	A
A-K-J, A-K-10, A-K *in 4-, 5-, or 6-card suit*	K, then A	Fourth best
A-Q-J-x *or longer*	A	Q
A-Q-10-9 *or longer*	A	10
A-J-10-x *or longer*	A	J
A-10-9-x *or longer*	A	10
A-x-x-x *or longer*	A	Fourth best
A-K-x	K, then A	K, then A
A-K *alone*	A, then K	Avoid
K-Q-J *alone or with others*	K, then J	K, then Q
K-Q-10 *alone or with others*	K	K
K-Q-x-x-x-x *(7 cards) or more*	K	K
K-Q-x-x-(x-x)	K	Fourth best
K-Q-x	K	K
K-Q *alone*	K	Avoid
K-J-10-x *or longer*	J	J
K-10-9-x *or longer*	10	10

* The lead of the Ace of an unbid suit against a notrump contract is *conventional*, requesting that partner follow suit with his highest card, even the King or Queen, unless dummy reveals that the sacrifice of such a card would eventually lose a trick. The lead of a King against notrump may be used to call conventionally for partner's second-highest card, but this convention is of doubtful value.

The Card to Lead (Continued)

HOLDING IN SUIT	LEAD AT SUIT-BIDS	LEAD AT NOTRUMP
Q-J-10 *alone or with others*	Q	Q
Q-J-9 *alone or with others*	Q	Q
Q-J-x-x-x-x (7 *cards*)	Q	Q
Q-J-x-x-(x-x)	Q	*Fourth best*
Q-J-x	Q	Q
Q-J *alone*	Q	Q
Q-10-9-x *or longer*	10	10
J-10-9 *alone or with others*	J	J
J-10-8 *alone or with others*	J	J
J-10-x	J	J
J-10 *alone*	J	J
J-10-x-x *or more*	J	*Fourth best*
10-9-8 *alone or with others*	10	10
10-9-7 *alone or with others*	10	10
10-9-x-x *or more*	10	*Fourth best*
10-9 *alone or* 10-9-x *alone*	10	10
Any 4-card or longer suit not listed above	*Fourth best*	*Fourth best*

LEADS IN PARTNER'S BID SUIT

A-x, K-x, Q-x, J-x, 10-x, *or any other* doubleton	*High card*	*High card*
J-10-x, 10-x-x *or* x-x-x	*Highest*	*Highest*
A-J-x, A-x-x, K-J-x, K-x-x, Q-10-x, Q-x-x, J-x-x	*Highest*	*Lowest*
Q-J-x-(x)	Q	Q
A-x-x-x *or better*	A	*Fourth best*
K-Q-x-(x)	K	K
Any other 4 or more cards	*Fourth best*	*Fourth best*

LEADS IN *UNBID* SHORT SUITS
At Trump or Notrump Contracts
The Card to Lead is Underlined

x̲-x	Q-x̲-x	K̲-x-x	K-10-9̲	A-10̲-9
x̲-x-x	Q-10-x̲	K-J̲-x	A-x̲-x	A-J̲-x
J̲-x-x	Q-10̲-9	K-10̲-x	A-10̲·x	A-J-10̲

Avoid leads from unbid short suits headed by an honor, except as *desperation* or *deceptive* leads.

CHAPTER FORTY-SIX

THE
DEFENDERS' GAME

With the opening lead the defenders inaugurate their campaign to defeat declarer's contract. The fact that they are called defenders does not mean that they cannot attack. Their line of defense may take one of two forms: A quick attempt to establish their tricks and cash them as soon as they get the lead with whatever stoppers they hold (the attacking game); and an attempt to prevent declarer from developing his own tricks by holding their stoppers until the lead comes to them (the protecting game).

Leads Against Notrump

Speed and number are the principal preoccupation in defense against notrump. Hence the following basic rule, which has few exceptions, governing leads against notrump: open your longest and best suit, regardless of tenaces.

When a hand contains two long suits, usually the longer should be opened if they are of unequal length and the stronger when they are of the same length. This general advice is modified, however, by considerations of speed and entries.

With one suit K Q J x and another suit 10 x x x x the stronger four-card suit is preferred because the long suit may never be established. Change the five-card holding to Q J x x x and the five-card suit is preferable. When the choice between the suits is about an even guess, but one is a major and the other a

minor, the major should usually be preferred. The opponents
in the course of their bidding might have gone to notrump
without ever mentioning a minor suit but would probably have
shown any biddable major suit.

With a seven-card suit headed by A K J or A K 10, or from
a six-card suit headed by A K Q, the Ace should be led; but
from a weaker long suit it is better to open fourth best rather
than high from an A-K combination, when the hand has no
entry. A doubleton and an entry in partner's hand will probably allow the suit to be brought in eventually. Even with
A K Q x x it is better to open fourth highest, on the chance
that partner will have a doubleton and declarer will hold J x x x,
unless there is danger that declarer can run his nine tricks
unless the entire five-card suit can be taken right away.

Short-Suit Leads

There are three situations which call for a short-suit lead
against notrump.

1. Warning short leads. You hold

♠ 7 5   ♥ 9 6 2   ♦ 8 4 3   ♣ J 7 6 4 3

Suppose you open your long club suit and your partner has a couple of entries and gets in to continue clubs.
Eventually you will establish the suit, perhaps, but you
will never get the lead to use it.

With such a hand it is preferable to open the ♥ 9
or ♦ 8 and hope you will be lucky enough to hit a
long suit in partner's hand and that he will have enough
entries, aided by the extra tempo you have given him
by the opening lead, to establish his suit.

2. Waiting short leads. With a hand containing distributed
strength but no suit long enough or strong enough to
be reasonably sure of establishing a long card, it is best
to open a worthless short suit and wait for the lead to
come to you in the other suits. A typical hand would
be—

♠ 9 7 3   ♥ Q 5   ♦ A Q 6 3   ♣ K J 7 5

The proper lead is the ♠ 9. The odds are against establishing the long card in either diamonds or clubs, and a lead away from either tenace may give declarer his precious ninth trick.

This does not apply when the strength in any suit is in a leadable sequence. There is no better waiting lead than a four-card or longer suit headed by a sequence.

3. Inferential short leads. The longest suit in a hand must sometimes be abandoned either because bidding information indicates that it cannot be established or because there will not be time to establish it before declarer has made his game.

For example, it is usually futile to open a long suit which the opponents have bid unless it is so solid that by leading it you cannot sacrifice a trick. There is also the typical case in which you can be sure declarer has a long six- or seven-card minor suit which he can run at once, and that he has your longest suit stopped. In such cases you may have to fall back on a desperation lead of a suit such as K J x in the hope that your partner has the other high cards in the suit and enough length to defeat the contract.

CHOICE OF SHORT SUITS

As between a three-card suit and a two-card suit, choose the three-card suit. You want the combined length of the suit to be as great as possible.

Avoid any doubleton or three-card suit headed by an honor. Any guarded honor may turn into a stopper in the course of play.

As a stab, a three-card suit headed by touching honors is often effective. K Q x and Q J x are dangerous leads, and should not be used except in desperate cases but J 10 x and 10 9 x are acceptable short-suit leads, often better than a worthless suit because they solidify any suit partner may hold and are very unlikely to sacrifice a trick or a stopper.

A K x has a value as two stoppers apart from its trick-winning value, and is strictly within the classification of desperation leads.

Leads Against Trump Bids

As a rule attacking leads are to be sought at trump bids when a good attacking lead is available. The best attacking leads are from any A K Q sequence, or from any five-card or longer suit headed by A-K. These, together with a singleton, doubleton, or three-card sequence in partner's bid suit, form a special class of preferred opening leads. They combine the finest timing (immediate winning of tricks) with least danger of sacrificing a stopper in a suit declarer will need to establish.

Inferior to these leads only in immediacy are those from solid sequences such as K Q J x, Q J 10 x, or high cards in partner's suit. Even a tenace remainder of partner's suit will, when combined with the high cards he undoubtedly holds in his suit, solidify his suit and make it a preferred opening lead.

Far below the sequence leads on the list of attacking leads are the four-card suits headed by a single honor. These suits should not be opened except when the situation definitely calls for action. If such a four-card suit *must* be opened, prefer K x x x to Q x x x, and as between Q 10 x x and Q x x x prefer the Q-10 suit, which any honor in partner's hand will probably protect.

Finally, when it comes to a suit headed by A-Q, A-J or K-J, we can almost state as a rule "do not open blindly from any tenace—try something else." And yet even here the necessity for cashing the setting tricks at once may force a desperation lead from such a holding.

The Ruffing Game

The defenders, like the declarer, have a third source of tricks at trump bids—the ruffers.

A singleton, A-x or K-x in a suit partner has bid are excellent introductions to a ruffing game, because partner is so likely to be able to win the trick and return the suit immediately before declarer can get in to draw trumps. The lead of a singleton or a doubleton Ace of an unbid suit is a justifiable lead only if the leader's hand contains A-x or K x x in trumps so that he can stop the suit and still have a worthless trump left for ruffing; or two or three small trumps if partner has shown strength and may be able either to win an immediate trick in the suit led or stop the trump suit in time to give the leader a ruff. Otherwise the singleton lead should be avoided except when the situation is desperate and immediate ruffing tricks are all that can be hoped for.

The Force Game

The object of the force game is to shorten declarer's trump suit and so weaken it that he will be unable to draw trumps. Favorable conditions for a force exist when the leader has, or infers in his partner's hand, four or more trumps plus a long side suit which can probably be established quickly.

Even the rule of not leading from suit and tenace positions is often disregarded when the bidding and texture of the player's hand indicate the advisability of trying the force game. Tenaces such as A Q x x x and A J x x should still be avoided, but from a five- or six-card suit headed by the Ace, King or Queen, there is a great deal of hope if the suit is started immediately. The following are typical hands for the force game, spades being trumps. The correct lead is underlined.

1.	♠ A J 7 4	2.	♠ 10 8 5 2	3.	♠ K 5 4 2
	♡ 8		♡ A 6		♡ 7
	◇ K 10 8 4 3		◇ Q 10 5 3		◇ K Q 7 5 4 3
	♣ 10 7 2		♣ A K 4		♣ 9 2

The technique of the force game is to establish the long suit as quickly as possible and then to lead it at every opportunity, each time making declarer use one of his long trumps to stop the suit.

The Waiting Lead

The lead of a worthless doubleton, despite its traditionally bad reputation, is an ideal waiting lead. In a hand such as ♠ K Q 8 ♡ 9 7 ◇ A Q 6 5 ♣ Q 9 6 2 it saves, at no risk, the valuable tenace positions in other suits, and has a further advantage of occasionally producing a ruffing trick. This is the reason a worthless doubleton should be preferred as a waiting lead to a three-card suit.

When the hand contains tenaces but no plain-suit double-ton, a trump from two or three small cards is an excellent waiting lead, and has this in common with the lead from any other worthless suit: it never costs a trick in the suit led. The worst it can do is save the declarer a guess on a two-way finesse. A singleton trump, however, is one of the worst leads in bridge, often trapping Q x x or J x x x in partner's hand when declarer, if unassisted by the lead, would have played for a drop rather than finesse.

A waiting trump lead should not be confused with the de-fenders' trump defense. In many hands a trump is the best opening lead to stop ruffers in dummy or to make declarer's and dummy's trumps fall together when he is planning a cross-ruff. A trump is led as part of the anti-ruff game in the follow-ing situations:

1. When the bidding shows that dummy's hand consists mainly of distributional strength, short suits and trumps.
2. When declarer has only a four-card suit and dummy has at most four trumps.
3. Against preëmptive bids, when the trump suit is prob-ably solid and it is desirable to throw declarer in and make him lead some other suits.

As effective as a worthless trump suit is a holding such as A x x or K x x, from which the small card can be led to remove declarer's trumps without great danger of sacrificing a trick.

Slam Leads

Against slam bids the choice between attacking and protect-ing leads becomes more difficult than ever because the amount of time available for suit establishment is usually so very small.

Against a trump small slam, when it is obvious or probable that declarer will have to give up a trick to establish an essen-tial suit, it is desirable to try to establish a trick on the opening lead to be cashed when the defenders get in with their lone stopper. A lead from a King or a Queen, in the hope that partner will hold the other honor, is therefore often preferable to the safer lead of a doubleton or a sequence such as J 10 9. A singleton is often the proper lead as the only hope.

Against a notrump slam an attacking lead of this type is too dangerous, since any guarded honor may turn out to be a stopper, and except with something like K-Q in one suit and Ace in another, seek a waiting lead. The worst lead against a notrump small slam is often an Ace.

See also "Lead-Directing Doubles" on page 522.

Later Leads and Defense

The old rule about leading to dummy's weakness is not a bad rule at all, though it is of course abandoned when a waiting lead, an entry-destroying play, the anti-ruff game or the force game is indicated. If you must lead to strength, when possible, lead up to a solid suit.

A lead through dummy's strength is likewise good if it does not aid declarer in the establishment of long cards. Thus, a lead through A Q x is proper, but a lead through A Q x x x should be avoided except when the object is to establish exactly one immediate trick.

Finessing Partner's Lead

An honor is most valuable when it can be used to capture an opponent's lower-ranking honor. On a lead through an honor in dummy, third-hand should try to save a higher honor whenever possible until such time as he may cover dummy's honor with it.

For this reason, in Figure 1 when dummy plays low East plays the Jack. It will not win the trick unless West has the Queen but the Ace is saved to capture the King later. If the Ace were played at once and South had the Queen he would win two tricks in the suit anyway. On the same reasoning, in Figure 2 East should finesse the 9, saving the King until dummy plays the Queen. In Figure 3, West does not put up the Ace but plays the 8 and lets dummy's King win a trick, for it would have won sooner or later in any case, and by saving his Ace West may prevent South's winning a second trick with the Queen if he has it.

1.

```
                 K 7 5
      West         N
      Leads   W    E    A J 6
        2           S
```

2.

```
                 Q 8 4
      West         N
      Leads   W    E    K 9 3
        2           S
```

3.

```
                 K 7 5
                   N         East
      A 10 8   W    E       Leads
                   S           2
```

South plays 6

DEFENDER'S TRUMP MANAGEMENT

A defender should not overruff with a high trump when that trump is valuable as a guard to a lower trump in the same hand.

1.   ♠ 7 2   2.   ♠ 8 7

           N   N

♠ Q 9 5 4 W   E ♠ 8   ♠ K 2 W   E ♠ J 10 9

           S   S

      ♠ A K J 10 6 3   ♠ A Q 6 5 4 3

In Figure 1 East leads a suit in which both South and West are void. South ruffs with the ♠ 10. West should not overruff. His ♠ Queen will never win but one trick, but he needs it in his hand as a guard to the ♠ 9. If West overruffs, South later draws his remaining trumps with the ♠ A K J; if West discards and saves all four spades he will later win two tricks. In Figure 2 spades are trumps and again East leads a suit in which both South and West are void. South ruffs with the ♠ 3. To many players it seems a shame to waste a King on a three but nevertheless West should overruff. There is no card in his hand which the King will serve to guard, and he may as well win a trick with it now as later. If West does not overruff South leads the Ace and a low spade and later clears the suit with the Queen. If West overruffs, East will win a trick later and the total trump tricks for East and West will be two instead of one.

Ruffing with a high trump may force declarer to overruff with one of his own high trumps at the cost of a trick.

               ♠ 6 5

               ♡ 9 8

               ◇ J 6

    ♠ Q   N   ♠ J 9 7 4 3

    ♡ 10 7 5 3 W   E ♡ 6

    ◇ A   S   ◇ —

               ♠ —

               ♡ A K Q J 4 2

               ◇ —

This example shows how a seemingly impregnable trump suit can be destroyed by a forced high overruff. South has plenty of trumps to draw West's supply. But it is West's lead and he leads the Ace of diamonds. It is a high card but East nevertheless ruffs with the ♡ 6. To overruff South must use one of his honors and now West's ten is sufficiently guarded and wins a trick.

In this case West had no choice but to lead the ◇ Ace and it took considerable perspicacity on East's part to ruff it. In such positions whenever possible a player who wishes his partner to ruff high should lead a low card so that his partner will not be tempted to discard.

CULBERTSON SYSTEM OF LEADS

Opening Leads
Against Trump Contracts

CLASSIFIED IN ORDER OF PREFERENCE

1. A-K-Q, A-K-J, A-K-x-x-x *with or without others.*
2. A trump *when declarer has bid strongly in two suits, of which dummy has supported only one.*
3. A *or* A-K *alone, with sure entry to partner's hand and at least one ruffer.*
4. K-Q-J (-x-x-x)
5. A-x, K *or singleton[1] of partner's suit.*
6. Singleton *with trump entry and at least one ruffer.*
7. Q-J-10 *or more, with no probable entry.*
8. Partner's suit, *with 4 or less.*
9. Q-J-10 *or more, with or without an entry.*
10. J-10-9-x *with or without others.*
11. A-K-x-x *or* A-K-x[2]
12. K-Q-10 *with or without others.*
13. Singleton *with 3 or more ruffers.*
14. Doubleton *containing no honor.*
15. A-x *with trump entry or when partner has bid strongly.*
16. A *or* A-K *alone.*
17. 10-9-8-x
18. J-10-8-x
19. Trump x-x-x, x-x, A-x-x, K-x-x—*not a singleton.*
20. *Any suit which your partner has supported.*[3]
21. J-10, J-10-x, *or* Q-J *alone.*
22. A-x-x—*under-lead* A-x-x, A-x-x-x *when bidding indicates that dummy has a strong hand with balanced distribution.*
23. 10-9-7-x
24. x-x-x
25. x-x-x-x
26. Q-J-9-x
27. K-Q-x-x-x

Opening Leads (Continued)

28. J-10-x-x
29. K-x-x-x-(x)
30. Q-x-x-x-(x)
31. 10-x-x-x-(x)
32. J-x-x-x-(x)

33. Q-J-x (x-x)
34. A-x-x-x-x or more.
35. K-x-x
36. Q-10-x
37. 10-x-x

[1] A singleton of partner's suit should not be led except when the object is to get a ruff.
[2] A-K-x is often not so good as other leads ranked below it in this classification.
[3] A suit headed by A-Q or A-J should usually not be opened, unless partner has supported it very strongly.

LEADS TO BE AVOIDED

A-Q or A-Q-J
Singleton trump
Q-x-x or J-x-x
Q-x or J-x
A-x except as in case 17

K-J-x or K-J-10-x
A-J-x or A-J-10
K-Q-x or K-Q-x-x
K-x
K alone

A suit bid by the opponents

LEADS AGAINST SLAM BIDS

Either six- or seven-bids. Exceptions are marked (*).
See also "Lead-Directing Doubles," page 522.

	SUIT SLAM	NOTRUMP
Singleton	Good*	Very bad
Sequence of 3 honors...........	Good	Good
Partner's suit	Good	Good
Ace	Fair†	Very bad†
Doubleton	Fair	Fair
Sequence of 2 honors...........	Fair*	Bad
Trump 10-x-x or x-x-x..........	Good	
Trump J-x, 10-x, x-x or x.......	Bad	
Q-x-x-x-x or lower............	Good	Fair
K-x-x-x or Q-x-x-x............	Fair*	Very bad
x-x-x or x-x-x-x...............	Fair	Fair

* Very bad against grand slams.   † Very good against grand slams.

Opening Leads
Against Notrump Contracts

CLASSIFIED IN ORDER OF PREFERENCE

The <u>CARD</u> to lead is underlined

1. An established suit *(lead the Ace).*
2. <u>A</u>-K-J-x-x-x-x *or better.*
3. <u>A</u>-K-Q-10-x, <u>A</u>-K-Q-x, <u>A</u>-K-Q-x-x. *But from A-K-Q-x-x lead fourth best with no entry* if partner probably has one.*
4. A-<u>Q</u>-J-10-x-x, A-<u>Q</u>-J-x-x-x-x. *But with a sure entry,* lead Ace.*
5. <u>K</u>-Q-J-x-(x-x)
6. A-<u>K</u>-x-x-x-x-x, <u>K</u>-Q-x-x-x-x-x, or <u>Q</u>-J-x-x-x-x-x *(7-card suit).*
7. <u>Q</u>-J-10-x-x *(or more).*
8. A-K-x-<u>x</u>-x, A-Q-x-<u>x</u>-x, A-J-x-<u>x</u>-x, K-Q-x-<u>x</u>-x *(5-card or 6-card suits).*
9. <u>Q</u>-J-10-x, <u>K</u>-Q-10-x, <u>Q</u>-J-9-x-x *or more.*
10. Any six-card suit *with an entry.**
11. Q-x-x-<u>x</u>-x, J-10-x-<u>x</u>-x *or better, with an entry.**
12. <u>J</u>-10-9-x, Q-10-x-<u>x</u>, x-x-x-<u>x</u>-x, *or better, with an entry.**
13. x-x-x-<u>x</u> *(from strong hands only).*
14. x-<u>x</u>-x, <u>10</u>-x-x, <u>J</u>-10-x.
15. <u>x</u>-x, <u>J</u>-10, <u>10</u>-x *(not Q-x or higher).*
16. <u>Q</u>-J-x, <u>K</u>-Q-x, <u>A</u>-K-x *(usually avoid).*

AVOID THE FOLLOWING LEADS

In the order named

(Except as gambling *desperation leads*).

1. Doubleton honor leads.
2. Three-card suits headed by one high honor, or two honors not in sequence.
3. Four-card suits headed by only the Ace, King or Queen, without Jack or 10.
4. Weak five-card suits in entryless hands.

---

* An Ace, a King, and often a Q-J-x is a reasonably certain entry.

THE INTERNATIONAL CODE

LAWS OF
CONTRACT BRIDGE

COPYRIGHT 1948 AND
PROMULGATED IN THE WESTERN HEMISPHERE
BY THE NATIONAL LAWS COMMISSION

AMERICAN EDITION

*Authorized Publishers in the Western Hemisphere and in the
Republic of the Philippines*
THE JOHN C. WINSTON COMPANY

PROMULGATING BODIES

THE NATIONAL LAWS COMMISSION

HAROLD S. VANDERBILT, GEOFFREY MOTT-SMITH, *Chairmen*

RUSSELL J. BALDWIN	ALBERT H. MOREHEAD
WALTER BEINECKE	HAROLD C. RICHARD
MAJ. GEN. ALFRED M. GRUENTHER U. S. A.	A. M. SOBEL
LEE HAZEN	WALDEMAR VON ZEDTWITZ

RUBBER BRIDGE COMMITTEE FOR THE PROMULGATION OF THE AMERICAN EDITION

HAROLD S. VANDERBILT	WALDEMAR VON ZEDTWITZ
WALTER BEINECKE	LEE HAZEN
HAROLD C. RICHARD	GEOFFREY MOTT-SMITH

MAJ. GEN. ALFRED M. GRUENTHER U. S. A.

CARD COMMITTEE OF THE PORTLAND CLUB

SIR A. NOEL MOBBS, K.C.V.O., O.B.E., *Chairman*

LT. COL. J. C. CRAIGIE, M.C.	H. H. RENSHAW
DR. N. WOOD HILL	J. O. HASTIE
ARNOLD WARD	F. E. PERRY
K. HURST-BROWN	GEOFFREY BUTLER
SIR GUY DOMVILLE, BT.	COL. G. G. J. WALSHE

BARON R. DE NEXON

EXECUTIVE COMMITTEE OF THE EUROPEAN BRIDGE LEAGUE

SIR A. NOEL MOBBS, K.C.V.O., O.B.E. (President and Chairman)	GREAT BRITAIN
BARON R. DE NEXON	FRANCE
EMILE HENRIQUES	SWEDEN
J. ODRY	BELGIUM
H. DEDICHEN (Honorary Secretary)	DENMARK

540

Preface to the American Edition

The new International Laws of Contract Bridge, effective as of October 1, 1948, replace the 1943 American edition of the Laws.

The first International Laws of Contract Bridge were promulgated in 1932 by The Whist Club, New York, the Portland Club, London, and the Commission Française du Bridge, Paris, and, in 1935, the same clubs issued a revised edition. In 1943 this code was replaced, in America, by a code promulgated jointly by The Whist Club and the National Laws Commission of the American Contract Bridge League.

By an agreement made in 1947 between The Whist Club and the American Contract Bridge League, the National Laws Commission, to whom The Whist Club delegated its title to prepare and publish the code presented herein, becomes the sole promulgating body of that code for America. The Portland Club and the European Bridge League have joined in the preparation and promulgation of the new International Code, temporarily suspended in 1943 owing to the war.

The National Laws Commission elected to its membership three members of The Whist Club committee on laws nominated by The Whist Club.

The Laws of Contract Bridge as presented in this book apply only to Rubber Bridge. Duplicate Bridge is governed by a separate International Code, also promulgated by the National Laws Commission. However, the two codes are identical in substance so far as the nature of the respective games makes it possible. When the 1948 edition of the Duplicate Bridge Laws is not available to a duplicate director he should follow the provisions of this book wherever they may apply, rather than any previous edition of the Duplicate Bridge Laws.

The National Laws Commission wishes to acknowledge the valuable contributions made in the preparation of the 1948 Laws by William E. McKenney, its chairman until 1948.

The Scope of the Laws

The Laws are designed to define correct procedure and to provide an adequate remedy in all cases where a player accidentally, carelessly or inadvertently disturbs the proper course of the game, or gains an unintentional but nevertheless unfair advantage. An offending player should be ready to pay a prescribed penalty graciously.

The Laws are not designed to prevent dishonorable practices and there are no penalties to cover intentional violations. In the absence of penalty, moral obligations are strongest. Ostracism is the ultimate remedy for intentional offenses.

The object of the Proprieties is twofold: to familiarize players with the customs and etiquette of the game, generally accepted over a long period of years; and to enlighten those who might otherwise fail to appreciate when or how they are improperly conveying information to their partners—often a far more reprehensible offense than a violation of a law.

When these principles are appreciated, arguments are avoided and the pleasure which the game offers is materially enhanced.

PART I

THE DRAW, THE SHUFFLE, THE CUT, THE DEAL

THE PACK—RANK OF CARDS AND SUITS

1. Contract Bridge is played by four players with a pack of 52 cards, comprising 13 cards in each of 4 suits. The suits rank downwards in the order—Spades (♠), Hearts (♡), Diamonds (♢), Clubs (♣). The cards of each suit rank downwards in the order—Ace, King, Queen, Jack, 10, 9, 8, 7, 6, 5, 4, 3, 2. When practicable, two packs with distinguishable backs are used.

THE DRAW*

2. Before every rubber, each player draws a card from a shuffled pack spread face downwards on the table. A drawn card should not be exposed until all players have drawn. If a player exposes more than one card, or draws one of the four cards at either end of the pack, or draws a card from the other pack, he must draw again. In drawing, equal cards rank according to suit.

PARTNERSHIPS

3. The two players who draw the highest cards play as partners against the other two. The player with the highest card deals first and has the right to choose his seat and the pack with which he will deal. He may consult his partner but, having announced his decision, must abide by it. His partner sits opposite him. Thereafter, the opponents may, after consultation, determine their respective occupancy of the two remaining seats.

THE SHUFFLE

4. The pack for each deal is prepared by the player on the left of its dealer, if practicable while the other pack is being dealt. Preparing a pack consists of collecting the cards, shuffling them, and placing the shuffled pack face downwards on the left of the next dealer. The cards should be shuffled thoroughly and in full view of all players, but without exposing the face of any card.

5. A properly prepared pack should not be disturbed until its dealer picks it up for his deal, at which time he is entitled to the final shuffle. No player may shuffle a pack other than its dealer and the player on his left.

THE CUT

6. A pack must always be cut immediately before it is dealt. The dealer presents it to the player on his right, who lifts off a portion and places it

---

* If more than four persons desire to play, it is customary to follow the Rules for Club Procedure (page 560) to determine which of them shall have the right to play.

on the table toward the dealer beside the bottom portion. Each portion must contain at least four cards. The dealer completes the cut by placing the bottom portion uppermost.

NEW SHUFFLE—NEW CUT

7. Before the first card is dealt, any player may demand a new shuffle or a new cut. There must be a new shuffle and cut if a card is faced in cutting, or if there is a redeal. When there is a new shuffle, only the dealer may shuffle.

THE DEAL

8. The dealer must deal the cards face downwards, one at a time in rotation into four separate hands of 13 cards each, the first card to the player on his left and the last card to himself. If he deals two cards simultaneously or consecutively to the same player, he may rectify the error, provided he does so promptly and to the satisfaction of his opponents.

9. The dealer must not allow the face of any card to be seen while he is dealing. Until the deal is completed, no player may look at the face of any card, and no one but the dealer may touch any card except to correct or preclude an irregularity.

CHANGING THE DEALER

10. The turn to deal passes in rotation unless there is a redeal, in which case the same dealer redeals.

CHANGING THE PACK

11. The packs should be used alternately unless there is a redeal. The pack originally belonging to a side must be restored if reclaimed, but a deal may not be stopped to restore a pack. A pack containing a distinguishable damaged card must be replaced.

PART II

GENERAL LAWS COVERING IRREGULARITIES

REDEAL

12. There must be a redeal:

(a) If, before the last card is dealt, a redeal is demanded because a player is dealing out of turn or with an uncut pack.

(b) If it is ascertained before the last card is dealt that the cards have not been dealt correctly, or that a card is faced in the pack or elsewhere.

(c) If it is ascertained before the first call is duly made that a player has picked up another player's hand and seen a card in it.

(d) If it is ascertained before the cards have been mixed together that one player has picked up too many cards, another too few; or that the pack, when the deal began, did not conform in every respect to the requirements of section 1.

(e) If the players have allowed their hands to be mixed together before finding a missing card, or in the belief that a redeal is in order.

There may not be a redeal except as provided above.

MISSING CARD

13. A missing card, when found, is deemed to belong to the deficient hand.

When clause (d) or (e) of section 12 applies, there must be a redeal.

When neither clause applies, the deal stands, and, if the missing card was found in a trick, the defective trick law (section 80 or 81) applies. The missing card may become a penalty card under section 26 or 67, or failure to have played it may constitute a revoke. It must be placed in the deficient hand unless it becomes a penalty card or is found in a trick that stands as played.

SURPLUS CARD

14. If a player has too many cards, there must be a redeal unless he has omitted to play to a trick, in which case the defective trick law (section 80 or 81) applies.

DRAWING ATTENTION TO AN IRREGULARITY

15. When an irregularity is committed, any player (except dummy if he has looked at another player's hand) may draw attention to it and give or obtain information as to the law covering it. The fact that the offending side draws attention to its own irregularity does not in any way affect the rights of the opponents.

ENFORCEMENT OF A PENALTY

16. Either opponent individually (but not dummy) may select or enforce a penalty. If the opponents consult as to penalty selection or enforcement, or if either opponent waives the penalty; the right to penalize is cancelled, but the rectification provisions (if any) of the applicable section still apply.

17. After attention has been called to an irregularity, no player may call or play until all questions in regard to rectification and penalty enforcement have been determined.

18. The penalty provisions of the laws apply only after agreement on the fact that an irregularity has been committed, and after specific statement of the penalty to be applied.

19. All questions as to what course to follow must be settled by the players before the game continues. A penalty once paid or other action once taken stands, even though at some later time it is discovered to have been incorrect.

IMPROPER REMARKS AND GESTURES

20. If by a remark or unmistakable gesture a player other than declarer: discloses his intentions or desires, or the nature of an unfaced hand, or the

presence or absence of a card in an unfaced hand; or improperly suggests a lead, play, or line of play; or improperly directs attention to the cards on a trick to which his partner has yet to play:

(a) If the offense occurred before the auction closed, (penalty) either opponent may require the offending side to pass whenever it is its turn to call; and if the offending side become defenders, declarer may require or forbid the opening lead of a specified suit.

(b) If the offense occurred after the auction closed, (penalty) declarer or either defender, as the case may be, may require the offender's partner to withdraw any lead or play which may have been suggested by the improper remark or gesture, and to substitute a card which does not conform to the improper suggestion. This penalty may be exacted on any trick subsequent to the offense but only on one such trick. The offender's partner may not be required to withdraw his card from a trick to which an opponent has played after him. Before this penalty may be enforced, a majority of the players must agree as to what lead, play or line of play has been improperly suggested.

PART III

THE AUCTION

DURATION OF AUCTION

21. The auction begins when the last card of a correct deal has been placed on the table. The dealer makes the first call, and thereafter each player calls in rotation. After the first call has been made, the auction continues until three players have passed in rotation. This closes the auction.

PROCEDURE AFTER AUCTION IS CLOSED

22. After the auction is closed:

(a) If no player has bid, the hands are abandoned and the turn to deal passes in rotation.

(b) If any player has bid, the last bid becomes the contract and the play begins.

BIDS

23. Each bid must name a number of odd tricks, from one to seven, and a denomination, and must supersede any previous bid by naming either a greater number of odd tricks or the same number in a higher denomination. A bid that supersedes the previous bid is sufficient; one that does not is insufficient. The denominations rank downwards in order: Notrump, Spades, Hearts, Diamonds, Clubs.

DOUBLES AND REDOUBLES

24. A player may double only if the last preceding bid was made by an opponent and no call other than a pass has intervened. A player may re-

double only if the last preceding call other than a pass was a double by an opponent.

25. All doubles and redoubles are nullified by a proper subsequent bid. If there is no subsequent bid, the scoring value of the contract is increased as provided in section 98.

CARD EXPOSED DURING THE AUCTION

26. If during the auction a player faces a card on the table, or sees the face of a card belonging to his partner:

(a) If an Ace, King, Queen or Jack, or a lower card prematurely led, or more than one card;* (penalty) the owner's partner must pass when next it is his turn to call. Every such card must be left face up on the table until the auction closes; and if its owner is then a defender, it becomes a penalty card.

(b) If a single card, lower than a Jack and not prematurely led, there is no penalty.

IMPROPER CALLS†

IMPROPER CALL PREMATURELY OVERCALLED IN ROTATION

27. If a player calls before the penalty for an improper call by his right-hand opponent has been enforced (see section 17), the auction proceeds as though it had been a proper call; except that if the improper call was a bid of more than seven, or a double or redouble made when only a pass or bid could be a proper call, the auction proceeds as though the improper call had been a pass.

CHANGING A CALL

28. If a player changes a call in any way and does so practically in the same breath, his last call stands. There is no penalty unless he has changed to an improper call, in which case the appropriate "improper calls" section applies.

29. If a player changes a call in any way, and does not do so practically in the same breath, the change of call is void, and:

(a) If the first call was improper, the appropriate "improper calls" section applies.

(b) If the first call was a proper call, either the offender must allow his first call to stand, in which case (penalty) his partner must pass when next it is his turn to call; or the offender must substitute any other proper call, in which case (penalty) his partner must pass whenever it is his turn to call.

---

* If two (or more) cards are faced or seen at different times, clause (a) applies to both of them even though one has been picked up as provided in clause (b).

† All possible improper calls are listed under this heading. Calls not recognized by nor dealt with in these laws are merely improper remarks. The auction proceeds as if an improper remark had not been made, unless the remark is sufficiently informative to warrant the imposition of a penalty under section 20 (a).

INSUFFICIENT BID

30. If a player makes an insufficient bid, he must substitute either a sufficient bid or a pass.[1] If he substitutes—

(a) The lowest sufficient bid in the same denomination, there is no penalty.

(b) Any other bid, (penalty) the offender's partner must pass whenever it is his turn to call.

(c) A pass, (penalty) the offender's partner must pass whenever it is his turn to call; and if the offending side become the defenders, declarer may require or forbid the opening lead of a specified suit.

CALL OUT OF ROTATION

31. A call out of rotation is void. The auction reverts to the player whose turn it is to call; and—

(a) If a player has passed out of rotation before any player has bid, or when it was the turn of the opponent on his right to call, (penalty) the offender must pass when next it is his turn to call.[2]

(b) If a player has made any call out of rotation other than a pass listed in (a), (penalty) the offender's partner must pass whenever it is his turn to call.[3]

32. A call is not out of rotation when made without waiting for the right-hand opponent to pass, if he is required to pass because of a law infringement.

33. If a player, whose turn it was to call, calls before attention has been drawn to a call out of rotation by his left-hand opponent, the auction proceeds as though that opponent had not called.

SIMULTANEOUS CALLS

34. A call made simultaneously with another player's proper call is deemed to be a subsequent call.

NAMING BID INCORRECTLY IN DOUBLING[4]

35. If a player in doubling or redoubling names an incorrect number of tricks or a wrong denomination, he is deemed to have doubled or redoubled the bid as made.

DOUBLING WHEN THE ONLY PROPER CALL IS A PASS OR BID

36. If a player doubles or redoubles a bid which his side has already doubled or redoubled, (penalty) he must substitute any proper call, and his partner must pass whenever it is his turn to call. In addition, if the

---

[1] As provided in section 18, a player is entitled to select his substituted call after the applicable penalties have been stated. Any call he may have substituted previously is void, unless his left-hand opponent has overcalled it, in which case section 27 applies.

[2] Example: North (dealer) 1 Heart, South pass. The pass is void, and the auction reverts to East. After East has called, South must pass. Thereafter, North and South may in rotation make any proper call.

[3] Example: North (dealer) 1 Heart, South 1 Spade. The 1-Spade bid is void, and the auction reverts to East. After East has called, South may make any proper call. Thereafter, North must pass whenever it is his turn to call, but South may make any proper call whenever it is his turn to call.

[4] It is improper to state the number of tricks or the denomination in doubling.

offender elects to pass, either opponent may cancel all previous doubles and redoubles.

37. If a player doubles his partner's bid, redoubles an undoubled bid, or doubles or redoubles when there has been no bid, (penalty) the offender must substitute any proper call, and his partner must pass whenever it is his turn to call.

BID, DOUBLE OR REDOUBLE WHEN REQUIRED TO PASS BID OF MORE THAN SEVEN

38. If a player bids more than seven, or bids, doubles or redoubles when required by law to pass; the offender is deemed to have passed, and (penalty) the offending side must pass whenever it is its turn to call, and if the offender becomes a defender, declarer may require or forbid the opening lead of a specified suit.

DOUBLY IMPROPER CALL

39. If a player makes a call subject to penalty under two or more "improper calls" sections, either section may be applied but not both.

CALL AFTER THE AUCTION IS CLOSED

40. A call made after the auction is closed is cancelled. If it is a pass by a defender, or any call by a contractor, there is no penalty. If it is a bid, double or redouble by a defender, (penalty) declarer may require or forbid the other defender to lead a specified suit when first it is the latter's turn to lead.

REVIEWING THE AUCTION

41. A player who does not hear a call distinctly may forthwith require it to be repeated. There is no redress for a call based on a misunderstanding or on misinformation.

42. A player is entitled to have previous calls restated either when it is his turn to call, or after the auction closes but before the opening lead has been duly made. His request should be responded to only by an opponent. Dummy, or a player required by law to pass, should not ask to have calls restated, but may review the auction at an opponent's request and should correct errors in restatement.

43. After the opening lead, calls may not be restated, but declarer or a defender is entitled to be informed what the contract is and whether, but not by whom, it was doubled or redoubled.

PART IV

THE PLAY

COMMENCEMENT OF PLAY

44. After the auction closes, the defender on declarer's left makes the opening lead. After the opening lead dummy spreads his hand in front of him on the table, face up and grouped in suits with the trumps on his right. Declarer plays both of the contractors' hands.

DUMMY'S RIGHTS

45. Dummy should refrain from all comment and from taking any active part in the play, except that he may:

(a) Give or obtain information as to fact or law.

(b) Question players regarding revokes as provided in section 71.

(c) Draw attention to an irregularity, or try to prevent one apparently about to be committed.*

Dummy forfeits these rights if he looks at a card in another player's hand.

DUMMY'S LIMITATIONS

46. Dummy should not exchange hands with declarer, lean over to see a defender's cards, leave his seat to watch declarer play, or, on his own initiative, look at the face of a card in any other player's hand. If dummy, as a result of any such act, sees a card in any other player's hand, and thereafter:

(a) Is the first to draw attention to a defender's irregularity, declarer may not enforce any penalty for the offense.

(b) Warns declarer not to lead from the wrong hand, (penalty) either defender may choose the hand from which declarer shall lead.

(c) Is the first to ask declarer if a play from his hand constitutes a revoke, and the revoke card is consequently withdrawn, (penalty) either defender may require declarer to substitute his highest or lowest correct card.

LEADS AND PLAYS

THE SEQUENCE AND PROCEDURE OF PLAY

47. The leader to a trick may play any card in his hand. After a lead, each other hand in rotation plays a card, and the four cards so played constitute a trick.

48. In playing to a trick, each player must if possible follow suit. This obligation overrides all other requirements of the laws. If unable to follow suit, a player may play any card.

49. A trick containing a trump is won by the hand playing the highest trump. A trick that does not contain a trump is won by the hand playing the highest card of the suit led. The hand winning a trick leads to the next trick.

PLAYED CARD

50. A card in any hand is played when named as the one a player proposes to play; but a player may change his designation if he does so practically in the same breath.

51. A card in any unfaced hand is played when it touches the table face upwards after being detached from the remaining cards with apparent intent to play; a defender's card so detached is also played as soon as his partner sees its face.

52. A card in dummy or any other faced hand is played when touched unless for a purpose other than play either manifest or mentioned.

---

* Example: He may warn declarer against leading from the wrong hand, but only when it is apparent that declarer is about to do so.

TAKING BACK PLAYED CARD

53. A played card may not be withdrawn except:
    (a) To comply with a penalty.
    (b) To correct a revoke.
    (c) To correct the error of playing more than one card to a trick.
    (d) To substitute another card after an opponent has corrected either a revoke or a failure to comply with a lead or play penalty.

PREMATURE LEAD OR PLAY BY A DEFENDER

54. If a defender leads to the next trick before his partner has played to the current trick, or plays out of rotation before his partner has played, (penalty) declarer may require the offender's partner to play:
    (a) His highest card of the suit led; or
    (b) His lowest card of the suit led; or
    (c) A card of another specified suit.
If declarer has played from both contractors' hands, a defender is not subject to penalty for playing before his partner.

LEAD OUT OF TURN

55. A lead out of turn may be treated as a correct lead. It must be so treated if the non-offending side plays a card before attention is drawn to the irregularity.*

56. If either defender requires declarer to retract his lead out of turn, the card wrongly led is replaced without penalty; and if declarer has led from the wrong hand, he must lead from the correct hand and (penalty), if he can, a card of the same suit. A defender's drawing attention to declarer's lead out of turn is equivalent to requiring its retraction.

57. If declarer requires a defender to retract his lead out of turn:
    (a) If it was a contractor's turn to lead, declarer leads from the correct hand and the card led out of turn becomes a penalty card.
    (b) If it was the other defender's turn to lead, (penalty) declarer may forbid the lead of that suit, in which case the card wrongly led is picked up; or may treat the card led out of turn as a penalty card, in which case any card may be led.

SIMULTANEOUS LEADS OR PLAYS

58. A lead or play made simultaneously with another player's proper lead or play is deemed to be subsequent to it. If a defender leads or plays two or more cards simultaneously, he may play either card, and the other card becomes a penalty card.

INABILITY TO LEAD OR PLAY AS REQUIRED

59. If a player is unable to lead or play as required to comply with a penalty, either because he has no card of the required suit or because of his obligation to follow suit, he may play any correct card. The penalty is satisfied, except in the case of a penalty card, which must be played at the first legal opportunity.

---

*If, after an opening lead by the wrong defender, declarer exposes his hand, see section **65.**

60. If declarer plays from either hand before enforcing a lead or play penalty, he is deemed to waive the penalty.

61. If a defender plays to a contractor's lead out of turn after declarer has been required to retract it, the defender's card becomes a penalty card.

62. A play by a member of the offending side, before a penalty has been enforced, does not affect the right of the non-offending side to enforce a penalty.

EXPOSED CARDS

DECLARER EXPOSING CARDS

63. Declarer is never subject to penalty for exposure of a card, and no card of declarer's ever becomes a penalty card.

64. If declarer plays more than one card he must designate which is his play, and must restore any other card to his hand.

65. If declarer exposes his hand after an opening lead by the wrong defender, and before dummy has spread any part of his hand, dummy becomes declarer.

66. If declarer intentionally exposes his hand otherwise than as provided in the preceding section, it is treated as a claim or concession of tricks and section 88 applies.

DEFENDER EXPOSING CARDS

67. If a defender faces a card on the table, or sees the face of a card belonging to his partner before he is entitled to see it in the normal course of play or penalty enforcement; any such card becomes a penalty card, except as otherwise provided in these laws.*

DISPOSITION OF A PENALTY CARD

68. A penalty card must be left face upwards on the table until played. A defender should not pick up a penalty card and restore it to his hand; but if he does so, and if declarer plays from his own hand or dummy before requiring that the card be faced on the table again, such card ceases to be a penalty card.

69. A penalty card must be played at the first opportunity, whether in leading, following suit, discarding or trumping. The play of a penalty card is always subject to the obligation to follow suit, or to comply with a lead or play penalty. If a defender can play two or more penalty cards, declarer may designate which one is to be played.

DEFENDER IMPROPERLY EXPOSING HIS HAND

70. If a defender improperly exposes his remaining card or cards, declarer may treat the remaining cards of either defender as penalty cards. The hand of the other defender, if exposed, may be picked up.

---

* Exceptions to section 67: A card led out of turn may be treated as a correct lead (section 55) or may be picked up (section 57-b). An exposed card may not be treated as a penalty card if dummy improperly (section 46-a) draws attention to it, or to the irregularity that caused its exposure.

THE REVOKE*

INQUIRIES REGARDING A REVOKE

71. Any player, including dummy, may ask a player who has failed to follow suit whether he has a card of the suit led, and may demand that an opponent correct his revoke.

CORRECTING A REVOKE

72. A player must correct his revoke—

(a) Made in any of the first eleven tricks, if aware of it before it becomes established.

(b) Made in the twelfth trick, if aware of it before the cards have been mixed together. There is no penalty for a revoke made in the twelfth trick and it never becomes established.

73. To correct a revoke, the offender withdraws the revoke card and follows suit with any card. A revoke card from a defender's unfaced hand becomes a penalty card; any other revoke card may be replaced without penalty. The non-offending side may withdraw any card it played after the revoke but before attention was drawn to it.

ACTS THAT ESTABLISH A REVOKE

74. A revoke in any of the first eleven tricks becomes established when the offender or his partner leads or plays to a subsequent trick or signifies his intention of doing so by naming a card, by claiming or conceding a trick, or by exposing a hand.

PROCEDURE WHEN A REVOKE IS ESTABLISHED

75. When a revoke is established, the revoke trick stands as played. It counts in transferring tricks as a trick won "after the revoke."

76. If a revoke becomes established, after play ceases two tricks are transferred to the non-offending side if the revoking side has won two or more tricks after the revoke. One trick only is transferred if the revoking side wins but one trick after the revoke. There is no penalty for an established revoke:

(a) If the revoking side wins no trick after the revoke.

(b) If it is a subsequent revoke in the same suit by the same player.

(c) If attention is first drawn to it after the cards have been mixed together.

(d) If it is made in failing to play any card faced on the table, including a card from dummy's hand or a penalty card.

TRICKS

GATHERING AND ARRANGING TRICKS

77. Each completed trick must be gathered and turned face down on the table by the side winning it. The cards of each turned trick should be kept

---

* The penalty provisions of the revoke law are subject to section 46 if dummy has forfeited his rights. A claim of revoke does not warrant inspection of turned tricks except as permitted in sections 78 and 79.

together so that the trick can be readily identified. All the tricks taken by a side should be arranged together in front of declarer or of one defender in such manner that their number and sequence are apparent.

INSPECTING TRICKS
MIXING CARDS BEFORE A CLAIM IS SETTLED

78. Declarer or either defender may, until his side has led or played a card to the next trick, inspect a trick and inquire what card each hand has played to it. Except as above provided or to account for a surplus or missing card, turned tricks may be inspected before play ceases only with the other side's consent.

79. After play ceases, the tricks and unplayed cards may be inspected to settle a claim of a revoke or of honors, or the number of tricks won or lost. If, after such claim, an opponent so mixes the cards that the claim cannot be proved, it must be allowed.

DEFECTIVE TRICK

80. If a hand has played too many cards to a trick, or has omitted to play to it, and if attention is drawn to the irregularity before a player of each side has played to the next trick, the error must be rectified. A card withdrawn from a defective trick, if played from a defender's unfaced hand, becomes a penalty card.

81. If attention is drawn to a defective trick after a player of each side has played to the next trick, the defective trick stands as played, and:

(a) A hand with too few cards plays the hand out with fewer cards than the other hands, does not play to the final trick (or tricks), and if it wins a trick with its last card the lead passes in rotation.

(b) A hand with too many cards forthwith faces and adds to the defective trick (but without changing its ownership) a card it could properly have played to it.

TRICK APPROPRIATED IN ERROR

82. A trick appropriated by the wrong side must be restored on demand to the side that played the winning card, and, in any case, its scoring value must be credited to that side, subject to section 93.

FAILURE TO COMPLY WITH A LEAD OR PLAY PENALTY

83. If a player is able to lead or play a penalty card, or a card or suit specified by an opponent in conformity with an agreed penalty, but instead plays an incorrect card:

(a) The offender must correct his error if aware of it before he or his partner plays another card. If the incorrect card was played from a defender's unfaced hand, it becomes a penalty card. A card played from the hand on the offender's left may be withdrawn if it was played after the error and before attention was drawn to it.

(b) After the offender or his partner has played another card, the incorrect card may not be withdrawn. After play ceases, (penalty) there is a transfer of tricks to the non-offending side as though the offense were an established revoke (section 76).

CLAIMS AND CONCESSIONS

CONCESSION OF TRICK WHICH CANNOT BE LOST

84. The concession of a trick which cannot be lost by any play of the cards is void if attention is called to the error before the cards have been mixed together.

CONCESSION OF TRICK WHICH HAS BEEN WON

85. If a player concedes a trick he has in fact won (as by claiming nine tricks when his side has already won ten, or conceding defeat of a contract his side has fulfilled), the concession is void. If the score has been entered it may be corrected as provided in section 93.

DEFENDER CLAIMING OR CONCEDING TRICKS

86. A defender may show any or all of his remaining cards to declarer for the purpose of establishing a claim or concession. If a defender makes a claim or concession in any other manner, he may be liable to penalty under section 20.

87. A concession of tricks by a defender is not valid unless his partner accedes. This provision does not preclude the enforcement of a penalty for a defender's irregularity.

DECLARER CLAIMING OR CONCEDING TRICKS

88. If declarer intentionally exposes his hand, specifically claims or concedes one or more of the remaining tricks, or suggests that play may be curtailed, it is deemed to be a claim by declarer; and—

(a) Play should cease; and declarer should place and leave his hand face upwards on the table and forthwith make an adequate statement of his intended line of play.

(b) At any time after declarer's claim a defender may face his hand and may suggest a play to his partner. Declarer may not enforce any penalty for an irregularity committed by a defender whose hand is so faced.

(c) Declarer's claim must be allowed if both defenders accede to it, or if either defender allows his hand to be mixed with other cards.

(d) Either defender may require that play continue, in which case section 89 applies.

89. If either defender requires that play continue after declarer's claim, declarer must play on, leaving his hand face upwards on the table. Declarer may make no play inconsistent with any statement he may have made. Unless declarer has stated his intention to do so at the time of making his claim—

(a) He may not lead a trump while either defender has a trump.

(b) He may not finesse either in the suit led or in trumping the suit led. If declarer attempts to make a play prohibited by this section, either defender may require him to withdraw it, provided neither defender has played a card after it.

PART V

THE SCORE

KEEPING SCORE

90. Each side has a trick score and a premium score. The scores of the respective sides for each rubber should be entered in two adjacent vertical columns, the trick points in descending order below a horizontal line separating the trick and premium scores, the premium points (i.e., all points other than trick points) in ascending order above this line. A scorer should enter scores made by his side in the left-hand column. Whenever a game is scored, a line should be drawn across the trick score of both sides and underneath all trick point entries made in that game, none of which carry over to the next game. Subsequent trick points should be entered only below lines so drawn. Lines drawn prematurely should be forthwith erased.

RECORDING THE SCORE

91. When play ceases, all four players are equally responsible to see that the number of tricks won by each side is correctly determined, and that all scores are promptly and correctly entered in the score or scores, in accordance with the scoring table (section 98).

SCORING TRANSFERRED TRICKS

92. A transferred trick ranks for all scoring purposes as a trick won in play by the side receiving it.

CORRECTING THE SCORE

93. A proven or admitted error in any score may be corrected at any time before the rubber score is agreed, except that: If each player keeping score has made an error in entering or failing to enter a part score, or in omitting to score a game or in awarding one; such an error may not be corrected after the last card of the second succeeding correct deal has been dealt, unless a majority of the players consent.

A GAME—THE RUBBER

94. A game is won by the side which first scores a total of 100 or more trick points for odd tricks bid and won.

95. A rubber ends when a side has won two games, and the winners of the final game add to their score: 500 points if their opponents have won one game, 700 points if their opponents have not won a game. At the end of the rubber the trick and premium points of each side are added. The side with the larger total score wins the rubber, irrespective of the number of games (if any) which it has won. The difference between the two totals represents the number of points won.

EFFECT OF INCORRECT PACK

96. Scores made as a result of hands played with an incorrect pack are not affected by the discovery of the imperfection after the cards have been mixed together.

SCORING AN UNFINISHED RUBBER
PLAYER OBLIGED TO LEAVE

97. If for any reason a rubber is not finished, the score is computed as follows: If but one game has been completed, the winners of that game score 300 points; if but one side has a part score (or scores) in an unfinished game, that side scores 50 points; the trick and premium points of each side are added, and the side with the larger total score wins the difference between the two totals.

98. CONTRACT BRIDGE SCORING TABLE

	Odd Tricks Bid and Won in		Undoubled	Doubled
TRICK POINTS FOR CONTRACTORS	Clubs or Diamonds, each		20	40
	Hearts or Spades, each		30	60
	No Trump { first		40	80
	{ each subsequent		30	60

Redoubling doubles the doubled points for Odd Tricks.
Vulnerability does not affect points for Odd Tricks.
100 Trick Points constitute a game.

	Overtricks	Not Vulnerable	Vulnerable
PREMIUM POINTS FOR CONTRACTORS — DEFENDERS	Undoubled, each	Trick Value	Trick Value
	Doubled, each	100	200
	Making Doubled or Redoubled Contract	50	50
	Undertricks		
	Undoubled, each	50	100
	Doubled { first	100	200
	{ each subsequent	200	300

Redoubling doubles the doubled points for Overtricks and Under-tricks, but does not affect the points for making Doubled Contracts.

PREMIUM POINTS FOR CONTRACTORS HOLDERS	Honors in One Hand { 4 Trump Honors		100
	{ 5 Trump Honors or 4 Aces at Notrump		150
	Slams Bid and Won { Little, not vulnerable 500, vulnerable		750
	{ Grand, not vulnerable 1000, vulnerable		1500
	Rubber Points { Two game		700
	{ Three game		500

Unfinished Rubber—Winners of one game score 300 points.
If but one side has a part score in an unfinished game, it scores 50 points.
Doubling and Redoubling do not affect Honor, Slam, or Rubber points.
Vulnerability does not affect points for Honors.

THE PROPRIETIES

(1) It is reprehensible to profit by information gained as a result of an irregularity committed by one's own side for which no penalty, or a penalty incommensurate with the information gained, is prescribed.

(2) It is improper to infringe a law deliberately, as by making an insufficient bid, whether or not a penalty is prescribed.

(3) A player should refrain from—

 a. Varying the formulae used in calling;*

 b. Calling with special emphasis, inflection or intonation;

 c. Passing or doubling with exceptional haste or reluctance;

 d. Making a call with undue delay which may result in conveying improper information to partner;

 e. Indicating in any way approval or disapproval of partner's call or play;

 f. Giving by word, manner or gesture an indication of the nature of the hand held;

 g. Making a remark or gesture or asking a question from which an inference may be drawn;

 h. Giving unauthorized information as to an incident of the auction or play;

 i. Volunteering information which should be given only in response to a question;

 j. Requesting, except for his own benefit, a review of calls or a placing of cards played to a trick;

 k. An unnecessary hesitation, remark or mannerism which may deceive the opponents;

 l. Attracting attention to the score, except when necessary to do so for his own information;

 m. Calling attention to the number of tricks needed to complete or defeat the contract or to the fact that it has already been fulfilled or defeated;

 n. Playing a card with special emphasis;

 o. Playing with undue delay when the play does not need consideration;

 p. Preparing to gather a trick before all four hands have played to it;

 q. Detaching a card from his hand before it is his turn to lead or play;

 r. Failing to keep the tricks in correct order and distinct from one another, or allowing some to be placed on the opposite side of the table;

 s. Watching the place in a player's hand from which he draws a card, and drawing any inference therefrom;

 t. Making gratuitous comments during the play as to the auction, the adequacy of the contract or the nature of the hand.

(4) It is improper to attempt to conceal a revoke by revoking again, or to conceal a revoke card if a hand is not played out, but there is no obligation to call attention to an established revoke or other irregularity committed by self or partner.

---

* The recommended calling formulae are: "Pass" (avoid "I pass" or "no bid"); "1 heart" (avoid "I bid"); "1 notrump" (avoid "without" or "without a trump"); "double" (avoid stating the number of tricks or the denomination doubled; "6 spades" (avoid "little slam").

(5) It is improper to play out of turn, carelessly or otherwise.

(6) While it is reprehensible to allow partner's hesitation, remark or manner to influence a call, lead or play, it is proper to draw inferences from an opponent's gratuitous hesitation, remark or manner, but such inferences are drawn at one's own risk.

(7) It is proper to warn partner against infringing a law of the game (e.g., against revoking, or against calling, leading or playing out of turn).

(8) All four players are responsible to see that each hand plays a card, and but one, to each trick, and should forthwith correct such an irregularity.

(9) Declarer should play out all hands in which there is any doubt as to the eventual outcome.

(10) Bystanders or members not playing should refrain from making gratuitous remarks. They should not call attention to any irregularity or mistake, or speak on any question of fact or law except when requested to give an opinion.

(11) It is improper to employ, without explaining its meaning to the opponents, a convention in calling or an unusual convention in play, the significance of which may not be clear to them. When applied to a call, the term convention covers a call designed to convey an arbitrary or artificial meaning, or used by a player with the assurance that his partner will not accept it in its natural sense. Such a call is not subject to penalty as an improper remark. It is necessary that a convention so used should be fully understood by the other side, and players using convention calls should be ready to reply fully to a proper inquiry by an opponent as to their meaning or use. Should it be necessary to make such an inquiry during the auction, the partner of the player who has made the convention call should reply. The committee of any Association, Tournament or Club, or a group of persons playing Contract Bridge, may prohibit or restrict the use of conventions which are both generally unrecognized and sufficiently intricate to cause unreasonable delay.

RULES FOR CLUB PROCEDURE

The following rules, governing membership in new and existing tables, have proven satisfactory in club use over a long period of years.

DEFINITIONS

MEMBER—An applicant who has acquired the right to play at a table either immediately or in his turn.

COMPLETE TABLE—A Table with six members.

INCOMPLETE TABLE—A Table with four or five members.

TIME LIMIT ON RIGHT TO PLAY

A. An applicant may not play in a rubber, unless he has become a member of a table before a card is duly drawn for the selection of players or partners.

NEWLY FORMED TABLES

B. If there are more than six applicants, the six highest-ranking ones become members. The four highest-ranking members play the first rubber. Those who have not played, ranked in their order of entry into the room, take precedence over those who have played. The latter rank equally, except that players leaving existing tables to join the new table rank lowest.*

EXISTING TABLES

C. An application establishes membership in a table either forthwith or (if the table is complete) as soon as a vacancy occurs, unless applications in excess of the number required to complete a table are made at the same time, in which case precedence between applicants is established as in the preceding rule.

D. After each rubber place must be made, by the member who has played the greatest number of consecutive rubbers at that table,* for any member who did not play the last rubber, except that a member who has left another existing table must draw cards for the right to play his first rubber with the member who would otherwise have played.

E. If a member breaks up a game by leaving three players at a table, he is not entitled to compete against them for entry at another table.

MEMBERSHIP LIMITED TO ONE TABLE

F. No one can be a member of more than one table at the same time, unless a member consents, on request, to make a fourth at another table and announces his intention of returning to his former table as soon as his place can be filled. Failure to announce such intention results in loss of membership at his former table.

The Laws of Progressive Bridge

The following laws are reprinted by permission of the National Laws Commission.

They are taken from The Laws of Duplicate Contract Bridge and Party Contract Bridge, published by The John C. Winston Company, Philadelphia.

LAW No. 1

ARRANGEMENT OF TABLES

The game is played by two or more tables of four players each. The tables are numbered consecutively from Table No. 1 to the highest number.

COMMENT

It is customary to provide each table with two decks of cards having different backs. The tables should be numbered conspicuously for the conven-

---

* Precedence between those of equal rank is determined by drawing cards, the drawer of the higher-ranking card obtaining precedence.

ience of the players, and each one should be provided with one or more pencils and a score pad showing Contract scoring.

LAW No. 2

TALLY CARDS

Prior to the beginning of play, the game director or committee prepares individual tally cards, one for each player. Each tally card bears a table number and designates a position (North, South, East or West) at the table.

The tally cards may be drawn at random by the players or assigned by the game director, as he prefers. When play is called, each player takes the position assigned by his tally card.

COMMENT

At mixed parties it is customary to arrange the tallies and seat assignments so that a gentleman will always have a lady as a partner and vice versa. This is accomplished by having tallies of two different kinds or colors, one for the ladies and the other for the gentlemen.

LAW No. 3

A ROUND

A round consists of four deals, one by each player. When all tables are through play, the game director gives a signal and the players move to their positions for the next round according to the type of progression used.

COMMENT

Each round should take about 20 minutes and the average session of play is from 6 to 7 rounds.

LAW No. 4

A DEAL PASSED OUT

Only four hands are dealt at each table, one by each player. If a deal is passed out (that is, if all four players pass at their first opportunity to declare), the deal passes to the left and both sides score zero for that deal.

LAW No. 5

METHOD OF PROGRESSION

At the conclusion of each round, the winning pair at Table No. 1 remain and the losing pair move to the last table. At all tables except Table No. 1, the losers remain and the winners move up one table toward Table No. 1.

COMMENT

The above is the standard method of progression, but this may be waived or altered to suit the wishes of the game director or the players. Special tallies may be arranged or obtained, assigning positions for each round in such a way as to give each player as wide a variety of partners as possible. Another method is to have the ladies progress one way and the gentlemen the other way.

LAW No. 6

SELECTION OF PARTNERS

At mixed parties, it is customary but not essential for a gentleman to play with a lady partner and vice versa. If the standard method of progression is used, the visiting lady at each table becomes the partner of the gentleman who remains.

If the players are all of the same sex, the four players at each table draw cards to determine partners at the start of each round. The two new arrivals at each table draw first, and the one drawing higher has choice of seats and is the first dealer; the one drawing lower sits at the left of the first dealer. The two players who remain at the table from the preceding round then draw, the higher becoming the partner of the dealer. Thus all players change partners after each round.

COMMENT

Since the chief function of progressive bridge is social, it is preferable to change partners at each round. However, if for some reason a pair contest is desired, the same partnerships may be retained throughout by simply progressing as described in Law No. 5 without changing partners at the next table. Another method is to have the original N-S pairs remain in the same positions throughout the game, and to have the E-W pairs progress one table at a time until they reach Table No. 1, and then go to the last table. In this case, the progression is followed automatically, regardless of which pair wins at each table.

LAW No. 7

DRAW FOR DEAL

Unless the dealer is already determined under Law No. 6, the four players at a table draw for first deal. The player who draws highest is the first dealer and may select either deck.

PROGRESSIVE BRIDGE SCORING
COMMENT

With the exceptions specifically mentioned below, the scoring for Progressive Bridge is the same as for rubber bridge (see the table on page 558). The most important points to remember about the scoring are:

Each deal is scored and recorded separately, and no trick points are carried over from one deal to the next. Rubbers are not scored.

Game is 100 points for tricks bid and made in one deal. The game premium is 300 points, if not vulnerable, and 500 points, if vulnerable, and it is allowed only when game is bid and made in one deal.

A premium of 50 points is scored for making any contract less than game. This premium is in addition to the value of the tricks made. Premiums for a small and grand slam are allowed only if bid for.

LAW No. 8

SCORING LIMITS

A side may not score more than 1,000 points in a single deal, except in the case of a slam contract fulfilled.

COMMENT

It is not correct to prohibit doubles or redoubles. The limitation of penalties avoids the necessity of this restriction.

LAW No. 9

VULNERABILITY

The first deal of each round shall be played and scored as if neither side were vulnerable.

The second and third deals of each round shall be played and scored as if the dealer's side were vulnerable and the other side not vulnerable.

The fourth deal of each round shall be played and scored as if both sides were vulnerable.

COMMENT

This is the most desirable method of determining vulnerability in Progressive Bridge, but if preferred all deals may be played as though neither side were vulnerable, or all deals as though both sides were vulnerable. In any event, the method should be announced before play starts.

LAW No. 10

RECORDING THE SCORE

One of the four players at each table is appointed to record the score. He enters the result of each deal on the score pad separately and, at the end of the round, totals all the points made by each side.

He enters on the individual tally of each player the points made by that player's side and also the points made by the opponents.

COMMENT

Correctly designed tallies provide spaces to record both "My Score" and "Opponents' Score." It is important that both be entered on the tally, for otherwise the record would be meaningless.

LAW No. 11

COMPUTING TOTAL SCORES

At the conclusion of the game, each player totals his score. He also totals the scores of his opponents, as recorded on his tally, and subtracts his opponents' total from his own. The difference, plus or minus as the case may be, is recorded in the space provided at the bottom of his tally.

COMMENT

Let us suppose that a player scores 2,460 points, and the opponents score 1,520 points against him. This makes his net score +940 for the entire session. On the other hand, if a player scores only 1,650 points, and the opponents score 1,940 points against him, then his net score for the session is −290 points. Do not make the mistake of recording only plus scores, for that method gives false results, and is likely to lead to improper doubling and redoubling.

LAW No. 12

DETERMINING THE WINNER

The player with the largest plus score is the winner. Other players with plus scores rank in descending order followed by the players with minus scores, the one with the largest minus being last.

COMMENT

The method of awarding prizes is left to the discretion of the game director. At mixed parties it is usual to award one or more prizes to the highest ladies and one or more prizes to the highest gentlemen.

How to Run a Tournament

The complete technique of tournament direction is very complex. Learn the laws thoroughly and obtain Duplicate trays and score-slips from a Bridge Supply firm. The simpler forms of tournaments can be run by following the directions in this chapter.

REPLAY

Shuffle the cards. Point the arrows North and bid as in Rubber Bridge. Record the bidding on a slip of paper and then have the player who will make the opening lead name the card on the slip and put the slip (folded) into the tray.

Point the arrows East and bid and play without keeping record except of the total number of points won and lost. Then point the arrows North again. Read the bidding aloud and have the recorded opening lead made. Proceed to replay and record the total.

Determining the winner: (1) Each pair compares its two results made on any deal. Award one match-point to the pair which wins more points in the play than it loses in the replay (or vice versa); award one-half match-point to each pair for tied boards. The pair with the greater number of match-points wins. (2) Each pair adds total for play and replay and compares totals. The pair wins whose grand total of points won is greater than its grand total of points lost.

Note: To minimize the possibility that memory of the play may affect the replay: allow a few days to elapse between play and replay; select boards at random (instead of consecutively) during replay.

TEAMS OF FOUR

Shuffle the cards. Seat one team North-South at one table and East-West at the other table. The other team takes the remaining seats. Place half the boards at each table and have them bid and played with arrows pointing North. Then exchange the boards and replay.

Determining the winner: (1) Compare totals made by North-South pairs. Award one match-point for the larger plus (or smaller minus); one-half match-point for a tie. The team wins whose North-South pair has most match-points. (2) Total all scores made by each North-South pair. The team wins whose North-South pair's grand total is the greater plus (or smaller minus).

PAIR TOURNAMENTS

Mitchell Movement: Assign half the pairs to North-South seats; the other half, East-West. With an odd number of tables, distribute boards evenly among the tables in order from Table 1 to the highest-numbered table. Each pair is known by the number of the table at which it starts. After each deal has been bid and played, the North player enters the score on the slip (see illustration, page 402). When all tables have finished play, the East-West pairs progress to the next higher-numbered table (and from the highest-numbered table to Table 1); the boards move to the next lower-numbered table (and from Table 1 to the highest-numbered table). Proceed thus until each East-West pair has played at each table.

When the number of tables is even, station one set of boards on a stand (called a "relay stand") between the two middle tables.

Thus, with four tables, put the relay stand between Tables 2 and 3. This stand is considered a table *for the movement of boards only*. If it is planned that each pair should play four boards against each other pair, Boards 1–4 are played simultaneously by Tables 1 and 4; Boards 5–8 are played at Table 2; Boards 9–12 are placed on the relay stand and are not played in the first round; and Boards 13–16 are played at Table 3. After these boards have been played, the boards progress from Table 3 to the relay stand and are not played during the next round; the boards which started at the relay stand go to Table 2 and are played there.

Howell Movement: Follow directions printed on Howell Guide Cards, obtainable at any Bridge Supply firm.

SCORING

The winner of a Duplicate Bridge pair contest may be determined either by match-point scoring (page 400) or by total-point scoring. If the Howell System is used, match-point scoring must be used. For the Mitchell System, either match-point or total-point scoring must be used.

Follow the Contract Bridge scoring table on page 558, except that rubbers are not scored. For bidding and making game, add a bonus of 500 points if vulnerable, 300 points if not vulnerable. For making a part-score add a bonus of 50 points whether vulnerable or not. Part-scores do not carry over to the next deal; every board is scored independently. *Honors do not count if match-point scoring is used, and do count if total-point scoring is used.*

In a Mitchell pair game there are two winners, one North-South pair and one East-West pair.

INDIVIDUAL TOURNAMENTS

Assign each player a number and starting position. To determine the winner, see match-point scoring, page 400. A schedule for an eight-player tournament follows:

SCHEDULE FOR EIGHT PLAYERS*

	Table 1					Table 2		
	N	S	E	W	Boards	N	S	E	W
1st Round	8	1	4	2	1 to 4	7	3	5	6
2nd Round	8	2	5	3	5 to 8	1	4	6	7
3rd Round	8	3	6	4	9 to 12	2	5	7	1
4th Round	8	4	7	5	13 to 16	3	6	1	2
5th Round	8	5	1	6	17 to 20	4	7	2	3
6th Round	8	6	2	7	21 to 24	5	1	3	4
7th Round	8	7	3	1	25 to 28	6	2	4	5

Both tables play the same boards in each round. Three boards may be played to the round (1, 2, 3 in the first round, 4, 5, 6 in the second round, etc.) if a shorter game is desired.

* Schedules for individual tournaments for larger entries can be obtained from any Bridge Supply firm.

INDEX

ASKING BIDS, NEW, 329-335
  after opening two-bid, 370-373
  agreed suit, 339-340
  Blackwood and, 352-358
  choice of, 343-352
  defined, 338-339
  first bid and responses, 341-344
  in opponents' suits, 363-370
  responses to, 341-344
  second bid and responses, 348-349
  sign-off, 345-347
  slam valuation and, 335-338
  special cases, 373-374
  third bid and responses, 349
  understanding the method, 343
  when opponent overcalls, 374-375

BATH COUP, 464
BIDDING
  asking bid, new, 329-375
  duplication in, 395
  forcing, 123-135
  free, 236-242
  goals in, 28
  information, effect of, 41
  intermediate zone, 216-235
  opening, 403-407
  part-score, 244-249
  play and, 31-32
  scoring and, 30-31
  slam, 297-328

  three-way valuation in, 34-35
  tricks in, 28-29
  valuation in; 33-35
BLACKWOOD CONVENTION
  asking bids and, 352-358
  fine points, 326-327
  grand-slam bidding, 326
  responses, 323, 325-326
  when used, 324-325
BLOCKING PLAYS, 466-467

COMMUNICATION PLAYS, 459
  Bath coup, 464, 470
  blocking plays, 466-467
  defenders' entry plays, 465-466
  Deschapelles coup, 468-469
  ducking, 461, 466, 471
  entry-killing plays, 462-464
  entry-making plays, 459-462
  entry timing, 465-466
  hidden trump entry, 467-468
  shutout play, 469
  unblocking, 460-461, 465
CONVENTIONAL LEADS AND PLAYS, 516-525
  alphabet of, 516-517
  following suit and discarding, 520
    discards, 520
    echo, 520-521
    lead-directing doubles, 522-523

Conventional Leads, Plays (Cont.)
  suit-preference signal, 521-522, 523-524
  trump echo, 521
  honor leads, 517-518
  long-suit leads, 518-519
  short-suit leads, 519-520
  table of leads, 526-527
CROSS-RUFF, 491-493
CUE-BIDS, 314-321
  of opponents' suit, 317-318
  psychic, 317
  signing off over, 316-317
  order of suits, 316
  to show aces, 314-315, 318-321
  when to make, 315-316

DECLARER'S PLANNING AND PLAY, 478-479
  advance planning, 479-484
  at notrump, 484-486
  card reading, 493-494
  cross-ruff, 491-493
  play, 495-497
  trump planning, 486-491
DEFENDERS' BIDDING, 250-255
  responding to overcall, 253-255
  strong and weak overcalls, 251-253
DEFENDERS' GAME, 528
  defense, 534-535
  force, 532
  leads
    against notrump, 528-530, 538
    against trump bids, 531, 536-537
    opening, 536-537
    slam, 533-534, 537
    to be avoided, 537
    waiting, 532-533
  ruffing, 531-532

DESCHAPELLES COUP, 468-469
DISCARDS, 520-524
DISTRIBUTION
  count. See Distributional count
  modern theory of, 427
    law of symmetry, 427-433
    typical hand-patterns, 430-431
  reading from bidding, 391-393
DISTRIBUTIONAL COUNT, 49-59
  declarer's hand, valuation of
    honor-winners, 53-54
    long-suit tricks, 53
    long-suit winners, 54-55
  playing trick, 51
  revaluation of hand, 59
  scale of bids, raises, and rebids, 51-53
  valuation, natural method of, 50-51
  valuation when raising partner's hand
    honor-winners, 57
    ruffing-trick table, 56-57
    side lengths not counted, 57-58
    trump winners, 55-56
DOUBLES
  in point-count method, 24-27
  penalty, 282-295
  takeout, 249, 256-276
DUCKING, 461-462, 466, 471
DUPLICATE BRIDGE BIDDING, 400
  choice of contracts, 409-411
  match-point scoring, 400-401
  opening bids, 403-407
  overcalls, 407-408
  raises, 406-407
  vulnerability, 408-409
DUPLICATION, 394-399
  of bids, 395
  of hand-patterns, 397

Duplication (Cont.)
  of values, 396
  rare bidding situations, 398-399
  warnings from bidding, 397-398

EIGHT, RULE OF, 36-48
  average game, slam expectancies
    of, 45-46
  balance of strength, how to de-
    termine, 43-44
  blank in partner's hand, when
    to expect, 45
  4-5-6 table of expectancies, 46-
    48
  psychic bids, detecting, 44
  slam bidding, 45
END-PLAYS
  Grand Coup, 508-509
  squeeze, 500
    explanation of, 506
    typical positions, 504-505
  stripping process, 499, 500-501
  "throw-ins," 499-500
  trump-reducing plays, 507-508
  Vienna Coup, 509-510
ENTRY-KILLING PLAYS, 462-464
  Bath Coup, 464
  hold-up, 463-464
  when not to hold up, 464
ENTRY-MAKING PLAYS, 459-462
  ducking, 461-462
  timing of, 462
  unblocking, 460-461

FINESSE
  backward, 458
  defined, 442
  direct and indirect, 442-443
  direct simple, 443-444
  double, 444-445
  two-way, 447
  value of honor-tricks, 38

FORCING BIDS, 123-135
  defenders', 131-132
  for one round, 129-130
  limited and unlimited, 129
  object of, 125-126
  principle of, 123-124
  summary of, 132-135
  to game, 126-127
FOUR-FIVE NOTRUMP SLAM CONVEN-
  TIONS, 322-328
FREE BIDS, 236-243
  free suit takeouts, 239-241
  notrump takeouts, 238-239
  over opponent's takeout double,
    242-243
  penalty double, 239
  rebids, 241-242

GRAND COUP, 508-509

HOLD-UP PLAYS, 463-464
HONOR-TRICKS, 36-48
  application of defensive table,
    41-42
  average game, slam expectancies
    of, 45-46
  average hand, value of, 42
  bidding information, effect of,
    41
  Culbertson table of, 38
  finesse value of, 37
  4-5-6 table of expectancies, 46-
    48
  honor values, equivalence of, 40-
    41
  plus values, 38-39
  rule of eight, 43
    balance of strength, how to
      determine, 43-44
    blank in partner's hand, when
      to expect, 45

Honor-Tricks (Cont.)
psychic bids, detecting, 44
slam bidding, 45
unbalanced distribution, value
of, 39-40

INFERENCE FROM PARTNERSHIP
STRATEGY, 60-65
INTERMEDIATE ZONE, 216-217
guiding the bidding, 229-230
hand valuation, 217-218
notrump hands, 220-221
preference bids, 224-226
reading the bidding
equivalent bids, 223-224
first sign of strength, 222-223
inferences from bidding level,
221-222
safe and unsafe hands, 219-220
sign-off of rescue bids, 226-229
when the zone changes, 233-235
where to bid game, 230-233

LAWS OF CONTRACT BRIDGE, 539-567
auction, 546-547
claims and concessions, 555
club procedure, 560-561
cut, 543-544
deal, 544
draw, 543
exposed cards, 552
improper calls, 547-548
irregularities, 545-546
leads and play, 550-552
penalty cards, 554
play, 549-550
progressive bridge, 561-565
proprieties, 559-560
revoke, 553
scope, 541-542
score, 556-558

shuffle, 543
tournament, 566-567
tricks, 553-554
LEADS
defenders', 528-538
honor, 517-518
laws of, 550-552
long-suit, 518-519
short-suit, 519-520
table of, 526-527
LIMIT FORCING TWO-BID, 146-153
ace-showing responses, 152
advantages of, 151-152
exception to, 146
requirements for, 147-149
responses to, 149-150
trump suit, 150-152
two-club, 152-153
"weak" or artificial, 152-153
LOW-CARD TRICKS, 448-458
backward finesse, 458
drop *vs.* finesse, 456
economy of honors, 457
finessing, 454-455
long-suit establishment, 448-449
probabilities in, 449, 453
short-suit establishment, 449-452

MATHEMATICS OF SCORING, 384-390

NOTRUMP OPENING BIDS
alternative theory of, 93-94
of four and more, 93
of one
distributional, 85-87
rebids by opener, 79-82
requirements for, 67-70
responses to, 71-78
when distribution is not used,
87-88

Notrump Opening Bids (Cont.)
　　when doubled or overcalled,
　　　83-85
　　of three, 91-92
　　slam tries over, 92-93
　　of two, 88-89
　　opener's rebids, 91
　　responses to, 89-90

OPENING. See also Suit-bids and
　　Pre-emptive bids
　　duplicate, 403-407
　　in point-count method, 7, 10, 12-
　　14
OVERCALLS, STRENGTH-SHOWING.
　　See Strength-showing overcalls

PART-SCORE BIDDING, 244-249
　　forcing, 244-246
　　panicky, 247
　　strategy and tactics, 246-247
　　takeout doubles, 249
PARTNERSHIP LANGUAGE OF INFER-
　　ENCES, 60-65
　　approach method, 62
　　limit-bid principle, 62-63
　　strategy, 63-65
PASSED HAND, 184-188
　　responses to opening bids, 184-
　　186
　　second-round bids by responder,
　　186-188
PENALTY DOUBLES, 282-295
　　light doubles, 284-287
　　of notrump bids, 288-291
　　principal situations, 293-295
　　tight doubles, 287-288
　　two-trick rule, 283-284
　　vs. trick scores, 282-283
　　when to redouble, 291-293

PERSONAL EQUATION, 420
　　marriage and, 424-425
　　opponents' psychology, 425-426
　　playing partner's game, 420-424
POINT-COUNT METHOD
　　babel of, 4-5
　　free bids, 17-18
　　of Culbertson, 2-3
　　mechanics of, 6-7
　　notrump and, 7-9
　　doubling, 25
　　opening bids of two and
　　　three, 10
　　raise requirements, 9, 14-15
　　responses to two and three,
　　　11-12
　　suit takeout, 18-19
　　opener's rebids, 20-21
　　opener's revaluation, 19-20
　　opening suit-bids and responses,
　　　12-13
　　opening two-bids, 23
　　penalty pass, 26
　　powerful hands in, 21-22
　　raise requirements, 15
　　rapid count, 5-6
　　rebids by doubler, 26-27
　　rebids by responder, 22-23
　　reopening with double, 27
　　requirements for opening of
　　　one, 13-14
　　responses in notrump, 26
　　responses to opening of one, 14
　　responses to takeout doubles, 24,
　　　25-26
　　responses to two-bids, 24
　　six-card suits, 19
　　suit takeout, valuing responder's
　　　hand for, 16-17
　　takeout doubles, 24
　　vs. honor-trick method, 3-4

PRE-EMPTIVE BIDS, 154-155
  five-bids, minor-suit, 160
  four-bids, opening, 158-159
    responses to, 159-160
  safety factor, 155
  third and fourth hand, 160-161
  three-bids, opening, 155-156
    responses to, 156-158
PROMOTION PRINCIPLE, 437
PSYCHOLOGY AND TACTICS, 412
  bids to misplace cards, 418-419
  concealing weakness, 412-414
  trapping
    over a takeout double, 417
    shift-bids, 416-417
    trap-pass over opponents' bid,
      415

RAISE REQUIREMENTS, 9, 15-16
REBIDS
  by the opener
    after one notrump, 196
    choosing the zone, 189-191
    jump, 197-198
    notrump, 195-196
    over a double raise, 193-194
    strong and very strong, 202-
      207
    to forcing takeout, 191-193
    weak, 200-201
    when partner raises, 198-199
  by the responder
    after one-notrump response,
      214
    after one-over-one responses,
      210-212
    after two-of-a-suit responses,
      212-213
    guide to game valuation, 215
    to jump rebids, 208-210

RESPONSES
  in point-count method
    notrump, 26
    opening suit-bids, 14-16
    takeout doubles, 25-26
    two and three notrump, 11-12
    two-bids, 24
  notrump takeout
    one notrump, 171-173
    three notrump, 174-175
    two notrump, 173-174
  raises
    double, 167-169
    single, 164-166
    triple, 169-170
  suit takeouts
    choice of, 181-182
    forcing, 179-180
    higher-ranking, 176-177
    lower-ranking, 177-178
    one-round force, 175
RUFFING, 56-57, 531-532

SACRIFICE BIDDING
  duplicate bridge, 408-409
  pre-emptive bids, 155
  scoring, 388-389
SAFETY FACTOR, 380-383
  rule of risk and gain, 381
  rule of 2 and 3, 381-383
SAFETY PLAYS AND TECHNIQUE, 511-
  515
SCORING
  and its mathematics, 384-387
  bidding and, 30-31
  duplicate match-point, 400-401
  game *vs.* equivalent penalty,
    387-388
  sacrifice bidding, 388-389

SHUTOUT PLAY, 469
SIGN-OFF
  in opening notrump, 76
  of rescue bids, 226-229
  over cue-bids, 316-317
SLAM BIDDING, 296
  asking bids, new and old. See
    Asking bids
  controls in, 305-307
  cue-bids, 315-321
  direct method of, 308-309
    slam zone, recognizing, 309-
      311
    tries, 311-313
  4–5 notrump conventions
    action by responder, 325-326
    Blackwood, 322-324
    fine points, 326-328
    grand-slam bidding, 326, 328
    when used, 324-325
  mathematics of, 297
  when to make try, 301-305
SQUEEZE PLAY, 500-506
STRENGTH-SHOWING OVERCALLS, 277
  immediate overcall, 279-281
  jump overcall, 277-279
STRIPPING PROCESS, 499-501
SUIT-BIDS OF ONE, 103-104
  choice of suits, 110
    length, 110-111
    rank, principle of, 112
    strength of the hand, 112-113
    unequal length, 111
  4–4–3–2 and 4–3–3–3 mini-
    mums, 121-122
  fourth hand, when to pass, 108-
    109
  playing strength, factor of, 107-
    108
  position, factor of, 108

preparedness, principle of, 115
  choice of four-card suits, 117
  distribution, 118-120
  how to use, 115-116
  partner's count of length, 117
  three-card suits, 121
  why we use, 115
psychology in, 106-107
raises, 164-170
requirements, minimum, 105-
  106
responses, 162-163
  free, 183. See also Free bids
  notrump takeout, 171-175
  pass, 163-164
  suit takeouts, 175-182
"reverse," 113-115
third-hand strategic bids, 109-
  110
trap pass, 107
SUIT-BIDS OF TWO, 136-138
  forcing, 138-141
    responses to, 143, 152
  freaks, 139-141
  limit forcing
    requirements for, 147-149
    responses to, 149-150
    trump suit, 150-152
    "weak" or artificial, 152-153
  rule of, 141-142
  specifications for, 138-139
  suit takeouts, 144-145
SYMMETRY IN DISTRIBUTION, LAW
  OF, 427-433

TAKEOUT DOUBLES, 256-257
  classification of, 256
  definition of, 257
  jump bid after doubling, 273-
    274
  of four bid, 275-276

Takeout Doubles (Cont.)
  of pre-emptive three-bids, 274-275
  penalty pass, 267-272
  rebids after, 272-273
  requirements for, 257-263
  responses to, 263-267
TIME FACTOR, 472-474
  hand valuation, 475-477
  long-suit valuation, 474-475
  ruffing and, 477
TOURNAMENT RULES, 566-567
TRAPPING, 414-418
  over takeout double, 417-418
  shift bids, 416-417
  trap-pass over opponents' bid, 415
TRUMP
  biddable suits, 96-102
  hidden entry, 467-468
  winners, 55-56
TRUMP SUITS, BIDDABLE, 96-97
  adequate support, 99-100
  bidding level, 100

conditional, 97
rebiddable, strong, 98-99
support for a rebid, 100
when a suit need not be biddable, 100-101

UNBLOCKING, 460-461, 465

VIENNA COUP, 509-510

WINNING OF TRICKS, 436-437
  Culbertson rule of five steps, 441-442
  economy of honors principle, 445-447
  finesse, 442-445
  guards and suit-distribution, 438
  position, 439-441
  promotion principle, 437
  stoppers, 438
  straight leads from sequences, 439